The Ultimate Docker Container Book

Build, test, ship, and run containers with Docker
and Kubernetes

Dr. Gabriel N. Schenker

BIRMINGHAM—MUMBAI

The Ultimate Docker Container Book

Group Product Manager: Preet Ahuja
Publishing Product Manager: Suwarna Rajput
Senior Editor: Sayali Pingale
Technical Editor: Rajat Sharma
Copy Editor: Safis Editing
Project Coordinator: Aryaa Joshi
Proofreader: Safis Editing
Indexer: Manju Arasan
Production Designer: Shyam Sundar Korumilli
DevRel Marketing Coordinator: Rohan Dobhal

First published: April 2018
Second edition: March 2020
Third edition: August 2023

Production reference: 1100823

Published by Packt Publishing Ltd.
Grosvenor House
11 St Paul's Square
Birmingham
B3 1RB, UK

ISBN 978-1-80461-398-6

www.packtpub.com

To my wonderful wife, Veronicah, for being my loving partner throughout our joint life journey.

– Gabriel Schenker

Contributors

About the author

Dr. Gabriel N. Schenker has more than 30 years of experience as an independent consultant, architect, leader, trainer, mentor, and developer. Currently, Gabriel works as a senior software engineering manager and VP at iptiQ by Swiss Re. Prior to that, Gabriel worked as a lead solution architect at Techgroup Switzerland. Despite loving his home country of Switzerland, Gabriel also lived and worked for almost 10 years in the US, where, among other companies, he worked for Docker and Confluent. Gabriel has a Ph.D. in physics, and he is a former Docker Captain, a Certified Docker Associate, a Certified Kafka Developer, a Certified Kafka Operator, and an ASP Insider. When not working, Gabriel enjoys spending time with his wonderful wife Veronicah, and his children.

I want to thank my wife, Veronicah, for her endless love and unconditional support.

About the reviewers

Mátyás Kovács is an enthusiastic IT consultant with more than 9 years of hands-on experience in architecting, automating, optimizing, and supporting mission-critical systems. He has worked in modern development practices, CI/CD, configuration management, virtualization technologies, and cloud services. He is currently working as a lead systems engineer and people team lead. He is an eager mentor and huge supporter of lifelong learning.

Jeppe Cramon, a seasoned software professional and owner of Cloud Create, is known for his pioneering work in building distributed systems, strategic monoliths, and microservices. His deep understanding of these fields is evident in his comprehensive blog posts, where he provides detailed insights into the nature of distributed systems and how they should be implemented.

Not just a practitioner, Cramon is also an educator, regularly sharing his insights on distributed systems in his blog and at conferences, driving the conversation on these topics and their implications for autonomous services.

Table of Contents

Part 2: Containerization Fundamentals

3

Mastering Containers   45

4

Creating and Managing Container Images   73

5

6

7

Testing Applications Running in Containers   187

8

Increasing Productivity with Docker Tips and Tricks   217

Part 3: Orchestration Fundamentals

9

Learning about Distributed Application Architecture   245

10

Using Single-Host Networking   263

11

Managing Containers with Docker Compose   293

12

Shipping Logs and Monitoring Containers   325

13

Introducing Container Orchestration 357

14

Introducing Docker Swarm 377

15

Deploying and Running a Distributed Application on Docker Swarm 409

Part 4: Docker, Kubernetes, and the Cloud

16

Introducing Kubernetes 441

17

Deploying, Updating, and Securing an Application with Kubernetes

481

18

Running a Containerized Application in the Cloud

519

19

Monitoring and Troubleshooting an Application Running in Production

549

Preface

In today's fast-paced world, developers are under constant pressure to build, modify, test, and deploy highly distributed applications quickly and efficiently. Operations engineers need a consistent deployment strategy that can handle their growing portfolio of applications, while stakeholders want to keep costs low. Docker containers, combined with a container orchestrator such as Kubernetes, provide a powerful solution to these challenges.

Docker containers streamline the process of building, shipping, and running highly distributed applications. They supercharge CI/CD pipelines and allow companies to standardize on a single deployment platform, such as Kubernetes. Containerized applications are more secure and can be run on any platform capable of running containers, whether on-premises or in the cloud. With Docker containers, developers, operations engineers, and stakeholders can achieve their goals and stay ahead of the curve.

Who this book is for

This book is designed for anyone who wants to learn about Docker and its capabilities. Whether you're a system administrator, operations engineer, DevOps engineer, developer, or business stakeholder, this book will guide you through the process of getting started with Docker from scratch.

With clear explanations and practical examples, you'll explore all the capabilities that this technology offers, ultimately providing you with the ability to deploy and run highly distributed applications in the cloud. If you're looking to take your skills to the next level and harness the power of Docker, then this book is for you.

What this book covers

Chapter 1, What Are Containers and Why Should I Use Them? focuses on the software supply chain and the friction within it. It then presents containers as a means to reduce this friction and add enterprise-grade security on top of it. In this chapter, we also look into how containers and the ecosystem around them are assembled. We specifically point out the distinction between the upstream OSS components (Moby) that form the building blocks of the downstream products of Docker and other vendors.

Chapter 2, Setting Up a Working Environment, discusses in detail how to set up an ideal environment for developers, DevOps, and operators that can be used when working with Docker containers.

Chapter 3, Mastering Containers, teaches you how to start, stop, and remove containers. This chapter also teaches you how to inspect containers to retrieve additional metadata from them. Furthermore, it explains how to run additional processes and how to attach to the main process in an already-running container. It also shows how to retrieve logging information from a container that is produced by the processes running inside it. Finally, the chapter introduces the inner workings of a container including such things as Linux namespaces and groups.

Chapter 4, Creating and Managing Container Images, presents different ways to create container images, which serve as templates for containers. It introduces the inner structure of an image and how it is built. This chapter also shows how to "lift and shift" an existing legacy application such that it runs in containers.

Chapter 5, Data Volumes and Configuration, discusses data volumes, which can be used by stateful components running in containers. This chapter also shows how you can define individual environment variables for the application running inside the container, as well as how to use files containing whole sets of configuration settings.

Chapter 6, Debugging Code Running in Containers, introduces techniques commonly used to allow you to evolve, modify, debug, and test your code while running in a container. With these techniques at hand, you will enjoy a frictionless development process for applications running in a container, similar to what you experience when developing applications that run natively.

Chapter 7, Testing Applications Running in Containers, discusses software testing for applications and application services running in containers. You will be introduced to the various test types that exist and understand how they can be optimally implemented and executed when using containers. The chapter explains how all tests can be run locally on a developer's machine or as individual quality gates of a fully automated CI/CD pipeline.

Chapter 8, Increasing Productivity with Docker Tips and Tricks, shows miscellaneous tips, tricks, and concepts that are useful when containerizing complex distributed applications, or when using Docker to automate sophisticated tasks. You will also learn how to leverage containers to run your whole development environment in them.

Chapter 9, Learning about Distributed Application Architecture, introduces the concept of a distributed application architecture and discusses the various patterns and best practices that are required to run a distributed application successfully. Finally, it discusses the additional requirements that need to be fulfilled to run such an application in production.

Chapter 10, Using Single-Host Networking, presents the Docker container networking model and its single host implementation in the form of the bridge network. The chapter introduces the concept of **Software-Defined Networks (SDNs)** and how they are used to secure containerized applications. It also covers how container ports can be opened to the public and thus make containerized components accessible from the outside world. Finally, it introduces Traefik, a reverse proxy, to enable sophisticated HTTP application-level routing between containers.

Chapter 11, Managing Containers with Docker Compose, introduces the concept of an application consisting of multiple services, each running in a container, and explains how Docker Compose allows us to easily build, run, and scale such an application using a declarative approach.

Chapter 12, Shipping Logs and Monitoring Containers, shows how the container logs can be collected and shipped to a central location where the aggregated log can then be parsed for useful information. You will also learn how to instrument an application so that it exposes metrics and how those metrics can be scraped and shipped again to a central location. Finally, the chapter teaches you how to convert those collected metrics into graphical dashboards that can be used to monitor a containerized application.

Chapter 13, Introducing Container Orchestration, elaborates on the concept of container orchestrators. It explains why orchestrators are needed and how they conceptually work. The chapter will also provide an overview of the most popular orchestrators and name a few of their respective pros and cons.

Chapter 14, Introducing Docker Swarm, introduces Docker's native orchestrator called SwarmKit. It elaborates on all the concepts and objects SwarmKit uses to deploy and run a distributed, resilient, robust, and highly available application in a cluster on-premises or in the cloud.

Chapter 15, Deploying and Running a Distributed Application on Docker Swarm, introduces routing mesh and demonstrates how to deploy a first application consisting of multiple services onto the Swarm.

Chapter 16, Introducing Kubernetes, presents the currently most popular container orchestrator, Kubernetes. It introduces the core Kubernetes objects that are used to define and run a distributed, resilient, robust, and highly available application in a cluster. Finally, it introduces minikube as a way to locally deploy a Kubernetes application and also covers the integration of Kubernetes with Docker Desktop.

Chapter 17, Deploying, Updating, and Securing an Application with Kubernetes, teaches you how to deploy, update, and scale applications into a Kubernetes cluster. It also shows you how to instrument your application services with liveness and readiness probes, to support Kubernetes in its health and availability checking. Furthermore, the chapter explains how zero downtime deployments are achieved to enable disruption-free updates and rollbacks of mission-critical applications. Finally, it introduces Kubernetes Secrets as a means to configure services and protect sensitive data.

Chapter 18, Running a Containerized Application in the Cloud, gives an overview of some of the most popular ways of running containerized applications in the cloud. Fully managed offerings on Microsoft Azure, Amazon AWS, and Google Cloud Engine are discussed. We will create a hosted Kubernetes cluster on each cloud and deploy a simple distributed application to each of those clusters. We will also compare the ease of setup and use of the three offerings.

Chapter 19, Monitoring and Troubleshooting an Application Running in Production, covers different techniques used to instrument and monitor an individual service or a whole distributed application running on a Kubernetes cluster. You will be introduced to the concept of alerting based on key metrics. The chapter also shows how you can troubleshoot an application service that is running in production without altering the cluster or the cluster nodes on which the service is running.

To get the most out of this book

Software/hardware covered in the book	Operating system requirements
Docker v23.x	Windows, macOS, or Linux
Docker Desktop	
Kubernetes	
Docker SwarmKit	

If you are using the digital version of this book, we advise you to type the code yourself or access the code from the book's GitHub repository (a link is available in the next section). Doing so will help you avoid any potential errors related to the copying and pasting of code.

Download the example code files

You can download the example code files for this book from GitHub at `https://github.com/PacktPublishing/The-Ultimate-Docker-Container-Book/`. If there's an update to the code, it will be updated in the GitHub repository.

We also have other code bundles from our rich catalog of books and videos available at `https://github.com/PacktPublishing/`. Check them out!

Conventions used

There are a number of text conventions used throughout this book.

`Code in text`: Indicates code words in text, database table names, folder names, filenames, file extensions, pathnames, dummy URLs, user input, and Twitter handles. Here is an example: "Once Chocolatey has been installed, test it with the `choco --version` command."

A block of code is set as follows:

```
while :
do
    curl -s http://jservice.io/api/random | jq '.[0].question'
    sleep 5
done
```

When we wish to draw your attention to a particular part of a code block, the relevant lines or items are set in bold:

```
...
secrets: demo-secret: "<<demo-secret-value>>"
other-secret: "<<other-secret-value>>"
yet-another-secret: "<<yet-another-secret-value>>"
...
```

Any command-line input or output is written as follows:

```
$ docker version
$ docker container run hello-world
```

Bold: Indicates a new term, an important word, or words that you see onscreen. For instance, words in menus or dialog boxes appear in **bold**. Here is an example: "From the menu, select **Dashboard**."

> **Tips or important notes**
> Appear like this.

Get in touch

Feedback from our readers is always welcome.

General feedback: If you have questions about any aspect of this book, email us at customercare@ packtpub.com and mention the book title in the subject of your message.

Errata: Although we have taken every care to ensure the accuracy of our content, mistakes do happen. If you have found a mistake in this book, we would be grateful if you would report this to us. Please visit www.packtpub.com/support/errata and fill in the form.

Piracy: If you come across any illegal copies of our works in any form on the internet, we would be grateful if you would provide us with the location address or website name. Please contact us at copyright@packt.com with a link to the material.

If you are interested in becoming an author: If there is a topic that you have expertise in and you are interested in either writing or contributing to a book, please visit authors.packtpub.com.

Share Your Thoughts

Once you've read *The Ultimate Docker Container Book*, we'd love to hear your thoughts! Scan the QR code below to go straight to the Amazon review page for this book and share your feedback.

https://packt.link/r/1804613983

Your review is important to us and the tech community and will help us make sure we're delivering excellent quality content.

Download a free PDF copy of this book

Thanks for purchasing this book!

Do you like to read on the go but are unable to carry your print books everywhere? Is your eBook purchase not compatible with the device of your choice?

Don't worry, now with every Packt book you get a DRM-free PDF version of that book at no cost.

Read anywhere, any place, on any device. Search, copy, and paste code from your favorite technical books directly into your application.

The perks don't stop there, you can get exclusive access to discounts, newsletters, and great free content in your inbox daily

Follow these simple steps to get the benefits:

1. Scan the QR code or visit the link below

https://packt.link/free-ebook/9781804613986

2. Submit your proof of purchase

3. That's it! We'll send your free PDF and other benefits to your email directly

Part 1: Introduction

The objective of *Part 1* is to introduce you to the concept of containers and explain why they are so extremely useful in the software industry. You will also be shown how to prepare your working environment for the use of Docker.

This section has the following chapters:

- *Chapter 1, What Are Containers and Why Should I Use Them?*
- *Chapter 2, Setting Up a Working Environment*

1

What Are Containers and Why Should I Use Them?

This first chapter will introduce you to the world of containers and their orchestration. This book starts from the very beginning, in that it assumes that you have limited prior knowledge of containers, and will give you a very practical introduction to the topic.

In this chapter, we will focus on the software supply chain and the friction within it. Then, we'll present containers, which are used to reduce this friction and add enterprise-grade security on top of it. We'll also look into how containers and the ecosystem around them are assembled. We'll specifically point out the distinctions between the upstream **Open Source Software** (**OSS**) components, united under the code name Moby, that form the building blocks of the downstream products of Docker and other vendors.

The chapter covers the following topics:

- What are containers?
- Why are containers important?
- What's the benefit of using containers for me or for my company?
- The Moby project
- Docker products
- Container architecture

After completing this chapter, you will be able to do the following:

- Explain what containers are, using an analogy such as physical containers, in a few simple sentences to an interested layperson
- Justify why containers are so important using an analogy such as physical containers versus traditional shipping, or apartment homes versus single-family homes, and so on, to an interested layperson

- Name at least four upstream open source components that are used by Docker products, such as Docker Desktop
- Draw a high-level sketch of the Docker container architecture

Let's get started!

What are containers?

A software container is a pretty abstract thing, so it might help to start with an analogy that should be pretty familiar to most of you. The analogy is a shipping container in the transportation industry. Throughout history, people have transported goods from one location to another by various means. Before the invention of the wheel, goods would most probably have been transported in bags, baskets, or chests on the shoulders of humans themselves, or they might have used animals such as donkeys, camels, or elephants to transport them. With the invention of the wheel, transportation became a bit more efficient as humans built roads that they could move their carts along. Many more goods could be transported at a time. When the first steam-driven machines, and later gasoline-driven engines, were introduced, transportation became even more powerful. We now transport huge amounts of goods on planes, trains, ships, and trucks. At the same time, the types of goods became more and more diverse, and sometimes complex to handle. In all these thousands of years, one thing hasn't changed, and that is the necessity to unload goods at a target location and maybe load them onto another means of transportation. Take, for example, a farmer bringing a cart full of apples to a central train station where the apples are then loaded onto a train, together with all the apples from many other farmers. Or think of a winemaker bringing their barrels of wine on a truck to the port where they are unloaded, and then transferred to a ship that will transport those barrels overseas.

This unloading from one means of transportation and loading onto another means of transportation was a really complex and tedious process. Every type of product was packaged in its own way and thus had to be handled in its own particular way. Also, loose goods faced the risk of being stolen by unethical workers or damaged in the process of being handled.

Figure 1.1 – Sailors unloading goods from a ship

Then, containers came along, and they totally revolutionized the transportation industry. A container is just a metallic box with standardized dimensions. The length, width, and height of each container are the same. This is a very important point. Without the world agreeing on a standard size, the whole container thing would not have been as successful as it is now. Now, with standardized containers, companies who want to have their goods transported from A to B package those goods into these containers. Then, they call a shipper, who uses a standardized means of transportation. This can be a truck that can load a container, or a train whose wagons can each transport one or several containers. Finally, we have ships that are specialized in transporting huge numbers of containers. Shippers never need to unpack and repackage goods. For a shipper, a container is just a black box, and they are not interested in what is in it, nor should they care in most cases. It is just a big iron box with standard dimensions. Packaging goods into containers is now fully delegated to the parties who want to have their goods shipped, and they should know how to handle and package those goods. Since all containers have the same agreed-upon shape and dimensions, shippers can use standardized tools to handle containers; that is, cranes that unload containers, say from a train or a truck, and load them onto a ship and vice versa. One type of crane is enough to handle all the containers that come along over time. Also, the means of transportation can be standardized, such as container ships, trucks, and trains. Because of all this standardization, all the processes in and around shipping goods could also be standardized and thus made much more efficient than they were before the introduction of containers.

Figure 1.2 – Container ship being loaded in a port

Now, you should have a good understanding of why shipping containers are so important and why they revolutionized the whole transportation industry. I chose this analogy purposefully since the software containers that we are going to introduce here fulfill the exact same role in the so-called software supply chain as shipping containers do in the supply chain of physical goods.

Let's then have a look at what this whole thing means when translated to the IT industry and software development, shall we? In the old days, developers would develop new applications. Once an application was completed in their eyes, they would hand that application over to the operations engineers, who were then supposed to install it on the production servers and get it running. If the operations engineers were lucky, they even got a somewhat accurate document with installation instructions from the developers. So far, so good, and life was easy. But things got a bit out of hand when, in an enterprise, there were many teams of developers that created quite different types of applications, yet all of them needed to be installed on the same production servers and kept running there. Usually, each application has some external dependencies, such as which framework it was built on, what libraries it uses, and so on. Sometimes, two applications use the same framework but of different versions that might or might not be compatible with each other. Our operations engineers' lives became much harder over time. They had to become really creative with how they loaded their ships, that is, their servers, with different applications without breaking something. Installing a new version of a certain application was now a complex project on its own, and often needed months of planning and testing beforehand. In other words, there was a lot of friction in the software supply chain.

But these days, companies rely more and more on software, and the release cycles need to become shorter and shorter. Companies cannot afford to just release application updates once or twice a year anymore. Applications need to be updated in a matter of weeks or days, or sometimes even multiple times per day. Companies that do not comply risk going out of business due to the lack of agility. So, what's the solution? One of the first approaches was to use **virtual machines** (**VMs**). Instead of running multiple applications all on the same server, companies would package and run a single application on each VM. With this, all the compatibility problems were gone, and life seemed to be good again. Unfortunately, that happiness didn't last long. VMs are pretty heavy beasts on their own since they all contain a full-blown operating system such as Linux or Windows Server, and all that for just a single application. This is as if you used a whole ship just to transport a single truckload of bananas in the transportation industry. What a waste! That would never be profitable. The ultimate solution to this problem was to provide something much more lightweight than VMs also able to perfectly encapsulate the goods it needed to transport. Here, the goods are the actual application that has been written by our developers, plus – and this is important – all the external dependencies of the application, such as its framework, libraries, configurations, and more. This holy grail of a software packaging mechanism is the **Docker container**.

Developers package their applications, frameworks, and libraries into Docker containers, and then they ship those containers to the testers or operations engineers. For testers and operations engineers, a container is just a black box. It is a standardized black box, though. All containers, no matter what application runs inside them, can be treated equally. The engineers know that if any container runs on their servers, then any other containers should run too. And this is actually true, apart from some edge cases, which always exist. Thus, Docker containers are a means to package applications and their dependencies in a standardized way. Docker then coined the phrase *Build, ship*, and *run anywhere*.

Why are containers important?

These days, the time between new releases of an application becomes shorter and shorter, yet the software itself does not become any simpler. On the contrary, software projects increase in complexity. Thus, we need a way to tame the beast and simplify the software supply chain. Also, every day, we hear that cyber-attacks are on the rise. Many well-known companies are and have been affected by security breaches. Highly sensitive customer data gets stolen during such events, such as social security numbers, credit card information, health-related information, and more. But not only is customer data compromised – sensitive company secrets are stolen too. Containers can help in many ways. In a published report, Gartner found that applications running in a container are more secure than their counterparts not running in a container. Containers use Linux security primitives such as Linux kernel **namespaces** to sandbox different applications running on the same computers and **control groups** (**cgroups**) to avoid the noisy-neighbor problem, where one bad application uses all the available resources of a server and starves all other applications. Since container images are immutable, as we will learn later, it is easy to have them scanned for **common vulnerabilities and exposures** (**CVEs**), and in doing so, increase the overall security of our applications. Another way to make our software supply chain more secure is to have our containers use **content trust**. Content trust ensures that the author of a container image is who they say they are and that the consumer of the container image has a guarantee that the image has not been tampered with in transit. The latter is known as a **man-in-the-middle (MITM)** attack.

Everything I have just said is, of course, technically also possible without using containers, but since containers introduce a globally accepted standard, they make it so much easier to implement these best practices and enforce them. OK, but security is not the only reason containers are important. There are other reasons too. One is the fact that containers make it easy to simulate a production-like environment, even on a developer's laptop. If we can containerize any application, then we can also containerize, say, a database such as Oracle, PostgreSQL, or MS SQL Server. Now, everyone who has ever had to install an Oracle database on a computer knows that this is not the easiest thing to do, and it takes up a lot of precious space on your computer. You would not want to do that to your development laptop just to test whether the application you developed really works end to end. With containers to hand, we can run a full-blown relational database in a container as easily as saying 1, 2, 3. And when we are done with testing, we can just stop and delete the container and the database will be gone, without leaving a single trace on our computer. Since containers are very lean compared to VMs, it is common to have many containers running at the same time on a developer's laptop without overwhelming the laptop. A third reason containers are important is that operators can finally concentrate on what they are good at – provisioning the infrastructure and running and monitoring applications in production. When the applications they must run on a production system are all containerized, then operators can start to standardize their infrastructure. Every server becomes just another **Docker host**. No special libraries or frameworks need to be installed on those servers – just an OS and a container runtime such as Docker. Furthermore, operators do not have to have intimate knowledge of the internals of applications anymore, since those applications run self-contained in containers that ought to look like black boxes to them like how shipping containers look to personnel in the transportation industry.

What is the benefit of using containers for me or for my company?

Somebody once said *"...today every company of a certain size has to acknowledge that they need to be a software company..."* In this sense, a modern bank is a software company that happens to specialize in the business of finance. Software runs all businesses, period. As every company becomes a software company, there is a need to establish a software supply chain. For the company to remain competitive, its software supply chain must be secure and efficient. Efficiency can be achieved through thorough automation and standardization. But in all three areas – security, automation, and standardization – containers have been shown to shine. Large and well-known enterprises have reported that when containerizing existing legacy applications (many call them traditional applications) and establishing a fully automated software supply chain based on containers, they can reduce the cost for the maintenance of those mission-critical applications by a factor of 50% to 60% and they can reduce the time between new releases of these traditional applications by up to 90%. That being said, the adoption of container technologies saves these companies a lot of money, and at the same time, it speeds up the development process and reduces the time to market.

The Moby project

Originally, when Docker (the company) introduced Docker containers, everything was open source. Docker did not have any commercial products then. Docker Engine, which the company developed, was a monolithic piece of software. It contained many logical parts, such as the container runtime, a network library, a RESTful (REST) API, a command-line interface, and much more. Other vendors or projects such as Red Hat or Kubernetes used Docker Engine in their own products, but most of the time, they were only using part of its functionality. For example, Kubernetes did not use the Docker network library for Docker Engine but provided its own way of networking. Red Hat, in turn, did not update Docker Engine frequently and preferred to apply unofficial patches to older versions of Docker Engine, yet they still called it Docker Engine.

For all these reasons, and many more, the idea emerged that Docker had to do something to clearly separate Docker's open source part from Docker's commercial part. Furthermore, the company wanted to prevent competitors from using and abusing the name Docker for their own gains. This was the main reason the Moby project was born. It serves as an umbrella for most of the open source components Docker developed and continues to develop. These open source projects do not carry the name Docker anymore. The Moby project provides components used for image management, secret management, configuration management, and networking and provisioning. Also, part of the Moby project are special Moby tools that are, for example, used to assemble components into runnable artifacts. Some components that technically belong to the Moby project have been donated by Docker to the **Cloud Native Computing Foundation** (**CNCF**) and thus do not appear in the list of components anymore. The most prominent ones are **notary**, **containerd**, and **runc**, where the first is used for content trust and the latter two form the container runtime.

In the words of Docker, "*... Moby is an open framework created by Docker to assemble specialized container systems without reinventing the wheel. It provides a "Lego set" of dozens of standard components and a framework for assembling them into custom platforms....*"

Docker products

In the past, up until 2019, Docker separated its product lines into two segments. There was the **Community Edition** (**CE**), which was closed source yet completely free, and then there was the **Enterprise Edition** (**EE**), which was also closed source and needed to be licensed yearly. These enterprise products were backed by 24/7 support and were supported by bug fixes.

In 2019, Docker felt that what they had were two very distinct and different businesses. Consequently, they split away the EE and sold it to Mirantis. Docker itself wanted to refocus on developers and provide them with the optimal tools and support to build containerized applications.

Docker Desktop

Part of the Docker offering are products such as Docker Toolbox and Docker Desktop with its editions for Mac, Windows, and Linux. All these products are mainly targeted at developers. Docker Desktop is an easy-to-install desktop application that can be used to build, debug, and test dockerized applications or services on a macOS, Windows, or Linux machine. Docker Desktop is a complete development environment that is deeply integrated with the hypervisor framework, network, and filesystem of the respective underlying operating system. These tools are the fastest and most reliable ways to run Docker on a Mac, Windows, or Linux machine.

> Note
>
> Docker Toolbox has been deprecated and is no longer in active development. Docker recommends using Docker Desktop instead.

Docker Hub

Docker Hub is the most popular service for finding and sharing container images. It is possible to create individual, user-specific accounts and organizational accounts under which Docker images can be uploaded and shared inside a team, an organization, or with the wider public. Public accounts are free while private accounts require one of several commercial licenses. Later in this book, we will use Docker Hub to download existing Docker images and upload and share our own custom Docker images.

Docker Enterprise Edition

Docker EE – now owned by Mirantis – consists of the **Universal Control Plane** (**UCP**) and the **Docker Trusted Registry** (**DTR**), both of which run on top of Docker Swarm. Both are Swarm applications. Docker EE builds on top of the upstream components of the Moby project and adds enterprise-grade features such as **role-based access control** (**RBAC**), multi-tenancy, mixed clusters of Docker Swarm and Kubernetes, a web-based UI, and content trust, as well as image scanning on top.

> Docker Swarm
>
> Docker Swarm provides a powerful and flexible platform for deploying and managing containers in a production environment. It provides the tools and features you need to build, deploy, and manage your applications with ease and confidence.

Container architecture

Now, let us discuss how a system that can run Docker containers is designed at a high level. The following diagram illustrates what a computer that Docker has been installed on looks like. Note that a computer that has Docker installed on it is often called a Docker host because it can run or host Docker containers:

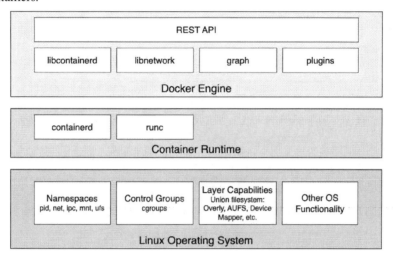

Figure 1.3 – High-level architecture diagram of Docker Engine

In the preceding diagram, we can see three essential parts:

- At the bottom, we have the **Linux Operating System**
- In the middle, we have the **Container Runtime**
- At the top, we have **Docker Engine**

Containers are only possible because the Linux OS supplies some primitives, such as namespaces, control groups, layer capabilities, and more, all of which are used in a specific way by the container runtime and Docker Engine. Linux kernel namespaces, such as process ID (pid) namespaces or network (net) namespaces, allow Docker to encapsulate or sandbox processes that run inside the container. Control groups make sure that containers do not suffer from noisy-neighbor syndrome, where a single application running in a container can consume most or all the available resources of the whole Docker host. Control groups allow Docker to limit the resources, such as CPU time or the amount of RAM, that each container is allocated. The container runtime on a Docker host consists of containerd and runc. runc is the low-level functionality of the container runtime such as container creation or management, while containerd, which is based on runc, provides higher-level functionality such as image management, networking capabilities, or extensibility via plugins. Both are open source and have been donated by Docker to the CNCF. The container runtime is responsible for the whole life cycle of a container. It pulls a container image (which is the template for a container) from a registry, if necessary, creates a container from that image, initializes and runs the container, and eventually stops and removes the container from the system when asked. Docker Engine provides additional functionality on top of the container runtime, such as network libraries or support for plugins. It also provides a REST interface over which all container operations can be automated. The Docker command-line interface that we will use often in this book is one of the consumers of this REST interface.

Summary

In this chapter, we looked at how containers can massively reduce friction in the software supply chain and, on top of that, make the supply chain much more secure. In the next chapter, we will familiarize ourselves with containers. We will learn how to run, stop, and remove containers and otherwise manipulate them. We will also get a pretty good overview of the anatomy of containers. For the first time, we are really going to get our hands dirty and play with these containers. So, stay tuned!

Further reading

The following is a list of links that lead to more detailed information regarding the topics we discussed in this chapter:

- *Docker overview*: `https://docs.docker.com/engine/docker-overview/`
- *The Moby project*: `https://mobyproject.org/`
- *Docker products*: `https://www.docker.com/get-started`
- *Docker Desktop*: `https://www.docker.com/products/docker-desktop/`
- *Cloud-Native Computing Foundation*: `https://www.cncf.io/`
- *containerd*: `https://containerd.io/`
- *Getting Started with Docker Enterprise 3.1*: `https://www.mirantis.com/blog/getting-started-with-docker-enterprise-3-1/`

Questions

Please answer the following questions to assess your learning progress:

1. Which statements are correct (multiple answers are possible)?

    A. A container is kind of a lightweight VM

    B. A container only runs on a Linux host

    C. A container can only run one process

    D. The main process in a container always has PID 1

    E. A container is one or more processes encapsulated by Linux namespaces and restricted
        by cgroups

2. In your own words, using analogies, explain what a container is.

3. Why are containers considered to be a game-changer in IT? Name three or four reasons.

4. What does it mean when we claim, if a container runs on a given platform, then it runs anywhere?
    Name two to three reasons why this is true.

5. Is the following claim true or false: *Docker containers are only useful for modern greenfield
    applications based on microservices*? Please justify your answer.

6. How much does a typical enterprise save when containerizing its legacy applications?

    A. 20%

    B. 33%

    C. 50%

    D. 75%

7. Which two core concepts of Linux are containers based on?

8. On which operating systems is Docker Desktop available?

Answers

1. The correct answers are *D* and *E*.

2. A Docker container is to IT what a shipping container is to the transportation industry. It defines
    a standard on how to package goods. In this case, goods are the application(s) developers write.
    The suppliers (in this case, the developers) are responsible for packaging the goods into the
    container and making sure everything fits as expected. Once the goods are packaged into a
    container, it can be shipped. Since it is a standard container, the shippers can standardize their
    means of transportation, such as lorries, trains, or ships. The shipper does not really care what
    is in the container. Also, the loading and unloading process from one means of transportation

to another (for example, train to ship) can be highly standardized. This massively increases the efficiency of transportation. Analogous to this is an operations engineer in IT, who can take a software container built by a developer and ship it to a production system and run it there in a highly standardized way, without worrying about what is in the container. It will just work.

3. Some of the reasons why containers are game-changers are as follows:

    - Containers are self-contained and thus if they run on one system, they run anywhere that a Docker container can run.

    - Containers run on-premises and in the cloud, as well as in hybrid environments. This is important for today's typical enterprises since it allows a smooth transition from on-premises to the cloud.

    - Container images are built or packaged by the people who know best – the developers.

    - Container images are immutable, which is important for good release management.

    - Containers are enablers of a secure software supply chain based on encapsulation (using Linux namespaces and cgroups), secrets, content trust, and image vulnerability scanning.

4. A container runs on any system that can host containers. This is possible for the following reasons:

    - Containers are self-contained black boxes. They encapsulate not only an application but also all its dependencies, such as libraries and frameworks, configuration data, certificates, and so on.

    - Containers are based on widely accepted standards such as OCI.

5. The answer is false. Containers are useful for modern applications and to containerize traditional applications. The benefits for an enterprise when doing the latter are huge. Cost savings in the maintenance of legacy apps of 50% or more have been reported. The time between new releases of such legacy applications could be reduced by up to 90%. These numbers have been publicly reported by real enterprise customers.

6. 50% or more.

7. Containers are based on Linux **namespaces** (network, process, user, and so on) and **cgroups**. The former help isolate processes running on the same machine, while the latter are used to limit the resources a given process can access, such as memory or network bandwidth.

8. Docker Desktop is available for macOS, Windows, and Linux.

2

Setting Up a Working Environment

In the previous chapter, we learned what Docker containers are and why they're important. We learned what kinds of problems containers solve in a modern software supply chain. In this chapter, we are going to prepare our personal or working environment to work efficiently and effectively with Docker. We will discuss in detail how to set up an ideal environment for developers, DevOps, and operators that can be used when working with Docker containers.

This chapter covers the following topics:

- The Linux command shell
- PowerShell for Windows
- Installing and using a package manager
- Installing Git and cloning the code repository
- Choosing and installing a code editor
- Installing Docker Desktop on macOS or Windows
- Installing Docker Toolbox
- Enabling Kubernetes on Docker Desktop
- Installing minikube
- Installing Kind

Technical requirements

For this chapter, you will need a laptop or a workstation with either macOS or Windows, preferably Windows 11, installed. You should also have free internet access to download applications and permission to install those applications on your laptop. It is also possible to follow along with this book if you have a Linux distribution as your operating system, such as Ubuntu 18.04 or newer. I will try to indicate where commands and samples differ significantly from the ones on macOS or Windows.

The Linux command shell

Docker containers were first developed on Linux for Linux. Hence, it is natural that the primary command-line tool used to work with Docker, also called a shell, is a Unix shell; remember, Linux derives from Unix. Most developers use the Bash shell. On some lightweight Linux distributions, such as Alpine, Bash is not installed and consequently, you must use the simpler Bourne shell, just called sh. Whenever we are working in a Linux environment, such as inside a container or on a Linux VM, we will use either /bin/bash or /bin/sh, depending on their availability.

Although Apple's macOS is not a Linux OS, Linux and macOS are both flavors of Unix and hence support the same set of tools. Among those tools are the shells. So, when working on macOS, you will probably be using the Bash or zsh shell.

In this book, we expect you to be familiar with the most basic scripting commands in Bash and PowerShell, if you are working on Windows. If you are an absolute beginner, then we strongly recommend that you familiarize yourself with the following cheat sheets:

- *Linux Command Line Cheat Sheet* by Dave Child at http://bit.ly/2mTQr8l
- *PowerShell Basic Cheat Sheet* at http://bit.ly/2EPHxze

PowerShell for Windows

On a Windows computer, laptop, or server, we have multiple command-line tools available. The most familiar is the command shell. It has been available on any Windows computer for decades. It is a very simple shell. For more advanced scripting, Microsoft has developed PowerShell. PowerShell is very powerful and very popular among engineers working on Windows. Finally, on Windows 10 or later, we have the so-called Windows Subsystem for Linux, which allows us to use any Linux tool, such as the Bash or Bourne shells. Apart from this, other tools install a Bash shell on Windows, such as the Git Bash shell. In this book, all commands will use Bash syntax. Most of the commands also run in PowerShell.

Therefore, we recommend that you either use PowerShell or any other Bash tool to work with Docker on Windows.

Installing and using a package manager

The easiest way to install software on a Linux, macOS, or Windows laptop is to use a good package manager. On macOS, most people use Homebrew, while on Windows, Chocolatey is a good choice. If you're using a Debian-based Linux distribution such as Ubuntu, then the package manager of choice for most is apt, which is installed by default.

Installing Homebrew on macOS

Homebrew is the most popular package manager on macOS, and it is easy to use and very versatile. Installing Homebrew on macOS is simple; just follow the instructions at `https://brew.sh/`:

1. In a nutshell, open a new Terminal window and execute the following command to install Homebrew:

    ```
    $ /usr/bin/ruby -e "$(curl -fsSL https://raw.
    githubusercontent.com/Homebrew/install/HEAD/install.sh)"
    ```

2. Once the installation has finished, test whether Homebrew is working by entering `brew --version` in the Terminal. You should see something like this:

    ```
    $ brew --version
    Homebrew 3.6.16
    Homebrew/homebrew-core (git revision 025fe79713b; last
    commit 2022-12-26)
    Homebrew/homebrew-cask (git revision 15acb0b64a; last
    commit 2022-12-26)
    ```

3. Now, we are ready to use Homebrew to install tools and utilities. If we, for example, want to install the iconic Vi text editor (note that this is not a tool we will use in this book; it serves just as an example), we can do so like this:

    ```
    $ brew install vim
    ```

This will download and install the editor for you.

Installing Chocolatey on Windows

Chocolatey is a popular package manager for Windows, built on PowerShell. To install the Chocolatey package manager, please follow the instructions at `https://chocolatey.org/` or open a new PowerShell window in admin mode and execute the following command:

```
PS> Set-ExecutionPolicy Bypass -Scope Process -Force; iex
((New-Object System.Net.WebClient).DownloadString('https://
chocolatey.org/install.ps1'))
```

> **Note**
>
> It is important to run the preceding command as an administrator; otherwise, the installation will not succeed. It is also important to note that the preceding command is one single line and has only been broken into several lines here due to the limited line width.

Once Chocolatey has been installed, test it with the `choco --version` command. You should see output similar to the following:

```
PS> choco --version
0.10.15
```

To install an application such as the Vi editor, use the following command:

```
PS> choco install -y vim
```

The `-y` parameter makes sure that the installation happens without Chocolatey asking for a reconfirmation. As mentioned previously, we will not use Vim in our exercises; it has only been used as an example.

> **Note**
>
> Once Chocolatey has installed an application, you may need to open a new PowerShell window to use that application.

Installing Git and cloning the code repository

We will be using Git to clone the sample code accompanying this book from its GitHub repository. If you already have Git installed on your computer, you can skip this section:

1. To install Git on macOS, use the following command in a Terminal window:

   ```
   $ brew install git
   ```

2. To install Git on Windows, open a PowerShell window and use Chocolatey to install it:

   ```
   PS> choco install git -y
   ```

3. Finally, on a Debian or Ubuntu machine, open a Bash console and execute the following command:

   ```
   $ sudo apt update && sudo apt install -y git
   ```

4. Once Git has been installed, verify that it is working. On all platforms, use the following command:

   ```
   $ git --version
   ```

   This should output the version of Git that's been installed. On the author's MacBook Air, the output is as follows:

   ```
   git version 2.39.1
   ```

> **Note**
>
> If you see an older version, then you are probably using the version that came installed with macOS by default. Use Homebrew to install the latest version by running $ `brew install git`.

5. Now that Git is working, we can clone the source code accompanying this book from GitHub. Execute the following command:

```
$ cd ~
$ git clone https://github.com/PacktPublishing/
The-Ultimate-Docker-Container-Book
```

This will clone the content of the main branch into your local folder, `~/The-Ultimate-Docker-Container-Book`. This folder will now contain all of the sample solutions for the labs we are going to do together in this book. Refer to these sample solutions if you get stuck.

Now that we have installed the basics, let's continue with the code editor.

Choosing and installing a code editor

Using a good code editor is essential to working productively with Docker. Of course, which editor is the best is highly controversial and depends on your personal preference. A lot of people use Vim, or others such as Emacs, Atom, Sublime, or **Visual Studio Code** (**VS Code**), to just name a few. VS Code is a completely free and lightweight editor, yet it is very powerful and is available for macOS, Windows, and Linux. According to Stack Overflow, it is currently by far the most popular code editor. If you are not yet sold on another editor, I highly recommend that you give VS Code a try.

But if you already have a favorite code editor, then please continue using it. So long as you can edit text files, you're good to go. If your editor supports syntax highlighting for Dockerfiles and JSON and YAML files, then even better. The only exception will be *Chapter 6*, *Debugging Code Running in Containers*. The examples presented in that chapter will be heavily tailored toward VS Code.

Installing VS Code on macOS

Follow these steps for installation:

1. Open a new Terminal window and execute the following command:

```
$ brew cask install visual-studio-code
```

2. Once VS Code has been installed successfully, navigate to your home directory:

```
$ cd ~
```

3. Now, open VS Code from within this folder:

```
$ code The-Ultimate-Docker-Container-Book
```

VS will start and open the The-Ultimate-Docker-Container-Book folder, where you just downloaded the repository that contains the source code for this book, as the working folder.

> **Note**
>
> If you already have VS Code installed without using brew, then the guide at https://code.visualstudio.com/docs/setup/mac#_launching-from-the-command-line will add code to your path.

4. Use VS Code to explore the code that you can see in the folder you just opened.

Installing VS Code on Windows

Follow these steps for installation:

1. Open a new PowerShell window in *admin mode* and execute the following command:

```
PS> choco install vscode -y
```

2. Close your PowerShell window and open a new one, to make sure VS Code is in your path.

3. Now, navigate to your home directory:

```
PS> cd ~
```

4. Now, open VS Code from within this folder:

```
PS> code The-Ultimate-Docker-Container-Book
```

VS will start and open the The-Ultimate-Docker-Container-Book folder, where you just downloaded the repository that contains the source code for this book, as the working folder.

5. Use VS Code to explore the code that you can see in the folder you just opened.

Installing VS Code on Linux

Follow these steps for installation:

1. On your Debian or Ubuntu-based Linux machine, you can use Snap to install VS Code. Open a Bash Terminal and execute the following statement to install VS Code:

```
$ sudo snap install --classic code
```

2. If you're using a Linux distribution that's not based on Debian or Ubuntu, then please follow the following link for more details: `https://code.visualstudio.com/docs/setup/linux`.

3. Once VS Code has been installed successfully, navigate to your home directory:

    ```
    $ cd ~
    ```

4. Now, open VS Code from within this folder:

    ```
    $ code The-Ultimate-Docker-Container-Book
    ```

    VS will start and open the `The-Ultimate-Docker-Container-Book` folder, where you just downloaded the repository that contains the source code for this book, as the working folder.

5. Use VS Code to explore the code that you can see in the folder you just opened.

Installing VS Code extensions

Extensions are what make VS Code such a versatile editor. On all three platforms (macOS, Windows, and Linux), you can install VS Code extensions the same way:

1. Open a Bash console (or PowerShell in Windows) and execute the following group of commands to install the most essential extensions we are going to use in the upcoming examples in this book:

    ```
    code --install-extension vscjava.vscode-java-pack
    code --install-extension ms-dotnettools.csharp
    code --install-extension ms-python.python
    code --install-extension ms-azuretools.vscode-docker
    code --install-extension eamodio.gitlens
    ```

    We are installing extensions that enable us to work with Java, C#, .NET, and Python much more productively. We're also installing an extension built to enhance our experience with Docker.

2. After the preceding extensions have been installed successfully, restart VS Code to activate the extensions. You can now click the **Extensions** icon in the **activity** pane on the left-hand side of VS Code to see all of the installed extensions.

3. To get a list of all installed extensions in your VS Code, use this command:

    ```
    $ code --list-extensions
    ```

Next, let's install Docker Desktop.

Installing Docker Desktop on macOS or Windows

If you are using macOS or have Windows 10 or later installed on your laptop, then we strongly recommend that you install Docker Desktop. Since early 2022, Docker has also released a version of Docker Desktop for Linux. Docker Desktop gives you the best experience when working with containers. Follow these steps to install Docker Desktop for your system:

1. No matter what OS you're using, navigate to the Docker start page at `https://www.docker.com/get-started`:

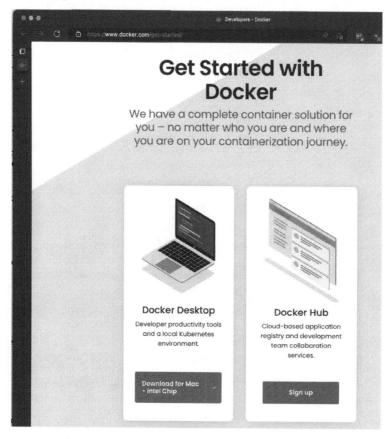

Figure 2.1 – Get Started with Docker

2. On the right-hand side of the view, you will find a blue **Sign up** button for Docker Hub. Click this button if you don't have an account on Docker Hub yet, then create one. It is free, but you need an account to download the software.

3. On the left-hand side of the view, you will find a blue button called **Download for <your OS>**, where **<your OS>** can be Linux, Mac, or Windows, depending on which OS you are working with. In the authors' case, it shows Mac as the target OS, but it got the CPU type wrong since the author is using a Mac with Apple's M1 chip.

    Click the small drop-down triangle on the right-hand side of the button to get the full list of available downloads:

Figure 2.2 – List of Docker Desktop targets

    Select the one that is appropriate for you and observe the installation package being downloaded.

4. Once the package has been completely downloaded, proceed with the installation, usually by double-clicking on the download package.

Testing Docker Engine

Now that you have successfully installed Docker Desktop, let's test it. We will start by running a simple Docker container directly from the command line:

1. Open a Terminal window and execute the following command:

    ```
    $ docker version
    ```

    You should see something like this:

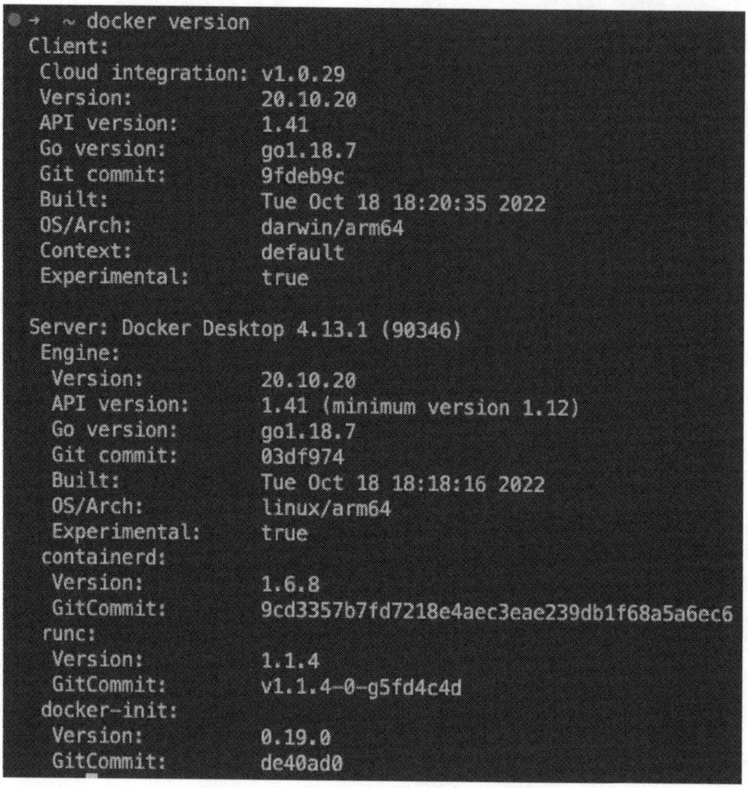

```
●  →   ~ docker version
Client:
 Cloud integration: v1.0.29
 Version:           20.10.20
 API version:       1.41
 Go version:        go1.18.7
 Git commit:        9fdeb9c
 Built:             Tue Oct 18 18:20:35 2022
 OS/Arch:           darwin/arm64
 Context:           default
 Experimental:      true

Server: Docker Desktop 4.13.1 (90346)
 Engine:
  Version:          20.10.20
  API version:      1.41 (minimum version 1.12)
  Go version:       go1.18.7
  Git commit:       03df974
  Built:            Tue Oct 18 18:18:16 2022
  OS/Arch:          linux/arm64
  Experimental:     true
 containerd:
  Version:          1.6.8
  GitCommit:        9cd3357b7fd7218e4aec3eae239db1f68a5a6ec6
 runc:
  Version:          1.1.4
  GitCommit:        v1.1.4-0-g5fd4c4d
 docker-init:
  Version:          0.19.0
  GitCommit:        de40ad0
```

Figure 2.3 – Docker version of Docker Desktop

In the preceding output, we can see that it consists of two parts – a client and a server. Here, the server corresponds to Docker Engine, which is responsible for hosting and running containers. At the time of writing, the version of Docker Engine is 20.10.21.

2. To see whether you can run containers, enter the following command into the Terminal window and hit *Enter*:

```
$ docker container run hello-world
```

If all goes well, your output should look something like the following:

```
● →  ~ docker container run hello-world
Unable to find image 'hello-world:latest' locally
latest: Pulling from library/hello-world
7050e35b49f5: Pull complete
Digest: sha256:e18f0a777aefabe047a671ab3ec3eed05414477c951ab1a6f352a06974245fe7
Status: Downloaded newer image for hello-world:latest

Hello from Docker!
This message shows that your installation appears to be working correctly.

To generate this message, Docker took the following steps:
 1. The Docker client contacted the Docker daemon.
 2. The Docker daemon pulled the "hello-world" image from the Docker Hub.
    (arm64v8)
 3. The Docker daemon created a new container from that image which runs the
    executable that produces the output you are currently reading.
 4. The Docker daemon streamed that output to the Docker client, which sent it
    to your terminal.

To try something more ambitious, you can run an Ubuntu container with:
 $ docker run -it ubuntu bash

Share images, automate workflows, and more with a free Docker ID:
 https://hub.docker.com/

For more examples and ideas, visit:
 https://docs.docker.com/get-started/
```

Figure 2.4 – Running Hello-World on Docker Desktop for macOS

If you read the preceding output carefully, you will have noticed that Docker didn't find an image called hello-world:latest and thus decided to download it from a Docker image registry. Once downloaded, Docker Engine created a container from the image and ran it. The application runs inside the container and then outputs all the text, starting with Hello from Docker!.

This is proof that Docker is installed and working correctly on your machine.

3. Let's try another funny test image that's usually used to check the Docker installation. Run the following command:

```
$ docker container run rancher/cowsay Hello
```

You should see this or a similar output:

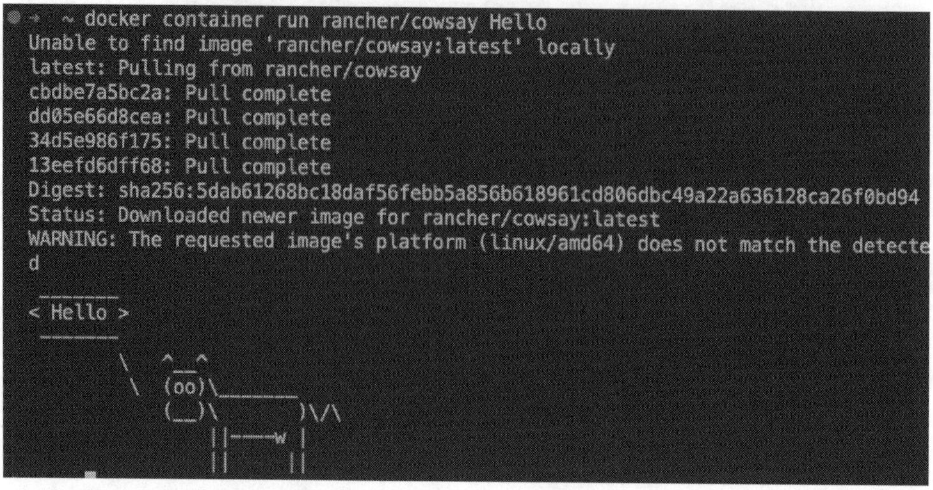

```
 ● →  ~ docker container run rancher/cowsay Hello
   Unable to find image 'rancher/cowsay:latest' locally
   latest: Pulling from rancher/cowsay
   cbdbe7a5bc2a: Pull complete
   dd05e66d8cea: Pull complete
   34d5e986f175: Pull complete
   13eefd6dff68: Pull complete
   Digest: sha256:5dab61268bc18daf56febb5a856b618961cd806dbc49a22a636128ca26f0bd94
   Status: Downloaded newer image for rancher/cowsay:latest
   WARNING: The requested image's platform (linux/amd64) does not match the detecte
   d
    _____
   < Hello >
    -----------
            \    ^__^
             \  (oo)_____
                (__)\          )\/\
                  ||----w |
                  ||      ||
```

Figure 2.5 – Running the cowsay image from Rancher

Great – we have confirmed that Docker Engine works on our local computer. Now, let's make sure the same is true for Docker Desktop.

Testing Docker Desktop

Depending on the operating system you are working with, be it Linux, Mac, or Windows, you can access the context menu for Docker Desktop in different areas. In any case, the symbol you are looking for is the little whale carrying containers. Here is the symbol as found on a Mac – 🐳 :

- **Mac**: You'll find the icon on the right-hand side of your menu bar at the top of the screen.
- **Windows**: You'll find the icon in the Windows system tray.
- **Linux**: *Here are the instructions for Ubuntu. On your distro, it may be different.* To start Docker Desktop for Linux, search for `Docker Desktop` via the **Applications** menu and open it. This will launch the Docker menu icon and open the Docker dashboard, reporting the status of Docker Desktop.

Once you have located the context menu for Docker Desktop on your computer, proceed with the following steps:

1. Click the *whale* icon to display the context menu of Docker Desktop. On the authors' Mac, it looks like this:

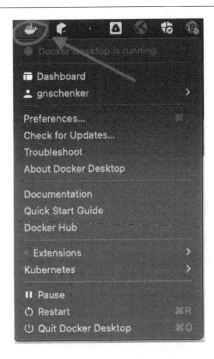

Figure 2.6 – Context menu for Docker Desktop

2.   From the menu, select **Dashboard**. The dashboard of Docker Desktop will open:

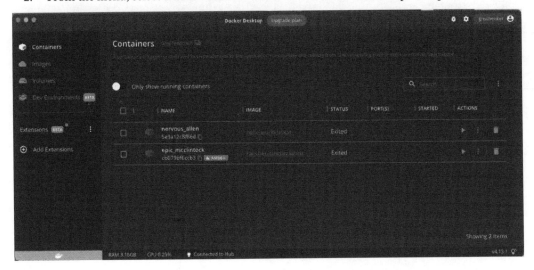

Figure 2.7 – Dashboard of Docker Desktop

We can see that the dashboard has multiple tabs, indicated on the left-hand side of the view. Currently, the **Containers** tab is active. Consequently, we can see the list of containers found in our system. Currently, on the author's system, two have been found. If you inspect this carefully, you will see that these are the containers that we previously created from the `hello-world` and `rancher/cowsay` Docker images. They both have a status of **Exited**.

Please take some time and explore this dashboard a bit. Don't worry if you get lost. It will all become much clearer as we proceed through the various chapters of this book.

3.   When you're done exploring, close the dashboard window.

> **Note**
>
> Closing the dashboard will not stop Docker Desktop. The application, as well as Docker Engine, will continue to run in the background. If for some reason you want to stop Docker on your system completely, you can select **Quit Docker Desktop** from the context menu shown in *Step 1*.

Congratulations, you have successfully installed and tested Docker Desktop on your working computer! Now, let's continue with a few other useful tools.

Installing Docker Toolbox

Docker Toolbox has been available for developers for a few years. It precedes newer tools such as Docker Desktop. Toolbox allows a user to work very elegantly with containers on any macOS or Windows computer. Containers must run on a Linux host. Neither Windows nor macOS can run containers natively. Hence, we need to run a Linux VM on our laptop, where we can then run our containers. Docker Toolbox installs VirtualBox on our laptop, which is used to run the Linux VMs we need.

> **Note**
>
> Docker Toolbox has been deprecated recently and thus we won't be discussing it further. For certain scenarios, it may still be of interest though, which is why we are mentioning it here.

Enabling Kubernetes on Docker Desktop

Docker Desktop comes with integrated support for Kubernetes.

> **What is Kubernetes?**
>
> Kubernetes is a powerful platform for automating the deployment, scaling, and management of containerized applications. Whether you're a developer, DevOps engineer, or system administrator, Kubernetes provides the tools and abstractions you need to manage your containers and applications in a scalable and efficient manner.

This support is turned off by default. But worry not – it is very easy to turn on:

1. Open the dashboard of Docker Desktop.

2. In the top-left corner, select the cog wheel icon. This will open the **settings** page.

3. On the left-hand side, select the **Kubernetes** tab and then check the **Enable Kubernetes** checkbox:

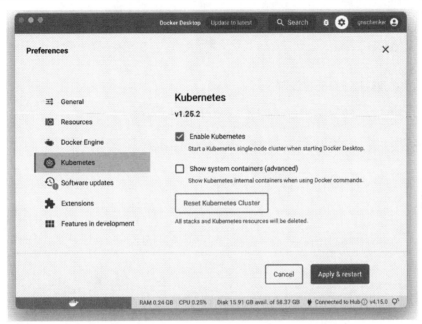

Figure 2.8 – Enabling Kubernetes on Docker Desktop

4. Click the **Apply & restart** button.

Now, you will have to be patient since Docker is downloading all the supporting infrastructure and then starting Kubernetes.

Once Docker has restarted, you are ready to use Kubernetes. Please refer to the *Installing minikube* section on how to test Kubernetes.

Installing minikube

If you are using Docker Desktop, you may not need minikube at all since the former already provides out-of-the-box support for Kubernetes. If you cannot use Docker Desktop or, for some reason, you only have access to an older version of the tool that does not yet support Kubernetes, then it is a good idea to install minikube. minikube provisions a single-node Kubernetes cluster on your workstation and is accessible through kubectl, which is the command-line tool used to work with Kubernetes.

Installing minikube on Linux, macOS, and Windows

To install minikube on Linux, macOS, or Windows, navigate to the following link: `https://kubernetes.io/docs/tasks/tools/install-minikube/`.

Follow the instructions carefully. Specifically, do the following:

1. Make sure you have a hypervisor installed, as described here:

    Documentation / Get Started!

    # minikube start

    minikube is local Kubernetes, focusing on making it easy to learn and develop for Kubernetes.

    All you need is Docker (or similarly compatible) container or a Virtual Machine environment, and Kubernetes is a single command away: `minikube start`

    ## What you'll need ⊝

    - 2 CPUs or more
    - 2GB of free memory
    - 20GB of free disk space
    - Internet connection
    - Container or virtual machine manager, such as: Docker, Hyperkit, Hyper-V, KVM, Parallels, Podman, VirtualBox, or VMware Fusion/Workstation

Figure 2.9 – Prerequisites for minikube

2. Under **1 Installation**, select the combination that is valid for you. As an example, you can see the authors' selection for a *MacBook Air M1 laptop* as the target machine:

Figure 2.10 – Selecting the configuration

Installing minikube for a MacBook Air M1 using Homebrew

Follow these steps:

1. In a Terminal window, execute the steps shown previously. In the authors' case, this is as follows:

    ```
    $ brew install minikube
    ```

2. Test the installation with the following command:

    ```
    $ brew version
    minikube version: v1.28.0
    commit: 986b1ebd987211ed16f8cc10aed7d2c42fc8392f
    ```

3. Now, we're ready to start a cluster. Let's start with the default:

    ```
    $ minikube start
    ```

> **Note**
>
> minikube allows you to define single and multi-node clusters.

4. The first time you do this, it will take a while since minikube needs to download all the Kubernetes binaries. When it's done, the last line of the output on your screen should be something like this:

```
Done! kubectl is now configured to use "minikube" cluster
and "default" namespace by default
```

Great, we have successfully installed minikube on our system! Let's try to play with minikube a bit by creating a cluster and running our first application in a container on it. Don't worry if the following commands do not make a lot of sense to you at this time. We will discuss everything in this book in the coming chapters.

Testing minikube and kubectl

Let's start. Please follow these steps carefully:

1. Let's try to access our cluster using kubectl. First, we need to make sure we have the correct context selected for kubectl. If you have previously installed Docker Desktop and now minikube, you can use the following command:

```
$ kubectl config get-contexts
```

You should see this:

```
● →  The-Ultimate-Docker-Container-Book git:(main) ✗ kubectl config get-contexts
CURRENT   NAME            CLUSTER         AUTHINFO        NAMESPACE
          docker-desktop  docker-desktop  docker-desktop
*         minikube        minikube        minikube        default
```

Figure 2.11 – List of contexts for kubectl after installing minikube

The asterisk next to the context called minikube tells us that this is the current context. Thus, when using kubectl, we will work with the new cluster created by minikube.

2. Now, let's see how many nodes our cluster has with this command:

```
$ kubectl get nodes
```

You should get something similar to this. Note that the version shown could differ in your case:

```
● →  The-Ultimate-Docker-Container-Book git:(main) ✗ kubectl get nodes
NAME       STATUS   ROLES          AGE    VERSION
minikube   Ready    control-plane  9m9s   v1.25.3
```

Figure 2.12 – Showing the list of cluster nodes for the minikube cluster

Here, we have a single-node cluster. The node's role is that of the control plane, which means it is a master node. A typical Kubernetes cluster consists of a few master nodes and many worker nodes. The version of Kubernetes we're working with here is v1.25.3.

3. Now, let's try to run something on this cluster. We will use Nginx, a popular web server for this. If you have previously cloned the GitHub repository accompanying this book to the `The-Ultimate-Docker-Container-Book` folder in your home directory (~), then you should find a folder setup inside this folder that contains a `.yaml` file, which we're going to use for this test:

    I.   Open a new Terminal window.

    II.   Navigate to the `The-Ultimate-Docker-Container-Book` folder:

    ```
    $ cd ~/The-Ultimate-Docker-Container-Book
    ```

    III. Create a pod running Nginx with the following command:

    ```
    $ kubectl apply -f setup/nginx.yaml
    ```

    You should see this output:

    ```
    pod/nginx created
    ```

    IV.   We can double-check whether the pod is running with kubectl:

    ```
    $ kubectl get pods
    ```

    We should see this:

    ```
    NAME       READY    STATUS     RESTARTS    AGE
    nginx      1/1      Running    0           11m
    ```

    This indicates that we have 1 pod with Nginx running and that it has been restarted 0 times.

4. To access the Nginx server, we need to expose the application running in the pod with the following command:

    ```
    $ kubectl expose pod nginx --type=NodePort --port=80
    ```

    This is the only way can we access Nginx from our laptop – for example, via a browser. With the preceding command, we're creating a Kubernetes service, as indicated in the output generated for the command:

    ```
    service/nginx exposed
    ```

5. We can use kubectl to list all the services defined in our cluster:

    ```
    $ kubectl get services
    ```

We should see this:

```
  → The-Ultimate-Docker-Container-Book git:(main) x kubectl get services
NAME         TYPE        CLUSTER-IP       EXTERNAL-IP   PORT(S)        AGE
kubernetes   ClusterIP   10.96.0.1        <none>        443/TCP        59m
nginx        NodePort    10.104.77.208    <none>        80:30373/TCP   11m
```

Figure 2.13 – List of services on the minikube cluster

In the preceding output, we can see the second service called Nginx, which we just created. The service is of the NodePort type; port 80 of the pod had been mapped to port 30373 of the cluster node of our Kubernetes cluster in minikube.

6. Now, we can use minikube to make a tunnel to our cluster and open a browser with the correct URL to access the Nginx web server. Use this command:

```
$ minikube service nginx
```

The output in your Terminal window will be as follows:

```
  → The-Ultimate-Docker-Container-Book git:(main) x minikube service nginx
|-----------|-------|-------------|---------------------------|
| NAMESPACE | NAME  | TARGET PORT |            URL            |
|-----------|-------|-------------|---------------------------|
| default   | nginx |          80 | http://192.168.49.2:30373 |
|-----------|-------|-------------|---------------------------|
  Starting tunnel for service nginx.
|-----------|-------|-------------|---------------------------|
| NAMESPACE | NAME  | TARGET PORT |            URL            |
|-----------|-------|-------------|---------------------------|
| default   | nginx |             | http://127.0.0.1:64171    |
|-----------|-------|-------------|---------------------------|
  Opening service default/nginx in default browser...
  Because you are using a Docker driver on darwin, the terminal needs to be open to run it.
```

Figure 2.14 – Opening access to the Kubernetes cluster on minikube

The preceding output shows that minikube created a tunnel for the nginx service listening on node port 30373 to port 64171 on the host, which is on our laptop.

7. A new browser tab should have been opened automatically and should have navigated you to http://127.0.0.1:64171. You should see the welcome screen for Nginx:

Figure 2.15 – Welcome screen of Nginx running on a Kubernetes cluster on minikube

Wonderful, we have successfully run and accessed an Nginx web server on our little single-node Kubernetes cluster on minikube! Once you are done playing around, it is time to clean up:

1. Stop the tunnel to the cluster by pressing *Ctrl + C* inside your Terminal window.

2. Delete the nginx service and pod on the cluster:

    ```
    $ kubectl delete service nginx
    $ kubectl delete pod nginx
    ```

3. Stop the cluster with the following command:

    ```
    $ minikube stop
    ```

4. You should see this:

    ```
    ● →  The-Ultimate-Docker-Container-Book git:(main) ✗ minikube stop
    ✋  Stopping node "minikube"  ...
    ●  Powering off "minikube" via SSH ...
    ●  1 node stopped.
    ```

Figure 2.16 – Stopping minikube

Working with a multi-node minikube cluster

At times, testing with a single-node cluster is not enough. Worry not – minikube has got you covered. Follow these instructions to create a true multi-node Kubernetes cluster in minikube:

1. If we want to work with a cluster consisting of multiple nodes in minikube, we can use this command:

    ```
    $ minikube start --nodes 3 -p demo
    ```

    The preceding command creates a cluster with three nodes and calls it demo.

2. Use kubectl to list all your cluster nodes:

    ```
    $ kubectl get nodes
    NAME          STATUS    ROLES           AGE    VERSION
    demo          Ready     control-plane   84s    v1.25.3
    demo-m02      Ready     <none>          45s    v1.25.3
    demo-m03      Ready     <none>          22s    v1.25.3
    ```

    We have a 3-node cluster where the demo node is a master node, and the two remaining nodes are work nodes.

3. We are not going to go any further with this example here, so use the following command to stop the cluster:

    ```
    $ minikube stop -p demo
    ```

4. Delete all the clusters on your system with this command:

    ```
    $ minikube delete --all
    ```

    This will delete the default cluster (called minikube) and the demo cluster in our case.

With this, we will move on to the next interesting tool useful when working with containers and Kubernetes. You should have this installed and readily available on your work computer.

Installing Kind

Kind is another popular tool that can be used to run a multi-node Kubernetes cluster locally on your machine. It is super easy to install and use. Let's go:

1. Use the appropriate package manager for your platform to install Kind. You can find more detailed information about the installation process here: https://kind.sigs.k8s.io/docs/user/quick-start/:

    I.   On MacOS, use Homebrew to install Kind with the following command:

    ```
    $ brew install kind
    ```

    II. On a Windows machine, use Chocolatey to do the same with this command:

```
$ choco install kind -y
```

III.   Finally, on a Linux machine, you can use the following script to install Kind from its binaries:

```
$ curl -Lo ./kind https://kind.sigs.k8s.io/dl/v0.17.0/
kind-linux-amd64
$ chmod +x ./kind
$ sudo mv ./kind /usr/local/bin/kind
```

2.   Once Kind has been installed, test it with the following command:

```
$ kind version
```

If you're on a Mac, it should output something like this:

```
kind v0.17.0 go1.19.2 darwin/arm64
```

3.   Now, try to create a simple Kubernetes cluster consisting of one master node and two worker nodes. Use this command to accomplish this:

```
$ kind create cluster
```

After some time, you should see this output:

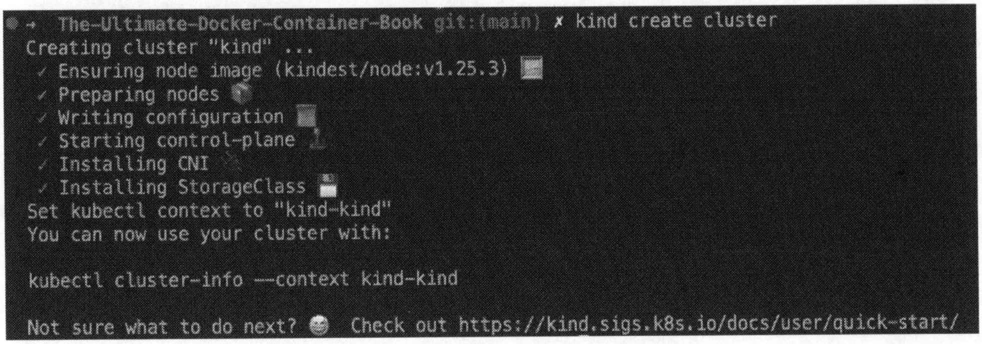

Figure 2.17 – Creating a cluster with Kind

4.   To verify that a cluster has been created, use this command:

```
$ kind get clusters
```

The preceding output shows that there is exactly one cluster called **kind**, which is the default name.

5.   We can create an additional cluster with a different name using the --name parameter, like so:

```
$ kind create cluster --name demo
```

6. Listing the clusters will then show this:

```
$ kind show clusters
Kind
demo
```

And this works as expected.

Testing Kind

Now that we have used kind to create two sample clusters, let's use kubectl to play with one of the clusters and run the first application on it. We will be using Nginx for this, similar to what we did with minikube:

1. We can now use **kubectl** to access and work with the clusters we just created. While creating a cluster, Kind also updated the configuration file for our kubectl. We can double-check this with the following command:

```
$ kubectl config get-contexts
```

It should produce the following output:

```
→  The-Ultimate-Docker-Container-Book git:(main) ✗ k config get-contexts
CURRENT   NAME               CLUSTER            AUTHINFO           NAMESPACE
          docker-desktop     docker-desktop     docker-desktop
*         kind-demo          kind-demo          kind-demo
          kind-kind          kind-kind          kind-kind
```

Figure 2.18 – List of contexts defined for kubectl

You can see that the kind and demo clusters are part of the list of known clusters and that the demo cluster is the current context for kubectl.

2. Use the following command to make the demo cluster your current cluster if the asterisk is indicating that another cluster is current:

```
$ kubectl config use-context kind-demo
```

3. Let's list all the nodes of the sample-cluster cluster:

```
$ kubectl get nodes
```

The output should be like this:

```
→  The-Ultimate-Docker-Container-Book git:(main) ✗ kubectl get nodes
NAME                  STATUS   ROLES           AGE     VERSION
demo-control-plane    Ready    control-plane   2m25s   v1.25.3
```

Figure 2.19 – Showing the list of nodes on the kind cluster

4. Now, let's try to run the first container on this cluster. We will use our trusted Nginx web server, as we did earlier. Use the following command to run it:

```
$ kubectl apply -f setup/nginx.yaml
```

The output should be as follows:

```
pod/nginx created
```

5. To access the Nginx server, we need to do port forwarding using kubectl. Use this command to do so:

```
$ kubectl port-forward nginx 8080 80
```

The output should look like this:

```
Forwarding from 127.0.0.1:8080 -> 80
Forwarding from [::1]:8080 -> 80
```

6. Open a new browser tab and navigate to http://localhost:8080; you should see the welcome screen of Nginx:

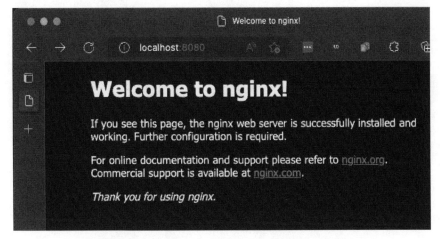

Figure 2.20 – Welcome screen of Nginx running on a Kind cluster

7. Once you've finished playing with Nginx, use this command to delete the pod from the cluster:

```
$ kubectl delete -f setup/nginx.yaml
```

8. Before we continue, let's clean up and delete the two clusters we just created:

```
$ kind delete cluster --name kind
$ kind delete cluster --name demo
```

With this, we have installed all the tools that we will need to successfully work with containers on our local machine.

Summary

In this chapter, we set up and configured our personal or working environment so that we can productively work with Docker containers. This equally applies to developers, DevOps, and operations engineers.

We started with a package manager that should be at the fingertip of every serious engineer. It makes installing and managing applications and tools so much easier. Next, we made sure that we used a good shell for scripting – a powerful editor. We then made sure to have Docker Desktop installed, which we can use to run and test containers natively. Finally, we installed and quickly tested minikube and Kind on our machine. The latter are tools that can be used to run and test our containers on a local Kubernetes cluster.

In the next chapter, we're going to learn important facts about containers. For example, we will explore how we can run, stop, list, and delete containers, but more than that, we will also dive deep into the anatomy of containers.

Further reading

Consider the following links for further reading:

- *Chocolatey – The Package Manager for Windows*: https://chocolatey.org/
- *Run Docker on Hyper-V with Docker Machine*: http://bit.ly/2HGMPiI
- *Developing inside a Container*: https://code.visualstudio.com/docs/remote/containers

Questions

Based on what was covered in this chapter, please answer the following questions:

1. Why would we care about installing and using a package manager on our local computer?
2. With Docker Desktop, you can develop and run Linux containers.

   A. True

   B. False

3. Why are good scripting skills (such as Bash or PowerShell) essential for the productive use of containers?

4. Name three to four Linux distributions on which Docker is certified to run.

5. You installed minikube on your system. What kind of tasks will you use this tool for?

Answers

The following are the answers to this chapter's questions:

1. Package managers such as `apk`, `apt`, or `yum` on Linux systems, Homebrew on macOS, and Chocolatey on Windows make it easy to automate the installation of applications, tools, and libraries. It is a much more repeatable process when an installation happens interactively, and the user has to click through a series of views.

2. The answer is *True*. Yes, with Docker Desktop, you can develop and run Linux containers. It is also possible, but not discussed in this book, to develop and run native Windows containers with this edition of Docker Desktop. With the macOS and Linux editions, you can only develop and run Linux containers.

3. Scripts are used to automate processes and hence avoid human errors. Building, testing, sharing, and running Docker containers are tasks that should always be automated to increase their reliability and repeatability.

4. The following Linux distros are certified to run Docker: **Red Hat Linux** (**RHEL**), CentOS, Oracle Linux, Ubuntu, and more.

5. minikube makes it possible to define and run a single or multi-node cluster on a local computer such as a developer's laptop. This way, using minikube, you can run and test containerized applications locally on your machine and do not have to rely on a remote Kubernetes cluster such as one running in the cloud on, say, AWS, Microsoft Azure, or Google cloud.

Part 2: Containerization Fundamentals

This part teaches you how to start, stop, and remove containers, and how to inspect containers to retrieve additional metadata from them. Furthermore, it explains how to run additional processes and how to attach to the main process in an already running container. It also covers how to retrieve logging information from a container, which is produced by the processes running inside it. Finally, this part introduces the inner workings of a container, including such things as Linux namespaces and groups.

- *Chapter 3, Mastering Containers*

- *Chapter 4, Creating and Managing Container Images*

- *Chapter 5, Data Volumes and Configuration*

- *Chapter 6, Debugging Code Running in Containers*

- *Chapter 7, Testing Applications Running in Containers*

- *Chapter 8, Increasing Productivity with Docker Tips and Tricks*

3

Mastering Containers

In the previous chapter, you learned how to optimally prepare your working environment for the productive and frictionless use of Docker. In this chapter, we are going to get our hands dirty and learn about everything that is important to know when working with containers.

Here are the topics we're going to cover in this chapter:

- Running the first container
- Starting, stopping, and removing containers
- Inspecting containers
- Exec into a running container
- Attaching to a running container
- Retrieving container logs
- The anatomy of containers

After finishing this chapter, you will be able to do the following things:

- Run, stop, and delete a container based on an existing image, such as Nginx, BusyBox, or Alpine
- List all containers on the system
- Inspect the metadata of a running or stopped container
- Retrieve the logs produced by an application running inside a container
- Run a process such as /bin/sh in an already-running container
- Attach a terminal to an already-running container
- Explain in your own words, to an interested layman, the underpinnings of a container

Technical requirements

For this chapter, you should have Docker Desktop installed on your Linux workstation, macOS, or Windows PC. If you are on an older version of Windows or are using Windows 10 Home Edition, then you should have Docker Toolbox installed and ready to use. On macOS, use the Terminal application, and on Windows, use the PowerShell console or Git Bash to try out the commands you will be learning.

Running the first container

Before we start, we want to make sure that Docker is installed correctly on your system and ready to accept your commands. Open a new terminal window and type in the following command (note: do not type the $ sign, as it is a placeholder for your prompt):

```
$ docker version
```

If everything works correctly, you should see the version of the Docker client and server installed on your laptop output in the terminal. At the time of writing, it looks like this:

```
→  The-Ultimate-Docker-Container-Book git:(main) docker version
Client:
 Cloud integration: v1.0.29
 Version:           20.10.20
 API version:       1.41
 Go version:        go1.18.7
 Git commit:        9fdeb9c
 Built:             Tue Oct 18 18:20:35 2022
 OS/Arch:           darwin/arm64
 Context:           default
 Experimental:      true

Server: Docker Desktop 4.13.1 (90346)
 Engine:
  Version:          20.10.20
  API version:      1.41 (minimum version 1.12)
  Go version:       go1.18.7
  Git commit:       03df974
  Built:            Tue Oct 18 18:18:16 2022
  OS/Arch:          linux/arm64
  Experimental:     true
 containerd:
  Version:          1.6.8
  GitCommit:        9cd3357b7fd7218e4aec3eae239db1f68a5a6ec6
 runc:
  Version:          1.1.4
  GitCommit:        v1.1.4-0-g5fd4c4d
 docker-init:
  Version:          0.19.0
  GitCommit:        de40ad0
```

Figure 3.1 – Output of the docker version command

As you can see, I have version 20.10.20 installed on my MacBook Air M1 laptop.

If this doesn't work for you, then something with your installation is not right. Please make sure that you have followed the instructions in the previous chapter on how to install Docker Desktop on your system.

So, you're ready to see some action. Please type the following command into your terminal window and hit the *Return* key:

```
$ docker container run alpine echo "Hello World"
```

When you run the preceding command the first time, you should see an output in your terminal window like this:

```
● → The-Ultimate-Docker-Container-Book git:(main) docker container run alpine echo "Hello World"
Unable to find image 'alpine:latest' locally
latest: Pulling from library/alpine
6875df1f5354: Pull complete
Digest: sha256:b95359c2505145f16c6aa384f9cc74eeff78eb36d308ca4fd902eeeb0a0b161b
Status: Downloaded newer image for alpine:latest
Hello World
```

Figure 3.2 – Running an Alpine container for the first time

Now that was easy! Let's try to run the very same command again:

```
$ docker container run alpine echo "Hello World"
```

The second, third, or nth time you run the preceding command, you should see only this output in your terminal:

```
Hello World
```

Try to reason why the first time you run a command you see a different output than all of the subsequent times. But don't worry if you can't figure it out; we will explain the reasons in detail in the following sections of this chapter.

Starting, stopping, and removing containers

You successfully ran a container in the previous section. Now, we want to investigate in detail what exactly happened and why. Let's look again at the command we used:

```
$ docker container run alpine echo "Hello World"
```

This command contains multiple parts. First and foremost, we have the word `docker`. This is the name of the Docker **Command-Line Interface** (**CLI**) tool, which we are using to interact with Docker Engine, which is responsible for running containers. Next, we have the word `container`, which indicates the context we are working with, such as `container`, `image`, or `volume`. As we want to run a container, our context is `container`. Next is the actual command we want to execute in the given context, which is `run`.

Let me recap – so far, we have `docker container run`, which means, "hey Docker, we want to run a container."

Now we also need to tell Docker which container to run. In this case, this is the so-called `alpine` container.

> **Alpine Linux**
>
> `alpine` is a minimal Docker image based on Alpine Linux with a complete package index and is only about 5 MB in size. It is an official image supported by the Alpine open source project and Docker.

Finally, we need to define what kind of process or task will be executed inside the container when it is running. In our case, this is the last part of the command, `echo "Hello World"`.

The following figure may help you to get a better idea of the whole thing:

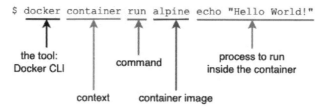

Figure 3.3 – docker run command explained

Now that we have understood the various parts of a command to run a container, let's try to run another container with a different process executed inside it. Type the following command into your terminal:

```
$ docker container run centos ping -c 5 127.0.0.1
```

You should see output in your terminal window similar to the following:

```
→  The-Ultimate-Docker-Container-Book git:(main) docker container run centos ping -c 5 127.0.0.1
Unable to find image 'centos:latest' locally
latest: Pulling from library/centos
52f9ef134af7: Pull complete
Digest: sha256:a27fd8080b517143cbbbab9dfb7c8571c40d67d534bbdee55bd6c473f432b177
Status: Downloaded newer image for centos:latest
PING 127.0.0.1 (127.0.0.1) 56(84) bytes of data.
64 bytes from 127.0.0.1: icmp_seq=1 ttl=64 time=0.837 ms
64 bytes from 127.0.0.1: icmp_seq=2 ttl=64 time=0.142 ms
64 bytes from 127.0.0.1: icmp_seq=3 ttl=64 time=0.207 ms
64 bytes from 127.0.0.1: icmp_seq=4 ttl=64 time=0.123 ms
64 bytes from 127.0.0.1: icmp_seq=5 ttl=64 time=0.144 ms

--- 127.0.0.1 ping statistics ---
5 packets transmitted, 5 received, 0% packet loss, time 4091ms
rtt min/avg/max/mdev = 0.123/0.290/0.837/0.275 ms
```

Figure 3.4 – Running the ping command inside a CentOS container

What changed is that this time, the container image we're using is centos and the process we're executing inside the centos container is ping -c 5 127.0.0.1, which pings the loopback IP address (127.0.0.1) five times until it stops.

CentOS

centos is the official Docker image for CentOS Linux, which is a community-supported distribution derived from sources freely provided to the public by Red Hat for **Red Hat Enterprise Linux (RHEL)**.

Let's analyze the output in detail. The first line is as follows:

```
Unable to find image 'centos:latest' locally
```

This tells us that Docker didn't find an image named centos:latest in the local cache of the system. So, Docker knows that it has to pull the image from some registry where container images are stored. By default, your Docker environment is configured so that images are pulled from Docker Hub at docker.io. This is expressed by the second line, as follows:

```
latest: Pulling from library/centos
```

The next three lines of output are as follows:

```
52f9ef134af7: Pull complete
Digest: sha256:a27fd8080b517143cbbbab9dfb7c8571c4...
Status: Downloaded newer image for centos:latest
```

This tells us that Docker has successfully pulled the centos:latest image from Docker Hub. All of the subsequent lines of the output are generated by the process we ran inside the container, which is the ping tool in this case. If you have been attentive so far, then you might have noticed the latest keyword occurring a few times. Each image has a version (also called tag), and if we don't specify a version explicitly, then Docker automatically assumes it is latest.

If we run the preceding container again on our system, the first five lines of the output will be missing since, this time, Docker will find the container image cached locally and hence won't have to download it first. Try it out and verify what I just told you.

Running a random trivia question container

For the subsequent sections of this chapter, we need a container that runs continuously in the background and produces some interesting output. That's why we have chosen an algorithm that produces random trivia questions. The API that produces free random trivia can be found at http://jservice.io/.

Now, the goal is to have a process running inside a container that produces a new random trivia question every 5 seconds and outputs the question to STDOUT. The following script will do exactly that:

```
while :
do
    curl -s http://jservice.io/api/random | jq '.[0].question'
    sleep 5
done
```

If you are using PowerShell, the preceding command can be translated to the following:

```
while ($true) {
    Invoke-WebRequest -Uri "http://jservice.io/api/random" -Method GET
-UseBasicParsing |
    Select-Object -ExpandProperty Content |
    ConvertFrom-Json |
    Select-Object -ExpandProperty 0 |
    Select-Object -ExpandProperty question
    Start-Sleep -Seconds 5
}
```

> **Note**
>
> The ConvertFrom-Json cmdlet requires that the Microsoft.PowerShell.Utility module be imported. If it's not already imported, you'll need to run Import-Module Microsoft.PowerShell.Utility before running the script.

Try it in a terminal window. Stop the script by pressing *Ctrl* + *C*. The output should look similar to this:

```
 ⊙ →  The-Ultimate-Docker-Container-Book git:(main) while :
do
    curl -s http://jservice.io/api/random | jq '.[0].question'
    sleep 5
done
"In his first screen role since 1939, he won the 1975 Best Supporting Actor Oscar for \"The Sunshine Boys\""
"(An empress) Died July 1918:Yekaterinburg, Russia"
"The George Eastman House in this city is home to the International Museum of Photography & Film"
"\"Devils Night Out\" was the first album by this ska-punk band out of Boston"
^C
```

Figure 3.5 – Output random trivia

Each response is a different trivia question. You may need to install jq first on your Linux, macOS, or Windows computer. jq is a handy tool often used to nicely filter and format JSON output, which increases its readability on screen. Use your package manager to install jq if needed. On Windows, using Chocolatey, the command would be as follows:

```
$ choco install jq
```

And on a Mac using Homebrew, you would type the following:

```
$ brew install jq
```

Now, let's run this logic in an `alpine` container. Since this is not just a simple command, we want to wrap the preceding script in a script file and execute that one. To make things simpler, I have created a Docker image called `fundamentalsofdocker/trivia` that contains all of the necessary logic so that we can just use it here. Later on, once we have introduced Docker images, we will analyze this container image further. For the moment, let's just use it as is. Execute the following command to run the container as a background service. In Linux, a background service is also called a daemon:

```
$ docker container run --detach \
    --name trivia fundamentalsofdocker/trivia:ed2
```

> **Important note**
>
> We are using the \ character to allow line breaks in a single logical command that does not fit on a single line. This is a feature of the shell script we use. In PowerShell, use the backtick (`) instead.
>
> Also note that on `zsh`, you may have to press *Shift + Enter* instead of only *Enter* after the \ character to start a new line. Otherwise, you will get an error.

In the preceding expression, we have used two new command-line parameters, `--detach` and `--name`. Now, `--detach` tells Docker to run the process in the container as a Linux daemon.

The `--name` parameter, in turn, can be used to give the container an explicit name. In the preceding sample, the name we chose is `trivia`. If we don't specify an explicit container name when we run a container, then Docker will automatically assign the container a random but unique name. This name will be composed of the name of a famous scientist and an adjective. Such names could be `boring_borg` or `angry_goldberg`. They're quite humorous, the Docker engineers, aren't they?

Finally, the container we're running is derived from the `fundamentalsofdocker/trivia:ed2` image. Note how we are also using a tag, `ed2`, for the container. This tag just tells us that this image was originally created for the second edition of this book.

One important takeaway is that the container name has to be unique on the system. Let's make sure that the trivia container is up and running:

```
$ docker container ls -l
```

This should give us something like this:

Figure 3.6 – Details of the last run container

An important part of the preceding output is the `STATUS` column, which in this case is `Up 6 minutes`. That is, the container has been up and running for 6 minutes now.

Don't worry if the previous Docker command is not yet familiar to you; we will come back to it in the next section.

To complete this section, let's stop and remove the `trivia` container with the following command:

```
$ docker rm --force trivia
```

The preceding command, while forcefully removing the `trivia` container from our system, will just output the name of the container, `trivia`, in the output.

Now, it is time to learn how to list containers running or dangling on our system.

Listing containers

As we continue to run containers over time, we get a lot of them in our system. To find out what is currently running on our host, we can use the `container ls` command, as follows:

```
$ docker container ls
```

This will list all currently running containers. Such a list might look similar to this:

```
●  +  The-Ultimate-Docker-Container-Book git:(main) docker container ls
CONTAINER ID   IMAGE                              COMMAND                CREATED          STATUS          PORTS     NAMES
8de7d43f0362   alpine                             "sleep 3600"           8 seconds ago    Up 7 seconds              laughing_torvalds
5a805de0ea1c   fundamentalsofdocker/trivia:ed2    "/bin/sh -c 'source …" 27 seconds ago   Up 26 seconds             trivia
8e713f2c037a   centos                             "ping 127.0.0.1"       50 seconds ago   Up 49 seconds             determined_lamarr
```

Figure 3.7 – List of all running containers on the system

By default, Docker outputs seven columns with the following meanings:

Column	Description
Container ID	This is a short version of the unique ID of the container. It is an SHA-256, where Secure Hash Algorithm 256-bit (SHA-256) is a widely used cryptographic hash function that takes an input and generates a fixed-size (256-bit) output, known as a hash. The full ID is 64 characters long.
Image	This is the name of the container image from which this container is instantiated.
Command	This is the command that is used to run the main process in the container.
Created	This is the date and time when the container was created.
Status	This is the status of the container (created, restarting, running, removing, paused, exited, or dead).
Ports	This is the list of container ports that have been mapped to the host.
Names	This is the name assigned to this container (note: multiple names for the same container are possible).

Table 3.1 – Description of the columns of the docker container ls command

If we want to list not just the currently running containers but all containers that are defined on our system, then we can use the `-a` or `--all` command-line parameter, as follows:

```
$ docker container ls --all
```

This will list containers in any state, such as `created`, `running`, or `exited`.

Sometimes, we want to just list the IDs of all containers. For this, we have the `-q` or `--quiet` parameter:

```
$ docker container ls --quiet
```

You might wonder when this is useful. I will show you a command where it is very helpful right here:

```
$ docker container rm --force $(docker container ls --all --quiet)
```

Lean back and take a deep breath. Then, try to find out what the preceding command does. Don't read any further until you find the answer or give up.

Here is the solution: the preceding command forcefully deletes all containers that are currently defined on the system, including the stopped ones. The `rm` command stands for "remove," and it will be explained soon.

In the previous section, we used the `-l` parameter in the list command, that is, `docker container ls -l`. Try to use the `docker help` command to find out what the `-l` parameter stands for. You can invoke help for the list command as follows:

```
$ docker container ls --help
```

Now that you know how to list created, running, or stopped containers on your system, let's learn how to stop and restart containers.

Stopping and starting containers

Sometimes, we want to (temporarily) stop a running container. Let's try this out with the trivia container we used previously:

1. Run the container again with this command:

    ```
    $ docker container run -d --name trivia fundamentalsofdocker/
    trivia:ed2
    ```

2. Now, if we want to stop this container, then we can do so by issuing this command:

    ```
    $ docker container stop trivia
    ```

When you try to stop the trivia container, you will probably notice that it takes a while until this command is executed. To be precise, it takes about 10 seconds. *Why is this the case?*

Docker sends a Linux SIGTERM signal to the main process running inside the container. If the process doesn't react to this signal and terminate itself, Docker waits for 10 seconds and then sends SIGKILL, which will kill the process forcefully and terminate the container.

In the preceding command, we have used the name of the container to specify which container we want to stop. But we could have also used the container ID instead.

How do we get the ID of a container? There are several ways of doing so. The manual approach is to list all running containers and find the one that we're looking for in the list. From there, we copy its ID. A more automated way is to use some shell scripting and environment variables. If, for example, we want to get the ID of the trivia container, we can use this expression:

```
$ export CONTAINER_ID=$(docker container ls -a | grep trivia | awk
'{print $1}')
```

The equivalent command in PowerShell would look like this:

```
$ CONTAINER_ID = docker container ls -a | Select-String "trivia" |
Select-Object -ExpandProperty Line | ForEach-Object { $_ -split ' ' }
| Select-Object -First 1
$ Write-Output $CONTAINER_ID
```

> **Note**
>
> We are using the -a (or --all) parameter with the docker container ls command to list all containers, even the stopped ones. This is necessary in this case since we stopped the trivia container a moment ago.

Now, instead of using the container name, we can use the $CONTAINER_ID variable in our expression:

```
$ docker container stop $CONTAINER_ID
```

Once we have stopped the container, its status changes to Exited.

If a container is stopped, it can be started again using the docker container start command. Let's do this with our trivia container. It is good to have it running again, as we'll need it in the subsequent sections of this chapter:

```
$ docker container start $CONTAINER_ID
```

We can also start it by using the name of the container:

```
$ docker container start trivia
```

It is now time to discuss what to do with stopped containers that we don't need anymore.

Removing containers

When we run the `docker container ls -a` command, we can see quite a few containers that are in the `Exited` status. If we don't need these containers anymore, then it is a good thing to remove them from memory; otherwise, they unnecessarily occupy precious resources. The command to remove a container is as follows:

```
$ docker container rm <container ID>
```

Here, `<container ID>` stands for the ID of the container – a SHA-256 code – that we want to remove. Another way to remove a container is the following:

```
$ docker container rm <container name>
```

Here, we use the name of the container.

> **Challenge**
>
> Try to remove one of your exited containers using its ID.

Sometimes, removing a container will not work as it is still running. If we want to force a removal, no matter what the condition of the container currently is, we can use the `-f` or `--force` command-line parameter:

```
$ docker container rm <container ID> --force
```

Now that we have learned how to remove containers from our system, let's learn how to inspect containers present in the system.

Inspecting containers

Containers are runtime instances of an image and have a lot of associated data that characterizes their behavior. To get more information about a specific container, we can use the `inspect` command. As usual, we have to provide either the container ID or the name to identify the container for which we want to obtain the data. So, let's inspect our sample container. First, if it is not already running, we have to run it:

```
$ docker container run --name trivia fundamentalsofdocker/ trivia:ed2
```

Then, use this command to inspect it:

```
$ docker container inspect trivia
```

The response is a big JSON object full of details. It looks similar to this:

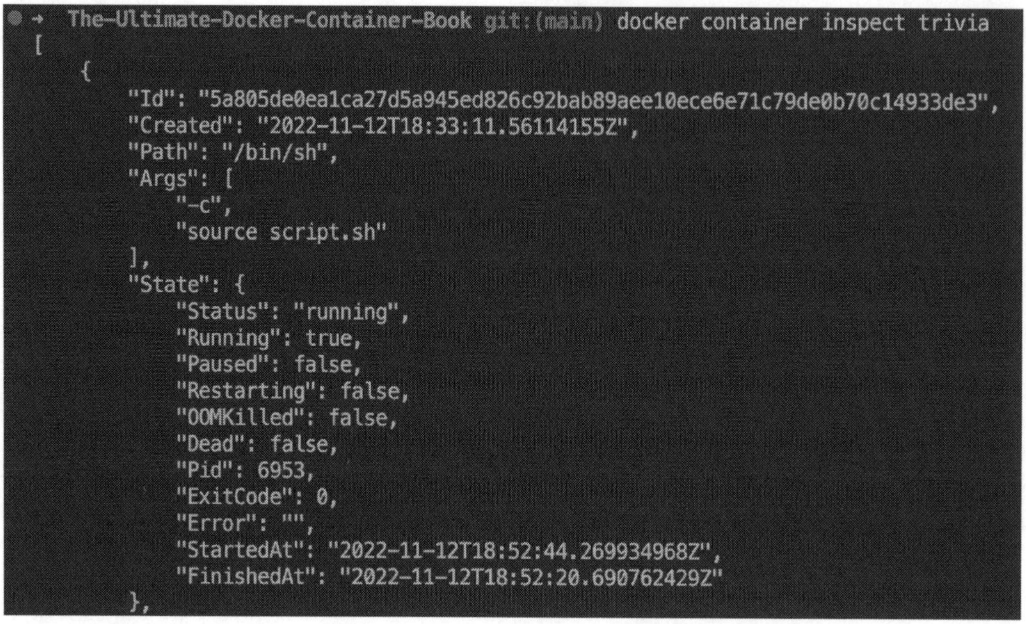

```
→ The-Ultimate-Docker-Container-Book git:(main) docker container inspect trivia
[
    {
        "Id": "5a805de0ea1ca27d5a945ed826c92bab89aee10ece6e71c79de0b70c14933de3",
        "Created": "2022-11-12T18:33:11.56114155Z",
        "Path": "/bin/sh",
        "Args": [
            "-c",
            "source script.sh"
        ],
        "State": {
            "Status": "running",
            "Running": true,
            "Paused": false,
            "Restarting": false,
            "OOMKilled": false,
            "Dead": false,
            "Pid": 6953,
            "ExitCode": 0,
            "Error": "",
            "StartedAt": "2022-11-12T18:52:44.269934968Z",
            "FinishedAt": "2022-11-12T18:52:20.690762429Z"
        },
```

Figure 3.8 – Inspecting the trivia container

Note that the preceding screenshot only shows the first part of a much longer output.

Please take a moment to analyze what you have. You should see information such as the following:

- The ID of the container
- The creation date and time of the container
- From which image the container is built

Many sections of the output, such as Mounts and NetworkSettings, don't make much sense right now, but we will discuss those in the upcoming chapters of this book. The data you're seeing here is also named the *metadata* of a container. We will be using the inspect command quite often in the remainder of this book as a source of information.

Sometimes, we need just a tiny bit of the overall information, and to achieve this, we can use either the grep tool or a filter. The former method does not always result in the expected answer, so let's look into the latter approach:

```
$ docker container inspect -f "{{json .State}}" trivia \
    | jq .
```

The -f or --filter parameter is used to define the "{{json .State}}" filter. The filter expression itself uses the Go template syntax. In this example, we only want to see the state part of the whole output in JSON format. To nicely format the output, we pipe the result into the jq tool:

```
    The-Ultimate-Docker-Container-Book git:(main) docker container inspect -f "{{json .State}}" trivia | jq .
{
  "Status": "running",
  "Running": true,
  "Paused": false,
  "Restarting": false,
  "OOMKilled": false,
  "Dead": false,
  "Pid": 6953,
  "ExitCode": 0,
  "Error": "",
  "StartedAt": "2022-11-12T18:52:44.269934968Z",
  "FinishedAt": "2022-11-12T18:52:20.690762429Z"
}
    The-Ultimate-Docker-Container-Book git:(main)
```

Figure 3.9 – The state node of the inspect output

After we have learned how to retrieve loads of important and useful meta information about a container, we want to investigate how we can execute it in a running container.

Exec into a running container

Sometimes, we want to run another process inside an already-running container. A typical reason could be to try to debug a misbehaving container. How can we do this? First, we need to know either the ID or the name of the container, and then we can define which process we want to run and how we want it to run. Once again, we use our currently running trivia container and we run a shell interactively inside it with the following command:

```
$ docker container exec -i -t trivia /bin/sh
```

The -i (or --interactive) flag signifies that we want to run the additional process interactively, and -t (or --tty) tells Docker that we want it to provide us with a TTY (a terminal emulator) for the command. Finally, the process we run inside the container is /bin/sh.

If we execute the preceding command in our terminal, then we will be presented with a new prompt, /app #. We're now in a Bourne shell inside the trivia container. We can easily prove that by, for example, executing the ps command, which will list all running processes in the context:

```
/app # ps
```

The result should look somewhat similar to this:

```
○ → The-Ultimate-Docker-Container-Book git:(main) docker container exec -i -t trivia /bin/sh
/app # ps
PID   USER     TIME  COMMAND
   1 root     0:00 {sh} /usr/bin/qemu-x86_64 /bin/sh /bin/sh -c source script.sh
1616 root     0:00 {sh} /usr/bin/qemu-x86_64 /bin/sh /bin/sh
1623 root     0:00 {sleep} /usr/bin/qemu-x86_64 /bin/sleep sleep 5
1626 root     0:00 ps
/app # █
```

Figure 3.10 – Executing into the running trivia container

We can clearly see that the process with PID 1 is the command that we have defined to run inside the trivia container. The process with PID 1 is also named the main process.

Exit the container by pressing *Ctrl + D*. We cannot only execute additional processes interactively in a container. Please consider the following command:

```
$ docker container exec trivia ps
```

The output evidently looks very similar to the preceding output:

```
● → The-Ultimate-Docker-Container-Book git:(main) x docker container exec trivia ps
PID   USER     TIME  COMMAND
   1 root     0:48 {sh} /usr/bin/qemu-x86_64 /bin/sh /bin/sh -c source script.sh
26901 root    0:00 {sleep} /usr/bin/qemu-x86_64 /bin/sleep sleep 5
26904 root    0:00 ps
```

Figure 3.11 – List of processes running inside the trivia container

The difference is that we did not use an extra process to run a shell but executed the ps command directly. We can even run processes as a daemon using the -d flag and define environment variables valid inside the container, using the -e or --env flag variables, as follows:

1. Run the following command to start a shell inside a trivia container and define an environment variable named MY_VAR that is valid inside this container:

   ```
   $ docker container exec -it \
       -e MY_VAR="Hello World" \
       trivia /bin/sh
   ```

2. You'll find yourself inside the trivia container. Output the content of the MY_VAR environment variable, as follows:

   ```
   /app # echo $MY_VAR
   ```

3. You should see this output in the terminal:

   ```
   Hello World
   ```

```
○ →  The-Ultimate-Docker-Container-Book git:(main) x docker container exec -it \
> -e MY_VAR="Hello World" \
> trivia /bin/sh
/app # echo $MY_VAR
Hello World
/app #
```

Figure 3.12 – Running a trivia container and defining an environment variable

4. To exit the trivia container, press *Ctrl + D*:

```
/app # <CTRL-d>
```

Great, we have learned how to execute into a running container and run additional processes. But there is another important way to work with a running container.

Attaching to a running container

We can use the `attach` command to attach our terminal's standard input, output, or error (or any combination of the three) to a running container using the ID or name of the container. Let's do this for our trivia container:

1. Open a new terminal window.

> **Tip**
>
> You may want to use another terminal than the integrated terminal of VS Code for this exercise, as it seems to cause problems with the key combinations that we are going to use. On Mac, use the Terminal app, as an example.

2. Run a new instance of the `trivia` Docker image in interactive mode:

```
$ docker container run -it \
    --name trivia2 fundamentalsofdocker/trivia:ed2
```

3. Open yet another terminal window and use this command to attach it to the container:

```
$ docker container attach trivia2
```

In this case, we will see, every 5 seconds or so, a new quote appearing in the output.

4. To quit the container without stopping or killing it, we can use the *Ctrl + P* + *Ctrl + Q* key combination. This detaches us from the container while leaving it running in the background.

5. Stop and remove the container forcefully:

```
$ docker container rm --force trivia2
```

Let's run another container, this time, an Nginx web server:

1. Run the Nginx web server as follows:

    ```
    $ docker run -d --name nginx -p 8080:80 nginx:alpine
    ```

> **Tip**
>
> Here, we run the Alpine version of Nginx as a daemon in a container named `nginx`. The `-p 8080:80` command-line parameter opens port `8080` on the host (that is, the user's machine) for access to the Nginx web server running inside the container. Don't worry about the syntax here as we will explain this feature in more detail in *Chapter 10, Using Single-Host Networking.*
>
> On Windows, you'll need to approve a prompt that Windows Firewall will pop up. You have to allow Docker Desktop on the firewall.

2. Let's see whether we can access Nginx using the `curl` tool by running this command:

    ```
    $ curl -4 localhost:8080
    ```

    If all works correctly, you should be greeted by the welcome page of Nginx:

```
→  The-Ultimate-Docker-Container-Book git:(main) ✗ curl -4 localhost:8080
<!DOCTYPE html>
<html>
<head>
<title>Welcome to nginx!</title>
<style>
html { color-scheme: light dark; }
body { width: 35em; margin: 0 auto;
font-family: Tahoma, Verdana, Arial, sans-serif; }
</style>
</head>
<body>
<h1>Welcome to nginx!</h1>
<p>If you see this page, the nginx web server is successfully installed and
working. Further configuration is required.</p>

<p>For online documentation and support please refer to
<a href="http://nginx.org/">nginx.org</a>.<br/>
Commercial support is available at
<a href="http://nginx.com/">nginx.com</a>.</p>

<p><em>Thank you for using nginx.</em></p>
</body>
</html>
```

Figure 3.13 – Welcome message of the Nginx web server

3. Now, let's attach our terminal to the Nginx container to observe what's happening:

    ```
    $ docker container attach nginx
    ```

4. Once you are attached to the container, you will not see anything at first. But now, open another terminal, and in this new terminal window, repeat the `curl` command a few times, for example, using the following script:

```
$ for n in {1..10} do; curl -4 localhost:8080 done;
```

Or, in PowerShell, use the following:

```
PS> 1..10 | ForEach-Object {C:\ProgramData\chocolatey\bin\curl.exe -4 localhost:8080}
```

You should see the logging output of Nginx, which looks similar to this:

```
○ →  The-Ultimate-Docker-Container-Book git:(main) ✗ docker container attach nginx
172.17.0.1 - - [13/Nov/2022:17:11:39 +0000] "GET / HTTP/1.1" 200 615 "-" "curl/7.79.1" "-"
172.17.0.1 - - [13/Nov/2022:17:11:39 +0000] "GET / HTTP/1.1" 200 615 "-" "curl/7.79.1" "-"
172.17.0.1 - - [13/Nov/2022:17:11:39 +0000] "GET / HTTP/1.1" 200 615 "-" "curl/7.79.1" "-"
172.17.0.1 - - [13/Nov/2022:17:11:39 +0000] "GET / HTTP/1.1" 200 615 "-" "curl/7.79.1" "-"
172.17.0.1 - - [13/Nov/2022:17:11:39 +0000] "GET / HTTP/1.1" 200 615 "-" "curl/7.79.1" "-"
172.17.0.1 - - [13/Nov/2022:17:11:39 +0000] "GET / HTTP/1.1" 200 615 "-" "curl/7.79.1" "-"
172.17.0.1 - - [13/Nov/2022:17:11:39 +0000] "GET / HTTP/1.1" 200 615 "-" "curl/7.79.1" "-"
172.17.0.1 - - [13/Nov/2022:17:11:39 +0000] "GET / HTTP/1.1" 200 615 "-" "curl/7.79.1" "-"
172.17.0.1 - - [13/Nov/2022:17:11:39 +0000] "GET / HTTP/1.1" 200 615 "-" "curl/7.79.1" "-"
172.17.0.1 - - [13/Nov/2022:17:11:39 +0000] "GET / HTTP/1.1" 200 615 "-" "curl/7.79.1" "-"
172.17.0.1 - - [13/Nov/2022:17:11:39 +0000] "GET / HTTP/1.1" 200 615 "-" "curl/7.79.1" "-"
□
```

Figure 3.14 – Output of Nginx

5. Quit the container by pressing *Ctrl + C*. This will detach your terminal and, at the same time, stop the Nginx container.

6. To clean up, remove the Nginx container with the following command:

```
$ docker container rm nginx
```

In the next section, we're going to learn how to work with container logs.

Retrieving container logs

It is a best practice for any good application to generate some logging information that developers and operators alike can use to find out what the application is doing at a given time, and whether there are any problems to help to pinpoint the root cause of the issue.

When running inside a container, the application should preferably output the log items to STDOUT and STDERR and not into a file. If the logging output is directed to STDOUT and STDERR, then Docker can collect this information and keep it ready for consumption by a user or any other external system:

1. Run a trivia container in `detach` mode:

```
$ docker container run --detach \
    --name trivia fundamentalsofdocker/trivia:ed2
```

Let it run for a minute or so so that it has time to generate a few trivia questions.

2. To access the logs of a given container, we can use the `docker container logs` command. If, for example, we want to retrieve the logs of our `trivia` container, we can use the following expression:

```
$ docker container logs trivia
```

This will retrieve the whole log produced by the application from the very beginning of its existence.

> **Note**
>
> Stop, wait a second – this is not quite true, what I just said. By default, Docker uses the so-called `json-file` logging driver. This driver stores logging information in a file. If there is a file rolling policy defined, then `docker container logs` only retrieves what is in the currently active log file and not what is in previous rolled files that might still be available on the host.

3. If we want to only get a few of the latest entries, we can use the `-t` or `--tail` parameter, as follows:

```
$ docker container logs --tail 5 trivia
```

This will retrieve only the last five items that the process running inside the container produced.

4. Sometimes, we want to follow the log that is produced by a container. This is possible when using the `-f` or `--follow` parameter. The following expression will output the last five log items and then follow the log as it is produced by the containerized process:

```
$ docker container logs --tail 5 --follow trivia
```

5. Press *Ctrl + C* to stop following the logs.

6. Clean up your environment and remove the trivia container with the following:

```
$ docker container rm --force trivia
```

Often, using the default mechanism for container logging is not enough. We need a different way of logging. This is discussed in the following section.

Logging drivers

Docker includes multiple logging mechanisms to help us to get information from running containers. These mechanisms are named logging drivers. Which logging driver is used can be configured at the Docker daemon level. The default logging driver is `json-file`. Some of the drivers that are currently supported natively are as follows:

Driver	Description
none	No log output for the specific container is produced.
json-file	This is the default driver. The logging information is stored in files, formatted as JSON.
journald	If the journald daemon is running on the host machine, we can use this driver. It forwards logging to the journald daemon.
syslog	If the syslog daemon is running on the host machine, we can configure this driver, which will forward the log messages to the syslog daemon.
gelf	When using this driver, log messages are written to a **Graylog Extended Log Format (GELF)** endpoint. Popular examples of such endpoints are Graylog and Logstash.
fluentd	Assuming that the fluentd daemon is installed on the host system, this driver writes log messages to it.
awslogs	The awslogs logging driver for Docker is a logging driver that allows Docker to send log data to Amazon CloudWatch Logs.
splunk	The Splunk logging driver for Docker allows Docker to send log data to Splunk, a popular platform for log management and analysis.

Table 3.2 – List of logging drivers

> **Note**
>
> If you change the logging driver, please be aware that the docker container logs command is only available for the json-file and journald drivers. Docker 20.10 and up introduce *dual logging*, which uses a local buffer that allows you to use the docker container logs command for any logging driver.

Using a container-specific logging driver

The logging driver can be set globally in the Docker daemon configuration file. But we can also define the logging driver on a container-by-container basis. In the following example, we run a busybox container and use the --logdriver parameter to configure the none logging driver:

1. Run an instance of the busybox Docker image and execute a simple script in it outputting a Hello message three times:

    ```
    $ docker container run --name test -it \
        --log-driver none \
        busybox sh -c 'for N in 1 2 3; do echo "Hello $N"; done'
    ```

We should see the following:

```
Hello 1
Hello 2
Hello 3
```

2. Now, let's try to get the logs of the preceding container:

```
$ docker container logs test
```

The output is as follows:

```
Error response from daemon: configured logging driver does not
support reading
```

This is to be expected since the none driver does not produce any logging output.

3. Let's clean up and remove the test container:

```
$ docker container rm test
```

To end this section about logging, we want to discuss a somewhat advanced topic, namely, how to change the default logging driver.

Advanced topic – changing the default logging driver

Let's change the default logging driver of a Linux host. The easiest way to do this is on a real Linux host. For this purpose, we're going to use Vagrant with an Ubuntu image. Vagrant is an open source tool developed by HashiCorp that is often used to build and maintain portable virtual software development environments. Please follow these instructions:

1. Open a new terminal window.

2. If you haven't done so before, on your Mac and Windows machine, you may need to install a hypervisor such as VirtualBox first. If you're using a Pro version of Windows, you can also use Hyper-V instead:

    *   To install VirtualBox on a Mac with an Intel CPU, use Homebrew as follows:

    ```
    $ brew install --cask virtualbox
    ```

    *   On Windows, with Chocolatey, use the following:

    ```
    $ choco install -y virtualbox
    ```

> **Note**
>
> On a Mac with an M1/M2 CPU, at the time of writing, you need to install the developer preview of VirtualBox. Please follow the instructions here: https://www.virtualbox.org/wiki/Downloads.

3. Install Vagrant on your computer using your package manager, such as Chocolatey on Windows or Homebrew on Mac. On my MacBook Air M1, the command looks like this:

```
$ brew install --cask vagrant
```

On a Windows machine, the corresponding command would be the following:

```
$ choco install -y vagrant
```

4. Once successfully installed, make sure Vagrant is available with the following command:

```
$ vagrant –version
```

At the time of writing, Vagrant replies with the following:

```
Vagrant 2.3.2
```

5. In your terminal, execute the following command to initialize an Ubuntu 22.04 VM with Vagrant:

```
$ vagrant init bento/ubuntu-22.04
```

Here is the generated output:

```
→  The-Ultimate-Docker-Container-Book git:(main) vagrant init bento/ubuntu-22.04
A `Vagrantfile` has been placed in this directory. You are now
ready to `vagrant up` your first virtual environment! Please read
the comments in the Vagrantfile as well as documentation on
`vagrantup.com` for more information on using Vagrant.
```

Figure 3.15 – Initializing a Vagrant VM based on Ubuntu 22.04

Vagrant will create a file called Vagrantfile in the current folder. Optionally, you can use your editor to analyze the content of this file.

> **Note**
>
> On a Mac with an M1/M2 CPU, at the time of writing, the bento/ubuntu-22.4 image does not work. An alternative that seems to work is illker/ubuntu-2004.

6. Now, start this VM using Vagrant:

```
$ vagrant up
```

7. Connect from your laptop to the VM using Secure Shell (ssh):

```
$ vagrant ssh
```

After this, you will find yourself inside the VM and can start working with Docker inside this VM.

8. Once inside the Ubuntu VM, we want to edit the Docker daemon configuration file and trigger the Docker daemon to reload the configuration file thereafter:

A. Navigate to the `/etc/docker` folder:

```
$ cd /etc/docker
```

B. Run `vi` as follows:

```
$ vi daemon.json
```

C. Enter the following content:

```
{
    "Log-driver": "json-log",
    "log-opts": {
        "max-size": "10m",
        "max-file": 3
    }
}
```

D. The preceding definition tells the Docker daemon to use the `json-log` driver with a maximum log file size of 10 MB before it is rolled, and the maximum number of log files that can be present on the system is three before the oldest file gets purged.

E. Save and exit `vi` by first pressing *Esc*, then typing `:w:q` (which means *write and quit*), and finally hitting the *Enter* key.

F. Now, we must send a `SIGHUP` signal to the Docker daemon so that it picks up the changes in the configuration file:

```
$ sudo kill -SIGHUP $(pidof dockerd)
```

G. Note that the preceding command only reloads the config file and does not restart the daemon.

9. Test your configuration by running a few containers and analyzing the log output.

10. Clean up your system once you are done experimenting with the following:

```
$ vagrant destroy [name|id]
```

Great! The previous section was an advanced topic and showed how you can change the log driver on a system level. Let's now talk a bit about the anatomy of containers.

The anatomy of containers

Many people wrongly compare containers to VMs. However, this is a questionable comparison. Containers are not just lightweight VMs. OK then, what is the correct description of a container?

Containers are specially encapsulated and secured processes running on the host system. Containers leverage a lot of features and primitives available on the Linux operating system. The most important ones are **namespaces** and **control groups** (**cgroups** for short). All processes running in containers only share the same Linux kernel of the underlying host operating system. This is fundamentally different from VMs, as each VM contains its own full-blown operating system.

The startup times of a typical container can be measured in milliseconds, while a VM normally needs several seconds to minutes to start up. VMs are meant to be long-living. It is a primary goal of each operations engineer to maximize the uptime of their VMs. Contrary to that, containers are meant to be ephemeral. They come and go relatively quickly.

Let's first get a high-level overview of the architecture that enables us to run containers.

Architecture

Here, we have an architectural diagram of how this all fits together:

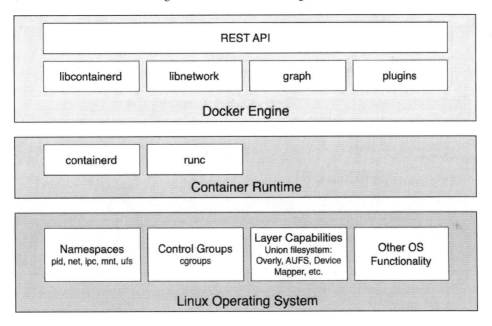

Figure 3.16 – High-level architecture of Docker

In the lower part of the preceding diagram, we have the Linux operating system with its cgroups, namespaces, and layer capabilities as well as other operating system functionality that we do not need to explicitly mention here. Then, there is an intermediary layer composed of `containerd` and `runc`. On top of all that now sits the Docker engine. The Docker engine offers a RESTful interface to the outside world that can be accessed by any tool, such as the Docker CLI, Docker Desktop, or Kubernetes, to name just a few.

Let's now describe the main building blocks in a bit more detail.

Namespaces

Linux namespaces were around for years before they were leveraged by Docker for their containers. A **namespace** is an abstraction of global resources such as filesystems, network access, and process trees (also named PID namespaces) or the system group IDs and user IDs. A Linux system is initialized with a single instance of each namespace type. After initialization, additional namespaces can be created or joined.

The Linux namespaces originated in 2002 in the 2.4.19 kernel. In kernel version 3.8, user namespaces were introduced, and with this, namespaces were ready to be used by containers.

If we wrap a running process, say, in a filesystem namespace, then this provides the illusion that the process owns its own complete filesystem. This, of course, is not true; it is only a virtual filesystem. From the perspective of the host, the contained process gets a shielded subsection of the overall filesystem. It is like a filesystem in a filesystem:

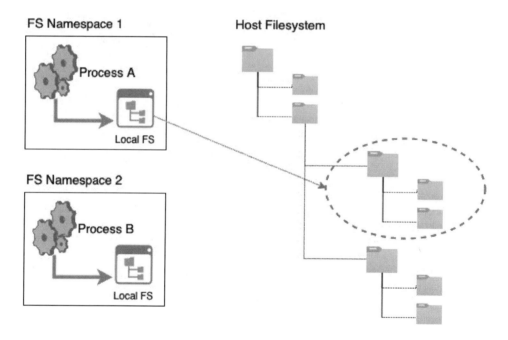

Figure 3.17 – Namespaces explained

The same applies to all of the other global resources for which namespaces exist. The user ID namespace is another example. Now that we have a user namespace, we can define a jdoe user many times on the system as long as it is living in its own namespace.

The PID namespace is what keeps processes in one container from seeing or interacting with processes in another container. A process might have the apparent PID 1 inside a container, but if we examine it from the host system, it will have an ordinary PID, say, 334:

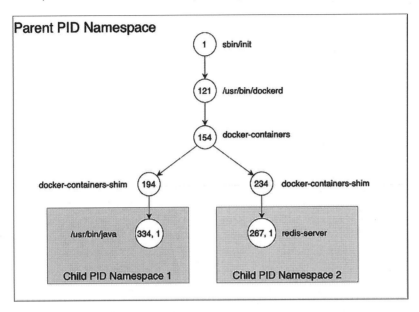

Figure 3.18 – Process tree on a Docker host

In each namespace, we can run one-to-many processes. That is important when we talk about containers, which we already experienced when we executed another process in an already-running container.

Control groups

Linux cgroups are used to limit, manage, and isolate the resource usage of collections of processes running on a system. Resources are the CPU time, system memory, network bandwidth, or combinations of these resources.

Engineers at Google originally implemented this feature in 2006. The cgroups functionality was merged into the Linux kernel mainline in kernel version 2.6.24, which was released in January 2008.

Using cgroups, administrators can limit the resources that containers can consume. With this, we can avoid, for example, the classic noisy neighbor problem, where a rogue process running in a container consumes all the CPU time or reserves massive amounts of RAM and, as such, starves all the other processes running on the host, whether they're containerized or not.

Union filesystem

Union filesystem (**unionfs**) forms the backbone of what is known as container images. We will discuss container images in detail in the next chapter. Currently, we want to just understand what unionfs is and how it works a bit better. unionfs is mainly used on Linux and allows files and directories of distinct filesystems to be overlaid to form a single coherent filesystem. In this context, the individual filesystems are called branches. Contents of directories that have the same path within the merged branches will be seen together in a single merged directory, within the new virtual filesystem. When merging branches, the priority between the branches is specified. In that way, when two branches contain the same file, the one with the higher priority is seen in the final filesystem.

Container plumbing

The foundation on top of which Docker Engine is built comprises two components, `runc` and `containerd`.

Originally, Docker was built in a monolithic way and contained all of the functionality necessary to run containers. Over time, this became too rigid, and Docker started to break out parts of the functionality into their own components. Two important components are `runc` and `containerd`.

runc

runc is a lightweight, portable container runtime. It provides full support for Linux namespaces as well as native support for all security features available on Linux, such as SELinux, AppArmor, seccomp, and cgroups.

runC is a tool for spawning and running containers according to the **Open Container Initiative** (**OCI**) specification. It is a formally specified configuration format, governed by the **Open Container Project** (**OCP**) under the auspices of the Linux Foundation.

containerd

runC is a low-level implementation of a container runtime; containerd builds on top of it and adds higher-level features, such as image transfer and storage, container execution, and supervision as well as network and storage attachments. With this, it manages the complete life cycle of containers. containerd is the reference implementation of the OCI specifications and is by far the most popular and widely used container runtime.

Containerd was donated to and accepted by the CNCF in 2017. There are alternative implementations of the OCI specification. Some of them are `rkt` by CoreOS, CRI-O by Red Hat, and LXD by Linux Containers. However, containerd is currently by far the most popular container runtime and is the default runtime of Kubernetes 1.8 or later and the Docker platform.

Summary

In this chapter, you learned how to work with containers that are based on existing images. We showed how to run, stop, start, and remove a container. Then, we inspected the metadata of a container, extracted its logs, and learned how to run an arbitrary process in an already-running container. Last but not least, we dug a bit deeper and investigated how containers work and what features of the underlying Linux operating system they leverage.

In the next chapter, you're going to learn what container images are and how we can build and share our own custom images. We'll also be discussing the best practices commonly used when building custom images, such as minimizing their size and leveraging the image cache. Stay tuned!

Further reading

The following articles give you some more information related to the topics we discussed in this chapter:

- Get started with containers at `https://docs.docker.com/get-started/`
- Get an overview of Docker container commands at `http://dockr.ly/2iLBV2I`
- Learn about isolating containers with a user namespace at `http://dockr.ly/2gmyKdf`
- Learn about limiting a container's resources at `http://dockr.ly/2wqN5Nn`

Questions

To assess your learning progress, please answer the following questions:

1. Which two important concepts of Linux are enabling factors for containers?
2. What are the possible states a container can be in?
3. Which command helps us to find out which containers are currently running on our Docker host?
4. Which command is used to list only the IDs of all containers?

Answers

Here are some sample answers to the questions presented in this chapter:

1. Linux had to first introduce **namespaces** and **cgroups** to make containers possible. Containers use those two concepts extensively. Namespaces are used to encapsulate and thus protect resources defined and/or running inside a container. cgroups are used to limit the resources processes running inside a container can use, such as memory, bandwidth, or CPU.

2. The possible states of a Docker container are as follows:

   - `created`: A container that has been created but not started

- `restarting`: A container that is in the process of being restarted
- `running`: A currently running container
- `paused`: A container whose processes have been paused
- `exited`: A container that ran and completed
- `dead`: A container that Docker Engine tried and failed to stop

3. We can use the following (or the old, shorter version, `docker ps`):

```
$ docker container ls
```

This is used to list all containers that are currently running on our Docker host. Note that this will *not* list the stopped containers, for which you need the extra `--all` (or `-a`) parameter.

4. To list all container IDs, running or stopped, we can use the following:

```
$ docker container ls -a -q
```

Here, `-q` stands for output ID only, and `-a` tells Docker that we want to see all containers, including stopped ones.

4

Creating and Managing Container Images

In the previous chapter, we learned what containers are and how to run, stop, remove, list, and inspect them. We extracted the logging information of some containers, ran other processes inside an already running container, and finally, we dived deep into the anatomy of containers. Whenever we ran a container, we created it using a container image. In this chapter, we will familiarize ourselves with these container images. We will learn what they are, how to create them, and how to distribute them.

This chapter will cover the following topics:

- What are images?
- Creating images
- Lift and shift – containerizing a legacy app
- Sharing or shipping images

After completing this chapter, you will be able to do the following:

- Name three of the most important characteristics of a container image
- Create a custom image by interactively changing the container layer and committing it
- Author a simple Dockerfile to generate a custom image
- Export an existing image using `docker image save` and import it into another Docker host using `docker image load`
- Write a two-step Dockerfile that minimizes the size of the resulting image by only including the resulting artifacts in the final image

What are images?

In Linux, everything is a file. The whole operating system is a filesystem with files and folders stored on the local disk. This is an important fact to remember when looking at what container images are. As we will see, an image is a big tarball containing a filesystem. More specifically, it contains a layered filesystem.

> **Tarball**
>
> A tarball (also known as a .tar archive) is a single file that contains multiple files or directories. It is a common archive format that is used to distribute software packages and other collections of files. The .tar archive is usually compressed using gzip or another compression format to reduce its size. Tarballs are commonly used in Unix-like operating systems, including Linux and macOS, and can be unpacked using the tar command.

The layered filesystem

Container images are templates from which containers are created. These images are not made up of just one monolithic block but are composed of many layers. The first layer in the image is also called the **base layer**. We can see this in the following figure:

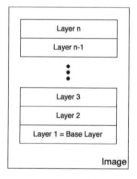

Figure 4.1 – The image as a stack of layers

Each layer contains files and folders. Each layer only contains the changes to the filesystem concerning the underlying layers. Docker uses a Union filesystem – as discussed in *Chapter 3, Mastering Containers* – to create a virtual filesystem out of the set of layers. A storage driver handles the details regarding the way these layers interact with each other. Different storage drivers are available that have advantages and disadvantages in different situations.

The layers of a container image are all immutable. Immutable means that once generated, the layer cannot ever be changed. The only possible operation affecting the layer is its physical deletion. This immutability of layers is important because it opens up a tremendous number of opportunities, as we will see.

In the following figure, we can see what a custom image for a web application, using Nginx as a web server, could look like:

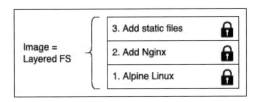

Figure 4.2 – A sample custom image based on Alpine and Nginx

Our base layer here consists of the Alpine Linux distribution. Then, on top of that, we have an **Add Nginx** layer where Nginx is added on top of Alpine. Finally, the third layer contains all the files that make up the web application, such as HTML, CSS, and JavaScript files.

As has been said previously, each image starts with a base image. Typically, this base image is one of the official images found on Docker Hub, such as a Linux distro, Alpine, Ubuntu, or CentOS. However, it is also possible to create an image from scratch.

> **Note**
> Docker Hub is a public registry for container images. It is a central hub ideally suited for sharing public container images. The registry can be found here: `https://hub.docker.com/`.

Each layer only contains the delta of changes regarding the previous set of layers. The content of each layer is mapped to a special folder on the host system, which is usually a subfolder of `/var/lib/docker/`.

Since layers are immutable, they can be cached without ever becoming stale. This is a big advantage, as we will see.

The writable container layer

As we have discussed, a container image is made of a stack of immutable or read-only layers. When Docker Engine creates a container from such an image, it adds a writable container layer on top of this stack of immutable layers. Our stack now looks as follows:

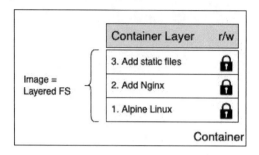

Figure 4.3 – The writable container layer

The container layer is marked as **read/write (r/w)**. Another advantage of the immutability of image layers is that they can be shared among many containers created from this image. All that is needed is a thin, writable container layer for each container, as shown in the following figure:

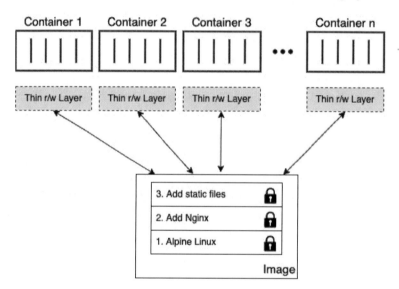

Figure 4.4 – Multiple containers sharing the same image layers

This technique, of course, results in a tremendous reduction in the resources that are consumed. Furthermore, this helps decrease the loading time of a container since only a thin container layer has to be created once the image layers have been loaded into memory, which only happens for the first container.

Copy-on-write

Docker uses the copy-on-write technique when dealing with images. Copy-on-write is a strategy for sharing and copying files for maximum efficiency. If a layer uses a file or folder that is available in one of the low-lying layers, then it just uses it. If, on the other hand, a layer wants to modify, say, a file from a low-lying layer, then it first copies this file up to the target layer and then modifies it. In the following figure, we can see what this means:

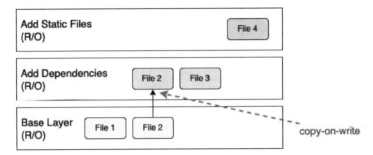

Figure 4.5 – Docker image using copy-on-write

The second layer wants to modify **File 2**, which is present in the base layer. Thus, it copies it up and then modifies it. Now, let's say that we're sitting in the top layer of the preceding graphic. This layer will use **File 1** from the base layer and **File 2** and **File 3** from the second layer.

Graph drivers

Graph drivers are what enable the Union filesystem. Graph drivers are also called storage drivers and are used when dealing with layered container images. A graph driver consolidates multiple image layers into a root filesystem for the mount namespace of the container. Or, put differently, the driver controls how images and containers are stored and managed on the Docker host.

Docker supports several different graph drivers using a pluggable architecture. The preferred driver is **overlay2,** followed by **overlay.**

Now that we understand what images are, we will learn how we can create a Docker image ourselves.

Creating Docker images

There are three ways to create a new container image on your system. The first one is by interactively building a container that contains all the additions and changes you desire, and then committing those changes into a new image. The second, and most important, way is to use a Dockerfile to describe what's in the new image, and then build the image using that Dockerfile as a manifest. Finally, the third way of creating an image is by importing it into the system from a tarball.

Now, let's look at these three ways in detail.

Interactive image creation

The first way we can create a custom image is by interactively building a container. That is, we start with a base image that we want to use as a template and run a container of it interactively. Let's say that this is the Alpine image:

1. The command to run the container would be as follows:

```
$ docker container run -it \
    --name sample \
    alpine:3.17 /bin/sh
```

The preceding command runs a container based on the `alpine:3.17` image.

2. We run the container interactively with an attached **teletypewriter** (**TTY**) using the `-it` parameter, name it `sample` with the `--name` parameter, and finally run a shell inside the container using `/bin/sh`.

In the Terminal window where you ran the preceding command, you should see something like this:

```
→  ch04 git:(main) x docker container run -it \
>  --name sample \
>  alpine:3.17 /bin/sh
Unable to find image 'alpine:3.17' locally
3.17: Pulling from library/alpine
261da4162673: Pull complete
Digest: sha256:8914eb54f968791faf6a8638949e480fef81e697984fba772b3976835194c6d4
Status: Downloaded newer image for alpine:3.17
/ #
```

Figure 4.6 – Alpine container in interactive mode

By default, the Alpine container does not have the `curl` tool installed. Let's assume we want to create a new custom image that has `curl` installed.

3. Inside the container, we can then run the following command:

```
/ # apk update && apk add curl
```

The preceding command first updates the Alpine package manager, `apk`, and then it installs the `curl` tool. The output of the preceding command should look approximately like this:

```
/ # apk update && apk add curl
fetch https://dl-cdn.alpinelinux.org/alpine/v3.17/main/aarch64/APKINDEX.tar.gz
fetch https://dl-cdn.alpinelinux.org/alpine/v3.17/community/aarch64/APKINDEX.tar.gz
v3.17.0-21-g62c4fc0981 [https://dl-cdn.alpinelinux.org/alpine/v3.17/main]
v3.17.0-24-geb334dcd4f [https://dl-cdn.alpinelinux.org/alpine/v3.17/community]
OK: 17672 distinct packages available
(1/5) Installing ca-certificates (20220614-r2)
(2/5) Installing brotli-libs (1.0.9-r9)
(3/5) Installing nghttp2-libs (1.51.0-r0)
(4/5) Installing libcurl (7.86.0-r1)
(5/5) Installing curl (7.86.0-r1)
Executing busybox-1.35.0-r29.trigger
Executing ca-certificates-20220614-r2.trigger
OK: 10 MiB in 20 packages
/ # 
```

Figure 4.7 – Installing curl on Alpine

4. Now, we can indeed use `curl`, as the following code snippet shows:

```
/ # curl -I https://google.com
HTTP/2 301
location: https://www.google.com/
content-type: text/html; charset=UTF-8
date: Sun, 27 Nov 2022 13:33:27 GMT
expires: Sun, 27 Nov 2022 13:33:27 GMT
cache-control: private, max-age=2592000
server: gws
content-length: 220
x-xss-protection: 0
x-frame-options: SAMEORIGIN
set-cookie: CONSENT=PENDING+438; expires=Tue, 26-Nov-2024 13:33:27 GMT; path=/; domain=.google.com; Sec
ure
p3p: CP="This is not a P3P policy! See g.co/p3phelp for more info."
alt-svc: h3=":443"; ma=2592000,h3-29=":443"; ma=2592000,h3-Q050=":443"; ma=2592000,h3-Q046=":443"; ma=2
592000,h3-Q043=":443"; ma=2592000,quic=":443"; ma=2592000; v="46,43"
```

Figure 4.8 – Using curl from within the container

With the preceding command, we have contacted the Google home page, and with the `-I` parameter, we have told `curl` to only output the response headers.

5. Once we have finished our customization, we can quit the container by typing `exit` at the prompt or hitting *Ctrl + D*.

6. Now, if we list all containers with the `docker container ls -a` command, we will see that our sample container has a status of `Exited`, but still exists on the system, as shown in the following code block:

```
$ docker container ls -a | grep sample
```

7. This should output something similar to this:

```
5266d7da377c    alpine:3.17      "/bin/sh"                 2 hours
ago       Exited (0) 48 seconds ago
```

8. If we want to see what has changed in our container concerning the base image, we can use the `docker container diff` command, as follows:

    ```
    $ docker container diff sample
    ```

9. The output should present a list of all modifications done on the filesystem of the container, as follows:

    ```
    → ch04 git:(main) ✗ docker container diff sample
    C /var
    C /var/cache
    C /var/cache/apk
    A /var/cache/apk/APKINDEX.ac15ed62.tar.gz
    A /var/cache/apk/APKINDEX.c3d4ed66.tar.gz
    A /-sSL
    C /etc
    C /etc/apk
    C /etc/apk/world
    C /etc/apk/protected_paths.d
    A /etc/apk/protected_paths.d/ca-certificates.list
    C /etc/ssl
    C /etc/ssl/certs
    A /etc/ssl/certs/fc5a8f99.0
    A /etc/ssl/certs/ca-cert-HiPKI_Root_CA_-_G1.pem
    A /etc/ssl/certs/ca-cert-NetLock_Arany_=Class_Gold=_Főtanúsítvány.pem
    A /etc/ssl/certs/ca-cert-Secure_Global_CA.pem
    A /etc/ssl/certs/ca-cert-GlobalSign_Root_CA_-_R6.pem
    A /etc/ssl/certs/ca-cert-SSL.com_EV_Root_Certification_Authority_ECC.pem
    A /etc/ssl/certs/0b1b94ef.0
    A /etc/ssl/certs/aee5f10d.0
    A /etc/ssl/certs/ca-cert-DigiCert_Assured_ID_Root_G2.pem
    ```

    Figure 4.9 – Output of the docker diff command (truncated)

    We have shortened the preceding output for better readability. In the list, A stands for added, and C stands for changed. If we had any deleted files, then those would be prefixed with D.

10. We can now use the `docker container commit` command to persist our modifications and create a new image from them, like this:

    ```
    $ docker container commit sample my-alpine
    ```

    The output generated by the preceding command on the author's computer is as follows:

    ```
    sha256:5287bccbb3012ded35e7e992a5ba2ded9b8b5d0...
    ```

    With the preceding command, we have specified that the new image will be called `my-alpine`. The output generated by the preceding command corresponds to the ID of the newly generated image.

11. We can verify this by listing all the images on our system, as follows:

    ```
    $ docker image ls
    ```

We can see this image ID as follows:

```
→  ch04 git:(main) x docker image ls
REPOSITORY                        TAG        IMAGE ID        CREATED             SIZE
my-alpine                         latest     5287bccbb301    About a minute ago  12.4MB
alpine                            3.17       d3156fec8bcb    4 days ago          7.46MB
nginx                             alpine     d0ddde8e3f4f    2 weeks ago         22.1MB
alpine                            latest     2b4661558fb8    2 weeks ago         5.29MB
busybox                           latest     2d0d8216f525    4 weeks ago         1.46MB
centos                            latest     e6a0117ec169    14 months ago       272MB
fundamentalsofdocker/trivia       ed2        bbc92c8f014d    3 years ago         7.94MB
```

Figure 4.10 – Listing all Docker images

We can see that the image named my-alpine has the expected ID of 5287bccbb301 (corresponding to the first part of the full hash code) and automatically got a tag of latest assigned. This happened since we did not explicitly define a tag ourselves. In this case, Docker always defaults to the latest tag.

12. If we want to see how our custom image has been built, we can use the history command, as follows:

```
$ docker image history my-alipine
```

This will print a list of the layers our image consists of, as follows:

```
→  ch04 git:(main) x docker image history my-alpine
IMAGE           CREATED         CREATED BY                                          SIZE     COMMENT
5287bccbb301    6 minutes ago   /bin/sh                                             4.98MB
d3156fec8bcb    4 days ago      /bin/sh -c #(nop)  CMD ["/bin/sh"]                  0B
<missing>       4 days ago      /bin/sh -c #(nop) ADD file:685b5edadf1d5bf0a…      7.46MB
```

Figure 4.11 – History of the my-alpine Docker image

The top layer – marked in red – in the preceding output is the one that we just created by adding the curl package. The other two lines stem from the original build of the Alpine 3.17 Docker image. It was created and uploaded 4 days ago.

Now that we have seen how we can interactively create a Docker image, let's look into how we can do the same declaratively using a Dockerfile.

Using Dockerfiles

Manually creating custom images, as shown in the previous section of this chapter, is very helpful when doing exploration, creating prototypes, or authoring feasibility studies. But it has a serious drawback: it is a manual process and thus is not repeatable or scalable. It is also error-prone, just like any other task executed manually by humans. There must be a better way.

This is where the so-called Dockerfile comes into play. A `Dockerfile` is a text file that, by default, is called `Dockerfile`. It contains instructions on how to build a custom container image. It is a declarative way of building images.

> **Declarative versus imperative**
>
> In computer science in general, and with Docker specifically, you often use a declarative way of defining a task. You describe the expected outcome and let the system figure out how to achieve this goal, rather than giving step-by-step instructions to the system on how to achieve this desired outcome. The latter is an imperative approach.

Let's look at a sample Dockerfile, as follows:

```
FROM python:3.12
RUN mkdir -p /app
WORKDIR /app
COPY ./requirements.txt /app/
RUN pip install -r requirements.txt
CMD ["python", "main.py"]
```

This is a Dockerfile as it is used to containerize a Python 3.12 application. As we can see, the file has six lines, each starting with a keyword such as FROM, RUN, or COPY.

> **Note**
>
> It is a convention to write the keywords in all caps, but that is not a must.

Each line of the Dockerfile results in a layer in the resulting image. In the following figure, the image is drawn upside down compared to the previous figures in this chapter, showing an image as a stack of layers. Here, the base layer is shown on top. Don't let yourself be confused by this. In reality, the base layer is always the lowest in the stack:

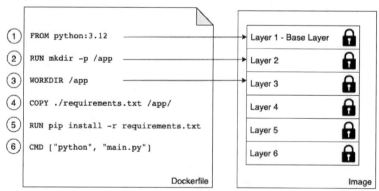

Figure 4.12 – The relationship between a Dockerfile and the layers in an image

Now, let's look at the individual keywords in more detail.

The FROM keyword

Every Dockerfile starts with the FROM keyword. With it, we define which base image we want to start building our custom image from. If we want to build starting with CentOS 7, for example, we would have the following line in the Dockerfile:

```
FROM centos:7
```

On Docker Hub, there are curated or official images for all major Linux distros, as well as for all important development frameworks or languages, such as Python, Node.js, Ruby, Go, and many more. Depending on our needs, we should select the most appropriate base image.

For example, if I want to containerize a Python 3.12 application, I might want to select the relevant official python:3.12 image.

If we want to start from scratch, we can also use the following statement:

```
FROM scratch
```

This is useful in the context of building super-minimal images that only – for example – contain a single binary: the actual statically linked executable, such as Hello-World. The scratch image is an empty base image.

FROM scratch, in reality, is a no-op in the Dockerfile, and as such does not generate a layer in the resulting container image.

The RUN keyword

The next important keyword is RUN. The argument for RUN is any valid Linux command, such as the following:

```
RUN yum install -y wget
```

The preceding command is using the yum CentOS package manager to install the wget package into the running container. This assumes that our base image is CentOS or **Red Hat Enterprise Linux (RHEL)**. If we had Ubuntu as our base image, then the command would look similar to the following:

```
RUN apt-get update && apt-get install -y wget
```

It would look like this because Ubuntu uses apt-get as a package manager. Similarly, we could define a line with RUN, like this:

```
RUN mkdir -p /app && cd /app
```

We could also do this:

```
RUN tar -xJC /usr/src/python --strip-components=1 -f python.tar.xz
```

Here, the former creates an /app folder in the container and navigates to it, and the latter un-tars a file to a given location. It is completely fine, and even recommended, for you to format a Linux command using more than one physical line, such as this:

```
RUN apt-get update \
    && apt-get install -y --no-install-recommends \
        ca-certificates \
        libexpat1 \
        libffi6 \
        libgdbm3 \
        libreadline7 \
        libsqlite3-0 \
    libssl1.1 \
    && rm -rf /var/lib/apt/lists/*
```

If we use more than one line, we need to put a backslash (\) at the end of the lines to indicate to the shell that the command continues on the next line.

> **Tip**
> Try to find out what the preceding command does.

The COPY and ADD keywords

The COPY and ADD keywords are very important since, in the end, we want to add some content to an existing base image to make it a custom image. Most of the time, these are a few source files of – say – a web application, or a few binaries of a compiled application.

These two keywords are used to copy files and folders from the host into the image that we're building. The two keywords are very similar, with the exception that the ADD keyword also lets us copy and unpack TAR files, as well as provide an URI as a source for the files and folders to copy.

Let's look at a few examples of how these two keywords can be used, as follows:

```
COPY . /app
COPY ./web /app/web
COPY sample.txt /data/my-sample.txt
ADD sample.tar /app/bin/
ADD http://example.com/sample.txt /data/
```

In the preceding lines of code, the following applies:

- The first line copies all files and folders from the current directory recursively to the app folder inside the container image
- The second line copies everything in the web subfolder to the target folder, /app/web
- The third line copies a single file, sample.txt, into the target folder, /data, and at the same time, renames it my-sample.txt
- The fourth statement unpacks the sample.tar file into the target folder, /app/bin
- Finally, the last statement copies the remote file, sample.txt, into the target file, /data

Wildcards are allowed in the source path. For example, the following statement copies all files starting with sample to the mydir folder inside the image:

```
COPY ./sample* /mydir/
```

From a security perspective, it is important to know that, by default, all files and folders inside the image will have a **user ID (UID)** and a **group ID (GID)** of 0. The good thing is that for both ADD and COPY, we can change the ownership that the files will have inside the image using the optional --chown flag, as follows:

```
ADD --chown=11:22 ./data/web* /app/data/
```

The preceding statement will copy all files starting with web and put them into the /app/data folder in the image, and at the same time assign user 11 and group 22 to these files.

Instead of numbers, we could also use names for the user and group, but then these entities would have to be already defined in the root filesystem of the image at /etc/passwd and /etc/group, respectively; otherwise, the build of the image would fail.

The WORKDIR keyword

The WORKDIR keyword defines the working directory or context that is used when a container is run from our custom image. So, if I want to set the context to the /app/bin folder inside the image, my expression in the Dockerfile would have to look as follows:

```
WORKDIR /app/bin
```

All activity that happens inside the image after the preceding line will use this directory as the working directory. It is very important to note that the following two snippets from a Dockerfile are not the same:

```
RUN cd /app/bin
RUN touch sample.txt
```

Compare the preceding code with the following code:

```
WORKDIR /app/bin
RUN touch sample.txt
```

The former will create the file in the root of the image filesystem, while the latter will create the file at the expected location in the /app/bin folder. Only the WORKDIR keyword sets the context across the layers of the image. The cd command alone is not persisted across layers.

> **Note**
>
> It is completely fine to change the current working directory multiple times in a Dockerfile.

The CMD and ENTRYPOINT keywords

The CMD and ENTRYPOINT keywords are special. While all other keywords defined for a Dockerfile are executed at the time the image is built by the Docker builder, these two are definitions of what will happen when a container is started from the image we define. When the container runtime starts a container, it needs to know what the process or application will be that has to run inside that container. That is exactly what CMD and ENTRYPOINT are used for – to tell Docker what the start process is and how to start that process.

Now, the differences between CMD and ENTRYPOINT are subtle, and honestly, most users don't fully understand them or use them in the intended way. Luckily, in most cases, this is not a problem and the container will run anyway; it's just handling it that is not as straightforward as it could be.

To better understand how to use these two keywords, let's analyze what a typical Linux command or expression looks like. Let's take the ping utility as an example, as follows:

```
$ ping -c 3 8.8.8.8
```

In the preceding expression, ping is the command, and -c 3 8.8.8.8 are the parameters of this command. Let's look at another expression here:

```
$ wget -O - http://example.com/downloads/script.sh
```

Again, in the preceding expression, wget is the command, and -O - http://example.com/ downloads/script.sh are the parameters.

Now that we have dealt with this, we can get back to CMD and ENTRYPOINT. ENTRYPOINT is used to define the command of the expression, while CMD is used to define the parameters for the command. Thus, a Dockerfile using Alpine as the base image and defining ping as the process to run in the container could look like this:

```
FROM alpine:3.17
ENTRYPOINT [ "ping" ]
CMD [ "-c", "3", "8.8.8.8" ]
```

For both `ENTRYPOINT` and `CMD`, the values are formatted as a JSON array of strings, where the individual items correspond to the tokens of the expression that are separated by whitespace. This is the preferred way of defining `CMD` and `ENTRYPOINT`. It is also called the exec form.

Alternatively, we can use what's called the shell form, as shown here:

```
CMD command param1 param2
```

We can now build an image called `pinger` from the preceding Dockerfile, as follows:

```
$ docker image build -t pinger .
```

Here is the output generated by the preceeding command:

Figure 4.13 – Building the pinger Docker image

Then, we can run a container from the pinger image we just created, like this:

```
$ docker container run --rm -it pinger
```

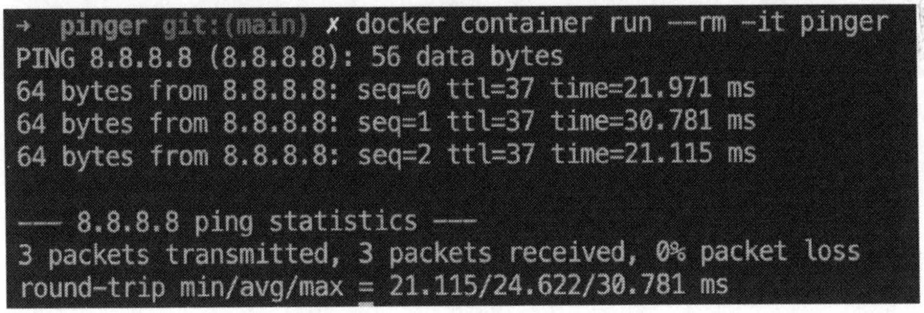

Figure 4.14 – Output of the pinger container

In the preceding command, we are using the `--rm` parameter, which defines that the container is automatically removed once the applications inside the container end.

The beauty of this is that I can now override the CMD part that I have defined in the Dockerfile (remember, it was `["-c", "3","8.8.8.8"]`) when I create a new container by adding the new values at the end of the `docker container run` expression, like this:

```
$ docker container run --rm -it pinger -w 5 127.0.0.1
```

This will cause the container to ping the loopback IP address (`127.0.0.1`) for 5 seconds.

If we want to override what's defined in `ENTRYPOINT` in the Dockerfile, we need to use the `--entrypoint` parameter in the `docker container run` expression. Let's say we want to execute a shell in the container instead of the `ping` command. We could do so by using the following command:

```
$ docker container run --rm -it --entrypoint /bin/sh pinger
```

We will then find ourselves inside the container. Type `exit` or press *Ctrl + D* to leave the container.

As I already mentioned, we do not necessarily have to follow best practices and define the command through `ENTRYPOINT` and the parameters through `CMD`; instead, we can enter the whole expression as a value of `CMD` and it will work, as shown in the following code block:

```
FROM alpine:3.17
CMD wget -O - http://www.google.com
```

Here, I have even used the shell form to define CMD. But what happens in this situation if `ENTRYPOINT` is undefined? If you leave `ENTRYPOINT` undefined, then it will have the default value of `/bin/sh -c`, and whatever the value of CMD is will be passed as a string to the shell command. The preceding definition would thereby result in entering the following code to run the process inside the container:

```
/bin/sh -c "wget -O - http://www.google.com"
```

Consequently, `/bin/sh` is the main process running inside the container, and it will start a new child process to run the `wget` utility.

A complex Dockerfile

So far, we have discussed the most important keywords commonly used in Dockerfiles. Now, let's look at a realistic and somewhat complex example of a Dockerfile. Those of you who are interested might note that it looks very similar to the first Dockerfile that we presented in this chapter. Here is its content:

```
FROM node:19-buster-slim
RUN mkdir -p /app
WORKDIR /app
COPY package.json /app/
RUN npm install
COPY . /app
```

```
ENTRYPOINT ["npm"]
CMD ["start"]
```

OK; so, what is happening here? This is a Dockerfile that is used to build an image for a Node.js application; we can deduce this from the fact that the node:19-buster-slim base image is used. Then, the second line is an instruction to create an /app folder in the filesystem of the image. The third line defines the working directory or context in the image to be this new /app folder. Then, on line four, we copy a package.json file into the /app folder inside the image. After this, on line five, we execute the npm install command inside the container; remember, our context is the /app folder, so npm will find the package.json file there that we copied on line four.

Once all the Node.js dependencies have been installed, we copy the rest of the application files from the current folder of the host into the /app folder of the image.

Finally, in the last two lines, we define what the startup command will be when a container is run from this image. In our case, it is npm start, which will start the Node.js application.

Building an image

Let's look at a concrete example and build a simple Docker image, as follows:

1. Navigate to the sample code repository. Normally, this should be located in your home folder:

    ```
    $ cd ~/The-Ultimate-Docker-Container-Book
    ```

2. Create a new subfolder for *Chapter 4* and navigate to it:

    ```
    $ mkdir ch04 && cd ch04
    ```

3. In the preceding folder, create a sample1 subfolder and navigate to it, like this:

    ```
    $ mkdir sample1 && cd sample1
    ```

4. Use your favorite editor to create a file called Dockerfile inside this sample folder, with the following content:

    ```
    FROM centos:7
    RUN yum install -y wget
    ```

5. Save the file and exit your editor.

6. Back in the Terminal window, we can now build a new container image using the preceding Dockerfile as a manifest or construction plan, like this:

    ```
    $ docker image build -t my-centos .
    ```

Please note that there is a period (.) at the end of the preceding command:

```
→  sample1 git:(main) x docker image build -t my-centos .
[+] Building 21.7s (7/7) FINISHED
 => [internal] load build definition from Dockerfile                                   0.0s
 => => transferring dockerfile: 80B                                                    0.0s
 => [internal] load .dockerignore                                                      0.0s
 => => transferring context: 2B                                                        0.0s
 => [internal] load metadata for docker.io/library/centos:7                            1.9s
 => [auth] library/centos:pull token for registry-1.docker.io                         0.0s
 => [1/2] FROM docker.io/library/centos:7@sha256:c73f515d06b0fa07bb18d8202035e739a494ce7  11.1s
 => => resolve docker.io/library/centos:7@sha256:c73f515d06b0fa07bb18d8202035e739a494ce76  0.0s
 => => sha256:c73f515d06b0fa07bb18d8202035e739a494ce760aa73129f60f4bf2bd2 1.20kB / 1.20kB  0.0s
 => => sha256:73f11afcbb50d8bc70eab9f0850b3fa30e61a419bc48cf426e63527d14a8373 530B / 530B  0.0s
 => => sha256:c9a1fdca3387618f8634949de4533419327736e2f5c618e3bfebe877aa3 2.77kB / 2.77kB  0.0s
 => => sha256:6717b8ec66cd6add0272c6391165585613c31314a43ff77d9751b53 108.37MB / 108.37MB  8.6s
 => => extracting sha256:6717b8ec66cd6add0272c6391165585613c31314a43ff77d9751b53010e531ec  2.4s
 => [2/2] RUN yum install -y wget                                                      8.4s
 => exporting to image                                                                 0.1s
 => => exporting layers                                                                0.1s
 => => writing image sha256:8eb6daefac9659b05b1774042cb50b543cf2081d5d42fd2ca5854f82451b4  0.0s
 => => naming to docker.io/library/my-centos                                           0.0s
```

Figure 4.15 – Building our first custom image from CentOS

The previous command means that the Docker builder creates a new image called my-centos using the Dockerfile that is present in the current directory. Here, the period at the end of the command specifies the current directory. We could also write the preceding command as follows, with the same result:

```
$ docker image build -t my-centos -f Dockerfile .
```

Here, we can omit the -f parameter since the builder assumes that the Dockerfile is called Dockerfile. We only ever need the -f parameter if our Dockerfile has a different name or is not located in the current directory.

Let's analyze the output shown in *Figure 4.15*. This output is created by the Docker build kit:

1. First, we have the following line:

    ```
    [+] Building 21.7s (7/7) FINISHED
    ```

    This line is generated at the end of the build process, although it appears as the first line. It tells us that the building took approximately 22 seconds and was executed in 7 steps.

2. Now, let's skip the next few lines until we reach this one:

    ```
    => [1/2] FROM docker.io/library/centos:7@sha256:c73f51...
    ```

    This line tells us which line of the Dockerfile the builder is currently executing (1 of 2). We can see that this is the FROM centos:7 statement in our Dockerfile. This is the declaration of the base image, on top of which we want to build our custom image. What the builder then does is pull this image from Docker Hub, if it is not already available in the local cache.

3. Now, follow the next step. I have shortened it even more than the preceding one to concentrate on the essential part:

```
=> [2/2] RUN yum install -y wget
```

This is our second line in the Dockerfile, where we want to use the yum package manager to install the wget utility.

4. The last few lines are as follows:

```
=> exporting to image                              0.1s
=> => exporting layers                             0.1s
=> => writing image sha256:8eb6daefac9659b05b17740...
=> => naming to docker.io/library/my-centos
```

Here, the builder finalizes building the image and provides the image with the sha256 code of 8eb6daefac9....

This tells us that the resulting custom image has been given an ID of 8eb6daefac9... and has been tagged with my-centos:latest.

Now that we have analyzed how the build process of a Docker image works and what steps are involved, let's talk about how to further improve this by introducing multi-step builds.

Multi-step builds

To demonstrate why a Dockerfile with multiple build steps is useful, let's make an example Dockerfile. Let's take a Hello World application written in C:

1. Open a new Terminal window and navigate to this chapter's folder:

```
$ cd The-Ultimate-Docker-Container-Book/ch04
```

2. Create a new folder called multi-step-build in your chapter folder:

```
$ mkdir multi-step-build
```

3. Open VS Code for this folder:

```
$ code multi-step-build
```

4. Create a file called hello.c in this folder and add the following code to it:

```
#include <stdio.h>
int main (void)
{
    printf ("Hello, world!\n");
    return 0;
}
```

5. Now, we want to containerize this application and write a Dockerfile with this content:

```
FROM alpine:3.12
RUN apk update && \
    apk add --update alpine-sdk
RUN mkdir /app
WORKDIR /app
COPY . /app
RUN mkdir bin
RUN gcc -Wall hello.c -o bin/hello
CMD /app/bin/hello
```

6. Next, let's build this image:

```
$ docker image build -t hello-world .
```

This gives us a fairly long output since the builder has to install the Alpine **Software Development Kit (SDK)**, which, among other tools, contains the C++ compiler we need to build the application.

7. Once the build is done, we can list the image and see the size that's been shown, as follows:

```
$ docker image ls | grep hello-world
```

In the author's case, the output is as follows:

```
hello-world    latest    42c0c7086fbf    2 minutes ago    215MB
```

With a size of 215 MB, the resulting image is way too big. In the end, it is just a Hello World application. The reason for it being so big is that the image not only contains the Hello World binary but also all the tools to compile and link the application from the source code. But this is not desirable when running the application, say, in production. Ideally, we only want to have the resulting binary in the image and not a whole SDK.

It is precisely for this reason that we should define Dockerfiles as multi-stage. We have some stages that are used to build the final artifacts, and then a final stage, where we use the minimal necessary base image and copy the artifacts into it. This results in very small Docker images. Let's do this:

1. Create a new Dockerfile to your folder called `Dockerfile.multi-step` with this content:

```
FROM alpine:3.12 AS build
RUN apk update && \
    apk add --update alpine-sdk
RUN mkdir /app
WORKDIR /app
COPY . /app
RUN mkdir bin
RUN gcc hello.c -o bin/hello

FROM alpine:3.12
```

```
COPY --from=build /app/bin/hello /app/hello
CMD /app/hello
```

Here, we have the first stage with an alias called `build`, which is used to compile the application; then, the second stage uses the same `alpine:3.12` base image but does not install the SDK, and only copies the binary from the `build` stage, using the `--from` parameter, into this final image.

2. Let's build the image again, as follows:

```
$ docker image build -t hello-world-small \
    -f Dockerfile.multi-step .
```

3. Let's compare the sizes of the images with this command:

```
$ docker image ls | grep hello-world
```

Here, we get the following output:

```
hello-world-small latest 72c... 20 seconds ago 5.34MB
hello-world       latest 42c... 10 minutes ago 215
```

We have been able to reduce the size from 215 MB down to 5.34 MB. This is a reduction in size by a factor of approximately 40. A smaller image has many advantages, such as a smaller attack surface area for hackers, reduced memory and disk consumption, faster startup times for the corresponding containers, and a reduction of the bandwidth needed to download the image from a registry, such as Docker Hub.

Dockerfile best practices

There are a few recommended best practices to consider when authoring a Dockerfile, which are as follows:

*   First and foremost, we need to consider that containers are meant to be ephemeral. By ephemeral, we mean that a container can be stopped and destroyed, and a new one built and put in place with the absolute minimum setup and configuration. That means that we should try hard to keep the time that is needed to initialize the application running inside the container at a minimum, as well as the time needed to terminate or clean up the application.

*   The next best practice tells us that we should order the individual commands in the Dockerfile so that we leverage caching as much as possible. Building a layer of an image can take a considerable amount of time – sometimes many seconds, or even minutes. While developing an application, we will have to build the container image for our application multiple times. We want to keep the build times at a minimum.

When we're rebuilding a previously built image, the only layers that are rebuilt are the ones that have changed, but if one layer needs to be rebuilt, all subsequent layers also need to be rebuilt. This is very important to remember. Consider the following example:

```
FROM node:19
RUN mkdir -p /app
WORKIR /app
COPY . /app
RUN npm install
CMD ["npm", "start"]
```

In this example, the npm install command on line five of the Dockerfile usually takes the longest. A classical Node.js application has many external dependencies, and those are all downloaded and installed in this step. It can take minutes until it is done. Therefore, we want to avoid running npm install each time we rebuild the image, but a developer changes their source code all the time during the development of an application. That means that line four, the result of the COPY command, changes every time, and thus this layer has to be rebuilt. But as we discussed previously, that also means that all subsequent layers have to be rebuilt, which – in this case – includes the npm install command. To avoid this, we can slightly modify the Dockerfile and have the following:

```
FROM node:19
RUN mkdir -p /app
WORKIR /app
COPY package.json /app/
RUN npm install
COPY . /app
CMD ["npm", "start"]
```

Here, on line four, we only copied the single file that the npm install command needs as a source, which is the package.json file. This file rarely changes in a typical development process. As a consequence, the npm install command also has to be executed only when the package. json file changes. All the remaining frequently changed content is added to the image after the npm install command.

A further best practice is to keep the number of layers that make up your image relatively small. The more layers an image has, the more the graph driver needs to work to consolidate the layers into a single root filesystem for the corresponding container. Of course, this takes time, and thus the fewer layers an image has, the faster the startup time for the container can be.

But how can we keep our number of layers low? Remember that in a Dockerfile, each line that starts with a keyword such as FROM, COPY, or RUN creates a new layer. The easiest way to reduce the number of layers is to combine multiple individual RUN commands into a single one. For example, say that we had the following in a Dockerfile:

```
...
RUN apt-get update
RUN apt-get install -y ca-certificates
RUN rm -rf /var/lib/apt/lists/*
...
```

We could combine these into a single concatenated expression, as follows:

```
...
RUN apt-get update \
    && apt-get install -y ca-certificates \
    && rm -rf /var/lib/apt/lists/*
...
```

The former will generate three layers in the resulting image, while the latter will only create a single layer.

The next three best practices all result in smaller images. Why is this important? Smaller images reduce the time and bandwidth needed to download the image from a registry. They also reduce the amount of disk space needed to store a copy locally on the Docker host and the memory needed to load the image. Finally, smaller images also mean a smaller attack surface for hackers. Here are the best practices mentioned:

- The first best practice that helps reduce the image size is to use a .dockerignore file. We want to avoid copying unnecessary files and folders into an image, to keep it as lean as possible. A .dockerignore file works in the same way as a .gitignore file, for those who are familiar with Git. In a .dockerignore file, we can configure patterns to exclude certain files or folders from being included in the context when building the image.

- The next best practice is to avoid installing unnecessary packages into the filesystem of the image. Once again, this is to keep the image as lean as possible.

- Last but not least, it is recommended that you use multi-stage builds so that the resulting image is as small as possible and only contains the absolute minimum needed to run your application or application service.

In the next section, we are going to learn how to create a Docker image from a previously saved image. In fact, it may look like restoring an image.

Saving and loading images

The third way to create a new container image is by importing or loading it from a file. A container image is nothing more than a tarball. To demonstrate this, we can use the docker image save command to export an existing image to a tarball, like this:

```
$ mkdir backup
$ docker image save -o ./backup/my-alpine.tar my-alpine
```

The preceding command takes our my-alpine image that we previously built and exports it into a file called ./backup/my-alpine.tar:

```
→  ch04 git:(main) x mkdir backup
→  ch04 git:(main) x docker image save -o ./backup/my-alpine.tar my-alpine
→  ch04 git:(main) x ls -al backup
total 25400
drwxr-xr-x  3 gabriel  staff        96 27 Nov 16:18 .
drwxr-xr-x  5 gabriel  staff       160 27 Nov 16:17 ..
-rw--------  1 gabriel  staff  13003264 27 Nov 16:18 my-alpine.tar
```

Figure 4.16 – Exporting an image as a tarball

If, on the other hand, we have an existing tarball and want to import it as an image into our system, we can use the docker image load command, as follows:

```
$ docker image load -i ./backup/my-alpine.tar
```

The output of the preceding command should be as follows:

```
Loaded image: my-alpine:latest
```

With this, we have learned how to build a Docker image in three different ways. We can do so interactively, by defining a Dockerfile, or by importing it into our system from a tarball.

In the next section, we will discuss how we can create Docker images for existing legacy applications, and thus run them in a container and profit from this.

Lift and shift – containerizing a legacy app

We can't always start from scratch and develop a brand-new application. More often than not, we find ourselves with a huge portfolio of traditional applications that are up and running in production and provide mission-critical value to the company or the customers of the company. Often, those applications are organically grown and very complex. Documentation is sparse, and nobody wants to touch such an application. Often, the saying *"Never touch a running system"* applies. Yet, the market needs change, and with that arises the need to update or rewrite those apps. Often, a complete rewrite is not possible due to the lack of resources and time, or due to the excessive cost. What are we going to do about those applications? Could we possibly Dockerize them and profit from the benefits introduced by containers?

It turns out we can. In 2017, Docker introduced a program called **Modernize Traditional Apps (MTA)** to their enterprise customers, which in essence promised to help those customers take their existing or traditional Java and .NET applications and containerize them, without the need to change a single line of code. The focus of MTA was on Java and .NET applications since those made up the lion's share of the traditional applications in a typical enterprise. But it can also be used for any application that was written in – say – C, C++, Python, Node.js, Ruby, PHP, or Go, to name just a few other languages and platforms.

Let's imagine such a legacy application for a moment. Let's assume we have an old Java application that was written 10 years ago and that was continuously updated during the following 5 years. The application is based on Java SE 6, which came out in December 2006. It uses environment variables and property files for configuration. Secrets such as usernames and passwords used in the database connection strings are pulled from a secrets keystore, such as HashiCorp Vault.

Now, let's describe each of the required steps to lift and shift a legacy application in more detail.

Analyzing external dependencies

One of the first steps in the modernization process is to discover and list all external dependencies of the legacy application:

- Does it use a database? If so, which one? What does the connection string look like?

- Does it use external APIs such as credit card approval or geo-mapping APIs? What are the API keys and key secrets?

- Is it consuming from or publishing to an **Enterprise Service Bus (ESB)**?

These are just a few possible dependencies that come to mind. Many more exist. These are the seams of the application to the outer world, and we need to be aware of them and create an inventory.

Source code and build instructions

The next step is to locate all the source code and other assets, such as images and CSS and HTML files that are part of the application. Ideally, they should be located in a single folder. This folder will be the root of our project and can have as many subfolders as needed. This project root folder will be the context during the build of the container image we want to create for our legacy application. Remember, the Docker builder only includes files in the build that are part of that context; in our case, that is the root project folder.

There is, though, an option to download or copy files during the build from different locations, using the COPY or ADD commands. Please refer to the online documentation for the exact details on how to use these two commands. This option is useful if the sources for your legacy application cannot be easily contained in a single, local folder.

Once we are aware of all the parts that contribute to the final application, we need to investigate how the application is built and packaged. In our case, this is most probably done by using **Maven**. Maven is the most popular build automation tool for Java, and has been – and still is – used in most enterprises that develop Java applications. In the case of a legacy .NET application, it is most probably done by using the MSBuild tool; and in the case of a C/C++ application, make would most likely be used.

Once again, let's extend our inventory and write down the exact build commands used. We will need this information later on when authoring the Dockerfile.

Configuration

Applications need to be configured. Information provided during configuration could be – for example – the type of application logging to use, connection strings to databases, and hostnames to services such as ESBs or URIs to external APIs, to name just a few.

We can differentiate a few types of configurations, as follows:

- **Build time**: This is the information needed during the build of the application and/or its Docker image. It needs to be available when we create the Docker images.

- **Environment**: This is configuration information that varies with the environment in which the application is running – for example, DEVELOPMENT versus STAGING or PRODUCTION. This kind of configuration is applied to the application when a container with the app starts – for example, in production.

- **Runtime**: This is information that the application retrieves during runtime, such as secrets to access an external API.

Secrets

Every mission-critical enterprise application needs to deal with secrets in some form or another. The most familiar secrets are part of the connection information needed to access databases that are used to persist the data produced by or used by the application. Other secrets include the credentials needed to access external APIs, such as a credit score lookup API. It is important to note that, here, we are talking about secrets that have to be provided by the application itself to the service providers the application uses or depends on, and not secrets provided by the users of the application. The actor here is our application, which needs to be authenticated and authorized by external authorities and service providers.

There are various ways traditional applications got their secrets. The worst and most insecure way of providing secrets is by hardcoding them or reading them from configuration files or environment variables, where they are available in cleartext. A much better way is to read the secrets during runtime from a special secret store that persists the secrets encrypted and provides them to the application over a secure connection, such as **Transport Layer Security** (**TLS**).

Once again, we need to create an inventory of all the secrets that our application uses and the way it procures them. Thus, we need to ask ourselves where we can get our secrets from: is it through environment variables or configuration files, or is it by accessing an external keystore, such as HashiCorp Vault, AWS Secrets Manager, or Azure Key Vault?

Authoring the Dockerfile

Once we have a complete inventory of all the items we discussed in the previous few sections, we are ready to author our Dockerfile. But I want to warn you: don't expect this to be a one-shot-and-go task.

You may need several iterations until you have crafted your final Dockerfile. The Dockerfile may be rather long and ugly-looking, but that's not a problem, so long as we get a working Docker image. We can always fine-tune the Dockerfile once we have a working version.

The base image

Let's start by identifying the base image we want to use and build our image from. Is there an official Java image available that is compatible with our requirements? Remember that our application is based on Java SE 6. If such a base image is available, then we should use that one. Otherwise, we will want to start with a Linux distro such as Red Hat, Oracle, or Ubuntu. In the latter case, we will use the appropriate package manager of the distro (`yum`, `apt`, or another) to install the desired versions of Java and Maven. For this, we can use the RUN keyword in the Dockerfile. Remember, RUN allows us to execute any valid Linux command in the image during the build process.

Assembling the sources

In this step, we make sure all the source files and other artifacts needed to successfully build the application are part of the image. Here, we mainly use the two keywords of the Dockerfile: COPY and ADD. Initially, the structure of the source inside the image should look the same as on the host, to avoid any build problems. Ideally, you would have a single COPY command that copies all of the root project folders from the host into the image. The corresponding Dockerfile snippet could then look as simple as this:

```
WORKDIR /app
COPY . .
```

> **Note**
>
> Don't forget to also provide a `.dockerignore` file, which is located in the project root folder, which lists all the files and (sub)folders of the project root folder that should not be part of the build context.

As mentioned earlier, you can also use the ADD keyword to download sources and other artifacts into the Docker image that are not located in the build context but somewhere reachable by a URI, as shown here:

```
ADD http://example.com/foobar ./
```

This would create a `foobar` folder in the image's working folder and copy all the contents from the URI.

Building the application

In this step, we make sure to create the final artifacts that make up our executable legacy application. Often, this is a JAR or WAR file, with or without some satellite JARs. This part of the Dockerfile should mimic the way you traditionally used to build an application before containerizing it. Thus, if you're using Maven as your build automation tool, the corresponding snippet of the Dockerfile could look as simple as this:

```
RUN mvn --clean install
```

In this step, we may also want to list the environment variables the application uses and provide sensible defaults. But never provide default values for environment variables that provide secrets to the application, such as the database connection string! Use the ENV keyword to define your variables, like this:

```
ENV foo=bar
ENV baz=123
```

Also, declare all ports that the application is listening on and that need to be accessible from outside of the container via the EXPOSE keyword, like this:

```
EXPOSE 5000
EXPOSE 15672/tcp
```

Next, we will explain the start command.

Defining the start command

Usually, a Java application is started with a command such as java -jar <mainapplication jar> if it is a standalone application. If it is a WAR file, then the start command may look a bit different. Therefore, we can either define ENTRYPOINT or CMD to use this command. Thus, the final statement in our Dockerfile could look like this:

```
ENTRYPOINT java -jar pet-shop.war
```

Often, though, this is too simplistic, and we need to execute a few pre-run tasks. In this case, we can craft a script file that contains the series of commands that need to be executed to prepare the environment and run the application. Such a file is often called docker-entrypoint.sh, but you are free to name it however you want. Make sure the file is executable – for example, run the following command on the host:

```
chmod +x ./docker-entrypoint.sh
```

The last line of the Dockerfile would then look like this:

```
ENTRYPOINT ./docker-entrypoint.sh
```

Now that you have been given hints on how to containerize a legacy application, it is time to recap and ask ourselves, is it worth the effort?

Why bother?

At this point, I can see you scratching your head and asking yourself: why bother? Why should you take on this seemingly huge effort just to containerize a legacy application? What are the benefits?

It turns out that the **return on investment (ROI)** is huge. Enterprise customers of Docker have publicly disclosed at conferences such as DockerCon 2018 and 2019 that they are seeing these two main benefits of Dockerizing traditional applications:

- More than a 50% saving in maintenance costs
- Up to a 90% reduction in the time between the deployments of new releases

The costs saved by reducing the maintenance overhead can be directly reinvested and used to develop new features and products. The time saved during new releases of traditional applications makes a business more agile and able to react to changing customer or market needs more quickly.

Now that we have discussed how to build Docker images at length, it is time to learn how we can ship those images through the various stages of the software delivery pipeline.

Sharing or shipping images

To be able to ship our custom image to other environments, we need to give it a globally unique name. This action is often called **tagging an image**. We then need to publish the image to a central location from which other interested or entitled parties can pull it. These central locations are called **image registries**.

In the following sections, we will describe how this works in more detail.

Tagging an image

Each image has a so-called tag. A tag is often used to version images, but it has a broader reach than just being a version number. If we do not explicitly specify a tag when working with images, then Docker automatically assumes we're referring to the latest tag. This is relevant when pulling an image from Docker Hub, as shown in the following example:

```
$ docker image pull alpine
```

The preceding command will pull the `alpine:latest` image from Docker Hub. If we want to explicitly specify a tag, we can do so like this:

```
$ docker image pull alpine:3.5
```

This will pull the Alpine image that has been tagged with `3.5`.

Demystifying image namespaces

So far, we have pulled various images and haven't worried so much about where those images originated from. Your Docker environment is configured so that, by default, all images are pulled from Docker Hub. We also only pulled so-called official images from Docker Hub, such as `alpine` or `busybox`.

Now, it is time to widen our horizons a bit and learn about how images are namespaced. The most generic way to define an image is by its fully qualified name, which looks as follows:

```
<registry URL>/<User or Org>/<name>:<tag>
```

Let's look at this in a bit more detail:

Namespace part	Description
`<registry URL>`	This is the URL to the registry from which we want to pull the image. By default, this is `docker.io`. More generally, this could be `https://registry.acme.com`. Other than Docker Hub, there are quite a few public registries out there that you could pull images from. The following is a list of some of them, in no particular order: • Google, at `https://cloud.google.com/container-registry` • Amazon AWS Amazon **Elastic Container Registry (ECR)**, at `https://aws.amazon.com/ecr/` • Microsoft Azure, at `https://azure.microsoft.com/en-us/services/container-registry/` • Red Hat, at `https://access.redhat.com/containers/` • Artifactory, at `https://jfrog.com/integration/artifactorydocker-registry/`
`<User>` or `<Org>`	This is the private Docker ID of either an individual or an organization defined on Docker Hub – or any other registry, for that matter, such as `microsoft` or `oracle`.
`<name>`	This is the name of the image, which is often also called a repository.
`<tag>`	This is the tag of the image.

Let's look at an example, as follows:

```
https://registry.acme.com/engineering/web-app:1.0
```

Here, we have an image, `web-app`, that is tagged with version `1.0` and belongs to the `engineering` organization on the private registry at `https://registry.acme.com`.

Now, there are some special conventions:

- If we omit the registry URL, then Docker Hub is automatically taken
- If we omit the tag, then the `latest` tag is taken
- If it is an official image on Docker Hub, then no user or organization namespace is needed

Here are a few samples in tabular form:

Image	Description
`alpine`	The official `alpine` image on Docker Hub with the `latest` tag.
`ubuntu:22.04`	The official `ubuntu` image on Docker Hub with the `22.04` tag or version.
`hashicorp/vault`	The `vault` image of an organization called `hashicorp` on Docker Hub with the `latest` tag.
`acme/web-api:12.0`	The `web-api` image version of `12.0` that's associated with the `acme` org. The image is on Docker Hub.
`gcr.io/jdoe/sample-app:1.1`	The `sample-app` image with the `1.1` tag belonging to an individual with the `jdoe` ID in Google's container registry.

Now that we know how the fully qualified name of a Docker image is defined and what its parts are, let's talk about some special images we can find on Docker Hub.

Explaining official images

In the preceding table, we mentioned "official image" a few times. This needs an explanation.

Images are stored in repositories on the Docker Hub registry. Official repositories are a set of repositories hosted on Docker Hub that are curated by individuals or organizations that are also responsible for the software packaged inside the image. Let's look at an example of what that means. There is an official organization behind the Ubuntu Linux distro. This team also provides official versions of Docker images that contain their Ubuntu distros.

Official images are meant to provide essential base OS repositories, images for popular programming language runtimes, frequently used data storage, and other important services.

Docker sponsors a team whose task is to review and publish all those curated images in public repositories on Docker Hub. Furthermore, Docker scans all official images for vulnerabilities.

Pushing images to a registry

Creating custom images is all well and good, but at some point, we want to share or ship our images to a target environment, such as a test, **quality assurance (QA)**, or production system. For this, we typically use a container registry. One of the most popular public registries out there is Docker Hub. It is configured as a default registry in your Docker environment, and it is the registry from which we have pulled all our images so far.

In a registry, we can usually create personal or organizational accounts. For example, the author's account at Docker Hub is gnschenker. Personal accounts are good for personal use. If we want to use the registry professionally, then we'll probably want to create an organizational account, such as acme, on Docker Hub. The advantage of the latter is that organizations can have multiple teams. Teams can have differing permissions.

To be able to push an image to my account on Docker Hub, I need to tag it accordingly. Let's say I want to push the latest version of the Alpine image to my account and give it a tag of 1.0. I can do this in the following way:

1. Tag the existing image, alpine:latest, with this command:

    ```
    $ docker image tag alpine:latest gnschenker/alpine:1.0
    ```

    Here, Docker does not create a new image but creates a new reference to the existing image, alpine:latest, and names it gnschenker/alpine:1.0.

2. Now, to be able to push the image, I have to log in to my account, as follows:

    ```
    $ docker login -u gnschenker -p <my secret password>
    ```

3. Make sure to replace gnschenker with your own Docker Hub username and <my secret password> with your password.

4. After a successful login, I can then push the image, like this:

    ```
    $ docker image push gnschenker/alpine:1.0
    ```

    I will see something similar to this in the Terminal window:

    ```
    The push refers to repository [docker.io/gnschenker/alpine]
    04a094fe844e: Mounted from library/alpine
    1.0: digest: sha256:5cb04fce... size: 528
    ```

For each image that we push to Docker Hub, we automatically create a repository. A repository can be private or public. Everyone can pull an image from a public repository. From a private repository, an image can only be pulled if you are logged in to the registry and have the necessary permissions configured.

Summary

In this chapter, we discussed what container images are and how we can build and ship them. As we have seen, there are three different ways that an image can be created – either manually, automatically, or by importing a tarball into the system. We also learned some of the best practices commonly used when building custom images. Finally, we got a quick introduction to how to share or ship custom images by uploading them to a container image registry such as Docker Hub.

In the next chapter, we're going to introduce Docker volumes, which can be used to persist the state of a container. We'll also show you how to define individual environment variables for the application running inside the container, as well as how to use files containing whole sets of configuration settings.

Questions

Please try to answer the following questions to assess your learning progress:

1. How would you create a Dockerfile that inherits from Ubuntu version 22.04, and that installs `ping` and runs `ping` when a container starts? The default address used to ping should be `127.0.0.1`.

2. How would you create a new container image that uses `alpine:latest` as a base image and installs `curl` on top of it? Name the new image `my-alpine:1.0`.

3. Create a Dockerfile that uses multiple steps to create an image of a Hello World app of minimal size, written in C or Go.

4. Name three essential characteristics of a Docker container image.

5. You want to push an image named `foo:1.0` to your `jdoe` personal account on Docker Hub. Which of the following is the right solution?

    A. `$ docker container push foo:1.0`

    B. `$ docker image tag foo:1.0 jdoe/foo:1.0`

    C. `$ docker image push jdoe/foo:1.0`

    D. `$ docker login -u jdoe -p <your password>`

    E. `$ docker image tag foo:1.0 jdoe/foo:1.0`

    F. `$ docker image push jdoe/foo:1.0`

    G. `$ docker login -u jdoe -p <your password>`

    H. `$ docker container tag foo:1.0 jdoe/foo:1.0`

    I. `$ docker container push jdoe/foo:1.0`

    J. `$ docker login -u jdoe -p <your password>`

    K. `$ docker image push foo:1.0 jdoe/foo:1.0`

Answers

Here are possible answers to this chapter's questions:

1. The Dockerfile could look like this:

```
FROM ubuntu:22.04
RUN apt-get update && \
apt-get install -y iputils-ping
CMD ping 127.0.0.1
```

Note that in Ubuntu, the ping tool is part of the iputils-ping package. You can build the image called pinger – for example – with the following command:

```
$ docker image build -t mypinger .
```

2. The Dockerfile could look like this:

```
FROM alpine:latest
RUN apk update && \
apk add curl
```

Build the image with the following command:

```
$ docker image build -t my-alpine:1.0 .
```

3. The Dockerfile for a Go application could look like this:

```
FROM golang:alpine
WORKDIR /app
ADD . /app
RUN go env -w GO111MODULE=off
RUN cd /app && go build -o goapp
ENTRYPOINT ./goapp
```

You can find the full solution in the ~/The-Ultimate-Docker-Container-Book/sample-solutions/ch04/answer03 folder.

4. A Docker image has the following characteristics:

   - It is immutable

   - It consists of one-to-many layers

   - It contains the files and folders needed for the packaged application to run

5. The correct answer is C. First, you need to log in to Docker Hub; then, you must tag your image correctly with the username. Finally, you must push the image.

5

Data Volumes and Configuration

In the previous chapter, we learned how to build and share our container images. Focus was placed on how to build images that are as small as possible by only containing artifacts that are needed by the containerized application.

In this chapter, we are going to learn how we can work with stateful containers – that is, containers that consume and produce data. We will also learn how to configure our containers at runtime and at image build time, using environment variables and config files.

Here is a list of the topics we're going to discuss:

- Creating and mounting data volumes
- Sharing data between containers
- Using host volumes
- Defining volumes in images
- Configuring containers

After working through this chapter, you will be able to do the following:

- Create, delete, and list data volumes
- Mount an existing data volume into a container
- Create durable data from within a container using a data volume
- Share data between multiple containers using data volumes
- Mount any host folder into a container using data volumes
- Define the access mode (read/write or read-only) for a container when accessing data in a data volume

- Configure environment variables for applications running in a container
- Parameterize a Dockerfile by using build arguments

Technical requirements

For this chapter, you need Docker Desktop installed on your machine. There is no code accompanying this chapter.

Before we start, we need to create a folder for *Chapter 5* inside our code repository:

1. Use this command to navigate to the folder where you checked out the code from GitHub:

```
$ cd ~/The-Ultimate-Docker-Container-Book
```

> **Note**
> If you did not check out the GitHub repository at the default location, the preceding command may vary for you.

2. Create a sub-folder for *Chapter 5* and navigate to it:

```
$ mkdir ch05 && cd ch05
```

Let's get started!

Creating and mounting data volumes

All meaningful applications consume or produce data. Yet containers are, ideally, meant to be stateless. How are we going to deal with this? One way is to use Docker volumes. Volumes allow containers to consume, produce, and modify a state. Volumes have a life cycle that goes beyond the life cycle of containers. When a container that uses a volume dies, the volume continues to exist. This is great for the durability of the state.

Modifying the container layer

Before we dive into volumes, let's first discuss what happens if an application in a container changes something in the filesystem of the container. In this case, the changes are all happening in the writable container layer that we introduced in *Chapter 4, Creating and Managing Container Images*. Let's quickly demonstrate this:

1. Run a container and execute a script in it that is creating a new file, like this:

```
$ docker container run --name demo \
```

```
alpine /bin/sh -c 'echo "This is a test" > sample.txt'
```

2. The preceding command creates a container named `demo`, and, inside this container, creates a file called `sample.txt` with the content `This is a test`. The container exits after running the `echo` command but remains in memory, available for us to do our investigations.

3. Let's use the `diff` command to find out what has changed in the container's filesystem concerning the filesystem of the original image, as follows:

```
$ docker container diff demo
```

The output should look like this:

```
A /sample.txt
```

4. A new file, as indicated by the letter `A`, has been added to the filesystem of the container, as expected. Since all layers that stem from the underlying image (Alpine, in this case) are immutable, the change could only happen in the writeable container layer.

Files that have changed compared to the original image will be marked with a `C` and those that have been deleted with a `D`.

Now, if we remove the container from memory, its container layer will also be removed, and with it, all the changes will be irreversibly deleted. If we need our changes to persist even beyond the lifetime of the container, this is not a solution. Luckily, we have better options, in the form of Docker volumes. Let's get to know them.

Creating volumes

When using Docker Desktop on a macOS or Windows computer, containers are not running natively on macOS or Windows but rather in a (hidden) VM created by Docker Desktop.

To demonstrate how and where the underlying data structures are created in the respective filesystem (macOS or Windows), we need to be a bit creative. If, on the other hand, we are doing the same on a Linux computer, things are straightforward.

Let's start with a simple exercise to create a volume:

1. Open a new Terminal window and type in this command:

```
$ docker volume create sample
```

You should get this response:

```
sample
```

Here, the name of the created volume will be the output.

The default volume driver is the so-called **local driver**, which stores the data locally in the host filesystem.

2. The easiest way to find out where the data is stored on the host is by using the `docker volume inspect` command on the volume we just created. The actual location can differ from system to system, so this is the safest way to find the target folder. So, let's use this command:

```
$ docker volume inspect sample
```

We should see something like this:

```
→  ch05 git:(main) x docker volume inspect sample
[
    {
        "CreatedAt": "2022-12-04T10:46:58Z",
        "Driver": "local",
        "Labels": {},
        "Mountpoint": "/var/lib/docker/volumes/sample/_data",
        "Name": "sample",
        "Options": {},
        "Scope": "local"
    }
]
```

Figure 5.1 – Inspecting the Docker volume called sample

The host folder can be found in the output under `Mountpoint`. In our case, the folder is `/var/lib/docker/volumes/sample/_data`.

3. Alternatively, we can create a volume using the dashboard of Docker Desktop:

    A. Open the Dashboard of Docker Desktop.

    B. On the left-hand side, select the **Volumes** tab.

    C. In the top-right corner, click the **Create** button, as shown in the following screenshot:

Figure 5.2 – Creating a new Docker volume with Docker Desktop

D. Type in `sample-2` as the name for the new volume and click **Create**. You should now see this:

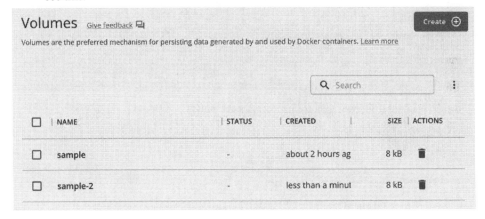

Figure 5.3 – List of Docker volumes shown in Docker Desktop

There are other volume drivers available from third parties, in the form of plugins. We can use the `--driver` parameter in the `create` command to select a different volume driver.

Other volume drivers use different types of storage systems to back a volume, such as cloud storage, **Network File System (NFS)** drives, software-defined storage, and more. The discussion of the correct usage of other volume drivers is beyond the scope of this book, though.

Mounting a volume

Once we have created a named volume, we can mount it into a container by following these steps:

1. For this, we can use the --volume or -v parameter in the docker container run command, like this:

    ```
    $ docker container run --name test -it \
        -v sample:/data \
        alpine /bin/sh
    ```

    If you are working on a clean Docker environment, then the output produced by this command should look similar to this:

    ```
    Unable to find image 'alpine:latest' locally latest:
    Pulling from library/alpine
    050382585609: Pull complete
    Digest: sha256: 8914eb54f968791faf6a86...
    Status: Downloaded newer image for alpine:latest
    / #
    ```

    Otherwise, you should just see the prompt of the Bourne shell running inside the Alpine container:

    ```
    / #
    ```

    The preceding command mounts the sample volume to the /data folder inside the container.

2. Inside the container, we can now create files in the /data folder, as follows:

    ```
    / # cd /data
    / # echo "Some data" > data.txt
    / # echo "Some more data" > data2.txt
    ```

3. If we were to navigate to the host folder that contains the data of the volume and list its content, we should see the two files we just created inside the container. But this is a bit more involved so long as we are working on a Mac or Windows computer and will be explained in detail in the *Accessing Docker volumes* section. Stay tuned.

4. Exit the tool container by pressing *Ctrl + D*.

5. Now, let's delete the dangling test container:

    ```
    $ docker container rm test
    ```

6. Next, we must run another one based on CentOS. This time, we are even mounting our volume to a different container folder, /app/data, like this:

```
$ docker container run --name test2 -it --rm \
    -v sample:/app/data \
    centos:7 /bin/bash
```

You should see an output similar to this:

```
Unable to find image 'centos:7' locally
7: Pulling from library/centos
8ba884070f61: Pull complete
Digest: sha256:a799dd8a2ded4a83484bbae769d9765...
Status: Downloaded newer image for centos:7
[root@275c1fe31ec0 /]#
```

The last line of the preceding output indicates that we are at the prompt of the Bash shell running inside the CentOS container.

7. Once inside the CentOS container, we can navigate to the /app/data folder to which we have mounted the volume and list its content, as follows:

```
[root@275c1fe31ec0 /]# cd /app/data
[root@275c1fe31ec0 /]# ls -l
```

As expected, we should see these two files:

```
-rw-r--r-- 1 root root 10 Dec  4 14:03 data.txt
-rw-r--r-- 1 root root 15 Dec  4 14:03 data2.txt
```

This is the definitive proof that data in a Docker volume persists beyond the lifetime of a container, as well as that volumes can be reused by other, even different, containers from the one that used it first.

It is important to note that the folder inside the container to which we mount a Docker volume is excluded from the Union filesystem. That is, each change inside this folder and any of its subfolders will not be part of the container layer but will be persisted in the backing storage provided by the volume driver. This fact is really important since the container layer is deleted when the corresponding container is stopped and removed from the system.

8. Exit the CentOS container with *Ctrl* + *D*.

Great – we have learned how to mount Docker volumes into a container! Next, we will learn how to delete existing volumes from our system.

Removing volumes

Volumes can be removed using the `docker volume rm` command. It is important to remember that removing a volume destroys the containing data irreversibly, and thus is to be considered a dangerous command. Docker helps us a bit in this regard, as it does not allow us to delete a volume that is still in use by a container. Always make sure before you remove or delete a volume that you either have a backup of its data or you don't need this data anymore. Let's learn how to remove volumes by following these steps:

1. The following command deletes the sample volume that we created earlier:

    ```
    $ docker volume rm sample
    ```

2. After executing the preceding command, double-check that the folder on the host has been deleted. You can use this command to list all volumes defined on your system:

    ```
    $ docker volume ls
    ```

    Make sure the `sample` volume has been deleted.

3. Now, also remove the `sample-2` volume from your system.

4. To remove all running containers to clean up the system, run the following command:

    ```
    $ docker container rm -v -f $(docker container ls -aq)
    ```

5. Note that by using the `-v` or `--volume` flag in the command you use to remove a container, you can ask the system to also remove any anonymous volume associated with that particular container. Of course, that will only work if the particular volume is only used by this container.

In the next section, we will show you how to access the backing folder of a volume when working with Docker Desktop.

Accessing Docker volumes

Now, let's for a moment assume that we are on a Mac with macOS. This operating system is not based on Linux but on a different Unix flavor. Let's see whether we can find the data structure for the `sample` and `sample-2` volumes, where the `docker volume inspect` command told us so:

1. First, let's create two named Docker volumes, either using the command line or doing the same via the dashboard of Docker Desktop:

    ```
    $ docker volume create sample
    $ docker volume create sample-2
    ```

2. In your Terminal, try to navigate to that folder:

    ```
    $ cd /var/lib/docker/volumes/sample/_data
    ```

On the author's MacBook Air, this is the response to the preceding command:

```
cd: no such file or directory: /var/lib/docker/volumes/
sample/_data
```

This was expected since Docker is not running natively on Mac but inside a slim VM, as mentioned earlier in this chapter.

Similarly, if you are using a Windows machine, you won't find the data where the inspect command indicated.

It turns out that on a Mac, the data for the VM that Docker creates can be found in the ~/Library/Containers/com.docker.docker/Data/vms/0 folder.

To access this data, we need to somehow get into this VM. On a Mac, we have two options to do so. The first is to use the terminal screen command. However, this is very specific to macOS and thus we will not discuss it here. The second option is to get access to the filesystem of Docker on Mac via the special nsenter command, which should be executed inside a Linux container such as Debian. This also works on Windows, and thus we will show the steps needed using this second option.

3. To run a container that can inspect the underlying host filesystem on your system, use this command:

```
$ docker container run -it --privileged --pid=host \
    debian nsenter -t 1 -m -u -n -i sh
```

When running the container, we execute the following command inside the container:

```
nsenter -t 1 -m -u -n -i sh
```

If that sounds complicated to you, don't worry; you will understand more as we proceed through this book. If there is one takeaway, then it is to realize how powerful the right use of containers can be.

4. From within this container, we can now list all the volumes that are defined with / # ls -l /var/lib/docker/volumes. What we get should look similar to this:

Figure 5.4 – List of Docker volumes via nsenter

5. Next, navigate to the folder representing the mount point of the volume:

```
/ # cd /var/lib/docker/volumes/sample/_data
```

6. And then list its content, as follows:

```
/var/lib/docker/volumes/sample/_data # ls -l
```

This should output the following:

```
total 0
```

The folder is currently empty since we have not yet stored any data in the volume.

7. Similarly, for our `sample-2` volume, we can use the following command:

```
/ # cd /var/lib/docker/volumes/sample-2/_data
/var/lib/docker/volumes/sample-2/ # ls -l
```

This should output the following:

```
total 0
```

Again, this indicates that the folder is currently empty.

8. Next, let's generate two files with data in the `sample` volume from within an Alpine container. First, open a new Terminal window, since the other one is blocked by our `nsenter` session.

9. To run the container and mount the `sample` volume to the `/data` folder of the container, use the following code:

```
$ docker container run --rm -it \
    -v sample:/data alpine /bin/sh
```

10. Generate two files in the `/data` folder inside the container, like this:

```
/ # echo "Hello world" > /data/sample.txt
/ # echo "Other message" > /data/other.txt
```

11. Exit the Alpine container by pressing *Ctrl + D*.

12. Back in the `nsenter` session, try to list the content of the sample volume again using this command:

```
/ # cd /var/lib/docker/volumes/sample/_data
/ # ls -l
```

This time, you should see this:

```
total 8
-rw-r--r--    1 root     root           10 Dec  4 14:03 data.txt
-rw-r--r--    1 root     root           15 Dec  4 14:03 data2.txt
```

This indicates that we have data written to the filesystem of the host.

13. Let's try to create a file from within this special container, and then list the content of the folder, as follows:

```
/ # echo "I love Docker" > docker.txt
```

14. Now, let's see what we got:

```
/ # ls -l
```

This gives us something like this:

```
total 12
-rw-r--r--    1 root     root    10 Dec   4 14:03 data.txt
-rw-r--r--    1 root     root    15 Dec   4 14:03 data2.txt
-rw-r--r--    1 root     root    14 Dec   4 14:25 docker.txt
```

15. Let's see whether we can see this new file from within a container mounting the sample volume. From within a new Terminal window, run this command:

```
$ docker container run --rm \
    -v sample:/data \
    centos:7 ls -l /data
```

That should output this:

```
total 12
-rw-r--r-- 1 root root 10 Dec   4 14:03 data.txt
-rw-r--r-- 1 root root 15 Dec   4 14:03 data2.txt
-rw-r--r-- 1 root root 14 Dec   4 14:25 docker.txt
```

The preceding output is showing us that we can add content directly to the host folder backing the volume and then access it from a container that has the volume mounted.

16. To exit our special privileged container with the nsenter tool, we can just press *Ctrl + D* twice.

We have now created data using two different methods:

- From within a container that has a sample volume mounted
- Using a special privileged folder to access the hidden VM used by Docker Desktop, and directly writing into the backing folder of the sample volume

In the next section, we will learn how to share data between containers.

Sharing data between containers

Containers are like sandboxes for the applications running inside them. This is mostly beneficial and wanted, to protect applications running in different containers from each other. It also means that the whole filesystem visible to an application running inside a container is private to this application, and no other application running in a different container can interfere with it.

At times, though, we want to share data between containers. Say an application running in **container A** produces some data that will be consumed by another application running in **container B**. How can we achieve this? Well, I'm sure you've already guessed it – we can use Docker volumes for this purpose. We can create a volume and mount it to container A, as well as to container B. In this way, both applications A and B have access to the same data.

Now, as always when multiple applications or processes concurrently access data, we have to be very careful to avoid inconsistencies. To avoid concurrency problems such as race conditions, we should ideally have only one application or process that is creating or modifying data, while all other processes concurrently accessing this data only read it.

> **Race condition**
>
> A race condition is a situation that can occur in computer programming when the output of a program or process is affected by the order and timing of events in ways that are unpredictable or unexpected. In a race condition, two or more parts of a program are trying to access or modify the same data or resource simultaneously, and the outcome depends on the timing of these events. This can result in incorrect or inconsistent output, errors, or crashes.

We can enforce a process running in a container to only be able to read the data in a volume by mounting this volume as read-only. Here's how we can do this:

1. Execute the following command:

    ```
    $ docker container run -it --name writer \
        -v shared-data:/data \
        .alpine /bin/sh
    ```

    Here, we are creating a container called `writer` that has a volume, `shared-data`, mounted in default read/write mode.

2. Try to create a file inside this container, like this:

    ```
    # / echo "I can create a file" > /data/sample.txt
    ```

    It should succeed.

3. Exit this container by pressing *Ctrl + D* or typing `exit` and hitting the *Enter* key at the prompt.

4. Then, execute the following command:

```
$ docker container run -it --name reader \
    -v shared-data:/app/data:ro \
    ubuntu:22.04 /bin/bash
```

Here we have a container called `reader` that has the same volume mounted as **read-only (ro)**.

5. First, make sure you can see the file created in the first container, like this:

```
$ ls -l /app/data
```

This should give you something like this:

```
total 4
-rw-r--r-- 1 root root 20 Jan 28 22:55 sample.txt
```

6. Then, try to create a file, like this:

```
# / echo "Try to break read/only" > /app/data/data.txt
```

It will fail with the following message:

```
bash: /app/data/data.txt: Read-only file system
```

This is expected since the volume was mounted as read-only.

7. Let's exit the container by typing `exit` at the command prompt. Back on the host, let's clean up all containers and volumes, as follows:

```
$ docker container rm -f $(docker container ls -aq)
$ docker volume rm $(docker volume ls -q)
```

Exercise: Analyze the preceding commands carefully and try to understand what exactly they do and how they work.

Next, we will show you how to mount arbitrary folders from the Docker host into a container.

Using host volumes

In certain scenarios, such as when developing new containerized applications or when a containerized application needs to consume data from a certain folder produced – say, by a legacy application – it is very helpful to use volumes that mount a specific host folder. Let's look at the following example:

```
$ docker container run --rm -it \
    -v $(pwd)/src:/app/src \
    alpine:latest /bin/sh
```

The preceding expression interactively starts an Alpine container with a shell and mounts the `src` subfolder of the current directory into the container at `/app/src`. We need to use `$(pwd)` (or pwd, for that matter), which is the current directory, as when working with volumes, we always need to use absolute paths.

Developers use these techniques all the time when they are working on their application that runs in a container and wants to make sure that the container always contains the latest changes to the code, without the need to rebuild the image and rerun the container after each change.

Let's make a sample to demonstrate how that works. Let's say we want to create a simple static website while using Nginx as our web server, as follows:

1. First, let's create a new subfolder on the host. The best place to do this is inside the chapter folder we created at the beginning of the chapter. There, we will put our web assets such as HTML, CSS, and JavaScript files. Use this command to create the subfolder and navigate to it:

    ```
    $ cd ~/The-Ultimate-Docker-Container-Book/ch05
    $ mkdir my-web && cd my-web
    ```

2. Then, create a simple web page, like this:

    ```
    $ echo "<h1>Personal Website</h1>" > index.html
    ```

3. Now, add a Dockerfile that will contain instructions on how to build the image containing our sample website. Add a file called `Dockerfile` to the folder, with this content:

    ```
    FROM nginx:alpine
    COPY . /usr/share/nginx/html
    ```

    The Dockerfile starts with the latest Alpine version of Nginx and then copies all files from the current host directory into the `/usr/share/nginx/html` containers folder. This is where Nginx expects web assets to be located.

4. Now, let's build the image with the following command:

    ```
    $ docker image build -t my-website:1.0 .
    ```

    Please do not forget the period (`.`) at the end of the preceding command. The output of this command will look similar to this:

```
→  my-web git:(main) ✗ docker image build -t my-website:1.0 .
[+] Building 0.2s (7/7) FINISHED
 => [internal] load build definition from Dockerfile      0.0s
 => => transferring dockerfile: 88B                        0.0s
 => [internal] load .dockerignore                          0.0s
 => => transferring context: 2B                            0.0s
 => [internal] load metadata for docker.io/library/ngin    0.0s
 => [internal] load build context                          0.0s
 => => transferring context: 148B                          0.0s
 => [1/2] FROM docker.io/library/nginx:alpine              0.0s
 => [2/2] COPY . /usr/share/nginx/htm                      0.0s
 => exporting to image                                     0.0s
 => => exporting layers                                    0.0s
 => => writing image sha256:84a23dd336b555db985abf2b8f5    0.0s
 => => naming to docker.io/library/my-website:1.0          0.0s
```

Figure 5.5 – Building a Docker image for a sample Nginx web server

5.   Finally, we will run a container from this image. We will run the container in detached mode, like this:

```
$ docker container run -d \
    --name my-site \
    -p 8080:80 \
    my-website:1.0
```

Note the `-p 8080:80` parameter. We haven't discussed this yet, but we will do so in detail in *Chapter 10, Using Single-Host Networking*. At the moment, just know that this maps the container port 80 on which Nginx is listening for incoming requests to port 8080 of your laptop, where you can then access the application.

6.   Now, open a browser tab and navigate to `http://localhost:8080/index.html`; you should see your website, which currently consists only of a title, **Personal Website**.

7.   Now, edit the `index.html` file in your favorite editor so that it looks like this:

```
<h1>Personal Website</h1>
<p>This is some text</p>
```

8.   Now, save it, and then refresh the browser. Oh! That didn't work. The browser still displays the previous version of the `index.html` file, which consists only of the title. So, let's stop and remove the current container, then rebuild the image and rerun the container, as follows:

```
$ docker container rm -f my-site
$ docker image build -t my-website:1.0 .
$ docker container run -d \
```

```
--name my-site \
-p 8080:80 \
my-website:1.0
```

9. Refresh the browser again. This time, the new content should be shown. Well, it worked, but there is way too much friction involved. Imagine having to do this every time that you make a simple change to your website. That's not sustainable.

10. Now is the time to use host-mounted volumes. Once again, remove the current container and rerun it with the volume mount, like this:

```
$ docker container rm -f my-site
$ docker container run -d \
    --name my-site \
    -v $(pwd):/usr/share/nginx/html \
    -p 8080:80 \
    my-website:1.0
```

> **Note**
>
> If you are working on Windows, a pop-up window will be displayed that says Docker wants to access the hard drive and that you have to click on the **Share access** button.

11. Now, append some more content to the index.html file and save it. Then, refresh your browser. You should see the changes. This is exactly what we wanted to achieve; we also call this an edit-and-continue experience. You can make as many changes in your web files and always immediately see the result in the browser, without having to rebuild the image and restart the container containing your website.

12. When you're done playing with your web server and wish to clean up your system, remove the container with the following command:

```
$ docker container rm -f my-site
```

It is important to note that the updates are now propagated bi-directionally. If you make changes on the host, they will be propagated to the container, and vice versa. It's also important to note that when you mount the current folder into the container target folder, /usr/share/nginx/html, the content that is already there is replaced by the content of the host folder.

In the next section, we will learn how to define volumes used in a Docker image.

Defining volumes in images

If we go back to what we have learned about containers in *Chapter 4, Creating and Managing Container Images*, for more moment, then we have this: the filesystem of each container, when started, is made up of the immutable layers of the underlying image, plus a writable container layer specific to this very container. All changes that the processes running inside the container make to the filesystem will be persisted in this container layer. Once the container is stopped and removed from the system, the corresponding container layer is deleted from the system and irreversibly lost.

Some applications, such as databases running in containers, need to persist their data beyond the lifetime of the container. In this case, they can use volumes. To make things a bit more explicit, let's look at a concrete example. MongoDB is a popular open source document database. Many developers use MongoDB as a storage service for their applications. The maintainers of MongoDB have created an image and published it on Docker Hub, which can be used to run an instance of the database in a container. This database will be producing data that needs to be persisted long term, but the MongoDB maintainers do not know who uses this image and how it is used. So, they can't influence the docker container run command with which the users of the database will start this container. So, how can they define volumes?

Luckily, there is a way of defining volumes in the Dockerfile. The keyword to do so is VOLUME, and we can either add the absolute path to a single folder or a comma-separated list of paths. These paths represent the folders of the container's filesystem. Let's look at a few samples of such volume definitions, as follows:

```
VOLUME /app/data
VOLUME /app/data, /app/profiles, /app/config
VOLUME ["/app/data", "/app/profiles", "/app/config"]
```

The first line in the preceding snippet defines a single volume to be mounted at /app/data. The second line defines three volumes as a comma-separated list. The last one defines the same as the second line, but this time, the value is formatted as a JSON array.

When a container is started, Docker automatically creates a volume and mounts it to the corresponding target folder of the container for each path defined in the Dockerfile. Since each volume is created automatically by Docker, it will have an SHA-256 as its ID.

At container runtime, the folders defined as volumes in the Dockerfile are excluded from the Union filesystem, and thus any changes in those folders do not change the container layer but are persisted to the respective volume. It is now the responsibility of the operations engineers to make sure that the backing storage of the volumes is properly backed up.

We can use the docker image inspect command to get information about the volumes defined in the Dockerfile. Let's see what MongoDB gives us by following these steps:

1. First, we will pull the image with the following command:

    ```
    $ docker image pull mongo:5.0
    ```

2. Then, we will inspect this image, and use the --format parameter to only extract the essential part from the massive amount of data, as follows:

    ```
    $ docker image inspect \
        --format='{{json .ContainerConfig.Volumes}}' \
        mongo:5.0 | jq .
    ```

    Note | jq . at the end of the command. We are piping the output of docker image inspect into the jq tool, which nicely formats the output.

    > **Tip**
    >
    > If you haven't installed jq yet on your system, you can do so with brew install jq on macOS or choco install jq on Windows.

    The preceding command will return the following result:

    ```
    {
        "/data/configdb": {},
        "/data/db": {}
    }
    ```

    As we can see, the Dockerfile for MongoDB defines two volumes at /data/configdb and /data/db.

3. Now, let's run an instance of MongoDB in the background as a daemon, as follows:

    ```
    $ docker run --name my-mongo -d mongo:5.0
    ```

4. We can now use the docker container inspect command to get information about the volumes that have been created, among other things. Use this command to just get the volume information:

    ```
    $ docker inspect --format '{{json .Mounts}}' my-mongo | jq .
    ```

    The preceding command should output something like this (shortened):

```
→ ch05 git:(main) x docker inspect --format '{{json .Mounts}}' my-mongo | jq .
[
  {
    "Type": "volume",
    "Name": "8006ec38c77553376c585833c1b8cf900e632e18f7ef722033e77266b632d77b",
    "Source": "/var/lib/docker/volumes/8006ec38c77553376c585833c1b8cf900e632e18f7ef722
033e77266b632d77b/_data",
    "Destination": "/data/configdb",
    "Driver": "local",
    "Mode": "",
    "RW": true,
    "Propagation": ""
  },
  {
    "Type": "volume",
    "Name": "f4f8c0b3a29c74280eb24cc954ddfaeb8abbfa65922712f5cc1dfe022d507089",
```

Figure 5.6 – Inspecting the MongoDB volumes

The Source field gives us the path to the host directory, where the data produced by MongoDB inside the container will be stored.

Before you leave, clean up the Mongo DB container with the following command:

```
$ docker rm -f my-mongo
```

That's it for the moment concerning volumes. In the next section, we will explore how we can configure applications running in containers, and the container image build process itself.

Configuring containers

More often than not, we need to provide some configuration to the application running inside a container. The configuration is often used to allow the same container to run in very different environments, such as in development, test, staging, or production environments. In Linux, configuration values are often provided via environment variables.

We have learned that an application running inside a container is completely shielded from its host environment. Thus, the environment variables that we see on the host are different from the ones that we see within a container.

Let's prove this by looking at what is defined on our host:

1. Use this command to display a list of all environment variables defined for your Terminal session:

```
$ export
```

On the author's macOS, the output is something like this (shortened):

```
...
COLORTERM=truecolor
```

```
COMMAND_MODE=unix2003
...
HOME=/Users/gabriel
HOMEBREW_CELLAR=/opt/homebrew/Cellar
HOMEBREW_PREFIX=/opt/homebrew
HOMEBREW_REPOSITORY=/opt/homebrew
INFOPATH=/opt/homebrew/share/info:/opt/homebrew/...:
LANG=en_GB.UTF-8
LESS=-R
LOGNAME=gabriel
...
```

2. Next, let's run a shell inside an Alpine container:

   A. Run the container with this command:

```
$ docker container run --rm -it alpine /bin/sh
```

   Just as a reminder, we are using the --rm command-line parameter so that we do not have to remove the dangling container once we stop it.

   B. Then, list the environment variables we can see there with this command:

```
/ # export
```

   This should produce the following output:

```
export HOME='/root'
export HOSTNAME='91250b722bc3'
export PATH='/usr/local/sbin:/usr/local/bin:...'
export PWD='/'
export SHLVL='1'
export TERM='xterm'
```

   The preceding output is different than what we saw directly on the host.

3. Hit *Ctrl + D* to leave and stop the Alpine container.

Next, let's define environment variables for containers.

Defining environment variables for containers

Now, the good thing is that we can pass some configuration values into the container at start time. We can use the --env (or the short form, -e) parameter in the form of --env <key>=<value> to do so, where <key> is the name of the environment variable and <value> represents the value to be associated with that variable. Let's assume we want the app that is to be run in our container to have access to an environment variable called `LOG_DIR`, with a value of `/var/log/my-log`. We can do so with this command:

```
$ docker container run --rm -it \
    --env LOG_DIR=/var/log/my-log \
    alpine /bin/sh
/ #
```

The preceding code starts a shell in an Alpine container and defines the requested environment inside the running container. To prove that this is true, we can execute this command inside the Alpine container:

```
/ # export | grep LOG_DIR
```

The output should be as follows:

```
export LOG_DIR='/var/log/my-log'
```

The output looks as expected. We now have the requested environment variable with the correct value available inside the container. We can, of course, define more than just one environment variable when we run a container. We just need to repeat the `--env` (or `-e`) parameter. Have a look at this sample:

```
$ docker container run --rm -it \
    --env LOG_DIR=/var/log/my-log \
    --env MAX_LOG_FILES=5 \
    --env MAX_LOG_SIZE=1G \
    alpine /bin/sh
```

After running the preceding command, we are left at the command prompt inside the Alpine container:

```
/ #
```

Let's list the environment variables with the following command:

```
/ # export | grep LOG
```

We will see the following:

```
export LOG_DIR='/var/log/my-log'
export MAX_LOG_FILES='5'
export MAX_LOG_SIZE='1G'
```

Now, let's look at situations where we have many environment variables to configure.

Using configuration files

Complex applications can have many environment variables to configure, and thus our command to run the corresponding container can quickly become unwieldy. For this purpose, Docker allows us to pass a collection of environment variable definitions as a file. We have the `--env-file` parameter in the `docker container run` command for this purpose.

Let's try this out, as follows:

1. Navigate to the source folder for `chapter 5` that we created at the beginning of this chapter:

    ```
    $ cd ~/The-Ultimate-Docker-Container-Book/ch05
    ```

2. Create a `config-file` subfolder and navigate to it, like this:

    ```
    $ mkdir config-file && cd config-file
    ```

3. Use your favorite editor to create a file called `development.config` in this folder. Add the following content to the file and save it, as follows:

    ```
    LOG_DIR=/var/log/my-log
    MAX_LOG_FILES=5
    MAX_LOG_SIZE=1G
    ```

    Notice how we have the definition of a single environment variable per line in <key>=<value> format, where, once again, <key> is the name of the environment variable, and <value> represents the value to be associated with that variable.

4. Now, from within the `config-file` subfolder, let's run an Alpine container, pass the file as an environment file, and run the `export` command inside the container to verify that the variables listed inside the file have indeed been created as environment variables inside the container, like this:

    ```
    $ docker container run --rm -it \
        --env-file ./development.config \
        alpine sh -c "export | grep LOG"
    ```

    And indeed, the variables are defined, as we can see in the output generated:

    ```
    export LOG_DIR='/var/log/my-log'
    export MAX_LOG_FILES='5'
    export MAX_LOG_SIZE='1G'
    ```

    This is exactly what we expected.

Next, let's look at how to define default values for environment variables that are valid for all container instances of a given Docker image.

Defining environment variables in container images

Sometimes, we want to define some default value for an environment variable that must be present in each container instance of a given container image. We can do so in the Dockerfile that is used to create that image by following these steps:

1. Navigate to the source folder for chapter 5 that we created at the beginning of this chapter:

   ```
   $ cd ~/The-Ultimate-Docker-Container-Book/ch05
   ```

2. Create a subfolder called config-in-image and navigate to it, like this:

   ```
   $ mkdir config-in-image && cd config-in-image
   ```

3. Use your favorite editor to create a file called Dockerfile in the config-in-image subfolder. Add the following content to the file and save it:

   ```
   FROM alpine:latest
   ENV LOG_DIR=/var/log/my-log
   ENV MAX_LOG_FILES=5
   ENV MAX_LOG_SIZE=1G
   ```

4. Create a container image called my-alpine using the preceding Dockerfile, as follows:

   ```
   $ docker image build -t my-alpine .
   ```

> **Note**
> Don't forget the period at the end of the preceding line!

5. Run a container instance from this image that outputs the environment variables defined inside the container, like this:

   ```
   $ docker container run --rm -it \
       my-alpine sh -c "export | grep LOG"
   ```

   You should see the following in your output:

   ```
   export LOG_DIR='/var/log/my-log'
   export MAX_LOG_FILES='5'
   export MAX_LOG_SIZE='1G'
   ```

This is exactly what we expected.

6. The good thing, though, is that we are not stuck with those variable values at all. We can override one or many of them by using the --env parameter in the docker container run command. Use this command:

```
$ docker container run --rm -it \
    --env MAX_LOG_SIZE=2G \
    --env MAX_LOG_FILES=10 \
    my-alpine sh -c "export | grep LOG"
```

7. Now, have a look at the following command and its output:

```
export LOG_DIR='/var/log/my-log'
export MAX_LOG_FILES='10'
export MAX_LOG_SIZE='2G'
```

8. We can also override default values by using environment files together with the --env-file parameter in the docker container run command. Please try it out for yourself.

In the next section, we are going to introduce environment variables that are used at the build time of a Docker image.

Environment variables at build time

Sometimes, we want to be able to define some environment variables that are valid at the time when we build a container image. Imagine that you want to define a BASE_IMAGE_VERSION environment variable that shall then be used as a parameter in your Dockerfile. Imagine the following Dockerfile:

```
ARG BASE_IMAGE_VERSION=12.7-stretch
FROM node:${BASE_IMAGE_VERSION}
WORKDIR /app
COPY packages.json .
RUN npm install
COPY . .
CMD npm start
```

We are using the ARG keyword to define a default value that is used each time we build an image from the preceding Dockerfile. In this case, that means that our image uses the node:12.7-stretch base image.

Now, if we want to create a special image for, say, testing purposes, we can override this variable at image build time using the --build-arg parameter, as follows:

```
$ docker image build \
```

```
    --build-arg BASE_IMAGE_VERSION=12.7-alpine \
    -t my-node-app-test .
```

In this case, the resulting `my-node-test:latest` image will be built from the `node:12.7-alpine` base image and not from the `node:12.7-stretch` default image.

To summarize, environment variables defined via `--env` or `--env-file` are valid at container runtime. Variables defined with `ARG` in the Dockerfile or `--build-arg` in the `docker container build` command are valid at container image build time. The former is used to configure an application running inside a container, while the latter is used to parameterize the container image build process.

And with that, we have come to the end of this chapter.

Summary

In this chapter, we introduced Docker volumes, which can be used to persist the state produced by containers and make them durable. We can also use volumes to provide containers with data originating from various sources. We learned how to create, mount, and use volumes. We also learned various techniques for defining volumes such as by name, by mounting a host directory, or by defining volumes in a container image.

In this chapter, we also discussed how we can configure environment variables that can be used by applications running inside a container. We have shown how to define those variables in the `docker container run` command, either explicitly, one by one, or as a collection in a configuration file. Finally, we learned how to parameterize the build process of container images by using build arguments.

In the next chapter, we are going to introduce techniques commonly used to allow a developer to evolve, modify, debug, and test their code while running in a container.

Further reading

The following articles provide more in-depth information:

- *Use volumes*: `http://dockr.ly/2EUjTml`
- *Manage data in Docker*: `http://dockr.ly/2EhBpzD`
- *Docker volumes* on **Play with Docker (PWD)**: `http://bit.ly/2sjIfDj`
- `nsenter` —Linux man page, at `https://bit.ly/2MEPG0n`
- *Set environment variables*: `https://dockr.ly/2HxMCjS`
- *Understanding how ARG and FROM interact*: `https://dockr.ly/2OrhZgx`

Questions

Please try to answer the following questions to assess your learning progress:

1. How would you create a named data volume with a name such as my-products using the default driver?

2. How would you run a container using the Alpine image and mount the my-products volume in read-only mode into the /data container folder?

3. How would you locate the folder that is associated with the my-products volume and navigate to it? Also, how would you create a file, sample.txt, with some content?

4. How would you run another Alpine container where you mount the my-products volume to the /app-data folder, in read/write mode? Inside this container, navigate to the /app-data folder and create a hello.txt file with some content.

5. How would you mount a host volume – for example, ~/my-project – into a container?

6. How would you remove all unused volumes from your system?

7. The list of environment variables that an application running in a container sees is the same as if the application were to run directly on the host.

    A. True

    B. False

8. Your application, which shall run in a container, needs a huge list of environment variables for configuration. What is the simplest method to run a container with your application and provide all this information to it?

Answers

Here are the answers to this chapter's questions:

1. To create a named volume, run the following command:

    ```
    $ docker volume create my-products
    ```

2. Execute the following command:

    ```
    $ docker container run -it --rm \
        -v my-products:/data:ro \
        alpine /bin/sh
    ```

3. To achieve this result, do this:

   A. To get the path on the host for the volume, use this command

   ```
   $ docker volume inspect my-products | grep Mountpoint
   ```

   B. This should result in the following output

   ```
   "Mountpoint": "/var/lib/docker/volumes/my-products/_data"
   ```

   i. Now, execute the following command to run a container and execute `nsenter` within it:

   ```
   $ docker container run -it --privileged --pid=host \
       debian nsenter -t 1 -m -u -n -i sh
   ```

   C. Navigate to the folder containing the data for the `my-products` volume:

   ```
   / # cd /var/lib/docker/volumes/my-products/_data
   ```

   D. Create a file containing the text `"I love Docker"` within this folder:

   ```
   / # echo "I love Docker" > sample.txt
   ```

   E. Exit `nsenter` and its container by pressing *Ctrl + D*.

   F. Execute the following command to verify that the file generated in the host filesystem is indeed part of the volume and accessible to the container to which we'll mount this volume:

   ```
   $ docker container run --rm \
       --volume my-products:/data \
       alpine ls -l /data
   ```

   The output of the preceding command should look similar to this:

   ```
   total 4
   -rw-r--r--    1 root     root    14 Dec  4 17:35 sample.
   txt
   ```

   And indeed, we can see the file.

   G. Optional: Run a modified version of the command to output the content of the `sample.txt` file.

4. Execute the following command:

   ```
   $ docker run -it --rm -v my-products:/data:ro alpine /
   bin/sh
   / # cd /data
   ```

```
/data # cat sample.txt
```

In another Terminal, execute this command:

```
$ docker run -it --rm -v my-products:/app-data alpine /
bin/sh
/ # cd /app-data
/app-data # echo "Hello other container" > hello.txt
/app-data # exit
```

5. Execute a command such as this:

```
$ docker container run -it --rm \
    -v $HOME/my-project:/app/data \
    alpine /bin/sh
```

6. Exit both containers and then, back on the host, execute this command:

```
$ docker volume prune
```

7. The answer is *False* (B). Each container is a sandbox and thus has its very own environment.

8. Collect all environment variables and their respective values in a configuration file, which you then provide to the container with the --env-file command-line parameter in the docker container run command, like so:

```
$ docker container run --rm -it \
    --env-file ./development.config \
    alpine sh -c "export"
```

6

Debugging Code Running in Containers

In the previous chapter, we learned how to work with stateful containers – that is, containers that consume and produce data. We also learned how to configure our containers at runtime and at image build time using environment variables and config files.

In this chapter, we're going to introduce techniques commonly used to allow a developer to evolve, modify, debug, and test their code while it's running in a container. With these techniques at hand, you will enjoy a frictionless development process for applications running in a container, similar to what you experience when developing applications that run natively.

Here is a list of the topics we're going to discuss:

- Evolving and testing code running in a container
- Auto-restarting code upon changes
- Line-by-line code debugging inside a container
- Instrumenting your code to produce meaningful logging information
- Using Jaeger to monitor and troubleshoot

After finishing this chapter, you will be able to do the following:

- Mount source code residing on the host in a running container
- Configure an application running in a container to auto-restart after a code change
- Configure **Visual Studio Code** (**VS Code**) to debug applications written in Java, Node.js, Python, or .NET running inside a container line by line
- Log important events from your application code
- Configure your multi-component application for distributed tracing using the OpenTracing standard and a tool such as Jaeger

Technical requirements

In this chapter, if you want to follow along with the code, you will need Docker Desktop on macOS or Windows and a code editor – preferably VS Code. The samples will also work on a Linux machine with Docker and VS Code installed.

To prepare your environment for the coming hands-on labs, follow these steps:

1. Please navigate to the folder where you have cloned the sample repository to. Normally, this should be `~/The-Ultimate-Docker-Container-Book`, so do the following:

    ```
    $ cd ~/The-Ultimate-Docker-Container-Book
    ```

2. Create a new subfolder called `ch06` and navigate to it:

    ```
    $ mkdir ch06 && cd ch06
    ```

A complete set of sample solutions for all the examples discussed in this chapter can be found in the `sample-solutions/ch06` folder or directly on GitHub: `https://github.com/PacktPublishing/The-Ultimate-Docker-Container-Book/tree/main/sample-solutions/ch06`.

Evolving and testing code running in a container

Make sure you have Node.js and npm installed on your computer before you continue. On Mac, use this command:

```
$ brew install node
```

On Windows, use the following command:

```
$ choco install -y nodejs
```

When developing code that will eventually be running in a container, the best approach is often to run the code in the container from the very beginning, to make sure there will be no surprises. But we have to do this in the right way so that we don't introduce any unnecessary friction to our development process. First, let's look at a naïve way we could run and test code in a container. We can do this using a basic Node.js sample application:

1. Create a new project folder and navigate to it:

    ```
    $ mkdir node-sample && cd node-sample
    ```

2. Let's use npm to create a new Node.js project:

    ```
    $ npm init
    ```

3. Accept all the defaults. Notice that a `package.json` file is created with the following content:

```
 1  {
 2      "name": "sample",
 3      "version": "1.0.0",
 4      "description": "",
 5      "main": "index.js",
 6      "scripts": {
 7          "test": "echo \"Error: no test specified\" && exit 1"
 8      },
 9      "author": "",
10      "license": "ISC",
11      "dependencies": {
12          "express": "^4.18.2"
13      }
14  }
```

Figure 6.1 – Content of the package.json file of the sample Node.js application

4. We want to use the `Express.js` library in our Node application; thus, use `npm` to install it:

```
$ npm install express –save
```

This will install the newest version of `Express.js` on our machine and, because of the `–save` parameter, add a reference to our `package.json` file that looks similar to this:

```
"dependencies": {
    "express": "^4.18.2"
}
```

Note that in your case, the version number of `express` may be different.

5. Start VS Code from within this folder:

```
$ code .
```

6. In VS Code, create a new file called `index.js` and add this code snippet to it. Do not forget to save:

```
1   const express = require('express');
2   const app = express();
3
4   app.listen(3000, '0.0.0.0', ()=>{
5     console.log('Application listening at 0.0.0.0:3000');
6   })
7
8   app.get('/', (req,res)=>{
9     res.send('Sample Application: Hello World!');
10  })
```

Figure 6.2 – Content of the index.js file of the sample Node.js application

7. From within your terminal window, start the application:

```
$ node index.js
```

> **Note**
>
> On Windows and Mac, when you execute the preceding command for the first time, a window
> will pop up, asking you to approve it on the firewall.

You should see this as the output:

```
Application listening at 0.0.0.0:3000
```

This means that the application is running and ready to listen at the 0.0.0.0:3000 endpoint.

> **Tip**
>
> You might be wondering what the meaning of the host address, 0.0.0.0, is and why we have
> chosen it. We will come back to this later when we run the application inside a container. For
> the moment, just know that 0.0.0.0 is a reserved IP address with a special meaning, similar
> to the loopback address, 127.0.0.1. The 0.0.0.0 address simply means all IPv4 addresses
> on the local machine. If a host has two IP addresses, say 52.11.32.13 and 10.11.0.1,
> and a server running on the host listens on 0.0.0.0, it will be reachable at both of those IPs.

8. Now, open a new tab in your favorite browser and navigate to http://localhost:3000.
    You should see this:

Figure 6.3 – Sample Node.js application running in a browser

Great – our Node.js application is running on our developer machine. Stop the application by pressing *Ctrl + C* in the terminal.

9. Now, we want to test the application we have developed so far by running it inside a container. To do this, we must create a Dockerfile so that we can build a container image, from which we can then run a container. Let's use VS Code again to add a file called `Dockerfile` to our project folder and give it the following content:

Figure 6.4 – Dockerfile for the sample Node.js application

10. We can then use this Dockerfile to build an image called `sample-app`, as follows:

```
$ docker image build -t sample-app .
```

It will take a few seconds for the base image to be downloaded and your custom image to be built on top of it.

11. After building, run the application in the container with this command:

```
$ docker container run --rm -it \
    --name my-sample-app \
    -p 3000:3000 \
    sample-app
```

The output will be as follows:

```
Application listening at 0.0.0.0:3000
```

> **Note**
>
> The preceding command runs a container called `my-sample-app` from the `sample-app` container image and maps the container's port, `3000`, to the equivalent host port. This port mapping is necessary; otherwise, we won't be able to access the application running inside the container from outside the container. We will learn more about port mapping in *Chapter 10, Using Single-Host Networking*. It is similar to when we ran the application directly on our host.

12. Refresh your previous browser tab (or open a new browser tab and navigate to `localhost:3000`, if you closed it). You should see that the application still runs and produces the same output as when running natively. This is good. We have just shown that our application not only runs on our host but also inside a container.

13. Stop and remove the container by pressing *Ctrl + C* in the terminal.

14. Now, let's modify our code and add some additional functionality. We will define another HTTP GET endpoint at `/hobbies`. Please add the following code snippet at the end of your `index.js` file:

```
const hobbies = [
    'Swimming', 'Diving', 'Jogging', 'Cooking', 'Singing'
];
app.get('/hobbies', (req,res)=>{
    res.send(hobbies);
})
```

15. We can test the new functionality on our host by running the app with the following command:

```
$ node index.js
```

Then, we can navigate to `http://localhost:3000/hobbies` in our browser. We should see the expected output – a JSON array with the list of hobbies – in the browser window. Don't forget to stop the application with *Ctrl + C* when you've finished testing.

16. Next, we need to test the code when it runs inside the container. So, first, we must create a new version of the container image:

```
$ docker image build -t sample-app .
```

This time, the build should be quicker than the first time we did this since the base image is already in our local cache.

17. Next, we must run a container from this new image:

```
$ docker container run --rm -it \
    --name my-sample-app \
    -p 3000:3000 \
    sample-app
```

18. Now, we can navigate to `http://localhost:3000/hobbies` in our browser and confirm that the application works as expected inside the container too.

19. Once again, don't forget to stop the container when you're done by pressing *Ctrl + C*.

We can repeat this sequence of tasks over and over again for each feature we add or any existing features we improve. It turns out that this is a lot of added friction compared to times when all the applications we developed always ran directly on the host.

However, we can do better. In the next section, we will look at a technique that allows us to remove most of this friction.

Mounting evolving code into the running container

What if, after a code change, we do not have to rebuild the container image and rerun a container? Wouldn't it be great if the changes would immediately, as we save them in an editor such as VS Code, be available inside the container too? Well, that is possible with volume mapping. In the previous chapter, we learned how to map an arbitrary host folder to an arbitrary location inside a container. We want to leverage that in this section. In *Chapter 5*, *Data Volumes and Configuration*, we learned how to map host folders as volumes in a container. For example, if we want to mount a host folder, `/projects/sample-app`, into a container at `/app`, the syntax for this will look as follows:

```
$ docker container run --rm -it \
    --volume /projects/sample-app:/app \
    alpine /bin/sh
```

Notice the `--volume <host-folder>:<container-folder>` line. The path to the host folder needs to be an absolute path, which in this example is `/projects/sample-app`.

Now, if we want to run a container from our `sample-app` container image and we do that from the project folder, we can map the current folder to the `/app` folder of the container, as follows:

```
$ docker container run --rm -it \
    --volume $(pwd):/app \
    -p 3000:3000 \
    sample-app
```

> **Note**
>
> Please note `$(pwd)` in place of the host folder path. `$(pwd)` equals the absolute path of the current folder, which comes in very handy.

Now, if we use the above volume mapping parameter, then whatever was in the /app folder of the sample-app container image will be overridden by the content of the mapped host folder, which in our case is the current folder. That's exactly what we want – we want the current source to be mapped from the host into the container. Let's test whether it works:

1. Stop the container if you have started it by pressing *Ctrl + C*.

2. Then, add the following snippet to the end of the index.js file:

    ```
    app.get('/status', (req,res)=>{
        res.send('OK');
    })
    ```

    Do not forget to save.

3. Then, run the container again – this time, without rebuilding the image first – to see what happens:

    ```
    $ docker container run --rm -it \
        --name my-sample-app \
        --volume $(pwd):/app \
        -p 3000:3000 \
        sample-app
    ```

4. In your browser, navigate to http://localhost:3000/status. You will see the OK output in your browser window. Alternatively, instead of using your browser, you could use curl in another terminal window to probe the /status endpoint, as follows:

    ```
    $ curl localhost:3000/status
    OK
    ```

> **Note**
>
> For all those working on Windows and/or Docker Desktop for Windows, you can use the PowerShell Invoke-WebRequest command or iwr for short instead of curl. In this case, the equivalent to the preceding command would be PS> iwr -Url http://localhost:3000/status.

5. Leave the application in the container running for the moment and make yet another change. Instead of just returning OK when navigating to /status, we want a message stating OK, all good to be returned. Make your modification and save your changes.

6. Then, execute the curl command again or, if you did use your browser, refresh the page. What do you see? Right – nothing happened. The change we made is not reflected in the running application.

7. Well, let's double-check whether the change has been propagated in the running container. To do this, let's execute the following command:

    ```
    $ docker container exec my-sample-app cat index.js
    ```

This executes the `cat index.js` command inside our already running container. We should see something like this – I have shortened the output for readability:

```
...
app.get('/hobbies', (req,res)=>{
    res.send(hobbies);
})
app.get('/status', (req,res)=>{
    res.send('OK, all good');
})
...
```

As we can see, our changes have been propagated into the container as expected. Why, then, are the changes not reflected in the running application? Well, the answer is simple: for changes to be applied to the application, the Node.js sample application has to be restarted.

8. Let's try that. Stop the container with the application running by pressing *Ctrl + C*. Then, re-execute the preceding `docker container run` command and use `curl` to probe the `http://localhost:3000/status` endpoint. This time, the following new message should be displayed:

```
$ curl http://localhost:3000/status
OK, all good
```

With that, we have significantly reduced the friction in the development process by mapping the source code in the running container. We can now add new codeor modify existing code and test it without having to build the container image first. However, a bit of friction has been left in play. We have to manually restart the container every time we want to test some new or modified code. Can we automate this? The answer is yes! We will demonstrate exactly this in the next section.

Auto-restarting code upon changes

In the previous section, we showed you how we can massively reduce friction by volume mapping the source code folder in the container, thus avoiding having to rebuild the container image and rerun the container over and over again. Yet we still feel some remaining friction. The application running inside the container does not automatically restart when a code change is made. Thus, we have to manually stop and restart the container to pick up these new changes.

In this section, we will learn how we can containerize our applications written in various languages, such as Node.js, Java, Python, and .NET, and have them restart automatically whenever a code change is detected. Let's start with Node.js.

Auto-restarting for Node.js

If you have been coding for a while, you will certainly have heard about helpful tools that can run your applications and restart them automatically whenever they discover a change in the code base. For Node.js applications, the most popular tool is nodemon. Let's take a look:

1. We can install nodemon globally on our system with the following command:

    ```
    $ npm install -g nodemon
    ```

2. Now that nodemon is available, instead of starting our application (for example, on the host) with node index.js, we can just execute nodemon and we should see the following:

    ```
    →  node-sample git:(main) x nodemon
    [nodemon] 2.0.20
    [nodemon] to restart at any time, enter `rs`
    [nodemon] watching path(s): *.*
    [nodemon] watching extensions: js,mjs,json
    [nodemon] starting `node index.js`
    Application listening at 0.0.0.0:3000
    ```

    Figure 6.5 – Running our Node.js sample application with nodemon

    > **Note**
    >
    > As we can see, from parsing our package.json file, nodemon has recognized that it should use node index.js as the starting command.

3. Now, try to change some code. For this example, add the following code snippet to the end of index.js and then save the file:

    ```
    app.get('/colors', (req,res)=>{
        res.send(['red','green','blue']);
    })
    ```

4. Look at the terminal window. Did you see something happen? You should see this additional output:

    ```
    [nodemon] restarting due to changes...
    [nodemon] starting `node index.js`
    Application listening at 0.0.0.0:3000
    ```

    This indicates that nodemon has recognized some changes and automatically restarted the application.

5. Try this out on your browser by navigating to localhost:3000/colors. You should see the following expected output in your browser:

    ```
    ["red", "green", "blue"]
    ```

This is cool – you got this result without having to manually restart the application. This makes us yet another bit more productive. Now, can we do the same within the container?

Yes, we can. However, we won't use the start command, `node index.js`, as defined in the last line of our Dockerfile:

```
CMD node index.js
```

We will use `nodemon` instead.

Do we have to modify our Dockerfile? Or do we need two different Dockerfiles, one for development and one for production?

Our original Dockerfile creates an image that unfortunately does not contain `nodemon`. Thus, we need to create a new Dockerfile:

1. Create a new file. Let's call it `Dockerfile.dev`. Its content should look like this:

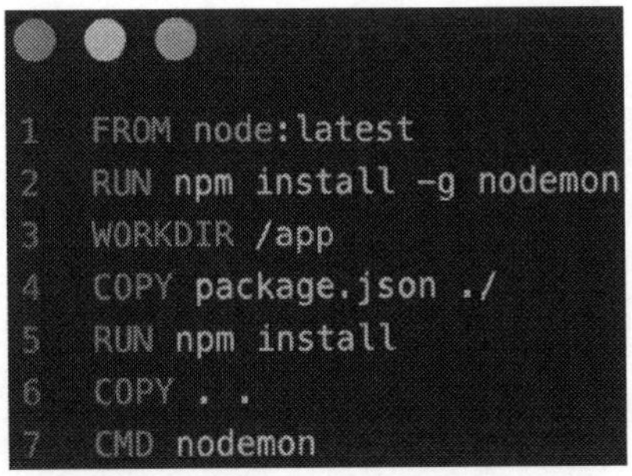

```
1  FROM node:latest
2  RUN npm install -g nodemon
3  WORKDIR /app
4  COPY package.json ./
5  RUN npm install
6  COPY . .
7  CMD nodemon
```

Figure 6.6 – Dockerfile used for developing our Node.js application

Comparing this with our original `Dockerfile`, we have added line 2, where we install `nodemon`. We have also changed the last line and are now using `nodemon` as our start command.

2. Let's build our development image, as follows:

```
$ docker image build \
    -f Dockerfile.dev \
    -t node-demo-dev .
```

Please note the `-f Dockerfile.dev` command-line parameter. We must use this since we are using a Dockerfile with a non-standard name.

3. Run a container, like this:

```
$ docker container run --rm -it \
    -v $(pwd):/app \
    -p 3000:3000 \
    node-demo-dev
```

4. Now, while the application is running in the container, change some code, save it, and notice that the application inside the container is automatically restarted. With this, we have achieved the same reduction in friction while running in a container as we did when running directly on the host.

5. Hit *Ctrl + C* when you're done to exit your container.

6. Use the following command to clean up your system and remove all running or dangling containers:

```
$ docker container rm -f $(docker container ls -aq)
```

You might be wondering, does this only apply to Node.js? No – fortunately, many popular languages support similar concepts.

Auto-restarting for Java and Spring Boot

Java and Spring Boot are still by far the most popular programming languages and libraries when developing **line of business** (**LOB**) type applications. Let's learn how to work as friction-free as possible when developing such an application and containerizing it.

For this example to work, you have to have Java installed on your computer. At the time of writing, the recommended version is Java 17. Use your favorite package manager to do so, such as Homebrew on Mac or Chocolatey on Windows.

You may also want to make sure you have *Extension Pack for Java* by Microsoft installed for VS Code. You can find more details here: `https://marketplace.visualstudio.com/items?itemName=vscjava.vscode-java-pack`.

Once you have the Java 17 SDK installed and ready on your computer, proceed as follows:

1. The easiest way to bootstrap a Spring Boot application is by using the **Spring Initializr** page:

   I.   Navigate to `https://start.spring.io`.

   II.   Under **Project**, select **Maven**.

   III. Under **Language**, select **Java**.

   IV.   Under **Spring Boot**, select **3.0.2** (or newer if available at the time of writing).

   V.   For **Packaging**, select **Jar**.

   VI.   Finally, for **Java**, select **17**.

   VII. Click **ADD DEPENDENCIES**, search for `Spring Web`, and select it (*do not* select **Spring Reactive Web**).

   Your page should look like this:

Figure 6.7 – Bootstrapping a new Java project with Spring Initializr

2. Click **GENERATE** and unpack the resulting ZIP file into a folder called `ch06/java-springboot-demo`.

3. Navigate to this folder:

```
$ cd ch06/java-springboot-demo
```

4. Open VS Code from within this folder by using the following command:

```
$ code .
```

5. Locate the main file of the project, which is called `DemoApplication.java`, and click on the **Run** hyperlink directly above the `main` method on line 9, as shown in the following screenshot:

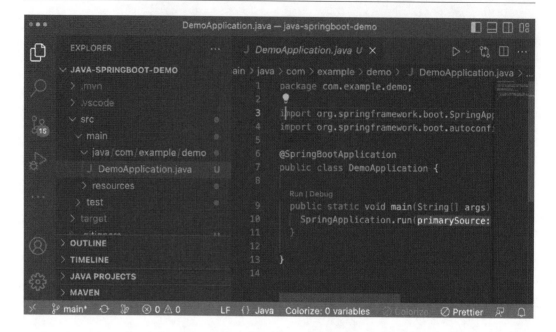

Figure 6.8 – Starting the Java Spring Boot application

6.   Observe that the application has been compiled and that a terminal window opens. Content similar to the following will be displayed:

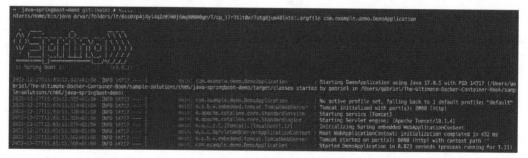

Figure 6.9 – Output generated by a running Spring Boot application

7.   On the second to last line of the preceding output, we can see that the application uses the Tomcat web server and is listening at port 8080.

8. Now, let's add an endpoint that we can then try to access:

    I.   Decorate the DemoApplication class with a @RestController annotation.

    II.   Add a getSpecies method that returns a list of strings

    III. Decorate the method with the following annotation:

    @GetMapping("/species")

    Don't forget to add the required import statements. The complete code will look like this:

```
1    package com.example.demo;
2
3    import java.util.List;
4
5    import org.springframework.boot.SpringApplication;
6    import org.springframework.boot.autoconfigure.SpringBootApplication;
7    import org.springframework.web.bind.annotation.GetMapping;
8    import org.springframework.web.bind.annotation.RestController;
9
10   @SpringBootApplication
11   @RestController
12   public class DemoApplication {
13
14       public static void main(String[] args) {
15           SpringApplication.run(DemoApplication.class, args);
16       }
17
18       @GetMapping("/species")
19       public List<String> getSpecies() {
20           return List.of("Elephant", "Mouse", "Cat");
21       }
22   }
23
```

Figure 6.10 – Complete demo code for the Spring Boot example

9. Use curl or the **Thunder Client** plugin for VS Code to try and access the /species endpoint:

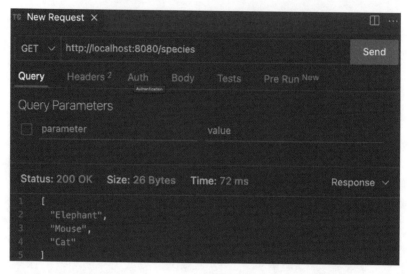

Figure 6.11 – Using the Thunder Client plugin to test the Java demo application

10. To add auto-restart support to our Java Spring Boot application, we need to add the so-called dev tools:

I.   Locate the `pom.xml` file in your Java project and open it in the editor.

II.   Add the following snippet to the dependencies section of the file:

```
23        </dependency>
24
25  ∨     <dependency>
26          <groupId>org.springframework.boot</groupId>
27          <artifactId>spring-boot-starter-test</artifactId>
28          <scope>test</scope>
29        </dependency>
30
31  ∨     <dependency>
32          <groupId>org.springframework.boot</groupId>
33          <artifactId>spring-boot-devtools</artifactId>
34          <version>3.0.1</version>
35          <optional>true</optional>
36        </dependency>
37
38      </dependencies>
```

Figure 6.12 – Adding a reference to the Spring Boot dev tools

Note that the version node in the dependency definition can be omitted as the project uses `spring-boot-starter-parent` as the parent.

11. Stop and rerun the application.

12. Modify line 20 of the `DemoApplication` class and add `Crocodile` as a fourth species to return to the caller.

13. Save your changes and observe that the application automatically rebuilds and restarts.

14. Use `curl` or Thunder Client again to access the `/species` endpoint. This time, a list of four species should be returned, including the just-added `Crocodile`.

Great – we have a Java Spring Boot application that automatically re-compiles and restarts when we change any code in it. Now, we need to dockerize the whole thing, as we did with the Node.js example:

1. Add a `Dockerfile` to the root of the project with the following content:

```
1   FROM eclipse-temurin:17-jdk-focal AS build
2   WORKDIR /app
3   COPY mvnw .
4   COPY .mvn .mvn
5   COPY pom.xml .
6   COPY src src
7
8   CMD ./mvnw spring-boot:run
```

Figure 6.13 – Dockerfile for the Java Spring Boot demo

> **Note**
> We have used the `eclipse-temurin` image with the `17-jdk-focal` tag for this example since this image, at the time of writing, works on the M1 or M2 processor used by modern MacBooks.

2. Create an image using the preceding Dockerfile with this command:

```
$ docker image build -t java-demo .
```

3. Create a container from this Docker image with the following command:

```
$ docker container run --name java-demo --rm \
    -p 8080:8080
    -v $(pwd)/.:/app
    java-demo
```

> **Note**
>
> The first time you run the container, it will take a while to compile since all the Maven dependencies need to be downloaded.

4. Try to access the `/species` endpoint, as you did previously.

5. Now, change some code – for example, add a fifth species to be returned to the `getSpecies` method, such as `Penguin`, and then save your changes.

6. Observe how the application running inside the container is rebuilt. Verify that the change has been incorporated by accessing the `/species` endpoint once again and asserting that five species are returned, including `Penguin`.

7. When you're done playing around, stop the container either via the dashboard of Docker Desktop or the Docker plugin in VS Code.

Well, that was quite straightforward, wasn't it? But let me tell you, setting up your development environment this way can make developing containerized applications much more enjoyable by eliminating much of the unnecessary friction.

> **Challenge**
>
> Try to find out how you could map your local Maven cache into the container, to accelerate the first startup of the container even further.

Next, we are going to show you how easy it is to do the same exercise in Python. Stay tuned.

Auto-restarting for Python

Let's look at how the same thing works for Python.

Prerequisites

For this example to work, you need to have Python 3.x installed on your computer. You can do this using your preferred package manager, such as Homebrew on Mac or Chocolatey on Windows.

On your Mac, use this command to install the latest Python version:

```
$ brew install python
```

On your Windows computer, use this command to do the same:

```
$ choco install python
```

Use this command to verify that the installation was successful:

```
$ python3 --version
```

In the author's case, the output looks like this:

```
Python 3.10.8
```

Let's begin:

1. First, create a new project folder for our sample Python application and navigate to it:

    ```
    $ mkdir python-demo && cd python-demo
    ```

2. Open VS Code from within this folder by using the following command:

    ```
    $ code .
    ```

3. We will create a sample Python application that uses the popular Flask library. Thus, add a file to this folder called `requirements.txt` that contains this content:

    ```
    flask
    ```

4. Next, add a `main.py` file and give it this content:

```python
1  from flask import Flask
2  app = Flask(__name__)
3  @app.route("/")
4  def hello():
5      return "Hello World!"
6
7  if __name__ == "__main__":
8      app.run(host="0.0.0.0", port=5000)
```

Figure 6.14 – Content of the main.py file of our sample Python application

This is a simple Hello World-type app that implements a single RESTful endpoint at `http://localhost:5000/`.

> **Note**
>
> The `host="0.0.0.0"` parameter in the `app.run` command is needed so that we can expose the port on which the Python app is listening (`5000`) to the host. We will need this later in this example.
>
> Please also note that some people have reported that, when running on a Mac and using port `5000`, an error stating "Address already in use. Port `5000` is in use by another program..." is triggered. In this case, just try to use a different port, such as `5001`.

5. Before we can run and test this application, we need to install the necessary dependencies – in our case, Flask. In the terminal, run the following command:

```
$ pip3 install -r requirements.txt
```

This should install Flask on your host. We are now ready to go.

6. When using Python, we can also use `nodemon` to have our application auto-restart when any changes are made to the code. For example, assume that your command to start the Python application is `python main.py`. In this case, you would just use `nodemon` like so:

```
$ nodemon --exec python3 main.py
```

You should see the following output:

```
→ python-demo git:(main) ✗ nodemon ---exec python3 main.py
[nodemon] 2.0.20
[nodemon] to restart at any time, enter `rs`
[nodemon] watching path(s): *.*
[nodemon] watching extensions: py,json
[nodemon] starting `python3 main.py`
 * Serving Flask app 'main'
 * Debug mode: off
WARNING: This is a development server. Do not use it in a production deployment.
 * Running on http://127.0.0.1:5000
Press CTRL+C to quit
```

Figure 6.15 – Using nodemon to auto-restart a Python 3 application

7. When using `nodemon` to start and monitor a Python application, we can test the application by using `curl`. Open another terminal window and enter this:

```
$ curl localhost:5000
```

You should see this in the output:

```
Hello World!
```

8. Now, let's modify the code by adding the following snippet to `main.py`, right after the definition of the `/` endpoint (that is, right after line 5), and save it:

```
from flask import jsonify
@app.route("/colors")
def colors():
    return jsonify(["red", "green", "blue"])
```

`nodemon` will discover the changes and restart the Python app, as we can see in the output produced in the terminal:

```
[nodemon] restarting due to changes...
[nodemon] starting `python3 main.py`
 * Serving Flask app 'main'
 * Debug mode: off
WARNING: This is a development server. Do not use it in a production deployment.
 * Running on http://127.0.0.1:5000
Press CTRL+C to quit
```

Figure 6.16 – nodemon discovering a change in the Python code

9. Once again, believing is good, but testing is better. Thus, let's use our friend `curl` once again to probe the new endpoint and see what we get:

    ```
    $ curl localhost:5000/colors
    ```

    The output should look like this:

    ```
    ["red", "green", "blue"]
    ```

    Nice – it works! With that, we have covered Python.

10. Now, it's time to containerize this application. Add a file called `Dockerfile` to the project with the following content:

    ```
    1  FROM nikolaik/python-nodejs:latest
    2  RUN npm install -g nodemon
    3  WORKDIR /app
    4  COPY requirements.txt .
    5  RUN pip install -r requirements.txt
    6  COPY . .
    7  CMD [ "nodemon", "--exec", "python", "main.py" ]
    ```

    Figure 6.17 – Dockerfile for the sample Python application

    Note that on line 1, we are using a special base image that contains both Python and Node.js code. Then, on line 2, we install the `nodemon` tool before we copy the `requirements.txt` file into the container and execute the `pip install` command. Next, we copy all other files into the container and define the start command for whenever an instance of this image – that is, a container – is created.

11. Let's build a Docker image with this command:

    ```
    $ docker image build -t python-sample .
    ```

12. Now, we can run a container from this image with the following code:

```
$ docker container run --rm \
    -p 5000:5000 \
    -v $(pwd)/.:/app \
    python-sample
```

We should have an output similar to what was produced by the application running inside the container in *step 6*, where we ran the application natively:

```
[nodemon] 2.0.20
[nodemon] to restart at any time, enter `rs`
[nodemon] watching path(s): *.*
[nodemon] watching extensions: py,json
[nodemon] starting `python main.py`
 * Serving Flask app 'main'
 * Debug mode: off
WARNING: This is a development server. Do not use it in a production deployment.
erver instead.    Follow link (cmd + click)
 * Running on
 * Running on http://127.0.0.1:5000
 * Running on http://172.17.0.2:5000
Press CTRL+C to quit
```

Figure 6.18 – Running the containerized Python sample application

Note how we have mapped the container port, 5000, to the equivalent host port so that we can access the application from outside. We have also mapped the content of the sample directory on the host to the /app folder inside the running container. This way, we can update the code and the containerized application will automatically restart.

13. Try to change the application code, and return a fourth color when the /colors endpoint is hit. Save the change and observe how the application running inside the container is restarted.

14. Use the curl command to verify that an array of four colors is returned.

15. When you're done playing with this example, hit *Ctrl + C* in the terminal window where you have the container running to stop the application and the container.

With this, we have shown a fully working example for Python that helps you massively reduce the friction of working with containers during the development process.

.NET is another popular platform. Let's see if we can do something like this when developing a C# application on .NET.

Auto-restarting for .NET

Our next candidate is a .NET application written in C#. Let's look at how dynamic code updates and auto-restarts work in .NET.

Prerequisites

If you have not done so before, please install .NET on your laptop or workstation. You can use your favorite package manager, such as Homebrew on Mac or Chocolatey on Windows, to do so.

On Mac, use this command to install the .NET 7 SDK:

```
$ brew install --cask dotnet-sdk
```

On a Windows machine, you can use this command:

```
$ choco install -y dotnet-sdk
```

Finally, use this command to verify your installation:

```
$ dotnet --version
```

On the author's machine, the output is as follows:

```
7.0.100
```

Let's begin:

1. In a new terminal window, navigate to this chapter's folder:

    ```
    $ cd ~/The-Ultimate-Docker-Container-Book/ch06
    ```

2. From within this folder, use the `dotnet` tool to create a new Web API and have it placed in the `dotnet` subfolder:

    ```
    $ dotnet new webapi -o csharp-sample
    ```

3. Navigate to this new project folder:

    ```
    $ cd csharp-sample
    ```

4. Open VS Code from within this folder:

    ```
    $ code .
    ```

> **Note**
>
> If this is the first time you have opened a .NET project with VS Code, then the editor may display a popup asking you to add the missing dependencies for our `dotnet` project. Click the **Yes** button in this case:

Required assets to build and debug are missing from 'csharp-sample'. Add them?
Source: C# (Extension)
Don't Ask Again
Not Now
Yes

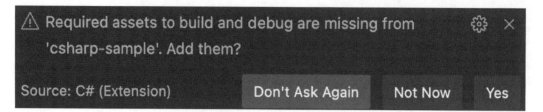

Figure 6.19 – Request to load missing assets for the .NET sample application

5. In the Project Explorer of VS Code, you should see this:

EXPLORER
CSHARP-SAMPLE
bin
Controllers
obj
Properties
appsettings.Development.json
appsettings.json
csharp-sample.csproj
Program.cs
WeatherForecast.cs
U
U
U
U
U

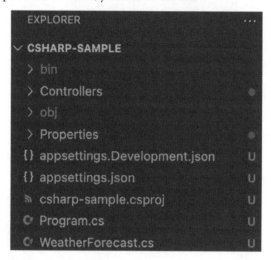

Figure 6.20 – The .NET sample application in the VS Code Project Explorer

6. Please note the `Controllers` folder with the `WeatherForecastController.cs` file in it. Open this file and analyze its content. It contains the definition for the `WeatherForecastController` class, which implements a simple RESTful controller with a GET endpoint at `/WeatherForecast`.

7. From your terminal, run the application with `dotnet run`. You should see something like this:

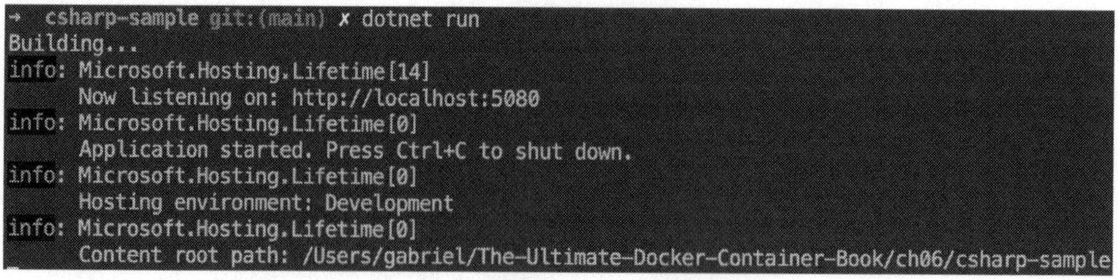

→ csharp-sample git:(main) ✗ dotnet run
Building...
info: Microsoft.Hosting.Lifetime[14]
Now listening on: http://localhost:5080
info: Microsoft.Hosting.Lifetime[0]
Application started. Press Ctrl+C to shut down.
info: Microsoft.Hosting.Lifetime[0]
Hosting environment: Development
info: Microsoft.Hosting.Lifetime[0]
Content root path: /Users/gabriel/The-Ultimate-Docker-Container-Book/ch06/csharp-sample

Figure 6.21 – Running the .NET sample Web API on the host

Please note the fourth line in the above output, where .NET tells us that the application is listening at `http://localhost:5080`. In your case, the port may be a different one. Use the one reported for you for all subsequent steps.

8. We can use `curl` to test the application, like so:

```
$ curl http://localhost:5080/WeatherForecast
```

This will output an array of five JSON objects containing random weather data:

```
→  csharp-sample git:(main) ✗ curl http://localhost:5080/weatherforecast
[{"date":"2022-12-11","temperatureC":14,"temperatureF":57,"summary":"Balmy"}
,{"date":"2022-12-12","temperatureC":53,"temperatureF":127,"summary":"Hot"},
{"date":"2022-12-13","temperatureC":6,"temperatureF":42,"summary":"Warm"},{"
date":"2022-12-14","temperatureC":-17,"temperatureF":2,"summary":"Chilly"},{
"date":"2022-12-15","temperatureC":32,"temperatureF":89,"summary":"Cool"}]
```

Figure 6.22 – Weather data produced by the .NET sample application

9. We can now try to modify the code in `WeatherForecastController.cs` and return, say, 10 instead of the default 5 items. Change line 24 so that it looks like this:

```
...
    return Enumerable.Range(1, 10).Select(...
...
```

10. Save your changes and rerun the `curl` command. Notice how the result does not contain the newly added value. This is the same problem that we observed for Node.js and Python. To see the newly updated return value, we need to (manually) restart the application.

11. Thus, in your terminal, stop the application with *Ctrl + C* and restart it with `dotnet run`. Try the `curl` command again. The result should now reflect your changes.

12. Luckily for us, the `dotnet` tool has the `watch` command. Stop the application by pressing *Ctrl + C* and execute this slightly modified command:

```
$ dotnet watch run
```

You should see output resembling the following (shortened):

```
dotnet watch ⚙ Started
info: Microsoft.Hosting.Lifetime[14]
      Now listening on: http://localhost:5080
info: Microsoft.Hosting.Lifetime[0]
      Application started. Press Ctrl+C to shut down.
info: Microsoft.Hosting.Lifetime[0]
      Hosting environment: Development
info: Microsoft.Hosting.Lifetime[0]
      Content root path: /Users/gabriel/The-Ultimate-Docker-Container-Book/ch06/csharp-sample
```

Figure 6.23 – Running the .NET sample application with the watch task

Notice the first line in the preceding output, which states that the running application is now watched for changes.

13. Make another change in `WeatherForecastController.cs`; for example, make the `GET` endpoint method return 100 weather items and then save your changes. Observe the output in the terminal. It should look something like this:

```
dotnet watch ⬚ File changed: ./Controllers/WeatherForecastController.cs.
dotnet watch 🔥 Hot reload of changes succeeded.
```

Figure 6.24 – Auto-restarting the running sample .NET Core application

14. By automatically restarting the application upon making changes to the code, the result is immediately available to us, and we can easily test it by running the following `curl` command:

```
$ curl http://localhost:5080/WeatherForecast
```

100 instead of 10 weather items should be output this time.

15. Now that we have auto-restart working on the host, we can author a `Dockerfile` that does the same for the application running inside a container. In VS Code, add a new file called `Dockerfile-dev` to the project and add the following content to it:

```
1   FROM mcr.microsoft.com/dotnet/sdk:7.0
2   WORKDIR /app
3   COPY csharp-sample.csproj ./
4   RUN dotnet restore
5   COPY . .
6   CMD dotnet watch run --urls "http://0.0.0.0:5000"
```

Figure 6.25 – Dockerfile for the .NET sample application

Note the `--urls` command-line parameter on line 6. This explicitly tells the application to listen on port `5000` at all endpoints inside the container (denoted by the special `0.0.0.0` IP address). If we were to leave the default of `localhost`, then we wouldn't be able to reach the application from outside the container.

Port is already in use

Please note that some people have reported that when running on a Mac and using port `5000`, an error stating "Address already in use. Port `5000` is in use by another program…" is triggered. In this case, just try to use a different port, such as `5001`.

Now, we're ready to build the container image:

1. Use the following command to build a container image for the .NET sample:

```
$ docker image build -f Dockerfile-dev \
    -t csharp-sample .
```

2. Once the image has been built, we can run a container from it:

```
$ docker container run --rm \
    --name csharp-sample \
    -p 5000:5000 \
    -v $(pwd):/app \
    csharp-sample
```

We should see a similar output to what we saw when running natively.

3. Let's test the application with our friend, `curl`:

```
$ curl localhost:5000/weatherforecast
```

We should get the array of weather forecast items. No surprises here – it works as expected.

4. Now, let's make a code change in the controller and save it. Observe what's happening in the terminal window. We should see an output like this:

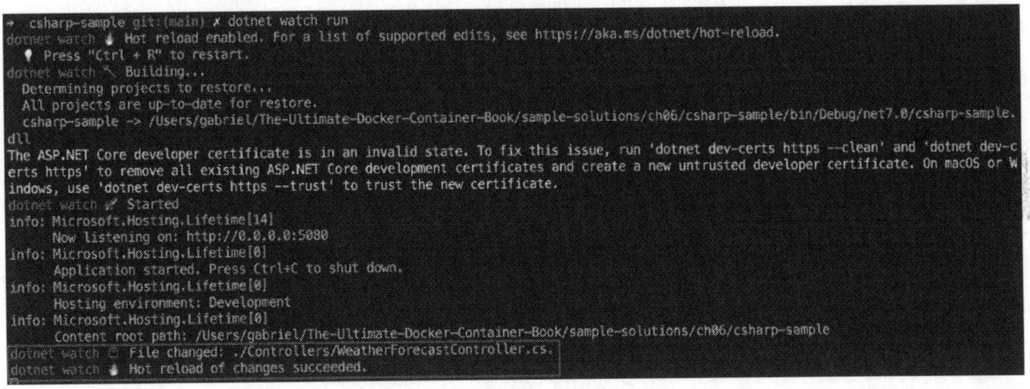

Figure 6.26 – Hot reloading the .NET sample application running inside a container

Well, that's exactly what we expected. With this, we have removed most of the friction that we introduced by using containers when developing a .NET application.

5. When you're done playing with the .NET sample application, open the dashboard of your Docker Desktop application. Locate the `csharp-sample` container and select it. Then, click the red **Delete** button to remove it from your system. This is the easiest way to do this since, unfortunately, just pressing *Ctrl + C* in the terminal window where you ran the container does not work. Alternatively, you can open another terminal window and use this command to get rid of the container:

```
$ docker container rm --force csharp-sample
```

That's it for now. In this section, we explored how we can reduce friction during development when working with containerized applications written in Node.js, Python, Spring Boot, Java, or .NET. Next, we are going to learn how we can debug an application running in a container line by line.

Line-by-line code debugging inside a container

Before we dive into this section about debugging code running inside a container line by line, let me make a disclaimer. What you will learn in this section should usually be your last resort if nothing else works. Ideally, when following a test-driven approach when developing your application, the code is mostly guaranteed to work since you have written unit and integration tests for it and run them against your code, which also runs in a container. Alternatively, if unit or integration tests don't provide you with enough insight and you need to debug your code line by line, you can do so by running your code directly on your host, thus leveraging the support of development environments such as VS Code, Eclipse, or IntelliJ, to name just a few IDEs.

With all this preparation, you should rarely need to manually debug your code as it is running inside a container. That said, let's see how you can do it anyways!

In this section, we are going to concentrate exclusively on how to debug when using VS Code. Other editors and IDEs may or may not offer similar capabilities.

Debugging a Node.js application

We'll start with the easiest one – a Node.js application. We will use our sample application in the `~/The-Ultimate-Docker-Container-Book/ch06/node-sample` folder, which we worked with earlier in this chapter:

1. Open a new terminal window and make sure that you navigate to this project folder:

```
$ cd ~/The-Ultimate-Docker-Container-Book/ch06/node-sample
```

2. Open VS Code from within this container:

```
$ code .
```

3. In the terminal window, from within the project folder, run a container with our sample Node.js application:

```
$ docker container run --rm -it \
    --name node-sample \
    -p 3000:3000 \
    -p 9229:9229 \
    -v $(pwd):/app \
    node-demo-dev node --inspect=0.0.0.0 index.js
```

> **Note**
>
> In the preceding command, we mapped port `9229` to the host. This port is used by the Node.js debugger, and VS Studio will communicate with our Node application via this port. Thus, it is important that you open this port – but only during a debugging session! Also, note that we overrode the standard start command that we defined in the Dockerfile (remember, it was just `node index.js`) with `node --inspect=0.0.0.0 index.js`. The `--inspect=0.0.0.0` command-line parameter tells Node to run in debug mode and listen on all IPv4 addresses in the container.

Now, we are ready to define a VS Code launch task for the scenario at hand – that is, our code running inside a container.

4. Add a folder called `.vscode` to your project (please note the leading period in the name of the folder). Within this folder, add a file called `launch.json` with the following content:

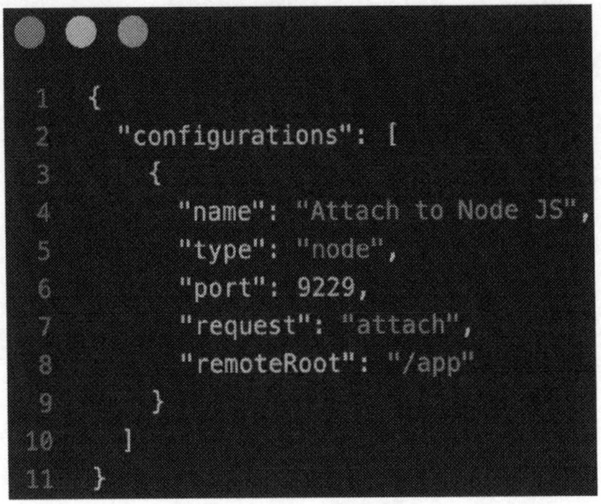

```json
 1  {
 2      "configurations": [
 3          {
 4              "name": "Attach to Node JS",
 5              "type": "node",
 6              "port": 9229,
 7              "request": "attach",
 8              "remoteRoot": "/app"
 9          }
10      ]
11  }
```

Figure 6.27 – The launch configuration to debug a Node.js application

5. To open the `launch.json` file, press *cmd + Shift + P* (or *Ctrl + Shift + P* on Windows) to open the command palette; look for **Debug:Open launch.json** and select it. The `launch.json` file should open in the editor.

6. Open the `index.js` file and click on the left sidebar on line 25 to set a breakpoint:

```
JS index.js U  ✕

JS index.js > ⊕ app.get('/status') callback
 20      app.get( /status ,  (req,res)=>{
 21        res.send('OK, all is definitely good');
 22      })
 23
 24      app.get('/colors', (req,res)=>{
 25        res.send(['red','green','blue']);
 26      })
```

Figure 6.28 – Setting a breakpoint in our Node.js sample application

7. Open the Debug view in VS Code by pressing *cmd + Shift + D* (or *Ctrl + Shift + D* on Windows).

8. Make sure you select the correct launch task in the dropdown next to the green start button at the top of the view. Select **Attach to Node JS** and specify the name of the launch configuration in the `launch.json` file. It should look like this:

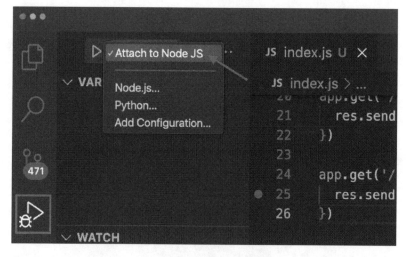

Figure 6.29 – Selecting the correct launch task to debug our Node.js application

9. Next, click on the green start button to attach VS Code to the Node.js application running in the container.

10. In another terminal window, use `curl` to navigate to the `/colors` endpoint:

```
$ curl localhost:3000/colors
```

Observe that the code's execution stops at the breakpoint:

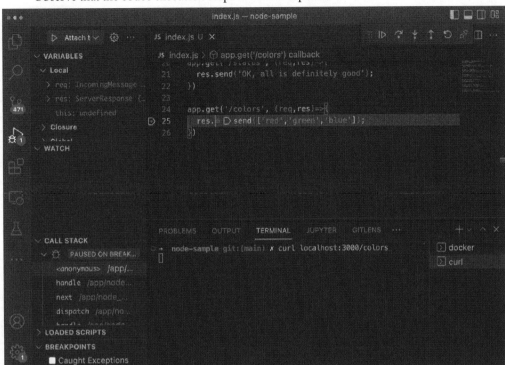

Figure 6.30 – The code's execution stops at the breakpoint

In the preceding screenshot, we can see a yellow bar, indicating that the code's execution has stopped at the breakpoint. In the top-right corner, we have a toolbar that allows us to navigate through the code step by step. On the left-hand side, we can see the **VARIABLES, WATCH,** and **CALL STACK** windows, which we can use to observe the details of our running application. The fact that we are debugging the code running inside the container can be verified by the fact that, in the terminal windows where we started the container, we can see that the output debugger is attached, which was generated the moment we started debugging inside VS Code.

11. To stop the container, enter the following command in the terminal window:

```
$ docker container rm --force node-sample
```

12. If we want to use nodemon for even more flexibility, then we have to change the container run command slightly:

```
$ docker container run --rm \
    --name node-sample \
    -p 3000:3000 \
    -p 9229:9229 \
```

```
        -v $(pwd):/app \
        node-sample-dev nodemon --inspect=0.0.0.0 index.js
```

Note how we use the start command, nodemon --inspect=0.0.0.0 index.js. This will have the benefit that, upon any code changes, the application running inside the container will restart automatically, as we learned earlier in this chapter. You should see the following:

```
→  node-sample git:(main) x docker container run --rm --name node-sample \
-p 3000:3000 -p 9229:9229 -v $(pwd):/app \
node-sample-dev nodemon --inspect=0.0.0.0 index.js
[nodemon] 2.0.20
[nodemon] to restart at any time, enter `rs`
[nodemon] watching path(s): *.*
[nodemon] watching extensions: js,mjs,json
[nodemon] starting `node --inspect=0.0.0.0 index.js`
Debugger listening on ws://0.0.0.0:9229/f2e524ea-2a27-4774-87d0-7d1993c89603
For help, see: https://nodejs.org/en/docs/inspector
Application listening at 0.0.0.0:3000
Debugger attached.  ◄───────────────────────
[nodemon] restarting due to changes...
[nodemon] starting `node --inspect=0.0.0.0 index.js`
Debugger listening on ws://0.0.0.0:9229/f9c3af87-c433-419b-8054-9b4918f68d6f
For help, see: https://nodejs.org/en/docs/inspector
Application listening at 0.0.0.0:3000
```

Figure 6.31 – Starting the Node.js application with nodemon and debugging turned on

13. Unfortunately, the consequence of an application restart is that the debugger loses its connection with VS Code. But don't worry – we can mitigate this by adding "restart": true to our launch task in the launch.json file. Modify the task so that it looks like this:

```
{
    "type": "node",
    "request": "attach",
    "name": "Docker: Attach to Node",
    "remoteRoot": "/app",
    "restart": true
},
```

14. After saving your changes, start the debugger in VS Code by clicking the green start button in the debug window. In the terminal, you should see that the debugger is attached, with a message as the output. In addition to that, VS Code will have an orange status bar at the bottom, indicating that the editor is in debug mode.

15. In a different terminal window, use curl and try to navigate to localhost:3000/colors to test that your line-by-line debugging still works. Make sure the code execution stops at any breakpoint you have set in the code.

16. Once you have verified that debugging still works, try to modify some code; for example, change the array of returned colors and add yet another color. Save your changes. Observe how nodemon restarts the application and that the debugger is automatically re-attached to the application running inside the container:

```
→  node-sample git:(main) ✗ docker container run —rm --name node-sample \
-p 3000:3000 -p 9229:9229 -v $(pwd):/app \
node-sample-dev nodemon --inspect=0.0.0.0 index.js
[nodemon] 2.0.20
[nodemon] to restart at any time, enter `rs`
[nodemon] watching path(s): *.*
[nodemon] watching extensions: js,mjs,json
[nodemon] starting `node --inspect=0.0.0.0 index.js`
Debugger listening on ws://0.0.0.0:9229/1873b319-40ca-4860-8e57-c8c6bb85a188
For help, see: https://nodejs.org/en/docs/inspector
Application listening at 0.0.0.0:3000
Debugger attached.
[nodemon] restarting due to changes...
[nodemon] starting `node --inspect=0.0.0.0 index.js`
Debugger listening on ws://0.0.0.0:9229/90543579-93e8-472f-8d39-b605502877ce
For help, see: https://nodejs.org/en/docs/inspector
Application listening at 0.0.0.0:3000
Debugger attached.
```

Figure 6.32 – nodemon restarting the application and the debugger
automatically re-attaching to the application

With that, we have everything assembled and can now work with code running inside a container as if the same code were running natively on the host. We have removed pretty much all of the friction that containers brought into the development process. We can now just enjoy the benefits of deploying our code in containers.

17. To clean up, stop the container by pressing *Ctrl* + *C* within the terminal window from where you started it.

Now that you've learned how to debug a Node.js application running in a container line by line, let's learn how to do the same for a .NET application.

Debugging a .NET application

In this section, we want to give you a quick run-through of how to debug a .NET application line by line. We will use the sample .NET application that we created earlier in this chapter:

1. Navigate to the project folder and open VS Code from within it:

```
$ cd ~/The-Ultimate-Docker-Container-Book/ch06/csharp-sample
```

2. Then, open VS Code with the following command:

```
$ code .
```

3. To work with the debugger, we can fully rely on the help of VS Code commands. Hit *cmd + Shift + P* (*Shift + Ctrl + P* on Windows) to open the command palette.

4. Search for `Docker: Add Docker Files to Workspace` and select it:

    I.   Select **.NET: ASP.NET Core** for the application platform when prompted.

    II. Select Linux when prompted to select the operating system.

    III. When you're asked if you want to add Docker Compose files, answer with **No** at this time. Later in this book, we will discover what Docker Compose files are.

    IV. Change the port to use for the application to `5000`.

    Once you have entered all the required information, a `Dockerfile` and a `.dockerignore` file will be added to the project. Take a moment to explore both. Notice that this `Dockerfile` is defined as a multistage build.

    The previous command also added the `launch.json` and `tasks.json` files to a new `.vscode` folder in the project. These will be used by VS Code to help it define what to do when we ask it to debug our sample application.

5. Let's put a breakpoint in the first GET request of the `WeatherForecastController.cs` file.

6. Locate the `.vscode/launch.json` file in the project and open it.

7. Locate the Docker .NET Core Launch debug configuration and add the snippet marked with the red rectangle to it:

```
{
    "name": "Docker .NET Core Launch",
    "type": "docker",
    "request": "launch",
    "dockerServerReadyAction": {
        "uriFormat": "%s://localhost:%s/WeatherForecast"
    },
    "preLaunchTask": "docker-run: debug",
    "netCore": {
        "appProject": "${workspaceFolder}/csharp-sample.csproj"
    }
}
```

Figure 6.33 – Modifying the Docker Launch configuration

The `dockerServerReadyAction` property in the `launch.json` file of a .NET project in VS Code is used to specify an action that should be taken when a Docker container is ready to accept requests.

8. Switch to the debug window of VS Code (use *Command + Shift + D* or *Ctrl + Shift + D* on Linux or Windows to open it, respectively). Make sure you have selected the correct debug launch task – its name is Docker .NET Core Launch:

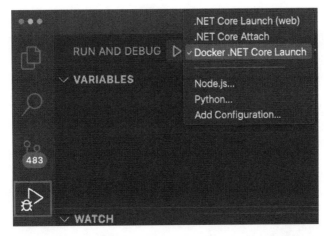

Figure 6.34 – Selecting the correct debug launch task in VS Code

9.   Now, click the green start button to start the debugger. VS Code will build the Docker images, run a container of them, and configure the container for debugging. The output will be shown in the terminal window of VS Code. A browser window will open and navigate to `http://localhost:5000/wetherforecast` since this is what we defined in the launch configuration (*step 6*). At the same time, the breakpoint in the application controller is hit, as shown here:

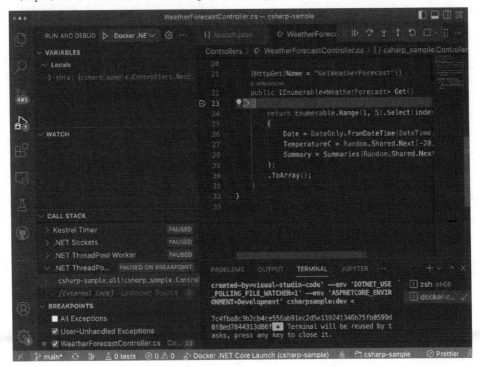

Figure 6.35 – Debugging a .NET Core application running inside a container line by line

10. We can now step through the code, define watches, or analyze the call stack of the application, similar to what we did with the sample Node.js application. Hit the **Continue** button on the debug toolbar or press *F5* to continue executing the code.

11. To stop the application, click the red stop button in the debugging toolbar, which is visible in the top-right corner of the preceding screenshot.

Now that we know how to debug code running in a container line by line, it is time to instrument our code so that it produces meaningful logging information.

Instrumenting your code to produce meaningful logging information

Once an application is running in production, it is impossible or strongly discouraged to interactively debug the application. Thus, we need to come up with other ways to find the root cause when the system is behaving unexpectedly or causing errors. The best way is to have the application generate detailed logging information that can then be used by the developers that need to track down any errors. Since logging is such a common task, all relevant programming languages or frameworks offer libraries that make the task of producing logging information inside an application straightforward.

It is common to categorize the information that's output by an application as logs into so-called severity levels. Here is a list of those severity levels with a short description of each:

Log Level	Description
TRACE	Very fine-grained information. At this level, you are looking at capturing every detail possible about your application's behavior.
DEBUG	Relatively granular and mostly diagnostic information that helps you pin down potential problems if they occur.
INFO	Normal application behavior or milestones, such as startup or shutdown information.
WARNING	The application might have encountered a problem, or you detected an unusual situation.
ERROR	The application encountered a serious issue. This most probably represents the failure of an important application task.
FATAL	The catastrophic failure of your application. The immediate shutdown of the application is advised.

Table 6.1 – A list of the severity levels used when generating logging information

Logging libraries usually allow a developer to define different log sinks – that is, destinations for the logging information. Popular sinks are file sinks or a stream to the console. When working with containerized applications, it is strongly recommended that you always direct logging output to the console or `STDOUT`. Docker will then make this information available to you via the `docker container logs` command. Other log collectors, such as Logstash, Fluentd, Loki, and others, can also be used to scrape this information.

Instrumenting a Python application

Let's try to instrument our existing Python sample application:

1. First, in your terminal, navigate to the project folder and open VS Code:

    ```
    $ cd ~/The-Ultimate-Docker-Container-Book/ch06/python-demo
    ```

2. Open VS Code with the following command:

    ```
    $ code .
    ```

3. Open the `main.py` file and add the following code snippet to the top of it:

```
1   import logging
2
3   logger = logging.getLogger("Python demo app")
4   logger.setLevel(logging.WARN)
5   # create a console handler
6   ch = logging.StreamHandler()
7   # create a formatter and add it to the handlers
8   formatter = logging.Formatter('%(asctime)s - %(name)s - %(levelname)s - %(message)s')
9   ch.setFormatter(formatter)
10  logger.addHandler(ch)
```

Figure 6.36 – Defining a logger for our Python sample application

On line 1, we import the standard logging library. We then define a logger for our sample application on line 3. On line 4, we define the filter for logging to be used. In this case, we set it to `WARN`. This means that all logging messages produced by the application with a severity equal to or higher than `WARN` will be output to the defined logging handlers or sinks, which is what we called them at the beginning of this section. In our case, only log messages with a log level of `WARN`, `ERROR`, or `FATAL` will be output.

On line 6, we create a logging sink or handler. In our case, it is `StreamHandler`, which outputs to `STDOUT`. Then, on line 8, we define how we want the logger to format the messages it outputs. Here, the format that we chose will output the time and date, the application (or logger) name, the log severity level, and finally, the actual message that we developers define in the code. On line 9, we add the formatter to the log handler, while on line 10, we add the handler to the logger.

> **Note**
>
> We can define more than one handler per logger.

Now, we are ready to use the logger.

4. Let's instrument the `hello` function, which is called when we navigate to the `/` endpoint:

```
1   @app.route("/")
2   def hello():
3       logger.info("Accessing endpoint '/'")
4       return "Hello World!"
```

Figure 6.37 – Instrumenting a method with logging

As shown in the preceding screenshot, we added line 3 to the preceding snippet, where we used the `logger` object to produce a logging message with the `INFO` log level. The message is `"Accessing endpoint '/'"`.

5. Let's instrument another function and output a message with the `WARN` log level:

```
1   @app.route("/colors")
2   def colors():
3       logger.warning("Warning, you are accessing /colors")
4       return jsonify(["red", "green", "blue"])
```

Figure 6.38 – Generating a warning

This time, we produced a message with the `WARN` log level on line 3 in the `colors` function. So far, so good – that wasn't hard!

6. Now, let's run the application and see what output we get:

```
$ python3 main.py
```

7. Then, in your browser, navigate to `localhost:5000/` first and then to `localhost:5000/colors`. You should see an output like this:

```
→  python-demo git:(main) x python3 main.py
 * Serving Flask app 'main'
 * Debug mode: off
WARNING: This is a development server. Do not use it in a production deployment. Use a production WSGI
erver instead.
 * Running on all addresses (0.0.0.0)
 * Running on http://127.0.0.1:5000
 * Running on http://192.168.1.54:5000
Press CTRL+C to quit
127.0.0.1 - - [28/Dec/2022 18:56:18] "GET / HTTP/1.1" 200 -
127.0.0.1 - - [28/Dec/2022 18:56:18] "GET /favicon.ico HTTP/1.1" 404 -
127.0.0.1 - - [28/Dec/2022 18:56:22] "GET / HTTP/1.1" 200 -
2022-12-28 18:56:24,030 - Python demo app - WARNING - Warning, you are accessing /colors
127.0.0.1 - - [28/Dec/2022 18:56:24] "GET /colors HTTP/1.1" 200 -
```

Figure 6.39 – Running the instrumented sample Python application

As you can see, only the warning is output to the console; the INFO message is not. This is due to the filter we set when defining the logger. Also, note how our logging message is formatted with the date and time at the beginning, then the name of the logger, the log level, and finally, the message that was defined on line 3 of the snippet shown in *Figure 6.39*.

8.   When you're done, stop the application by pressing *Ctrl + C*.

Now that we've learned how to instrument a Python application, let's learn how to do the same for .NET.

Instrumenting a .NET C# application

Let's instrument our sample C# application:

1.   First, navigate to the project folder, from where you'll open VS Code:

```
$ cd ~/The-Ultimate.Docker-Container-Book/ch06/csharp-sample
```

2.   Open VS Code with the following command:

```
$ code .
```

3.   Next, we need to add a NuGet package containing the logging library to the project:

```
$ dotnet add package Microsoft.Extensions.Logging
```

This should add the following line to your dotnet.csproj project file:

```
<PackageReference Include="Microsoft.Extensions.Logging"
Version="7.0.0" />
```

4.   Open the Program.cs class and notice that we have the following statement on line 1:

```
var builder = WebApplication.CreateBuilder(args);
```

This method call, by default, adds a few logging providers to the application, among which is the console logging provider. This comes in very handy and frees us from having to do any complicated configuration first. You can, of course, override the default setting at any time with your own settings.

5. Next, open the `WeatherForecastController.cs` file in the `Controllers` folder and add the following:

    I.   Add an instance variable, `logger`, of the `ILogger` type.

    II. Add a constructor that has a parameter of the `ILogger< WeatherForecastController >` type. Assign this parameter to the `logger` instance variable:

```
1   [ApiController]
2   [Route("[controller]")]
3   public class WeatherForecastController : ControllerBase
4   {
5       private ILogger logger;
6       public WeatherForecastController(ILogger<WeatherForecastController> logger)
7       {
8           this.logger = logger;
9       }
```

Figure 6.40 – Defining a logger for the Web API controller

6. Now, we're ready to use the logger in the controller methods. Let's instrument the `Get` method with an *info* message (line 4 in the following code):

```
1       [HttpGet(Name = "GetWeatherForecast")]
2       public IEnumerable<WeatherForecast> Get()
3       {
4           logger.LogInformation("Accessing the /weatherforecast endpoint.");
5           return Enumerable.Range(1, 10).Select(index => new WeatherForecast
6           {
7
```

Figure 6.41 – Logging an INFO message from the API controller

7. Now, let's add a method that implements a `/warning` endpoint right after the `Get` method and instrument it (line 4 here):

```
1   [HttpGet("/warning")]
2   public string ShowWarning()
3   {
4       logger.LogWarning("This endpoint shows a warning!");
5       return "Just a warning";
6   }
```

Figure 6.42 – Logging messages with the WARN log level

8. Let's run the application by using the following command:

```
$ dotnet run
```

9. We should see the following output when in a new browser tab. To do so, we must navigate to `localhost:3000/weatherforecast` and then `localhost:3000/warning`:

```
→ csharp-sample git:(main) ✗ dotnet run
Building...
info: Microsoft.Hosting.Lifetime[14]
      Now listening on: http://0.0.0.0:5080
info: Microsoft.Hosting.Lifetime[0]
      Application started. Press Ctrl+C to shut down.
info: Microsoft.Hosting.Lifetime[0]
      Hosting environment: Development
info: Microsoft.Hosting.Lifetime[0]
      Content root path: /Users/gabriel/The-Ultimate-Docker-Container-Book/sample-solutions/ch06/csharp-sample
warn: Microsoft.AspNetCore.HttpsPolicy.HttpsRedirectionMiddleware[3]
      Failed to determine the https port for redirect.
info: csharp_sample.Controllers.WeatherForecastController[0]
      Accessing the /weatherforecast endpoint. ◄──────────
warn: csharp_sample.Controllers.WeatherForecastController[0]
      This endpoint shows a warning! ◄──────────
```

Figure 6.43 – The log output of our sample .NET application

We can see the output of our log message, which is of the `info` and `warn` types, marked by red arrows. All the other log items have been produced by the ASP.NET library. You can see that there is a lot of helpful information available if you need to debug the application.

10. When you're done, end the application with *Ctrl + C*.

Now that we have learned how to instrument code to simplify how we can find the root cause of an issue when running in production, next, we will look at how we can instrument a distributed application using the Open Tracing standard for distributed tracing and then use Jaeger as a tool.

Using Jaeger to monitor and troubleshoot

When we want to monitor and troubleshoot transactions in a complex distributed system, we need something a bit more powerful than what we have just learned. Of course, we can and should continue to instrument our code with meaningful logging messages, yet we need something more on top of that. This *more* is the capability to trace a single request or transaction end to end, as it flows through a system consisting of many application services. Ideally, we also want to capture other interesting metrics, such as the time spent on each component versus the total time that the request took.

Luckily, we do not have to reinvent the wheel. There is battle-tested open source software out there that helps us achieve the aforementioned goals. One example of such an infrastructure component or software is Jaeger (`https:/ www.jaegertracing.io/`). When using Jaeger, you run a central Jaeger server component and each application component uses a Jaeger client that will forward debug and tracing information transparently to the Jaeger server component. There are Jaeger clients for all major programming languages and frameworks, such as Node.js, Python, Java, and .NET.

We will not go into all the intimate details of how to use Jaeger in this book, but we will provide a high-level overview of how it works conceptually:

1. First, we must define a Jaeger tracer object. This object coordinates the whole process of tracing a request through our distributed application. We can use this tracer object and also create a logger object from it, which our application code can use to generate log items, similar to what we did in the previous Python and .NET examples.

2. Next, we must wrap each method in the code that we want to trace with what Jaeger calls a span. This span has a name and provides us with a scope object.

3. Let's look at some C# pseudocode that illustrates this:

```
1  public void SayHello(string helloTo) {
2      using(var scope = _tracer.BuildSpan("sayhello").
3          StartActive(true)) {
4          // here is the actual logic of the method
5          ...
6          var helloString = FormatString(helloTo);
7          ...
8      }
9  }
```

Figure 6.44 – Defining a span in Jaeger – pseudocode

As you can see, we're instrumenting the `SayHello` method. With a `using` statement creating a span, we're wrapping the whole application code of this method. We have called the span `sayhello`; this will be the ID with which we can identify the method in the trace log produced by Jaeger.

Note that the method calls another nested method, `FormatString`. This method will look quite similar to the code needed to instrument it.

Using Jaeger to monitor and troubleshoot

The span that our tracer object builds in this method will be a child span of the calling method. This child span is called `format-string`. Also, note that we are using the logger object in the preceding method to explicitly generate a log item of the `INFO` log level:

```
1   public void string Format(string helloTo) {
2       using(var scope = _tracer.BuildSpan("format-string").StartActive(true))
3       {
4           // here is the actual logic of the method
5           ...
6           _logger.LogInformation(helloTo);
7           return
8       ...
9       }
10  }
```

Figure 6.45 – Creating a child span in Jaeger – pseudocode

In the code included with this chapter, you can find a complete sample application written in Java and Spring Boot consisting of a Jaeger server container and two application containers called `api` and `inventory` that use the Jaeger client library to instrument the code. Follow these steps to rebuild this solution:

1. Navigate to the **Spring Initializr** page at `https://start.spring.io` and create bootstrap code for a project called `api`, as follows:

Figure 6.46 – Bootstrapping the API component of the Jaeger sample

Note how we are using Spring Boot 2.7.7 for this example since, at the time of writing, the Jaeger and Open Tracing integration does not yet work with Spring Boot 3. Also, note how we have added the Spring Web reference to the project.

2. Click **GENERATE**. A ZIP file called `api.zip` will be downloaded to your computer.

3. Repeat the same steps but this time change the **Artifact** and **Name** entries to `inventory`. Then, click **GENERATE** again; a file called `inventory.zip` containing the bootstrap code will be downloaded to your computer.

4. Navigate to the source folder for this chapter:

```
$ cd ~/The-Ultimate-Docker-Container-Book/ch06
```

5. Then, create a subfolder called `jaeger-demo` in it:

```
$ mkdir jaeger-demo
```

6. Extract the two ZIP files into the `jaeger-demo` folder. Make sure the subfolders are called `api` and `inventory`, respectively.

7. Open VS Code from within this folder:

```
$ code .
```

8. Next, create a `docker-compose.yml` file in the root with this content:

```
1   version: "3"
2   services:
3     jaeger:
4       image: jaegertracing/all-in-one:latest
5       container_name: jaeger
6       environment:
7         COLLECTOR_ZIPKIN_HTTP_PORT: 9411
8       ports:
9         - 5775:5775/udp
10        - 6831:6831/udp
11        - 6832:6832/udp
12        - 5778:5778
13        - 16686:16686
14        - 14268:14268
15        - 9411:9411
```

Figure 6.47 – The Docker Compose file for the Jaeger demo

We will explain what a `docker-compose` file is in detail in *Chapter 11, Managing Containers with Docker Compose*.

9. Run Jaeger with this command:

```
$ docker compose up -d
```

10. In a new browser tab, navigate to the Jaeger UI at `http://localhost:16686`.

11. Locate the two `pom.xml` files for the `api` and `inventory` projects in your VS Code. Add the Jaeger integration component to each file by adding this snippet to their `dependencies` sections:

```
18    <dependencies>
19        <dependency>
20            <groupId>org.springframework.boot</groupId>
21            <artifactId>spring-boot-starter-web</artifactId>
22            <version>2.7.5</version>
23        </dependency>
24
25        <dependency>
26            <groupId>io.opentracing.contrib</groupId>
27            <artifactId>opentracing-spring-jaeger-cloud-starter</artifactId>
28            <version>3.3.1</version>
29        </dependency>
30
31        <dependency>
32            <groupId>org.springframework.boot</groupId>
33            <artifactId>spring-boot-starter-test</artifactId>
```

Figure 6.48 – Adding integration with Jaeger to the Java project(s)

12. In the `inventory` project, locate the start class, `InventoryApplication`, and add a bean to it that generates an instance of `RestTemplate`. We will use this to access an external API to download some data. The code snippet should look like this:

```
@Bean
RestTemplate restTemplate() {
    return new RestTemplate();
}
```

13. Do the same for the start class of the `api` project, called `ApiApplication`.

14. Now, let's go back to the `inventory` project. Add a new file called `Todo.java` as a sibling next to the start class. The file will have the following content:

```
1   package com.schenker.api;
2
3   public class Todo {
4       private int id;
5       private int userId;
6       private String title;
7       private boolean completed;
8
9       public int getUserId() {
10          return userId;
11      }
12
13      public void setUserId(int userId) {
14          this.userId = userId;
15      }
16
17      public String getTitle() {
18          return title;
19      }
20
21      public void setTitle(String title) {
22          this.title = title;
23      }
24
25      public boolean isCompleted() {
26          return completed;
27      }
28
29      public void setCompleted(boolean completed) {
30          this.completed = completed;
31      }
32
33      public int getId() {
34          return id;
35      }
36
37      public void setId(int id) {
38          this.id = id;
39      }
40
41  }
42
```

Figure 6.49 – The Todo class in the api project for the Jaeger demo

This is a really simple POJO class that we are using as a data container.

15. Do the same in the `api` project.

16. Go to the `inventory` project and add a new file called `TodosController.java` with the following content:

```
1   package com.schenker.inventory;
2
3   import org.springframework.web.bind.annotation.GetMapping;
4   import org.springframework.web.bind.annotation.RequestMapping;
5   import org.springframework.web.bind.annotation.RestController;
6   import org.springframework.web.client.RestTemplate;
7
8   @RestController
9   @RequestMapping("/api/todos")
10  public class TodosController {
11      private final RestTemplate restTemplate;
12
13      public TodosController(RestTemplate restTemplate) {
14          this.restTemplate = restTemplate;
15      }
16
17      @GetMapping
18      public Todo[] getTodos() {
19          var response = restTemplate.getForEntity("https://jsonplaceholder.typicode.com/todos", Todo[].class);
20          return response.getBody();
21      }
22  }
23
```

Figure 6.50 – The TodosController class for the Jaeger demo

Notice how, on line 19, we reach out to the public **JSONPlaceholder API** to download a list of todo items and return those items to the caller on line 20. There's nothing fancy here.

17. For the `api` project, add a new file called `HelloController.java` with the following content:

```
1     package com.schenker.api;
2
3     import org.slf4j.Logger;
4     import org.slf4j.LoggerFactory;
5     import org.springframework.web.bind.annotation.GetMapping;
6     import org.springframework.web.bind.annotation.RestController;
7     import org.springframework.web.client.RestTemplate;
8
9     @RestController
10    public class HelloController {
11        private static final Logger logger = LoggerFactory.getLogger(HelloController.class);
12        private RestTemplate restTemplate;
13
14        public HelloController(RestTemplate restTemplate) {
15            this.restTemplate = restTemplate;
16        }
17
18        @GetMapping("/hello")
19        public String hello() {
20            logger.info("Requesting hello world!");
21            return "Hello World!";
22        }
23
24
25        @GetMapping("/todos")
26        public Todo[] getTodos() {
27            logger.info("Requesting list of todos!");
28            var todos = restTemplate.getForEntity("http://localhost:8090/api/todos", Todo[].class);
29            return todos.getBody();
30        }
31    }
32
```

Figure 6.51 – The HelloController class for the Jaeger demo

Notice how the first method, which is listening on the /hello endpoint, just returns a string. However, the second endpoint, which is listening on the /todos endpoint, reaches out to the api service and its endpoint, /api/todos. The api service will send back the list of todos that it downloaded from the JSON Placeholder API. This way, we have a real distributed application ready to demonstrate the power of Jaeger and Open Tracing.

18. We are not quite done yet. We need to configure both projects via their respective applications. properties files:

19. Locate the application.properties file in the api project and add the following line to it:

```
spring.application.name=jaeger-demo:api
```

The preceding code defines the name of the service and how Jaeger will report it.

20. Locate the same file in the `inventory` project and add the following two lines to it:

```
server.port=8090
spring.application.name=jaeger-demo:inventory
```

21. The first line makes sure the inventory service is listening at port `8090` and not at the default port of `8080` to avoid any conflict with the `api` service, which will run on the default port.

    The second line defines the name of the service and how Jaeger will report it.

22. Now, start the `inventory` and `api` projects from within VS Code by clicking the **Run** hyperlink and decorating the `main` methods of their respective start classes.

23. Use `curl` or Thunder Client to access the exposed endpoint of the inventory service at `http://localhost:8090/api/todos`. You can also do the same in a new browser tab. You should receive a list of 100 random todo items.

24. Next, try to access the `api` service at the `http://localhost:8080/todos` endpoint. The same list of todos should be returned, but this time, they should originate from the `api` service and not directly from the JSON Placeholder API.

25. Now, go back to the browser tab where you opened the Jaeger UI.

26. Make sure you are on the **Search** tab.

27. From the **Services** drop-down list, select **jaeger-demo:api**.

28. Click **Find Traces**. You should see something like this:

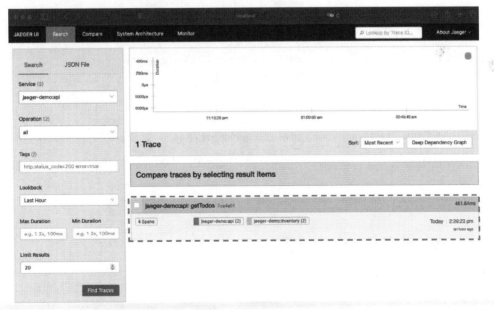

Figure 6.52 – Jaeger trace for the api service

29. Click on the trace to expand it. You should see this:

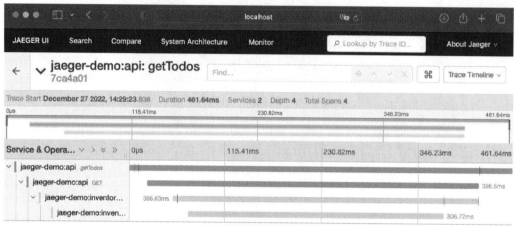

Figure 6.53 – Details of the Jaeger trace for the api service

Here, we can see how the call is reaching out from the `api` service to the `inventory` service. We can also see the time that's been spent on each component.

30. To clean up, stop the Jaeger server container:

```
$ docker compose down
```

31. Also, stop the API with *Ctrl + C*.

In this demo, we saw that without any special code, by just adding a component that integrates our Spring Boot applications with Jaeger and Open Tracing, we have gained a lot of insight. However, we're only just scratching the surface of what is possible.

Challenge: Try to containerize the `api` and `inventory` services using a similar `Dockerfile` for each, as we did in the Java demo application earlier in this chapter. The respective `Dockerfile` should be in the root of the `api` and `inventory` projects.

Then, amend the `docker-compose.yml` file. When you're done, run the whole application with this command:

```
$ docker compose up -d
```

Don't worry if you're not familiar with Docker Compose yet. We will discuss this very useful tool in *Chapter 11, Managing Containers with Docker Compose.*

Summary

In this chapter, we learned how to run and debug Node.js, Python, Java, and .NET code running inside a container. We started by mounting the source code from the host into the container to avoid the container image being rebuilt each time the code changes. Then, we smoothed out the development process further by enabling automatic application restarts inside the container upon code changes. Next, we learned how to configure VS Code to enable full interactive code debugging when code is running inside a container.

Finally, we learned how we can instrument our applications so that they generate logging information that can help us do root cause analysis on failures of misbehaving applications or application services running in production. We started by instrumenting our code using a logging library. Then, we used the Open Tracing standard for distributed tracing and the Jaeger tool to instrument a Java and Spring Boot application and gain valuable insight into the application's inner workings.

In the next chapter, we are going to show you how using Docker containers can supercharge your automation, from running a simple automation task in a container to using containers to build a CI/CD pipeline.

Questions

Try to answer the following questions to assess your learning progress:

1. Name two methods that help reduce the friction in the development process that's introduced by using containers.
2. How can you achieve live code inside a container?
3. When and why would you debug code line by line when running inside a container?
4. Why is instrumenting code with good debugging information paramount?

Answers

Here are the answers to this chapter's questions:

1. Possible answers:

    *   Volume-mount your source code in the container
    *   Use a tool that automatically restarts the app running inside the container when code changes are detected
    *   Configure your container for remote debugging

2. You can mount the folder containing the source code on your host in the container.

3. If you cannot cover certain scenarios easily with unit or integration tests and if the observed behavior of the application cannot be reproduced when the application runs on the host. Another scenario is a situation where you cannot run the application on the host directly due to a lack of the necessary language or framework.

4. Once an application is running in production, we cannot easily gain access to it as developers. If the application shows unexpected behavior or even crashes, logs are often the only source of information we have to help us reproduce the situation and pinpoint the root cause of the bug.

7

Testing Applications Running in Containers

In the previous chapters, we have learned how we can containerize our applications written in any language, such as Node.js, Python, Java, C#, and .NET. We all know that just writing code and then shipping it to production is not enough. We also need to guarantee that the code is error-free and that it does what it is supposed to do. This is commonly subsumed under the term **quality assurance**, or **QA** for short.

It has been proven in practice over and over again that fixing a bug in an application that has been discovered in production as opposed to during development is very costly. We want to avoid this. The most cost-effective way to do so is to have the developer who writes the code also write automated tests that make sure the new or changed code is of high quality and performs exactly as specified in the acceptance criteria of the business requirement or feature specification.

Here is a list of the topics we are going to discuss in this chapter:

- The benefits of testing applications running in containers
- Different types of testing
- Commonly used tools and technologies
- Best practices for setting up a testing environment
- Tips for debugging and troubleshooting issues
- Challenges and considerations when testing applications running in containers
- Case studies

After reading this chapter, you will be able to do the following:

- Explain the benefits of testing applications running in containers to an interested layperson
- Set up a productive environment that allows you to write and execute tests for applications or services running in containers
- Develop unit and integration tests for code running in a container
- Run your unit and integration tests in a container with the application code under test
- Run a dedicated container with functional tests that act on your application as a black box
- Manage application dependencies and create test data

Technical requirements

In this chapter, you need Docker Desktop, a terminal, and VS Code installed on your Mac, Windows, or Linux machine. As we will work with code, you should prepare a chapter folder in the code repository you cloned from GitHub:

1. Navigate to the folder to which you cloned the GitHub repository accompanying this book. Normally, you do this as follows:

```
$ cd ~/The-Ultimate-Docker-Container-Book
```

2. Create a chapter folder in this directory and navigate to it:

```
$ mkdir ch07 && cd ch07
```

As always, you can find complete sample solutions for all the exercises we will do in this chapter in the `sample-solutions/ch07` subfolder.

Benefits of testing applications in containers

In this section, we are discussing the benefits of testing applications in containers, including the ability to replicate production environments, ease of configuration and setup, and faster test execution.

But before we start, let's pause for a second and ask ourselves, why do we care to test at all?

Why do we test?

Every person working in any role in software development is aware that one needs to implement and ship new or changed application features at a fast cadence. There is constant pressure to implement new code and ship it as quickly as possible to production. But business analysts that write the feature specifications and software engineers that write the actual code implementing the specifications are just human beings. Human beings working under a lot of pressure tend to make mistakes. These mistakes can be subtle, or they can be quite substantial. Those mistakes will manifest themselves in the application running in production. Our customers will discover them, and this will have consequences.

Manual versus automated testing

Most companies that write commercial applications will have a team of manual software testers. These people will take the newest version of the application that product engineering has prepared for them and execute a suite of manual regression tests against this application. If a manual tester discovers a bug, they will report it in a tool such as Jira as a bug ticket, where they will ideally write down all the necessary details that matter for the developer who will have to fix the bug. This includes the exact version of the application tested, the steps that the tester took before the bug was detected, and some evidence of the bug, such as screenshots, error messages, stack traces, and log entries. These tickets written by manual testers will become part of the backlog of product engineering.

Product engineering will then, together with the testers, triage all the new bug tickets on a regular basis, say daily, and decide how quickly a particular bug needs to be addressed. Usually, the classification of P1, P2, P3, and P4 is used, where P1 is a defect of the highest severity that needs to be fixed immediately, and P4 is a bug that is of low priority and can be dealt with whenever the team has time.

If the application is a typical enterprise application consisting of many services all running in the cloud, then the testers need a special environment where they can perform their regression testing. This environment is often called **user acceptance testing**, or **UAT** for short. A full test suite for such an enterprise application usually consists of several hundred test cases. To perform a single test case takes a manual tester a considerable amount of time. It is not unheard of that a team of dedicated manual testers needs a couple of weeks to perform a full test run. During this time, the UAT environment is blocked. No new version can be deployed to this environment, because otherwise the testers would have to restart their regression testing. Each change in the application can introduce new bugs, and we can only be certain to catch them all if we execute the whole suite of regression tests on each new version.

Only after the manual testers have run through all regression tests, and only if no more severe bugs have been discovered, can the current version of the application be shipped to production.

I bet you can imagine that having UAT blocked for several weeks at a time can introduce some significant problems in the software development process. Your many product engineering teams will have accumulated a lot of new code in the form of new features and bug fixes that are blocked from being shipped to production since the manual testers are still testing the previous version. But accumulating a lot of code changes does, at the same time, increase risk. To ship a piece of software that has undergone many changes is riskier than if we continuously ship new versions with minimal changes to production.

The only real solution to this problem is to shorten the regression test cycle. We need to shorten it from weeks to minutes or a small number of hours. This way, we can test and ship small batches of changes in a continuous fashion. But no human being is able to test so fast. The solution is to exclusively use automated testing. And yes, I mean it: we should rely exclusively on automated regression and acceptance testing.

What did we learn? Manual testing is not scalable, it is super boring, since the testers have to repeat the same tests over and over again, and it is error prone, since everything humans do is not automated and thus not exactly repeatable every time.

Does this mean we have to fire all manual testers? Not necessarily. Manual testers should not perform acceptance and regression tests but rather exploratory tests. Manual testers are human beings, and they should leverage that fact and their creativity to discover yet undiscovered potential defects in the application. As the term *exploratory testing* implies, these tests are not following a particular script, but are rather random and only guided by the professional experience of the tester and their understanding of the business domain for which the application has been written. If the tester discovers a bug, they write a ticket for it, which then will be triaged and flown into the backlog of the development teams.

Why do we test in containers?

There are several reasons why it is often useful to run tests in containers:

- **Isolation**: Running tests in containers can provide a level of isolation between the test environment and the host system, which can be useful for ensuring that the test results are consistent and repeatable.

- **Environment consistency**: Containers allow you to package the entire test environment (including dependencies, libraries, and configuration) in a self-contained unit, which can help to ensure that the test environment is consistent across different development environments.

- **Ease of use**: Containers can make it easier to set up and run tests, as you don't have to manually install and configure all of the required dependencies and libraries on the host system.

- **Portability**: Containers can be easily moved between different environments, which can be useful for running tests in different environments or on different platforms.

- **Scalability**: Containers can make it easier to scale up your test infrastructure by allowing you to run tests in parallel or on multiple machines.

Overall, running tests in containers can help to improve the reliability, consistency, and scalability of the testing process and can make it easier to set up and maintain a testing environment that is isolated from the host system.

Different types of testing

This section gives an overview of different types of testing that can be performed on applications running in containers, including unit tests, integration tests, and acceptance tests.

Unit tests

A unit test's primary objective is to validate the functionality of a *unit*, or tiny, isolated portion of code. In order to check that the code is accurate and operates as expected, developers frequently build unit tests as they create or modify the code. These tests are then routinely executed as part of the development process.

With no reliance on other resources or components, unit tests are made to test distinct pieces of code in isolation. This enables developers to find and quickly solve bugs in their code and makes them quick and simple to run.

Typically, tools and testing frameworks that facilitate the creation, running, and reporting of unit tests are used to generate unit tests. These tools frequently offer capabilities such as automatic test discovery, test execution, and test results reporting, and they enable developers to create unit tests using a particular syntax or structure.

A thorough testing approach should include unit tests, since they enable developers to verify that their code is valid and works as intended at the most granular level. Normally, they are executed as a part of a **continuous integration** (**CI**) process, which is a workflow in which code changes are automatically executed each time they are committed to a version control system.

Integration tests

Software testing called *integration testing* examines how well various systems or components function together as a whole. It usually follows unit testing and entails examining how various parts of an application or system interact with one another.

Integration tests are created to examine how well various units or components interact together. They are frequently used to confirm that an application's or system's various components can function as intended. Testing the integration of several software components or the integration of a software program with external resources such as databases or APIs are examples of this.

As many components or systems need to be set up and configured in order to execute the tests, integration tests are typically more complicated and time-consuming than unit tests. In order to enable the execution and reporting of the tests, they could also call for the employment of specialist testing tools and frameworks.

Integration tests, like unit tests, are a crucial component of a thorough testing approach, because they enable developers to confirm that several systems or components can function together as intended.

Acceptance tests

Software testing of this kind, known as *acceptance testing*, ensures that a system or application is suitable for its intended use and that it satisfies all of the requirements. It usually comes after all other types of testing (such as unit testing and integration testing) and is the last step in the testing procedure.

Acceptance tests are typically developed and carried out by a different team or group of testers who are tasked with assessing the system or application from the viewpoint of the end user. These tests are intended to make sure that the system or program is simple to use, fits the demands of the intended users, and is user-friendly.

Functional testing (to ensure that the application or system performs the required functions correctly), usability testing (to make sure that the application or system is easy to use), and performance testing are just a few examples of the different types of testing that may be included in acceptance tests (to verify that the application or system performs well under different load conditions).

Acceptance testing is a crucial step in the software development process, since it enables developers to confirm that the system or application is ready for deployment and satisfies the needs of the intended customers. Although it is highly recommended to employ automated acceptance testing technologies to assist the testing process, it is often carried out manually by testers.

In this chapter, we will look at a special type of acceptance test called *black box tests*. The main differentiator compared to unit and integration tests is that these black box tests look at the system under tests from a decidedly business-oriented perspective. Ideally, acceptance tests, and with it black box tests, reflect the acceptance criteria to be found in the feature specifications written by business analysts or product owners. Most often, acceptance tests are written in a way that they look at the component to be tested as a black box. The internals of this component do not and should not matter. The test code only ever accesses the component or system under test via its public interfaces. Typically, public interfaces are APIs or messages that the component consumes or produces.

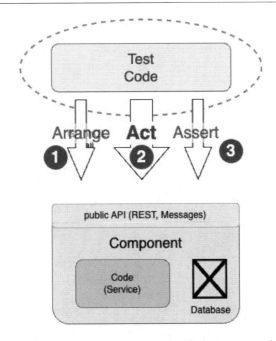

Figure 7.1 – Acceptance test interacting with the system under test

In the preceding figure, we can see how the test code is structured in the popular format of **Arrange-Act-Assert**, or **AAA**. First, we set up the boundary conditions (arrange). Next, we specify the action to exercise on the system under test (act). Finally, we verify that the outcome of the action is as expected (assert). The **system under test (SUT)** is the component that has a public interface in the form of either a REST API and/or messages that it consumes from a message bus. The SUT, in most cases, also has a database where it stores it state.

In the next section, we will present tools and technologies used for testing.

Commonly used tools and technologies

Let's now discuss the tools and technologies that are commonly used for testing applications running in containers, such as Docker, Kubernetes, and **continuous integration and delivery (CI/CD)** platforms.

Implementing a sample component

In this section, we want to implement a sample component that we are later going to use to demonstrate how we can write and execute tests for, and, specifically, how we can combine the advantage of automated tests and the use of Docker containers. We will implement the sample component using recent versions of Java and Spring Boot.

This sample component represents a simple REST API with some CRUD logic behind it. The tasks of creating and managing lists of animal species and associated races are simple enough to not warrant more complicated modeling. For simplicity, we are working with the in-memory database H2. This means that upon each restart of the component, the previous data is wiped out. If you want to change this, you can configure H2 to use a backing file for persistence instead:

1. Use the **spring initializr** page at `https://start.spring.io` to bootstrap the Java project. After configuring everything, the page should look like this:

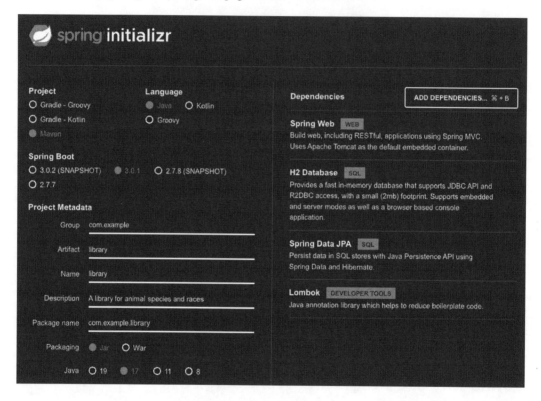

Figure 7.2 – Bootstrapping the library project

Note how we have added the four dependencies listed on the right-hand side of the preceding figure.

2. Download the bootstrap code and unzip the file into the chapter folder, `.../ch07`. You should now have a subfolder called `library` containing the code we can use as a starting point to implement our API.

3. Open the project in VS Code.

4. Locate the `LibraryApplication.java` file in the `src/main/java/com/example/library` folder. It's the typical start class containing the `main` function for a Spring Boot-based Java application.

5. Inside this folder, create three subfolders called `controllers`, `models`, and `repositories`, respectively. They will contain the logic for our library.

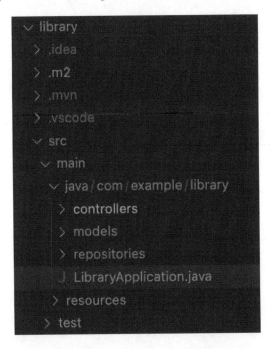

Figure 7.3 – Project structure of the library API

6. Let's first define the models we're using in our application. To the `models` folder, add the following simple data classes:

   I. To a file called `Race.java`, add the following content:

```
1   package com.example.library.models;
2
3   import jakarta.persistence.Entity;
4   import jakarta.persistence.Id;
5   import lombok.AllArgsConstructor;
6   import lombok.Data;
7   import lombok.NoArgsConstructor;
8
9   @Data
10  @AllArgsConstructor
11  @NoArgsConstructor
12  @Entity
13  public class Race {
14    @Id
15    private Integer id;
16    private Integer speciesId;
17    private String name;
18    private String description;
19  }
```

Figure 7.4 – The Race data class

II.   To a file called Species.java, add this content:

```
1   package com.example.library.models;
2
3   import jakarta.persistence.Entity;
4   import jakarta.persistence.Id;
5   import lombok.AllArgsConstructor;
6   import lombok.Data;
7   import lombok.NoArgsConstructor;
8
9   @Data
10  @AllArgsConstructor
11  @NoArgsConstructor
12  @Entity
13  public class Species {
14    @Id
15    private int id;
16    private String name;
17    private String description;
18  }
```

Figure 7.5 – The Species data class

Note how we use the @Entity annotation to mark these classes as (database) entities, and we decorate their respective id properties with the @Id annotation to tell Spring Boot that this property represents the unique ID of each entity.

7. Next, we are going to implement the repositories we're going to use to persist data to and retrieve data from our database. To the repositories folder, add the following:

A.   A file called RaceRepository.java with this content:

```java
package com.example.library.repositories;

import java.util.List;

import org.springframework.data.repository.CrudRepository;

import com.example.library.models.Race;

public interface RaceRepository extends CrudRepository<Race, Integer> {
  List<Race> findBySpeciesId(Integer speciesId);
}
```

Figure 7.6 – Code for the race repository

Note how on line 10, we add a custom findBySpeciesId method, which will allow us to retrieve all races assigned to a given speciesId.

B.   A file called SpeciesRepository.java with the following content:

```java
package com.example.library.repositories;

import org.springframework.data.repository.CrudRepository;

import com.example.library.models.Species;

public interface SpeciesRepository extends CrudRepository<Species, Integer> {

}
```

Figure 7.7 – Code for the species repository

8. Then, we define the two REST controllers through which we can interact with the application. To the `controllers` folder, add the following:

    A. A file called `RacesController.java` with this content:

```java
package com.example.library.controllers;

import org.springframework.http.ResponseEntity;
import org.springframework.web.bind.annotation.GetMapping;
import org.springframework.web.bind.annotation.PathVariable;
import org.springframework.web.bind.annotation.PostMapping;
import org.springframework.web.bind.annotation.PutMapping;
import org.springframework.web.bind.annotation.RequestBody;
import org.springframework.web.bind.annotation.RestController;

import com.example.library.models.Race;
import com.example.library.repositories.RaceRepository;

@RestController
public class RacesController {
    private final RaceRepository repository;

    public RacesController(RaceRepository repository) {
        this.repository = repository;
    }

    @GetMapping("/races")
    public Iterable<Race> index() {
        return repository.findAll();
    }

    @GetMapping("/races/{id}")
    public ResponseEntity<Race> getById(@PathVariable("id") Integer id) {
        var race = repository.findById(id);
        return race
            .map(r -> ResponseEntity.ok().body(r))
            .orElseGet(() -> ResponseEntity.notFound().build());
    }

    @GetMapping("/species/{speciesId}/races")
    public Iterable<Race> getBySpecies(@PathVariable("speciesId") Integer speciesId) {
        return repository.findBySpeciesId(speciesId);
    }

    @PostMapping("/races")
    public Race add(@RequestBody Race race) {
        return repository.save(race);
    }

    @PutMapping("/races/{id}")
    public ResponseEntity<Race> update(@PathVariable("id") Integer id, @RequestBody Race updatedRace) {
        var race = repository.findById(id);
        if(!race.isPresent())
            return ResponseEntity.notFound().build();

        updatedRace.setId(id);
        repository.save(updatedRace);
        return ResponseEntity.ok().body(updatedRace);
    }
}
```

Figure 7.8 – Code for the races controller

You can find the full code here: `https://github.com/PacktPublishing/The-Ultimate-Docker-Container-Book/blob/main/sample-solutions/ch07/library/src/main/java/com/example/library/controllers/RacesController.java`.

B.   A file called `SpeciesController.java` with this code:

```java
package com.example.library.controllers;

import org.springframework.http.ResponseEntity;
import org.springframework.web.bind.annotation.GetMapping;
import org.springframework.web.bind.annotation.PathVariable;
import org.springframework.web.bind.annotation.PostMapping;
import org.springframework.web.bind.annotation.PutMapping;
import org.springframework.web.bind.annotation.RequestBody;
import org.springframework.web.bind.annotation.RestController;

import com.example.library.models.Species;
import com.example.library.repositories.SpeciesRepository;

@RestController
public class SpeciesController {
    private final SpeciesRepository repository;

    public SpeciesController(SpeciesRepository repository) {
        this.repository = repository;
    }

    @GetMapping("/species")
    public Iterable<Species> index() {
        return repository.findAll();
    }

    @GetMapping("/species/{id}")
    public ResponseEntity<Species> getById(@PathVariable("id") Integer id) {
        var species = repository.findById(id);
        return species
            .map(r -> ResponseEntity.ok().body(r))
            .orElseGet(() -> ResponseEntity.notFound().build());
    }

    @PostMapping("/species")
    public Species add(@RequestBody Species species) {
        return repository.save(species);
    }

    @PutMapping("/species/{id}")
    public ResponseEntity<Species> update(@PathVariable("id") Integer id, @RequestBody Species updatedSpecies) {
        var race = repository.findById(id);
        if(!race.isPresent())
            return ResponseEntity.notFound().build();

        updatedSpecies.setId(id);
        repository.save(updatedSpecies);
        return ResponseEntity.ok().body(updatedSpecies);
    }
}
```

Figure 7.9 – Code for the species controller

You can find the full code here: `https://github.com/PacktPublishing/The-Ultimate-Docker-Container-Book/blob/main/sample-solutions/ch07/library/src/main/java/com/example/library/controllers/SpeciesController.java`.

9. Finally, we need to do some application configuration. We can do so in the `application.properties` file, which you can find in the `src/main/resources` folder. Add this content to it, which configures the database we are going to use for this example:

```
1   spring.datasource.url=jdbc:h2:mem:inventory
2   spring.datasource.driverClassName=org.h2.Driver
3   spring.datasource.username=sa
4   spring.datasource.password=
5   spring.jpa.database-platform=org.hibernate.dialect.H2Dialect
6   spring.h2.console.enabled=true
```

Figure 7.10 – Application configuration

We are using the H2 in-memory database with a username of `sa` and no password. We are also making sure to enable the H2 console in our application to have an easy way to inspect the data from our browser (line 6).

10. Now open the `LibraryApplication` class and click the **Run** link above the main method to start the application. Observe the output generated in the terminal:

Figure 7.11 – Logging the output of the running library application

Read through the log output and try to make sense of each line. The second-to-last line of the preceding output is telling us that the application can be accessed at port 8080, which is the default for Spring Boot applications. Also note the line where it says H2 console available at '/h2-console'. Database available at 'jdbc:h2:mem:inventory'. This indicates that we can now open a browser at localhost:8080/h2-console to open the H2 console and, through it, access our in-memory database.

11. Use the Thunder client in VS Code, Postman, or the curl command in the terminal to add a species to the database. Here we are using curl:

```
$ curl -X POST -d '{"id": 1, "name": "Elephant"}' \
    -H 'Content-Type: application/json' \
    localhost:8080/species
```

The response should look like this:

```
{"id":1,"name":"Elephant","description":null}
```

12. Use curl (or any other tool) again to list the species stored in the system:

```
$ curl localhost:8080/species
```

The output should look like this:

```
[{"id":1,"name":"Elephant","description":null}]
```

It is a JSON array with exactly one element.

13. Try all the other REST calls that the two controllers we implemented support, such as PUT to update an existing species and GET, POST, and PUT for the /races endpoint.

14. When done, make sure to stop the application.

Next, we need to package the application into a container and run it:

1. Add a Dockerfile to the root of the library project with this content:

```
1   FROM eclipse-temurin:17-jdk-focal AS build
2   WORKDIR /app
3   COPY mvnw .
4   COPY .mvn .mvn
5   COPY pom.xml .
6   COPY src src
7
8   CMD ./mvnw spring-boot:run
```

Figure 7.12 – Dockerfile for the library component

2. Create a Docker image using this Dockerfile with this command executed from within the `ch07` folder:

```
$ docker image build -t library library
```

3. Run a container with this command:

```
$ docker container run -d --rm \
    -p 8080:8080 library
```

4. Test that the component now running inside a container still works as expected by using the same commands as in the previous section.

5. When done, stop the container with the library component. We suggest that you use the Docker plugin of VS Code to do so or the dashboard of Docker Desktop.

Now that we have a working example application, we can continue and discuss how we can test this REST API using unit, integration, and black box tests. Let's start with the unit and/or integration tests.

Implementing and running unit and integration tests

Now that we have a working component, it is time to write some tests for it. In this section, we concentrate on unit and integration tests. Spring Boot makes it really simple to get started:

1. To the `src/test/java/com/example/library` folder, add a `LibraryUnitTests.java` file with the following content:

```
1   package com.example.library;
2
3   import static org.junit.jupiter.api.Assertions.assertEquals;
4
5   import org.junit.jupiter.api.Test;
6   import org.springframework.boot.test.context.SpringBootTest;
7
8   @SpringBootTest
9   class LibraryUnitTests {
10
11      // *** This is our system under test (SUT) ***
12      class Calculator {
13        public int add(int a, int b) {
14          return a + b;
15        }
16      }
17
18      @Test
19      public void assertCanAddNumbers() {
20        // arrange
21        var calc = new Calculator();
22        var expected = 6;
23        // act
24        var result = calc.add(1, 5);
25        // assert
26        assertEquals(expected, result);
27      }
28  }
```

Figure 7.13 – Sample unit test written for the library project

Note how we have added a private `Calculator` class to our `Test` class. This is for demonstration purposes only and makes it easier to show how to write a unit test. Normally, one would test classes and their methods that are part of the code base.

> **Tip**
>
> It is a good idea to always structure your tests in a similar way and make it easier for others (and yourself) to read and comprehend those tests. In this case, we have chosen the triple-A (AAA) syntax consisting of Arrange, Act, and Assert. Alternatively, you could use the Given-When-Then syntax.

2. If you have the **Test Runner for Java** extension installed on your VS Code editor, you should now see a green triangle next to the test method (line 19 in the preceding figure). Click it to run the test. As a result, you should see something like this:

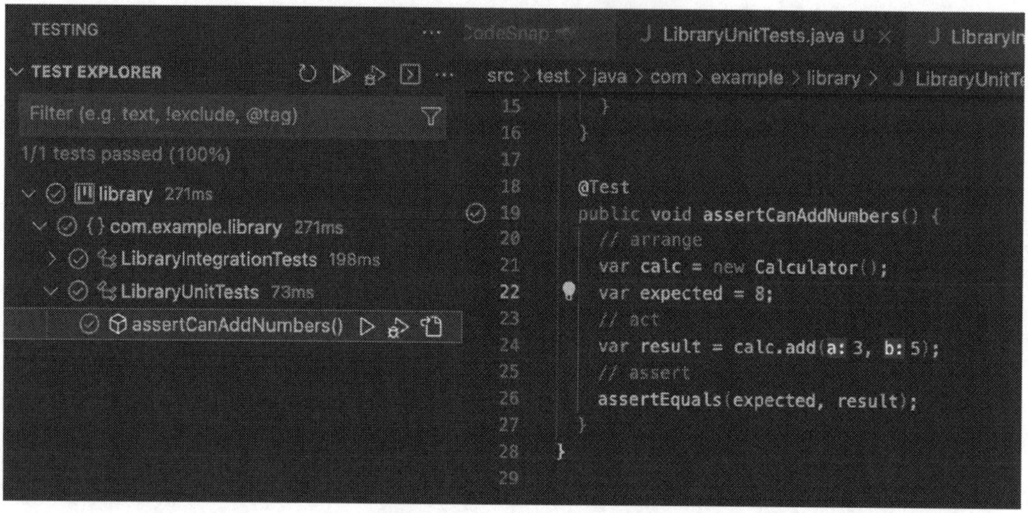

Figure 7.14 – Results of a first test run

> **Note**
>
> Alternatively, you can run the tests from the command line with this command:
>
> `$ ./mvnw test`

3. Now let's add a sample integration test. For this, add a file called `LibraryIntegrationTests. java` in the same folder as where you have put the unit tests. We will implement a test using the `MockMvc` helper class provided by Spring Boot to simulate that our application runs on a web server and we're accessing it through its REST endpoints. Add the following content to the test class:

```
1   package com.example.library;
2
3   import org.junit.jupiter.api.Test;
4   import org.springframework.beans.factory.annotation.Autowired;
5   import org.springframework.boot.test.autoconfigure.web.servlet.AutoConfigureMockMvc;
6   import org.springframework.boot.test.context.SpringBootTest;
7   import org.springframework.http.MediaType;
8   import org.springframework.test.web.servlet.MockMvc;
9
10  import static org.springframework.test.web.servlet.request.MockMvcRequestBuilders.post;
11  import static org.springframework.test.web.servlet.result.MockMvcResultMatchers.jsonPath;
12  import static org.springframework.test.web.servlet.result.MockMvcResultMatchers.status;
13
14  @SpringBootTest
15  @AutoConfigureMockMvc
16  class LibraryIntegrationTests {
17
18      @Autowired
19      private MockMvc mockMvc;
20
21      @Test
22      void testAddSpecies() throws Exception {
23        var body = "{\"id\":\"1\", \"name\":\"Elephant\"}";
24        mockMvc.perform(post("/species")
25          .contentType(MediaType.APPLICATION_JSON)
26          .content(body))
27          .andExpect(status().isOk())
28          .andExpect(jsonPath("$.id").exists())
29          .andExpect(jsonPath("$.name").value("Elephant"));
30      }
31  }
32
```

Figure 7.15 – Sample Integration Test written for the library project

4. Run the preceding test the same way as you did with the unit test. Make sure the test passes.

We have finished our preparation and are now ready to package the component into a container and run the unit and integration tests inside the same container. To do this, follow these steps:

1. Let's add a Dockerfile with the following content to the root of our library project. The content is the same that we already used in the previous Java example:

```
1 FROM eclipse-temurin:17-jdk-focal AS build
2 WORKDIR /app
3 COPY mvnw .
4 COPY .mvn .mvn
5 COPY pom.xml .
6 COPY src src
7
8 CMD ./mvnw spring-boot:run
```

Figure 7.16 – Dockerfile for the library project

2. Then, let's build an image using this Dockerfile:

```
$ docker image build -t library .
```

3. Run the tests in the container with the following command:

```
$ docker container run --rm \
    -v $HOME/.m2:/root/.m2
    library ./mvnw test
```

Note the volume mapping we are using. We are sharing our local Maven repository at `$HOME/.m2` with the container, so when building the application, Maven does not have to download all dependencies first as they are already in our local cache. This improves the overall experience massively.

Also note how we override the `CMD` command in our Dockerfile (line 8 in the preceding figure) with `./mvnw test` to run the tests instead of running the application.

4. Observe the output generated. The last few lines of the output should look like this, indicating that tests were run:

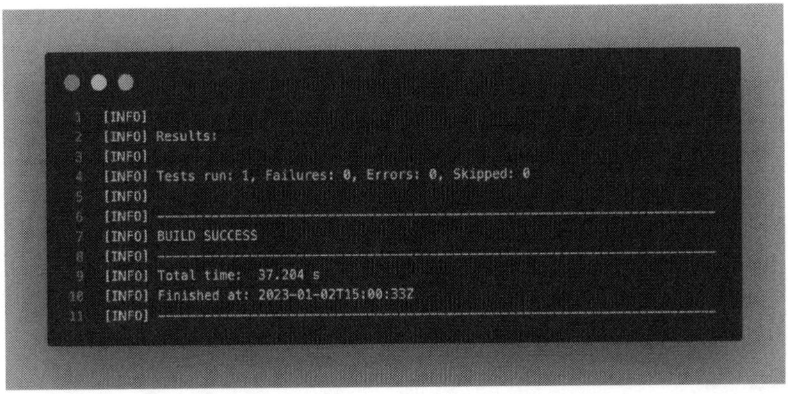

Figure 7.17 – Output of a test run inside the container

In the same way that you have now run the unit and integration tests inside a container locally on your laptop, you can also run it during the CI phase of your CI/CD pipeline. A simple shell script is enough to automate what you just did manually.

Implementing and running black box tests

Since black box tests have to deal with the SUT as a closed system, the tests should not run inside the same container as the component itself. It is instead recommended to run the test code in its own dedicated test container.

It is also recommended to not intermingle the code of black box tests and the component but to keep them strictly separate. We will demonstrate this by writing the tests in a different language than the component. This time, we will use C#. Any language will do such as Kotlin, Node.js, or Python.

In this example, we will use .NET and C# to implement the component tests:

1. From within the ch07 folder, execute the following command to create a test project:

```
$ dotnet new xunit -o library-component-tests
```

This will create a test project in the library-component-tests subfolder using the popular xunit test library.

2. Try to run the tests with the following command:

```
$ dotnet test library-component-tests
```

The (shortened) output should look like this:

```
Passed!  - Failed:  0, Passed:  1, Skipped:  0, Total:  1, …
```

This indicates that all tests passed. Of course, by default, there exists only an empty sample test in the project at this time.

3. Open this project in VS Code with the following:

```
$ code library-component-tests
```

4. Locate the `UnitTest1.cs` file and open it. At the top of the file, add this statement:

```
using System.Text.Json;
```

5. Right after the `namespace` declaration, add this record definition:

```
public record Species(int id, string name, string description);
```

6. Now add a new method called `can_add_species`, looking like this:

```
1   [Fact]
2       public async Task can_add_species()
3       {
4           // Arrange
5           var client = new HttpClient();
6           var url = "http://localhost:8080/species";
7           var species = new Species(1, "Elephant", "The big gray mammal");
8           var json = JsonSerializer.Serialize(species);
9           var body = new StringContent(json, System.Text.Encoding.UTF8, "application/json");
10
11          // act
12          var response = await client.PostAsync(url, body);
13
14          // assert
15          Assert.Equal(System.Net.HttpStatusCode.OK, response.StatusCode);
16      }
```

Figure 7.18 – Component test to add a species

Here we are using the `HttpClient` class to post a data object of type `Species` to the `/species` endpoint. We are then asserting that the HTTP response code for the operation is `OK (200)`. Note how we are using the AAA convention to structure our test.

7. Add another method called `can_get_a_species_by_id` with the following content:

```
1    [Fact]
2    public async Task can_get_a_species_by_id()
3    {
4        // Arrange
5        var client = new HttpClient();
6        var species = new Species(2, "Dog", "Human's best friend");
7        var json = JsonSerializer.Serialize(species);
8        var body = new StringContent(json, System.Text.Encoding.UTF8, "application/json");
9        var res = await client.PostAsync("http://localhost:8080/species", body);
10
11       // Act
12       var response = await client.GetAsync("http://localhost:8080/species/2");
13
14       // Assert
15       var stream = await response.Content.ReadAsStreamAsync();
16       var data = await JsonSerializer.DeserializeAsync<Species>(stream);
17       System.Console.WriteLine(data);
18       Assert.NotNull(data);
19       Assert.Equal(species, data);
20   }
21
```

Figure 7.19 – Component test to read a species by ID

8. Before you proceed and run the tests, make sure the `library` component is running and listening at port `8080`. Otherwise, the tests will fail, since nobody is listening at the expected endpoints. Use this command:

```
$ docker container run --rm \
    -v $HOME/.m2:/root/.m2
    library
```

9. Run the tests with this command:

```
$ dotnet test
```

Make sure the two tests pass.

10. **Optional**: Add additional component tests testing the other endpoints of the `library` component.

11. When done, stop the `library` component.

Next, we are going to show how we can run the tests in a container:

1. Add a Dockerfile with the following content to the root of the .NET test project:

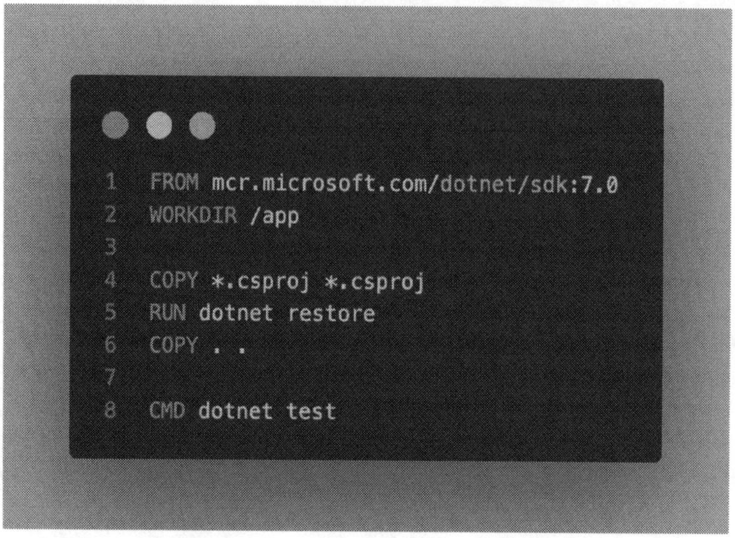

```
1   FROM mcr.microsoft.com/dotnet/sdk:7.0
2   WORKDIR /app
3
4   COPY *.csproj *.csproj
5   RUN dotnet restore
6   COPY . .
7
8   CMD dotnet test
```

Figure 7.20 – Dockerfile for the component tests

2. Create an image with this Dockerfile. From within the ch07 folder, use this command:

```
$ docker image build -t library-component-tests \
    library-component-tests
```

3. Double-check that we already have a Docker image created for the library component. If not, use this command to do so from within the ch07 folder:

```
$ docker image build -t library library
```

4. Now that we have a Docker image for the library component and one for the component tests, we need to run a container of each:

    I.   To run the library component, use this:

```
$ docker container run -d --rm \
    -p 8080:8080 library
```

    II. To run the component tests, use this command:

```
$ docker container run library-component-tests
```

Observe that the tests are executed and are all passing.

5. When done, remove the two containers. Use your Docker plugin in VS Code or the dashboard of Docker Desktop to do so.

Well, that was quite a run. We have shown how to write unit and integration tests for a component written in Java and using Spring Boot 3. We ran the tests natively on our laptop and also inside a container. Then we showed how to create some black box tests in .NET 7, C# and ran them against our library component. We did this again natively on our laptop and then ran the component and the black box tests each in their own container.

Next, we are going to discuss how to best set up a testing environment.

Best practices for setting up a testing environment

In this section, we want to list a few best practices for setting up a testing environment for applications running in containers, including considerations for network isolation, data management, and resource constraints:

- **Use a separate testing environment**: It is generally a good idea to use a separate testing environment for running tests in containers rather than running tests on the same host as your production environment. This can help to prevent any potential issues or disruptions from affecting your production environment.

- **Isolate the testing network**: To ensure that your testing environment is isolated from your production environment, it is a good idea to use a separate network for testing. This can be achieved by using a separate virtual network or by using network namespaces or overlays in your container runtime.

- **Manage test data carefully**: When testing applications in containers, it is important to manage test data carefully to ensure that your tests are reliable and repeatable. This can involve using test data generation tools, snapshotting the test data, or using a separate test database.

- **Use resource constraints**: To ensure that your tests are reliable and consistent, it is a good idea to use resource constraints (e.g., CPU, memory) to limit the resources available to your containers. This can help to prevent resource contention and ensure that your tests are not impacted by external factors such as the load on the host system.

- **Use a container orchestration tool**: To manage a large number of containers and ensure that they are deployed and scaled consistently, it is a good idea to use a container orchestration tool such as Kubernetes or Docker Swarm. These tools can help to automate the process of deploying and scaling containers and can provide features such as automatic rollbacks and self-healing.

- **Monitor the testing environment**: To ensure that your testing environment is running smoothly and to identify any issues that may arise, it is a good idea to use monitoring tools to track the performance and resource usage of your containers. This can help you to identify and fix any issues that may affect the reliability of your tests.

Now when testing, you may face some troubles and hard-to-explain test failures. In the next section, we're going to provide a few tips about what you can do in such a situation.

Tips for debugging and troubleshooting issues

As we are running automated tests in our containerized environments, we may from time to time face seemingly weird behaviors and mysteriously failing tests. Here are some tips for debugging and troubleshooting issues that may arise when testing applications in containers:

- **Check the logs**: The first step in debugging any issue is to check the logs for any error messages or other clues about the cause of the problem. In a containerized environment, you can use tools such as `docker container logs` to view the logs for a specific container.

- **Use a debugger**: If the error message or log output is not sufficient to diagnose the problem, you can use a debugger to inspect the state of the application at runtime. Many IDEs, such as VS Code, which we use all the time, Visual Studio, and IntelliJ, have built-in support for debugging applications running in containers.

- **Inspect the container environment**: If the issue appears to be related to the container environment itself (e.g., a missing dependency or configuration issue), you can use tools such as `docker container exec` to run commands inside the container and inspect its environment.

- **Use a container runtime debugger**: Some container runtimes, such as Docker, provide tools for debugging issues with the container itself (e.g., resource usage and networking issues). These tools can be helpful for diagnosing issues that are specific to the container runtime.

- **Use a containerized debugging environment**: If you are having difficulty reproducing the issue in a local development environment, you can use a containerized debugging environment (e.g., a debugger container) to replicate the production environment more closely.

- **Check for known issues**: If you are using third-party libraries or dependencies in your application, it is worth checking whether there are any known issues or bugs that could be causing the problem. Many libraries and dependencies maintain lists of known issues and workarounds on their website or in their documentation.

- **Get help**: If you are unable to diagnose the issue on your own, don't hesitate to seek help from the community, for example, from Stack Overflow or the maintainers of the libraries and tools you are using. There are many resources available online.

Now let's discuss a few challenges that may occur during testing and what we should consider when testing.

Challenges and considerations when testing applications running in containers

Next to all the many advantages that testing applications running in containers brings to the table, we need to also have a brief discussion of the challenges and considerations involved in this type of testing, such as dealing with dependencies and managing test data:

- **Isolation**: Testing applications in containers can provide a level of isolation between the test environment and the host system, which can be useful for ensuring that the test results are consistent and repeatable. However, this isolation can also make it more difficult to debug issues and identify the root cause of problems, as you may not have access to the host system and its resources.

- **Environment consistency**: Ensuring that the test environment is consistent across different development environments can be a challenge when using containers. Differences in the host system, container runtime, and network configuration can all impact the behavior of the application and the test results.

- **Data management**: Managing test data in a containerized environment can be challenging, as you may need to ensure that the test data is consistent and available to all containers, or that it is properly isolated and not shared between tests.

- **Resource constraints**: Testing applications in containers can be resource-intensive, as you may need to run multiple containers in parallel to test different scenarios. This can lead to resource contention and may require careful resource management to ensure that your tests are reliable and consistent.

- **Integration testing**: Testing the integration between multiple containers can be challenging, as you may need to coordinate the startup and shutdown of multiple containers and ensure that they can communicate with each other.

- **Performance testing**: Testing the performance of applications running in containers can be difficult, as the performance may be impacted by the host system, the container runtime, and the network configuration.

Overall, testing applications running in containers requires careful planning and consideration to ensure that the test environment is consistent and reliable, and to ensure that the test results are meaningful and actionable.

Before we end this chapter, let's look at a few case studies where companies are using containerized tests.

Case studies

In this last section of the chapter, we present a few case studies and examples of organizations that have successfully implemented testing strategies for applications running in containers:

1. An automated testing technique was introduced by a well-known online shop to boost the effectiveness and efficiency of its software development process. The company was able to considerably reduce the time and effort needed to test its applications by automating the execution of functional, integration, and acceptance tests. As a result, it was able to provide customers with new features and upgrades more rapidly and reliably.

2. Automated testing was used by a financial services company to enhance the dependability and stability of their trading platform. The business was able to find and fix problems early in the development process by automating the execution of unit, integration, and acceptance tests, minimizing the risk of downtime and enhancing customer satisfaction.

3. Automated testing was used by a healthcare organization to guarantee the precision and dependability of its **electronic medical record** (**EMR**) system. The business was able to swiftly identify and address problems by automating the execution of functional and acceptability tests, increasing the EMR system's dependability and trustworthiness, and lowering the risk of mistakes and patient harm.

The advantages of automated testing, such as better quality, quicker development and deployment cycles, increased reliability, and higher customer happiness, are illustrated by these case studies.

Summary

In this chapter, we learned about the benefits of testing applications running in containers, discussed the different types of testing, presented some of the tools and technologies commonly used for testing, as well as best practices for setting up a testing environment. We also presented a list of tips for debugging and troubleshooting issues, talked about challenges and considerations when testing applications running in containers, and concluded the chapter with a list of case studies.

In the next chapter, we will introduce miscellaneous tips, tricks, and concepts useful when containerizing complex distributed applications or when using Docker to automate sophisticated tasks.

Questions

To assess your learning, please try to answer the following questions before you proceed to the next chapter:

1. How do we run unit tests for an application inside a container?

2. Should the Docker images that we use in production contain test code? Justify your answer.

3. Where do we typically run unit and integration tests that run inside a container?

4. List a few advantages of running unit and integration tests in containers.

5. What are a few challenges you may face if running tests in containers?

Answers

Here are sample answers to the questions of this chapter:

1. We have learned how to run an application in a container. We have seen examples written in Node.js, Python, Java, and .NET C#. We have learned how the Dockerfile must look to create an image. Specifically, we have learned how to define the startup command to execute when a container is created from such an image. In the case of a Java application, this could be as follows:

   ```
   CMD java -jar /app/my-app.jar
   ```

   For a Node.js application, it could be as follows:

   ```
   CMD node index.js
   ```

   To run the unit tests for the application, we just have to use a different startup command.

2. We strongly advise against shipping test code to a production environment. Tests bloat the Docker image, which has several negative side effects, such as the following:

   • Providing a bigger surface for hacker attacks

   • Longer startup times for the container since it takes longer to load an image from storage into the memory of the container host

   • Longer download times and higher network usage due to the increased size of the image

3. Unit and integration tests are typically run on the developer's local machine before they push code to a code repository such as GitHub. Once the code is pushed to GitHub or any other remote code repository, usually the CI/CD pipeline kicks in and the CI stage is executed. Part of this stage is the execution of all unit and integration tests against the application. Usually, this is performed on a so-called build agent. In many cases, this is a sandbox environment where Docker containers can be run. Thus, the CI stage uses the same technique to run the tests in the build agent as a developer would do locally. It is important to note that tests other than some special smoke tests are never run in a production environment, since this could have undesired side effects.

4. One of the most important advantages of running tests in containers is the isolation aspect. We can run the tests on any environment able to run containers and do not have to worry about installing frameworks or libraries on the hosting machine first.

    Another important advantage is that running tests in containers makes them repeatable out of the box. Each time a container containing the application code and the tests are started, the boundary conditions are the same. With this, we guarantee consistency in the test execution. Were we to run the tests natively on the host, we would have a harder time guaranteeing this consistency.

5. Some challenges we may face when running our tests inside containers are as follows:

    -   It may be harder to troubleshoot and debug failing tests

    -   Integration testing can be more challenging when several containers are involved in the necessary setup

    -   Resources such as CPU, RAM, and network bandwidth can be limited in a containerized environment (via cgroup settings) and thus negatively impact your test runs

8

Increasing Productivity with Docker Tips and Tricks

This chapter introduces miscellaneous tips, tricks, and concepts that are useful when containerizing complex distributed applications or when using Docker to automate sophisticated tasks. You will also learn how to leverage containers to run your whole development environment in them. Here is the list of topics we are going to discuss:

- Keeping your Docker environment clean
- Using a `.dockerignore` file
- Executing simple admin tasks in a container
- Limiting the resource usage of a container
- Avoiding running a container as `root`
- Running Docker from within Docker
- Optimizing your build process
- Scanning for vulnerabilities and secrets
- Running your development environment in a container

After reading this chapter, you will have learned how to do the following:

- Successfully restore your Docker environment after it has been messed up completely
- Use a `.dockerignore` file to speed up builds, reduce image size, and enhance security
- Run various tools to perform tasks on your computer without installing them
- Limit the number of resources a containerized application uses during runtime
- Harden your system by not running containers as root

- Enable advanced scenarios by running Docker inside of a Docker container

- Accelerate and improve the build process of your custom Docker images

- Scan your Docker images for common vulnerabilities and exposures and the accidental inclusion of secrets

- Run a whole development environment inside a container running locally or remotely

Let's get started!

Technical requirements

In this chapter, if you want to follow along with the code, you need Docker Desktop installed on your local machine as well as the Visual Studio Code editor.

Before we start, let's create a folder for the samples that we will be using during this part of the book. Open a new terminal window and navigate to the folder you clone the sample code to. Usually, this is ~/The-Ultimate-Docker-Container-Book:

```
$ cd ~/The-Ultimate-Docker-Container-Book
```

Create a new subfolder for *Chapter 8* called ch08 and navigate to it:

```
$ mkdir ch08 && cd ch08
```

Now that you are ready, let's start with the tips and tricks on how to keep our Docker environment clean.

You can find the sample code here: https://github.com/PacktPublishing/The-Ultimate-Docker-Container-Book/tree/main/sample-solutions/ch08.

Keeping your Docker environment clean

First, we want to learn how we can delete dangling images. A dangling Docker image is an unused image that has no association with any tagged images or containers. It usually occurs when a new image is built using the same tag as an existing image. Instead of removing the old image, Docker preserves it but removes the tag reference, leaving the image without a proper tag.

Dangling images are not referenced by any container or tagged image, and they consume disk space without providing any benefit. They can accumulate over time, especially in environments with frequent image builds and updates. Thus, it is better to remove them from time to time. Here is the command to do so:

```
$ docker image prune -f
```

Please note that we have added the -f (or --force) parameter to the prune command. This is to prevent the CLI from asking you to confirm that you really want to delete those superfluous layers.

Stopped containers can waste precious resources too. If you're sure that you don't need these containers anymore, then you should remove them. You can remove them individually with the following command:

```
$ docker container rm <container-id|container-name>
```

You can also remove them as a batch by using this command:

```
$ docker container prune --force
```

In the command for removing them individually, `<container-id|container-name>` means that we can either use the container ID or its name to identify the container.

Unused Docker volumes can also quickly fill up disk space. It is good practice to tender your volumes, specifically in a development or **Continuous Integration (CI)** environment where you create a lot of mostly temporary volumes. But I have to warn you, Docker volumes are meant to store data. Often, this data must live longer than the life cycle of a container. This is specifically true in a production or production-like environment where the data is often mission-critical. Hence, be 100% sure of what you're doing when using the following command to prune volumes on your Docker host:

```
$ docker volume prune
    WARNING! This will remove all local volumes not used by at least
one container.
    Are you sure you want to continue? [y/N]
```

We recommend using this command without the `-f` (or `--force`) flag. It is a dangerous and terminal operation and it's better to give yourself a second chance to reconsider your action. Without the flag, the CLI outputs the warning you see in the preceding command. You have to explicitly confirm by typing y and pressing the *Enter* key.

On production or production-like systems, you should abstain from the preceding command and rather delete unwanted volumes one at a time by using this command:

```
$ docker volume rm <volume-name>
```

I should also mention that there is a command to prune Docker networks. But since we have not yet officially introduced networks, I will defer this to *Chapter 10, Using Single-Host Networking*.

In the next section, we are going to show how we can exclude some folders and files from being included in the build context for a Docker image.

Using a .dockerignore file

The `.dockerignore` file is a text file that tells Docker to ignore certain files and directories when building a Docker image from a Dockerfile. This is similar to how the `.gitignore` file works in Git.

The primary benefit of using a `.dockerignore` file is that it can significantly speed up the Docker build process. When Docker builds an image, it first sends all of the files in the current directory (known as the "build context") to the Docker daemon. If this directory contains large files or directories that aren't necessary for building the Docker image (such as log files, local environment variables, cache files, etc.), these can be ignored to speed up the build process.

Moreover, using a `.dockerignore` file can help to improve security and maintain clean code practices. For instance, it helps prevent potentially sensitive information (such as `.env` files containing private keys) from being included in the Docker image. It can also help to keep the Docker image size minimal by avoiding unnecessary files, which is particularly beneficial when deploying the image or transferring it across networks.

Here's an example of a `.dockerignore` file:

```
# Ignore everything
**
# Allow specific directories
!my-app/
!scripts/
# Ignore specific files within allowed directories
my-app/*.log
scripts/temp/
```

In this example, all files are ignored except those in the `my-app/` and `scripts/` directories. However, log files within `my-app/` and all files in the `scripts/temp/` subdirectory are ignored. This level of granularity provides developers with fine control over what is included in the Docker build context.

In conclusion, the use of a `.dockerignore` file is a best practice for Docker builds, helping to speed up builds, reduce image size, and enhance security by excluding unnecessary or sensitive files from the build context. In the next section, we are going to show how to execute simple administrative tasks within a Docker container.

Executing simple admin tasks in a container

In this section, we want to provide a few examples of tasks you may want to run in a container instead of natively on your computer.

Running a Perl script

Let's assume you need to strip all leading whitespaces from a file and you found the following handy Perl script to do exactly that:

```
$ cat sample.txt | perl -lpe 's/^\s*//'
```

As it turns out, you don't have Perl installed on your working machine. What can you do? Install Perl on the machine? Well, that would certainly be an option, and it's exactly what most developers or system admins do. But wait a second, you already have Docker installed on your machine. Can't we use Docker to circumvent the need to install Perl? And can't we do this on any operating system supporting Docker? Yes, we can. This is how we're going to do it:

1. Navigate to the chapter's code folder:

   ```
   $ cd ~/The-Ultimate-Docker-Container-Book/ch08
   ```

2. Create a new subfolder called `simple-task`, and navigate to it:

   ```
   $ mkdir simple-task && cd simple-task
   ```

3. Open VS Code from within this folder:

   ```
   $ code .
   ```

4. In this folder, create a `sample.txt` file with the following content:

   ```
           1234567890
       This is some text
        another line of text
     more text
   final line
   ```

   Please note the whitespaces at the beginning of each line. Save the file.

5. Now, we can run a container with Perl installed in it. Thankfully, there is an official Perl image on Docker Hub. We are going to use the slim version of the image. The primary difference between the normal Perl Docker image and the slim version lies in their size and the components included in the images. Both images provide the Perl runtime environment, but they are optimized for different use cases:

   ```
   $ docker container run --rm -it \
       -v $(pwd):/usr/src/app \
       -w /usr/src/app \
       perl:slim sh -c "cat sample.txt | perl -lpe 's/^\s*//'"
   ```

   The preceding command runs a Perl container (`perl:slim`) interactively, maps the content of the current folder into the `/usr/src/app` folder of the container, and sets the working folder inside the container to `/usr/src/app`. The command that is run inside the container is as follows:

   ```
   sh -c "cat sample.txt | perl -lpe 's/^\s*//'"
   ```

   It basically spawns a Bourne shell and executes our desired Perl command.

6.   Analyze the output generated by the preceding command. It should look like this:

```
1234567890
This is some text
another line of text
more text
final line
```

That is, all trailing blanks have been removed.

Without needing to install Perl on our machine, we were able to achieve our goal. The nice thing is that, after the script has run, the container is removed from your system without leaving any traces because we used the `--rm` flag in the `docker container run` command, which automatically removes a stopped container.

> **Tip**
>
> If that doesn't convince you yet because, if you're on macOS, you already have Perl installed, then consider you're looking into running a Perl script named `your-old-perl-script.pl` that is old and not compatible with the newest release of Perl that you happen to have installed on your system. Do you try to install multiple versions of Perl on your machine and potentially break something? No, you just run a container with the (old) version of Perl that is compatible with your script, as in this example:
>
> ```
> $ docker container run -it --rm \
>     -v $(pwd):/usr/src/app \
>     -w /usr/src/app \
>     perl:<old-version> perl your-old-perl-script.pl
> ```
>
> Here, `<old-version>` corresponds to the tag of the version of Perl that you need to run your script.

In the next section, we are going to demonstrate how to run a Python script.

Running a Python script

A lot of people use quick and dirty Python scripts or mini apps to automate tasks that are not easily coded with, say, Bash. Now, if the Python script has been written in Python 3.x and you only happen to have Python 2.7 installed or no version at all on your machine, then the easiest solution is to execute the script inside a container. Let's assume a simple example where the Python script counts lines, words, and letters in a given file and outputs the result to the console:

1.   Still in the `simple-task` folder, add a `stats.py` file and add the following content:

```
1   import sys
2
3   fname = sys.argv[1]
4   lines = 0
5   words = 0
6   letters = 0
7   for line in open(fname):
8       lines += 1
9       letters += len(line)
10      pos = 'out'
11      for letter in line:
12          if letter != ' ' and pos == 'out':
13              words += 1
14              pos = 'in'
15          elif letter == ' ':
16              pos = 'out'
17
18  print("Lines:", lines)
19  print("Words:", words)
20  print("Letters:", letters)
```

Figure 8.1 – Python script to calculate statistics of a sample text

2. After saving the file, you can run it with the following command:

```
$ docker container run --rm -it \
    -v $(pwd):/usr/src/app \
    -w /usr/src/app \
    python:3-alpine python stats.py sample.txt
```

3. Note that, in this example, we are reusing the sample.txt file from the previous *Running a Perl script* section. The output in my case is as follows:

```
Lines: 5
Words: 13
Letters: 121
```

The beauty of this approach is that the Perl script before and this last Python script will now run on any computer with any OS installed, as long as the machine is a Docker host and hence, can run containers.

Next, we are going to learn how to limit the number of resources a container running on the system can consume.

Limiting the resource usage of a container

One of the great features of a container, apart from encapsulating application processes, is the possibility of limiting the resources a single container can consume at most. This includes CPU and memory consumption. Let's have a look at how limiting the amount of memory (RAM) works:

```
$ docker container run --rm -it \
        --name stress-test \
        --memory 512M \
        ubuntu:22.04 /bin/bash
```

Once inside the container, install the `stress` tool, which we will use to simulate memory pressure:

```
/# apt-get update && apt-get install -y stress
```

Open another terminal window and execute the `docker stats` command to observe the resource consumption of all running Docker containers. You should see something like this:

```
CONTAINER ID   NAME          CPU %    MEM USAGE / LIMIT   MEM %    NET I/O        BLOCK I/O       PIDS
367274a0f48c   stress-test   0.00%    36.57MiB / 512MiB   7.14%    24.4MB / 411kB  45.1kB / 61.8MB  1
```

Figure 8.2 – The Docker stats showing a resource-limited container

Look at MEM USAGE and LIMIT. Currently, the container uses only 36.57MiB memory and has a limit of 512MiB. The latter corresponds to what we have configured for this container. Now, let's use the `stress` tool to simulate three workers, which will allocate memory using the `malloc()` function in blocks of 256MiB. Run this command inside the container to do so:

```
/# stress -m 3
```

The preceding command puts stress on the system's memory by creating three child processes that will `malloc()` and touch memory until the system runs out of memory. In the terminal running Docker stats, observe how the value for MEM USAGE approaches but never exceeds LIMIT. This is exactly the behavior we expected from Docker. Docker uses Linux **cgroups** to enforce those limits.

> **What are cgroups?**
>
> Linux **cgroups**, short for **control groups**, is a kernel-level feature that allows you to organize processes into hierarchical groups, and to allocate, restrict, and monitor system resources such as CPU, memory, disk I/O, and network among these groups. Cgroups provide a way to manage and limit the resource usage of processes, ensuring fair distribution and preventing individual processes from monopolizing system resources.

We could similarly limit the amount of CPU a container can consume with the `--cpu` switch.

With this operation, engineers can avoid the noisy neighbor problem on a busy Docker host, where a single container starves all of the others by consuming an excessive amount of resources.

Avoiding running a container as root

Most applications or application services that run inside a container do not need `root` access. To tighten security, it is helpful in those scenarios to run these processes with minimal necessary privileges. These applications should not be run as `root` nor assume that they have `root`-level privileges.

Once again, let's illustrate what we mean with an example. Assume we have a file with top-secret content. We want to secure this file on our Unix-based system using the `chmod` tool so that only users with `root` permissions can access it. Let's assume I am logged in as `demo` on the dev host and hence my prompt is `demo@dev $`. I can use `sudo su` to impersonate a superuser. I have to enter the superuser password though:

```
demo@dev $ sudo su
    Password: <root password>
    root@dev $
```

Now, as the `root` user, I can create this file called `top-secret.txt` and secure it:

```
root@dev $ echo "You should not see this." > top-secret.txt
root@dev $ chmod 600 ./top-secret.txt
root@dev $ exit
demo@dev $
```

If I try to access the file as user `demo`, the following happens:

```
cat: ./top-secret.txt: Permission denied
```

I get a `Permission denied` message, which is what we wanted. No other user except `root` can access this file. Now, let's build a Docker image that contains this secured file and when a container is created from it, tries to output the content of the `secrets` file. The Dockerfile could look like this:

```
FROM ubuntu:22.04
COPY ./top-secret.txt /secrets/
# simulate use of restricted file
CMD cat /secrets/top-secret.txt
```

We can build an image from that Dockerfile (as `root`!) with the following:

```
demo@dev $ sudo su
Password: <root password>
root@dev $ docker image build -t demo-image .
root@dev $ exit
demo@dev $
```

Then, by running a container with the image built in the previous step, we get the following:

```
demo@dev $ docker container run demo-image
```

The preceding command will generate this output:

```
You should not see this.
```

OK, so although I am impersonating the demo user on the host and running the container under this user account, the application running inside the container automatically runs as root, and hence has full access to protected resources. That's bad, so let's fix it! Instead of running with the default, we define an explicit user inside the container. The modified Dockerfile looks like this:

```
FROM ubuntu:22.04
RUN groupadd -g 3000 demo-group |
        && useradd -r -u 4000 -g demo-group demo-user
USER demo-user
COPY ./top-secret.txt /secrets/
# simulate use of restricted file
CMD cat /secrets/top-secret.txt
```

We use the groupadd tool to define a new group, demo-group, with the ID 3000. Then, we use the useradd tool to add a new user, demo-user, to this group. The user has the ID 4000 inside the container. Finally, with the USER demo-user statement, we declare that all subsequent operations should be executed as demo-user.

Rebuild the image—again, as root—and then try to run a container from it:

```
demo@dev $ sudo su
Password: <root password>
root@dev $ docker image build -t demo-image .
root@dev $ exit
demo@dev $ docker container run demo-image \
    cat: /secrets/top-secret.txt:
Permission denied
```

And as you can see on the last line, the application running inside the container runs with restricted permissions and cannot access resources that need root-level access. By the way, what do you think would happen if I ran the container as root? Try it out!

In the next section, we are going to show how we can automate Docker from within a container.

Running Docker from within Docker

At times, we may want to run a container hosting an application that automates certain Docker tasks. How can we do that? Docker Engine and the Docker CLI are installed on the host, yet the application runs inside the container. Well, from early on, Docker has provided a means to bind-mount Linux sockets from the host into the container. On Linux, sockets are used as very efficient data communications endpoints between processes that run on the same host. The Docker CLI uses a socket to communicate with Docker Engine; it is often called the **Docker socket**. If we can give access to the Docker socket to an application running inside a container, then we can just install the Docker CLI inside this container, and we will then be able to run an application in the same container that uses this locally installed Docker CLI to automate container-specific tasks.

> **Important note**
>
> Here, we are not talking about running Docker Engine inside the container but rather only the Docker CLI and bind-mounting the Docker socket from the host into the container so that the CLI can communicate with Docker Engine running on the host computer. This is an important distinction.
>
> Running Docker Engine inside a container is generally not recommended due to several reasons, including security, stability, and potential performance issues. This practice is often referred to as **Docker-in-Docker** or **DinD**. The main concerns are as follows:
>
> - **Security**: Running Docker Engine inside a container requires elevated privileges, such as running the container in privileged mode or mounting the Docker socket. This can expose the host system to potential security risks, as a compromised container could gain control over the host's Docker daemon and escalate privileges, affecting other containers and the host itself.
>
> - **Stability**: Containers are designed to be isolated, lightweight, and ephemeral. Running Docker Engine inside a container can create complex dependencies and increase the chances of conflicts or failures, particularly when managing storage, networking, and process namespaces between the host and the nested container environment.
>
> - **Performance**: Running Docker Engine inside a container can introduce performance overhead, as it adds another layer of virtualization, particularly in terms of storage and networking. This can lead to increased latency and reduced throughput, particularly when managing large numbers of containers or when working with high-performance applications.
>
> - **Resource management**: Docker-in-Docker can make it challenging to manage and allocate resources effectively, as nested containers may not inherit resource limits and restrictions from their parent container, leading to potential resource contention or over-commitment on the host.

To illustrate the concept, let's look at an example using the preceding technique. We are going to use a copy of the `library` component we built in the previous chapter (*Chapter 7*) for this:

1. Navigate to the chapter folder:

    ```
    $ cd ~/The-Ultimate-Docker-Container-Book/ch08
    ```

2. Copy the `library` component from the `ch07` directory to this folder:

    ```
    $ cp -r ../ch07/library .
    ```

3. Open the component in VS Code:

    ```
    $ code library
    ```

4. Add a new file called `pipeline.sh` to the root of the project and add the following code to it, which automates the building, testing, and pushing of a Docker image:

```bash
1   #! /bin/bash
2
3   # *** Sample script to build, test & push       ***
4   # *** containerized Java/Spring Boot applications ***
5
6   # build the Docker image
7   docker image build -t $HUB_USER/$REPOSITORY:$TAG .
8   # Run all unit tests
9   docker container run $HUB_USER/$REPOSITORY:$TAG ./mvnw test
10  # Login to Docker Hub
11  docker login -u $HUB_USER -p $HUB_PWD
12  # Push the image to Docker Hub
13  docker image push $HUB_USER/$REPOSITORY:$TAG
```

Figure 8.3 – Script to build, test, and push a Java application

Note that we're using four environment variables: `$HUB_USER` and `$HUB_PWD` being the credentials for Docker Hub, and `$REPOSITORY` and `$TAG` being the name and tag of the Docker image we want to build. Eventually, we will have to pass values for those environment variables in the `docker container run` command, so that they are available for any process running inside the container.

5. Save the file and make it an executable:

```
$ chmod +x ./pipeline.sh
```

We want to run the `pipeline.sh` script inside a builder container. Since the script uses the Docker CLI, our builder container must have the Docker CLI installed, and to access Docker Engine, the builder container must have the Docker socket bind-mounted.

Let's start creating a Docker image for such a builder container:

1. Add a file called `Dockerfile.builder` to the root of the project and add the following content to it:

```
1   FROM eclipse-temurin:17-jdk-focal AS build
2
3   RUN apt-get update \
4       && apt-get install -y ca-certificates curl gnupg lsb-release \
5       && mkdir -p /etc/apt/keyrings \
6       && curl -fsSL https://download.docker.com/linux/ubuntu/gpg | \
7           gpg --dearmor -o /etc/apt/keyrings/docker.gpg \
8       && echo \
9           "deb [arch=$(dpkg --print-architecture) signed-by=/etc/apt/keyrings/docker.gpg] \
10          https://download.docker.com/linux/ubuntu $(lsb_release -cs) stable" \
11          | tee /etc/apt/sources.list.d/docker.list > /dev/null \
12      && apt-get update \
13      && apt-get install -y docker-ce docker-ce-cli containerd.io docker-compose-plugin
14
15  WORKDIR /app
16  COPY mvnw .
17  COPY .mvn .mvn
18  COPY pom.xml .
19  COPY src src
20  COPY pipeline.sh .
21
22  CMD ./mvnw spring-boot:run
```

Figure 8.4 – Dockerfile for the builder

Note the long RUN command on line 3 onward. This is needed to install Docker in the container. For more details about this command, you may want to consult the Docker online documentation here: `https://docs.docker.com/engine/install/ubuntu/`.

2. Building a Docker image with this Dockerfile is straightforward:

```
$ docker image build -f Dockerfile.builder -t builder .
```

3. We are now ready to try the `builder` command with a real Java application; for example, let's take the sample app we defined in the `ch08/library` folder. Make sure you replace `<user>` and `<password>` with your own credentials for Docker Hub:

```
1   docker container run --rm \
2       --name builder \
3       -v /var/run/docker.sock:/var/run/docker.sock \
4       -v "$PWD":/usr/src/app \
5       -e HUB_USER=<user> \
6       -e HUB_PWD=<password> \
7       -e REPOSITORY=ch08-library \
8       -e TAG=1.0 \
9       builder
```

Figure 8.5 – Docker run command for the builder

Notice how, in the preceding command, we mounted the Docker socket into the container with `-v /var/run/docker.sock:/var/run/docker.sock`. If everything goes well, you should have a container image built for the sample application, the test should have been run, and the image should have been pushed to Docker Hub. This is only one of the many use cases where it is very useful to be able to bind-mount the Docker socket.

A special notice to those of you who want to try Windows containers on a Windows computer: on Docker Desktop for Windows, you can create a similar environment by bind-mounting Docker's **named pipe** instead of a socket. A named pipe on Windows is roughly the same as a socket on a Unix- based system. Assuming you're using a PowerShell terminal, the command to bind-mount a named pipe when running a Windows container hosting Jenkins looks like this:

```
PS> docker container run `
        --name jenkins `
        -p 8080:8080 `
        -v \\.\pipe\docker_engine:\\.\pipe\docker_engine `
        friism/jenkins
```

Note the special syntax, `\\.\pipe\docker_engine`, to access Docker's named pipe.

In this section, we have shown how to run Docker from within Docker by mounting the Docker socket into the respective container.

Next, we are going to revisit the topic of how to make your Docker build as fast as possible to reduce friction in the development cycle.

Optimizing your build process

The Docker build process can and should be optimized. This will remove a lot of friction in the software development life cycle.

Many Docker beginners make the following mistake when crafting their first Dockerfile:

Figure 8.6 – Unoptimized Dockerfile for a Node.js application

Can you spot the weak point in this typical Dockerfile for a Node.js application? In *Chapter 4, Creating and Managing Container Images*, we learned that an image consists of a series of layers. Each (logical) line in a Dockerfile creates a layer, except the lines with the CMD and/or ENTRYPOINT keywords. We also learned that the Docker builder tries to do its best by caching layers and reusing them if they have not changed between subsequent builds. But the caching only uses cached layers that occur before the first changed layer. All subsequent layers need to be rebuilt. That said, the preceding structure of the Dockerfile invalidates – or as we often hear said – *busts* the image layer cache!

Why? Well, from experience, you certainly know that the npm install command can be a pretty expensive operation in a typical Node.js application with many external dependencies. The execution of this command can take from seconds to many minutes. That said, each time one of the source files changes, and we know that happens frequently during development, line 3 in the Dockerfile causes the corresponding image layer to change. Hence, the Docker builder cannot reuse this layer from the cache, nor can it reuse the subsequent layer created by RUN npm install. Any minor change in code causes a complete rerun of npm install. That can be avoided. The package. json file containing the list of external dependencies rarely changes. With all of that information, let's fix the Dockerfile:

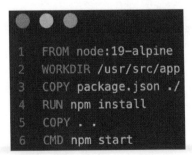

Figure 8.7 – Optimized Dockerfile for a Node.js application

This time, on line 3, we only copy the `package.json` file into the container, which rarely changes. Hence, the subsequent `npm install` command has to be executed equally rarely. The `COPY` command on line 5 is then a very fast operation and hence rebuilding an image after some code has changed only needs to rebuild this last layer. Build times reduce to merely a fraction of a second.

The very same principle applies to most languages or frameworks, such as Python, .NET, or Java. Avoid busting your image layer cache!

Scanning for vulnerabilities and secrets

What exactly are vulnerabilities, or to be more accurate, **Common Vulnerabilities and Exposures** (CVE)?

A database of information security problems that have been made publicly known is called **Common Vulnerabilities and Exposures**. A number uniquely identifies each vulnerability from the list of all other entries in the database. This list is continuously reviewed and updated by experts who include any new vulnerabilities or exposures as soon as they are found.

Now, we can scan the various layers of our Docker images using specialist software, such as Snyk, to find software libraries that are known to have such CVE. If we find that our image is flawed, we should and can repair the issue by switching to a more recent version of the flawed library. The image will then need to be rebuilt.

But our work is not yet done. Security experts frequently find new CVE, as was already mentioned previously. As a result, a software library that was previously secure may suddenly be vulnerable as a result of newly revealed CVE.

This means that we must ensure that all of our active Docker images are routinely inspected, notify our developers and security experts about the issue, and take other steps to ensure a speedy resolution of the issue.

There are a few ways to scan a Docker image for vulnerabilities and secrets:

- Use a vulnerability scanner such as Clair, Anchore, or Trivy. These tools can scan a Docker image and check it against a database of known vulnerabilities in order to identify any potential security risks.

- Use a tool such as Aquasec or Sysdig to scan the image for secrets. These tools can detect and alert on sensitive information such as private keys, passwords, and other sensitive data that may have been accidentally committed to the image.

- Use a combination of both tools, for example, Docker Bench for Security, which checks for dozens of common best practices around deploying Docker containers in production.

- Use a tool such as OpenSCAP, which can perform vulnerability scans, security configuration assessments, and compliance checks on a Docker image.

It's important to note that it's always good practice to keep your images updated and only use official and trusted images.

In the next section, we will investigate how we can discover vulnerabilities inside our Docker images.

Using Snyk to scan a Docker image

Snyk is a security platform that can be used to scan Docker images for vulnerabilities. Here is an example of how to use Snyk to scan a Docker image for vulnerabilities:

1. First, we have to install the Snyk CLI on our machine. We can do this by running the following command:

    ```
    $ npm install -g snyk
    ```

2. Once Snyk is installed, we can authenticate with our Snyk account by running the following command and following the prompts:

    ```
    $ snyk auth
    ```

3. Next, we can run the following command to scan a specific Docker image for vulnerabilities:

    ```
    $ snyk test --docker <image-name>
    ```

    The preceding command will perform a vulnerability scan on the specified Docker image and print the results in the console. The results will show the number of vulnerabilities found, the severity of each vulnerability, and the package and version that is affected.

4. We can also use the `--file` flag to scan a Dockerfile instead of a built image:

    ```
    $ snyk test --file=path/to/Dockerfile
    ```

5. Additionally, we can also use the `--org` flag to specify an organization, if we're a member of multiple organizations:

    ```
    $ snyk test --docker <image-name> --org=my-org
    ```

6. Finally, we can use the `--fix` flag to automatically fix the vulnerabilities found by running the following command:

    ```
    $ snyk protect --docker <image-name>
    ```

    Please note that this feature is only available for images that are built using a Dockerfile and it will update the Dockerfile with the new package versions, and you will need to rebuild the image to take advantage of the fix.

> **Note**
>
> The Snyk free plan is limited to a certain number of scans, and it does not include the *Protect* feature. You will have to upgrade to a paid plan to have access to this feature.

Using docker scan to scan a Docker image for vulnerabilities

In this section, we are once again going to use Snyk to scan a Docker image for vulnerabilities. Snyk should be included with your Docker Desktop installation:

1. Check by using this command:

    ```
    $ docker scan --version
    ```

    The output should look similar to this:

    ```
    Version:    v0.22.0
    Git commit: af9ca12
    Provider:   Snyk (1.1054.0)
    ```

2. Let's try to scan a sample `whoami` application from the author's Docker Hub account. First, make sure you have the `whoami` image in your local cache:

    ```
    $ docker image pull gnschenker/whoami:1.0
    ```

3. Scan the image for vulnerabilities:

    ```
    $ docker scan gnschenker/whoami:1.0
    ```

4. You will be asked the following:

    ```
    Docker Scan relies upon access to Snyk, a third party provider,
    do you consent to proceed using Snyk? (y/N)
    ```

    Please answer this with `y`.

    The result of the preceding scan looks like this on my computer:

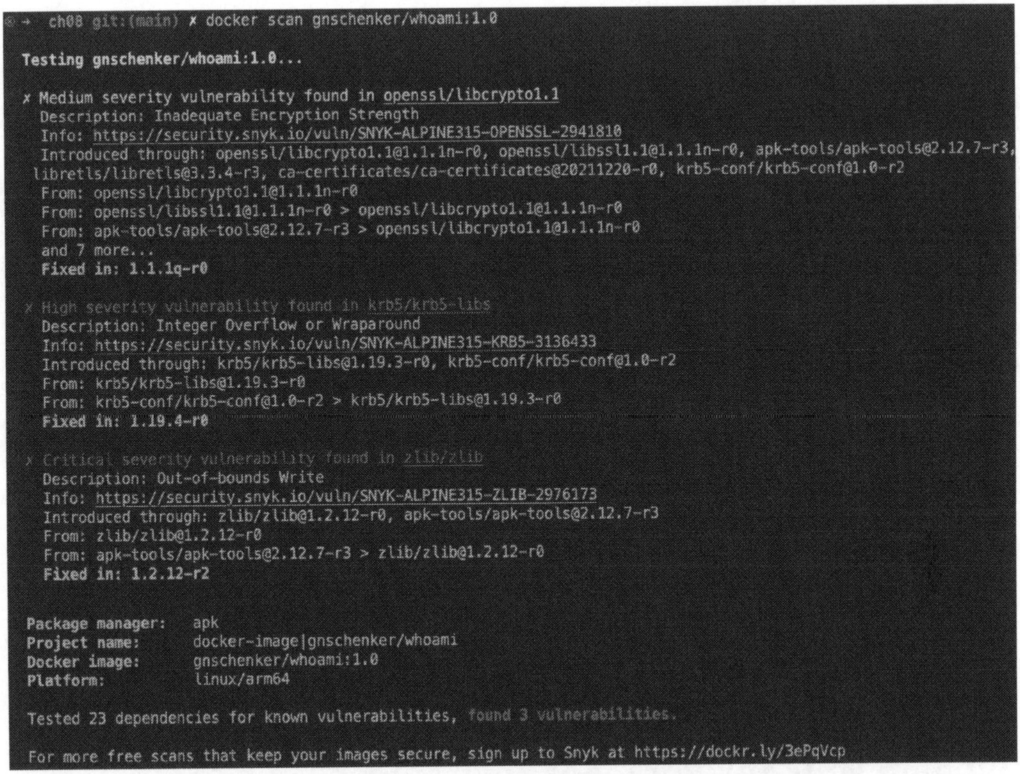
```
→  ch08 git:(main) ✗ docker scan gnschenker/whoami:1.0

Testing gnschenker/whoami:1.0...

✗ Medium severity vulnerability found in openssl/libcrypto1.1
  Description: Inadequate Encryption Strength
  Info: https://security.snyk.io/vuln/SNYK-ALPINE315-OPENSSL-2941810
  Introduced through: openssl/libcrypto1.1@1.1.1n-r0, openssl/libssl1.1@1.1.1n-r0, apk-tools/apk-tools@2.12.7-r3,
 libretls/libretls@3.3.4-r3, ca-certificates/ca-certificates@20211220-r0, krb5-conf/krb5-conf@1.0-r2
  From: openssl/libcrypto1.1@1.1.1n-r0
  From: openssl/libssl1.1@1.1.1n-r0 > openssl/libcrypto1.1@1.1.1n-r0
  From: apk-tools/apk-tools@2.12.7-r3 > openssl/libcrypto1.1@1.1.1n-r0
  and 7 more...
  Fixed in: 1.1.1q-r0

✗ High severity vulnerability found in krb5/krb5-libs
  Description: Integer Overflow or Wraparound
  Info: https://security.snyk.io/vuln/SNYK-ALPINE315-KRB5-3136433
  Introduced through: krb5/krb5-libs@1.19.3-r0, krb5-conf/krb5-conf@1.0-r2
  From: krb5/krb5-libs@1.19.3-r0
  From: krb5-conf/krb5-conf@1.0-r2 > krb5/krb5-libs@1.19.3-r0
  Fixed in: 1.19.4-r0

✗ Critical severity vulnerability found in zlib/zlib
  Description: Out-of-bounds Write
  Info: https://security.snyk.io/vuln/SNYK-ALPINE315-ZLIB-2976173
  Introduced through: zlib/zlib@1.2.12-r0, apk-tools/apk-tools@2.12.7-r3
  From: zlib/zlib@1.2.12-r0
  From: apk-tools/apk-tools@2.12.7-r3 > zlib/zlib@1.2.12-r0
  Fixed in: 1.2.12-r2

Package manager:   apk
Project name:      docker-image|gnschenker/whoami
Docker image:      gnschenker/whoami:1.0
Platform:          linux/arm64

Tested 23 dependencies for known vulnerabilities, found 3 vulnerabilities.

For more free scans that keep your images secure, sign up to Snyk at https://dockr.ly/3ePqVcp
```

Figure 8.8 – Scanning the gnschenker/whoami:1.0 Docker image

As you can see, there were three vulnerabilities found in this version of the image: one of *medium*, one of *high*, and one of *critical* severity. It is clear that we should address critical vulnerabilities as soon as possible. Let's do this now:

1. First, we copy over the original `whoami` project including the Dockerfile we used to build this image. You can find the copy in your `~/The-Ultimate-Docker-Container-Book/sample-solutions/ch14` folder.
2. Open the Dockerfile and inspect it. We used version `6.0-alpine` for both the .NET SDK and the runtime. Let's see whether Microsoft has updated the vulnerabilities in this version already.
3. Navigate to your .../`ch08/whoami` folder.
4. Build a new version of the Docker image with this command:

```
$ docker image build -t gnschenker/whoami:1.0.1 .
```

Note, you may want to replace `gnschenker` with your own Docker account name.

5. Scan the new image:

```
$ docker scan gnschenker/whoami:1.0.1
```

This time, the output should look like this:

```
 ⬢ → ch08 git:(main) ✗ docker scan gnschenker/whoami:1.0.1

Testing gnschenker/whoami:1.0.1...

Package manager:    apk
Project name:       docker-image|gnschenker/whoami
Docker image:       gnschenker/whoami:1.0.1
Platform:           linux/arm64

✔ Tested 24 dependencies for known vulnerabilities, no vulnerable paths found.

For more free scans that keep your images secure, sign up to Snyk at https://dockr.ly/3ePqVcp
```

Figure 8.9 – Scanning the rebuilt whoami Docker image

As you can see, this time, the image is free from any vulnerabilities. We should now instruct our DevOps to use this new version of the image. We can use a rolling update in production and should be just fine, as the application itself did not change.

In the next section, we are going to learn how to run a complete development environment inside a container.

Running your development environment in a container

Imagine that you only have access to a workstation with Docker Desktop installed, but no possibility to add or change anything else on this workstation. Now you want to do some proofs of concept and code some sample applications using Java. Unfortunately, Java and SpringBoot are not installed on your computer. What can you do? What if you could run a whole development environment inside a container, including a code editor and debugger? What if, at the same time, you could still have your code files on your host machine?

Containers are awesome, and genius engineers have come up with solutions for exactly this kind of problem.

> **Note**
>
> Microsoft and the community are continuously updating VS Code and the plugins. Thus your version of VS Code may be newer than the one used during the writing of this book. As such, expect a slightly different experience. Refer to the official documentation for more details on how to work with Dev containers: `https://code.visualstudio.com/docs/devcontainers/containers`.

We will be using Visual Studio Code, our favorite code editor, to show how to run a complete Java development environment inside a container:

1. But first, we need to install the necessary VS Code extension. Open VS Code and install the extension called **Remote Development**:

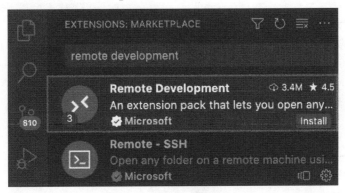

Figure 8.10 – Adding the Remote Development extension to VS Code

2. Then, click the green quick actions status bar item in the lower-left of the Visual Studio Code window. In the popup, select **Remote-Containers | Open Folder in Container...**:

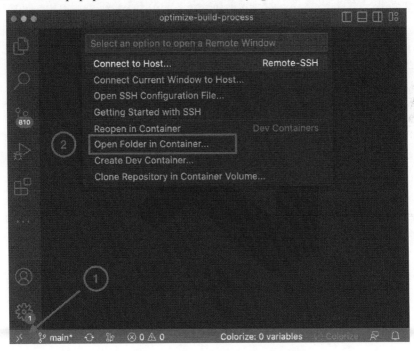

Figure 8.11 – Open Folder in Container

3. Select the project folder you want to work with in the container. In our case, we selected the
    `~/The-Ultimate-Docker-Container-Book/ch08/library` folder.

4. A popup will appear asking you to define how you want to create the development container.
    From the list, select **From 'Dockerfile'**:

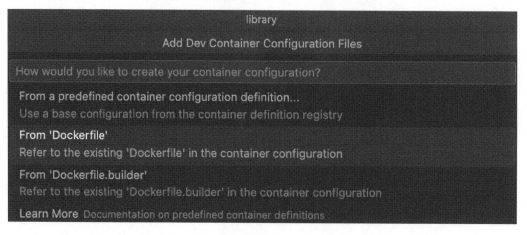

Figure 8.12 – Selecting the method to create the development container

5. When asked to add additional features to install, just click **OK** to continue. At this time, we
    do not need anything special.

    VS Code will now start preparing the environment, which, the very first time, can take a couple
    of minutes or so.

6. Once the environment is ready, you should notice that in the lower-left corner, the prompt has
    changed to the following:

    ```
    Dev Container: Existing Dockerfile @ <folder-path>
    ```

    This indicates that VS Code has indeed run a container based on the Dockerfile found in the
    library folder and is allowing you to work within it.

7. You will be asked to install the extension pack for Java since VS Code has recognized that this
    is a Java project. Click **Install**. Note, the VS Code server is running inside the dev container
    and only the UI is still running on your laptop. Thus, the extension pack will be installed for
    the engine inside the container. You will notice this when you open the **EXTENSIONS** panel
    and find a list of remote extensions under **DEV CONTAINER**. In our case, by installing the
    Java extensions pack, we now have the following eight remote extensions installed:

Figure 8.13 – Remote extensions installed on the dev container

8. Open a Terminal inside VS Code with *Shift + Ctrl + '* and notice the prompt revealing that the terminal session is inside the dev container and that we are *not* running directly on our Docker host:

```
root@c96b82891be7:/workspaces/.../ch08/library#
```

Note that for readability, we have shortened the preceding prompt.

9. Now, try to run the Java application by locating the main method in the LibraryApplication class and clicking the **Run** link just above the method. The application should start as normal, but notice that our context is inside the dev container and not directly on our working machine.

Alternatively, we could have started the application from the command line with this command:

```
$ ./mvnw spring-boot:run
```

10. Now, add a file called `DefaultController.java` to the `controllers` folder and give it this content:

```
1   package com.example.library.controllers;
2
3   import org.springframework.web.bind.annotation.GetMapping;
4   import org.springframework.web.bind.annotation.RestController;
5
6   @RestController
7   public class DefaultController {
8     @GetMapping("/")
9     public String index() {
10        return "Library component";
11    }
12  }
13
```

Figure 8.14 – Adding a default controller while working inside the dev container

11. Restart the application and open a browser as `http://localhost:8080`. The message `Library component` should be displayed as expected.

12. When done experimenting, click on the green area in the lower-left corner of VS Code and select **Open folder locally** from the pop-up menu to quit the dev container and open the project locally.

13. Observe that a new folder, `.devcontainer`, has been added to the project containing a `devcontainer.json` file. This file contains the configuration needed to run a dev container from this project. Please read the documentation of VS Code to familiarize yourself with the possibilities this file offers to you.

These have been a few tips and tricks for pros that are useful in the day-to-day usage of containers. There are many more. Google them. It is worth it.

Summary

In this chapter, we presented miscellaneous tips, tricks, and concepts that are useful when containerizing complex distributed applications or when using Docker to automate sophisticated tasks. We also learned how to leverage containers to run a whole development environment inside of them.

In the next chapter, we will introduce the concept of a distributed application architecture and discuss the various patterns and best practices that are required to run a distributed application successfully.

Questions

Here are a few questions you should try to answer to assess your progress:

1. Name the reasons why you would want to run a complete development environment inside a container.

2. Why should you avoid running applications inside a container as `root`?

3. Why would you ever bind-mount the Docker socket into a container?

4. When pruning your Docker resources to make space, why do you need to handle volumes with special care?

5. Why would you want to run certain admin tasks inside a Docker container and not natively on the host machine?

Answers

Here are sample answers for the questions in this chapter:

1. You could be working on a workstation with limited resources or capabilities, or your workstation could be locked down by your company so that you are not allowed to install any software that is not officially approved. Sometimes, you might need to do proofs of concept or experiments using languages or frameworks that are not yet approved by your company (but might be in the future if the proof of concept is successful).

2. Bind-mounting a Docker socket into a container is the recommended method when a containerized application needs to automate some container-related tasks. This can be an application such as an automation server (such as Jenkins) that you are using to build, test, and deploy Docker images.

3. Most business applications do not need `root`-level authorizations to do their job. From a security perspective, it is therefore strongly recommended to run such applications with the least necessary access rights to their job. Any unnecessary elevated privileges could possibly be exploited by hackers in a malicious attack. By running the application as a non-`root` user, you make it more difficult for potential hackers to compromise your system.

4. Volumes contain data and the lifespan of data most often needs to go far beyond the life cycle of a container, or an application, for that matter. Data is often mission-critical and needs to be stored safely for days, months, or even years. When you delete a volume, you irreversibly delete the data associated with it. Hence, make sure you know what you're doing when deleting a volume.

5. There are several reasons why you might want to run certain admin tasks inside a Docker container, rather than natively on the host machine:

    *   **Isolation**: Containers provide a level of isolation from the host machine, so running admin tasks inside a container can help to prevent conflicts with other processes or dependencies on the host machine.

    *   **Portability**: Containers are designed to be lightweight and portable, which allows for easy deployment of admin tasks across different environments. This can be particularly useful for tasks that need to be run in multiple environments or on multiple machines.

    *   **Consistency**: Containers provide a consistent environment for running admin tasks, regardless of the underlying host machine's configuration. This can be useful for ensuring that tasks are run in a predictable and repeatable manner, which can help to minimize errors and improve efficiency.

    *   **Versioning**: Containers allow for easy versioning of admin tasks, which allows for rollbacks and roll forward of the tasks. This can be useful for testing, troubleshooting, and production environments.

    *   **Security**: Running admin tasks inside a container can help to improve security by isolating the task from the host machine, and by making it easier to limit the permissions and access that the task has.

    *   **Scalability**: Containers can be easily scaled up and down, allowing you to increase or decrease the resources that the admin task needs.

    Please note that this is not a comprehensive list and different use cases may require different approaches. It's important to weigh the pros and cons of running admin tasks inside a container versus natively on the host machine and to choose the approach that best fits your particular use case.

Part 3: Orchestration Fundamentals

By the end of *Part 3*, you will be familiar with the concepts of a Dockerized distributed application and container orchestrators, and be able to use Docker Swarm to deploy and run your applications.

9

Learning about Distributed Application Architecture

This chapter introduces the concept of distributed application architecture and discusses the various patterns and best practices that are required to run a distributed application successfully. It will also discuss the additional requirements that need to be fulfilled to run such an application in production. You might be wondering, what does this have to do with Docker containers? And you are right to ask. At first glance, these are not related to each other. But as you will soon see, when introducing containers that host an application or application service, your application will quickly consist of several containers that will be running on different nodes of a cluster of computers or VMs; and voilà – you are dealing with a distributed application. We thought that it makes sense to provide you with a sense of the complexity that distributed applications introduce and help you avoid the most common pitfalls.

Here is the list of topics we are going to discuss:

- What is a distributed application architecture?
- Patterns and best practices
- Running in production

After reading this chapter, you will be able to do the following:

- Draft a high-level architecture diagram of a distributed application while pointing out key design patterns
- Identify the possible pitfalls of a poorly designed distributed application
- Name commonly used patterns for dealing with the problems of a distributed system
- Name at least four patterns that need to be implemented for a production-ready distributed application

Let's get started!

What is a distributed application architecture?

In this section, we are going to explain what we mean when we talk about distributed application architecture. First, we need to make sure that all the words or acronyms we use have a meaning and that we are all talking in the same language.

Defining the terminology

In this and subsequent chapters, we will talk a lot about concepts that might not be familiar to everyone. To make sure we are all talking the same language, let's briefly introduce and describe the most important of these concepts or words:

Keyword	Description
VM	A virtual machine (VM) is a software simulation of a physical computer that runs on a host computer. It provides a separate operating system and resources, allowing multiple operating systems to run on a single physical machine.
Cluster	A cluster is a group of connected servers that work together as a single system to provide high availability, scalability, and increased performance for applications. The nodes in a cluster are connected through a network and share resources to provide a unified, highly available solution.
Node	A cluster node is a single server within a cluster computing system. It provides computing resources and works together with other nodes to perform tasks as a unified system, providing high availability and scalability for applications.
Network	A network is a group of interconnected devices that can exchange data and information. Networks can be used to connect computers, servers, mobile devices, and other types of devices and allow them to communicate with each other and share resources, such as printers and storage. More specifically in our case, these are physical and software-defined communication paths between individual nodes of a cluster and programs running on those nodes.
Port	A port is a communication endpoint in a network-attached device, such as a computer or server. It allows the device to receive and send data to other devices on the network through a specific network protocol, such as TCP or UDP. Each port has a unique number that is used to identify it, and different services and applications use specific ports to communicate.
Service	Unfortunately, this is a very overloaded term and its real meaning depends on the context that it is used in. If we use the term service in the context of an application, such as an application service, then it usually means that this is a piece of software that implements a limited set of functionalities that are then used by other parts of the application. As we progress through this book, other types of services that have slightly different definitions will be discussed.

Naively said, a distributed application architecture is the opposite of a monolithic application architecture, but it is not unreasonable to look at this monolithic architecture first. Traditionally, most business applications are written in such a way that the result can be seen as a single, tightly coupled program that runs on a named server somewhere in a data center. All its code is compiled into a single binary, or a few very tightly coupled binaries that need to be co-located when running the application. The fact that the server – or more generally – the host, that the application is running on has a well-defined name or static IP address is also important in this context. Let's look at the following diagram, which illustrates this type of application architecture a bit more precisely:

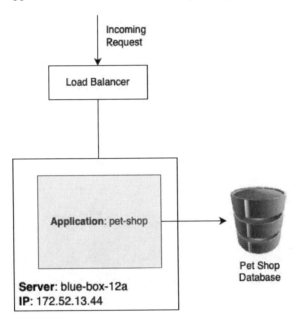

Figure 9.1 – Monolithic application architecture

In the preceding diagram, we can see a server named `blue-box-12a` with an IP address of `172.52.13.44` running an application called `pet-shop`, which is a monolith consisting of a main module and a few tightly coupled libraries.

Now, let's look at the following diagram:

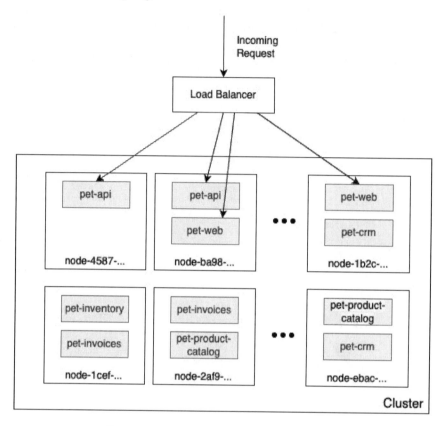

Figure 9.2 – Distributed application architecture

Here, all of a sudden, we do not have just a single named server anymore; instead, we have a lot of them, and they do not have human-friendly names, but rather some unique IDs that can be something such as a **Universal Unique Identifier** (**UUID**). Now, the pet shop application does not consist of a single monolithic block anymore, but rather a plethora of interacting, yet loosely coupled, services such as `pet-api`, `pet-web`, and `pet-inventory`. Furthermore, each service runs in multiple instances in this cluster of servers or hosts.

You might be wondering why we are discussing this in a book about Docker containers, and you are right to ask. While all the topics we're going to investigate apply equally to a world where containers do not (yet) exist, it is important to realize that containers and container orchestration engines help address all these problems in a much more efficient and straightforward way. Most of the problems that used to be very hard to solve in a distributed application architecture become quite simple in a containerized world.

Patterns and best practices

A distributed application architecture has many compelling benefits, but it also has one very significant drawback compared to a monolithic application architecture – the former is way more complex. To tame this complexity, the industry has come up with some important best practices and patterns. In the following sections, we are going to investigate some of the most important ones in more detail.

Loosely coupled components

The best way to address a complex subject has always been to divide it into smaller subproblems that are more manageable. As an example, it would be insanely complex to build a house in a single step. It is much easier to build a house from simple parts that are then combined into the final result.

The same also applies to software development. It is much easier to develop a very complex application if we divide this application into smaller components that interoperate and make up the overall application. Now, it is much easier to develop these components individually if they are loosely coupled with each other. What this means is that component A makes no assumptions about the inner workings of, say, components B and C, and is only interested in how it can communicate with those two components across a well-defined interface.

If each component has a well-defined and simple public interface through which communication with the other components in the system and the outside world happens, then this enables us to develop each component individually, without implicit dependencies on other components. During the development process, other components in the system can easily be replaced by stubs or mocks to allow us to test our components.

Stateful versus stateless

Every meaningful business application creates, modifies, or uses data. In IT, a synonym for data is **state**. An application service that creates or modifies persistent data is called a **stateful component**. Typical stateful components are database services or services that create files. On the other hand, application components that do not create or modify persistent data are called **stateless components**.

In a distributed application architecture, stateless components are much simpler to handle than stateful components. Stateless components can easily be scaled up and down. Furthermore, they can be quickly and painlessly torn down and restarted on a completely different node of the cluster – all because they have no persistent data associated with them.

Given this, it is helpful to design a system in a way that most of the application services are stateless. It is best to push all the stateful components to the boundaries of the application and limit how many are used. Managing stateful components is hard.

Service discovery

As we build applications that consist of many individual components or services that communicate with each other, we need a mechanism that allows the individual components to find each other in the cluster. Finding each other usually means that you need to know on which node the target component is running, and on which port it is listening for communication. Most often, nodes are identified by an **IP address** and a **port**, which is just a number in a well-defined range.

Technically, we could tell **Service A**, which wants to communicate with a target, **Service B**, what the IP address and port of the target are. This could happen, for example, through an entry in a configuration file:

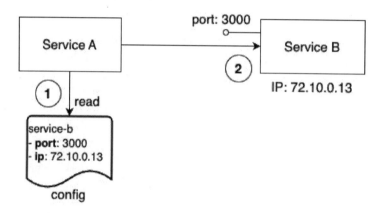

Figure 9.3 – Components are hardwired

While this might work very well in the context of a monolithic application that runs on one or only a few well-known and curated servers, it falls apart in a distributed application architecture. First of all, in this scenario, we have many components, and keeping track of them manually becomes a nightmare. This is not scalable. Furthermore, typically, Service A should or will never know on which node of the cluster the other components run. Their location may not even be stable as component B could be moved from node X to another node, Y, due to various reasons external to the application. Thus, we need another way in which Service A can locate Service B, or any other service, for that matter. Commonly, an external authority that is aware of the topology of the system at any given time is used.

This external authority or service knows all the nodes and their IP addresses that currently pertain to the cluster; it knows about all the services that are running and where they are running. Often, this kind of service is called a **DNS service**, where DNS stands for **Domain Name System**. As we will see, Docker has a DNS service implemented as part of its underlying engine. Kubernetes – the number one container orchestration system, which we'll discuss in *Chapter 13, Introducing Container Orchestration* – also uses a DNS service to facilitate communication between components running in a cluster:

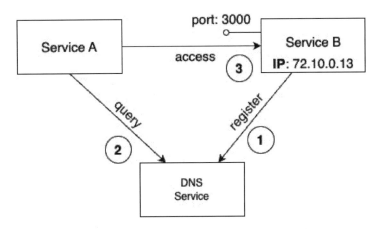

Figure 9.4 – Components consulting an external locator service

In the preceding diagram, we can see how Service A wants to communicate with Service B, but it can't do this directly. First, it has to query the external authority, a registry service (here, this is called **DNS Service**), about the whereabouts of Service B. The registry service will answer with the requested information and hand out the IP address and port number that Service A can use to reach Service B. Service A then uses this information and establishes communication with Service B. Of course, this is a naive picture of what's happening at a low level, but it is a good picture to help us understand the architectural pattern of service discovery.

Routing

Routing is the mechanism of sending packets of data from a source component to a target component. Routing is categorized into different types. The so-called OSI model (see the reference to this in the *Further reading* section at the end of this chapter for more information) is used to distinguish between different types of routing. In the context of containers and container orchestration, routing at layers 2, 3, 4, and 7 are relevant. We will look at routing in more detail in subsequent chapters. For now, let's just say that layer 2 routing is the most low-level type of routing, which connects a MAC address to another MAC address, while layer 7 routing, which is also called application-level routing, is the most high-level one. The latter is, for example, used to route requests that have a target identifier – that is, a URL such as `https://acme.com/pets` – to the appropriate target component in our system.

Load balancing

Load balancing is used whenever **Service A** needs to communicate with **Service B**, such as in a request-response pattern, but the latter is running in more than one instance, as shown in the following diagram:

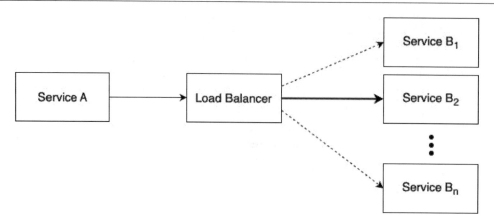

Figure 9.5 – The request of Service A is being load balanced to Service B

If we have multiple instances of a service such as Service B running in our system, we want to make sure that every one of those instances gets an equal amount of workload assigned to it. This task is a generic one, which means that we don't want the caller to have to do the load balancing but, rather, an external service that intercepts the call and takes over the role of deciding which of the target service instances to forward the call to. This external service is called a load balancer. Load balancers can use different algorithms to decide how to distribute incoming calls to target service instances. The most common algorithm that's used is called round-robin. This algorithm assigns requests repetitively, starting with instance 1, then 2, until instance n. After the last instance has been served, the load balancer starts over with instance number 1.

In the preceding example, a load balancer also facilitates high availability since a request from Service A will be forwarded to a healthy instance of Service B. The load balancer also takes the role of periodically checking the health of each instance of B.

Defensive programming

When developing a service for a distributed application, it is important to remember that this service is not going to be standalone and that it's dependent on other application services or even on external services provided by third parties, such as credit card validation services or stock information services, to just name two. All these other services are external to the service we are developing. We have no control over their correctness or their availability at any given time. Thus, when coding, we always need to assume the worst and hope for the best. Assuming the worst means that we have to deal with potential failures explicitly.

Retries

When there is a possibility that an external service might be temporarily unavailable or not responsive enough, then the following procedure can be used. When the call to the other service fails or times out, the calling code should be structured in such a way that the same call is repeated after a short wait time. If the call fails again, the wait should be a bit longer before the next trial. The calls should be repeated up to a maximum number of times, each time increasing the wait time. After that, the service should give up and provide a degraded service, which could mean returning some stale cached data or no data at all, depending on the situation.

Logging

Important operations that are performed on a service should always be logged. Logging information needs to be categorized to be of any real value. A common list of categories includes *debug, info, warning, error*, and *fatal*. Logging information should be collected by a central log aggregation service and not stored on an individual node of the cluster. Aggregated logs are easy to parse and filter for relevant information. This information is essential to quickly pinpoint the root cause of a failure or unexpected behavior in a distributed system consisting of many moving parts, running in production.

Error handling

As we mentioned earlier, each application service in a distributed application is dependent on other services. As developers, we should always expect the worst and have appropriate error handling in place. One of the most important best practices is to fail fast. Code the service in such a way that unrecoverable errors are discovered as early as possible and, if such an error is detected, have the service fail immediately. But don't forget to log meaningful information to STDERR or STDOUT, which can be used by developers or system operators later to track malfunctions in the system. Also, return a helpful error to the caller, indicating as precisely as possible why the call failed.

One sample of fail fast is always checking the input values provided by the caller. Are the values in the expected ranges and complete? If not, then do not try to continue processing; instead, immediately abort the operation.

Redundancy

A mission-critical system has to be available at all times, around the clock, 365 days a year. Downtime is not acceptable since it might result in a huge loss of opportunities or reputation for the company. In a highly distributed application, the likelihood of a failure of at least one of the many involved components is non-neglectable. We can say that the question is not whether a component will fail, but rather when a failure will occur.

To avoid downtime when one of the many components in the system fails, each part of the system needs to be redundant. This includes the application components, as well as all infrastructure parts. What that means is that if we have a payment service as part of our application, then we need to run this service redundantly. The easiest way to do that is to run multiple instances of this very service on different nodes of our cluster. The same applies, say, to an edge router or a load balancer. We cannot afford for these to ever go down. Thus, the router or load balancer must be redundant.

Health checks

We have mentioned various times that in a distributed application architecture, with its many parts, the failure of an individual component is highly likely and that it is only a matter of time until it happens. For that reason, we must run every single component of the system redundantly. Load balancers then distribute the traffic across the individual instances of a service.

But now, there is another problem. How does the load balancer or router know whether a certain service instance is available? It could have crashed, or it could be unresponsive. To solve this problem, we can use so-called **health checks**. The load balancer, or some other system service on behalf of it, periodically polls all the service instances and checks their health. The questions are basically, *Are you still there? Are you healthy?* The answer to each question is either *Yes* or *No*, or the health check times out if the instance is not responsive anymore.

If the component answers with *No* or a timeout occurs, then the system kills the corresponding instance and spins up a new instance in its place. If all this happens in a fully automated way, then we say that we have an auto-healing system in place. Instead of the load balancer periodically polling the status of the components, responsibility can also be turned around. The components could be required to periodically send live signals to the load balancer. If a component fails to send live signals over a predefined, extended period, it is assumed to be unhealthy or dead.

There are situations where either of the described ways is more appropriate.

Circuit breaker pattern

A circuit breaker is a mechanism that is used to avoid a distributed application going down due to the cascading failure of many essential components. Circuit breakers help us avoid one failing component tearing down other dependent services in a domino effect. Like circuit breakers in an electrical system, which protect a house from burning down due to the failure of a malfunctioning plugged-in appliance by interrupting the power line, circuit breakers in a distributed application interrupt the connection from **Service A** to **Service B** if the latter is not responding or is malfunctioning.

This can be achieved by wrapping a protected service call in a circuit breaker object. This object monitors for failures. Once the number of failures reaches a certain threshold, the circuit breaker trips. All subsequent calls to the circuit breaker will return with an error, without the protected call being made at all:

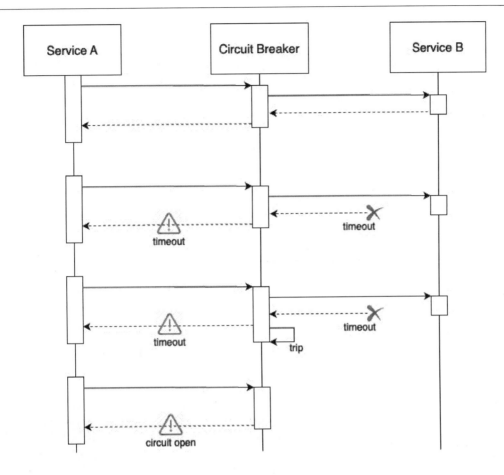

Figure 9.6 – Circuit breaker pattern

In the preceding diagram, we have a circuit breaker that tips over after the second timeout is received when calling **Service B**.

Rate limiter

In the context of a circuit breaker, a rate limiter is a technique that's used to control the rate at which requests are processed by a system or service. By limiting the number of requests allowed within a specific time window, rate limiters help prevent overloading and ensure the stability and availability of the service. This mechanism proves useful in mitigating the impact of sudden traffic spikes, protecting backend systems from being overwhelmed, and avoiding cascading failures throughout a distributed system. By integrating rate limiting with circuit breakers, systems can effectively maintain optimal performance and gracefully handle unexpected surges in demand.

Bulkhead

In addition to that, and still in the context of a circuit breaker, a bulkhead is a resilience pattern that's used to isolate components or resources within a system, ensuring that a failure in one area does not cause a cascading effect on the entire system. By partitioning resources and segregating operations into separate, independent units, bulkheads help prevent a single point of failure from bringing down the entire service. This mechanism is useful in maintaining system stability, improving fault tolerance, and ensuring that critical operations can continue functioning, even in the event of localized failures. When combined with circuit breakers, bulkheads contribute to a more robust and resilient system, capable of handling failures and maintaining overall system performance.

Running in production

To successfully run a distributed application in production, we need to consider a few more aspects beyond the best practices and patterns that were presented in the preceding sections. One specific area that comes to mind is introspection and monitoring. Let's go through the most important aspects in detail.

Logging

Once a distributed application is in production, it is not possible to live debug it. But how can we then find out what the root cause of the application malfunctioning is? The solution to this problem is that the application produces abundant and meaningful logging information while running. We briefly discussed this topic in an earlier section. But due to its importance, it is worth reiterating. Developers need to instrument their application services in such a way that they output helpful information, such as when an error occurs or a potentially unexpected or unwanted situation is encountered. Often, this information is output to STDOUT and STDERR, where it is then collected by system daemons that write the information to local files or forward it to a central log aggregation service.

If there is sufficient information in the logs, developers can use those logs to track down the root cause of the errors in the system.

In a distributed application architecture, with its many components, logging is even more important than in a monolithic application. The paths of execution of a single request through all the components of the application can be very complex. Also, remember that the components are distributed across a cluster of nodes. Thus, it makes sense to log everything of importance and add things to each log entry, such as the exact time when it happened, the component in which it happened, and the node on which the component ran, to name just a few. Furthermore, the logging information should be aggregated in a central location so that it is readily available for developers and system operators to analyze.

Tracing

Tracing is used to find out how an individual request is funneled through a distributed application and how much time is spent overall on the request and in every individual component. This information, if collected, can be used as one of the sources for dashboards that show the behavior and health of the system.

Monitoring

Operation engineers like to have dashboards showing live key metrics of the system, which show them the overall health of the application at a glance. These metrics can be nonfunctional metrics, such as memory and CPU usage, the number of crashes of a system or application component, and the health of a node, as well as functional and, hence, application-specific metrics, such as the number of checkouts in an ordering system or the number of items out of stock in an inventory service.

Most often, the base data that's used to aggregate the numbers that are used for a dashboard is extracted from logging information. This can either be system logs, which are mostly used for non-functional metrics, or application-level logs, for functional metrics.

Application updates

One of the competitive advantages for a company is to be able to react promptly to changing market situations. Part of this is being able to quickly adjust an application to fulfill new and changed needs or to add new functionality. The faster we can update our applications, the better. Many companies these days roll out new or changed features multiple times per day.

Since application updates are so frequent, these updates have to be non-disruptive. We cannot allow the system to go down for maintenance when upgrading. It all has to happen seamlessly and transparently.

Rolling updates

One way of updating an application or an application service is to use rolling updates. The assumption here is that the particular piece of software that has to be updated runs in multiple instances. Only then can we use this type of update.

What happens is that the system stops one instance of the current service and replaces it with an instance of the new service. As soon as the new instance is ready, it will be served traffic. Usually, the new instance is monitored for some time to see whether it works as expected; if it does, the next instance of the current service is taken down and replaced with a new instance. This pattern is repeated until all the service instances have been replaced.

Since there are always a few instances running at any given time, current or new, the application is operational all the time. No downtime is needed.

Blue-green deployments

In blue-green deployments, the current version of the application service, called **blue**, handles all the application traffic. We then install the new version of the application service, called **green**, on the production system. This new service is not wired with the rest of the application yet.

Once the green service has been installed, we can execute **smoke tests** against this new service. If those succeed, the router can be configured to funnel all traffic that previously went to blue to the new service, green. The behavior of the green service is then observed closely and, if all success criteria are met, the blue service can be decommissioned. But if, for some reason, the green service shows some unexpected or unwanted behavior, the router can be reconfigured to return all traffic to the blue service. The green service can then be removed and fixed, and a new blue-green deployment can be executed with the corrected version:

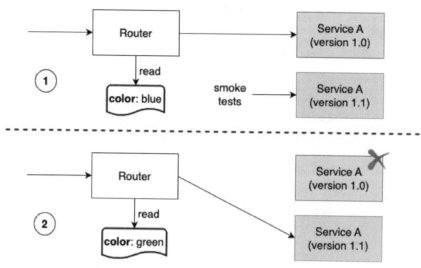

Figure 9.7 – Blue-green deployment

Next, let's look at canary releases.

Canary releases

Canary releases are releases where we have the current version of the application service and the new version installed on the system in parallel. As such, they resemble blue-green deployments. At first, all traffic is still routed through the current version. We then configure a router so that it funnels a small percentage, say 1%, of the overall traffic to the new version of the application service. Subsequently, the behavior of the new service is monitored closely to find out whether it works as expected. If all the criteria for success are met, then the router is configured to funnel more traffic, say 5% this time, through the new service. Again, the behavior of the new service is closely monitored and, if it is successful, more and more traffic is routed to it until we reach 100%. Once all the traffic has been routed to the new service and it has been stable for some time, the old version of the service can be decommissioned.

Why do we call this a canary release? It is named after coal miners who would use canary birds as an early warning system in mines. Canaries are particularly sensitive to toxic gas and if such a bird died, the miners knew they had to abandon the mine immediately.

Irreversible data changes

If part of our update process is to execute an irreversible change in our state, such as an irreversible schema change in a backing relational database, then we need to address this with special care. It is possible to execute such changes without downtime if we use the right approach. It is important to recognize that, in such a situation, we cannot deploy the code changes that require the new data structure in the data store at the same time as the changes to the data. Rather, the whole update has to be separated into three distinct steps. In the first step, we roll out a backward-compatible schema and data change. If this is successful, then we roll out the new code in the second step. Again, if that is successful, we clean up the schema in the third step and remove the backward compatibility:

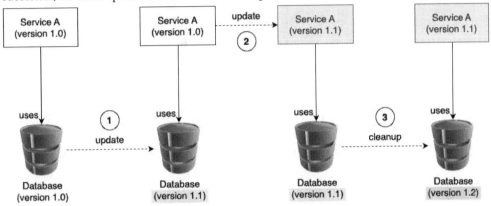

Figure 9.8 – Rolling out an irreversible data or schema change

The preceding diagram shows how the data and its structure are updated, how the application code is updated, and how the data and data structure are cleaned up.

Changing the data structure at scale

Over time, an application may produce an enormous amount of data. Changing the data structure at scale refers to the process of altering the format, organization, or layout of large amounts of data stored in a database or other type of data storage system. This can involve adding, removing, or modifying fields, tables, or other elements within the data structure. The goal is to optimize the data for a specific use case or business requirement while preserving the data's accuracy and integrity. This process typically involves analyzing the existing data structure, planning and testing the changes, and then executing the update in a controlled manner. In large-scale data structure changes, it is important to have a well-defined strategy, a robust testing and validation process, and adequate resources, including technical expertise and backup systems, to minimize the risk of data loss or corruption during the migration process.

In a dynamic data migration scenario, data is constantly updated in real time as it is being used, making the migration process more complex and challenging. This type of migration requires a more sophisticated approach to ensure data consistency and integrity throughout the migration process. The solution should be able to keep track of changes made to the data in the source system and replicate them in the target system while minimizing downtime and data loss. This may involve using specialized tools, such as data replication or mirroring software, or employing a multi-step process that includes data synchronization and reconciliation. Additionally, it is essential to have robust testing and validation procedures in place, as well as a clear rollback plan, to minimize the risk of data loss or corruption during the migration process.

Rollback and roll forward

If we have frequent updates for our application services that run in production, sooner or later, there will be a problem with one of those updates. Maybe a developer, while fixing a bug, introduced a new one, which was not caught by all the automated, and maybe manual, tests, so the application is misbehaving. In this case, we must roll back the service to the previous good version. In this regard, a rollback is a recovery from a disaster.

Again, in a distributed application architecture, it is not a question of whether a rollback will ever be needed, but rather when a rollback will have to occur. Thus, we need to be sure that we can always roll back to a previous version of any service that makes up our application. Rollbacks cannot be an afterthought; they have to be a tested and proven part of our deployment process.

If we are using blue-green deployments to update our services, then rollbacks should be fairly simple. All we need to do is switch the router from the new green version of the service back to the previous blue version.

If we adhere to continuous delivery and the main branch of our code is always in a deployable state, then we can also consider rolling forward instead of rolling back. Often, it is faster to fix a production issue and roll out the fix immediately instead of trying to roll back our system to a previous state. The technique of rolling forward is of particular interest if the previous change introduced some backward incompatibility.

Summary

In this chapter, we learned what a distributed application architecture is and what patterns and best practices are helpful or needed to successfully run a distributed application. We also discussed what is needed to run such an application in production.

In the next chapter, we will dive into networking limited to a single host. We are going to discuss how containers living on the same host can communicate with each other and how external clients can access containerized applications if necessary.

Further reading

The following articles provide more in-depth information regarding what was covered in this chapter:

- *Circuit breakers*: `http://bit.ly/1NU1sgW`
- *The OSI model explained*: `http://bit.ly/1UCcvMt`
- *Blue-green deployments*: `http://bit.ly/2r2IxNJ`

Questions

Please answer the following questions to assess your understanding of this chapter's content:

1. When and why does every part in a distributed application architecture have to be redundant? Explain this in a few short sentences.

2. Why do we need DNS services? Explain this in three to five sentences.

3. What is a circuit breaker and why is it needed?

4. What are some of the important differences between a monolithic application and a distributed or multi-service application?

5. What is a blue-green deployment?

Answers

Here are the possible answers to this chapter's questions:

1. In a distributed application architecture, every piece of the software and infrastructure needs to be redundant in a production environment, where the continuous uptime of the application is mission-critical. A highly distributed application consists of many parts and the likelihood of one of the pieces failing or misbehaving increases with the number of parts. It is guaranteed that, given enough time, every part will eventually fail. To avoid outages of the application, we need redundancy in every part, be it a server, a network switch, or a service running on a cluster node in a container.

2. In highly distributed, scalable, and fault-tolerant systems, individual services of the application can move around due to scaling needs or due to component failures. Thus, we cannot hardwire different services with each other. Service A, which needs access to Service B, should not have to know details about Service B, such as its IP address. It should rely on an external provider for this information. TheDNS is such a provider of location information. Service A just tells it that it wants to talk to Service B and the DNS service will figure out the details.

3. A circuit breaker is a means to avoid cascading failures if a component in a distributed application is failing or misbehaving. Similar to a circuit breaker in electric wiring, a software-driven circuit breaker cuts the communication between a client and a failed service. The circuit breaker will directly report an error back to the client component if the failed service is called. This allows the system to recover or heal from failure.

4. A monolithic application is easier to manage than a multi-service application since it consists of a single deployment package. On the other hand, a monolith is often harder to scale to account for increased demand in one particular area of the application. In a distributed application, each service can be scaled individually and each service can run on optimized infrastructure, while a monolith needs to run on infrastructure that is OK for all or most of the features implemented in it. However, over time, this has become less of a problem since very powerful servers and/or VMs are made available by all major cloud providers. These are relatively cheap and can handle the load of most average line-of-business or web applications with ease.

    Maintaining and updating a monolith, if not well modularized, is much harder than a multi-service application, where each service can be updated and deployed independently. The monolith is often a big, complex, and tightly coupled pile of code. Minor modifications can have unexpected side effects. (Micro) Services, in theory, are self-contained, simple components that behave like black boxes. Dependent services know nothing about the inner workings of the service and thus do not depend on it.

> **Note**
>
> The reality is often not so nice – in many cases, microservices are hard coupled and behave like distributed monoliths. Sadly, the latter is the worst place a team or a company can be in as it combines the disadvantages of both worlds, with the monolith on one side and the distributed application on the other.

5. A blue-green deployment is a form of software deployment that allows for zero downtime deployments of new versions of an application or an application service. If, say, Service A needs to be updated with a new version, then we call the currently running blue version. The new version of the service is deployed into production, but not yet wired up with the rest of the application. This new version is called green. Once the deployment succeeds and smoke tests have shown it's ready to go, the router that funnels traffic to the blue version is reconfigured to switch to the green version. The behavior of the green version is observed for a while and if everything is OK, the blue version is decommissioned. On the other hand, if the green version causes difficulties, the router can simply be switched back to the blue version, and the green version can be fixed and later redeployed.

10

Using Single-Host Networking

In the previous chapter, we learned about the most important architectural patterns and best practices that are used when dealing with distributed application architecture.

In this chapter, we will introduce the Docker container networking model and its single-host implementation in the form of the bridge network. This chapter also introduces the concept of **Software Defined Networks** (**SDNs**) and how they are used to secure containerized applications. Furthermore, we will demonstrate how container ports can be opened to the public and thus make containerized components accessible to the outside world. Finally, we will introduce Traefik, a reverse proxy, which can be used to enable sophisticated HTTP application-level routing between containers.

This chapter covers the following topics:

- Dissecting the container network model
- Network firewalling
- Working with the bridge network
- The host and null network
- Running in an existing network namespace
- Managing container ports
- HTTP-level routing using a reverse proxy

After completing this chapter, you will be able to do the following:

- Create, inspect, and delete a custom bridge network
- Run a container attached to a custom bridge network
- Isolate containers from each other by running them on different bridge networks
- Publish a container port to a host port of your choice
- Add Traefik as a reverse proxy to enable application-level routing

Technical requirements

For this chapter, the only thing you will need is a Docker host that is able to run Linux containers. You can use your laptop with Docker Desktop for this purpose.

To start with, let's first create a folder for this chapter where we are going to store the code for our examples:

1. Navigate to the folder where you have cloned the repository accompanying this book. Usually, this is the following:

    ```
    $ cd ~/The-Ultimat-Docker-Container-Book
    ```

2. Create a subfolder for this chapter and navigate to it:

    ```
    $ mkdir ch10 && cd ch10
    ```

Let's get started!

Dissecting the container network model

So far, we have mostly worked with single containers, but in reality, a containerized business application consists of several containers that need to collaborate to achieve a goal. Therefore, we need a way for individual containers to communicate with each other. This is achieved by establishing pathways, which we can use to send data packets back and forth between containers. These pathways are called networks. Docker has defined a very simple networking model, the so-called **container network model (CNM)**, to specify the requirements that any software that implements a container network has to fulfill. The following is a graphical representation of the CNM:

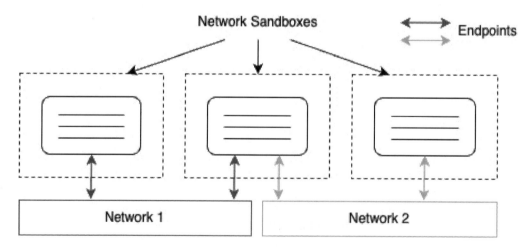

Figure 10.1 – The Docker CNM

The CNM has three elements – sandboxes, endpoints, and networks:

- **Network Sandboxes**: The sandbox perfectly isolates a container from the outside world. No inbound network connection is allowed into the sandboxed container, but it is very unlikely that a container will be of any value in a system if absolutely no communication with it is possible. To work around this, we have element number two, which is the endpoint.

- **Endpoint**: An endpoint is a controlled gateway from the outside world into the network's sandbox, which shields the container. The endpoint connects the network sandbox (but not the container) to the third element of the model, which is the network.

- **Network**: The network is the pathway that transports the data packets of an instance of communication from endpoint to endpoint or, ultimately, from container to container.

It is important to note that a network sandbox can have zero to many endpoints, or, said differently, each container living in a network sandbox can either be attached to no network at all or it can be attached to multiple different networks at the same time. In the preceding diagram, the middle one of the three **Network Sandboxes** is attached to both **Network 1** and **Network 2** using an endpoint.

This networking model is very generic and does not specify where the individual containers that communicate with each other over a network run. All containers could, for example, run on the same host (local) or they could be distributed across a cluster of hosts (global).

Of course, the CNM is just a model describing how networking works among containers. To be able to use networking with our containers, we need real implementations of the CNM. For both local and global scopes, we have multiple implementations of the CNM. In the following table, we've given a short overview of the existing implementations and their main characteristics. The list is in no particular order:

Network	Company	Scope	Description
Bridge	Docker	Local	Simple network based on Linux bridges to allow networking on a single host
Macvlan	Docker	Local	Configures multiple layer-2 (that is, MAC) addresses on a single physical host interface
Overlay	Docker	Global	Multi-node capable container network based on Virtual Extensible LAN (VXLan)
Weave Net	Weaveworks	Global	Simple, resilient, multi-host Docker networking
Contiv Network Plugin	Cisco	Global	Open source container networking

Table 10.1 – Network types

All network types not directly provided by Docker can be added to a Docker host as a plugin.

In the next section, we will describe how network firewalling works.

Network firewalling

Docker has always had the mantra of security first. This philosophy had a direct influence on how networking in a single- and multi-host Docker environment was designed and implemented. SDNs are easy and cheap to create, yet they perfectly firewall containers that are attached to this network from other non-attached containers, and from the outside world. All containers that belong to the same network can freely communicate with each other, while others have no means to do so.

In the following diagram, we have two networks called **front** and **back**. Attached to the **front** network, we have containers **c1** and **c2**, and attached to the **back** network, we have containers **c3** and **c4**. **c1** and **c2** can freely communicate with each other, as can **c3** and **c4**, but **c1** and **c2** have no way to communicate with either **c3** or **c4**, and vice versa:

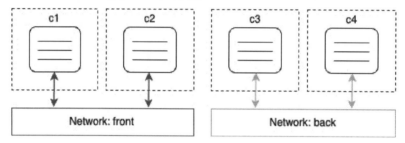

Figure 10.2 – Docker networks

Now, what about a situation in which we have an application consisting of three services: webAPI, productCatalog, and database? We want webAPI to be able to communicate with productCatalog, but not with the database, and we want productCatalog to be able to communicate with the database service. We can solve this situation by placing webAPI and the database on different networks and attaching productCatalog to both of these networks, as shown in the following diagram:

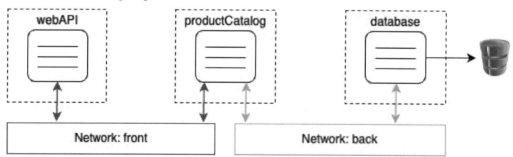

Figure 10.3 – Container attached to multiple networks

Since creating SDNs is cheap, and each network provides added security by isolating resources from unauthorized access, it is highly recommended that you design and run applications so that they use multiple networks and only run services on the same network that absolutely need to communicate with each other. In the preceding example, there is absolutely no need for the webAPI component to ever communicate directly with the database service, so we have put them on different networks. If the worst-case scenario happens and a hacker compromises webAPI, they won't be able to access the database from there without also hacking the productCatalog service.

Now we are ready to discuss the first implementation of the CNM, the bridge network.

Working with the bridge network

The Docker bridge network is the first implementation of the CNM that we're going to look at in detail. This network implementation is based on the Linux bridge.

When the Docker daemon runs for the first time, it creates a Linux bridge and calls it docker0. This is the default behavior and can be changed by changing the configuration.

Docker then creates a network with this Linux bridge and calls it the network bridge. All the containers that we create on a Docker host and that we do not explicitly bind to another network lead to Docker automatically attaching the containers to this bridge network.

To verify that we indeed have a network called bridge of the bridge type defined on our host, we can list all the networks on the host with the following command:

```
$ docker network ls
```

This should provide an output similar to the following:

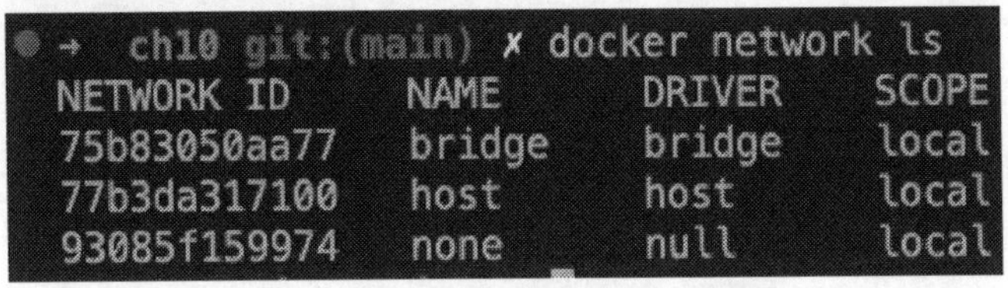

Figure 10.4 – Listing all the Docker networks available by default

In your case, the IDs will be different, but the rest of the output should look the same. We do indeed have a first network called bridge using the bridge driver. The scope being local just means that this type of network is restricted to a single host and cannot span across multiple hosts. In *Chapter 14, Introducing Docker Swarm*, we will also discuss other types of networks that have a global scope, meaning they can span whole clusters of hosts.

Now, let's look a little bit deeper into what this bridge network is all about. For this, we are going to use the Docker `inspect` command:

```
$ docker network inspect bridge
```

When executed, this outputs a big chunk of detailed information about the network in question. This information should look as follows:

```
● →  ch10 git:(main) ✗ docker network inspect bridge
[
    {
        "Name": "bridge",
        "Id": "75b83050aa772bdfed2f0de1ce5243276e22bd35eda514a24ae6fa4f330e587b",
        "Created": "2023-02-15T16:23:15.807986084Z",
        "Scope": "local",
        "Driver": "bridge",
        "EnableIPv6": false,
        "IPAM": {
            "Driver": "default",
            "Options": null,
            "Config": [
                {
                    "Subnet": "172.17.0.0/16",
                    "Gateway": "172.17.0.1"
                }
            ]
        },
        "Internal": false,
        "Attachable": false,
        "Ingress": false,
        "ConfigFrom": {
            "Network": ""
        },
        "ConfigOnly": false,
        "Containers": {},
        "Options": {
            "com.docker.network.bridge.default_bridge": "true",
            "com.docker.network.bridge.enable_icc": "true",
            "com.docker.network.bridge.enable_ip_masquerade": "true",
            "com.docker.network.bridge.host_binding_ipv4": "0.0.0.0",
            "com.docker.network.bridge.name": "docker0",
            "com.docker.network.driver.mtu": "1500"
        },
        "Labels": {}
    }
]
```

Figure 10.5 – Output generated when inspecting the Docker bridge network

We saw the `ID`, `Name`, `Driver`, and `Scope` values when we listed all the networks, so that is nothing new, but let's have a look at the **IP address management (IPAM)** block.

IPAM is a piece of software that is used to track the IP addresses that are used on a computer. The important part of the IPAM block is the *config* node with its values for the subnet and gateway. The subnet for the bridge network is defined by default as 172.17.0.0/16. This means that all containers attached to this network will get an IP address assigned by Docker that is taken from the given range, which is 172.17.0.2 to 172.17.255.255. The 172.17.0.1 address is reserved for the router of this network whose role in this type of network is taken by the Linux bridge. We can expect that the very first container that will be attached to this network by Docker will get the 172.17.0.2 address. All subsequent containers will get a higher number; the following diagram illustrates this fact:

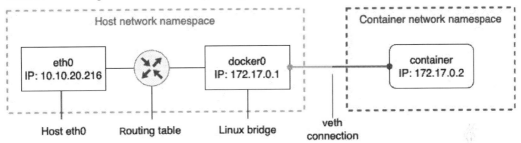

Figure 10.6 – The bridge network

In the preceding diagram, we can see the network namespace of the host, which includes the host's eth0 endpoint, which is typically an NIC if the Docker host runs on bare metal or a virtual NIC if the Docker host is a VM. All traffic to the host comes through eth0. The Linux bridge is responsible for routing the network traffic between the host's network and the subnet of the bridge network.

> **What is a NIC?**
>
> A **Network Interface Card** (**NIC**), sometimes referred to as a network interface connector, is a hardware component that enables a computer or device to connect to a network. It serves as an interface between the computer and the network, allowing data to be transmitted and received. NICs are typically built-in components on motherboards or installed as expansion cards and support various types of network connections, such as Ethernet, Wi-Fi, or fiber-optic connections.

By default, only egress traffic is allowed, and all ingress is blocked. What this means is that while containerized applications can reach the internet, they cannot be reached by any outside traffic. Each container attached to the network gets its own **virtual ethernet** (**veth**) connection to the bridge. This is illustrated in the following diagram:

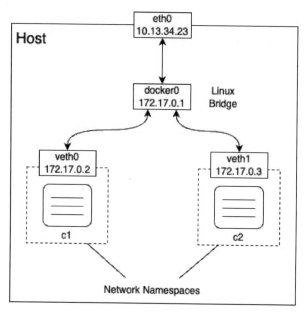

Figure 10.7 – Details of the bridge network

The preceding diagram shows us the world from the perspective of the host. We will explore what this situation looks like from within a container later on in this section. We are not limited to just the bridge network, as Docker allows us to define our own custom bridge networks. This is not just a feature that is nice to have; it is a recommended best practice not to run all containers on the same network. Instead, we should use additional bridge networks to further isolate containers that have no need to communicate with each other. To create a custom bridge network called `sample-net`, use the following command:

```
$ docker network create --driver bridge sample-net
```

If we do this, we can then inspect what subnet Docker has created for this new custom network, as follows:

```
$ docker network inspect sample-net | grep Subnet
```

This returns the following value:

```
"Subnet": "172.18.0.0/16",
```

Evidently, Docker has just assigned the next free block of IP addresses to our new custom bridge network. If, for some reason, we want to specify our own subnet range when creating a network, we can do so by using the --subnet parameter:

```
$ docker network create --driver bridge --subnet "10.1.0.0/16" test-
net
```

> **Note**
> To avoid conflicts due to duplicate IP addresses, make sure you avoid creating networks with overlapping subnets.

Now that we have discussed what a bridge network is and how we can create a custom bridge network, we want to understand how we can attach containers to these networks.

First, let's interactively run an Alpine container without specifying the network to be attached:

```
$ docker container run --name c1 -it --rm alpine:latest /bin/sh
```

In another Terminal window, let's inspect the c1 container:

```
$ docker container inspect c1
```

In the vast output, let's concentrate for a moment on the part that provides network-related information. This can be found under the `NetworkSettings` node. I have it listed in the following output:

```
 1   "NetworkSettings": {
 2       "Bridge": "",
 3       "SandboxID": "841910ccff0bed554bdb4c0f577c6fb5863ecd687e99824d85e82830b00730ac",
 4       "HairpinMode": false,
 5       "LinkLocalIPv6Address": "",
 6       "LinkLocalIPv6PrefixLen": 0,
 7       "Ports": {},
 8       "SandboxKey": "/var/run/docker/netns/841910ccff0b",
 9       "SecondaryIPAddresses": null,
10       "SecondaryIPv6Addresses": null,
11       "EndpointID": "ee156f9601de95f77aec273edd8362ce22b4ab3a29460215d2c4538539d3ad0d",
12       "Gateway": "172.17.0.1",
13       "GlobalIPv6Address": "",
14       "GlobalIPv6PrefixLen": 0,
15       "IPAddress": "172.17.0.2",
16       "IPPrefixLen": 16,
17       "IPv6Gateway": "",
18       "MacAddress": "02:42:ac:11:00:02",
19       "Networks": {
20           "bridge": {
21               "IPAMConfig": null,
22               "Links": null,
23               "Aliases": null,
24               "NetworkID": "d172692adf8641abc3a22b0e35df20c86bd8eb23bcc44e04533a3a95379eb9b7",
25               "EndpointID": "ee156f9601de95f77aec273edd8362ce22b4ab3a29460215d2c4538539d3ad0d",
26               "Gateway": "172.17.0.1",
27               "IPAddress": "172.17.0.2",
28               "IPPrefixLen": 16,
29               "IPv6Gateway": "",
30               "GlobalIPv6Address": "",
31               "GlobalIPv6PrefixLen": 0,
32               "MacAddress": "02:42:ac:11:00:02",
33               "DriverOpts": null
34           }
35       }
36   }
```

Figure 10.8 – The NetworkSettings section of the container metadata

In the preceding output, we can see that the container is indeed attached to the bridge network since `NetworkID` is equal to `d172692...`, which we can see from the preceding code being the ID of the bridge network. We can also see that the container was assigned the IP address of `172.17.0.2` as expected and that the gateway is at `172.17.0.1`.

Please note that the container also had a `MacAddress` associated with it. This is important as the Linux bridge uses the `MacAddress` for routing.

So far, we have approached this from the outside of the container's network namespace. Now, let's see what the situation looks like when we're not only inside the container but inside the container's network namespace. Inside the `c1` container, let's use the `ip` tool to inspect what's going on. Run the `ip addr` command and observe the output that is generated, as follows:

```
/ # ip addr
1: lo: <LOOPBACK,UP,LOWER_UP> mtu 65536 qdisc noqueue state UNKNOWN qlen 1000
    link/loopback 00:00:00:00:00:00 brd 00:00:00:00:00:00
    inet 127.0.0.1/8 scope host lo
       valid_lft forever preferred_lft forever
2: tunl0@NONE: <NOARP> mtu 1480 qdisc noop state DOWN qlen 1000
    link/ipip 0.0.0.0 brd 0.0.0.0
3: ip6tnl0@NONE: <NOARP> mtu 1452 qdisc noop state DOWN qlen 1000
    link/tunnel6 00:00:00:00:00:00:00:00:00:00:00:00:00:00:00:00 brd 00:00:00:00:00:00:00:00:00:00:00:00:00:00:00:00
54: eth0@if55: <BROADCAST,MULTICAST,UP,LOWER_UP,M-DOWN> mtu 1500 qdisc noqueue state UP
    link/ether 02:42:ac:11:00:02 brd ff:ff:ff:ff:ff:ff
    inet 172.17.0.2/16 brd 172.17.255.255 scope global eth0
       valid_lft forever preferred_lft forever
```

Figure 10.9 – Container namespace, as seen by the IP tool

The interesting part of the preceding output is `54:`, that is, the `eth0` endpoint. The `veth0` endpoint that the Linux bridge created outside of the container namespace is mapped to `eth0` inside the container. Docker always maps the first endpoint of a container network namespace to `eth0`, as seen from inside the namespace. If the network namespace is attached to an additional network, then that endpoint will be mapped to `eth1`, and so on.

Since at this point, we're not really interested in any endpoint other than `eth0`, we could have used a more specific variant of the command, which would have given us the following:

```
/ # ip addr show eth0
54: eth0@if55: <BROADCAST,MULTICAST,UP,LOWER_UP,M-DOWN> mtu 1500 qdisc noqueue state UP
    link/ether 02:42:ac:11:00:02 brd ff:ff:ff:ff:ff:ff
    inet 172.17.0.2/16 brd 172.17.255.255 scope global eth0
       valid_lft forever preferred_lft forever
```

Figure 10.10 – eth0 endpoint as seen from inside of the container

In the output, we can also see what MAC address (`02:42:ac:11:00:02`) and what IP (`172.17.0.2`) have been associated with this container network namespace by Docker.

We can also get some information about how requests are routed by using the `ip route` command:

```
/ # ip route
```

This gives us the following output:

```
default via 172.17.0.1 dev eth0
172.17.0.0/16 dev eth0 scope link  src 172.17.0.2
```

This output tells us that all the traffic to the gateway at 172.17.0.1 is routed through the eth0 device.

Now, let's run another container called c2 on the same network and in detach mode:

```
$ docker container run --name c2 -d --rm alpine:latest ping 127.0.0.1
```

The c2 container will also be attached to the bridge network since we have not specified any other network. Its IP address will be the next free one within the subnet, which is 172.17.0.3, as we can readily test with the following command:

```
$ docker container inspect --format "{{.NetworkSettings.IPAddress}}"
c2
```

This results in the following output:

```
172.17.0.3
```

Now, we have two containers attached to the bridge network. We can try to inspect this network once again to find a list of all containers attached to it in the output:

```
$ docker network inspect bridge
```

This information can be found under the Containers node:

```
1   "Containers": {
2       "58058230363c64cbf53a0d0df295750c0b8708ead5717234cae0710d24e91ed1": {
3           "Name": "c2",
4           "EndpointID": "1d5e50a8da428f11f01a705c4d9d1125bd91c495f0252aec6f6385d427d08640",
5           "MacAddress": "02:42:ac:11:00:03",
6           "IPv4Address": "172.17.0.3/16",
7           "IPv6Address": ""
8       },
9       "c3cadb88145edfc435c522df616215b1c0b0c9b7131767769960668dd28d8a03": {
10          "Name": "c1",
11          "EndpointID": "ee156f9601de95f77aec273edd8362ce22b4ab3a29460215d2c4538539d3ad0d",
12          "MacAddress": "02:42:ac:11:00:02",
13          "IPv4Address": "172.17.0.2/16",
14          "IPv6Address": ""
15      }
16  },
```

Figure 10.11 – The Containers section of the output of the Docker network inspect bridge

Once again, we have shortened the output to the relevant part for readability.

Now, let's create two additional containers, c3 and c4, and attach them to sample-net, which we created earlier. For this, we'll use the --network parameter:

```
$ docker container run --name c3 --rm -d \
    --network sample-net \
    alpine:latest ping 127.0.0.1

$ docker container run --name c4 --rm -d \
    --network sample-net \
    alpine:latest ping 127.0.0.1
```

Let's inspect the sample-net network and confirm that c3 and c4 are indeed attached to it:

```
$ docker network inspect sample-net
```

This will give us the following output for the Containers section:

```
 1   "Containers": {
 2       "852c4ff38de3c2029b25c4c6076a7bbb28aeea48eeea603d2c4eeccda0b50dc1": {
 3           "Name": "c3",
 4           "EndpointID": "36fff74b9b5138ffa04e1d031e5a0cd7a33b334289e9cf578c6dd885f3ad4a9f",
 5           "MacAddress": "02:42:ac:14:00:02",
 6           "IPv4Address": "172.20.0.2/16",
 7           "IPv6Address": ""
 8       },
 9       "cca95c07251705c33631fa8c08b3070fd3e79c1612dfa5c350b3fde97600a312": {
10           "Name": "c4",
11           "EndpointID": "0c4e0b4daf99e16d12957297d07d2f2c440c8252646d7a45794b0f7f3d64efbf",
12           "MacAddress": "02:42:ac:14:00:03",
13           "IPv4Address": "172.20.0.3/16",
14           "IPv6Address": ""
15       }
16   },
```

Figure 10.12 – The Containers section of the Docker network inspect test-net command

The next question we're going to ask ourselves is whether the c3 and c4 containers can freely communicate with each other. To demonstrate that this is indeed the case, we can exec into the c3 container:

```
$ docker container exec -it c3 /bin/sh
```

Once inside the container, we can try to ping container c4 by name and by IP address:

```
/ # ping c4
```

We should get this output:

```
PING c4 (172.20.0.3): 56 data bytes
64 bytes from 172.20.0.3: seq=0 ttl=64 time=3.092 ms
64 bytes from 172.20.0.3: seq=1 ttl=64 time=0.481 ms
...
```

Instead of the container name, here, we use c4's IP address:

```
/ # ping 172.20.0.3
```

We should see the following result:

```
PING 172.20.0.3 (172.20.0.3): 56 data bytes
64 bytes from 172.20.0.3: seq=0 ttl=64 time=0.200 ms
64 bytes from 172.20.0.3: seq=1 ttl=64 time=0.172 ms
...
```

The answer in both cases confirms to us that the communication between containers attached to the same network is working as expected. The fact that we can even use the name of the container we want to connect to shows us that the name resolution provided by the Docker DNS service works inside this network.

Now, we want to make sure that the bridge and sample-net networks are firewalled from each other. To demonstrate this, we can try to ping the c2 container from the c3 container, either by its name or by its IP address. Let's start with pinging by name:

```
/ # ping c2
```

This results in the following output:

```
ping: bad address 'c2'
```

The following is the result of the ping using the IP address of the c2 container instead:

```
/ # ping 172.17.0.3
```

It gives us this output:

```
PING 172.17.0.3 (172.17.0.3): 56 data bytes
^C
--- 172.17.0.3 ping statistics ---
11 packets transmitted, 0 packets received, 100% packet loss
```

The preceding command remained hanging and I had to terminate the command with *Ctrl + C*. From the output of pinging c2, we can also see that the name resolution does not work across networks. This is the expected behavior. Networks provide an extra layer of isolation, and thus security, to containers.

Earlier, we learned that a container can be attached to multiple networks. Let's first create a network called `test-net`. Note that the following command does not define the driver of the network; thus, the default driver is used, which happens to be the bridge driver:

```
$ docker network create test-net
```

Then, we attach a container, `c5`, to our `sample-net` network:

```
$ docker container run --name c5 --rm -d \
    --network sample-net
    alpine:latest ping 127.0.0.1
```

Then, we attach the `c6` container to the `sample-net` and `test-net` networks at the same time:

```
$ docker container run --name c6 --rm -d \
    --network sample-net \
    alpine:latest ping 127.0.0.1
$ docker network connect test-net c6
```

Now, we can test that `c6` is reachable from the `c5` container attached to the `test-net` network, as well as from the `c3` container attached to the `sample-net` network. The result will show that the connection indeed works.

If we want to remove an existing network, we can use the `docker network rm` command, but note that we cannot accidentally delete a network that has containers attached to it:

```
$ docker network rm test-net
```

It results in this output:

```
Error response from daemon: network test-net id 455c922e... has active
endpoints
```

Before we continue, let's clean up and remove all the containers:

```
$ docker container rm -f $(docker container ls -aq)
```

Now, we can remove the two custom networks that we created:

```
$ docker network rm sample-net
$ docker network rm test-net
```

Alternatively, we could remove all the networks that no container is attached to with the `prune` command:

```
$ docker network prune --force
```

I used the `--force` (or `-f`) argument here to prevent Docker from reconfirming that I really want to remove all unused networks.

Double-check with the docker network ls command that you are only left with the three default networks provided by Docker.

The next network types we are going to inspect a bit are the host and null network types.

The host and null networks

In this section, we are going to look at two predefined and somewhat unique types of networks, the host and the null networks. Let's start with the former.

The host network

There are occasions when we want to run a container in the network namespace of the host. This may be necessary when we need to run some software in a container that is used to analyze or debug the host network's traffic, but keep in mind that these are very specific scenarios. When running business software in containers, there is no good reason to ever run the respective containers attached to the host's network. For security reasons, it is strongly recommended that you do not run any such container attached to the host network in a production or production-like environment.

That said, how can we run a container inside the network namespace of the host? Simply by attaching the container to the host network:

1. Run an Alpine container and attach it to the host network:

    ```
    $ docker container run --rm -it \
        --network host \
        alpine:latest /bin/sh
    ```

2. Use the ip tool to analyze the network namespace from within the container. You will see that we get exactly the same picture as we would if we were running the ip tool directly on the host. For example, I inspect the eth0 device on my laptop with the following:

    ```
    / # ip addr show eth0
    ```

    As a result, I get this:

    ```
    / # ip addr show eth0
    8: eth0@if7: <BROADCAST,MULTICAST,UP,LOWER_UP,M-DOWN> mtu 1500 qdisc noqueue state UP
        link/ether de:36:11:0b:28:23 brd ff:ff:ff:ff:ff:ff
        inet 192.168.65.4 peer 192.168.65.5/32 scope global eth0
           valid_lft forever preferred_lft forever
        inet6 fe80::dc36:11ff:fe0b:2823/64 scope link
           valid_lft forever preferred_lft forever
    ```

    Figure 10.13 – Showing the eth0 device from inside a container

    Here, I can see that 192.168.65.3 is the IP address that the host has been assigned and that the MAC address shown here also corresponds to that of the host.

3. We can also inspect the routes:

```
/ # ip route
```

On my MacBook Air M1, this is what I get:

```
/ # ip route
default via 192.168.65.5 dev eth0
172.17.0.0/16 dev docker0 scope link  src 172.17.0.1
192.168.65.5 dev eth0 scope link  src 192.168.65.4
```

Figure 10.14 – Routes from within a container

Before we move on to the next section of this chapter, I want to once again point out that running a container on the host network can be dangerous due to potential security vulnerabilities and conflicts:

- **Security risks**: By using the host network, the container has the same network access as the host machine. This means that if an application running within the container has a vulnerability that is exploited, the attacker could gain access to the host network and potentially compromise other services or data.

- **Port conflicts**: When a container uses the host network, it shares the same network namespace as the host. This means that if your containerized application and a host application listen on the same port, there can be conflicts.

- **Isolation**: One of the major benefits of using Docker is the isolation it provides at various levels (process, filesystem, or network). By using the host network, you lose this level of isolation, which could lead to unforeseen issues.

Therefore, it's generally recommended to use a user-defined network instead of the host network when running Docker containers, as it provides better isolation and reduces the risk of conflicts and security vulnerabilities.

The null network

Sometimes, we need to run a few application services or jobs that do not need any network connection at all to execute the task at hand. It is strongly advised that you run those applications in a container that is attached to the none network. This container will be completely isolated and is thus safe from any outside access. Let's run such a container:

```
$ docker container run --rm -it \
    --network none \
    alpine:latest /bin/sh
```

Once inside the container, we can verify that there is no eth0 network endpoint available:

```
/ # ip addr show eth0
ip: can't find device 'eth0'
```

There is also no routing information available, as we can demonstrate by using the following command:

```
/ # ip route
```

This returns nothing.

In the following section, we are going to learn how we can run a container inside the existing network namespace of another container.

Running in an existing network namespace

Normally, Docker creates a new network namespace for each container we run. The network namespace of the container corresponds to the sandbox of the container network model we described earlier on. As we attach the container to a network, we define an endpoint that connects the container network namespace to the actual network. This way, we have one container per network namespace.

Docker provides an additional way for us to define the network namespace that a container runs in. When creating a new container, we can specify that it should be attached to (or maybe we should say included in) the network namespace of an existing container. With this technique, we can run multiple containers in a single network namespace:

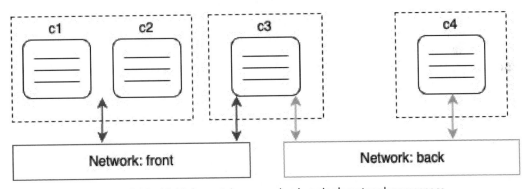

Figure 10.15 – Multiple containers running in a single network namespace

In the preceding diagram, we can see that in the leftmost network namespace, we have two containers. The two containers, since they share the same namespace, can communicate on localhost with each other. The network namespace (and not the individual containers) is then attached to the **front** network.

This is useful when we want to debug the network of an existing container without running additional processes inside that container. We can just attach a special utility container to the network namespace of the container to inspect. This feature is also used by Kubernetes when it creates a Pod. We will learn more about Kubernetes and Pods in subsequent chapters of this book.

Now, let's demonstrate how this works:

1. First, we create a new `bridge` network:

```
$ docker network create --driver bridge test-net
```

2. Next, we run a container attached to this network:

```
$ docker container run --name web -d \
    --network test-net \
    nginx:alpine
```

3. Finally, we run another container and attach it to the network of our web container:

```
$ docker container run -it --rm \
    --network container:web \
    alpine:latest /bin/sh
```

Specifically, note how we define the network: `--network container:web`. This tells Docker that our new container will use the same network namespace as the container called web.

4. Since the new container is in the same network namespace as the web container running nginx, we're now able to access nginx on `localhost`! We can prove this by using the wget tool, which is part of the Alpine container, to connect to nginx. We should see the following:

```
/ # wget -qO - localhost
<!DOCTYPE html>
<html>
<head>
<title>Welcome to nginx!</title>
...
</html>
```

Note that we have shortened the output for readability. Please also note that there is an important difference between running two containers attached to the same network and two containers running in the same network namespace. In both cases, the containers can freely communicate with each other, but in the latter case, the communication happens over `localhost`.

5. To clean up the container and network, we can use the following command:

```
$ docker container rm --force web
$ docker network rm test-net
```

In the next section, we are going to learn how to expose container ports on the container host.

Managing container ports

Now that we know how we can isolate firewall containers from each other by placing them on different networks, and that we can have a container attached to more than one network, we have one problem that remains unsolved. How can we expose an application service to the outside world? Imagine a container running a web server hosting our webAPI from before. We want customers from the internet to be able to access this API. We have designed it to be a publicly accessible API. To achieve this, we have to, figuratively speaking, open a gate in our firewall through which we can funnel external traffic to our API. For security reasons, we don't just want to open the doors wide; we want to have a single controlled gate that traffic flows through.

We can create this kind of gate by mapping a container port to an available port on the host. We're also calling this container port to publish a port. Remember that the container has its own virtual network stack, as does the host. Therefore, container ports and host ports exist completely independently and by default have nothing in common at all, but we can now wire a container port with a free host port and funnel external traffic through this link, as illustrated in the following diagram:

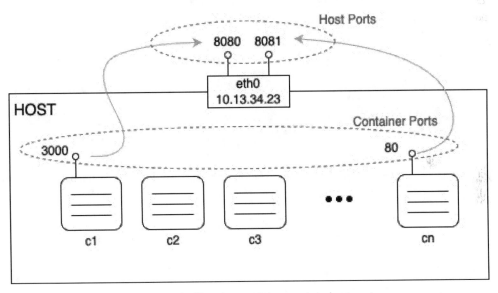

Figure 10.16 – Mapping container ports to host ports

But now, it is time to demonstrate how we can actually map a container port to a host port. This is done when creating a container. We have different ways of doing so:

1. First, we can let Docker decide which host port our container port should be mapped to. Docker will then select one of the free host ports in the range of 32xxx. This automatic mapping is done by using the -P parameter:

    ```
    $ docker container run --name web -P -d nginx:alpine
    ```

The preceding command runs an nginx server in a container. nginx is listening at port 80 inside the container. With the -P parameter, we're telling Docker to map all the exposed container ports to a free port in the 32xxx range. We can find out which host port Docker is using by using the docker container port command:

```
$ docker container port web
80/tcp -> 0.0.0.0:32768
```

The nginx container only exposes port 80, and we can see that it has been mapped to the host port 32768. If we open a new browser window and navigate to localhost:32768, we should see the following screen:

Figure 10.17 – The welcome page of nginx

2. An alternative way to find out which host port Docker is using for our container is to inspect it. The host port is part of the NetworkSettings node:

```
$ docker container inspect web | grep HostPort
        "HostPort": "32768"
```

3. Finally, the third way of getting this information is to list the container:

```
$ docker container ls
CONTAINER ID IMAGE ... PORTS NAMES
56e46a14b6f7 nginx:alpine ... 0.0.0.0:32768->80/tcp web
```

Please note that in the preceding output, the /tcp part tells us that the port has been opened for communication with the TCP protocol, but not for the UDP protocol. TCP is the default, and if we want to specify that we want to open the port for UDP, then we have to specify this explicitly. The special (IP) address, 0.0.0.0, in the mapping tells us that traffic from any host IP address can now reach container port 80 of the web container.

4. Sometimes, we want to map a container port to a very specific host port. We can do this by using the -p parameter (or --publish). Let's look at how this is done with the following command:

```
$ docker container run --name web2 -p 8080:80 -d nginx:alpine
```

The value of the -p parameter is in the form of <host port>:<container port>. Therefore, in the preceding case, we map container port 80 to host port 8080. Once the web2 container runs, we can test it in the browser by navigating to localhost:8080, and we should be greeted by the same nginx welcome page that we saw in the previous example that dealt with automatic port mapping.

When using the UDP protocol for communication over a certain port, the publish parameter will look like so: -p 3000:4321/udp. Note that if we want to allow communication with both TCP and UDP protocols over the same port, then we have to map each protocol separately.

In the next section, we will talk about HTTP routing using a reverse proxy.

HTTP-level routing using a reverse proxy

Imagine you have been tasked with containerizing a monolithic application. The application has organically evolved over the years into an unmaintainable behemoth. Changing even a minor feature in the source code may break other features due to the tight coupling that exists in the code base. Releases are rare due to their complexity and require the whole team to be on board. The application has to be taken down during the release window, which costs the company a lot of money due to lost opportunities, not to mention their loss of reputation.

Management has decided to put an end to that vicious cycle and improve the situation by containerizing the monolith. This alone will lead to a massively decreased time between releases, as witnessed within the industry. As a later step, the company wants to break out every piece of functionality from the monolith and implement it as a microservice. This process will continue until the monolith has been completely starved.

But it is this second point that leads to some head-scratching for the team involved. How will we break down the monolith into loosely coupled microservices without affecting all the many clients of the monolith out there? The public API of the monolith, though very complex, has a well-structured design. Public URIs were carefully crafted and should not be changed at any cost. For example, there is a product catalog function implemented in the app that can be accessed via https://acme.com/catalog?category=bicycles so that we can access a list of bicycles offered by the company.

On the other hand, there is a URL called https://acme.com/checkout that we can use to initiate the checkout of a customer's shopping cart, and so on. I hope it is clear where we are going with this.

Containerizing the monolith

Let's start with the monolith. I have prepared a simple code base that has been implemented in Python 3.7 and uses Flask to implement the public REST API. The sample app is not really a full-blown application but just complex enough to allow for some redesign. The sample code can be found in the ch10/e-shop folder. Inside this folder is a subfolder called monolith containing the Python application. Follow these steps:

1. In a new Terminal window, navigate to that folder, install the required dependencies, and run the application:

```
$ cd ~/The-Ultimate-Docker-Container-Book
$ cd ch10/e-shop/monolith
$ pip install -r requirements.txt
$ export FLASK_APP=main.py
$ flask run
```

The application will start and listen on localhost on port 5000:

```
→ monolith-solved git:(main) ✗ flask run
 * Serving Flask app 'main.py'
 * Debug mode: off
WARNING: This is a development server. Do not use it in a production deployment. Use a production WSGI server instead.
 * Running on http://127.0.0.1:5000
Press CTRL+C to quit
```

Figure 10.18 – Running the Python monolith

2. We can use curl to test the app. Open another Terminal window and use the following command to retrieve a list of all the bicycles the company offers:

```
$ curl localhost:5000/catalog?type=bicycle
```

This results in the following output:

```
[{"id": 1, "name": "Mountanbike Driftwood 24", "unitPrice":
199},
{"id": 2, "name": "Tribal 100 Flat Bar Cycle Touring Road Bike",
"unitPrice": 300}, {"id": 3, "name": "Siech Cycles Bike (58
cm)",
"unitPrice": 459}]
```

Here, we have a JSON-formatted list of three types of bicycles. OK – so far, so good.

3. Now, let's change the hosts file, add an entry for acme.com, and map it to 127.0.0.1, the loop-back address. This way, we can simulate a real client accessing the app at http://acme.com/catalog?type=bicycle instead of using localhost. You need to use sudo to edit the /etc/hosts file on a macOS or on Linux. You should add a line to the hosts file that looks like this:

```
127.0.0.1 acme.com
```

> **Windows host file**
>
> On Windows, you can edit the file by, for example, running Notepad as an administrator, opening the `c:\Windows\System32\Drivers\etc\hosts` file, and modifying it.

4. Save your changes and assert that it works by pinging `acme.com`:

```
$ ping acme.com
PING acme.com (127.0.0.1): 56 data bytes
64 bytes from 127.0.0.1: icmp_seq=0 ttl=55 time<1 ms
64 bytes from 127.0.0.1: icmp_seq=1 ttl=55 time<1 ms
64 bytes from 127.0.0.1: icmp_seq=2 ttl=55 time<1 ms
...
```

After all this, it is time to containerize the application. The only change we need to make to the application is ensuring that we have the application web server listening on `0.0.0.0` instead of `localhost`.

5. We can do this easily by modifying the application and adding the following start logic at the end of `main.py`:

```
if __name__ == '__main__':
    app.run(host='0.0.0.0', port=5000)
```

6. Then, we can start the application as follows:

```
$ python main.py.
```

7. Now, add a Dockerfile to the monolith folder with the following content:

```
1  FROM python:3.7-alpine
2  WORKDIR /app
3  COPY requirements.txt ./
4  RUN pip install -r requirements.txt
5  COPY . .
6  EXPOSE 5000
7  CMD python main.py
```

Figure 10.19 – The Dockerfile for the monolith

8. In your Terminal window, from within the monolith folder, execute the following command to build a Docker image for the application:

```
$ docker image build -t acme/eshop:1.0 .
```

9. After the image has been built, try to run the application:

```
$ docker container run --rm -it \
    --name eshop \
    -p 5000:5000 \
    acme/eshop:1.0
```

Notice that the output from the app now running inside a container is indistinguishable from what we got when running the application directly on the host. We can now test whether the application still works as before by using the two `curl` commands to access the catalog and the checkout logic:

```
● → The-Ultimate-Docker-Container-Book git:(main) x curl http://acme.com:5000/catalog\?type\=bicycle
[{"id": 1, "name": "Mountanbike Driftwood 24\"", "unitPrice": 199}, {"id": 2, "name": "Tribal 100 Flat Bar Cycl
e Touring Road Bike", "unitPrice": 300}, {"id": 3, "name": "Siech Cycles Bike (58 cm)", "unitPrice": 459}]
● → The-Ultimate-Docker-Container-Book git:(main) x curl http://acme.com:5000/checkout
Starting checkout of your shopping cart...
○ → The-Ultimate-Docker-Container-Book git:(main) x █
```

Figure 10.20 – Testing the monolith while running in a container

Evidently, the monolith still works exactly the same way as before, even when using the correct URL, that is, `http://acme.com`. Great! Now, let's break out part of the monolith's functionality into a Node.js microservice, which will be deployed separately.

Extracting the first microservice

The team, after some brainstorming, has decided that the catalog product is a good candidate for the first piece of functionality that is cohesive yet self-contained enough to be extracted from the monolith. They decide to implement the product catalog as a microservice implemented in Node.js.

You can find the code they came up with and the Dockerfile in the `catalog` subfolder of the project folder, that is, `e-shop`. It is a simple Express.js application that replicates the functionality that was previously available in the monolith. Let's get started:

1. In your Terminal window, from within the `catalog` folder, build the Docker image for this new microservice:

    ```
    $ docker image build -t acme/catalog:1.0 .
    ```

2. Then, run a container from the new image you just built:

    ```
    $ docker run --rm -it --name catalog -p 3000:3000 \
        acme/catalog:1.0
    ```

3. From a different Terminal window, try to access the microservice and validate that it returns the same data as the monolith:

    ```
    $ curl http://acme.com:3000/catalog?type=bicycle
    ```

Please notice the differences in the URL compared to when accessing the same functionality in the monolith. Here, we are accessing the microservice on port 3000 (instead of 5000).

But we said that we didn't want to have to change the clients that access our e-shop application. What can we do? Luckily, there are solutions to problems like this. We need to reroute incoming requests. We'll show you how to do this in the next section.

Using Traefik to reroute traffic

In the previous section, we realized that we would have to reroute incoming traffic with a target URL starting with `http://acme.com:5000/catalog` to an alternative URL such as `product-catalog:3000/catalog`. We will be using Traefik to do exactly that.

Traefik is a cloud-native edge router and it is open source, which is great for our specific case. It even has a nice web UI that you can use to manage and monitor your routes. Traefik can be combined with Docker in a very straightforward way, as we will see in a moment.

To integrate well with Docker, Traefik relies on the metadata found for each container or service. This metadata can be applied in the form of labels that contain the routing information:

1. First, let's look at how to run the `catalog` service. Here is the Docker run command:

```
$ docker container run --rm -d \
    --name catalog \
    --label traefik.enable=true \
    --label traefik.port=3000 \
    --label traefik.priority=10 \
    --label traefik.http.routers.catalog.rule=\
            "Host(\"acme.com\") && PathPrefix(\"/catalog\")" \
    acme/catalog:1.0
```

Let's quickly look at the four labels we define:

- `traefik.enable=true`: This tells Traefik that this particular container should be included in the routing (the default is `false`).

- `traefik.port=3000`: The router should forward the call to port 3000 (which is the port that the Express.js app is listening on).

- `traefik.priority=10`: This gives this route high priority. We will see why in a second.

- `traefik.http.routers.catalog.rule="Host(\"acme.com\") && PathPrefix(\"/catalog\")"`: The route must include the hostname, `acme.com`, and the path must start with `/catalog` in order to be rerouted to this service. As an example, `acme.com/catalog?type=bicycles` would qualify for this rule.

- Please note the special form of the fourth label. Its general form is `traefik.http.routers.<service name>.rule`.

2. Now, let's look at how we can run the `eshop` container:

```
$ docker container run --rm -d \
    --name eshop \
    --label traefik.enable=true \
    --label traefik.port=5000 \
    --label traefik.priority=1 \
    --label traefik.http.routers.eshop.rule=\
            "Host(\"acme.com\")" \
    acme/eshop:1.0
```

Here, we forward any matching calls to port `5000`, which corresponds to the port where the `eshop` application is listening. Pay attention to the priority, which is set to `1` (low). This, in combination with the high priority of the catalog service, allows us to filter out all URLs starting with `/catalog` and redirect them to the `catalog` service, while all other URLs will go to the `eshop` service.

3. Now, we can finally run Traefik as the edge router that will serve as a reverse proxy in front of our application. This is how we start it:

```
$ docker run -d \
    --name traefik \
    -p 8080:8080 \
    -p 80:80 \
    -v /var/run/docker.sock:/var/run/docker.sock \
    traefik:v2.0 --api.insecure=true --providers.docker
```

Note how we mount the Docker socket into the container using the `-v` (or `--volume`) parameter so that Traefik can interact with the Docker engine. We will be able to send web traffic to port `80` of Traefik, from where it will be rerouted according to our rules in the routing definitions found in the metadata of the participating container. Furthermore, we can access the web UI of Traefik via port `8080`.

4. Now that everything is running, that is, the monolith, the first microservice called `catalog`, and Traefik, we can test whether everything works as expected. Use `curl` once again to do so:

```
$ curl http://acme.com/catalog?type=bicycles
$ curl http://acme.com/checkout
```

As we mentioned earlier, we are now sending all traffic to port `80`, which is the port Traefik is listening on. This proxy will then reroute the traffic to the correct destination.

5. Before proceeding, stop and remove all containers:

```
$ docker container rm -f traefik eshop catalog
```

That's it for this chapter.

Summary

In this chapter, we learned about how containers running on a single host can communicate with each other. First, we looked at the CNM, which defines the requirements of a container network, and then we looked at several implementations of the CNM, such as the bridge network. We then looked at how the bridge network functions in detail and also what kind of information Docker provides us with about the networks and the containers attached to those networks. We also learned about adopting two different perspectives, from both outside and inside the container.

In the next chapter, we're going to introduce Docker Compose. We will learn about creating an application that consists of multiple services, each running in a container, and how Docker Compose allows us to easily build, run, and scale such an application using a declarative approach.

Further reading

Here are some articles that describe the topics that were presented in this chapter in more detail:

- *Docker networking overview*: `http://dockr.ly/2sXGzQn`
- *What is a bridge?*: `https://bit.ly/2HyC3Od`
- *Using bridge networks*: `http://dockr.ly/2BNxjRr`
- *Using Macvlan networks*: `http://dockr.ly/2ETjy2x`
- *Networking using the host network*: `http://dockr.ly/2F4aI59`

Questions

To assess the skills that you have gained from this chapter, please try to answer the following questions:

1. Name the three core elements of the **container network model** (**CNM**).
2. How do you create a custom `bridge` network called, for example, `frontend`?
3. How do you run two `nginx:alpine` containers attached to the frontend network?
4. For the frontend network, get the following:
   - The IPs of all the attached containers
   - The subnet associated with the network
5. What is the purpose of the `host` network?
6. Name one or two scenarios where the use of the `host` network is appropriate.
7. What is the purpose of the `none` network?

8. In what scenarios should the none network be used?

9. Why would we use a reverse proxy such as Traefik together with our containerized application?

Answers

Here are example answers for the questions of this chapter:

1. The three core elements of the Docker CNM are as follows:

    -   **Sandbox**: A network namespace for a container where its network stack resides

    -   **Endpoint**: An interface that connects a container to a network

    -   **Network**: A collection of endpoints that can communicate with each other directly

2. To create a custom Docker bridge network called frontend, you can use the docker network create command with the --driver flag set to bridge (which is the default driver) and the --subnet flag to specify the subnet for the network. Here's an example command:

    ```
    $ docker network create --driver bridge \
        --subnet 172.25.0.0/16 frontend
    ```

    This will create a bridge network named frontend with a subnet of 172.25.0.0/16. You can then use this network when starting containers with the --network option:

    ```
    $ docker run --network frontend <docker-image>
    ```

3. To run two nginx:alpine containers attached to the frontend network that we created earlier, you can use the following docker run commands:

    ```
    $ docker run --name nginx1 --network frontend -d nginx:alpine
    $ docker run --name nginx2 --network frontend -d nginx:alpine
    ```

    These commands will start two containers named nginx1 and nginx2 with the nginx:alpine image and attach them to the frontend network. The -d flag runs the containers in the background as daemons. You can then access the containers by their container names (nginx1 and nginx2) or their IP addresses within the frontend network.

4. Here is the solution:

    A. To get the IPs of all the containers attached to the frontend Docker network, you can use the docker network inspect command, followed by the network name. Here's an example command:

        ```
        $ docker network inspect frontend --format='{{range
        .Containers}}{{.IPv4Address}} {{end}}'
        ```

    B. This will output the IPv4 addresses of all the containers attached to the frontend network, separated by spaces.

    C.   To get the subnet associated with the `frontend` network, you can again use the `docker network inspect` command followed by the network name. Here's an example command:

```
$ docker network inspect frontend --format='{{json .IPAM.
Config}}' | jq -r '.[].Subnet'
```

    D.   This will output the subnet associated with the `frontend` network in CIDR notation (e.g., `172.25.0.0/16`). The `jq` command is used here to parse the output of the `docker network inspect` command and extract the subnet.

5.   The Docker `host` network is a networking mode that allows a Docker container to use the host's networking stack instead of creating a separate network namespace. In other words, containers running in `host` network mode can directly access the network interfaces and ports of the Docker host machine.

    The purpose of using the `host` network mode is to improve network performance since it avoids the overhead of containerization and network virtualization. This mode is often used for applications that require low-latency network communication or need to listen on a large number of ports.

    However, using the `host` network mode can also present security risks since it exposes the container's services directly on the Docker host's network interfaces, potentially making them accessible to other containers or hosts on the same network.

6.   The Docker `host` network mode is appropriate for scenarios where network performance is critical and where network isolation is not a requirement. For example, see the following:

- In cases where the containerized application needs to communicate with other services running on the host machine, such as a database or cache service, the use of the `host` network mode can improve performance by eliminating the need for **network address translation** (**NAT**) and routing between containers.

- In scenarios where the containerized application needs to listen on a large number of ports, the `host` network mode can simplify network configuration and management by allowing the container to use the same network interfaces and IP addresses as the host machine, without the need to manage port mapping between the container and host network namespaces.

7.   The purpose of the Docker `none` network is to completely disable networking for a container. When a container is started with the `none` network mode, it does not have any network interfaces or access to the network stack of the host machine. This means that the container cannot communicate with the outside world or any other container.

    The `none` network mode is useful in scenarios where the container does not require network connectivity, such as when running a batch process or a single-use container that performs a specific task and then exits. It can also be used for security purposes, to isolate the container from the network and prevent any potential network-based attacks.

It's important to note that when a container is started with the none network mode, it can still access its own filesystem and any volumes that are mounted to it. However, if the container requires network access later on, it must be stopped and restarted with a different network mode.

8. The Docker none network mode is useful in scenarios where the container does not require network connectivity, such as the following:

    - Running a batch process or a single-use container that performs a specific task and then exits

    - Running a container that does not need to communicate with other containers or the host machine

    - Running a container that has no need for external network access, such as a container that is used only for testing or debugging

    - Running a container that requires high security and isolation from the network

9. There are several reasons why we might use a reverse proxy such as Traefik together with our containerized application:

    - **Load balancing**: A reverse proxy can distribute incoming traffic across multiple instances of our application running on different containers, ensuring that no single instance becomes overwhelmed with requests.

    - **Routing**: With a reverse proxy, we can route incoming requests to the appropriate container based on the URL or domain name. This allows us to run multiple applications on the same host, each with its own unique domain or URL.

    - **SSL/TLS termination**: A reverse proxy can terminate SSL/TLS connections and handle certificate management, eliminating the need for our application to do this itself. This can simplify our application code and reduce the risk of security vulnerabilities.

    - **Security**: A reverse proxy can act as a buffer between our application and the public internet, providing an additional layer of security. For example, it can block certain types of traffic or filter out malicious requests.

    - **Scalability**: By using a reverse proxy such as Traefik, we can quickly and easily scale our application up or down by adding or removing containers. The reverse proxy can automatically route traffic to the appropriate containers, making it easy to manage our application's infrastructure.

11

Managing Containers with Docker Compose

In the previous chapter, we learned a lot about how container networking works on a single Docker host. We introduced the **Container Network Model** (**CNM**), which forms the basis of all networking between Docker containers, and then we dove deep into different implementations of the CNM, specifically the bridge network. Finally, we introduced Traefik, a reverse proxy to enable sophisticated HTTP application-level routing between containers.

This chapter introduces the concept of an application consisting of multiple services, each running in a container, and how Docker Compose allows us to easily build, run, and scale such an application using a declarative approach.

This chapter covers the following topics:

- Demystifying declarative versus imperative orchestration of containers
- Running a multi-service application
- Building images with Docker Compose
- Running an application with Docker Compose
- Scaling a service
- Building and pushing an application
- Using Docker Compose overrides

After completing this chapter, you will be able to do the following:

- Explain, in a few short sentences, the main differences between an imperative and declarative approach for defining and running an application
- Describe, in your own words, the difference between a container and a Docker Compose service

- Author a Docker Compose YAML file for a simple multi-service application
- Build, push, deploy, and tear down a simple multi-service application using Docker Compose
- Use Docker Compose to scale an application service up and down
- Define environment-specific Docker Compose files using overrides

Technical requirements

The code accompanying this chapter can be found at `https://github.com/PacktPublishing/The-Ultimate-Docker-Container-Book/tree/main/sample-solutions/ch11`.

Before we start, let's make sure we have a folder ready for the code you are going to implement in this chapter:

1. Navigate to the folder in which you cloned the previously listed code repository accompanying this book. Normally, this is the `The-Ultimate-Docker-Container-Book` folder in your home folder:

```
$ cd ~/The-Ultimate-Docker-Container-Book
```

2. Create a subfolder called `ch11` and navigate to it:

```
$ mkdir ch11 && cd ch11
```

In the past, you needed to have a separate docker-compose tool installed on your system. This is not the case anymore as the Docker CLI has recently been extended such that it contains all the functionality and more than the docker-compose tool previously offered.

If you are curious, you can find detailed installation instructions for the old `docker-compose` tool here: `https://docs.docker.com/compose/install/`.

Demystifying declarative versus imperative orchestration of containers

Docker Compose is a tool provided by Docker that is mainly used when you need to run and orchestrate containers running on a single Docker host. This includes, but is not limited to, development, **continuous integration (CI)**, automated testing, manual QA, or demos. Since very recently, Docker Compose is embedded in the normal Docker CLI.

Docker Compose uses files formatted in YAML as input. By default, Docker Compose expects these files to be called `docker-compose.yml`, but other names are possible. The content of a `docker-compose.yml` file is said to be a declarative way of describing and running a containerized application potentially consisting of more than a single container.

So, what is the meaning of declarative?

First of all, declarative is the antonym of imperative. Well, that doesn't help much. Now that I have introduced another definition, I need to explain both:

- **Imperative**: This is a way in which we can solve problems by specifying the exact procedure that has to be followed by the system.

  If I tell a system, such as the Docker daemon, imperatively how to run an application, then that means that I must describe, step by step, what the system has to do and how it must react if some unexpected situation occurs. I must be very explicit and precise in my instructions. I need to cover all edge cases and how they need to be treated.

- **Declarative**: This is a way in which we can solve problems without requiring the programmer to specify an exact procedure to be followed.

  A declarative approach means that I tell the Docker engine what my desired state for an application is and it has to figure out on its own how to achieve this desired state and how to reconcile it if the system deviates from it.

Docker clearly recommends the declarative approach when dealing with containerized applications. Consequently, the Docker Compose tool uses this approach.

Running a multi-service app

In most cases, applications do not consist of only one monolithic block, but rather of several application services that work together. When using Docker containers, each application service runs in its own container. When we want to run such a multi-service application, we can, of course, start all the participating containers with the well-known `docker container run` command, and we have done this in previous chapters. But this is inefficient at best. With the Docker Compose tool, we are given a way to define the application in a declarative way in a file that uses the YAML format.

Let's create and analyze a simple `docker-compose.yml` file:

1. Inside the chapter's folder (`ch11`), create a subfolder called `step1` and navigate to it:

    ```
    $ mkdir step1 && cd step1
    ```

2.   Inside this folder, add a file called `docker-compose.yml` and add the following snippet to it:

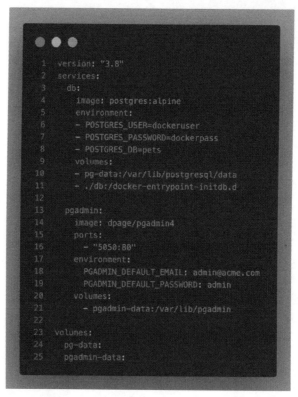

```
1   version: "3.8"
2   services:
3     db:
4       image: postgres:alpine
5       environment:
6         - POSTGRES_USER=dockeruser
7         - POSTGRES_PASSWORD=dockerpass
8         - POSTGRES_DB=pets
9       volumes:
10        - pg-data:/var/lib/postgresql/data
11        - ./db:/docker-entrypoint-initdb.d
12
13    pgadmin:
14      image: dpage/pgadmin4
15      ports:
16        - "5050:80"
17      environment:
18        PGADMIN_DEFAULT_EMAIL: admin@acme.com
19        PGADMIN_DEFAULT_PASSWORD: admin
20      volumes:
21        - pgadmin-data:/var/lib/pgadmin
22
23  volumes:
24    pg-data:
25    pgadmin-data:
```

Figure 11.1 – Simple Docker Compose file

The lines in the file are explained as follows:

- Line 1: `version` – On this line, we specify the version of the Docker Compose format we want to use. At the time of writing, this is version 3.8.

- Lines 2–21: `services` – In this section, we specify the services that make up our application in the `services` block. In our sample, we have two application services, and we call them db and pgadmin.

- Lines 3–11: db – The db service is using the image name `postgres:alpine`, which is the latest version of the Alpine Linux-based PostgreSQL database:

  - Line 4: `image` – Here, we define which Docker image to use for the service. As mentioned previously, we're using the curated `postgres` image with a tag of `alpine`. Since we're not specifying a version number, it will take the latest stable version of the Alpine-based PostgreSQL image.

- Lines 5–8: `environment` – Here, we are defining the environment variables that will be accessible from within the running PostgreSQL service. In this case, we define the default username, password, and database name.

- Lines 9–11: `volumes` – We are defining two volume mappings.

- Line 10: We are mapping a volume called `pg-data` to the `/var/lib/postgresql/data` container folder. This is where PostgreSQL by default stores the data. This way, the data is persisted into the `pg-data` volume and will survive a restart of the `db` service.

- Line 11: In this case, we are mapping the host folder, `./db`, into a container folder called `/docker-entrypoint-initdb.d`. This is the folder where PostgreSQL expects any initialization files that are run upon the first start of the database. In our case, we'll use it to define a database initialization script called `init-db.sql`.

- Lines 13–21: `pgadmin` – The `pgadmin` service uses a Docker image containing the popular administration tool for PostgreSQL and similar databases called `Pg4Admin`. We are mounting a volume called `pgadmin-data` into the container of the `db` service:

  - Line 14: `image` – This service is using the `dpage/pgadmin4` image. Note we're not defining any tags for the image, so we'll automatically work with the latest version.

  - Lines 15–16: `ports` – Here, we define which container ports we want to map to the host. In this case, we map the default `Pg4Admin` port `80` to the host port `5050`. This way, we can access the admin tool on this latter port from a browser window, as we will see shortly.

  - Lines 17–19: `environment` – Here, we are defining the environment variables that will be accessible from within the running `Pg4Admin` tool container. It is the email and password we will need to log in to the tool.

  - Lines 20–21: `volumes` – We are mapping a Docker volume called `pgadmin-data` to the `/var/lib/pgadmin` folder inside the container. This is the place where the tool stores its data and makes it possible to survive a restart of the tool container.

- Lines 23–25: `volumes` – The volumes used by any of the services must be declared in this section. In our sample, this is the last section of the file. The first time the application is run, volumes called `pg-data` and `pgadmin-data` will be created by Docker and then, in subsequent runs, if the volumes are still there, they will be reused. This could be important if the application, for some reason, crashes and must be restarted. Then, the previous data is still around and ready to be used by the restarted database service.

3. Create a folder called db in the step1 folder and add a file called init-db.sql to it with
    the following content:

```sql
1   CREATE TABLE images
2   (
3       imageid serial UNIQUE PRIMARY KEY,
4       description character varying(10485760) NOT NULL,
5       url character varying(255) NOT NULL
6   );
7
8   ALTER TABLE images
9       OWNER TO dockeruser;
10  ALTER ROLE dockeruser CONNECTION LIMIT -1;
11
12  -- add image data
13  INSERT INTO images (description, url) VALUES('vulture on tree', 'images/vulture.png');
14  INSERT INTO images (description, url) VALUES('female lions', 'images/3-female-lions.png');
15  INSERT INTO images (description, url) VALUES('antelopes', 'images/antelopes.png');
16  INSERT INTO images (description, url) VALUES('birds', 'images/birds.png');
17  INSERT INTO images (description, url) VALUES('buffalo', 'images/buffalo.png');
18  INSERT INTO images (description, url) VALUES('cheetah', 'images/cheetah.png');
19  INSERT INTO images (description, url) VALUES('elephants', 'images/elephants.png');
20  INSERT INTO images (description, url) VALUES('jackal', 'images/jackal.png');
21  INSERT INTO images (description, url) VALUES('giraffe', 'images/giraffe.png');
22  INSERT INTO images (description, url) VALUES('hippos', 'images/hippos.png');
23  INSERT INTO images (description, url) VALUES('male lion', 'images/male-lion.png');
24  INSERT INTO images (description, url) VALUES('zebra', 'images/zebra.png');
```

Figure 11.2 – Database initialization script

If you don't want to type in all of the preceding, you can find the file here: https://github.
com/PacktPublishing/The-Ultimate-Docker-Container-Book/blob/
main/sample-solutions/ch11/step1/db/init-db.sql. As you will see later,
this file will be used to initialize our database with some initial schema and some data.

4. Next, let's see how we can run the services with the help of Docker Compose. Execute the
    following command from within your step1 folder where the docker-compose.yml
    file resides:

```
$ docker compose up
```

Let's analyze the output generated by the preceding command:

- The first few lines are telling us that Docker is pulling the images for the db and
  pgadmin services

- The next few lines indicate that Docker is automatically creating a new network called step1_
  default

- Two volumes called step1_pgadmin-data and step1-pg-data

- Two container instances called step1-db-1 and step1-pgadmin-1

```
 # 4b376ac95f0c Pull complete
[+] Running 5/5
 # Network step1_default                    Created
 # Volume "step1_pgadmin-data"              Created
 # Volume "step1_pg-data"                   Created
 # Container step1-db-1                     Created
 # Container step1-pgadmin-1                Created
```

Figure 11.3 – Creating the resources for the Docker Compose application

Note the step1_ prefix added to all the preceding resources. This is the folder name within which the docker-compose.yml exists and from where the app was started, combined with the underscore character.

- Now, let's look at the third part of the output in blue. Here, the database is started up:

```
Attaching to step1-db-1, step1-pgadmin-1
step1-db-1    | The files belonging to this database system will be owned by user "postgres".
step1-db-1    | This user must also own the server process.
step1-db-1    |
step1-db-1    | The database cluster will be initialized with locale "en_US.utf8".
step1-db-1    | The default database encoding has accordingly been set to "UTF8".
step1-db-1    | The default text search configuration will be set to "english".
step1-db-1    |
step1-db-1    | Data page checksums are disabled.
step1-db-1    |
step1-db-1    | fixing permissions on existing directory /var/lib/postgresql/data ... ok
step1-db-1    | creating subdirectories ... ok
step1-db-1    | selecting dynamic shared memory implementation ... posix
step1-db-1    | selecting default max_connections ... 100
step1-db-1    | selecting default shared_buffers ... 128MB
step1-db-1    | selecting default time zone ... UTC
step1-db-1    | creating configuration files ... ok
step1-db-1    | running bootstrap script ... ok
step1-db-1    | sh: locale: not found
step1-db-1    | 2023-03-19 10:20:36.847 UTC [30] WARNING:  no usable system locales were found
step1-db-1    | performing post-bootstrap initialization ... ok
step1-db-1    | initdb: warning: enabling "trust" authentication for local connections
```

Figure 11.4 – Starting up the database

- The second part of the initialization of the database looks like this:

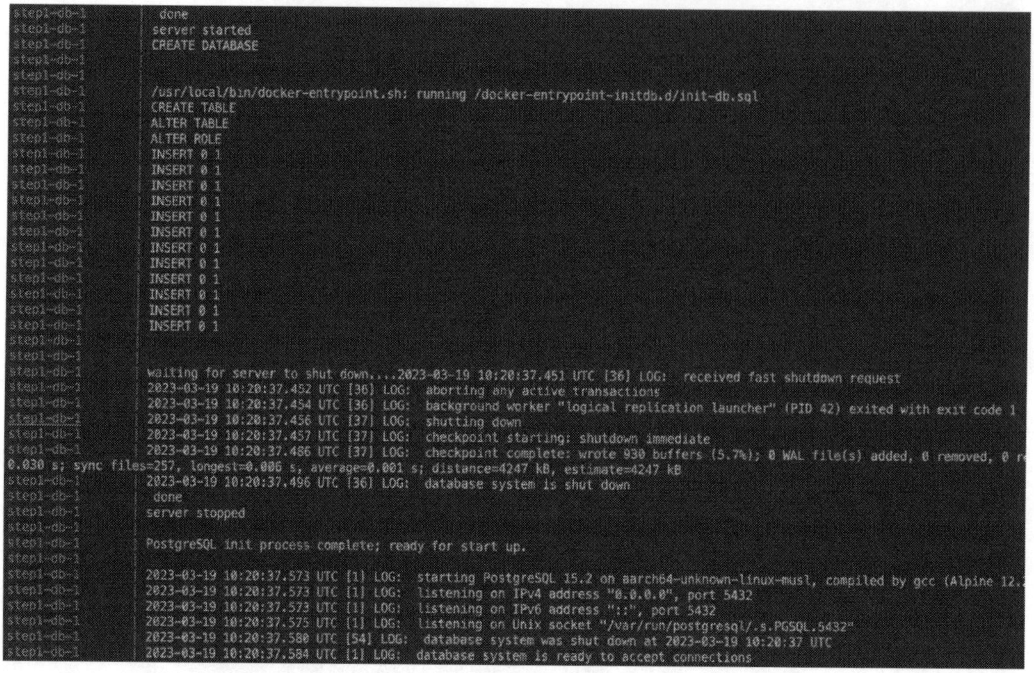

Figure 11.5 – Initializing the database using the provided script

- We have shortened the second part of the output a bit. It shows us how the database finalizes its initialization. We can specifically see how our initialization script, `init-db.sql`, is applied, which defines a database and seeds it with some data.

- The last line in the output tells us that the PostgreSQL database is now up and running and ready to accept an incoming connection. The connection is expected to happen at port 5432, as indicated by the fourth and fifth last lines in the preceding output.

Hint

If for some reason your volume mapping does not work – you may have a typo or so in the volume mapping part – you can start over by using the `docker compose down -v` command, where the `-v` parameter instructs Docker to remove any volumes associated with this application.

- Lastly, we have the initialization of the `pgamin` tool, shown in yellow:

```
step1-pgadmin-1  | NOTE: Configuring authentication for SERVER mode.
step1-pgadmin-1  |
step1-pgadmin-1  | pgAdmin 4 - Application Initialisation
step1-pgadmin-1  | ======================================
step1-pgadmin-1  |
step1-pgadmin-1  | [2023-03-19 10:20:44 +0000] [1] [INFO] Starting gunicorn 20.1.0
step1-pgadmin-1  | [2023-03-19 10:20:44 +0000] [1] [INFO] Listening at: http://[::]:80 (1)
step1-pgadmin-1  | [2023-03-19 10:20:44 +0000] [1] [INFO] Using worker: gthread
step1-pgadmin-1  | [2023-03-19 10:20:44 +0000] [91] [INFO] Booting worker with pid: 91
```

Figure 11.6 – Starting up the pgadmin tool

5. We are now ready to roll. Let's open a new browser window and navigate to `http://localhost:5050`. When asked, log in using the username (email) and password defined for the `pgadmin` tool in the `docker-compose.yml` file, namely `admin@acme.com` for the email and `admin` for the password. Add a server called `demo` and fill out the connection details as follows:

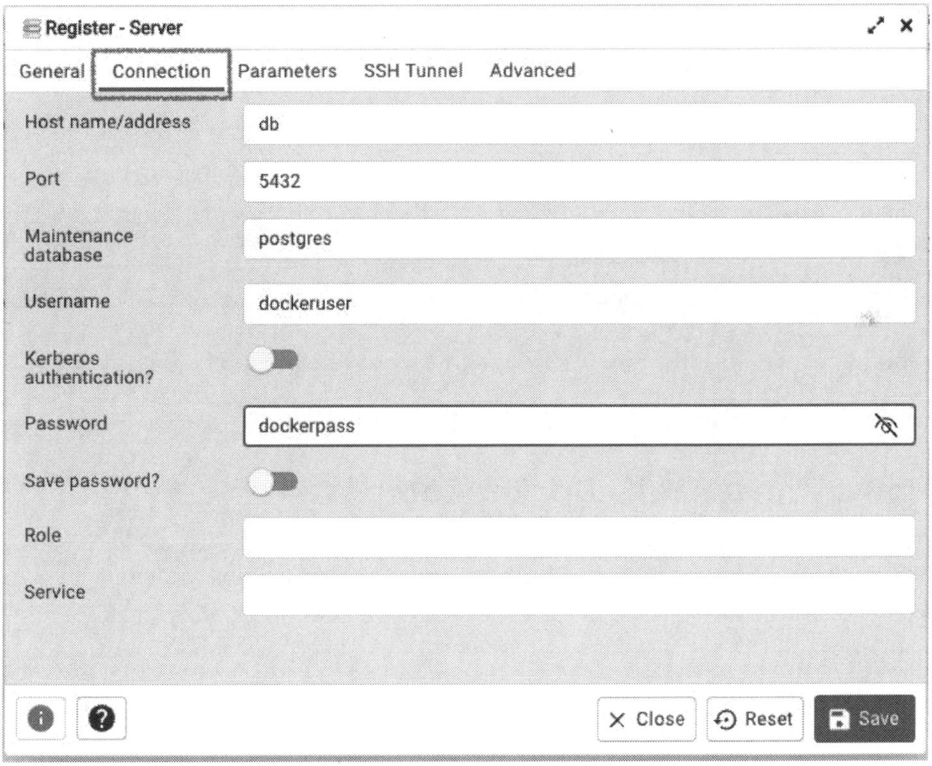

Figure 11.7 – Pg4Admin connection details

Note that the hostname/address, db, corresponds to the name of the database service in our docker-compose file. Port 5432 is the default port used by a PostgreSQL database and the username and password correspond to what we have defined in our docker-compose file for the database as well.

6. Once connected to the database, make sure that you can locate the pets database and within it the images table. Use the tool to retrieve all the records in the images table. You should find the 12 records that we defined in the init-db.sql initialization script.

7. Before you continue, you can stop the application by pressing *Ctrl + C* in the terminal window where the application still runs. After that, run the following:

```
$ docker compose down -v
```

This is to make sure the application container, the network, and the volumes are removed. You should see the following output in your terminal:

```
[+] Running 5/5
 ⁝⁝ Container step1-pgadmin-1    Removed              0.0s
 ⁝⁝ Container step1-db-1         Removed              0.0s
 ⁝⁝ Volume step1_pgadmin-data    Removed              0.0s
 ⁝⁝ Volume step1_pg-data         Removed              0.1s
 ⁝⁝ Network step1_default        Removed              0.1s
```

Specifically, notice the use of the -v command-line parameter, which tells Docker to forcibly remove volumes that were created and used by the application. Use this parameter wisely as it will destroy all data that has been persisted into those volumes.

Great, that worked. You have learned how to use the docker-compose.yml file to declaratively define an application made up of more than one service and start it with a simple docker compose up command.

Next, you will learn how you can use Docker Compose to build your own custom images.

Building images with Docker Compose

To demonstrate how to build a Docker image using Docker Compose, we need a small application. Proceed as follows:

1. In the chapter's folder (ch11), create a subfolder, step2, and navigate to it:

```
mkdir step2 && cd step2
```

2. From the previous exercise, copy the db folder containing the database initialization script to the step2 folder and also copy the docker-compose.yml file:

```
$ cp -r ../step1/db .
$ cp ../docker-compose.yml .
```

3. Create a folder called web in the step2 folder. This folder will contain a simple Express.js web application.

4. Add a file called package.json to the folder with this content:

```
1  {
2      "name": "wild-animals",
3      "version": "2.0.0",
4      "description": "Wild Animals of Massai Mara National Park",
5      "main": "src/server.js",
6      "scripts": {
7          "start": "node src/server.js"
8      },
9      "dependencies": {
10          "express": "^4.18.2",
11          "mustache-express": "^1.3.2",
12          "pg": "^8.10.0"
13      }
14  }
```

Figure 11.8 – The package.json file of the sample web application

> **Note**
>
> If you prefer not to type yourself, you can always download the files from the sample solution: https://github.com/PacktPublishing/The-Ultimate-Docker-Container-Book/tree/main/sample-solutions/ch11/step2.

5. Create a folder called src inside the web folder.

6.   Add a file called `server.js` to the `src` folder with this content:

```
1   const express = require('express');
2   const mustacheExpress = require('mustache-express');
3   const os = require('os');
4   const { Pool } = require('pg');
5
6   const app = express();
7   app.use(express.static('public'))
8   app.set('view engine', 'html');
9   app.engine('html', mustacheExpress());              // register file extension
10  app.set('views', __dirname);
11
12  const port = 3000;
13  const dbhost = process.env.DB_HOST || 'localhost';
14  console.log(`DB_HOST: ${dbhost}`);
15  const pool = new Pool({
16      host: dbhost,
17      user: 'dockeruser',
18      password: 'dockerpass',
19      database: 'pets',
20      port: 5432,
21  })
22
23  app.get('/', (req,res) => {
24      res.status(200).send('Wild Animals of Massai Mara National Park');
25  });
26
27  app.get('/images', async (req, res) => {
28      const result = await pool.query('SELECT * FROM images');
29      res.status(200).json({ info: result.rows });
30  })
31
32  app.get('/animal', async (req,res) => {
33      const imageId = getRandomInt(12) + 1;
34      const result = await pool.query('SELECT * FROM images WHERE imageid=$1', [imageId]);
35      const url = result.rows[0].url;
36      res.render('index', {
37              url: url,
38              hostname: os.hostname()
39          });
40  });
41
42  function getRandomInt(max) {
43      return Math.floor(Math.random() * Math.floor(max));
44  }
45
46  app.listen(port, '0.0.0.0', () => {
47      console.log(`Application listening on port ${port}`)
48  })
```

Figure 11.9 – The server.js file of the sample web application

This file contains the complete logic for our simple web application. Of interest is specifically the logic for the `/animal` endpoint on lines 32 to 40. Also note how we connect to the PostgreSQL database using a constant `pool` of type `Pool` (lines 15 to 21). The username, password, and database name should match the ones we define for the database.

7. Add another file called `index.html` to the `src` folder with this content:

```
1   <html>
2   <head>
3       <link rel="stylesheet" href="css/main.css">
4   </head>
5   <body>
6       <div class="container">
7           <h4>Animal of the day</h4>
8           <img src="{{url}}"" />
9           <p><small>Photo taken at <a href="https://www.maasaimara.com/">Massai Mara National Park</a></small></p>
10          <p>Delivered to you by container {{hostname}}<p>
11      </div>
12  </body>
13  </html>
```

Figure 11.10 – The index.html file of the sample web application

This file serves as a template to display the image of a wild animal.

8. Add a folder called `public/css` to the `web` folder:

```
mkdir -p public/css
```

9. Add a file called `main.css` to this `public/css` folder, which we will use to style our sample web application. Add this content to the file:

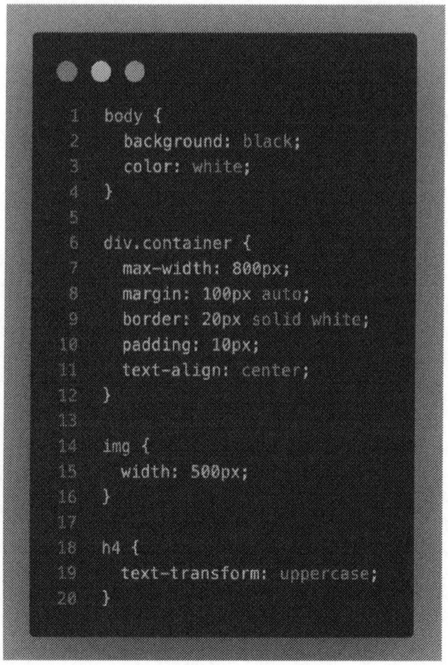

```
body {
  background: black;
  color: white;
}

div.container {
  max-width: 800px;
  margin: 100px auto;
  border: 20px solid white;
  padding: 10px;
  text-align: center;
}

img {
  width: 500px;
}

h4 {
  text-transform: uppercase;
}
```

Figure 11.11 – The main.css file of the sample web application

10. Now we need some real images to display. The easiest way is to copy our sample images from GitHub:

    A. Create a folder called `images` in the `public` folder.

    B. Then, download all images into this `images` folder, which you can find here: `https://github.com/PacktPublishing/The-Ultimate-Docker-Container-Book/tree/main/sample-solutions/ch11/step2/web/public/images`.

11. We now need to make a small addition to the `docker-compose.yml` file that we have copied from the `step1` folder. Locate the `docker-compose.yml` file in the `step2` folder, open it, and after line 4, add this snippet:

```
ports:
- 5432:5432
```

The result should look like this:

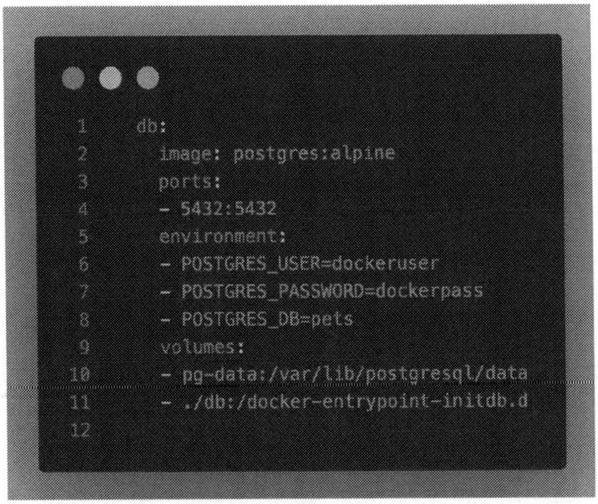

```
1    db:
2        image: postgres:alpine
3        ports:
4          - 5432:5432
5        environment:
6          - POSTGRES_USER=dockeruser
7          - POSTGRES_PASSWORD=dockerpass
8          - POSTGRES_DB=pets
9        volumes:
10          - pg-data:/var/lib/postgresql/data
11          - ./db:/docker-entrypoint-initdb.d
12
```

Figure 11.12 – Add host port mapping to the db service

This way, we can actually access the database from any application running on the host. We will use this possibility in the coming steps.

12. Now, we are ready to run and test this application:

A. Run the database using the docker-compose file and this command:

```
$ docker compose up db --detach
```

We are telling Docker Compose to only start the db service and to run it in detach mode, indicated by the --detach parameter.

B. Navigate to the web folder:

```
$ cd web
```

C. Install all dependencies with the following:

```
$ npm install
```

D. Run the application using the following:

```
$ npm run start
```

You should see this:

```
○ →  web git:(main) ✗ npm run start

> wild-animals@2.0.0 start
> node src/server.js

DB_HOST: localhost
Application listening on port 3000
```

Figure 11.13 – Running the web application natively

13. Open a browser tab and navigate to `http://localhost:3000/animal` and you should see something like this:

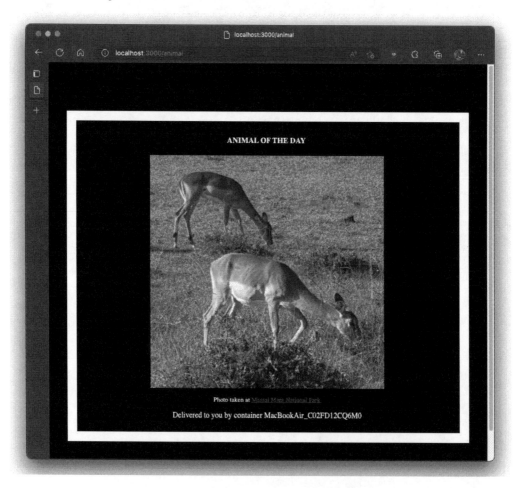

Figure 11.14 – The web application running and displaying a wild animal

14. Refresh the browser a few times and notice that each time, a new random animal is displayed.

15. Before you leave, make sure to stop the web application and stop the other containers with `docker compose down`.

Great, now we can move on to the next step, where we will Dockerize the web application and use Docker Compose to build the image:

1. Add a file called `Dockerfile` to the web folder and add this snippet:

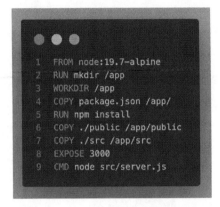

Figure 11.15 – Dockerfile for the web application

Analyze this Dockerfile and try to understand what it does exactly. Refer to what you learned in *Chapter 4, Creating and Managing Container Images*, if needed.

2. Open the `docker-compose.yml` file from the `step2` folder and add the definition of the web service, right after the `db` and `pgadmin` services and before the `volumes` section (that is, after line 24). The snippet to add should look like this:

```
1  web:
2     image: gnschenker/ch11-web:1.0
3     build: web
4     ports:
5     - 3000:3000
6     environment:
7     - DB_HOST=db
8     depends_on:
9     - db
10
```

Figure 11.16 – Defining the service called web in the docker-compose.yml file

Make sure that on line 2, you replace the `gnschenker` username with your own Docker Hub username.

3. Build the image using this command:

```
$ docker compose build web
```

The preceding command assumes that you are in the `step2` folder and that there is a `docker-compose.yml` file located in that folder.

When building the image, Docker looks for and uses a Dockerfile in the `web` folder, as instructed by the `build: web` instruction on line 3 in the preceding snippet.

To build images using Docker Compose, use the following instructions:

1. Open a terminal window.

2. Make sure that you are in the `ch11/step2` subfolder of the `The-Ultimate-Docker-Container-Book` folder:

```
$ cd ~/ The-Ultimate-Docker-Container-Book/ch11/step2
```

3. Then, build the images:

```
$ docker compose build
```

If we enter the preceding command, then the tool will assume that there must be a file in the current directory called `docker-compose.yml` and it will use that one to run. In our case, this is indeed the case, and the tool will build the images.

4. Observe the output in your terminal window. You should see something like this:

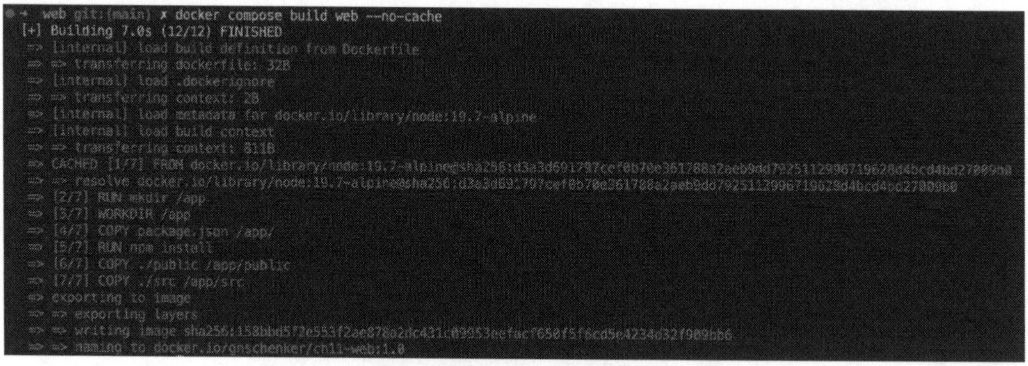

Figure 11.17 – Building the Docker image for the web service

In the preceding screenshot, you can see that docker-compose first downloads the base image, `node:19.7-alpine`, for the web image we're building from Docker Hub. Subsequently, it uses the Dockerfile found in the web folder to build the image and names it `gnschenker/ch11-web:2.0`.

After building the Docker image for the web service, we are ready to use Docker Compose to run the whole multi-service application.

Running an application with Docker Compose

Once we have built our images, we can start the application using Docker Compose:

```
$ docker compose up
```

The output, similar to the output we discussed in the previous section for the db and pgadmin services, will look as follows for the web service:

```
step2-web-1        | DB_HOST: db
step2-web-1        | Application listening on port 3000
```

This indicates that the containerized web service is ready and is listening on port 3000. Coincidentally, we have mapped container port 3000 to the same port 3000 on the host in our docker-compose.yml file. Thus, we can just open a new browser tab and navigate to the URL http://localhost:3000/animal; we should once again see a wild animal displayed.

Refresh the browser a few times to see other animal images. The application selects the current image randomly from a set of 12 images whose URLs are stored in the database.

As the application is running in interactive mode and, thus, the terminal where we ran Docker Compose is blocked, we can cancel the application by pressing *Ctrl + C*. If we do so, we will see the following:

```
^CGracefully stopping... (press Ctrl+C again to force)
Aborting on container exit...
[+] Running 3/3
⠿ Container step2-pgadmin-1   Stopped                          1.4s
⠿ Container step2-web-1       Stopped                         10.2s
⠿ Container step2-db-1        Stopped                          0.1s
canceled
```

We will notice that the db and web services stop immediately. Sometimes, though, some services will take about 10 seconds to do so. The reason for this is that the db and the web service listen, and react, to the SIGTERM signal sent by Docker, while other services might not, and so Docker kills them after a predefined timeout interval of 10 seconds.

If we run the application again with docker compose up, the startup will be much faster as the database didn't have to initialize from scratch, but it was just reusing the data that was already present in the pg-data volume from the previous run.

We can also run the application in the background. All containers will run as daemons. For this, we just need to use the -d parameter, as shown in the following code:

```
$ docker compose up -d
```

Docker Compose offers us many more commands than just up. We can also use the tool to list all services that are part of the application:

```
$ docker compose ps
```

We should see this:

Figure 11.18 – Output of docker compose ps

This command is similar to docker container ls, with the only difference being that docker-compose only lists containers or services that are part of the application.

To stop and clean up the application, we use the docker compose down command:

```
$ docker compose down
```

This should result in an output similar to this:

```
⁝ Container step2-web-1       Removed                                    10.2s
⁝ Container step2-pgadmin-1   Removed                                     0.9s
⁝ Container step2-db-1        Removed                                     0.1s
⁝ Network step2_default       Removed                                     0.1s
```

If we also want to remove the volumes for the database, then we can use the following command:

```
$ docker volume rm step2_pd-data step2_pgadmin-data
```

Alternatively, instead of using the two commands, docker compose down and docker volume rm <volume name>, we can combine them into a single command:

```
$ docker compose down -v
```

Here, the argument -v (or --volumes) removes named volumes declared in the volumes section of the Docker Compose file and anonymous volumes attached to containers.

Why is there a `step2` prefix in the name of the volume? In the `docker-compose.yml` file, we have called the volumes to use `pg-data` and `pgadmin-data`. But, as we have already mentioned, Docker Compose prefixes all names with the name of the parent folder of the `docker-compose.yml` file plus an underscore. In this case, the parent folder is called `step2`. If you don't like this approach, you can define a project name explicitly, for example, as follows:

```
$ docker compose  --project-name demo up --detach
```

This way, all resources (containers, networks, and volumes) will be prefixed by the project name, in this case, called `demo`.

Scaling a service

Now, let's, for a moment, assume that our sample application has been live on the web and become very successful. Loads of people want to see our cute animal images. But now we're facing a problem: our application has started to slow down. To overcome this problem, we want to run multiple instances of the web service. With Docker Compose, this is readily done.

Running more instances is also called scaling out. We can use this tool to scale our `web` service up to, say, three instances:

```
$ docker compose up --scale web=3
```

If we do this, we are in for a surprise. The output will look as in the following screenshot:

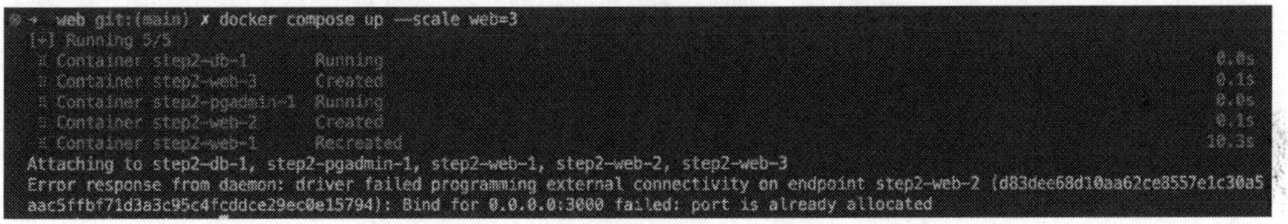

Figure 11.19 – Output of docker-compose --scale

The second and third instances of the `web` service fail to start. The error message tells us why we cannot use the same host port, `3000`, more than once. When instances 2 and 3 try to start, Docker realizes that port `3000` is already taken by the first instance. What can we do? Well, we can just let Docker decide which host port to use for each instance.

If, in the `ports` section of the Docker Compose file, we only specify the container port and leave out the host port, then Docker automatically selects an ephemeral port. Let's do exactly this:

1. First, let's tear down the application:

```
$ docker compose down
```

2. Then, we modify the `docker-compose.yml` file. The port mapping of the web service originally looks like this:

```
ports:
- 3000:3000
```

We change it to simply the following:

```
ports:
- 3000
```

This way, Docker will allocate the host port dynamically.

3. Now, we can start the application again and scale it up immediately after that:

```
$ docker compose up -d
$ docker compose up -d --scale web=3
```

And we should see this:

```
[+] Running 5/5
 :: Container step2-pgadmin-1   Started                    0.3s
 :: Container step2-db-1        Started                    0.3s
 :: Container step2-web-1       Started                    0.6s
 :: Container step2-web-3       Started                    0.8s
 :: Container step2-web-2       Started                    1.0s
```

4. If we now execute `docker compose ps`, we should see what is in the following screenshot:

Figure 11.20 – Output of the docker compose ps command

Note that in your case, the host ports may be different than those shown in the preceding screenshot. There, we have a mapping to ports `590076`, `59078`, and `59077` for the three instances of `web`.

5. We can try to see whether those port mappings work, for example, using `curl`. Let's test the third instance, `step2_web-3`:

```
$ curl -4 localhost:59077
```

We should see the following:

```
Wild Animals of Massai Mara National Park%
```

The answer tells us that, indeed, our application is still working as expected. Try it out for the other two instances to be sure.

In the next section, we are going to learn how to build and subsequently push the application container images to an image registry.

Building and pushing an application

We saw earlier that we can also use the `docker-compose build` command to just build the images of an application defined in the underlying `docker-compose` file. But to make this work, we'll have to add the build information to the `docker-compose` file:

1. Open a new browser window and navigate to the chapter's folder (`ch11`):

    ```
    $ cd ~/The-Ultimate-Docker-Container-Book/ch11
    ```

2. Create a subfolder called `step3` and navigate to it:

    ```
    $ mkdir step3 && cd step3
    ```

3. Copy the `docker-compose.yml` file from the `step2` folder to this new folder:

    ```
    $ cp ../step2/docker-compose.yml .
    ```

4. Open the copied file and please note the `build` key for the web service on line 3 in the following screenshot. The value of that key indicates the context or folder where Docker is expecting to find the Dockerfile to build the corresponding image.

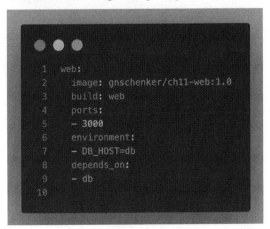

Figure 11.21 – The build key in the web service of the docker-compose.yml file

Please note the `depends_on` section on lines 8 and 9. This instructs Docker Compose to make sure that the `db` service is started before the `web` service.

5. If we wanted to use a Dockerfile that is named differently, say `Dockerfile.dev`, for the web service, then the `build` block in the `docker-compose` file would look like this:

```
build:
    context: web
    dockerfile: Dockerfile.dev
```

A. Copy the `web` and the `db` folder and their contents from the `step2` folder into the `step3` folder:

```
$ cp -r ../step2/web .
$ cp -r ../step2/db .
```

B. Create a file called `Dockerfile.dev` in the `web` folder, which is just a copy of the existing Dockerfile:

```
$ cp web/Dockerfile web/Dockerfile.dev
```

C. To the `step3` folder, add a new file, `docker-compose.dev.yml`, which is a copy of the `docker-compose.yml` file:

```
$ cp ../step2/docker-compose.yml docker-compose.dev.yml
```

D. Modify the `build` block according to the preceding snippet.

6. Let's use that alternative `docker-compose.dev.yml` file now:

```
$ docker-compose -f docker-compose.dev.yml build
```

The `-f` parameter will tell the Docker Compose application which Docker Compose file to use.

7. To push all images to Docker Hub, we can use `docker compose push`:

A. We need to be logged in to Docker Hub so that this succeeds; otherwise, we get an authentication error while pushing. Thus, in my case, I do the following:

```
$ docker login -u gnschenker -p <password>
```

B. Assuming the login succeeds, I can then push the following code:

```
$ docker-compose -f docker-compose.dev.yml push
```

This may take a while, depending on the bandwidth of your internet connection. While pushing, your screen may look like this:

```
● →  step3 git:(main) x docker compose -f docker-compose.dev.yml push
[+] Running 2/12
 ⋮ db Skipped
 ⋮ pgadmin Skipped
 ⋮ Pushing web: d05f4f266045 Pushed
 ⋮ Pushing web: 867f76229ddd Pushed
 ⋮ Pushing web: f55045ef6e3f Pushed
 ⋮ Pushing web: 8d457daa88e7 Pushed
 ⋮ Pushing web: 5f70bf18a086 Mounted from axoniq/axonserver
 ⋮ Pushing web: e4eae9e23651 Pushed
 ⋮ Pushing web: fcc2e8e52b6c Mounted from library/node
 ⋮ Pushing web: f3d76c8a1bb5 Mounted from library/node
 ⋮ Pushing web: fe3516b3bd7c Mounted from library/node
 ⋮ Pushing web: edf70074bd40 Mounted from dpage/pgadmin4
```

Figure 11.22 – Pushing images with docker-compose to Docker Hub

The preceding command pushes the Docker image for the web service to the gnschenker account on Docker Hub. The other two services, db and pgadmin, in the Docker Compose file are ignored.

> **Note**
>
> Make sure you are using your own Docker Hub account instead of gnschenker.

The last feature of Docker Compose we want to discuss is overrides.

Using Docker Compose overrides

Sometimes, we want to run our applications in different environments that need specific configuration settings. Docker Compose provides a handy capability to address exactly this issue.

Let's illustrate the with a specific sample:

1. Open a new browser window and navigate to the chapter's folder (ch11):

    ```
    $ cd ~/The-Ultimate-Docker-Container-Book/ch11
    ```

2. Create a subfolder called step4 and navigate to it:

    ```
    $ mkdir step4 && cd step4
    ```

3. Copy the web and db folder and their contents from the step2 folder into the step4 folder:

    ```
    $ cp -r ../step2/web .
    $ cp -r ../step2/db .
    ```

4. We can define a base Docker Compose file and then define environment-specific overrides. Let's assume we have a file called `dockercompose.base.yml` with the following content:

```
1   version: "3.8"
2   services:
3     db:
4       image: postgres:alpine
5       volumes:
6       - pg-data:/var/lib/postgresql/data
7       - ./db:/docker-entrypoint-initdb.d
8
9     pgadmin:
10      image: dpage/pgadmin4
11      volumes:
12        - pgadmin-data:/var/lib/pgadmin
13
14    web:
15      image: gnschenker/ch11-web:1.0
16      depends_on:
17      - db
18
19  volumes:
20    pg-data:
21    pgadmin-data:
```

Figure 11.23 – Docker Compose file used as a base

This only defines the part that should be the same in all environments. All specific settings have been taken out.

5. Now assume we want to run the application in **Continuous Integration** (**CI**). Let's call the corresponding override file `docker-compose.ci.yml` and add this snippet of code:

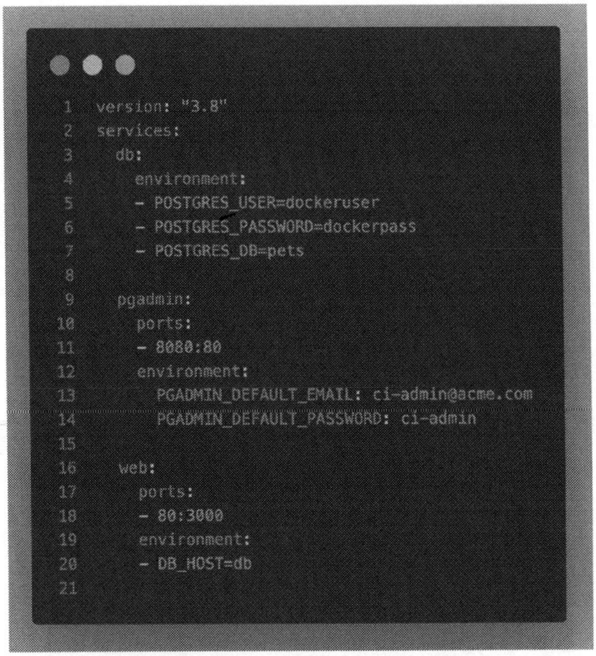

```
version: "3.8"
services:
  db:
    environment:
      - POSTGRES_USER=dockeruser
      - POSTGRES_PASSWORD=dockerpass
      - POSTGRES_DB=pets

  pgadmin:
    ports:
      - 8080:80
    environment:
      PGADMIN_DEFAULT_EMAIL: ci-admin@acme.com
      PGADMIN_DEFAULT_PASSWORD: ci-admin

  web:
    ports:
      - 80:3000
    environment:
      - DB_HOST=db
```

Figure 11.24 – Docker Compose file for CI

6.   We can run this application with the following command:

```
$ docker compose -f docker-compose.base.yml \
    -f docker-compose.ci.yml up \
    -d --build
```

Note that with the first -f parameter, we provide the base Docker Compose file, and with the second one, we provide the override. The --build parameter instructs Docker Compose to rebuild all Docker images before starting them.

Warning

When using environment variables, note the following:

1) Declaring them in the Docker file defines a default value

2) Declaring the same variable in the Docker Compose file overrides the value from the Dockerfile

---

With this, we have reached the end of this chapter about Docker Compose. But before we finish, we have the following tip for you.

> **Tip**
>
> Had we followed the standard naming convention and called the base file just `docker-compose.yml` and the override file `docker-compose.overrid.yml` instead, then we could have started the application with `docker-compose up -d` without explicitly naming the Docker Compose files. In any other case, we need to use the following full and more verbose syntax:
>
> ```
> $ docker compose -f <base compose file> -f <override compose file> up
> ```

Summary

In this chapter, we introduced the docker-compose tool. This tool is mostly used to run and scale multi-service applications on a single Docker host. Typically, developers and CI servers work with single hosts, and those two are the main users of Docker Compose. The tool uses YAML files as input, which contain the description of the application in a declarative way.

The tool can also be used to build and push images, among many other helpful tasks.

In the next chapter, we will discuss why logging and monitoring is important and show how container logs can be collected and shipped to a central location where the aggregated logs can then be parsed to gain useful information.

You will also learn how to instrument an application, so that it exposes metrics, and how those metrics can be scraped and shipped again to a central location. Finally, you will learn how to convert those collected metrics into graphical dashboards that can be used to monitor a containerized application.

Further reading

The following links provide additional information on the topics discussed in this chapter:

- *The official YAML website*: `http://www.yaml.org/`

- *The Docker Compose documentation*: `http://dockr.ly/1FL2VQ6`

- *Docker Compose file version 2 reference*: `https://docs.docker.com/compose/compose-file/compose-file-v2/`

- *Docker Compose file version 3 reference*: `https://docs.docker.com/compose/compose-file/compose-file-v3/`

- *Share Docker Compose configurations between files and projects*: `https://docs.docker.com/compose/extends/`

Questions

To assess your learning of Docker Compose, please answer the following questions:

1. What is Docker Compose, and what is it used for?

2. What is a Docker Compose file, and what are some of the key elements it can contain?

3. How can you use Docker Compose to start and stop an application, and what are some of the key command-line options?

4. What are some of the benefits of using Docker Compose to manage multi-container applications?

5. How do you use docker-compose to run an application in daemon mode?

6. How do you use docker-compose to display the details of the running service?

7. How do you scale up a particular web service to, say, three instances?

Answers

Here are some sample answers to the questions of *Chapter 11*:

1. Docker Compose is a tool for defining and running multi-container Docker applications. It allows you to define the services that make up your application in a YAML file, and then run and manage those services with a single command.

2. A Docker Compose file is a YAML file that defines the services that make up a Docker application, along with any associated configuration options. Some of the key elements that a Docker Compose file can contain include the following:

    - `version`: The version of the Docker Compose file syntax to use. This field is mandatory.

    - `services`: A list of the services that make up the application, along with any associated configuration options.

    - `ports`: A list of ports that need to be opened for the respective service and mapped to a corresponding container port.

    - `networks`: Any custom networks that need to be created for the application. Note that a service can be attached to more than one network at the same time.

    - `volumes`: Any volumes that need to be created for the application.

    Here is a (shortened) example `docker-compose.yml` file using more than one network:

    ```
    services:
      web:
        image: <some image>
        network:
    ```

```
       - front
  accounting:
    image: <some other image>
    network:
    - front
    - back
  db:
    image: postgres:latest
    network:
    - back
networks:
  front:
  back:
```

3. To start an application with Docker Compose, you can use the `docker compose up` command. This command reads the Docker Compose file, creates any necessary containers, and starts the services. To stop an application, you can use the `docker compose down` command. Some of the key command-line options that can be used with these commands include the following:

    - `-d` or `--detach`: Run containers in the background and print new container names

    - `-p` or `--project-name`: Specify an alternate project name

    - `--build`: Build images before starting containers

4. Some of the benefits of using Docker Compose to manage multi-container applications include the following:

    - **Simplifying the deployment process**: Docker Compose allows you to define your application's services and configurations in a single file, which can simplify the deployment process and make it easier to manage complex applications

    - **Enabling collaboration**: By using a Docker Compose file to define an application, developers can easily share their development environments with others and collaborate more effectively

    - **Enabling portability**: Docker Compose allows you to define an application's environment and dependencies in a portable way, which can make it easier to move applications between different environments and infrastructure providers

5. To run the application services in daemon (or `detach`) mode, use the following:

```
$ docker compose up --detach
```

6. To display the details of the running services in a Docker Compose application, use the following:

```
$ docker compose ps
```

7. To scale, for example, the web service of a Docker Compose application to three instances, use the following command:

```
$ docker compose up web --scale 3
```

12

Shipping Logs and Monitoring Containers

In the previous chapter, we introduced the Docker Compose tool. We learned that this tool is mostly used to run and scale multi-service applications on a single Docker host. Typically, developers and CI servers work with single hosts and they are the main users of Docker Compose. We saw that the tool uses YAML files as input, which contain the description of the application in a declarative way. We investigated many useful tasks the tool can be used for, such as building and pushing images, to just name the most important ones.

This chapter discusses why logging and monitoring are so important and shows how container logs can be collected and shipped to a central location where the aggregated log can then be parsed for useful information.

You will also learn how to instrument an application so that it exposes metrics and how those metrics can be scraped and shipped again to a central location. Finally, you will learn how to convert those collected metrics into graphical dashboards that can be used to monitor a containerized application.

We will be using Filebeat as an example to collect logs from a default location where Docker directs the logs at `/var/lib/docker/containers`. This is straightforward on Linux. Luckily, on a production or production-like system, we mostly find Linux as the OS of choice.

Collecting metrics on a Windows or Mac machine, on the other hand, is a bit more involved than on a Linux machine. Thus, we will generate a special Docker Compose stack, including Filebeat, that can run on a Mac or Windows computer by using the workaround of redirecting the standard log output to a file whose parent folder is mapped to a Docker volume. This volume is then mounted to Filebeat, which, in turn, forwards the logs to Elasticsearch.

This chapter covers the following topics:

- Why is logging and monitoring important?
- Shipping container and Docker daemon logs
- Querying a centralized log
- Collecting and scraping metrics
- Monitoring a containerized application

After reading this chapter, you should be able to do the following:

- Define a log driver for your containers
- Install an agent to collect and ship your container and Docker daemon logs
- Execute simple queries in the aggregate log to pinpoint interesting information
- Instrument your application services so that they expose infrastructure and business metrics
- Convert the collected metrics into dashboards to monitor your containers

Technical requirements

The code accompanying this chapter can be found at `https://github.com/PacktPublishing/The-Ultimate-Docker-Container-Book/tree/main/sample-solutions/ch12`.

Before we start, let's make sure you have a folder ready for the code you are going to implement in this chapter.

Navigate to the folder where you cloned the code repository that accompanies this book. Normally, this is the `The-Ultimate-Docker-Container-Book` folder in your home folder:

```
$ cd ~/The-Ultimate-Docker-Container-Book
```

Create a subfolder called `ch12` and navigate to it:

```
$ mkdir ch12 && cd ch12
```

Without further ado, let's dive into the first topic of shipping containers and daemon logs.

Why is logging and monitoring important?

When working with a distributed mission-critical application in production or any production-like environment, it is of utmost importance to gain as much insight as possible into the inner workings of those applications. Have you ever had a chance to investigate the cockpit of an airplane or the command center of a nuclear power plant? Both, an airplane and a power plant are examples of highly complex systems that deliver mission-critical services. If a plane crashes or a power plant shuts down unexpectedly, a lot of people are negatively affected, to say the least. Thus, the cockpit and the command center are full of instruments showing the current or past state of some parts of the system. What you see there is the visual representation of some sensors that are placed in strategic parts of the system and constantly collect data such as the temperature or the flow rate.

Similar to an airplane or a power plant, our application needs to be instrumented with "sensors" that can feel the "temperature" of our application services or the infrastructure they run on. I put the word temperature in double quotes since it is only a placeholder for things that matter in an application, such as the number of requests per second on a given RESTful endpoint, or the average latency of requests to the same endpoint.

The resulting values or readings that we collect, such as the average latency of requests, are often called **metrics**. It should be our goal to expose as many meaningful metrics as possible of the application services we build. Metrics can be both functional and non-functional. Functional metrics are values that say something business-relevant about the application service, such as how many checkouts are performed per minute if the service is part of an e-commerce application, or what are the 5 most popular songs over the last 24 hours if we are talking about a streaming application.

Non-functional metrics are important values that are not specific to the kind of business the application is used for, such as the average latency of a particular web request, how many 4xx status codes are returned per minute by another endpoint, or how much RAM or how many CPU cycles a given service is consuming.

In a distributed system where each part is exposing metrics, some overarching service should be collecting and aggregating the values periodically from each component. Alternatively, each component should forward its metrics to a central metrics server. Only if the metrics for all components of our highly distributed system are available for inspection in a central location are they of any value. Otherwise, monitoring the system becomes impossible. That's why pilots of an airplane never have to go and inspect individual and critical parts of the airplane in person during a flight; all necessary readings are collected and displayed in the cockpit.

Today, one of the most popular services that is used to expose, collect, and store metrics is **Prometheus**. It is an open source project and has been donated to the **Cloud Native Computing Foundation (CNCF)**. Prometheus has first-class integration with Docker containers, Kubernetes, and many other systems and programming platforms. In this chapter, we will use Prometheus to demonstrate how to instrument a simple service that exposes important metrics.

In the next section, we are going to show you how to ship containers and Docker daemon logs to a central location.

Shipping containers and Docker daemon logs

In the world of containerization, understanding the logs generated by your Docker environment is crucial for maintaining a healthy and well-functioning system. This section will provide an overview of two key types of logs you will encounter: shipping **container logs** and **Docker daemon logs**.

Shipping container logs

As applications run within containers, they generate log messages that provide valuable insights into their performance and any potential problems.

Container logs can be accessed using the `docker logs` command, followed by the container's ID or name. These logs can help developers and system administrators diagnose issues, monitor container activities, and ensure the smooth operation of deployed applications. Centralizing and analyzing container logs is essential for optimizing resource usage, identifying performance bottlenecks, and troubleshooting application issues.

Some best practices for managing shipping container logs include the following:

- Configuring log rotation and retention policies to prevent excessive disk space usage
- Using a log management system to centralize logs from multiple containers
- Setting up log filtering and alerting mechanisms to identify critical events and anomalies

Let's look at these recommendations in detail, starting with log rotation and retention policies.

Configuring log rotation and retention policies

Configuring log rotation and retention policies for container logs is essential for preventing excessive disk space usage and maintaining optimal performance. Here's a step-by-step guide on how to set up these policies for Docker container logs.

Configuring the logging driver

Docker supports various logging drivers, such as `json-file`, `syslog`, `journald`, and more. To configure the logging driver, you can either set it up globally for the entire Docker daemon or individually for each container. For this example, we'll use the `json-file` logging driver, which is the default driver for Docker.

Globally setting the log driver

To set the logging driver globally, edit the `/etc/docker/daemon.json` configuration file (create it if it doesn't exist) and do the following:

1. Open the dashboard of Docker Desktop and navigate to **Settings**, then **Docker Engine**. You should see something similar to this:

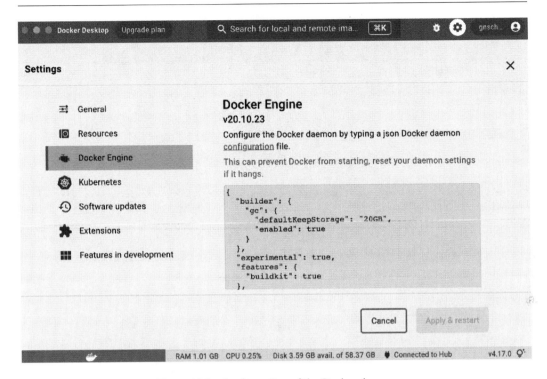

Figure 12.1 – Configuration of the Docker daemon

2. Analyze the existing configuration and add the following key-value pair to it, if not present already:

```
"log-driver": "json-file"
```

Here, the (shortened) result will look like this:

```
{
  ...
  "experimental": true,
  "features": {
    "buildkit": true
  },
  "metrics-addr": "127.0.0.1:9323",
  "log-driver": "json-file"
}
```

3. Restart the Docker daemon to apply the changes.

Locally setting the log driver

If you prefer to set the logging driver for an individual container instead of globally, then use the `--log-driver` option when starting the container:

```
docker run --log-driver=json-file <image_name>
```

Now, let's learn how to specify log rotation and retention policies.

Setting log rotation and retention policies

We can configure log rotation and retention policies by specifying the `max-size` and `max-file` options for the logging driver:

- `max-size`: This option limits the size of each log file. When a log file reaches the specified size, Docker creates a new file and starts logging into it. For example, to limit each log file to 10 MB, set `max-size=10m`.

- `max-file`: This option limits the number of log files to keep. When the limit is reached, Docker removes the oldest log file. For example, to keep only the last five log files, set `max-file=5`.

To set these options globally, add them to the `/etc/docker/daemon.json` configuration file. We can add the `log-opts` section to the daemon configuration right after the `log-driver` node that we added earlier:

```
{
  ...
  "log-driver": "json-file",
  "log-opts": {
    "max-size": "10m",
    "max-file": "5"
  }
}
```

We suggest that you modify the daemon configuration once again via the dashboard of Docker Desktop. Once you have modified the configuration, restart the Docker daemon to apply the changes.

To set these options for an individual container, use the `--log-opt` option when starting the container:

```
docker run --log-driver=json-file \
    --log-opt max-size=10m \
    --log-opt max-file=5 \
    <image_name>
```

By configuring log rotation and retention policies, you can prevent excessive disk space usage and maintain a well-functioning Docker environment. Remember to choose appropriate values for `max-size` and `max-file` based on your specific use case and storage capacity.

Using a log management system

Using a log management system to centralize logs from multiple containers is essential for efficient monitoring and troubleshooting in a Docker environment. This allows you to aggregate logs from all containers, analyze them in one place, and identify patterns or issues. In this chapter, we'll use the **Elasticsearch, Logstash, and Kibana (ELK)** Stack as an example log management system.

The ELK Stack

The ELK Stack, also known as the Elastic Stack, is a collection of open source software products that facilitate the ingestion, storage, processing, searching, and visualization of large volumes of data.

ELK is an acronym that stands for Elasticsearch, Logstash, and Kibana, which are the main components of the stack.

Elasticsearch: Elasticsearch is a distributed, RESTful search and analytics engine built on top of Apache Lucene. It provides a scalable and near real-time search platform with powerful full-text search capabilities, as well as support for aggregations and analytics. Elasticsearch is commonly used for log and event data analysis, application search, and various other use cases that require high-performance searching and indexing capabilities.

Logstash: Logstash is a flexible, server-side data processing pipeline that ingests, processes, and forwards data to various outputs, including Elasticsearch. Logstash supports multiple input sources, such as log files, databases, and message queues, and can transform and enrich data using filters before forwarding it. Logstash is often used to collect and normalize logs and events from various sources, making it easier to analyze and visualize the data in Elasticsearch.

Kibana: Kibana is a web-based data visualization and exploration tool that provides a user interface for interacting with Elasticsearch data. Kibana offers various visualization types, such as bar charts, line charts, pie charts, and maps, as well as support for creating custom dashboards to display and analyze data. Kibana also includes features such as Dev Tools for Elasticsearch query testing, monitoring, and alerting capabilities, and machine learning integration.

Note that the following description applies to a Linux system. If you happen to be one of the lucky people running Linux natively on your developer machine, then go for it and start right away with *Step 1 – setting up the ELK Stack on Linux*.

If, on the other hand, you are using a Mac or Windows machine for work, then we have created some step-by-step instructions on how to test the setup. Of special notice is *Step 2 – installing and configuring Filebeat*. See the part that matches your setup and give it a try.

Step 1 – setting up the ELK Stack on Linux

Deploy ELK using Docker containers or install them directly on your system. For detailed instructions, refer to the official ELK Stack documentation: `https://www.elastic.co/guide/index.html`.

Ensure that Elasticsearch and Kibana are properly configured and running. Verify this by accessing the Kibana dashboard through a web browser.

Step 2 – installing and configuring Filebeat

Filebeat is a lightweight log shipper that forwards logs from your Docker containers to the ELK Stack. Install Filebeat on the Docker host machine and configure it to collect container logs:

1. Install Filebeat using the official installation guide for your specific operating system. You can find the docs here: `https://www.elastic.co/guide/en/beats/filebeat/current/filebeat-installation-configuration.html`.

2. Configure Filebeat by editing the `filebeat.yml` configuration file (usually located in `/etc/filebeat` on Linux systems). Add the following configuration to collect Docker container logs:

    ```
    filebeat.inputs:
    - type: container
      paths:
        - '/var/lib/docker/containers/*/*.log'
    ```

3. Set up the output to forward logs to Elasticsearch. Replace `<elasticsearch_host>` and `<elasticsearch_port>` with the appropriate values:

    ```
    output.elasticsearch:
      hosts: ["<elasticsearch_host>:<elasticsearch_port>"]
    ```

4. Save the configuration file and start Filebeat:

    ```
    $  sudo systemctl enable filebeat
    $  sudo systemctl start filebeat
    ```

Note that this setup is strictly for Linux systems. On Mac or Windows, the situation is slightly more complicated given the fact that Docker runs in a VM on both systems and, as such, accessing the Docker logs that live inside this VM is slightly more involved. Please consult the documentation if you want to install Filebeat natively on your Mac or Windows machine as this is outside the scope of this book.

Alternatively, we can run Filebeat in a container, side by side with the ELK Stack.

Here is a complete Docker Compose file that will run the ELK Stack and Filebeat on a Linux computer:

```
1  version: '3.8'
2
3  services:
4    elasticsearch:
5      image: docker.elastic.co/elasticsearch/elasticsearch:7.15.2
6      container_name: elasticsearch
7      environment:
8        - discovery.type=single-node
9        - bootstrap.memory_lock=true
10       - "ES_JAVA_OPTS=-Xms512m -Xmx512m"
11     ulimits:
12       memlock:
13         soft: -1
14         hard: -1
15     volumes:
16       - esdata:/usr/share/elasticsearch/data
17     ports:
18       - 9200:9200
19
20   logstash:
21     image: docker.elastic.co/logstash/logstash:7.15.2
22     container_name: logstash
23     volumes:
24       - ./logstash/logstash.conf:/usr/share/logstash/pipeline/logstash.conf
25     ports:
26       - 5044:5044
27     depends_on:
28       - elasticsearch
29
30   kibana:
31     image: docker.elastic.co/kibana/kibana:7.15.2
32     container_name: kibana
33     ports:
34       - 5601:5601
35     depends_on:
36       - elasticsearch
37
38   filebeat:
39     image: docker.elastic.co/beats/filebeat:7.15.2
40     container_name: filebeat
41     user: root
42     volumes:
43       - ./filebeat/filebeat.yaml:/usr/share/filebeat/filebeat.yaml
44       - /var/lib/docker/containers:/var/lib/docker/containers:ro
45       - /var/run/docker.sock:/var/run/docker.sock:ro
46     depends_on:
47       - logstash
48
49 volumes:
50   esdata:
51     driver: local
52
```

Figure 12.2 – Docker Compose file for the ELK Stack and Filebeat

Now that we have learned how to run Filebeat on a Linux computer or server, we want to show how Filebeat can be used on a Mac or Windows computer, which is important during development.

Running the sample on a Mac or Windows computer

The preceding example will not run on a Mac or Windows computer since Docker is transparently running inside a VM and thus the Docker log files will not be found at `/var/lib/docker/containers`.

We can navigate around this problem by using a workaround: we can configure all our containers to write their respective logs into a file that is part of a Docker volume. Then, we can mount that volume into the Filebeat container instead of what we did on line 44 of the preceding Docker Compose file.

Here is a sample that uses a simple Node.js/Express.js application to demonstrate this. Please follow these steps:

1. Create a folder called `mac-or-windows` in your `ch12` chapter folder.

2. Inside this folder, create a subfolder called `app` and navigate to it.

3. Inside the `app` folder, initialize the Node.js application with the following command:

    ```
    $ npm init
    ```

    Accept all the defaults.

4. Install Express.js with the following command:

    ```
    $ npm install --save express
    ```

5. Modify the `package.json` file and add a script called `start` with its value set to `node index.js`.

6. Add a file called `index.js` to the folder with the following content:

```
1   const express = require('express');
2   const app = express();
3   const port = 3000;
4
5   app.use((req, res, next) => {
6       console.log(`[${new Date().toISOString()}] Incoming request: ${req.method} ${req.path}`);
7       next();
8   });
9
10  app.get('/', (req, res) => {
11      console.log('Handling request for the root path');
12      res.send('Hello, World!');
13  });
14
15  app.get('/test', (req, res) => {
16      console.log('Handling request for the /test path');
17      res.send('This is the /test route')
18  });
19
20  app.use((req, res) => {
21      console.log('Handle 4040 not found');
22      res.status(404).send('Not Found');
23  });
24
25  app.listen(port, '0.0.0.0', () => {
26      console.log(`Server is running at http://0.0.0.0:${port}`);
27  });
28
```

Figure 12.3 – The index.js application file

This simple Express.js application has two routes, / and /test. It also has middleware to log incoming requests and logs when handling specific routes or a 404 Not Found error.

7. Add a script file called entrypoint.sh to the folder with this content:

```
1   #!/bin/sh
2   set -e
3   echo $LOGGING_FILE
4   if [ -n "$LOGGING_FILE" ]; then
5       mkdir -p $(dirname "$LOGGING_FILE")
6       touch "$LOGGING_FILE"
7       exec npm start 2>&1 | tee -a "$LOGGING_FILE"
8   else
9       exec npm start 2>&1
10  fi
11
```

Figure 12.4 – The entrypoint.sh file for the sample application

This script will be used to run our sample application and redirect its logs to the specified LOGGING_FILE.

Make the preceding file executable with the following command:

```
$ chmod +x ./entrypoint.sh
```

8. Add a Dockerfile to the folder with this content:

```
1   FROM node:16-alpine
2   WORKDIR /usr/src/app
3   COPY package*.json ./
4   RUN npm ci
5   COPY . .
6   EXPOSE 3000
7   ENTRYPOINT [ "./entrypoint.sh" ]
```

Figure 12.5 – The Dockerfile for the sample application

9. Add a file called `docker-compose.yml` to the `mac-or-windows` folder with this content:

```
1   version: "3.9"
2   services:
3     app:
4       image: gnschenker/ch12-app
5       build: app
6       ports:
7         - 3000:3000
8       environment:
9         - "LOGGING_FILE=/usr/src/app/logs/app.log"
10      volumes:
11        - app_logs:/usr/src/app/logs
12
13    elasticsearch:
14      image: docker.elastic.co/elasticsearch/elasticsearch:7.17.1-arm64
15      environment:
16        - "discovery.type=single-node"
17      ports:
18        - "9200:9200"
19
20    filebeat:
21      image: docker.elastic.co/beats/filebeat:7.17.1-arm64
22      depends_on:
23        - elasticsearch
24      volumes:
25        - app_logs:/usr/src/app/logs
26        - ./filebeat.yml:/usr/share/filebeat/filebeat.yml
27
28    kibana:
29      image: docker.elastic.co/kibana/kibana:7.17.1-arm64
30      depends_on:
31        - elasticsearch
32      ports:
33        - "5601:5601"
34
35  volumes:
36    app_logs:
37
```

Figure 12.6 – Docker Compose file for the Mac or Windows use case

Note the environment variable on line 9, which defines the name and location of the log file generated by the Node.js/Express.js application. Also, note the volume mapping on line 11, which will make sure the log file is funneled to the Docker `app_logs` volume. This volume is then mounted to the `filebeat` container on line 25. This way, we make sure Filebeat can collect the logs and forward them to Kibana.

10. Also, add a file called `filebeat.yml` to the `mac-or-windows` folder that contains the following configuration for Filebeat:

```
1  filebeat.inputs:
2  - type: log
3    enabled: true
4    paths:
5      - '/usr/src/app/logs/*.log'
6
7  output.elasticsearch:
8    hosts: ["elasticsearch:9200"]
```

Figure 12.7 – Configuration for Filebeat on Mac or Windows

11. From within the folder where the `docker-compose.yml` file is located, build the Node.js application image with the following command:

```
$ docker compose build app
```

12. Now, you are ready to run the stack, like so:

```
$ docker compose up --detach
```

13. Use a REST client to access the `http://localhost:3000` and `http://localhost:3000/test` endpoints a few times to have the application generate a few log outputs.

Now, we are ready to explore the collected logs centrally in Kibana.

Step 3 – visualizing logs in Kibana

Access the Kibana dashboard through a web browser at `http://localhost:5601`.

For more details, refer to the *Querying a centralized log* section later in this chapter. Here is a quick rundown.

Go to the **Management** section and create an index pattern for Filebeat (for example, `filebeat-*`) to start analyzing the collected logs.

Navigate to the **Discover** section to search, filter, and visualize the logs from your Docker containers.

Once you have configured your Kibana dashboard, you should see something like this:

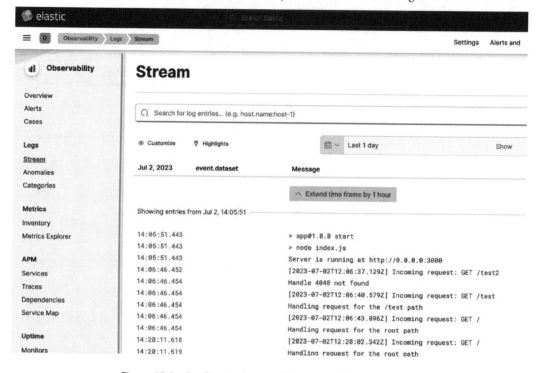

Figure 12.8 – Application logs in Kibana provided by Filebeat

By following these steps, you'll have a centralized log management system that aggregates logs from multiple Docker containers, allowing you to analyze and monitor your containerized applications efficiently. Note that there are other log management systems and log shippers available, such as Splunk, Graylog, and Fluentd. The process of setting up these systems will be similar but may require different configuration steps.

Setting up log filtering and alerting mechanisms

Setting up log filtering and alerting mechanisms helps you focus on important log messages, minimize noise, and respond to potential issues proactively. Here, we will use the ELK Stack along with the ElastAlert plugin to demonstrate log filtering and alerting.

Step 1 – setting up the Elastic Stack

First, follow the instructions provided in the *Setting up the ELK Stack* section to set up the Elastic Stack for centralized logging. This includes running Elasticsearch, Logstash, and Kibana in Docker containers.

Step 2 – setting up log filtering with Logstash

Configure Logstash to filter logs based on specific conditions, such as log levels, keywords, or patterns. Update your `logstash.conf` file with appropriate filters in the `filter` section. For example, to filter logs based on log level, you can use the following configuration:

```
filter {
  if [loglevel] == "ERROR" {
    mutate {
      add_tag => ["error"]
    }
  }
}
```

This configuration checks whether the log level is ERROR and adds a tag of `error` to the log event. Restart the Logstash container to apply the new configuration:

```
docker restart logstash
```

Step 3 – setting up ElastAlert for alerting

ElastAlert is a simple framework for alerting anomalies, spikes, or other patterns of interest found in data stored in Elasticsearch. Let's set it up:

1. Clone the ElastAlert repository and navigate to the ElastAlert directory:

    ```
    git clone https://github.com/Yelp/elastalert.git
    cd elastalert
    ```

2. Install ElastAlert:

    ```
    pip install elastalert
    ```

3. Create a configuration file for ElastAlert, `config.yaml`, and update it with the following contents:

    ```
    es_host: host.docker.internal
    es_port: 9200

    rules_folder: rules
    run_every:
      minutes: 1

    buffer_time:
      minutes: 15

    alert_time_limit:
      days: 2
    ```

4. Create a `rules` directory and define your alerting rules. For example, to create an alert for logs with the `error` tag, create a file called `error_logs.yaml` in the `rules` directory with the following contents:

```
name: Error Logs
index: logstash-*
type: frequency
num_events: 1
timeframe:
  minutes: 1

filter:
- term:
    tags: "error"

alert:
- "email"

email:
- "you@example.com"
```

This rule triggers an email alert if there is at least one log event with the `error` tag within a 1-minute timeframe.

5. Start ElastAlert:

```
elastalert --config config.yaml --verbose
```

Now, ElastAlert will monitor the Elasticsearch data based on your defined rules and send alerts when the conditions are met.

Step 4 – monitoring and responding to alerts

With log filtering and alerting mechanisms in place, you can focus on critical log messages and respond to potential issues proactively. Monitor your email or other configured notification channels for alerts and investigate the root causes to improve your application's reliability and performance.

Keep refining your Logstash filters and ElastAlert rules to minimize noise, detect important log patterns, and respond to potential issues more effectively.

In the next section, we will discuss how to ship Docker daemon logs.

Shipping Docker daemon logs

Docker daemon logs pertain to the overall functioning of the Docker platform. The Docker daemon is responsible for managing all Docker containers, and its logs record system-wide events and messages. These logs help in identifying issues related to the Docker daemon itself, such as networking problems, resource allocation errors, and container orchestration challenges.

Depending on the operating system, the location and configuration of Docker daemon logs may differ. For instance, on a Linux system, daemon logs are usually found in `/var/log/docker.log`, while on Windows, they are located in `%programdata%\docker\logs\daemon.log`.

> **Note**
> Daemon logs on Mac will be covered in the next section.

To effectively manage Docker daemon logs, consider the following best practices:

- Regularly review daemon logs to identify potential issues and anomalies
- Set up log rotation and retention policies to manage disk space usage
- Use a log management system to centralize and analyze logs for better visibility into the overall Docker environment

In conclusion, both shipping containers and Docker daemon logs play vital roles in monitoring and maintaining a healthy Docker environment. By effectively managing these logs, system administrators and developers can ensure optimal performance, minimize downtime, and resolve issues promptly.

Docker daemon logs on Mac

On a Mac with Docker Desktop installed, you can view the Docker daemon logs using the `log stream` command provided by the macOS log utility. Follow these steps:

1. Open the Terminal application.
2. Run the following command:

```
log stream --predicate 'senderImagePath CONTAINS "Docker"'
```

This command will display a real-time stream of logs related to Docker Desktop, including the Docker daemon logs. You can stop the stream by pressing *Ctrl + C*.

3. Alternatively, you can use the following command to view the Docker daemon logs in a file format:

```
log show --predicate 'senderImagePath CONTAINS "Docker"' \
    --style syslog --info \
    --last 1d > docker_daemon_logs.log
```

This command will create a file named `docker_daemon_logs.log` in the current directory, containing the Docker daemon logs from the last 1 day. You can change the `--last 1d` option to specify a different time range (for example, `--last 2h` for the last 2 hours). Open the `docker_daemon_logs.log` file with any text editor to view the logs.

Please note that you may need administrator privileges to execute these commands. If you encounter permission issues, prepend the commands with `sudo`.

Docker daemon logs on a Windows computer

On a Windows 11 machine with Docker Desktop installed, the Docker daemon logs are stored as text files. You can access these logs by following these steps:

1. Open File Explorer.
2. Navigate to the following directory:

    ```
    C:\ProgramData\DockerDesktop\service
    ```

    In this directory, you'll find the `DockerDesktopVM.log` file, which contains the Docker daemon logs.

3. Open the `DockerDesktopVM.log` file with any text editor to view the logs.

    Please note that the `C:\ProgramData` folder might be hidden by default. To display hidden folders in File Explorer, click on the **View** tab and check the **Hidden items** checkbox.

Alternatively, you can use PowerShell to read the logs:

1. Open PowerShell.
2. Execute the following command:

    ```
    Get-Content -Path "C:\ProgramData\DockerDesktop\service\
    DockerDesktopVM.log" -Tail 50
    ```

    This command will display the last 50 lines of the Docker daemon log file. You can change the number after `-Tail` to display a different number of lines.

Next, we are going to learn how to query a centralized log.

Querying a centralized log

Once your containerized application logs have been collected and stored in the ELK Stack, you can query the centralized logs using Elasticsearch's Query **Domain Specific Language** (**DSL**) and visualize the results in Kibana.

Step 1 – accessing Kibana

Kibana provides a user-friendly interface for querying and visualizing Elasticsearch data. In the provided `docker-compose.yml` file, Kibana can be accessed on port `5601`. Open your browser and navigate to `http://localhost:5601`.

Step 2 – setting up an index pattern

Before you can query the logs, you need to create an index pattern in Kibana to identify the Elasticsearch indices containing the log data. Follow these steps to create an index pattern:

1. The first time you access Kibana, you will be asked to add integrations. You can safely ignore this as we are using Filebeat to ship the logs.

2. Instead, locate the "hamburger menu" in the top left of the view and click it.

3. Locate the **Management** tab in the left-hand navigation menu and select **Stack Management**:

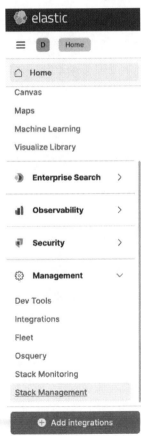

Figure 12.9 – The Management tab in Kibana

4.   Under the **Kibana** section, click **Index Patterns**:

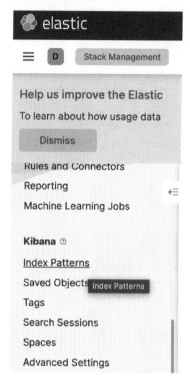

Figure 12.10 – The Index Patterns entry of Kibana

5.   Click the **Create index pattern** button.

6.   Enter the index pattern that matches your Logstash indices. For example, if your Logstash configuration uses the `logstash-%{+YYYY.MM.dd}` index pattern, enter `logstash-*` in the **Name** field.

7.   In the **Time Filter** field name dropdown, select the `@timestamp` field.

8.   Click **Create index pattern**.

Now, we are ready to query our container logs.

Step 3 – querying the logs in Kibana

Now, you're ready to query the logs using Kibana's **Discover** feature. Follow these steps:

1.   Once again, locate the "hamburger menu" in the top left of the view and click it.

2.   Locate the **Analytics** tab and select **Discover**.

3. Select the index pattern you created earlier from the drop-down menu in the top-left corner.

4. Use the time filter in the top-right corner to choose a specific time range for your query.

5. To search for specific log entries, enter your query in the search bar and press *Enter*. Kibana uses the Elasticsearch Query DSL to perform searches.

Here are some example queries:

- To find logs containing the word "error": `error`

- To find logs with a specific field value: `container.name: "my-container"`

- To use a wildcard search (for example, logs with a `container.name` starting with "app"): `container.name: "app*"`

- To use Boolean operators for more complex queries: `error AND container.name: "my-container"`

Step 4 – visualizing the logs

You can create visualizations and dashboards in Kibana to analyze the logs more effectively. To create a visualization, follow these steps:

1. Click on the **Visualize** tab in the left-hand navigation menu.

2. Click the **Create visualization** button.

3. Choose a visualization type (for example, pie chart, bar chart, line chart, and so on).

4. Select the index pattern you created earlier.

5. Configure the visualization by selecting the fields and aggregation types.

6. Click **Save** to save your visualization.

You can create multiple visualizations and add them to a dashboard for a comprehensive view of your log data. To create a dashboard, do the following:

1. Click on the **Dashboard** tab in the left-hand navigation menu.

2. Click the **Create dashboard** button.

3. Click **Add** to add visualizations to the dashboard.

4. Resize and rearrange the visualizations as needed.

5. Click **Save** to save your dashboard.

Now, you have a centralized view of your containerized application logs and you can query, analyze, and visualize the logs using Kibana.

In the following section, we will learn how to collect and scrape metrics exposed by Docker and your application.

Collecting and scraping metrics

To collect and scrape metrics from containers running on a system with Docker Desktop installed, you can use Prometheus and **Container Advisor (cAdvisor)**. Prometheus is a powerful open source monitoring and alerting toolkit, while cAdvisor provides container users with an understanding of the resource usage and performance characteristics of their running containers.

In this section, we'll provide a step-by-step guide to setting up Prometheus and cAdvisor to collect and scrape metrics from containers running on Docker Desktop.

Step 1 – running cAdvisor in a Docker container

cAdvisor is a Google-developed tool that collects, processes, and exports container metrics. Let's take a look:

1. In the chapter folder, ch12, create a new subfolder called metrics:

    ```
    mkdir metrics
    ```

2. In this folder, create a file called docker-compose.yml and add the following snippet to it:

    ```
    version: '3.8'
    services:
      cadvisor:
        image: gcr.io/cadvisor/cadvisor:v0.45.0
        container_name: cadvisor
        restart: always
        ports:
        - 8080:8080
        volumes:
        - /:/rootfs:ro
        - /var/run:/var/run:rw
        - /sys:/sys:ro
        - /var/lib/docker/:/var/lib/docker:ro
    ```

3. Run cAdvisor in a Docker container using the following command:

    ```
    docker compose up cadvisor --detach
    ```

    Replace v0.45.0 with the latest cAdvisor version available on the cAdvisor repository.

    This command mounts the necessary directories from the host system and exposes cAdvisor's web interface on port 8080.

> **Attention**
>
> A version lower than the one shown here will not run, for example, on a Mac with an M1 or M2 processor.

4. You can access the cAdvisor web interface by navigating to `http://localhost:8080` in your browser.

Step 2 – setting up and running Prometheus

Next, let's set up Prometheus using the following step-by-step instructions:

1. Create a subfolder called `prometheus` in the `metrics` folder.

2. In this new folder, create a `prometheus.yml` configuration file with the following contents:

```yaml
global:
  scrape_interval: 15s

scrape_configs:
  - job_name: 'prometheus'
    static_configs:
      - targets: ['localhost:9090']

  - job_name: 'cadvisor'
    static_configs:
      - targets: ['host.docker.internal:8080']
```

This configuration specifies the global scrape interval and two scrape jobs: one for Prometheus itself and another for cAdvisor running on port 8080.

3. Add the following snippet to the end of the `docker-compose.yml` file:

```yaml
prometheus:
  image: prom/prometheus:latest
  container_name: prometheus
  restart: always
  ports:
    - 9090:9090
  volumes:
    - ./prometheus:/etc/prometheus
    - prometheus_data:/prometheus
```

This instruction mounts the `prometheus.yml` configuration file and exposes Prometheus on port 9090.

4. The preceding `prometheus` service uses a volume called `prometheus_data`. To define this, please add the following two lines to the end of the `docker-compose.yml` file:

```
volumes:
  prometheus_data:
```

5. You can access the Prometheus web interface by navigating to `http://localhost:9090` in your browser.

Once Prometheus is up and running, you can verify that it's successfully scraping metrics from cAdvisor:

1. Open the Prometheus web interface at `http://localhost:9090`.
2. Click on **Status** in the top navigation bar, then select **Targets**.
3. Ensure that both the `prometheus` and `cadvisor` targets are listed with **State** set to UP.

Now, Prometheus can collect and store metrics from the containers running on your Docker Desktop system. You can use Prometheus' built-in expression browser to query metrics or set up Grafana for advanced visualization and dashboarding:

1. In the `query text` field, enter something like `container_start_time_seconds` to get the value for the startup time of all containers.
2. To refine the query and only get the value for the cAdvisor container, enter `container_start_time_seconds{job="cadvisor"}`.

Note that in the `query text` field, you get IntelliSense, which is convenient when you do not remember all the details of a command and its parameters.

Before you continue, stop cAdvisor and Prometheus with the following command:

```
docker compose down -v
```

In the last section of this chapter, you will learn how to monitor a containerized application using a tool such as Grafana.

Monitoring a containerized application

Monitoring a containerized application is crucial for understanding the application's performance, resource usage, and potential bottlenecks. This section will detail a step-by-step process for monitoring a containerized application using Prometheus, Grafana, and cAdvisor.

Step 1 – setting up Prometheus

Follow the instructions from the previous section to set up Prometheus and cAdvisor to collect and scrape metrics from containers running on Docker Desktop.

Step 2 – instrumenting your application with Prometheus metrics

To monitor a containerized application, you need to instrument the application with Prometheus metrics. This involves adding Prometheus client libraries to your application code and exposing metrics on an HTTP endpoint, usually `/metrics`.

Choose the appropriate Prometheus client library for your application's programming language from the official list: `https://prometheus.io/docs/instrumenting/clientlibs/`.

Add the library to your application while following the library's documentation and examples.

Expose the `/metrics` endpoint, which will be scraped by Prometheus.

Example using Kotlin and Spring Boot

To expose Prometheus metrics from a Kotlin and Spring Boot API, you need to follow these steps:

1. Create a new Kotlin Spring Boot project.
2. Add the necessary dependencies.
3. Implement the API and expose Prometheus metrics.
4. Expose the actuator endpoints.
5. Create a Dockerfile.
6. Integrate with the Docker Compose file.

Step 1 – creating a new Kotlin Spring Boot project

You can use Spring Initializr (`https://start.spring.io/`) to create a new Kotlin Spring Boot project. Name the artifact `kotlin-api`. Then, select Kotlin as the language, choose the packaging type (JAR or WAR), and add the necessary dependencies. For this example, select **Web**, **Actuator**, and **Prometheus** under the **Dependencies** section.

Download the generated project and extract it.

Step 2 – verifying the necessary dependencies

In your `build.gradle.kts` file, assert that the following dependencies are included:

```
implementation("org.springframework.boot:spring-boot-starter-web")
implementation("org.springframework.boot:spring-boot-starter-
actuator")
implementation("io.micrometer:micrometer-registry-prometheus")
```

Step 3 – implementing the API and exposing Prometheus metrics

Locate the Kotlin `KotlinApiApplication.kt` file in the `src/main/kotlin/com/example/kotlinapi/` subfolder and replace its existing content with the following:

```kotlin
package com.example.kotlinapi

import io.micrometer.core.instrument.MeterRegistry
import org.springframework.boot.autoconfigure.SpringBootApplication
import org.springframework.boot.runApplication
import org.springframework.context.annotation.Bean
import org.springframework.web.bind.annotation.GetMapping
import org.springframework.web.bind.annotation.RestController
import java.util.concurrent.atomic.AtomicInteger

@SpringBootApplication
class KotlinApiApplication {
    @Bean
    fun counter() = AtomicInteger(0)
}

fun main(args: Array<String>) {
    runApplication<KotlinApiApplication>(*args)
}

@RestController
class DemoController(private val counter: AtomicInteger, private val meterRegistry: MeterRegistry) {
    @GetMapping("/")
    fun hello(): String {
        val count = counter.incrementAndGet()
        meterRegistry.counter("api_requests_total", "path", "/").increment()
        return "Hello, World! Request count: $count"
    }
}
```

Figure 12.11 – Code in the KotlinApiApplication.kt file

You can also find this code in the `sample-solutions/ch12/kotlin-api` subfolder if you prefer not to type the example yourself.

In this example, a simple REST API with a single endpoint, /, was implemented. The endpoint increments a counter and exposes the count as a Prometheus metric named `api_requests_total`.

Add the following line to the `application.properties` file to use a different port than the default port, `8080`, which is already taken by cAdvisor in our stack. In our example, the port is `7000`:

```
server.port=7000
```

Step 4 – exposing metrics

Add the following line to the `application.properties` file:

```
management.endpoints.web.exposure.
include=health,info,metrics,prometheus
```

> **Note**
>
> The above configuration should be all on a single line. It is shown on two lines here due to space limitations.

This will expose the respective metrics on the `/actuator/health`, `/actuator/info`, `/actuator/metrics`, and `/actuator/prometheus` endpoints.

Step 5 – creating a Dockerfile

Create a `multistage` Dockerfile in the project's root directory with the following content:

```
1   # Build stage
2   FROM gradle:jdk17 AS build
3   WORKDIR /app
4   COPY . /app
5   RUN gradle clean build --no-daemon
6
7   # Runtime stage
8   FROM openjdk:17-oracle
9   COPY --from=build /app/build/libs/kotlin-api-0.0.1-SNAPSHOT.jar app.jar
10  EXPOSE 8080
11  ENTRYPOINT ["java", "-jar", "/app.jar"]
```

Figure 12.12 – Dockerfile for the Kotlin API

In this `multistage` Dockerfile, we have two stages:

- **Build stage**: This stage uses the `gradle:jdk17` base image to build the Kotlin Spring Boot application. It sets the working directory, copies the source code, and runs the Gradle `build` command. This stage is named `build` using the `AS` keyword.

- **Runtime stage**: This stage uses the `openjdk:17-oracle` base image for the runtime environment, which is a smaller image without the JDK. It copies the built JAR file from the build stage and sets the entry point to run the Spring Boot application.

This multi-stage Dockerfile allows you to build the Kotlin Spring Boot application and create the final runtime image in one go. It also helps reduce the final image size by excluding unnecessary build tools and artifacts.

Step 6 – integrating with the Docker Compose file

Update your existing `docker-compose.yml` file so that it includes the Kotlin Spring Boot API service, which resides in the `kotlin-api` subfolder:

```
version: '3.8'

services:
  # ... other services (Elasticsearch, Logstash, Kibana, etc.) ...

  kotlin-spring-boot-api:
    build: ./kotlin-api
    container_name: kotlin-spring-boot-api
    ports:
      - 7000:7000
```

Now, you can run `docker compose up -d` to build and start the Kotlin Spring Boot API service, along with the other services. The API will be accessible on port `8080`, and the Prometheus metrics can be collected.

Next, we will configure Prometheus to scrape all the metrics from our setup, including the Kotlin API we just created.

Step 3 – configuring Prometheus to scrape your application metrics

Update your `prometheus.yml` configuration file from the previous section so that it includes a new scrape job for your application. For example, since our Kotlin API sample application is running in a Docker container and exposing metrics on port `7000`, we will add the following to the `scrape_configs` section:

```
- job_name: 'kotlin-api'
  static_configs:
    - targets: ['host.docker.internal:7000']
  metrics_path: /actuator/prometheus
```

Step 4 – setting up Grafana for visualization

Grafana is a popular open source visualization and analytics tool that can integrate with Prometheus to create interactive dashboards for your containerized application:

1. To the `docker-compose.yml` from the previous section, add this snippet to define a service for Grafana:

    ```
    grafana:
      image: grafana/grafana:latest
    ```

```
container_name: grafana
restart: always
ports:
  - 3000:3000
volumes:
  - grafana_data:/var/lib/grafana
```

2. In the `volumes:` section, add a volume called `grafana_data`.

3. Run cAdvisor, Prometheus, and Grafana with this command:

```
docker compose up --detach
```

4. Access Grafana by navigating to `http://localhost:3000` in your browser. The default username is `admin` and the default password is also `admin`.

5. Add **Prometheus** as a data source.

6. Click on the gear icon (**Configuration**) in the left sidebar.

7. Select **Data Sources** and then click **Add data source**.

8. Choose **Prometheus** and enter `http://host.docker.internal:9090` as the URL.

9. Click **Save & Test** to verify the connection.

10. Create a dashboard and panels to visualize your application metrics.

11. Click on the + icon (**Create**) in the left sidebar and choose **Dashboard**.

12. Click **Add new panel** to start creating panels for your metrics.

13. Use the query editor to build queries based on your application metrics, and customize the visualization type, appearance, and other settings.

14. Save the dashboard by clicking the disk icon in the top-right corner.

With Grafana, you can create interactive dashboards that provide real-time insights into your containerized application's performance, resource usage, and other critical metrics.

Step 5 – setting up alerting (optional)

Grafana and Prometheus can be used to set up alerts based on your application metrics. This can help you proactively address issues before they impact your users:

1. In Grafana, create a new panel or edit an existing one.

2. Switch to the **Alert** tab in the panel editor.

3. Click **Create Alert** and configure the alerting rules, conditions, and notification settings.

4. Save the panel and dashboard.

You may also need to configure Grafana's notification channels to send alerts via email, Slack, PagerDuty, or other supported services. To do this, follow these steps:

1. In Grafana, click on the bell icon (**Alerting**) in the left sidebar.
2. Choose **Notification channels** and click **Add channel**.
3. Fill in the required information for your preferred notification service and click **Save**.

Now, when the alerting conditions specified in your panel are met, Grafana will send notifications through the configured channel.

Step 6 – monitoring your containerized application

With Prometheus, Grafana, and cAdvisor set up, you can now effectively monitor your containerized application. Keep an eye on your Grafana dashboards, set up appropriate alerting rules, and use the collected data to identify performance bottlenecks, optimize resource usage, and improve the overall health of your application.

Remember to continuously iterate and improve your monitoring setup by refining your application's instrumentation, adjusting alerting rules, and adding new visualizations to your dashboards as your application evolves and grows.

Summary

In this chapter, we learned why logging and shipping the log to a central location is important. We then showed you how to set up an ELK Stack locally on our computer that can serve as a hub for logs. We generated a special version of this stack, including Filebeat, which can run on a Mac or Windows computer using the workaround of redirecting the standard log output to a file whose parent folder is mapped to a Docker volume. This volume is then mounted to Filebeat, which, in turn, forwards the logs to ElasticSearch. On a production or production-like system, the applications run on Linux servers or VMs and thus Filebeat can directly collect the logs from the default location, where Docker directs the logs at `/var/lib/docker/containers`.

We also learned how to use Prometheus and Grafana to scrape, collect, and display the metrics of your applications centrally on a dashboard. We used a simple Kotlin application that exposed a counter to demonstrate this.

Lastly, we briefly mentioned how to define alerts based on the values of collected metrics.

In the next chapter, we will introduce the concept of container orchestrators. It will teach us why orchestrators are needed, and how they work conceptually. The chapter will also provide an overview of the most popular orchestrators and list a few of their pros and cons.

Questions

Here are a few questions that you should try to answer to self-assess your learning progress:

1. What are Docker container logs, and why are they important?

2. What is a daemon log in Docker, and how is it different from a container log?

3. How can you monitor Docker containers?

4. How can you view the logs of a running Docker container?

5. What are some best practices for logging and monitoring Docker containers?

6. How can you collect logs from multiple Docker containers?

Answers

Here are some sample answers to the questions for this chapter:

1. Docker container logs are records of the events and messages generated by the applications running within a container. They are essential for monitoring performance, troubleshooting issues, and ensuring the smooth operation of the applications deployed in Docker containers.

2. A daemon log in Docker refers to the log files generated by the Docker daemon, which manages Docker containers. These logs record system-wide events and messages related to the overall functioning of the Docker platform. In contrast, container logs are specific to individual containers and their applications.

3. Monitoring Docker containers can be done using various methods, including command-line tools such as docker stats, third-party monitoring solutions such as Prometheus, and Docker's built-in APIs. These tools help track resource usage, performance metrics, and the health status of containers.

4. You can view the logs of a running Docker container using the `docker logs` command, followed by the container's ID or name. This command retrieves the log messages generated by the container, which can help diagnose issues or monitor the container's activities.

5. Some best practices for logging and monitoring Docker containers include the following:

    *   Centralize logs using a log management system

    *   Configure log rotation and retention policies

    *   Set up log filtering and alerting mechanisms

    *   Monitor containers using a combination of built-in and third-party tools

    *   Regularly review logs and metrics for anomalies

6. To collect logs from multiple Docker containers, you can use a log management system such as the ELK Stack or Splunk. You can also use tools such as Fluentd or Logspout to aggregate and forward logs from all containers to a centralized log management system for analysis and visualization.

Introducing Container Orchestration

In the previous chapter, we showed how container logs can be collected and shipped to a central location where the aggregated logs can then be parsed for useful information. We also learned how to instrument an application so that it exposes metrics and how those metrics can be scraped and shipped again to a central location. Finally, the chapter taught us how to convert those collected metrics into graphical dashboards that can be used to monitor a containerized application.

This chapter introduces the concept of orchestrators. It teaches us why orchestrators are needed, and how they work conceptually. This chapter will also provide an overview of the most popular orchestrators and list a few of their pros and cons.

In this chapter, we will cover the following topics:

- What are orchestrators and why do we need them?
- The tasks of an orchestrator
- Overview of popular orchestrators

After finishing this chapter, you will be able to do the following:

- Name three to four tasks for which an orchestrator is responsible
- List two to three of the most popular orchestrators
- Explain to an interested lay person, in your own words, and with appropriate analogies, why we need container orchestrators

What are orchestrators and why do we need them?

In *Chapter 9, Learning about Distributed Application Architecture*, we learned which patterns and best practices are commonly used to successfully build, ship, and run a highly distributed application. Now, if our distributed application is containerized, then we're facing the exact same problems or challenges that a non-containerized distributed application faces. Some of these challenges are those that were discussed in that chapter, namely service discovery, load balancing, scaling, and so on.

Similar to what Docker did with containers—standardizing the packaging and shipping of software with the introduction of those containers—we would like to have some tool or infrastructure software that handles all or most of the challenges mentioned. This software turns out to be what we call container orchestrators or, as we also call them, orchestration engines.

If what I just said doesn't make much sense to you yet, then let's look at it from a different angle. Take an artist who plays an instrument. They can play wonderful music to an audience all on their own—just the artist and their instrument. But now take an orchestra of musicians. Put them all in a room, give them the notes of a symphony, ask them to play it, and leave the room. Without any director, this group of very talented musicians would not be able to play this piece in harmony; it would more or less sound like a cacophony. Only if the orchestra has a conductor, who orchestrates the group of musicians, will the resulting music of the orchestra be enjoyable to our ears.

Instead of musicians, we now have containers, and instead of different instruments, we have containers that have different requirements for the container hosts to run. And instead of the music being played at varying tempos, we have containers that communicate with each other in particular ways and have to scale up and scale down to account for changing load imposed on our applications. In this regard, a container orchestrator has very much the same role as a conductor in an orchestra. It makes sure that the containers and other resources in a cluster play together in harmony.

I hope that you can now see more clearly what a container orchestrator is, and why we need one. Assuming that you understand this question, we can now ask ourselves how the orchestrator is going to achieve the expected outcome, namely, to make sure that all the containers in the cluster play in harmony. Well, the answer is that the orchestrator has to execute very specific tasks, similar to how the conductor of an orchestra also has a set of tasks that they execute to tame and, at the same time, elevate the orchestra.

The tasks of an orchestrator

So, what are the tasks that we expect an orchestrator worth its money to execute for us? Let's look at them in detail. The following list shows the most important tasks that, at the time of writing, enterprise users typically expect from their orchestrator.

Reconciling the desired state

When using an orchestrator, you tell it, preferably in a declarative way, how you want it to run a given application or application service. We learned what declarative versus imperative means in *Chapter 11, Managing Container with Docker Compose*. Part of this declarative way of describing the application service that we want to run includes elements such as which container image to use, how many instances of this service to run, which ports to open, and more. This declaration of the properties of our application service is what we call the desired state.

So, when we now tell the orchestrator to create a new application service based on the declaration for the first time, then the orchestrator makes sure to schedule as many containers in the cluster as requested. If the container image is not yet available on the target nodes of the cluster where the containers are supposed to run, then the scheduler makes sure that they're first downloaded from the image registry. Next, the containers are started with all the settings, such as networks to attach to or ports to expose. The orchestrator works as hard as it can to exactly match, in reality, the cluster to the declaration.

Once our service is up and running as requested, that is, it is running in the desired state, then the orchestrator continues to monitor it. Every time the orchestrator discovers a discrepancy between the actual state of the service and its desired state, it again tries its best to reconcile the desired state.

What could such a discrepancy between the actual and desired states of an application service be? Well, let's say one of the replicas of the service, that is, one of the containers, crashes due to, say, a bug; then the orchestrator will discover that the actual state differs from the desired state in terms of the number of replicas: there is one replica missing. The orchestrator will immediately schedule a new instance to another cluster node, which replaces the crashed instance. Another discrepancy could be that there are too many instances of the application service running if the service has been scaled down. In this case, the orchestrator will just randomly kill as many instances as needed in order to achieve parity between the actual and the desired number of instances. Yet another discrepancy can be when the orchestrator discovers that there is an instance of the application service running a wrong (maybe old) version of the underlying container image. By now, you should get the picture, right?

Thus, instead of us actively monitoring our application's services running in the cluster and correcting any deviations from the desired state, we delegate this tedious task to the orchestrator. This works very well provided that we use a declarative and not an imperative way of describing the desired state of our application services.

Replicated and global services

There are two quite different types of services that we might want to run in a cluster that is managed by an orchestrator. They are replicated and global services. A **replicated service** is a service that is required to run across a specific number of instances, say 10. A **global service**, in turn, is a service that is required to have exactly one instance running on every single worker node of the cluster. I have used the term worker node here. In a cluster that is managed by an orchestrator, we typically have two types of nodes: managers and workers.

A **manager node** is usually exclusively used by the orchestrator to manage the cluster and does not run any other workload. Worker nodes, in turn, run the actual applications. So, the orchestrator makes sure that, for a global service, an instance of it is running on every single worker node, no matter how many there are. We do not care about the number of instances but only that on each node, a single instance of the service is guaranteed to run.

Once again, we can fully rely on the orchestrator to handle this. In a replicated service, we will always be guaranteed to find the exact desired number of instances, while for a global service, we can be assured that on every worker node, exactly one instance of the service will always run. The orchestrator will always work as hard as it can to guarantee this desired state. In Kubernetes, a global service is also called a **DaemonSet**.

Service discovery

When we describe an application service in a declarative way, we are never supposed to tell the orchestrator on which cluster nodes the different instances of the service have to run. We leave it up to the orchestrator to decide which nodes best fit this task.

It is, of course, technically possible to instruct the orchestrator to use very deterministic placement rules, but this would be an anti-pattern and is not recommended at all, other than in very special edge cases.

So, if we now assume that the orchestration engine has complete and free will as to where to place individual instances of the application service and, furthermore, that instances can crash and be rescheduled by the orchestrator on different nodes, then we will realize that it is a futile task for us to keep track of where the individual instances are running at any given time. Even better, we shouldn't even try to know this since it is not important.

OK, you might say, but what about if I have two services, A and B, and Service A relies on Service B; shouldn't any given instance of Service A know where it can find an instance of Service B?

Here, I have to say loudly and clearly—no, it shouldn't. This kind of knowledge is not desirable in a highly distributed and scalable application. Rather, we should rely on the orchestrator to provide us with the information that we need in order to reach the other service instances that we depend on. It is a bit like in the old days of telephony, when we could not directly call our friends and had to call the phone company's central office, where some operator would then route us to the correct destination. In our case, the orchestrator plays the role of the operator, routing a request coming from an instance of Service A to an available instance of Service B. This whole process is called service discovery.

Routing

We have learned so far that in a distributed application, we have many interacting services. When Service A interacts with Service B, this occurs through the exchange of data packets. These data packets need to somehow be funneled from Service A to Service B. This process of funneling the data packets from a source to a destination is also called *routing*. As authors or operators of an application, we do expect the orchestrator to take over this task of routing. As we will see in later chapters, routing can happen on different levels. It is like in real life. Suppose you're working in a big company in one of its office buildings. Now, you have a document that needs to be forwarded to another employee in the company. The internal post service will pick up the document from your outbox and take it to the post office located in the same building. If the target person works in the same building, the document can then be directly forwarded to that person. If, on the other hand, the person works in another building of the same block, the document will be forwarded to the post office in that target building, from which it is then distributed to the receiver through the internal post service. Thirdly, if the document is targeted at an employee working in another branch of the company located in a different city or even a different country, then the document is forwarded to an external postal service such as UPS, which will transport it to the target location, from where, once again, the internal post service takes over and delivers it to the recipient.

Similar things happen when routing data packets between application services that are running in containers. The source and target containers can be located on the same cluster node, which corresponds to the situation in which both employees work in the same building.

The target container may run on a different cluster node, which corresponds to the situation in which the two employees work in different buildings on the same block. Finally, the third situation is when a data packet comes from outside of the cluster and has to be routed to the target container that is running inside the cluster.

All these situations, and more, have to be handled by the orchestrator.

Load balancing

In a highly available distributed application, all components have to be redundant. That means that every application service has to be run in multiple instances so that if one instance fails, the service as a whole is still operational.

To make sure that all instances of a service are actually doing work and are not just sitting around idle, you have to make sure that the requests for service are distributed equally to all the instances. This process of distributing the workload across service instances is called load balancing. Various algorithms exist that dictate how the workload can be distributed.

Usually, a load balancer works using the so-called round-robin algorithm, which makes sure that the workload is distributed equally across the instances using a cyclic algorithm. Once again, we expect the orchestrator to take care of the load-balancing requests from one service to another or from external sources to internal services.

Scaling

When running our containerized, distributed application in a cluster that is managed by an orchestrator, we also want an easy way to handle expected or unexpected increases in workload. To handle an increased workload, we usually just schedule additional instances of a service that is experiencing this increased load. Load balancers will then automatically be configured to distribute the workload over more available target instances.

But in real-life scenarios, the workload varies over time. If we look at a shopping site such as Amazon, it might have a high load during peak hours in the evening, when everyone is at home and shopping online; it may experience extreme loads during special days such as Black Friday; and it may experience very little traffic early in the morning. Thus, services need to not just be able to scale up but also to scale down when the workload goes down.

We also expect orchestrators to distribute service instances meaningfully when scaling up or down. It would not be wise to schedule all instances of the service on the same cluster node, since, if that node goes down, the whole service goes down. The scheduler of the orchestrator, which is responsible for the placement of the containers, needs to also consider not placing all instances in the same rack of computers since, if the power supply of the rack fails, again, the whole service is affected. Furthermore, service instances of critical services should also be distributed across data centers in order to avoid outages. All these decisions, and many more, are the responsibility of the orchestrator.

In the cloud, instead of computer racks, the term "availability zones" is often used.

Self-healing

These days, orchestrators are very sophisticated and can do a lot for us to maintain a healthy system. Orchestrators monitor all the containers that are running in the cluster and they automatically replace crashed or unresponsive ones with new instances. Orchestrators monitor the health of cluster nodes and take them out of the scheduler loop if a node becomes unhealthy or is down. A workload that was located on those nodes is automatically rescheduled to different available nodes.

All these activities, where the orchestrator monitors the current state and automatically repairs the damage or reconciles the desired state, lead to a so-called self-healing system.

We do not, in most cases, have to actively engage and repair the damage. The orchestrator will do this for us automatically. However, there are a few situations that the orchestrator cannot handle without our help. Imagine a situation where we have a service instance running in a container. The container is up and running and, from the outside, looks perfectly healthy, but the application running inside it is in an unhealthy state. The application did not crash; it just is not able to work as it was originally designed anymore. How could the orchestrator possibly know about this without us giving it a hint? It can't! Being in an unhealthy or invalid state means something completely different for each application service. In other words, the health status is service-dependent. Only the authors of the service, or its operators, know what health means in the context of a service.

Now, orchestrators define seams or probes, over which an application service can communicate to the orchestrator about what state it is in. Two fundamental types of probes exist:

- The service can tell the orchestrator whether it is healthy or not
- The service can tell the orchestrator whether it is ready or temporarily unavailable

How the service determines either of the preceding answers is totally up to the service. The orchestrator only defines how it is going to ask, for example, through an HTTP GET request, or what type of answers it is expecting, for example, OK or NOT OK.

If our services implement logic in order to answer the preceding health or availability questions, then we have a truly self-healing system since the orchestrator can kill unhealthy service instances and replace them with new healthy ones, and it can take service instances that are temporarily unavailable out of the load balancer's round robin.

Data persistence and storage management

Data persistence and storage management are crucial aspects of container orchestration. They ensure that data is preserved across container restarts and failures, allowing applications to maintain their state and continue functioning as expected.

In a containerized environment, data storage can be divided into two main categories – ephemeral storage and persistent storage:

- **Ephemeral storage**: This type of storage is tied to the life cycle of the container. When a container is terminated or fails, the data stored in its ephemeral storage is lost. Ephemeral storage is useful for temporary data, caching, or other non-critical information that can be regenerated.

- **Persistent storage**: Persistent storage decouples data from the container's life cycle, allowing it to persist even after the container is terminated or fails. This type of storage is essential for preserving critical application data, such as user-generated content, database files, or configuration data.

Container orchestration engines handle data persistence and storage management by providing mechanisms for attaching persistent storage to containers. These mechanisms usually involve the creation and management of storage volumes, which can be mounted to containers as needed.

Most container orchestration engines support various types of storage backends, including block storage, file storage, and object storage. They also provide integrations with popular storage solutions, such as cloud-based storage services, network-attached storage, and distributed storage systems such as Ceph or GlusterFS.

Additionally, container orchestration engines handle storage provisioning and management, automating tasks such as volume creation, resizing, and deletion. They also allow users to define storage classes and policies, making it easier to manage storage resources across a distributed environment.

In summary, data persistence and storage management in container orchestration engines ensure that applications maintain their state across container restarts and failures. They provide mechanisms for attaching persistent storage to containers and automate storage provisioning and management tasks, simplifying the process of managing storage resources in a containerized environment.

Zero downtime deployments

These days, it gets harder and harder to justify downtime for a mission-critical application that needs to be updated. Not only does that mean missed opportunities but it can also result in a damaged reputation for the company. Customers using the application are no longer prepared to accept the inconvenience and will turn away quickly.

Furthermore, our release cycles get shorter and shorter. Where, in the past, we would have one or two new releases per year, these days, a lot of companies update their applications multiple times a week, or even multiple times per day.

The solution to that problem is to come up with a zero-downtime application update strategy. The orchestrator needs to be able to update individual application services, batch-wise. This is also referred to as rolling updates. At any given time, only one or a few of the total number of instances of a given service are taken down and replaced by the new version of the service. Only if the new instances are operational, and do not produce any unexpected errors or show any misbehavior, will the next batch of instances be updated. This is repeated until all instances are replaced with their new version. If, for some reason, the update fails, then we expect the orchestrator to automatically roll the updated instances back to their previous version.

Other possible zero-downtime deployments are blue-green deployments and canary releases. In both cases, the new version of a service is installed in parallel with the current, active version. But initially, the new version is only accessible internally. Operations can then run smoke tests against the new version, and when the new version seems to be running just fine, then, in the case of a blue-green deployment, the router is switched from the current blue version to the new green version. For some time, the new green version of the service is closely monitored and, if everything is fine, the old blue version can be decommissioned. If, on the other hand, the new green version does not work as expected, then it is only a matter of setting the router back to the old blue version in order to achieve a complete rollback.

In the case of a canary release, the router is configured in such a way that it funnels a tiny percentage, say 1%, of the overall traffic through the new version of the service while 99% of the traffic is still routed through the old version. The behavior of the new version is closely monitored and compared to the behavior of the old version. If everything looks good, then the percentage of the traffic that is funneled through the new service is slightly increased. This process is repeated until 100% of the traffic is routed through the new service. If the new service has run for a while and everything looks good, then the old service can be decommissioned.

Most orchestrators support at least the rolling update type of zero-downtime deployment out of the box. Blue-green deployments and canary releases are often quite easy to implement.

Affinity and location awareness

Sometimes, certain application services require the availability of dedicated hardware on the nodes on which they run. For example, I/O-bound services require cluster nodes with an attached high-performance **Solid-State Drive (SSD)**, while some services that are used for machine learning, or similar, require an **Accelerated Processing Unit (APU)**.

Orchestrators allow us to define node affinities per application service. The orchestrator will then make sure that its scheduler only schedules containers on cluster nodes that fulfill the required criteria.

Defining an affinity on a particular node should be avoided; this will introduce a single point of failure and thus compromise high availability. Always define a set of multiple cluster nodes as the target for an application service.

Some orchestration engines also support what is called location awareness or geo awareness. What this means is that you can ask the orchestrator to equally distribute service instances across a set of different locations. You could, for example, define a data center label, with possible west, center, and east values, and apply the label to all of the cluster nodes with the value that corresponds to the geographical region in which the respective node is located. Then, you instruct the orchestrator to use this label for the geo awareness of a certain application service. In this case, if you request nine replicas of the service, then the orchestrator will make sure that three instances are deployed to the nodes in each of the three data centers—west, center, and east.

Geo awareness can even be defined hierarchically; for example, you can have a data center as the top-level discriminator, followed by the availability zone.

Geo awareness, or location awareness, is used to decrease the probability of outages due to power supply failures or data center outages. If the application instances are distributed across nodes, availability zones, or even data centers, it is extremely unlikely that everything will go down at once. One region will always be available.

Security

These days, security in IT is a very hot topic. Cyber warfare is at an all-time high. Most high-profile companies have been victims of hacker attacks, with very costly consequences.

One of the worst nightmares of every **chief information officer (CIO)** or **chief technology officer (CTO)** is to wake up in the morning and hear in the news that their company has become a victim of a hacker attack and that sensitive information has been stolen or compromised.

To counter most of these security threats, we need to establish a secure software supply chain and enforce security defense in depth. Let's look at some of the tasks that you can expect from an enterprise-grade orchestrator.

Secure communication and cryptographic node identity

First and foremost, we want to make sure that our cluster that is managed by the orchestrator is secure. Only trusted nodes can join the cluster. Every node that joins the cluster gets a cryptographic node identity, and all communication between the nodes must be encrypted. For this, nodes can use **Mutual Transport Layer Security (MTLS)**. In order to authenticate nodes of the cluster with each other, certificates are used. These certificates are automatically rotated periodically, or on request, to protect the system in case a certificate is leaked.

The communication that happens in a cluster can be separated into three types. You talk about communication planes—management, control, and data planes:

- The management plane is used by the cluster managers, or masters, to, for example, schedule service instances, execute health checks, or create and modify any other resources in the cluster, such as data volumes, secrets, or networks.

- The control plane is used to exchange important state information between all the nodes in a cluster. This kind of information is, for example, used to update the local IP tables on clusters, which are used for routing purposes.

- The data plane is where the actual application services communicate with each other and exchange data.

Normally, orchestrators mainly care about securing the management and control plane. Securing the data plane is left to the user, although the orchestrator may facilitate this task.

Secure networks and network policies

When running application services, not every service needs to communicate with every other service in the cluster. Thus, we want the ability to sandbox services from each other and only run services in the same networking sandbox that absolutely need to communicate with each other. All other services and all network traffic coming from outside of the cluster should have no way to access the sandboxed services.

There are at least two ways in which this network-based sandboxing can happen. We can either use a **software-defined network** (**SDN**) to group application services or we can have one flat network and use network policies to control who does and does not have access to a particular service or group of services.

Role-based access control (RBAC)

One of the most important tasks (next to security) that an orchestrator must fulfill in order to be enterprise-ready is to provide RBAC to the cluster and its resources.

RBAC defines how subjects, users, or groups of users of the system, organized into teams, and so on, can access and manipulate the system. It makes sure that unauthorized personnel cannot do any harm to the system, nor can they see any of the available resources in the system that they're not supposed to know of or see.

A typical enterprise might have user groups such as Development, QA, and Prod, and each of those groups can have one or many users associated with it. John Doe, the developer, is a member of the Development group and, as such, can access resources that are dedicated to the development team, but he cannot access, for example, the resources of the Prod team, of which Ann Harbor is a member. She, in turn, cannot interfere with the Development team's resources.

One way of implementing RBAC is through the definition of grants. A grant is an association between a subject, a role, and a resource collection. Here, a role comprises a set of access permissions to a resource. Such permissions can be to create, stop, remove, list, or view containers; to deploy a new application service; to list cluster nodes or view the details of a cluster node; and many other things.

A resource collection is a group of logically related resources of the cluster, such as application services, secrets, data volumes, or containers.

Secrets

In our daily life, we have loads of secrets. Secrets are information that is not meant to be publicly known, such as the username and password combination that you use to access your online bank account, or the code to your cell phone or your locker at the gym.

When writing software, we often need to use secrets, too. For example, we need a certificate to authenticate our application service with the external service that we want to access, or we need a token to authenticate and authorize our service when accessing some other API.

In the past, developers, for convenience, just hardcoded those values or put them in cleartext in some external configuration files. There, this very sensitive information was accessible to a broad audience, which, in reality, should never have had the opportunity to see those secrets.

Luckily, these days, orchestrators offer what's called secrets to deal with sensitive information in a highly secure way. Secrets can be created by authorized or trusted personnel. The values of these secrets are then encrypted and stored in a highly available cluster state database. The secrets, since they are encrypted, are now secure at rest. Once a secret is requested by an authorized application service, the secret is only forwarded to the cluster nodes that actually run an instance of that particular service, and the secret value is never stored on the node but mounted into the container in a tmpfs RAM-based volume.

Only inside the respective container is the secret value available in clear text. We already mentioned that the secrets are secure at rest. Once they are requested by a service, the cluster manager, or master, decrypts the secret and sends it over the wire to the target nodes. So, what about the secrets remaining secure in transit? Well, we learned earlier that the cluster nodes use MTLS for their communication, and so the secret, although transmitted in clear text, is still secure since data packets will be encrypted by MTLS. Thus, secrets are secure both at rest and in transit. Only services that are authorized to use secrets will ever have access to those secret values.

> **Secrets in Kubernetes**
>
> Note that, although secrets used in Kubernetes are fairly safe, still, the documentation recommends using them in conjunction with an even safer service, namely a secrets manager such as AWS Secrets Manager or Hashicorp's Vault.

Content trust

For added security, we want to make sure that only trusted images run in our production cluster. Some orchestrators allow us to configure a cluster so that it can only ever run signed images. Content trust and signing images are all about making sure that the authors of the image are the ones that we expect them to be, namely, our trusted developers or, even better, our trusted CI server. Furthermore, with content trust, we want to guarantee that the image that we get is fresh, and is not an old and maybe vulnerable image. And finally, we want to make sure that the image cannot be compromised by malicious hackers in transit. The latter is often called a **man-in-the-middle (MITM)** attack.

By signing images at the source and validating the signature at the target, we can guarantee that the images that we want to run are not compromised.

Reverse uptime

The last point I want to discuss in the context of security is reverse uptime. What do we mean by that? Imagine that you have configured and secured a production cluster. On this cluster, you're running a few mission-critical applications of your company. Now, a hacker has managed to find a security hole in one of your software stacks and has gained root access to one of your cluster nodes. That alone is already bad enough but, even worse, this hacker could now mask their presence on this node and pretend to be root on the machine, after all, and then use it as a base to attack other nodes in your cluster.

Root access in Linux or any Unix-type operating system means that you can do anything on that system. It is the highest level of access that someone can have. In Windows, the equivalent role is that of an administrator.

But what if we leverage the fact that containers are ephemeral and cluster nodes are quickly provisioned, usually in a matter of minutes if fully automated? We just kill each cluster node after a certain uptime of, say, one day. The orchestrator is instructed to drain the node and then exclude it from the cluster. Once the node is out of the cluster, it is torn down and replaced by a freshly provisioned node.

That way, the hacker has lost their base and the problem has been eliminated. This concept is not yet broadly available, though, but to me, it seems to be a huge step toward increased security, and, as far as I have discussed it with engineers who are working in this area, it is not difficult to implement.

Introspection

So far, we have discussed a lot of tasks for which the orchestrator is responsible and that it can execute in a completely autonomous way. However, there is also the need for human operators to be able to see and analyze what's currently running on the cluster, and in what state or health the individual applications are. For all this, we need the possibility of introspection. The orchestrator needs to surface crucial information in a way that is easily consumable and understandable.

The orchestrator should collect system metrics from all the cluster nodes and make them accessible to the operators. Metrics include CPU, memory and disk usage, network bandwidth consumption, and more. The information should be easily available on a node-per-node basis, as well as in an aggregated form.

We also want the orchestrator to give us access to logs that are produced by service instances or containers. Even more, the orchestrator should provide us with `exec` access to every container if we have the correct authorization to do so. With exec access to containers, you can then debug misbehaving containers.

In highly distributed applications, where each request to the application goes through numerous services until it is completely handled, tracing requests is a really important task.

Ideally, the orchestrator supports us in implementing a tracing strategy or gives us some good guidelines to follow.

Finally, human operators can best monitor a system when working with a graphical representation of all the collected metrics and logging and tracing information. Here, we are speaking about dashboards. Every decent orchestrator should offer at least a basic dashboard with a graphical representation of the most critical system parameters.

However, human operators are not the only ones concerned about introspection. We also need to be able to connect external systems with the orchestrator in order to consume this information. There needs to be an API available, over which external systems can access data such as the cluster state, metrics, and logs, and use this information to make automated decisions, such as creating pager or phone alerts, sending out emails, or triggering an alarm siren if certain thresholds are exceeded by the system.

Overview of popular orchestrators

At the time of writing, there are many orchestration engines out there and in use, but there are a few clear winners. The number one spot is clearly held by Kubernetes, which reigns supreme. A distant second is Docker's own SwarmKit, followed by others such as Apache Mesos, AWS **Elastic Container Service (ECS)**, and Microsoft **Azure Container Service (ACS)**.

Kubernetes

Kubernetes was originally designed by Google and later donated to the **Cloud Native Computing Foundation (CNCF)**. Kubernetes was modeled after Google's proprietary Borg system, which has run containers on a supermassive scale for years. Kubernetes was Google's attempt to go back to the drawing board, completely start over, and design a system that incorporates all the lessons that were learned with Borg.

Contrary to Borg, which is proprietary technology, Kubernetes was open sourced early on. This was a very wise choice by Google since it attracted a huge number of contributors from outside of the company and, over only a couple of years, an even more massive ecosystem evolved around Kubernetes.

You can rightfully say that Kubernetes is the darling of the community in the container orchestration space. No other orchestrator has been able to produce so much hype and attract so many talented people who are willing to contribute in a meaningful way to the success of the project as contributors or early adopters.

In that regard, Kubernetes in the container orchestration space looks to me very much like what Linux has become in the server operating system space. Linux has become the de facto standard for server operating systems. All relevant companies, such as Microsoft, IBM, Amazon, Red Hat, and even Docker, have embraced Kubernetes.

And there is one thing that cannot be denied: Kubernetes was designed from the very beginning for massive scalability. After all, it was designed with Google Borg in mind.

One negative aspect that could be voiced against Kubernetes is that it is still complex to set up and manage, at least at the time of writing. There is a significant hurdle to overcome for newcomers. The first step is steep, but once you have worked with this orchestrator for a while, it all makes sense. The overall design is carefully thought through and executed very well.

In release 1.10 of Kubernetes, whose **general availability** (**GA**) was enacted in March 2018, most of the initial shortcomings compared to other orchestrators such as Docker Swarm have been eliminated. For example, security and confidentiality are now not only an afterthought but an integral part of the system.

New features are implemented at a tremendous speed. New releases happen every 3 months or so, more precisely, about every 100 days. Most of the new features are demand-driven, that is, companies using Kubernetes to orchestrate their mission-critical applications can voice their needs. This makes Kubernetes enterprise-ready. It would be wrong to assume that this orchestrator is only for start-ups and not for risk-averse enterprises. The contrary is the case. On what do I base this claim? Well, my claim is justified by the fact that companies such as Microsoft, Docker, and Red Hat, whose clients are mostly big enterprises, have fully embraced Kubernetes, and provide enterprise-grade support for it if it is used and integrated into their enterprise offerings.

Kubernetes supports both Linux and Windows containers.

Docker Swarm

It is well known that Docker popularized and commoditized software containers. Docker did not invent containers, but standardized them and made them broadly available, not least by offering the free image registry—Docker Hub. Initially, Docker focused mainly on the developer and the development life cycle. However, companies that started to use and love containers soon also wanted to use them not just during the development or testing of new applications but also to run those applications in production.

Initially, Docker had nothing to offer in that space, so other companies jumped into that vacuum and offered help to the users. But it didn't take long, and Docker recognized that there was a huge demand for a simple yet powerful orchestrator. Docker's first attempt was a product called Classic Swarm. It was a standalone product that enabled users to create a cluster of Docker host machines that could be used to run and scale their containerized applications in a highly available and self-healing way.

The setup of Docker Classic Swarm, though, was hard. A lot of complicated manual steps were involved. Customers loved the product but struggled with its complexity. So, Docker decided it could do better. It went back to the drawing board and came up with SwarmKit.

SwarmKit was introduced at DockerCon 2016 in Seattle and was an integral part of the newest version of Docker Engine. Yes, you got that right; SwarmKit was, and still is to this day, an integral part of Docker Engine. Thus, if you install a Docker host, you automatically have SwarmKit available with it.

SwarmKit was designed with simplicity and security in mind. The mantra was, and still is, that it has to be almost trivial to set up a swarm and that the swarm has to be highly secure out of the box. Docker Swarm operates on the assumption of least privilege.

Installing a complete, highly available Docker swarm is literally as simple as starting with `docker swarm init` on the first node in the cluster, which becomes the so-called leader, and then `docker swarm join <join-token>` on all other nodes. `<join-token>` is generated by the leader during initialization. The whole process takes fewer than 5 minutes on a swarm with up to 10 nodes. If it is automated, it takes even less time.

As I already mentioned, security was top on the list of must-haves when Docker designed and developed SwarmKit. Containers provide security by relying on Linux kernel namespaces and cgroups, as well as Linux syscall whitelisting (**seccomp**), and the support of Linux capabilities and the **Linux security module** (**LSM**). Now, on top of that, SwarmKit adds MTLS and secrets that are encrypted at rest and in transit.

Furthermore, Swarm defines the so-called **container network model** (**CNM**), which allows for SDNs that provide sandboxing for application services that are running on the swarm. Docker SwarmKit supports both Linux and Windows containers.

Apache Mesos and Marathon

Apache Mesos is an open source project, and was originally designed to make a cluster of servers or nodes look like one single big server from the outside. Mesos is software that makes the management of computer clusters simple. Users of Mesos do not have to care about individual servers but just assume they have a gigantic pool of resources at their disposal, which corresponds with the aggregate of all the resources of all the nodes in the cluster.

Mesos, in IT terms, is already pretty old, at least compared to the other orchestrators. It was first publicly presented in 2009, but at that time, of course, it wasn't designed to run containers since Docker didn't even exist yet. Similar to what Docker does with containers, Mesos uses Linux cgroups to isolate resources such as CPU, memory, or disk I/O for individual applications or services.

Mesos is really the underlying infrastructure for other interesting services built on top of it. From the perspective of containers specifically, Marathon is important. Marathon is a container orchestrator that runs on top of Mesos, which is able to scale to thousands of nodes.

Marathon supports multiple container runtimes, such as Docker or its own Mesos containers. It supports not only stateless but also stateful application services, for example, databases such as PostgreSQL or MongoDB. Similar to Kubernetes and Docker SwarmKit, it supports many of the features that were described earlier in this chapter, such as high availability, health checks, service discovery, load balancing, and location awareness, to name but a few of the most important ones.

Although Mesos and, to a certain extent, Marathon are rather mature projects, their reach is relatively limited. It seems to be most popular in the area of big data, that is, for running data-crunching services such as Spark or Hadoop.

Amazon ECS

If you are looking for a simple orchestrator and have already heavily bought into the AWS ecosystem, then Amazon's ECS might be the right choice for you. It is important to point out one very important limitation of ECS: if you buy into this container orchestrator, then you lock yourself into AWS. You will not be able to easily port an application that is running on ECS to another platform or cloud.

Amazon promotes its ECS service as a highly scalable, fast container management service that makes it easy to run, stop, and manage Docker containers on a cluster. Next to running containers, ECS gives direct access to many other AWS services from the application services that run inside the containers. This tight and seamless integration with many popular AWS services is what makes ECS compelling for users who are looking for an easy way to get their containerized applications up and running in a robust and highly scalable environment. Amazon also provides its own private image registry.

With AWS ECS, you can use Fargate to have it fully manage the underlying infrastructure, allowing you to concentrate exclusively on deploying containerized applications, and you do not have to care about how to create and manage a cluster of nodes. ECS supports both Linux and Windows containers.

In summary, ECS is simple to use, highly scalable, and well integrated with other popular AWS services, but it is not as powerful as, say, Kubernetes or Docker SwarmKit, and it is only available on Amazon AWS.

AWS EKS

Amazon **Elastic Kubernetes Service** (**EKS**) is a managed Kubernetes service provided by AWS. It simplifies the deployment, management, and scaling of containerized applications using Kubernetes, allowing developers and operations teams to focus on building and running applications without the overhead of managing the Kubernetes control plane.

EKS integrates seamlessly with various AWS services, such as Elastic Load Balancing, Amazon RDS, and Amazon S3, making it easy to build a fully managed, scalable, and secure infrastructure for containerized applications. It also supports the Kubernetes ecosystem, allowing users to leverage existing tools, plugins, and extensions to manage and monitor their applications.

With Amazon EKS, the Kubernetes control plane is automatically managed by AWS, ensuring high availability, automatic updates, and security patches. Users are only responsible for managing their worker nodes, which can be deployed using Amazon EC2 instances or AWS Fargate.

Microsoft ACS and AKS

Similar to what we said about ECS, we can claim the same for Microsoft's ACS. It is a simple container orchestration service that makes sense if you are already heavily invested in the Azure ecosystem. I should say the same as I have pointed out for Amazon ECS: if you buy into ACS, then you lock yourself into the offerings of Microsoft. It will not be easy to move your containerized applications from ACS to any other platform or cloud.

ACS is Microsoft's container service, which supports multiple orchestrators such as Kubernetes, Docker Swarm, and Mesos DC/OS. With Kubernetes becoming more and more popular, the focus of Microsoft has clearly shifted to that orchestrator. Microsoft has even rebranded its service and called it **Azure Kubernetes Service** (**AKS**) in order to put the focus on Kubernetes.

AKS manages a hosted Kubernetes, Docker Swarm, or DC/OS environment in Azure for you so that you can concentrate on the applications that you want to deploy, and you don't have to worry about configuring the infrastructure. Microsoft, in its own words, claims the following:

> *"AKS makes it quick and easy to deploy and manage containerized applications without container orchestration expertise. It also eliminates the burden of ongoing operations and maintenance by provisioning, upgrading, and scaling resources on demand, without taking your applications offline."*

Summary

This chapter demonstrated why orchestrators are needed in the first place, and how they work conceptually. It pointed out which orchestrators are the most prominent ones at the time of writing, and discussed the main commonalities and differences between the various orchestrators.

The next chapter will introduce Docker's native orchestrator, SwarmKit. It will elaborate on all the concepts and objects that SwarmKit uses to deploy and run a distributed, resilient, robust, and highly available application in a cluster—on-premises or in the cloud.

Further reading

The following links provide some deeper insight into orchestration-related topics:

- *Kubernetes—production-grade orchestration*: https://kubernetes.io/

- *An overview of Docker Swarm mode*: `https://docs.docker.com/engine/swarm/`
- *Mesosphere—container orchestration services*: `http://bit.ly/2GMpko3`
- *Containers and orchestration explained*: `http://bit.ly/2DFoQgx`

Questions

Answer the following questions to assess your learning progress:

1. What is a container orchestration engine?
2. Why do we need container orchestration engines?
3. What are the main tasks of container orchestration engines?
4. What are some popular container orchestration engines?
5. How does container orchestration improve application reliability?
6. How do container orchestration engines help with application scaling?
7. What are the main differences between Kubernetes and Docker Swarm?
8. How do container orchestration engines handle service discovery?

Answers

Here are some possible answers to the questions:

1. A container orchestration engine is a system that automates the deployment, scaling, management, and networking of containers. It helps developers and operations teams manage large numbers of containers, ensuring that they run efficiently and reliably across multiple hosts in a distributed environment.

2. As the number of containers and services in an application grows, it becomes difficult to manage them manually. Container orchestration engines automate the process of managing containers, enabling efficient resource usage, high availability, fault tolerance, and seamless scaling of containerized applications.

3. The main tasks of container orchestration engines include the following:

   - **Container deployment**: Deploying containers to the appropriate hosts based on resource requirements and constraints

   - **Scaling**: Automatically increasing or decreasing the number of containers based on application demand

   - **Load balancing**: Distributing network traffic across containers to ensure optimal performance

   - **Service discovery**: Enabling containers to find and communicate with each other

- **Health monitoring**: Monitoring container health and automatically replacing unhealthy containers

- **Data persistence and storage management**: Managing storage volumes and ensuring data persistence across container restarts and failures

- **Security and access control**: Managing container security, network policies, and access control.

4. Some popular container orchestration engines include Kubernetes, Docker Swarm, Apache Mesos, Microsoft ACS, Microsoft AKS, and Amazon ECS.

5. Container orchestration engines improve application reliability by ensuring that containers are deployed on appropriate hosts, monitoring container health, and automatically replacing unhealthy or failed containers. They also help maintain application availability by distributing network traffic across containers, allowing the system to handle failures and spikes in traffic gracefully.

6. Container orchestration engines can automatically scale applications by adding or removing containers based on demand, resource usage, and predefined rules. This ensures that applications can handle varying levels of traffic and workload while optimizing resource usage.

7. Kubernetes and Docker Swarm are both container orchestration engines, but they have some key differences:

- Kubernetes is more feature-rich and flexible, offering a wide range of functionality and extensibility. Docker Swarm is simpler and easier to set up, focusing on ease of use and integration with the Docker ecosystem.

- Kubernetes uses a declarative approach, allowing users to describe the desired state of the system, while Docker Swarm uses a more imperative approach.

- Kubernetes has a steeper learning curve compared to Docker Swarm, which has a shallower learning curve and is more straightforward for users already familiar with Docker.

- Kubernetes has a larger community, extensive documentation, and a broader range of third-party integrations compared to Docker Swarm.

8. Container orchestration engines handle service discovery by providing mechanisms for containers to find and communicate with each other. They usually assign unique network addresses or hostnames to containers and maintain a registry of these addresses. Containers can then use these addresses to communicate with other services within the application. Some orchestration engines also provide built-in load balancing and DNS-based service discovery to simplify this process.

14
Introducing Docker Swarm

In the last chapter, we introduced orchestrators. Like a conductor in an orchestra, an orchestrator makes sure that all our containerized application services play together nicely and contribute harmoniously to a common goal. Such orchestrators have quite a few responsibilities, which we discussed in detail. Finally, we provided a short overview of the most important container orchestrators on the market.

This chapter introduces Docker's native orchestrator, **SwarmKit**. It elaborates on all of the concepts and objects SwarmKit uses to deploy and run distributed, resilient, robust, and highly available applications in a cluster on-premises or in the cloud. This chapter also introduces how SwarmKit ensures secure applications by using a **Software-Defined Network** (**SDN**) to isolate containers. We will learn how to create a Docker Swarm locally, in a special environment called **Play with Docker** (**PWD**), and in the cloud. Lastly, we will deploy an application that consists of multiple services related to Docker Swarm.

These are the topics we are going to discuss in this chapter:

- The Docker Swarm architecture
- Stacks, services, and tasks
- Multi-host networking
- Creating a Docker Swarm
- Deploying a first application

After completing this chapter, you will be able to do the following:

- Sketch the essential parts of a highly available Docker Swarm on a whiteboard
- Explain what a (Swarm) service is in two or three simple sentences to an interested layman
- Create a highly available Docker Swarm in AWS, Azure, or GCP consisting of three manager and two worker nodes
- Successfully deploy a replicated service such as Nginx on a Docker Swarm
- Scale a running Docker Swarm service up and down

- Retrieve the aggregated log of a replicated Docker Swarm service
- Write a simple stack file for a sample application consisting of at least two interacting services
- Deploy a stack into a Docker Swarm

Let's get started!

The Docker Swarm architecture

The architecture of a Docker Swarm from a 30,000-foot view consists of two main parts—a raft consensus group of an odd number of manager nodes, and a group of worker nodes that communicate with each other over a gossip network, also called the **control plane**. The following diagram illustrates this architecture:

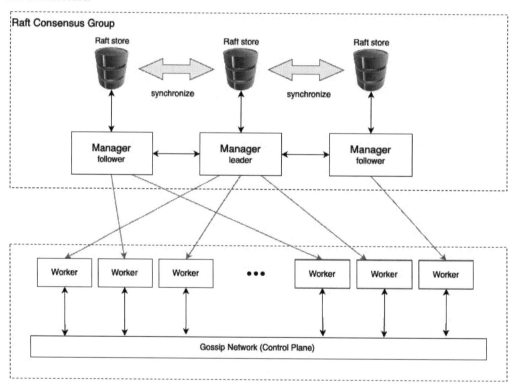

Figure 14.1 – High-level architecture of a Docker Swarm

The manager nodes manage the swarm while the worker nodes execute the applications deployed into the swarm. Each manager has a complete copy of the full state of the Swarm in its local raft store. Managers synchronously communicate with each other, and their raft stores are always in sync.

The workers, on the other hand, communicate with each other asynchronously for scalability reasons. There can be hundreds if not thousands of worker nodes in a Swarm.

Now that we have a high-level overview of what a Docker Swarm is, let's describe all of the individual elements of a Docker Swarm in more detail.

Swarm nodes

A Swarm is a collection of nodes. We can classify a node as a physical computer or **Virtual Machine** (**VM**). Physical computers these days are often referred to as bare metal. People say we're running on bare metal to distinguish from running on a VM.

When we install Docker on such a node, we call this node a Docker host. The following diagram illustrates a bit better what a node and a Docker host are:

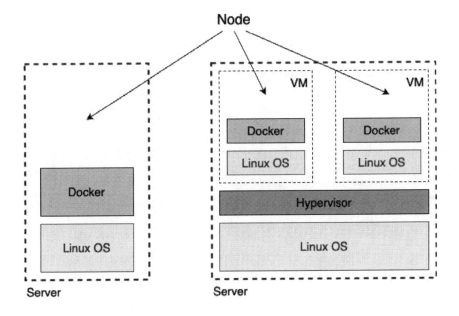

Figure 14.2 – Bare-metal and VM types of Docker Swarm nodes

To become a member of a Docker Swarm, a node must be a Docker host. A node in a Docker Swarm can have one of two roles: it can be a manager or it can be a worker. Manager nodes do what their name implies; they manage the Swarm. The worker nodes, in turn, execute the application workload.

Technically, a manager node can also be a worker node and hence run the application workload—although that is not recommended, especially if the Swarm is a production system running mission-critical applications.

Swarm managers

Each Docker Swarm needs to include at least one manager node. For high-availability reasons, we should have more than one manager node in a Swarm. This is especially true for production or production-like environments. If we have more than one manager node, then these nodes work together using the Raft consensus protocol. The Raft consensus protocol is a standard protocol that is often used when multiple entities need to work together and always need to agree with each other as to which activity to execute next.

To work well, the Raft consensus protocol asks for an odd number of members in what is called the **consensus group**. Hence, we should always have 1, 3, 5, 7, and so on manager nodes. In such a consensus group, there is always a leader. In the case of Docker Swarm, the first node that starts the Swarm initially becomes the leader. If the leader goes away, then the remaining manager nodes elect a new leader. The other nodes in the consensus group are called followers.

Raft leader election

Raft uses a heartbeat mechanism to trigger leader election. When servers start up, they begin as followers. A server remains in the follower state as long as it receives valid **Remote Procedure Calls (RPCs)** from a leader or candidate. Leaders send periodic heartbeats to all followers in order to maintain their authority. If a follower receives no communication over a period of time called the election timeout, then it assumes there is no viable leader and begins an election to choose a new leader. During the election, each server will start a timer with a random time chosen. When this timer fires, the server turns itself from a follower into a candidate. At the same time, it increments the term and sends messages to all its peers asking for a vote and waits for the responses back.

In the context of the Raft consensus algorithm, a "term" corresponds to a round of election and serves as a logical clock for the system, allowing Raft to detect obsolete information such as stale leaders. Every time an election is initiated, the term value is incremented.

When a server receives a vote request, it casts its vote only if the candidate has a higher term or the candidate has the same term. Otherwise, the vote request will be rejected. One peer can only vote for one candidate for one term, but when it receives another vote request with a higher term than the candidate it voted for, it will discard its previous vote.

In the context of Raft and many other distributed systems, "logs" refer to the state machine logs or operation logs, not to be confused with traditional application logs.

If the candidate doesn't receive enough votes before the next timer fires, the current vote will be void and the candidate will start a new election with a higher term. Once the candidate receives votes from the majority of their peers, it turns itself from candidate to leader and immediately broadcasts the authorities to prevent other servers from starting the leader election. The leader will periodically broadcast this information. Now, let's assume that we shut down the current leader node for maintenance reasons. The remaining manager nodes will elect a new leader. When the previous leader node comes back online, it will now become a follower. The new leader remains the leader.

All of the members of the consensus group communicate synchronously with each other. Whenever the consensus group needs to make a decision, the leader asks all followers for agreement. If the majority of the manager nodes gives a positive answer, then the leader executes the task. That means if we have three manager nodes, then at least one of the followers has to agree with the leader. If we have five manager nodes, then at least two followers have to agree with the leader.

Since all manager follower nodes have to communicate synchronously with the leader node to make a decision in the cluster, the decision-making process gets slower and slower the more manager nodes we have forming the consensus group. The recommendation of Docker is to use one manager for development, demo, or test environments. Use three managers nodes in small to medium-sized Swarms and use five managers in large to extra-large Swarms. Using more than five managers in a Swarm is hardly ever justified.

The manager nodes are not only responsible for managing the Swarm but also for maintaining the state of the Swarm. What do we mean by that? When we talk about the state of the Swarm, we mean all the information about it—for example, how many nodes are in the Swarm and what the properties of each node are, such as the name or IP address. We also mean what containers are running on which node in the Swarm and more. What, on the other hand, is not included in the state of the Swarm is data produced by the application services running in containers on the Swarm. This is called **application data** and is definitely not part of the state that is managed by the manager nodes:

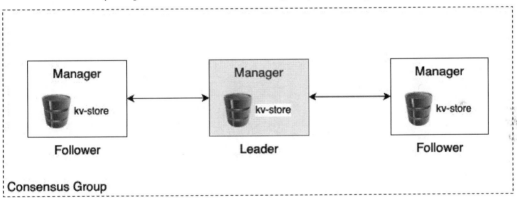

Figure 14.3 – A Swarm manager consensus group

All of the Swarm states are stored in a high-performance **key-value store** (**kv-store**) on each manager node. That's right, each manager node stores a complete replica of the whole Swarm state. This redundancy makes the Swarm highly available. If a manager node goes down, the remaining managers all have the complete state at hand.

If a new manager joins the consensus group, then it synchronizes the Swarm state with the existing members of the group until it has a complete replica. This replication is usually pretty fast in typical Swarms but can take a while if the Swarm is big and many applications are running on it.

Swarm workers

As we mentioned earlier, a Swarm worker node is meant to host and run containers that contain the actual application services we're interested in running on our cluster. They are the workhorses of the Swarm. In theory, a manager node can also be a worker. But, as we already said, this is not recommended on a production system. On a production system, we should let managers be managers.

Worker nodes communicate with each other over the so-called control plane. They use the gossip protocol for their communication. This communication is asynchronous, which means that, at any given time, it is likely that not all worker nodes are in perfect sync.

Now, you might ask—what information do worker nodes exchange? It is mostly information that is needed for service discovery and routing, that is, information about which containers are running on with nodes and more:

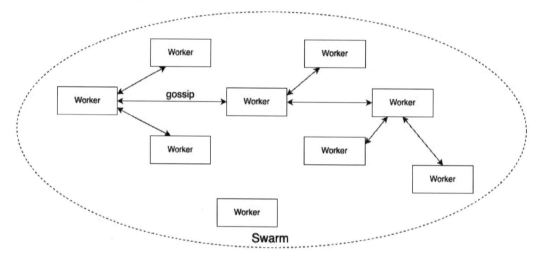

Figure 14.4 – Worker nodes communicating with each other

In the preceding diagram, you can see how workers communicate with each other. To make sure the gossiping scales well in a large Swarm, each worker node only synchronizes its own state with three random neighbors. For those who are familiar with Big O notation, that means that the synchronization of the worker nodes using the gossip protocol scales with $O(0)$.

Big O notation explained

Big O notation is a way to describe the speed or complexity of a given algorithm. It tells you the number of operations an algorithm will make. It's used to communicate how fast an algorithm is, which can be important when evaluating other people's algorithms, and when evaluating your own.

For example, let's say you have a list of numbers and you want to find a specific number in the list. There are different algorithms you can use to do this, such as simple search or binary search. Simple search checks each number in the list one by one until it finds the number you're looking for. Binary search, on the other hand, repeatedly divides the list in half until it finds the number you're looking for.

Now, let's say you have a list of 100 numbers. With simple search, in the worst case, you'll have to check all 100 numbers, so it takes 100 operations. With binary search, in the worst case, you'll only have to check about 7 numbers (because $\log_2(100)$ is roughly 7), so it takes 7 operations.

In this example, binary search is faster than simple search. But what if you have a list of 1 billion numbers? Simple search would take 1 billion operations, while binary search would take only about 30 operations (because $\log_2(1 \text{ billion})$ is roughly 30). So, as the list gets bigger, binary search becomes much faster than simple search.

Big O notation is used to describe this difference in speed between algorithms. In Big O notation, simple search is described as $O(n)$, which means that the number of operations grows linearly with the size of the list (n). Binary search is described as $O(\log n)$, which means that the number of operations grows logarithmically with the size of the list.

Worker nodes are kind of passive. They never actively do anything other than run the workloads they get assigned by the manager nodes. The worker makes sure, though, that it runs these workloads to the best of its capabilities. Later on in this chapter, we will get to know more about exactly what workloads the worker nodes are assigned by the manager nodes.

Now that we know what master and worker nodes in a Docker Swarm are, we are going to introduce stacks, services, and tasks next.

Stacks, services, and tasks

When using a Docker Swarm versus a single Docker host, there is a paradigm change. Instead of talking about individual containers that run processes, we are abstracting away to services that represent a set of replicas of each process, and, in this way, become highly available. We also do not speak anymore of individual Docker hosts with well-known names and IP addresses to which we deploy containers; we'll now be referring to clusters of hosts to which we deploy services. We don't care about an individual host or node anymore. We don't give it a meaningful name; each node rather becomes a number to us.

We also don't care about individual containers and where they are deployed any longer—we just care about having a desired state defined through a service. We can try to depict that as shown in the following diagram:

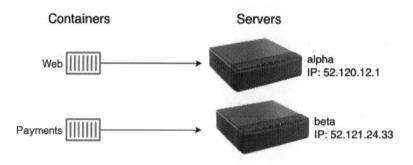

Figure 14.5 – Containers are deployed to well-known servers

Instead of deploying individual containers to well-known servers like in the preceding diagram, where we deploy the web container to the alpha server with the IP address 52.120.12.1, and the payments container to the beta server with the IP 52.121.24.33, we switch to this new paradigm of services and Swarms (or, more generally, clusters):

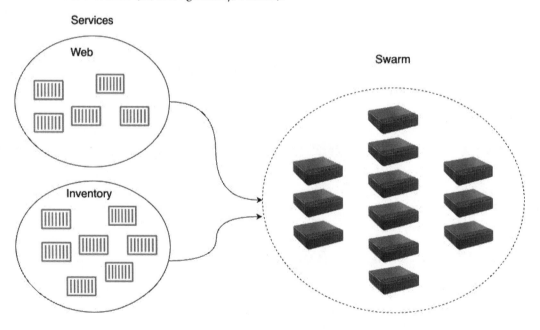

Figure 14.6 – Services are deployed to Swarms

In the preceding diagram, we see that a web service and an inventory service are both deployed to a Swarm that consists of many nodes. Each of the services has a certain number of replicas: five for web and seven for inventory. We don't really care which node the replicas will run on; we only care that the requested number of replicas is always running on whatever nodes the Swarm scheduler decides to put them on.

That said, let's now introduce the concept of a service in the context of a Docker swarm.

Services

A Swarm service is an abstract thing. It is a description of the desired state of an application or application service that we want to run in a Swarm. The Swarm service is like a manifest describing things such as the following:

- The name of the service
- The image from which to create the containers
- The number of replicas to run
- The network(s) that the containers of the service are attached to
- The ports that should be mapped

Having this service manifest, the Swarm manager then makes sure that the described desired state is always reconciled if the actual state should ever deviate from it. So, if, for example, one instance of the service crashes, then the scheduler on the Swarm manager schedules a new instance of this particular service on a node with free resources so that the desired state is re-established.

Now, what is a task? This is what we're going to learn next.

Tasks

We have learned that a service corresponds to a description of the desired state in which an application service should be at all times. Part of that description was the number of replicas the service should be running. Each replica is represented by a task. In this regard, a Swarm service contains a collection of tasks. On Docker Swarm, a task is an atomic unit of deployment. Each task of a service is deployed by the Swarm scheduler to a worker node. The task contains all of the necessary information that the worker node needs to run a container based on the image, which is part of the service description. Between a task and a container, there is a one-to-one relation. The container is the instance that runs on the worker node, while the task is the description of this container as a part of a Swarm service.

Finally, let's talk about a stack in the context of a Docker swarm.

Stacks

Now that we have a good idea about what a Swarm service is and what tasks are, we can introduce the stack. A stack is used to describe a collection of Swarm services that are related, most probably because they are part of the same application. In that sense, we could also say that a stack describes an application that consists of one-to-many services that we want to run on the Swarm.

Typically, we describe a stack declaratively in a text file that is formatted using the YAML format and that uses the same syntax as the already known Docker Compose file. This leads to a situation where people sometimes say that a stack is described by a Docker Compose file. A better wording would be that a stack is described in a stack file that uses similar syntax to a Docker Compose file.

Let's try to illustrate the relationship between the stack, services, and tasks in the following diagram and connect it with the typical content of a stack file:

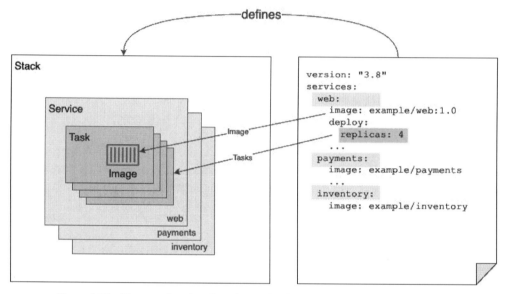

Figure 14.7 – Diagram showing the relationship between stack, services, and tasks

In the preceding diagram, we see on the right-hand side a declarative description of a sample Stack. The Stack consists of three services, called `web`, `payments`, and `inventory`. We also see that the web service uses the `example/web:1.0` image and has four replicas. On the left-hand side of the diagram, we see that the Stack embraces the three services mentioned. Each service, in turn, contains a collection of Tasks, as many as there are replicas. In the case of the web service, we have a collection of four Tasks. Each Task contains the name of the Image from which it will instantiate a container once the Task is scheduled on a Swarm node.

Now that you have a good understanding of the main concepts of a Docker swarm, such as nodes, stack, services, and tasks, let's look a bit more closely into the networking used in a swarm.

Multi-host networking

In *Chapter 10, Using Single-Host Networking*, we discussed how containers communicate on a single Docker host. Now, we have a Swarm that consists of a cluster of nodes or Docker hosts. Containers that are located on different nodes need to be able to communicate with each other. Many techniques can help us to achieve this goal. Docker has chosen to implement an overlay network driver for Docker Swarm. This overlay network allows containers attached to the same overlay network to discover each other and freely communicate with each other. The following is a schema for how an overlay network works:

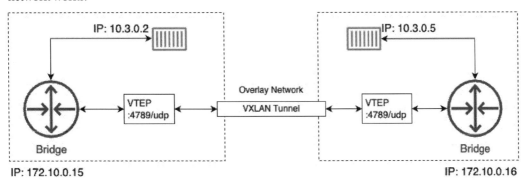

Figure 14.8 – The overlay network

We have two nodes or Docker hosts with the IP addresses 172.10.0.15 and 172.10.0.16. The values we have chosen for the IP addresses are not important; what is important is that both hosts have a distinct IP address and are connected by a physical network (a network cable), which is called the **underlay network**.

On the node on the left-hand side, we have a container running with the IP address 10.3.0.2, and on the node on the right-hand side, we have another container with the IP address 10.3.0.5. Now, the former container wants to communicate with the latter. How can this happen? In *Chapter 10, Using Single-Host Networking*, we saw how this works when both containers are located on the same node—by using a Linux bridge. But Linux bridges only operate locally and cannot span across nodes. So, we need another mechanism. Linux VXLAN comes to the rescue. VXLAN has been available on Linux since way before containers were a thing.

> **VXLAN explained**
>
> **VXLAN**, or **Virtual eXtensible Local Area Network**, is a networking protocol that allows for the creation of virtual layer 2 domains over an IP network using the UDP protocol. It was designed to solve the problem of limited VLAN IDs (4,096) in IEEE 802.1q by expanding the size of the identifier to 24 bits (16,777,216).
>
> In simpler terms, VXLAN allows for the creation of virtual networks that can span across different physical locations. For example, certain VMs that are running on different hosts can communicate over a VXLAN tunnel. The hosts can be in different subnets or even in different data centers around the world. From the perspective of the VMs, other VMs in the same VXLAN are within the same layer 2 domain.

When the left-hand container in *Figure 14.8* sends a data packet, the bridge realizes that the target of the packet is not on this host. Now, each node participating in an overlay network gets a so-called **VXLAN Tunnel Endpoint** (**VTEP**) object, which intercepts the packet (the packet at that moment is an OSI layer 2 data packet), wraps it with a header containing the target IP address of the host that runs the destination container (this now makes it an OSI layer 3 data packet), and sends it over the VXLAN tunnel. The VTEP on the other side of the tunnel unpacks the data packet and forwards it to the local bridge, which in turn forwards it to the destination container.

The overlay driver is included in SwarmKit and is in most cases the recommended network driver for Docker Swarm. There are other multi-node-capable network drivers available from third parties that can be installed as plugins in each participating Docker host. Certified network plugins are available from the Docker store.

Great, we have all the basic knowledge about a Docker swarm. So, let's create one.

Creating a Docker Swarm

Creating a Docker Swarm is almost trivial. It is so easy that if you know how orchestrators work, it might even seem unbelievable. But it is true, Docker has done a fantastic job in making Swarms simple and elegant to use. At the same time, Docker Swarm has been proven to be very robust and scalable when used by large enterprises.

Creating a local single-node swarm

So, enough imagining—let's demonstrate how we can create a Swarm. In its most simple form, a fully functioning Docker Swarm consists only of a single node. If you're using Docker Desktop, or even if you're using Docker Toolbox, then your personal computer or laptop is such a node. Hence, we can start right there and demonstrate some of the most important features of a Swarm.

Let's initialize a Swarm. On the command line, just enter the following command:

```
$ docker swarm init
```

After an incredibly short time, you should see an output like the following:

```
Swarm initialized: current node (zqzxn4bur43lywp55fysnymd4) is now a
manager.
To add a worker to this swarm, run the following command:
    docker swarm join --token SWMTKN-1-57ayqfyc8cdg09hi9tzuztzcg2gk2rd
6abu71ennaide3r20q5-21j3wpm8scytn9u5n1jrvlbzf 192.168.0.13:2377
To add a manager to this swarm, run 'docker swarm join-token manager'
and follow the instructions.
```

Our computer is now a Swarm node. Its role is that of a manager and it is the leader (of the managers, which makes sense since there is only one manager at this time). Although it took only a very short time to finish `docker swarm init`, the command did a lot of things during that time. Some of them are as follows:

- It created a root **Certificate Authority (CA)**
- It created a kv-store that is used to store the state of the whole Swarm

Now, in the preceding output, we can see a command that can be used to join other nodes to the Swarm that we just created. The command is as follows:

```
$ docker swarm join --token <join-token> <IP address>:2377
```

Here, we have the following:

- `<join-token>` is a token generated by the Swarm leader at the time the Swarm was initialized
- `<IP address>` is the IP address of the leader

Although our cluster remains simple, as it consists of only one member, we can still ask the Docker CLI to list all of the nodes of the Swarm using the `docker node ls` command. This will look similar to the following screenshot:

```
[node1] (local) root@192.168.0.13 ~
$ docker node ls
ID                            HOSTNAME  STATUS  AVAILABILITY  MANAGER STATUS  ENGINE VERSION
zqzxn4bur43lywp55fysnymd4 *   node1     Ready   Active        Leader          20.10.17
```

Figure 14.9 – Listing the nodes of the Docker Swarm

In this output, we first see the ID that was given to the node. The star (*) that follows the ID indicates that this is the node on which `docker node ls` was executed—basically saying that this is the active node. Then, we have the (human-readable) name of the node and its status, availability, and manager status. As mentioned earlier, this very first node of the Swarm automatically became the leader, which is indicated in the preceding screenshot. Lastly, we see which version of Docker Engine we're using.

To get even more information about a node, we can use the `docker node inspect` command, as shown in the following truncated output:

```
$ docker node inspect node1
[
    {
        "ID": "zqzxn4bur43lywp55fysnymd4",
        "Version": {
            "Index": 9
        },
        "CreatedAt": "2023-04-21T06:48:06.434268546Z",
        "UpdatedAt": "2023-04-21T06:48:06.955837213Z",
        "Spec": {
```

```
            "Labels": {},
            "Role": "manager",
            "Availability": "active"
        },
        "Description": {
            "Hostname": "node1",
            "Platform": {
                "Architecture": "x86_64",
                "OS": "linux"
            },
            "Resources": {
                "NanoCPUs": 8000000000,
                "MemoryBytes": 33737699328
            },
            "Engine": {
                "EngineVersion": "20.10.17",
                "Plugins": [
                    {
                        "Type": "Log",
                        "Name": "awslogs"
                    },
...
        }
    ]
```

There is a lot of information generated by this command, so we have only presented a shortened version of the output. This output can be useful, for example, when you need to troubleshoot a misbehaving cluster node.

Before you continue, don't forget to shut down or dissolve the swarm by using the following command:

```
$ docker swarm leave --force
```

In the next section, we will use the PWD environment to generate and use a Docker Swarm.

Using PWD to generate a Swarm

To experiment with Docker Swarm without having to install or configure anything locally on our computer, we can use PWD. PWD is a website that can be accessed with a browser and that offers us the ability to create a Docker Swarm consisting of up to five nodes. It is definitely a playground, as the name implies, and the time for which we can use it is limited to four hours per session. We can open as many sessions as we want, but each session automatically ends after four hours. Other than that, it is a fully functional Docker environment that is ideal for tinkering with Docker or demonstrating some features.

Let's access the site now. In your browser, navigate to the website `https://labs.play-with-docker.com`. You will be presented with a welcome and login screen. Use your Docker ID to log in. After successfully doing so, you will be presented with a screen that looks like the following screenshot:

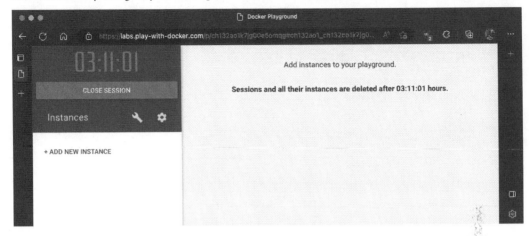

Figure 14.10 – PWD window

As we can see immediately, there is a big timer counting down from four hours. That's how much time we have left to play in this session. Furthermore, we see an + **ADD NEW INSTANCE** link. Click it to create a new Docker host. When you do that, your screen should look as in the following screenshot:

Figure 14.11 – PWD with one new node

On the left-hand side, we see the newly created node with its IP address (192.168.0.13) and its name (node1). On the right-hand side, we have some additional information about this new node in the upper half of the screen and a terminal in the lower half. Yes, this terminal is used to execute commands on this node that we just created. This node has the Docker CLI installed, and hence we can execute all of the familiar Docker commands on it, such as the Docker version. Try it out.

But now we want to create a Docker Swarm. Execute the following command in the terminal in your browser:

```
$ docker swarm init --advertise-addr=eth0
```

The output generated by the preceding command is similar to the one we saw when creating a local Docker Swarm. The important thing to note is the join command, which is what we want to use to join additional nodes to the cluster we just created.

You might have noted that we specified the --advertise-addr parameter in the Swarm init command. Why is that necessary here? The reason is that the nodes generated by PWD have more than one IP address associated with them. We can easily verify that by executing the ip command on the node. This command will show us that there are indeed two endpoints, eth0 and eth1, present. We hence have to specify explicitly to the new to-be swarm manager which one we want to use. In our case, it is eth0.

Create four additional nodes in PWD by clicking four times on the + **ADD NEW INSTANCE** link. The new nodes will be called node2, node3, node4, and node5 and will all be listed on the left-hand side. If you click on one of the nodes on the left-hand side, then the right-hand side shows the details of the respective node and a terminal window for that node.

Select each node (2 to 5) and execute the docker swarm join command that you have copied from the leader node (node1) in the respective terminal:

```
$ docker swarm join --token SWMTKN-1-4o1ybxxg7cv... 192.168.0.13:2377
```

This node joined the swarm as a worker.

Once you have joined all four nodes to the Swarm, switch back to node1 and list all nodes:

```
$ docker node ls
```

This, unsurprisingly, results in this (slightly reformatted for readability):

```
ID              HOSTNAME STATUS  AVAIL. MANAGER ST. ENGINE VER.
Nb16ey2p... *   node1    Ready   Active  Leader     20.10.17
Kdd0yv15...     node2    Ready   Active             20.10.17
t5iw0clx...     node3    Ready   Active             20.10.17
Nr6ngsgs...     node4    Ready   Active             20.10.17
thbiwgft...     node5    Ready   Active             20.10.17
```

Still on `node1`, we can now promote, say, `node2` and `node3`, to make the Swarm highly available:

```
$ docker node promote node2 node3
```

This results in this output:

```
Node node2 promoted to a manager in the swarm.
Node node3 promoted to a manager in the swarm.
```

With this, our Swarm on PWD is ready to accept a workload. We have created a highly available Docker Swarm with three manager nodes that form a Raft consensus group and two worker nodes.

Creating a Docker Swarm in the cloud

All of the Docker Swarms we have created so far are wonderful to use in development, to experiment with, or to use for demonstration purposes. If we want to create a Swarm that can be used as a production environment where we run our mission-critical applications, though, then we need to create a—I'm tempted to say—real Swarm in the cloud or on-premises. In this book, we are going to demonstrate how to create a Docker Swarm in AWS.

We can manually create a Swarm through the AWS console:

1. Log in to your AWS account. If you do not have one yet, create a free one.

2. First, we create an AWS **Security Group (SG)** and call it `aws-docker-demo-sg`:

    I.   Navigate to your default VPC.

    II.   On the left-hand side, select **Security groups**.

    III. Click the **Create Security Group** button.

    IV.   Call the SG `aws-docker-demo-sg`, as mentioned, and add a description such as `A SG for our Docker demo`.

    V.   Now, click the **Create security group** button.

    VI.   Add some inbound rules to the new SG by clicking the **Edit inbound rules** button on the overview page of the new SG.

    VII. For each rule you want to add, click **Add rule** and fill in the settings as follows:

          i.   **Type**: Custom TCP, **Protocol**: TCP, **Port range**: 2377, **Source**: Custom

          ii.   For the value, select the SG just created (in the author's case, it is `sg-030d0...`)

          iii. **Type**: Custom UDP, **Protocol**: UDP, **Port range**: 7946, **Source**: Custom

          iv.   For the value, select the SG just created

          v.   **Type**: Custom TCP, **Protocol**: TCP, **Port range**: 7946, **Source**: Custom

vi.   For the value select the SG just created

vii. **Type**: Custom TCP, **Protocol**: TCP, **Port range**: 4789, **Source**: Custom

viii. For the value, select the SG just created

ix.   **Type**: Custom TCP, **Protocol**: TCP, **Port range**: 22, **Source**: My IP

x.   This last rule is to be able to access the instances from your host via SSH

Docker Swarm ports

TCP port 2377: This is the main communication port for swarm mode. The Swarm management and orchestration commands are communicated over this port. It's used for communication between nodes and plays a crucial role in the Raft consensus algorithm, which ensures that all the nodes in a swarm act as a single system.

TCP and UDP port 7946: This port is used for communication among nodes (container network discovery). It helps the nodes in the swarm to exchange information about the services and tasks running on each of them.

UDP port 4789: This port is used for overlay network traffic. When you create an overlay network for your services, Docker Swarm uses this port for the data traffic between the containers.

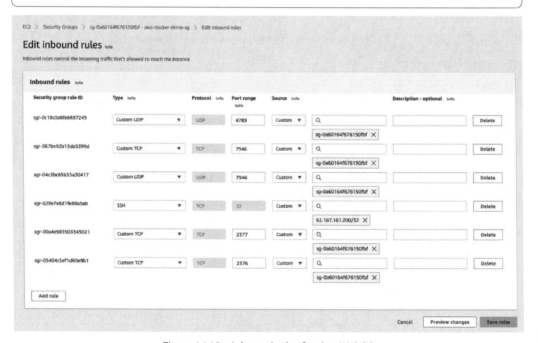

Figure 14.12 – Inbound rules for the AWS SG

xi.   When done, click **Save rules**.

3. Go to the EC2 dashboard.

4. First, we create a key pair for all EC2 instances we are going to create next:

    I.   Locate and click the **Key Pairs** item on the left-hand side.

    II. Click the **Create key pair** button.

    III. Enter a name for the key pair, such as `aws-docker-demo`.

    IV. Make sure the private key file format is `.pem`.

    V.   Click the **Create key pair** button.

    VI. The key pair is added to the list of existing key pairs and downloaded to your machine.

    VII. Store the downloaded `.pem` file in a safe location.

5. Back on the EC2 dashboard, launch a new EC2 instance with the following settings:

    I.   Name the instance `manager1`.

    II. Select the **Ubuntu Server 22.04 LTS** AMI (it should be eligible for the free tier).

    III. Use `t2.micro` as the instance type.

    IV. Use the key pair that we created before, called `aws-docker-demo`.

    V.   Select the existing SG, `aws-docker-demo-sg`, that we created previously.

    VI. Then, click the **Launch** button.

6. Repeat the previous step to create two worker nodes and call them `worker1` and `worker2`, respectively.

7. Go to the list of EC2 instances. You may have to wait a few minutes until they are all ready.

8. Start with the `manager1` instance by selecting it and then clicking the **Connect** button. A view will open, explaining the steps needed to connect to the instance via `ssh`. Follow those instructions carefully.

9. Once connected to the `manager1` instance, let's install Docker:

    ```
    $ sudo apt-get update && sudo apt -y install docker.io
    ```

    This may take a couple of minutes to finish.

10. Now, make sure you can use Docker without having to use the `sudo` command:

    ```
    $ sudo usermod -aG docker $USER
    ```

11. To apply the preceding command, you have to quickly exit from the AWS instance:

    ```
    $ exit
    ```

    Then, immediately connect again using the `ssh` command from *step 6*.

12. Back on the EC2 instance, make sure you can access Docker with the following:

```
$ docker version
```

If everything is installed and configured correctly, you should see the version information of the Docker client and engine.

13. Now repeat *steps 6* to *10* for the other two EC2 instances, `worker1` and `worker2`.

14. Now go back to your `manager1` instance and initialize a Docker swarm on it:

```
$ docker swarm init
```

The output should be the same as you saw for the case when you created a swarm locally or on PWD.

15. Copy the `docker swarm join` command from the preceding output.

16. Go to each worker node and run the command. The node should respond with the following:

```
This node joined a swarm as a worker.
```

17. Go back to the `manager1` node and run the following command to list all nodes of the swarm:

```
$ docker node ls
```

What you should see is similar to this:

```
ubuntu@ip-172-31-32-21:~$ docker node ls
ID                            HOSTNAME            STATUS   AVAILABILITY   MANAGER STATUS   ENGINE VERSION
bf962v1k2g2b297l7emo4s5we *   ip-172-31-32-21     Ready    Active         Leader           20.10.21
s6e4z5w4zopp4hzj41dm1sddi     ip-172-31-32-189    Ready    Active                          20.10.21
rmb4uj3aq8wljapv0fl8lju1m     ip-172-31-47-124    Ready    Active                          20.10.21
```

Figure 14.13 – List of swarm nodes on AWS

Now that we have a Docker swarm in the (AWS) cloud, let's deploy a simple application to it.

Deploying a first application

We have created a few Docker Swarms on various platforms. Once created, a Swarm behaves the same way on any platform. The way we deploy and update applications on a Swarm is not platform-dependent. It has been one of Docker's main goals to avoid vendor lock-in when using a Swarm. Swarm-ready applications can be effortlessly migrated from, say, a Swarm running on-premises to a cloud-based Swarm. It is even technically possible to run part of a Swarm on-premises and another part in the cloud. It works, yet we have, of course, to consider possible side effects due to the higher latency between nodes in geographically distant areas.

Now that we have a highly available Docker Swarm up and running, it is time to run some workloads on it. I'm using the swarm just created on AWS. We'll start by first creating a single service. For this, we need to SSH into one of the manager nodes. I selected the swarm node on the `manager1` instance:

```
$ ssh -i "aws-docker-demo.pem" <public-dns-name-of-manager1>
```

We start the deployment of our first application to the swarm by creating a service.

Creating a service

A service can be created either as part of a stack or directly using the Docker CLI. Let's first look at a sample stack file that defines a single service:

1. Use the Vi editor to create a new file called `stack.yml` and add this content:

    ```
    version: "3.7"
    services:
      whoami:
        image: training/whoami:latest
        networks:
        - test-net
        ports:
        - 81:8000
        deploy:
          replicas: 6
          update_config:
            parallelism: 2
            delay: 10s
          labels:
            app: sample-app
            environment: prod-south
    networks:
      test-net:
        driver: overlay
    ```

2. Exit the Vi editor by first pressing the *Esc* key, then typing `:wq`, and then pressing *Enter*. This will save the code snippet and exit vi.

Note

If you are not familiar with Vi, you can also use nano instead.

In the preceding example, we see what the desired state of a service called `whoami` is:

- It is based on the `training/whoami:latest` image

- Containers of the service are attached to the `test-net` network

- The container port `8000` is published to port `81`

- It is running with six replicas (or tasks)

- During a rolling update, the individual tasks are updated in batches of two, with a delay of 10 seconds between each successful batch

- The service (and its tasks and containers) is assigned the two labels, `app` and `environment`, with the values `sample-app` and `prod-south`, respectively

There are many more settings that we could define for a service, but the preceding ones are some of the more important ones. Most settings have meaningful default values. If, for example, we do not specify the number of replicas, then Docker defaults it to `1`. The name and image of a service are, of course, mandatory. Note that the name of the service must be unique in the Swarm.

3. To create the preceding service, we use the `docker stack deploy` command. Assuming that the file in which the preceding content is stored is called `stack.yaml`, we have the following:

```
$ docker stack deploy -c stack.yaml sample-stack
```

Here, we have created a stack called `sample-stack` that consists of one service, `whoami`.

4. We can list all stacks on our Swarm:

```
$ docker stack ls
```

Upon doing so, we should get this:

```
NAME                          SERVICES
sample-stack                  1
```

5. We can list the services defined in our Swarm, as follows:

```
$ docker service ls
```

We get the following output:

```
ubuntu@ip-172-31-32-21:~$ docker service ls
ID            NAME                  MODE         REPLICAS   IMAGE                    PORTS
nllohee42loz  sample-stack_whoami   replicated   6/6        training/whoami:latest   *:81->8000/tcp
```

Figure 14.14 – List of all services running in the Swarm

In the output, we can see that currently, we have only one service running, which was to be expected. The service has an ID. The format of the ID, contrary to what you have used so far for containers, networks, or volumes, is alphanumeric (in the latter cases, it was always SHA-256). We can also see that the name of the service is a combination of the service name we defined in the stack file and the name of the stack, which is used as a prefix. This makes sense since we want to be able to deploy multiple stacks (with different names) using the same stack file into our Swarm. To make sure that service names are unique, Docker decided to combine the service name and stack name.

In the third column, we see the mode, which is replicated. The number of replicas is shown as 6 / 6. This tells us that six out of the six requested replicas are running. This corresponds to the desired state. In the output, we also see the image that the service uses and the port mappings of the service.

Inspecting the service and its tasks

In the preceding output, we cannot see the details of the six replicas that have been created.

To get some deeper insight into that, we can use the `docker service ps <service-id>` command. If we execute this command for our service, we will get the following output:

```
ubuntu@ip-172-31-32-21:~$ docker service ps n1lohee
ID              NAME                   IMAGE                    NODE              DESIRED STATE    CURRENT STATE           ERROR    PORTS
5ae1aacbaq4j    sample-stack_whoami.1  training/whoami:latest   ip-172-31-47-124  Running          Running 2 minutes ago
mo6k4om7umfw    sample-stack_whoami.2  training/whoami:latest   ip-172-31-32-189  Running          Running 2 minutes ago
nqxqsjjp8jg5    sample-stack_whoami.3  training/whoami:latest   ip-172-31-32-21   Running          Running 2 minutes ago
ahzyah17llky    sample-stack_whoami.4  training/whoami:latest   ip-172-31-47-124  Running          Running 2 minutes ago
uh7zjzzt3rib    sample-stack_whoami.5  training/whoami:latest   ip-172-31-32-189  Running          Running 2 minutes ago
w90b8xmkdw53    sample-stack_whoami.6  training/whoami:latest   ip-172-31-32-21   Running          Running 2 minutes ago
```

Figure 14.15 – Details of the whoami service

In the preceding output, we can see the list of six tasks that corresponds to the requested six replicas of our whoami service. In the **NODE** column, we can also see the node to which each task has been deployed. The name of each task is a combination of the service name plus an increasing index. Also note that, similar to the service itself, each task gets an alphanumeric ID assigned.

In my case, apparently tasks 3 and 6, with the names sample-stack_whoami.3 and sample-stack_whoami.6, have been deployed to ip-172-31-32-21, which is the leader of our Swarm. Hence, I should find a container running on this node. Let's see what we get if we list all containers running on ip-172-31-32-21:

```
ubuntu@ip-172-31-32-21:~$ docker container ls
CONTAINER ID    IMAGE                    COMMAND       CREATED        STATUS         PORTS        NAMES
e0911d17425c    training/whoami:latest   "/app/http"   5 minutes ago  Up 5 minutes   8000/tcp     sample-stack_whoami.3.nqxqsjjp8jg51xq5kbhvd41at
ae8a50b5b058    training/whoami:latest   "/app/http"   5 minutes ago  Up 5 minutes   8000/tcp     sample-stack_whoami.6.w90b8xmkdw539j9g469l76hwm
```

Figure 14.16 – List of containers on node ip-172-31-32-21

As expected, we find a container running from the `training/whoami:latest` image with a name that is a combination of its parent task name and ID. We can try to visualize the whole hierarchy of objects that we generated when deploying our sample stack:

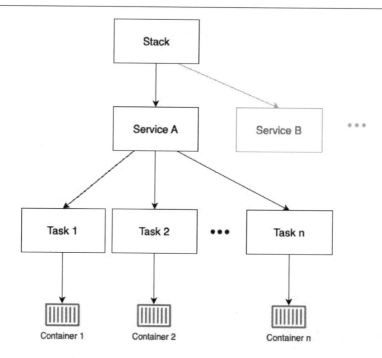

Figure 14.17 – Object hierarchy of a Docker Swarm stack

A stack can consist of one-to-many services. Each service has a collection of tasks. Each task has a one-to-one association with a container. Stacks and services are created and stored on the Swarm manager nodes. Tasks are then scheduled to Swarm worker nodes, where the worker node creates the corresponding container. We can also get some more information about our service by inspecting it. Execute the following command:

```
$ docker service inspect sample-stack_whoami
```

This provides a wealth of information about all of the relevant settings of the service. This includes those we have explicitly defined in our stack.yaml file, but also those that we didn't specify and that, therefore, got their default values assigned. We're not going to list the whole output here, as it is too long, but I encourage you to inspect it on your own machine. We will discuss part of the information in more detail in the *The swarm routing mesh* section in *Chapter 15*.

Testing the load balancing

To see that the swarm load balances incoming requests to our sample whoami application, we can use the curl tool. Execute the following command a few times and observe how the answer changes:

```
$ for i in {1..7}; do curl localhost:81; done
```

This results in an output like this:

```
I'm ae8a50b5b058
I'm 1b6b507d900c
I'm 83864fb80809
I'm 161176f937cf
I'm adf340def231
I'm e0911d17425c
I'm ae8a50b5b058
```

Note that after the sixth item, the sequence is repeating. This is due to the fact that the Docker swarm is load balancing calls using a round-robin algorithm.

Logs of a service

In an earlier chapter, we worked with the logs produced by a container. Here, we're concentrating on a service. Remember that, ultimately, a service with many replicas has many containers running. Hence, we would expect that, if we asked the service for its logs, Docker would return an aggregate of all logs of those containers belonging to the service. And indeed, we'll see this when we use the `docker service logs` command:

```
$ docker service logs sample-stack_whoami
```

This is what we get:

```
ubuntu@ip-172-31-32-21:~$ docker service logs sample-stack_whoami
sample-stack_whoami.6.w90b8xmkdw53@ip-172-31-32-21    | Listening on :8000
sample-stack_whoami.3.nqxqsjjp8jg5@ip-172-31-32-21    | Listening on :8000
sample-stack_whoami.2.mo6k4om7umfw@ip-172-31-32-189   | Listening on :8000
sample-stack_whoami.5.uh7zjzzt3rib@ip-172-31-32-189   | Listening on :8000
sample-stack_whoami.4.ahzyah17llky@ip-172-31-47-124   | Listening on :8000
sample-stack_whoami.1.5ae1aacbaq4j@ip-172-31-47-124   | Listening on :8000
```

Figure 14.18 – Logs of the whoami service

There is not much information in the logs at this point, but it is enough to discuss what we get. The first part of each line in the log always contains the name of the container combined with the node name from which the log entry originates. Then, separated by the vertical bar (|), we get the actual log entry. So, if we were to, say, ask for the logs of the first container in the list directly, we would only get a single entry, and the value we would see in this case would be `Listening on :8000`.

The aggregated logs that we get with the `docker service logs` command are not sorted in any particular way. So, if the correlation of events is happening in different containers, you should add information to your log output that makes this correlation possible.

Typically, this is a timestamp for each log entry. But this has to be done at the source; for example, the application that produces a log entry needs to also make sure a timestamp is added.

We can also query the logs of an individual task of the service by providing the task ID instead of the service ID or name. So, say we queried the logs from task 6 with the following:

```
$ docker service logs w90b8
```

This gives us the following output:

```
sample-stack_whoami.6.w90b8xmkdw53@ip-172-31-32-21    | Listening on
:8000
```

In the next section, we are investigating how the swarm reconciles the desired state.

Reconciling the desired state

We have learned that a Swarm service is a description or manifest of the desired state that we want an application or application service to run in. Now, let's see how Docker Swarm reconciles this desired state if we do something that causes the actual state of the service to be different from the desired state. The easiest way to do this is to forcibly kill one of the tasks or containers of the service.

Let's do this with the container that has been scheduled on `node-1`:

```
$ docker container rm -f sample-stack_whoami.3. nqxqs...
```

If we do that and then run `docker service ps` right afterward, we will see the following output:

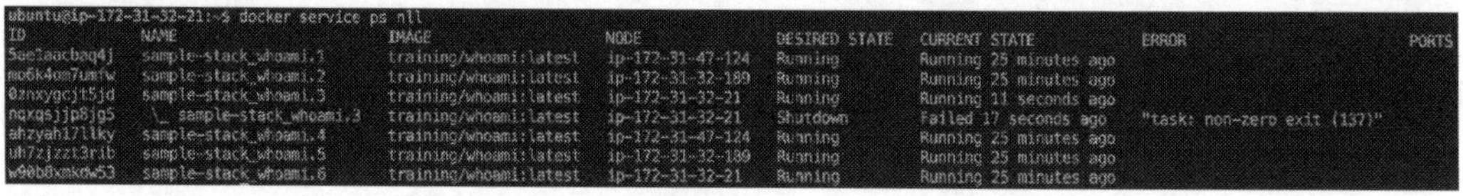
```
ubuntu@ip-172-31-32-21:~$ docker service ps nll
ID             NAME                       IMAGE                     NODE               DESIRED STATE   CURRENT STATE             ERROR                              PORTS
5ae1aacbaq4j   sample-stack_whoami.1      training/whoami:latest    ip-172-31-47-124   Running         Running 25 minutes ago
mo6k4om7umfw   sample-stack_whoami.2      training/whoami:latest    ip-172-31-32-189   Running         Running 25 minutes ago
0znxygcjt5jd   sample-stack_whoami.3      training/whoami:latest    ip-172-31-32-21    Running         Running 11 seconds ago
nqxqsjjp8jg5    \_ sample-stack_whoami.3  training/whoami:latest    ip-172-31-32-21    Shutdown        Failed 17 seconds ago     "task: non-zero exit (137)"
ahzyah17llky   sample-stack_whoami.4      training/whoami:latest    ip-172-31-47-124   Running         Running 25 minutes ago
uh7zjzzt3rib   sample-stack_whoami.5      training/whoami:latest    ip-172-31-32-189   Running         Running 25 minutes ago
w90b8xmkdw53   sample-stack_whoami.6      training/whoami:latest    ip-172-31-32-21    Running         Running 25 minutes ago
```

Figure 14.19 – Docker Swarm reconciling the desired state after one task failed

We see that task 2 failed with exit code `137` and that the Swarm immediately reconciled the desired state by rescheduling the failed task on a node with free resources. In this case, the scheduler selected the same node as the failed tasks, but this is not always the case. So, without us intervening, the Swarm completely fixed the problem, and since the service is running in multiple replicas, at no time was the service down.

Let's try another failure scenario. This time, we're going to shut down an entire node and are going to see how the Swarm reacts. Let's take node `ip-172-31-47-124` for this, as it has two tasks (tasks 1 and 4) running on it. For this, we can head over to the AWS console and in the EC2 dashboard, stop the instance called `ip-172-31-47-124`.

Note that I had to go into the details of each worker instance to find out which one has the hostname ip-172-31-47-124; in my case, it was worker2.

Back on the master node, we can now again run docker service ps to see what happened:

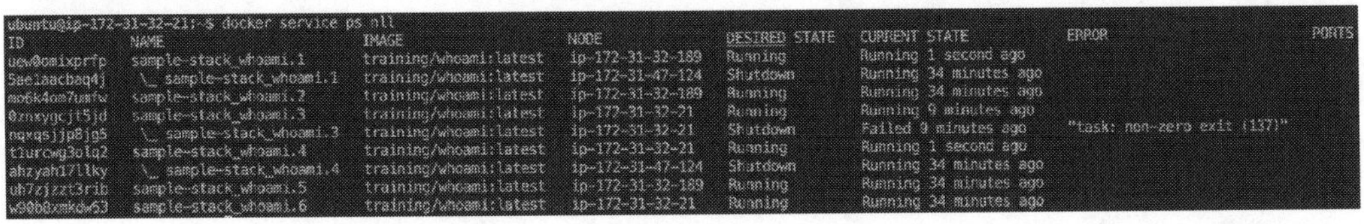

Figure 14.20 – Swarm reschedules all tasks of a failed node

In the preceding screenshot, we can see that immediately, task 1 was rescheduled on node ip-172-31-32-189, while task 4 was rescheduled on node ip-172-31-32-21. Even this more radical failure is handled gracefully by Docker Swarm.

It is important to note though that if node ip-172-31-47-124 ever comes back online in the Swarm, the tasks that had previously been running on it will not automatically be transferred back to it.

But the node is now ready for a new workload.

Deleting a service or a stack

If we want to remove a particular service from the Swarm, we can use the docker service rm command. If, on the other hand, we want to remove a stack from the Swarm, we analogously use the docker stack rm command. This command removes all services that are part of the stack definition. In the case of the whoami service, it was created by using a stack file and hence we're going to use the latter command:

```
$ docker stack rm sample-stack
```

This gives us this output:

```
Removing service sample-stack_whoami
Removing network sample-stack_test-net
```

The preceding command will make sure that all tasks of each service of the stack are terminated, and the corresponding containers are stopped by first sending SIGTERM, and then, if not successful, SIGKILL after 10 seconds of timeout.

It is important to note that the stopped containers are not removed from the Docker host.

Hence, it is advised to purge containers from time to time on worker nodes to reclaim unused resources. Use `docker container purge -f` for this purpose.

Question: Why does it make sense to leave stopped or crashed containers on the worker node and not automatically remove them?

Deploying a multi-service stack

In *Chapter 11, Managing Containers with Docker Compose*, we used an application consisting of two services that were declaratively described in a Docker Compose file. We can use this Compose file as a template to create a stack file that allows us to deploy the same application into a Swarm:

1. Create a new file called `pets-stack.yml`, and add this content to it:

```
version: "3.7"
services:
  web:
    image: fundamentalsofdocker/ch11-web:2.0
    networks:
    - pets-net
    ports:
    - 3000:3000
    deploy:
      replicas: 3

  db:
    image: fundamentalsofdocker/ch11-db:2.0
    networks:
    - pets-net
    volumes:
    - pets-data:/var/lib/postgresql/data

volumes:
  pets-data:

networks:
  pets-net:
    driver: overlay
```

We request that the web service has three replicas, and both services are attached to the overlay network, `pets-net`.

2. We can deploy this application using the `docker stack deploy` command:

```
$ docker stack deploy -c pets-stack.yml pets
```

This results in this output:

```
Creating network pets_pets-net
Creating service pets_db
Creating service pets_web
```

Docker creates the `pets_pets-net` overlay network and then the two services, `pets_web` and `pets_db`.

3. We can then list all of the tasks in the `pets` stack:

```
ubuntu@ip-172-31-32-21:~$ docker stack ps pets
ID            NAME          IMAGE                              NODE              DESIRED STATE   CURRENT STATE               ERROR   PORTS
s5xqwk68pq5n  pets_db.1     fundamentalsofdocker/ch11-db:2.0   ip-172-31-32-21   Running         Running about a minute ago
2z9odo62c10i  pets_web.1    fundamentalsofdocker/ch11-web:2.0  ip-172-31-47-124  Running         Running 2 minutes ago
4w5b0o56sqdb  pets_web.2    fundamentalsofdocker/ch11-web:2.0  ip-172-31-32-189  Running         Running 2 minutes ago
2y35ksgnh9vc  pets_web.3    fundamentalsofdocker/ch11-web:2.0  ip-172-31-32-21   Running         Running about a minute ago
```

Figure 14.21 – List of all of the tasks in the pets stack

4. Finally, let's test the application using `curl` to retrieve an HTML page with a pet. And, indeed, the application works as expected, as the expected page is returned:

```
ubuntu@ip-172-31-32-21:~$ curl localhost:3000/pet
<html>
<head>
    <link rel="stylesheet" href="css/main.css">
</head>
<body>
    <div class="container">
        <h4>Animal of the day</h4>
        <img src="images&#x2F;3-female-lions.png"" />
        <p><small>Photo taken at <a href="https://www.maasaimara.com/">Massai Mara National Park</a></small></p>
        <p>Delivered to you by container d01e2f1f87df<p>
    </div>
</body>
```

Figure 14.22 – Testing the pets application using curl

The container ID is in the output, where it says `Delivered to you by container d01e2f1f87df`. If you run the `curl` command multiple times, the ID should cycle between three different values. These are the IDs of the three containers (or replicas) that we have requested for the web service.

5. Once we're done, we can remove the stack with `docker stack rm pets`.

Once we're done with the swarm in AWS, we can remove it.

Removing the swarm in AWS

To clean up the Swarm in the AWS cloud and avoid incurring unnecessary costs, we can use the following command:

```
$ for NODE in `seq 1 5`; do
    docker-machine rm -f aws-node-${NODE}
done
```

Next, let's summarize what we have learned in this chapter.

Summary

In this chapter, we introduced Docker Swarm, which, next to Kubernetes, is the second most popular orchestrator for containers. We looked into the architecture of a Swarm, discussed all of the types of resources running in a Swarm, such as services, tasks, and more, and we created services in the Swarm. We learned how to create a Docker Swarm locally, in a special environment called PWD, as well as in the cloud. Lastly, we deployed an application that consists of multiple services related to Docker Swarm.

In the next chapter, we are going to introduce the routing mesh, which provides layer 4 routing and load balancing in a Docker Swarm. After that, we will demonstrate how to deploy a first application consisting of multiple services onto the Swarm. We will also learn how to achieve zero downtime when updating an application in the swarm and finally how to store configuration data in the swarm and how to protect sensitive data using Docker secrets. Stay tuned.

Questions

To assess your learning progress, please try to answer the following questions:

1. What is Docker Swarm?
2. What are the main components of a Docker Swarm?
3. How do you initialize a Docker Swarm?
4. How do you add nodes to a Docker Swarm?
5. What is a Docker Service in the context of Docker Swarm?
6. How do you create and update services in Docker Swarm?
7. What is Docker Stack and how does it relate to Docker Swarm?
8. How do you deploy a Docker Stack in Docker Swarm?
9. What are the networking options in Docker Swarm?
10. How does Docker Swarm handle container scaling and fault tolerance?

Answers

Here are sample answers to the preceding questions:

1. Docker Swarm is a native container orchestration tool built into Docker Engine that allows you to create, manage, and scale a cluster of Docker nodes, orchestrating the deployment, scaling, and management of containers across multiple hosts.

2. A Docker Swarm consists of two primary components: the manager nodes, which are responsible for managing the cluster's state, orchestrating tasks, and maintaining the desired state of services, and the worker nodes, which execute the tasks and run the container instances.

3. You can initialize a Docker Swarm by running the `docker swarm init` command on a Docker host, which will become the first manager node of the Swarm. The command will provide a token that can be used to join other nodes to the Swarm.

4. To add nodes to a Docker Swarm, use the `docker swarm join` command on the new node, along with the token and the IP address of the existing manager node.

5. A Docker Service is a high-level abstraction that represents a containerized application or microservice in a Docker Swarm. It defines the desired state of the application, including the container image, number of replicas, network, and other configuration options.

6. You can create a new service using the `docker service create` command, and update an existing service using the `docker service update` command, followed by the desired configuration options.

7. A Docker Stack is a collection of services that is deployed together and shares dependencies, defined in a Docker Compose file. Docker Stacks can be deployed in a Docker Swarm to manage and orchestrate multi-service applications.

8. To deploy a Docker Stack in Docker Swarm, use the `docker stack deploy` command, followed by the stack name and the path to the Docker Compose file.

9. Docker Swarm supports various networking options, including the default ingress network for load balancing and routing, overlay networks for container-to-container communication across nodes, and custom networks for specific use cases.

10. Docker Swarm automatically manages container scaling by adjusting the number of replicas based on the desired state specified in the service definition. It also monitors the health of containers and replaces any failed instances to maintain fault tolerance.

15

Deploying and Running a Distributed Application on Docker Swarm

In the last chapter, we got a detailed introduction to Docker's native orchestrator called SwarmKit. SwarmKit is part of Docker Engine, and no extra installation is needed once you have Docker installed on your system. We learned about the concepts and objects SwarmKit uses to deploy and run distributed, resilient, robust, and highly available applications in a cluster, which can either run on-premises or in the cloud. We also showed how Docker's orchestrator secures applications using SDNs. We learned how to create a Docker Swarm locally, in a special environment called Play with Docker, and also in the cloud. Finally, we discovered how to deploy an application that consists of multiple related services to Docker Swarm.

In this chapter, we are going to introduce the routing mesh, which provides layer-4 routing and load balancing. Next, we are going to demonstrate how to deploy a first application consisting of multiple services onto the Swarm. We are also learning how to achieve zero downtime when updating an application in the swarm and finally how to store configuration data in the swarm and how to protect sensitive data using Docker secrets.

These are the topics we are going to discuss in this chapter:

- The Swarm routing mesh
- Zero-downtime deployment
- Storing configuration data in the swarm
- Protecting sensitive data with Docker Secrets

After completing this chapter, you will be able to do the following:

- List two to three different deployment strategies commonly used to update a service without downtime

- Update a service in batches without causing a service interruption

- Define a rollback strategy for a service that is used if an update fails

- Store non-sensitive configuration data using Docker configs

- Use a Docker secret with a service

- Update the value of a secret without causing downtime

Let's get started!

The swarm routing mesh

If you have paid attention, then you might have noticed something interesting in the last chapter. We had the pets application deployed and it resulted in an instance of the web service being installed on the three nodes – node-1, node-2, and node-3.

Yet, we were able to access the web service on node-1 with localhost and we reached each container from there. How is that possible? Well, this is due to the so-called Swarm routing mesh. The routing mesh makes sure that when we publish a port of a service, that port is then published on all nodes of the Swarm. Hence, network traffic that hits any node of the Swarm and requests to use a specific port will be forwarded to one of the service containers by routing the mesh. Let's look at the following diagram to see how that works:

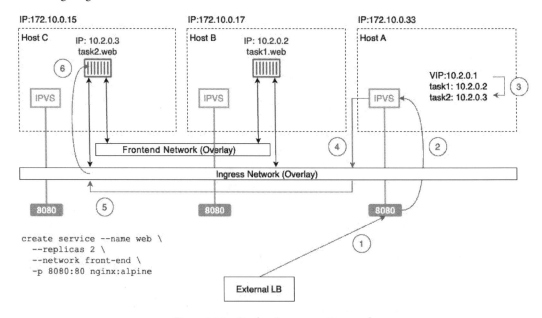

Figure 15.1 – Docker Swarm routing mesh

In this situation, we have three nodes, called **Host A**, **Host B**, and **Host C**, with the IP addresses 172.10.0.15, 172.10.0.17, and 172.10.0.33. In the lower-left corner of the diagram, we see the command that created a web service with two replicas. The corresponding tasks have been scheduled on **Host B** and **Host C**. **task1** landed on **Host B** while **task2** landed on **Host C**.

When a service is created in Docker Swarm, it automatically gets a **Virtual IP (VIP)** address assigned. This IP address is stable and reserved during the whole life cycle of the service. Let's assume that in our case the VIP is 10.2.0.1.

If now a request for port 8080 coming from an external **Load Balancer (LB)** is targeted at one of the nodes of our Swarm, then this request is handled by the Linux **IP Virtual Server (IPVS)** service on that node. This service makes a lookup with the given port 8080 in the IP table and will find that this corresponds to the VIP of the web service.

Now, since the VIP is not a real target, the IPVS service will load-balance the IP addresses of the tasks that are associated with this service. In our case, it picked **task2**, with the IP address 10.2.0.3. Finally, **Ingress Network (Overlay)** is used to forward the request to the target container on **Host C**.

It is important to note that it doesn't matter which Swarm node the external request is forwarded to by **External LB**. The routing mesh will always handle the request correctly and forward it to one of the tasks of the targeted service.

We have learned a lot about networking in a Docker swarm. The next topic that we are going to learn about is how can we deploy an application without causing any system downtime.

Zero-downtime deployment

One of the most important aspects of a mission-critical application that needs frequent updates is the ability to do updates in a fashion that requires no outage at all. We call this a zero-downtime deployment. At all times, the application that is updated must be fully operational.

Popular deployment strategies

There are various ways to achieve this. Some of them are as follows:

- Rolling updates
- Blue-green deployments
- Canary releases

Docker Swarm supports rolling updates out of the box. The other two types of deployments can be achieved with some extra effort on our part.

Rolling updates

In a mission-critical application, each application service has to run in multiple replicas. Depending on the load, that can be as few as two to three instances and as many as dozens, hundreds, or thousands of instances. At any given time, we want to have a clear majority when it comes to all the service instances running. So, if we have three replicas, we want to have at least two of them up and running at all times. If we have 100 replicas, we can be content with a minimum of, say, 90 replicas, available. By doing this, we can define the batch size of replicas that we may take down to upgrade. In the first case, the batch size would be 1, and in the second case, it would be 10.

When we take replicas down, Docker Swarm will automatically take those instances out of the load-balancing pool and all traffic will be load-balanced across the remaining active instances. Those remaining instances will thus experience a slight increase in traffic. In the following diagram, prior to the start of the rolling update, if **Task A3** wanted to access **Service B**, it could be load-balanced to any of the three tasks of **Service B** by SwarmKit. Once the rolling update started, SwarmKit took down **Task B1** for updates.

Automatically, this task is then taken out of the pool of targets. So, if **Task A3** now requests to connect to **Service B**, load balancing will only select from the remaining tasks, that is, **Task B2** and **Task B3**. Thus, those two tasks might experience a higher load temporarily:

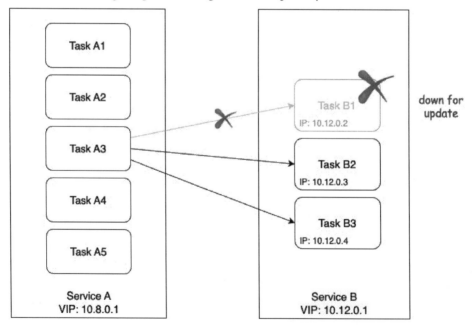

Figure 15.2 – Task B1 is taken down to be updated

The stopped instances are then replaced by an equivalent number of new instances of the new version of the application service. Once the new instances are up and running, we can have the Swarm observe them for a given period of time and make sure they're healthy. If all is well, then we can continue by taking down the next batch of instances and replacing them with instances of the new version. This process is repeated until all the instances of the application service have been replaced.

In the following diagram, we can see that **Task B1** of **Service B** has been updated to version 2. The container of **Task B1** was assigned a new IP address, and it was deployed to another worker node with free resources:

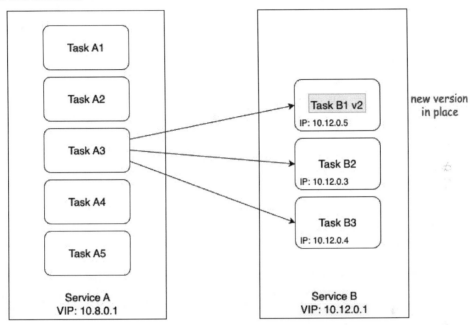

Figure 15.3 – The first batch being updated in a rolling update

It is important to understand that when the task of a service is updated, in most cases, it gets deployed to a worker node other than the one it used to live on, but that should be fine as long as the corresponding service is stateless. If we have a stateful service that is location- or node-aware and we'd like to update it, then we have to adjust our approach, but this is outside of the scope of this book.

Now, let's look at how we can actually instruct the Swarm to perform a rolling update of an application service. When we declare a service in a `stack` file, we can define multiple options that are relevant in this context. Let's look at a snippet of a typical `stack` file:

```
version: "3.5"
services:
  web:
    image: nginx:alpine
    deploy:
```

```
    replicas: 10
    update_config:
      parallelism: 2
      delay: 10s
...
```

In this snippet, we can see a section, update_config, with parallelism and delay properties. parallelism defines the batch size of how many replicas are going to be updated at a time during a rolling update. delay defines how long Docker Swarm is going to wait between updating individual batches. In the preceding case, we have 10 replicas that are being updated in two instances at a time and, between each successful update, Docker Swarm waits for 10 seconds.

Let's test such a rolling update. Navigate to the ch14 subfolder of our sample-solutions folder and use the web-stack.yaml file to create a web service that's been configured for a rolling update. The service uses an Alpine-based Nginx image whose version is 1.12-alpine. We will update the service to a newer version, that is, 1.13-alpine.

To start, we will deploy this service to the swarm that we created in AWS.

Let's take a look:

1. SSH into the master1 instance of your Docker swarm on AWS:

    ```
    $ ssh -i "aws-docker-demo.pem" <public-dns-of-manager1-
    instance>
    ```

2. Create a file called web-stack.yml using vi or nano with this content:

    ```
    version: "3.7"
    services:
      whoami:
        image: nginx:1.12-alpine
        ports:
        - 81:80
        deploy:
          replicas: 10
          update_config:
            parallelism: 2
            delay: 10s
    ```

3. Now, we can deploy the service using the stack file:

    ```
    $ docker stack deploy -c web-stack.yaml web
    ```

The output of the preceding command looks like this:

```
Creating network web_default
Creating service web_web
```

4. Once the service has been deployed, we can monitor it using the following command:

```
$ watch docker stack ps web
```

We will see the following output:

```
Every 2.0s: docker stack ps web

ID             NAME         IMAGE               NODE            DESIRED STATE   CURRENT STATE
fvh7kuxi1o62   web_web.1    nginx:1.12-alpine   ip-172-31-47-124   Running      Running about a minute ago
kdpnrg5gc5nx   web_web.2    nginx:1.12-alpine   ip-172-31-47-124   Running      Running about a minute ago
u35rewuz63j2   web_web.3    nginx:1.12-alpine   ip-172-31-32-21    Running      Running about a minute ago
owtcj2r6q8hb   web_web.4    nginx:1.12-alpine   ip-172-31-47-124   Running      Running about a minute ago
ylk1l1kidkn8e  web_web.5    nginx:1.12-alpine   ip-172-31-47-124   Running      Running about a minute ago
tig3dpg61j9m   web_web.6    nginx:1.12-alpine   ip-172-31-32-189   Running      Running about a minute ago
oz2t1wihtjtw   web_web.7    nginx:1.12-alpine   ip-172-31-32-189   Running      Running about a minute ago
x7fcsa0d2flh   web_web.8    nginx:1.12-alpine   ip-172-31-32-189   Running      Running about a minute ago
40ntqqtdo6df   web_web.9    nginx:1.12-alpine   ip-172-31-32-21    Running      Running about a minute ago
ipsm4h1anjd0   web_web.10   nginx:1.12-alpine   ip-172-31-32-21    Running      Running about a minute ago
```

Figure 15.4 – Service web of the web stack running in Swarm with 10 replicas

The previous command will continuously update the output and provide us with a good overview of what happens during the rolling update.

5. Now, we need to open a second Terminal and configure it for remote access for the manager node of our swarm. Once we have done that, we can execute the docker command, which will update the image of the web service of the stack, also called web:

```
$ docker service update --image nginx:1.13-alpine web_web
```

The preceding command leads to the following output, indicating the progress of the rolling update:

```
ubuntu@ip-172-31-32-21:~$ docker service update --image nginx:1.13-alpine web_web
web_web
overall progress: 4 out of 10 tasks
1/10: running   [==================================================>]
2/10: running   [==================================================>]
3/10: running   [==================================================>]
4/10: running   [==================================================>]
5/10:
6/10:
7/10:
8/10:
9/10:
10/10:
```

Figure 15.5 – Screen showing the progress of the rolling update

The preceding output indicates that the first two batches, each with two tasks, have been successful and that the third batch is about to be prepared.

In the first Terminal window, where we're watching the `stack`, we should now see how Docker Swarm updates the service batch by batch with an interval of 10 seconds. After the first batch, it should look like the following screenshot:

```
Every 2.0s: docker stack ps web                                                                    ip-

ID             NAME             IMAGE                NODE               DESIRED STATE   CURRENT STATE
z1cxecab6t13   web_web.1        nginx:1.12-alpine    ip-172-31-32-21    Running         Running 43 seconds ago
dfa8xtauti92   web_web.2        nginx:1.13-alpine    ip-172-31-47-124   Running         Running 9 seconds ago
7807rlpmvyek    \_ web_web.2    nginx:1.12-alpine    ip-172-31-47-124   Shutdown        Shutdown 11 seconds ago
6bpzygwztnu5   web_web.3        nginx:1.12-alpine    ip-172-31-32-21    Running         Running 43 seconds ago
qea1w8nv1723   web_web.4        nginx:1.12-alpine    ip-172-31-47-124   Running         Running 43 seconds ago
w9dkf3d0mhh2   web_web.5        nginx:1.12-alpine    ip-172-31-32-21    Running         Running 43 seconds ago
sl1m2leypjpv   web_web.6        nginx:1.12-alpine    ip-172-31-32-189   Running         Running 42 seconds ago
np9agclpwxrp   web_web.7        nginx:1.12-alpine    ip-172-31-32-189   Running         Running 42 seconds ago
wez3vagmgsfl   web_web.8        nginx:1.12-alpine    ip-172-31-32-189   Running         Running 42 seconds ago
upkizrpph2es   web_web.9        nginx:1.12-alpine    ip-172-31-47-124   Running         Running 43 seconds ago
o2ib7s4b9ovk   web_web.10       nginx:1.13-alpine    ip-172-31-47-124   Running         Running 9 seconds ago
ncvhpkkr9t59    \_ web_web.10   nginx:1.12-alpine    ip-172-31-32-189   Shutdown        Shutdown 11 seconds ago
```

Figure 15.6 – Rolling update for a service in Docker Swarm

In the preceding screenshot, we can see that the first batch of the two tasks, 2 and 10, has been updated. Docker Swarm is waiting for 10 seconds to proceed with the next batch.

It is interesting to note that in this particular case, SwarmKit deploys the new version of the task to the same node as the previous version. This is accidental since we have five nodes and two tasks on each node. SwarmKit always tries to balance the workload evenly across the nodes.

So, when SwarmKit takes down a task, the corresponding node has a smaller workload than all the others, so the new instance is scheduled to it. Normally, you cannot expect to find a new instance of a task on the same node. Just try it out yourself by deleting the `stack` with `docker stack rm web` and changing the number of replicas to say, seven, and then redeploy and update it.

Once all the tasks have been updated, the output of our `docker stack ps web` command will look similar to the following screenshot:

```
ubuntu@ip-172-31-32-21:~$ docker stack ps web
ID             NAME            IMAGE              NODE             DESIRED STATE  CURRENT STATE
p6m0qy0exrul   web_web.1       nginx:1.13-alpine  ip-172-31-32-189 Running        Running about a minute ago
z1cxecab6t13    \_ web_web.1   nginx:1.12-alpine  ip-172-31-32-189 Shutdown       Shutdown about a minute ago
dfa8xtauti92   web_web.2       nginx:1.13-alpine  ip-172-31-47-124 Running        Running 3 minutes ago
7807rlpmvyek    \_ web_web.2   nginx:1.12-alpine  ip-172-31-47-124 Shutdown       Shutdown 3 minutes ago
c9rqe1kc5lo0   web_web.3       nginx:1.13-alpine  ip-172-31-32-21  Running        Running about a minute ago
6bpzygwztnu5    \_ web_web.3   nginx:1.12-alpine  ip-172-31-32-21  Shutdown       Shutdown about a minute ago
hw03s2m0u0e2   web_web.4       nginx:1.13-alpine  ip-172-31-32-189 Running        Running 2 minutes ago
qea1w8nv1723    \_ web_web.4   nginx:1.12-alpine  ip-172-31-47-124 Shutdown       Shutdown 2 minutes ago
u0hnqvmxg5y4   web_web.5       nginx:1.13-alpine  ip-172-31-47-124 Running        Running 46 seconds ago
w9dkf3d0mhh2    \_ web_web.5   nginx:1.12-alpine  ip-172-31-32-21  Shutdown       Shutdown 46 seconds ago
j8l6nouakj2v   web_web.6       nginx:1.13-alpine  ip-172-31-47-124 Running        Running about a minute ago
s11m2leypjpv    \_ web_web.6   nginx:1.12-alpine  ip-172-31-32-189 Shutdown       Shutdown about a minute ago
i6n4x5jt4fm0   web_web.7       nginx:1.13-alpine  ip-172-31-32-189 Running        Running 2 minutes ago
np9agclpwxrp    \_ web_web.7   nginx:1.12-alpine  ip-172-31-32-189 Shutdown       Shutdown 2 minutes ago
y94yf3sdongu   web_web.8       nginx:1.13-alpine  ip-172-31-32-21  Running        Running about a minute ago
wez3vagmgsfl    \_ web_web.8   nginx:1.12-alpine  ip-172-31-32-189 Shutdown       Shutdown about a minute ago
ttkucj7cdd9s   web_web.9       nginx:1.13-alpine  ip-172-31-32-21  Running        Running 45 seconds ago
upkizrpph2es    \_ web_web.9   nginx:1.12-alpine  ip-172-31-47-124 Shutdown       Shutdown 46 seconds ago
o2ib7s4b9ovk   web_web.10      nginx:1.13-alpine  ip-172-31-47-124 Running        Running 3 minutes ago
ncvhpkkr9t59    \_ web_web.10  nginx:1.12-alpine  ip-172-31-32-189 Shutdown       Shutdown 3 minutes ago
```

Figure 15.7 – All tasks have been updated successfully

Please note that SwarmKit does not immediately remove the containers of the previous versions of the tasks from the corresponding nodes. This makes sense as we might want to, for example, retrieve the logs from those containers for debugging purposes, or we might want to retrieve their metadata using `docker container inspect`. SwarmKit keeps the four latest terminated task instances around before it purges older ones so that it doesn't clog the system with unused resources.

We can use the `--update-order` parameter to instruct Docker to start the new container replica before stopping the old one. This can improve application availability. Valid values are `start-first` and `stop-first`.

The latter is the default.

Once we're done, we can tear down the `stack` using the following command:

```
$ docker stack rm web
```

Although using `stack` files to define and deploy applications is the recommended best practice, we can also define the update behavior in a `service create` statement. If we just want to deploy a single service, this might be the preferred way of doing things. Let's look at such a `create` command:

```
$ docker service create --name web \
    --replicas 10 \
    --update-parallelism 2 \
    --update-delay 10s \
    nginx:alpine
```

This command defines the same desired state as the preceding `stack` file. We want the service to run with 10 replicas and we want a rolling update to happen in batches of two tasks at a time, with a 10-second interval between consecutive batches.

Health checks

To make informed decisions, for example, during a rolling update of a Swarm service regarding whether or not the just-installed batch of new service instances is running OK or whether a rollback is needed, SwarmKit needs a way to know about the overall health of the system. On its own, SwarmKit (and Docker) can collect quite a bit of information, but there is a limit. Imagine a container containing an application. The container, as seen from the outside, can look absolutely healthy and carry on just fine, but that doesn't necessarily mean that the application running inside the container is also doing well. The application could, for example, be in an infinite loop or be in a corrupt state, yet still be running. However, as long as the application runs, the container runs, and, from the outside, everything looks perfect.

Thus, SwarmKit provides a seam where we can provide it with some help. We, the authors of the application services running inside the containers in the swarm, know best whether or not our service is in a healthy state. SwarmKit gives us the opportunity to define a command that is executed against our application service to test its health. What exactly this command does is not important to Swarm; the command just needs to return *OK, NOT OK*, or *time out*. The latter two situations, namely NOT OK or timeout, will tell SwarmKit that the task it is investigating is potentially unhealthy.

Here, I am writing potentially on purpose, and we will see why later:

```
FROM alpine:3.6
...
HEALTHCHECK --interval=30s \
    --timeout=10s
    --retries=3
    --start-period=60s
    CMD curl -f http://localhost:3000/health || exit 1
...
```

In the preceding snippet from a Dockerfile, we can see the `HEALTHCHECK` keyword. It has a few options or parameters and an actual command, that is, `CMD`. Let's discuss the options:

- `--interval`: Defines the wait time between health checks. Thus, in our case, the orchestrator executes a check every 30 seconds.

- `--timeout`: This parameter defines how long Docker should wait if the health check does not respond until it times out with an error. In our sample, this is 10 seconds. Now, if one health check fails, SwarmKit retries a couple of times until it gives up and declares the corresponding task as unhealthy and opens the door for Docker to kill this task and replace it with a new instance.

- The number of retries is defined by the `--retries` parameter. In the preceding code, we want to have three retries.

- Next, we have the start period. Some containers take some time to start up (not that this is a recommended pattern, but sometimes it is inevitable). During this startup time, the service instance might not be able to respond to health checks. With the start period, we can define how long SwarmKit should wait before it executes the very first health check and thus give the application time to initialize. To define the startup time, we use the `--start-period` parameter. In our case, we do the first check after 60 seconds. How long this start period needs to be depends on the application and its startup behavior. The recommendation is to start with a relatively low value and, if you have a lot of false positives and tasks that are restarted many times, you might want to increase the time interval.

- Finally, we define the actual probing command on the last line with the CMD keyword. In our case, we are defining a request to the `/health` endpoint of `localhost` at port `3000` as a probing command. This call is expected to have three possible outcomes:

  - The command succeeds

  - The command fails

  - The command times out

The latter two are treated the same way by SwarmKit. This is the orchestrator telling us that the corresponding task might be unhealthy. I did say *might* with intent since SwarmKit does not immediately assume the worst-case scenario but assumes that this might just be a temporary fluke of the task and that it will recover from it. This is the reason why we have a `--retries` parameter. There, we can define how many times SwarmKit should retry before it can assume that the task is indeed unhealthy, and consequently kill it and reschedule another instance of this task on another free node to reconcile the desired state of the service.

Why can we use `localhost` in our probing command? This is a very good question, and the reason is that SwarmKit, when probing a container running in the Swarm, executes this probing command inside the container (that is, it does something such as `docker container exec <containerID> <probing command>`). Thus, the command executes in the same network namespace as the application running inside the container. In the following diagram, we can see the life cycle of a service task from its beginning:

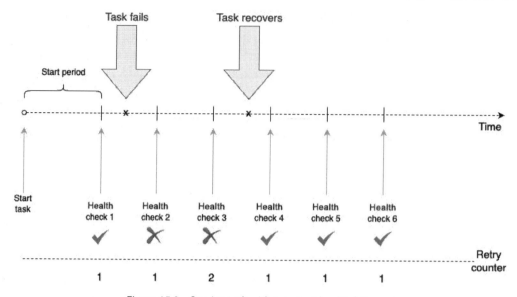

Figure 15.8 – Service task with transient health failure

First, SwarmKit waits to probe until the start period is over. Then, we have our first health check. Shortly thereafter, the task fails when probed. It fails two consecutive times but then it recovers. Thus, **health check 4** is successful and SwarmKit leaves the task running.

Here, we can see a task that is permanently failing:

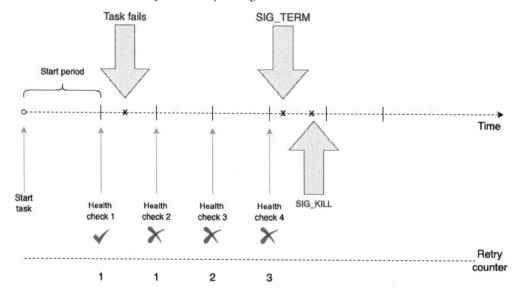

Figure 15.9 – Permanent failure of a task

We have just learned how we can define a health check for a service in the Dockerfile of its image, but this is not the only way we can do this. We can also define the health check in the stack file that we use to deploy our application into Docker Swarm. Here is a short snippet of what such a stack file would look like:

```
version: "3.8"
services:
  web:
    image: example/web:1.0
    healthcheck:
      test: ["CMD", "curl", "-f", http://localhost:3000/health]
      interval: 30s
      timeout: 10s
      retries: 3
      start_period: 60s
...
```

In the preceding snippet, we can see how the health check-related information is defined in the stack file. First and foremost, it is important to realize that we have to define a health check for every service individually. There is no health check at an application or global level.

Similar to what we defined previously in the Dockerfile, the command that is used to execute the health check by SwarmKit is curl -f http://localhost:3000/health. We also have definitions for interval, timeout, retries, and start_period. These four key-value pairs have the same meaning as the corresponding parameters we used in the Dockerfile. If there are health check-related settings defined in the image, then the ones defined in the stack file override the ones from the Dockerfile.

Now, let's try to use a service that has a health check defined:

1. Use vi or nano to create a file called stack-health.yml with the following content:

```
version: "3.8"
services:
  web:
    image: nginx:alpine
    deploy:
      replicas: 3
    healthcheck:
      test: ["CMD", "wget", "-qO", "-", "http://
localhost"]
```

```
          interval: 5s
          timeout: 2s
          retries: 3
          start_period: 15s
```

2. Let's deploy this:

```
$ docker stack deploy -c stack-health.yml myapp
```

3. We can find out where the single task was deployed to each cluster node using `docker stack ps myapp`. Thus, on any particular node, we can list all the containers to find one of our stacks. In my example, task 3 had been deployed to node `ip-172-31-32-21`, which happens to be the master.

4. Now, list the containers on that node:

Figure 15.10 – Displaying the health status of a running task instance

The interesting thing in this screenshot is the **STATUS** column. Docker, or more precisely, SwarmKit, has recognized that the service has a health check function defined and is using it to determine the health of each task of the service.

Next, let's see what happens if something goes wrong.

Rolling back

Sometimes, things don't go as expected. A last-minute fix to an application release may have inadvertently introduced a new bug, or the new version significantly may have significantly decreased the throughput of the component, and so on. In such cases, we need to have a plan B, which in most cases means the ability to roll back the update to the previous good version.

As with the update, the rollback has to happen so that it does not cause any outages in terms of the application; it needs to cause zero downtime. In that sense, a rollback can be looked at as a reverse update. We are installing a new version, yet this new version is actually the previous version.

As with the update behavior, we can declare, either in our `stack` files or in the Docker `service create` command, how the system should behave in case it needs to execute a rollback. Here, we have the `stack` file that we used previously, but this time with some rollback-relevant attributes:

```
version: "3.8"
services:
  web:
```

```
        image: nginx:1.12-alpine
        ports:
        - 80:80
        deploy:
          replicas: 10
        update_config:
          parallelism: 2
          delay: 10s
          failure_action: rollback
          monitor: 10s
        healthcheck:
          test: ["CMD", "wget", "-qO", "-", http://localhost]
          interval: 2s
          timeout: 2s
          retries: 3
          start_period: 2s
```

We can create a stack file named stack-rollback.yaml, and add the preceding content to it. In this content, we define the details of the rolling update, the health checks, and the behavior during rollback. The health check is defined so that after an initial wait time of 2 seconds, the orchestrator starts to poll the service on http://localhost every 2 seconds and retries 3 times before it considers a task unhealthy.

If we do the math, then it takes at least 8 seconds until a task will be stopped if it is unhealthy due to a bug. So, now under deploy, we have a new entry called monitor. This entry defines how long newly deployed tasks should be monitored for health and whether or not to continue with the next batch in the rolling update. Here, in this sample, we have given it 10 seconds. This is slightly more than the 8 seconds we calculated it takes to discover that a defective service has been deployed, so this is good.

We also have a new entry, failure_action, which defines what the orchestrator will do if it encounters a failure during the rolling update, such as the service being unhealthy. By default, the action is just to stop the whole update process and leave the system in an intermediate state. The system is not down since it is a rolling update and at least some healthy instances of the service are still operational, but an operations engineer would be better at taking a look and fixing the problem.

In our case, we have defined the action to be a rollback. Thus, in case of failure, SwarmKit will automatically revert all tasks that have been updated back to their previous version.

Blue-green deployments

In *Chapter 9, Learning about Distributed Application Architecture*, we discussed what blue-green deployments are, in an abstract way. It turns out that, on Docker Swarm, we cannot really implement blue-green deployments for arbitrary services. The service discovery and load balancing between two services running in Docker Swarm are part of the Swarm routing mesh and cannot be (easily) customized.

If **Service A** wants to call **Service B**, then Docker does this implicitly. Docker, given the name of the target service, will use the Docker DNS service to resolve this name to a VIP address. When the request is then targeted at the VIP, the Linux IPVS service will do another lookup in the Linux kernel IP tables with the VIP and load-balance the request to one of the physical IP addresses of the tasks of the service represented by the VIP, as shown in the following diagram:

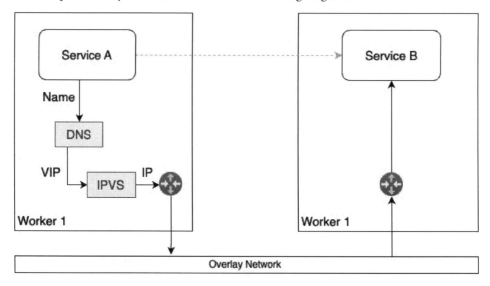

Figure 15.11 – How service discovery and load balancing work in Docker Swarm

Unfortunately, there is no easy way to intercept this mechanism and replace it with custom behavior, but this would be needed to allow for a true blue-green deployment of **Service B**, which is the target service in our example. As we will see in *Chapter 17, Deploying, Updating, and Securing an Application with Kubernetes*, Kubernetes is more flexible in this area.

That being said, we can always deploy the public-facing services in a blue-green fashion. We can use the **interlock 2** product and its layer-7 routing mechanism to allow for a true blue-green deployment.

Canary releases

Technically speaking, rolling updates are a kind of canary release, but due to their lack of seams, where you can plug customized logic into the system, rolling updates are only a very limited version of canary releases.

True canary releases require us to have more fine-grained control over the update process. Also, true canary releases do not take down the old version of the service until 100% of the traffic has been funneled through the new version. In that regard, they are treated like blue-green deployments.

In a canary release scenario, we don't just want to use things such as health checks as deciding factors regarding whether or not to funnel more and more traffic through the new version of the service; we also want to consider external input in the decision-making process, such as metrics that are collected and aggregated by a log aggregator or tracing information. An example that could be used as a decision-maker includes conformance to **Service Level Agreements** (**SLAs**), namely whether the new version of the service shows response times that are outside of the tolerance band. This can happen if we add new functionality to an existing service yet this new functionality degrades the response time.

Now that we know how to deploy an application causing zero downtime, we want to discuss how we can store configuration data used by the applications in the swarm.

Storing configuration data in the swarm

If we want to store non-sensitive data such as configuration files in Docker Swarm, then we can use Docker configs. Docker configs are very similar to Docker secrets, which we will discuss in the next section. The main difference is that config values are not encrypted at rest, while secrets are. Like Docker secrets, Docker configs can only be used in Docker Swarm – that is, they cannot be used in your non-Swarm development environment. Docker configs are mounted directly into the container's filesystem. Configuration values can either be strings or binary values up to a size of 500 KB.

With the use of Docker configs, you can separate the configuration from Docker images and containers. This way, your services can easily be configured with environment-specific values. The production swarm environment has different configuration values from the staging swarm, which in turn has different config values from the development or integration environment.

We can add configs to services and also remove them from running services. Configs can even be shared among different services running in the swarm.

Now, let's create some Docker configs:

1. First, we start with a simple string value:

    ```
    $ echo "Hello world" | docker config create hello-config -
    ```

Please note the hyphen at the end of the `docker config create` command. This means that Docker expects the value of the config from standard input. This is exactly what we're doing by piping the `Hello world` value into the `create` command.

The preceding command results in an output like this:

```
941xbaen80tdycup0wm01nspr
```

The preceding command creates a config named `hello-config` with the value "`Hello world`." The output of this command is the unique ID of this new config that's being stored in the swarm.

2. Let's see what we got and use the `list` command to do so:

```
$ docker config ls
```

This will output the following (which has been shortened):

```
ID         NAME         CREATED             UPDATED
rrin36..   hello-config About a minute ago  About a minute ago
```

The output of the `list` command shows the `ID` and `NAME` information for the config we just created, as well as its `CREATED` and (last) updated time. However, configs are non-confidential.

3. For that reason, we can do more and even output the content of a config, like so:

```
$ docker config inspect hello-config
```

The output looks like this:

```
[
    {
        "ID": "941xbaen80tdycup0wm01nspr",
        "Version": {
            "Index": 557
        },
        "CreatedAt": "2023-05-01T15:58:15.873515031Z",
        "UpdatedAt": "2023-05-01T15:58:15.873515031Z",
        "Spec": {
            "Name": "hello-config",
            "Labels": {},
            "Data": "SGVsbG8gd29ybGQK"
        }
    }
]
```

Hmmm, interesting. In the `Spec` subnode of the preceding JSON-formatted output, we have the `Data` key with a value of `SGVsbG8gd29ybGQK`. Didn't we just say that the config data is not encrypted at rest?

4.   It turns out that the value is just our string encoded as `base64`, as we can easily verify:

```
$ echo 'SGVsbG8gd29ybGQK' | base64 --decode
```

We get the following:

```
Hello world
```

So far, so good.

Now, let's define a somewhat more complicated Docker config. Let's assume we are developing a Java application. Java's preferred way of passing configuration data to the application is the use of so-called `properties` files. A `properties` file is just a text file containing a list of key-value pairs. Let's take a look:

1.   Let's create a file called `my-app.properties` and add the following content to it:

```
username=pguser
database=products
port=5432
dbhost=postgres.acme.com
```

2.   Save the file and create a Docker config called `app.properties` from it:

```
$ docker config create app.properties ./my-app.properties
```

This gives us an output like this:

```
2yzl73cg4cwny95hyft7fj80u
```

3.   To prepare the next command, first, install the `jq` tool:

```
$ sudo apt install -y jq
```

4.   Now, we can use this (somewhat contrived) command to get the cleartext value of the config we just created:

```
$ docker config inspect app.properties | jq .[].Spec.Data
| xargs echo | base64 --decode
```

We get this output:

```
username=pguser
database=products
```

```
port=5432
dbhost=postgres.acme.com
```

This is exactly what we expected.

5. Now, let's create a Docker service that uses the preceding config. For simplicity, we will be using the nginx image to do so:

```
$ docker service create \
     --name nginx \
     --config source=app.properties,target=/etc/myapp/
conf/app.properties,mode=0440 \
     nginx:1.13-alpine
```

This results in an output similar to the following:

```
svf9vmsjdttq4tx0cuy83hpgf
overall progress: 1 out of 1 tasks
1/1: running [=============================================
=======>]
verify: Service converged
```

The interesting part in the preceding service create command is the line that contains the --config parameter. With this line, we're telling Docker to use the config named app. properties and mount it as a file at /etc/myapp/conf/app.properties inside the container. Furthermore, we want that file to have mode 0440 assigned to it to give the owner (root) and the group read permission.

Let's see what we got:

```
$ docker service ps nginx
ID    NAME       IMAGE            NODE             DESIRED STATE
   CURRENT STATE          ERROR        PORTS
pvj   nginx.1   nginx:1.13-alpine   ip-172-31-32-21
   Running   Running 2 minutes ago
```

In the preceding output, we can see that the only instance of the service is running on node ip-172-31-32-21. On this node, I can now list the containers to get the ID of the nginx instance:

```
$ docker container ls
CONTAINER ID     IMAGE          COMMAND
   CREATED          STATUS          PORTS …
44417e1a70a1     nginx:1.13-alpine   "nginx -g 'daemon of…"
   5 minutes ago    Up 5 minutes         80/tcp …
```

Finally, we can `exec` into that container and output the value of the `/etc/myapp/conf/app.properties` file:

```
$ docker exec 44417 cat /etc/my-app/conf/app.properties
```

Note that `44417` in the preceding command represents the first part of the container hash.

This then will give us the expected values:

```
username=pguser
database=products
port=5432
dbhost=postgres.acme.com
```

No surprise here; this is exactly what we expected.

Docker configs can, of course, also be removed from the swarm, but only if they are not being used. If we try to remove the config we were just using previously, without first stopping and removing the service, we would get the following output:

```
$ docker config rm app.properties
```

Oh no, that did not work, as we can see from the following output:

```
Error response from daemon: rpc error: code = InvalidArgument
desc = config 'app.properties' is in use by the following
service: nginx
```

We get an error message in which Docker is nice enough to tell us that the config is being used by our service called nginx. This behavior is somewhat similar to what we are used to when working with Docker volumes.

Thus, first, we need to remove the service and then we can remove the config:

```
$ docker service rm nginx
nginx
```

And now it should work:

```
$ docker config rm app.properties
app.properties
```

It is important to note once more that Docker configs should never be used to store confidential data such as secrets, passwords, or access keys and key secrets.

In the next section, we will discuss how to handle confidential data.

Protecting sensitive data with Docker secrets

Secrets are used to work with confidential data in a secure way. Swarm secrets are secure at rest and in transit. That is, when a new secret is created on a manager node, and it can only be created on a manager node, its value is encrypted and stored in the raft consensus storage. This is why it is secure at rest. If a service gets a secret assigned to it, then the manager reads the secret from storage, decrypts it, and forwards it to all the containers that are instances of the swarm service that requested the secret. Since node-to-node communication in Docker Swarm uses **Mutual Transport Layer Security (mTLS)**, the secret value, although decrypted, is still secure in transit. The manager forwards the secret only to the worker nodes that a service instance is running on. Secrets are then mounted as files into the target container. Each secret corresponds to a file. The name of the secret will be the name of the file inside the container, and the value of the secret is the content of the respective file. Secrets are never stored in the filesystem of a worker node and are instead mounted using tmpFS into the container. By default, secrets are mounted into the container at /run/secrets, but you can change that to any custom folder.

It is important to note that secrets will not be encrypted on Windows nodes since there is no concept similar to tmpfs. To achieve the same level of security that you would get on a Linux node, the administrator should encrypt the disk of the respective Windows node.

Creating secrets

First, let's see how we can actually create a secret:

```
$ echo "sample secret value" | docker secret create sample-
secret -
```

This command creates a secret called sample-secret with a value of sample secret value. Please note the hyphen at the end of the docker secret create command. This means that Docker expects the value of the secret from standard input. This is exactly what we're doing by piping sample secret value into the create command.

Alternatively, we can use a file as the source for the secret value:

1. Create a secret-value.txt file as follows:

    ```
    $ echo "other secret" > secret-value.txt
    ```

2. Create the Docker secret from this file with the following:

    ```
    $ docker secret create other-secret ./secret-value.txt
    ```

Here, the value of the secret with the name `other-secret` is read from a file called `./secret-value.txt`.

3. Once a secret has been created, there is no way to access the value of it. We can, for example, list all our secrets to get the following output:

```
ubuntu@ip-172-31-32-21:~$ docker secret ls
ID                          NAME            DRIVER   CREATED          UPDATED
05iueidjipqcoyyaxptdswykk   other-secret             22 seconds ago   22 seconds ago
okrwum7y2mtqma4fvbj0qj9lo   sample-secret            5 minutes ago    5 minutes ago
```

Figure 15.12 – List of all secrets

In this list, we can only see the `ID` and `NAME` info for the secret, plus some other metadata, but the actual value of the secret is not visible.

4. We can also use `inspect` on a secret, for example, to get more information about `other-secret`:

```
ubuntu@ip-172-31-32-21:~$ docker secret inspect other-secret
[
    {
        "ID": "05iueidjipqcoyyaxptdswykk",
        "Version": {
            "Index": 572
        },
        "CreatedAt": "2023-05-01T16:24:27.1642861452",
        "UpdatedAt": "2023-05-01T16:24:27.1642861452",
        "Spec": {
            "Name": "other-secret",
            "Labels": {}
        }
    }
]
```

Figure 15.13 – Inspecting a swarm secret

Even here, we do not get the value of the secret back. This is, of course, intentional: a secret is a secret and thus needs to remain confidential. We can assign labels to secrets if we want and we can even use a different driver to encrypt and decrypt the secret if we're not happy with what Docker delivers out of the box.

Using a secret

Secrets are used by services that run in the swarm. Usually, secrets are assigned to a service at creation time. Thus, if we want to run a service called web and assign it a secret, say, api-secret-key, the syntax would look as follows:

```
$ docker service create --name web \
    --secret api-secret-key \
    --publish 8000:8000 \
    training/whoami:latest
```

This command creates a service called web based on the fundamentalsofdocker/whoami:latest image, publishes the container port 8000 to port 8000 on all swarm nodes, and assigns it the secret called api-secret-key.

This will only work if the secret called api-secret-key is defined in the swarm; otherwise, an error will be generated with the following text:

```
secret not found: api-secret-key.
```

Thus, let's create this secret now:

```
$ echo "my secret key" | docker secret create api-secret-key -
```

Now, if we rerun the service create command, it will succeed.

Now, we can use docker service ps web to find out on which node the sole service instance has been deployed, and then exec into this container. In my case, the instance has been deployed to node ip-172-31-32-21, which coincidentally happens to be the manager1 EC2 instance on which I am already working. Otherwise, I would have to SSH into the other node first.

Then, I list all my containers on that node with docker container ls to find the one instance belonging to my service and copy its container ID. We can then run the following command to make sure that the secret is indeed available inside the container under the expected filename containing the secret value in cleartext:

```
$ docker exec -it <container ID> cat /run/secrets/api-secret-
key
```

Once again, in my case, the output generated is as follows:

```
my secret key
```

This is evidently what we expected. We can see the secret in cleartext.

If, for some reason, the default location where Docker mounts the secrets inside the container is not acceptable to you, you can define a custom location. In the following command, we mount the secret to `/app/my-secrets`:

```
$ docker service create --name web \
    --name web \
    -p 8000:8000 \
    --secret source=api-secret-key,target=/run/my-secrets/
api-secret-key \
    fundamentalsofdocker/whoami:latest
```

In this command, we are using the extended syntax to define a secret that includes the destination folder.

Simulating secrets in a development environment

When working in development, we usually don't have a local swarm on our machine. However, secrets only work in a swarm. So, what can we do? Well, luckily, this answer is really simple.

Since secrets are treated as files, we can easily mount a volume that contains the secrets into the container to the expected location, which by default is at `/run/secrets`.

Let's assume that we have a folder called `./dev-secrets` on our local workstation. For each secret, we have a file named the same as the secret name and with the unencrypted value of the secret as the content of the file. For example, we can simulate a secret called `demo-secret` with a secret value of `demo secret value` by executing the following command on our workstation:

```
$ echo "demo secret value" > ./dev-secrets/sample-secret
```

Then, we can create a container that mounts this folder, like this:

```
$ docker container run -d --name whoami \
    -p 8000:8000 \
    -v $(pwd)/dev-secrets:/run/secrets \
    fundamentalsofdocker/whoami:latest
```

The process running inside the container will be unable to distinguish these mounted files from the ones originating from a secret. So, for example, `demo-secret` is available as a file called `/run/secrets/demo-secret` inside the container and has the expected value, `demo secret value`. Let's take a look at this in more detail in the following steps:

1. To test this, we can `exec` a shell inside the preceding container:

    ```
    $ docker container exec -it whoami /bin/bash
    ```

2. Now, we can navigate to the `/run/secrets` folder and display the content of the `demo-secret` file:

```
/# cd /run/secrets
/# cat demo-secret
demo secret value
```

Next, we will look at secrets and legacy applications.

Secrets and legacy applications

Sometimes, we want to containerize a legacy application that we cannot easily, or do not want to, change. This legacy application might expect a secret value to be available as an environment variable. How are we going to deal with this now? Docker presents us with the secrets as files, but the application is expecting them in the form of environment variables.

In this situation, it is helpful to define a script that runs when the container is started (a so-called entry point or startup script). This script will read the secret value from the respective file and define an environment variable with the same name as the file, assigning the new variable the value read from the file. In the case of a secret called `demo-secret` whose value should be available in an environment variable called DEMO_SECRET, the necessary code snippet in this startup script could look like this:

```
export DEMO_SECRET=$(cat /run/secrets/demo-secret)
```

Similarly, let's say we have a legacy application that expects the secret values to be present as an entry in, say, a YAML configuration file located in the `/app/bin` folder and called `app.config`, whose relevant part looks like this:

```
...
secrets:
demo-secret: "<<demo-secret-value>>"
other-secret: "<<other-secret-value>>"
yet-another-secret: "<<yet-another-secret-value>>"
...
```

Our initialization script now needs to read the secret value from the secret file and replace the corresponding placeholder in the config file with the secret value. For `demo_secret`, this could look like this:

```
file=/app/bin/app.conf
demo_secret=$(cat /run/secret/demo-secret)
sed -i "s/<<demo-secret-value>>/$demo_secret/g" "$file"
```

In the preceding snippet, we're using the `sed` tool to replace a placeholder with a value in place. We can use the same technique for the other two secrets in the config file.

We put all the initialization logic into a file called `entrypoint.sh`, make this file executable and, for example, add it to the root of the container's filesystem. Then, we define this file as ENTRYPOINT in the Dockerfile, or we can override the existing ENTRYPOINT of an image in the `docker container run` command.

Let's make a sample. Let's assume that we have a legacy application running inside a container defined by the `fundamentalsofdocker/whoami:latest` image that expects a secret called `db_password` to be defined in a file, `whoami.conf`, in the application folder.

Let's take a look at these steps:

1. We can define a file, `whoami.conf`, on our local machine that contains the following content:

    ```
    database:
        name: demo
        db_password: "<<db_password_value>>"
    others:
        val1=123
        val2="hello world"
    ```

    The important part is line 3 of this snippet. It defines where the secret value has to be put by the startup script.

2. Let's add a file called `entrypoint.sh` to the local folder that contains the following content:

    ```
    file=/app/whoami.conf
    db_pwd=$(cat /run/secret/db-password)
    sed -i "s/<<db_password_value>>/$db_pwd/g" "$file" /app/
    http
    ```

    The last line in the preceding script stems from the fact that this is the start command that was used in the original Dockerfile.

3. Now, change the mode of this file to an executable:

    ```
    $ sudo chmod +x ./entrypoint.sh
    ```

4. Now, we define a Dockerfile that inherits from the `fundamentalsofdocker/whoami:latest` image. Add a file called `Dockerfile` to the current folder that contains the following content:

    ```
    FROM fundamentalsofdocker/whoami:latest
    COPY ./whoami.conf /app/
    ```

```
COPY ./entrypoint.sh /
CMD ["/entrypoint.sh"]
```

5. Let's build the image from this Dockerfile:

    ```
    $ docker image build -t secrets-demo:1.0 .
    ```

6. Once the image has been built, we can run a service from it, but before we can do that, we need to define the secret in Swarm:

    ```
    $ echo "passw0rD123" | docker secret create demo-secret -
    ```

7. Now, we can create a service that uses the following secret:

    ```
    $ docker service create --name demo \
    --secret demo-secret \
    secrets-demo:1.0
    ```

Updating secrets

At times, we need to update a secret in a running service since secrets could be leaked out to the public or be stolen by malicious people, such as hackers. In this case, we need to change our confidential data since the moment it is leaked to a non-trusted entity, it has to be considered insecure.

Updating secrets, like any other update, requires zero downtime. Docker SwarmKit supports us in this regard.

First, we create a new secret in the swarm. It is recommended to use a versioning strategy when doing so. In our example, we use a version as a postfix of the secret name. We originally started with the secret named db-password and now the new version of this secret is called db-password-v2:

```
$ echo "newPassw0rD" | docker secret create db-password-v2 -
```

Let's assume that the original service that used the secret had been created like this:

```
$ docker service create --name web \
    --publish 80:80
    --secret db-password
    nginx:alpine
```

The application running inside the container was able to access the secret at /run/secrets/db-password. Now, SwarmKit does not allow us to update an existing secret in a running service, so we have to remove the now obsolete version of the secret and then add the new one. Let's start with removal with the following command:

```
$ docker service update --secret-rm db-password web
```

Now, we can add the new secret with the following command:

```
$ docker service update \
    --secret-add source=db-password-v2,target=db-password \
    web
```

Please note the extended syntax of `--secret-add` with the source and target parameters.

Summary

In this chapter, we introduced the routing mesh, which provides layer-4 routing and load balancing to a Docker Swarm. We then learned how SwarmKit allows us to update services without requiring downtime. Furthermore, we discussed the current limits of SwarmKit in regard to zero-downtime deployments. Then, we showed how to store configuration data in the Swarm, and in the last part of this chapter, we introduced secrets as a means to provide confidential data to services in a highly secure way.

In the next chapter, we will introduce the currently most popular container orchestrator, Kubernetes. We'll discuss the objects that are used to define and run a distributed, resilient, robust, and highly available application in a Kubernetes cluster. Furthermore, this chapter will familiarize us with MiniKube, a tool that's used to locally deploy a Kubernetes application, and also demonstrate the integration of Kubernetes with Docker Desktop.

Questions

To assess your learning progress, please try to answer the following questions:

1. In a few simple sentences, explain to an interested lay person what zero-downtime deployment means.

2. How does SwarmKit achieve zero-downtime deployments?

3. Contrary to traditional (non-containerized) systems, why does a rollback in Docker Swarm just work? Explain this in a few short sentences.

4. Describe two to three characteristics of a Docker secret.

5. You need to roll out a new version of the inventory service. What does your command look like? Here is some more information:

    -   The new image is called `acme/inventory:2.1`

    -   We want to use a rolling update strategy with a batch size of two tasks

    -   We want the system to wait for one minute after each batch

6. You need to update an existing service named `inventory` with a new password that is provided through a Docker secret. The new secret is called `MYSQL_PASSWORD_V2`. The code in the service expects the secret to be called `MYSQL_PASSWORD`. What does the update command look like? (Note that we do not want the code of the service to be changed!)

Answers

Here are sample answers to the preceding questions:

1. Zero-downtime deployment means that a new version of a service in a distributed application is updated to a new version without the application needing to stop working. Usually, with Docker SwarmKit or Kubernetes (as we will see), this is done in a rolling fashion. A service consists of multiple instances and those are updated in batches so that the majority of the instances are up and running at all times.

2. By default, Docker SwarmKit uses a rolling updated strategy to achieve zero-downtime deployments.

3. Containers are self-contained units of deployment. If a new version of a service is deployed and does not work as expected, we (or the system) only need to roll back to the previous version. The previous version of the service is also deployed in the form of self-contained containers. Conceptually, there is no difference between rolling forward (an update) or backward (a rollback). One version of a container is replaced by another one. The host itself is not affected by such changes in any way.

4. Docker secrets are encrypted at rest. They are only transferred to the services and containers that use the secrets. Secrets are transferred encrypted due to the fact that the communication between swarm nodes uses mTLS. Secrets are never physically stored on a worker node.

5. The command to achieve this is as follows:

```
$ docker service update \
    --image acme/inventory:2.1 \
    --update-parallelism 2 \
    --update-delay 60s \
    inventory
```

6. First, we need to remove the old secret from the service, and then we need to add the new version to it (directly updating a secret is not possible):

```
$ docker service update \
    --secret-rm MYSQL_PASSWORD \
    inventory
$ docker service update \
    --secret-add source=MYSQL_PASSWORD_V2, target=MYSQL_
PASSWORD \
    inventory
```

Part 4:
Docker, Kubernetes,
and the Cloud

This part introduces the currently most popular container orchestrator. It introduces the core Kubernetes objects that are used to define and run a distributed, resilient, robust, and highly available application in a cluster. Finally, it introduces minikube as a way to locally deploy a Kubernetes application and also covers the integration of Kubernetes with Docker for Mac and Docker Desktop.

- *Chapter 16, Introducing Kubernetes*
- *Chapter 17, Deploying, Updating, and Securing an Application with Kubernetes*
- *Chapter 18, Running a Containerized Application in the Cloud*
- *Chapter 19, Monitoring and Troubleshooting an Application Running in Production*

16

Introducing Kubernetes

This chapter introduces the current most popular container orchestrator. It introduces the core Kubernetes objects that are used to define and run a distributed, resilient, robust, and highly available application in a cluster. Finally, it introduces minikube as a way to locally deploy a Kubernetes application and also the integration of Kubernetes with Docker Desktop.

We will discuss the following topics:

- Understanding Kubernetes architecture
- Kubernetes master nodes
- Cluster nodes
- Introduction to Play with Kubernetes
- Kubernetes support in Docker Desktop
- Introduction to pods
- Kubernetes ReplicaSets
- Kubernetes Deployment
- Kubernetes Service
- Context-based routing
- Comparing SwarmKit with Kubernetes

After reading this chapter, you should have acquired the following skills:

- Drafting the high-level architecture of a Kubernetes cluster on a napkin
- Explaining three to four main characteristics of a Kubernetes pod
- Describing the role of Kubernetes ReplicaSets in two to three short sentences
- Explaining the two to three main responsibilities of a Kubernetes service
- Creating a pod in minikube

- Configuring Docker Desktop to use Kubernetes as an orchestrator

- Creating a Deployment in Docker Desktop

- Creating a Kubernetes Service to expose an application service internally (or externally) to the cluster

Technical requirements

In this chapter, if you want to follow along with the code, you need Docker Desktop and a code editor—preferably Visual Studio Code:

1. Please navigate to the folder in which you have cloned the sample repository. Normally, this should be ~/The-Ultimate-Docker-Container-Book:

```
$ cd ~/The-Ultimate-Docker-Container-Book
```

2. Create a new subfolder called ch16 and navigate to it:

```
$ mkdir ch16 && cd ch16
```

A complete set of sample solutions to all the examples discussed in this chapter can be found in the sample-solutions/ch16 folder or directly on GitHub: https://github.com/PacktPublishing/The-Ultimate-Docker-Container-Book/tree/main/sample-solutions/ch16.

Understanding Kubernetes architecture

A Kubernetes cluster consists of a set of servers. These servers can be VMs or physical servers. The latter is also called bare metal. Each member of the cluster can have one of two roles. It is either a Kubernetes master or a (worker) node. The former is used to manage the cluster, while the latter will run an application workload. I have put worker in parentheses since, in Kubernetes parlance, you only talk about a node when you're talking about a server that runs application workloads. But in Docker and Swarm parlance, the equivalent is a worker node. I think that the notion of a worker node better describes the role of the server than a simple node.

In a cluster, you have a small and odd number of masters and as many worker nodes as needed. Small clusters might only have a few worker nodes, while more realistic clusters might have dozens or even hundreds of worker nodes. Technically, there is no limit to how many worker nodes a cluster can have. In reality, though, you might experience a significant slowdown in some management operations when dealing with thousands of nodes.

On the Kubernetes worker nodes, we run pods. This is a new concept not present in Docker or Docker Swarm. A pod is an atomic unit of execution on a Kubernetes cluster. In many cases, a pod contains a single container, but a pod can consist of many containers running co-located. We will describe pods in much more detail later in this section.

All members of the cluster need to be connected by a physical network, the so-called **underlay network**. Kubernetes defines one flat network for the whole cluster. Kubernetes does not provide any networking implementation out of the box. Instead, it relies on plugins from third parties.

Kubernetes just defines the **Container Network Interface** (**CNI**) and leaves the implementation to others. The CNI is pretty simple. It states that each pod running in the cluster must be able to reach any other pod also running in the cluster without any **Network Address Translation** (**NAT**) happening in between. The same must be true between cluster nodes and pods, that is, applications or daemons running directly on a cluster node must be able to reach each pod in the cluster and vice versa.

The following diagram illustrates the high-level architecture of a Kubernetes cluster:

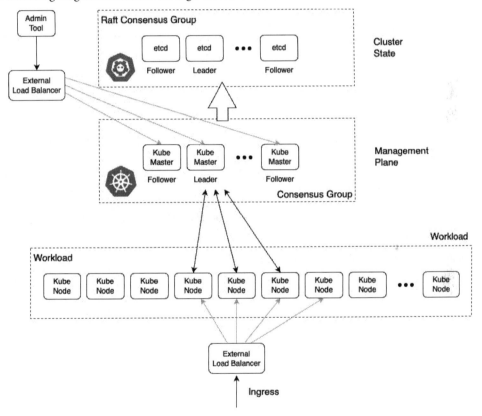

Figure 16.1 – High-level architecture diagram of Kubernetes

The preceding diagram is explained as follows.

In the top box, in the middle, we have a cluster of `etcd` nodes. An `etcd` node is a distributed key-value store that, in a Kubernetes cluster, is used to store all the states of the cluster. The number of `etcd` nodes has to be odd, as mandated by the Raft consensus protocol, which states which nodes are used to coordinate among themselves. When we talk about the Cluster State, we do not include data that is produced or consumed by applications running in the cluster. Instead, we're talking about all the information on the topology of the cluster, what services are running, network settings, secrets used, and more. That said, this `etcd` cluster is mission-critical to the overall cluster and thus, we should never run only a single `etcd` server in a production environment or any environment that needs to be highly available.

Then, we have a cluster of Kubernetes master nodes, which also form a Consensus Group among themselves, similar to the `etcd` nodes. The number of master nodes also has to be odd. We can run clusters with a single master but we should never do that in a production or mission-critical system. There, we should always have at least three master nodes. Since the master nodes are used to manage the whole cluster, we are also talking about the management plane.

Master nodes use the `etcd` cluster as their backing store. It is good practice to put a **load balancer** (**LB**) in front of master nodes with a well-known **Fully Qualified Domain Name** (**FQDN**), such as `https://admin.example.com`. All tools that are used to manage the Kubernetes cluster should access it through this LB rather than using the public IP address of one of the master nodes. This is shown on the upper left side of the preceding diagram.

Toward the bottom of the diagram, we have a cluster of worker nodes. The number of nodes can be as low as one and does not have an upper limit.

Kubernetes master and worker nodes communicate with each other. It is a bidirectional form of communication that is different from the one we know from Docker Swarm. In Docker Swarm, only manager nodes communicate with worker nodes and never the other way around. All ingress traffic accessing applications running in the cluster should go through another load balancer.

This is the application load balancer or reverse proxy. We never want external traffic to directly access any of the worker nodes.

Now that we have an idea about the high-level architecture of a Kubernetes cluster, let's delve a bit more deeply and look at the Kubernetes master and worker nodes.

Kubernetes master nodes

Kubernetes master nodes are used to manage a Kubernetes cluster. The following is a high-level diagram of such a master:

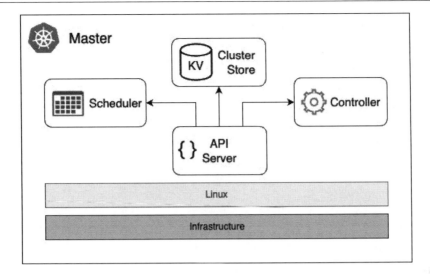

Figure 16.2 – Kubernetes master

At the bottom of the preceding diagram, we have the infrastructure, which can be a VM on-premises or in the cloud or a server (often called bare metal) on-premises or in the cloud.

Currently, Kubernetes masters only run on Linux. The most popular Linux distributions, such as RHEL, CentOS, and Ubuntu, are supported. On this Linux machine, we have at least the following four Kubernetes services running:

- **API Server**: This is the gateway to Kubernetes. All requests to list, create, modify, or delete any resources in the cluster must go through this service. It exposes a REST interface that tools such as `kubectl` use to manage the cluster and applications in the cluster.

- **Controller**: The controller, or more precisely the controller manager, is a control loop that observes the state of the cluster through the API server and makes changes, attempting to move the current or effective state toward the desired state if they differ.

- **Scheduler**: The scheduler is a service that tries its best to schedule pods on worker nodes while considering various boundary conditions, such as resource requirements, policies, quality-of-service requirements, and more.

- **Cluster Store**: This is an instance of `etcd` that is used to store all information about the state of the cluster. To be more precise, `etcd`, which is used as a cluster store, does not necessarily have to be installed on the same node as the other Kubernetes services. Sometimes, Kubernetes clusters are configured to use standalone clusters of `etcd` servers, as shown in *Figure 16.1*. But which variant to use is an advanced management decision and is outside the scope of this book.

We need at least one master, but to achieve high availability, we need three or more master nodes. This is very similar to what we have learned about the manager nodes of a Docker Swarm. In this regard, a Kubernetes master is equivalent to a Swarm manager node.

Kubernetes masters never run application workloads. Their sole purpose is to manage the cluster. Kubernetes masters build a Raft consensus group. The Raft protocol is a standard protocol used in situations where a group of members needs to make decisions. It is used in many well-known software products such as MongoDB, Docker SwarmKit, and Kubernetes. For a more thorough discussion of the Raft protocol, see the link in the *Further reading* section.

> **Running workload on master**
>
> At times, specifically in development and test scenarios, it can make sense to work with a single-node Kubernetes cluster, which then naturally becomes a master and a worker node at the same time. But this scenario should be avoided in production.

As we mentioned in the previous section, the state of the Kubernetes cluster is stored in an `etcd` node. If the Kubernetes cluster is supposed to be highly available, then the `etcd` node must also be configured in HA mode, which normally means that we have at least three `etcd` instances running on different nodes.

Let's state once again that the whole cluster state is stored in an `etcd` node. This includes all the information about all the cluster nodes, all the ReplicaSets, Deployments, secrets, network policies, routing information, and so on. It is therefore crucial that we have a robust backup strategy in place for this key-value store.

Now, let's look at the nodes that will be running the actual workload of the cluster.

Cluster nodes

Cluster nodes are the nodes with which Kubernetes schedules application workloads. They are the workhorses of the cluster. A Kubernetes cluster can have a few, dozens, hundreds, or even thousands of cluster nodes. Kubernetes has been built from the ground up for high scalability. Don't forget that Kubernetes was modeled on Google Borg, which has run tens of thousands of containers for years:

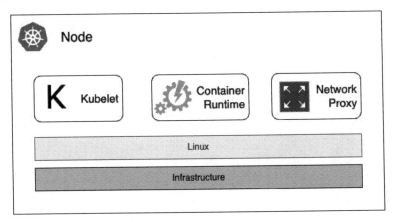

Figure 16.3 – Kubernetes worker node

A worker node – which is a cluster node, as are the master nodes – can run on a VM, bare metal, on-premises, or in the cloud. Originally, worker nodes could only be configured on Linux. But since version 1.10 of Kubernetes, worker nodes can also run on Windows Server 2010 or later. It is perfectly fine to have a mixed cluster with Linux and Windows worker nodes.

On each node, we have three services that need to run, as follows:

- **Kubelet**: This is the first and foremost service. Kubelet is the primary node agent. The Kubelet service uses pod specifications to make sure all of the containers of the corresponding pods are running and healthy. Pod specifications are files written in YAML or JSON format and they declaratively describe a pod. We will get to know what pods are in the next section. PodSpecs is provided to Kubelet primarily through the API server.

- **Container runtime**: The second service that needs to be present on each worker node is a container runtime. Kubernetes, by default, has used containerd since version 1.9 as its container runtime. Prior to that, it used the Docker daemon. Other container runtimes, such as rkt or CRI-O, can be used. The container runtime is responsible for managing and running the individual containers of a pod.

- **kube-proxy**: Finally, there is kube-proxy. It runs as a daemon and is a simple network proxy and load balancer for all application services running on that particular node.

Now that we have learned about the architecture of Kubernetes and the master and worker nodes, it is time to introduce the tooling that we can use to develop applications targeted at Kubernetes.

Introduction to Play with Kubernetes

Play with Kubernetes is a free playground sponsored by Docker, where users can learn how to use Docker containers and deploy them to Kubernetes:

1. Navigate to `https://labs.play-with-k8s.com/`.

2. Log in using your GitHub or Docker credentials.

3. Once successfully logged in, create a first cluster node or instance by clicking the + **ADD NEW INSTANCE** button on the left side of the screen.

4. Follow the instructions on the screen to create a first master node for your Kubernetes sandbox cluster.

5. Initialize the cluster master node with the command as indicated in *step 1* of the instructions in the terminal window. It's best if you directly copy the command from there. It should look like this:

```
$ kubeadm init --apiserver-advertise-address \
    $(hostname -i) --pod-network-cidr 10.5.0.0/16
```

The first command argument uses the name of the host to advertise the address of the Kubernetes API server and the second one defines the subnet the cluster is supposed to use.

6. Next, as indicated in Point 2 of the instructions in the console, initialize networking in our Kubernetes cluster (note, the following command should be on a single line):

```
$ kubectl apply -f https://raw.githubusercontent.com/
cloudnativelabs/kube-router/master/daemonset/kubeadm-
kuberouter.yaml
```

7. Create a second cluster node by again clicking the **ADD NEW INSTANCE** button.

8. Once the node is ready, run the `join` command that was output during *step 4*, where `<token-1>` and `<token-2>` are specific to your cluster:

```
$ kubeadm join 192.168.0.13:6443 --token <token-1> \
>       --discovery-token-ca-cert-hash <token-2>
```

It is best if you just copy the correct command from your command line in Play with Kubernetes.

9. Once the second node has joined the cluster, run the following command on the first node, where you initialized the cluster, to list the set of nodes in your new cluster:

```
$ kubectl get nodes
```

The output should look similar to this:

```
NAME     STATUS    ROLES                   AGE     VERSION
node1    Ready     control-plane,master    6m28s   v1.20.1
node2    Ready     <none>                  32s     v1.20.1
```

Note how Play with Kubernetes, at the time of writing, uses version 1.20.1 of Kubernetes, which even now is a rather old version. The latest stable version available is currently 1.27.x. But worry not; for our example version, 1.20.x, is enough.

Now let's try to deploy a pod to this cluster. Don't worry about what a *pod* is for now; we will delve into all the details about it later in this chapter. For the moment, just take it as is.

1. In your chapter code folder, create a new file called `sample-pod.yaml` and add the following content:

    ```yaml
    apiVersion: v1
    kind: Pod
    metadata:
      name: nginx
      labels:
        app: nginx
    spec:
      containers:
      - name: nginx
        image: nginx:alpine
        ports:
        - containerPort: 80
        - containerPort: 443
    ```

2. Now, to run the aforementioned pod on Play with Kubernetes, we need to copy the content of the preceding `yaml` file and create a new file on `node1` of our cluster:

3. Use `vi` to create a new file called `sample-pod.yaml`.

4. Hit *I* (the letter "i") to switch into the insert mode of `vi`.

5. Paste the copied code snippet with *Ctrl + V* (or *Command + V* on a Mac) into this file.

6. Press *Esc* to go into the command mode of `vi`.

7. Input `:wq` and hit *Enter* to save the file and quit `vi`.

Tip

Why are we using the Vi editor in our examples? It's the editor that is installed on any Linux (or Unix) distribution and is thus always available. You can find a quick tutorial for the Vi editor here: `https://www.tutorialspoint.com/unix/unix-vi-editor.htm`.

---

8. Now let's use the Kubernetes CLI called `kubectl` to deploy this pod. The `kubectl` CLI is already installed on each of the cluster nodes of your Play with Kubernetes cluster:

    ```
    $ kubectl create -f sample-pod.yaml
    ```

Doing so results in this output:

```
pod/nginx created
```

9. Now we list all of the pods:

```
$ kubectl get pods
```

We should see the following:

```
NAME      READY    STATUS      RESTARTS    AGE
nginx     1/1      Running     0           51s
```

10. To be able to access this pod, we need to create a Service. Let's use the `sample-service.yaml` file, which has the following content:

```
apiVersion: v1
kind: Service
metadata:
  name: nginx-service
spec:
  type: NodePort
  selector:
    app: nginx
  ports:
  - name: nginx-port
    protocol: TCP
    port: 80
    targetPort: http-web-svc
```

Again, don't worry about what exactly a *Service* is at this time. We'll explain this later.

11. Let's just create this Service:

```
$ kubectl create -f sample-service.yaml
```

12. Now let's see what Kubernetes created and list all Services defined on the cluster:

```
$ kubectl get services
```

We should see something similar to this:

```
[node1 ~]$ kubectl get services
NAME            TYPE         CLUSTER-IP       EXTERNAL-IP    PORT(S)        AGE
kubernetes      ClusterIP    10.96.0.1        <none>         443/TCP        46m
nginx-service   NodePort     10.110.128.176   <none>         80:31384/TCP   10m
```

Figure 16.4 – List of services

Please note the PORT(S) column. In my case, Kubernetes mapped the 80 container port of Nginx to the 31384 node port. We will use this port in the next command. Make sure you use the port number assigned on your system instead!

13. Now, we can use `curl` to access the service:

```
$ curl -4 http://localhost:31384
```

We should receive the Nginx welcome page as an answer.

14. Before you continue, please remove the two objects you just created:

```
$ kubectl delete po/nginx
$ kubectl delete svc/nginx-service
```

Note that in the aforementioned commands, the `po` shortcut is equivalent to `pod` or `pods`. The `kubectl` tool is very flexible and allows such abbreviations. Similarly, `svc` is a shortcut for `service` or `services`.

In the next section, we are going to use Docker Desktop and its support for Kubernetes to run the same pod and service as we did in this section.

Kubernetes support in Docker Desktop

Starting from version 18.01-ce, Docker Desktop started to support Kubernetes out of the box. Developers who want to deploy their containerized applications to Kubernetes can use this orchestrator instead of SwarmKit. Kubernetes support is turned off by default and has to be enabled in the settings. The first time Kubernetes is enabled, Docker Desktop will need a moment to download all the components that are needed to create a single-node Kubernetes cluster. Contrary to minikube, which is also a single-node cluster, the version provided by the Docker tools uses **containerized** versions of all Kubernetes components:

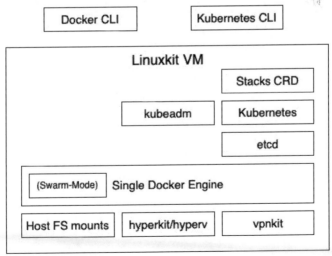

Figure 16.5 – Kubernetes support in Docker Desktop

The preceding diagram gives us a rough overview of how Kubernetes support has been added to Docker Desktop. Docker Desktop for macOS uses hyperkit to run a LinuxKit-based VM. Docker Desktop for Windows uses Hyper-V to achieve the result. Inside the VM, Docker Engine is installed. Part of the engine is SwarmKit, which enables Swarm mode. Docker Desktop uses the `kubeadm` tool to set up and configure Kubernetes in that VM. The following three facts are worth mentioning: Kubernetes stores its cluster state in `etcd`; thus, we have `etcd` running on this VM. Then, we have all the services that make up Kubernetes and, finally, some services that support the Deployment of Docker stacks from the Docker CLI into Kubernetes. This Service is not part of the official Kubernetes distribution, but it is Docker-specific.

All Kubernetes components run in containers in the LinuxKit VM. These containers can be hidden through a setting in Docker Desktop. Later in this section, we'll provide a complete list of Kubernetes system containers that will be running on your laptop, if you have Kubernetes support enabled.

One big advantage of Docker Desktop with Kubernetes enabled over minikube is that the former allows developers to use a single tool to build, test, and run a containerized application targeted at Kubernetes. It is even possible to deploy a multi-service application into Kubernetes using a Docker Compose file.

Now let's get our hands dirty:

1. First, we have to enable Kubernetes. On macOS, click on the Docker icon in the menu bar. On Windows, go to the command tray and select **Preferences**. In the dialog box that opens, select **Kubernetes**, as shown in the following screenshot:

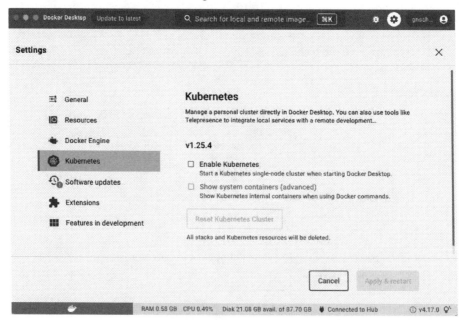

Figure 16.6 – Enabling Kubernetes in Docker Desktop

2. Then, tick the **Enable Kubernetes** checkbox. Also, tick the **Show system containers (advanced)** checkboxes.

3. Then, click the **Apply & restart** button. Installing and configuring Kubernetes takes a few minutes. It's time to take a break and enjoy a nice cup of tea.

4. Once the installation is finished (which Docker notifies us of by showing a green status icon in the **Settings** dialog), we can test it. Since we had multiple Kubernetes clusters running on our laptop such as minikube, Kind, and Docker Desktop, we need to configure `kubectl` to access the latter.

5. First, let's list all the contexts that we have. We can use the following command for this:

```
$ kubectl config get-contexts
```

In the case of the author's laptop, we get this output:

```
 ● → ch15 git:(main) ✗ kubectl config get-contexts
CURRENT   NAME              CLUSTER           AUTHINFO          NAMESPACE
          docker-desktop    docker-desktop    docker-desktop
    *     kind-demo         kind-demo         kind-demo
          kind-kind         kind-kind         kind-kind
```

Figure 16.7 – List of contexts for kubectl

Here, we can see that, on the author's laptop, we have three contexts, two of them stemming from his use of `kind`. Currently, the `kind` context with the `kind-demo` name is still active, flagged by the asterisk in the CURRENT column.

6. We can switch to the `docker-desktop` context using the following command:

```
$ kubectl config use-context docker-desktop
```

Doing so results in this ouput:

```
Switched to context "docker-desktop"
```

7. Now we can use `kubectl` to access the cluster that Docker Desktop just created:

```
$ kubectl get nodes
```

We should see something simliar to the following:

```
NAME    STATUS    ROLES           AGE      VERSION
node1   Ready     control-plane   6m28s    v1.25.9
```

OK, this looks very familiar. It is pretty much the same as what we saw when working with Play with Kubernetes. The version of Kubernetes that the author's Docker Desktop is using is 1.25.9. We can also see that the node is a `master` node, indicated by the role `control-plane`.

8. If we list all the containers that are currently running on our Docker Desktop, we get the list shown in the following screenshot (note that we use the `--format` argument to output the container ID and names of the containers):

```
$ docker container list --format "table {{.ID}}\t{{.Names}}"
```

This will result in the following output:

```
docker container list --format "table {{.ID}}\t{{.Names}}"
CONTAINER ID   NAMES
f561d030427c   demo-cluster-control-plane
ade15b460514   k8s_vpnkit-controller_vpnkit-controller_kube-system_633e1489-900f-42a2-8ebc-f95427562ba0_0
b08a3164a01d   k8s_storage-provisioner_storage-provisioner_kube-system_f723eb73-e930-4c2e-b062-598fd0de68fb_0
d494d79713fd   k8s_POD_vpnkit-controller_kube-system_633e1489-900f-42a2-8ebc-f95427562ba0_0
bcb40c4a3006   k8s_POD_storage-provisioner_kube-system_f723eb73-e930-4c2e-b062-598fd0de68fb_0
5ad04d668e2b   k8s_coredns_coredns-565d847f94-lsjr5_kube-system_431a0bd8-b3bb-4eaa-a148-4d6b0b3cd61b_0
271973e1ffb2   k8s_coredns_coredns-565d847f94-dgltw_kube-system_0fc46e43-d456-4089-8891-582e56afafd3_0
d8e5d5dc4268   k8s_POD_coredns-565d847f94-dgltw_kube-system_0fc46e43-d456-4089-8891-582e56afafd3_0
beb3726043ec   k8s_POD_coredns-565d847f94-lsjr5_kube-system_431a0bd8-b3bb-4eaa-a148-4d6b0b3cd61b_0
42c33c8b56df   k8s_kube-proxy_kube-proxy-ntgxj_kube-system_cd0c1774-240f-4d18-bbfc-13ca512998dc_0
d96e1786ce4e   k8s_POD_kube-proxy-ntgxj_kube-system_cd0c1774-240f-4d18-bbfc-13ca512998dc_0
3c7e05a6068a   k8s_etcd_etcd-docker-desktop_kube-system_daab091f7b57c624d51aae7ab076cb00_0
5777f1a40a66   k8s_kube-controller-manager_kube-controller-manager-docker-desktop_kube-system_861008677140df5bf14684241a098812_0
2c057a952451   k8s_kube-scheduler_kube-scheduler-docker-desktop_kube-system_42b55bbd22a41e1e397a84692d259b1e_0
567362aca936   k8s_kube-apiserver_kube-apiserver-docker-desktop_kube-system_8b71cd624d40d0ffecf5822890467a47_0
0b1930740fdc   k8s_POD_kube-controller-manager-docker-desktop_kube-system_861008677140df5bf14684241a098812_0
032abbb973c6   k8s_POD_kube-apiserver-docker-desktop_kube-system_8b71cd624d40d0ffecf5822890467a47_0
dc49ee6e9944   k8s_POD_etcd-docker-desktop_kube-system_daab091f7b57c624d51aae7ab076cb00_0
58e40d1c618a   k8s_POD_kube-scheduler-docker-desktop_kube-system_42b55bbd22a41e1e397a84692d259b1e_0
```

Figure 16.8 – List of Kubernetes system containers

In the preceding list, we can identify all the now-familiar components that make up Kubernetes, as follows:

- API server
- `etcd`
- `kube-proxy`
- DNS service
- `kube-controller`
- `kube-scheduler`

Normally, we don't want to clutter our list of containers with these system containers. Therefore, we can uncheck the **Show system containers (advanced)** checkbox in the settings for Kubernetes.

Now let's try to deploy a Docker Compose application to Kubernetes.

1. Navigate to the `ch16` subfolder of our `~/The-Ultimate-Docker-Container-Book` folder.

2. Copy the `docker-compose.yml` file from the sample solutions to this location:

    ```
    $ cp ../sample-solutions/ch16/docker-compose.yml .
    ```

3. Install the `kompose` tool on your machine by following the instructions on `https://kompose.io/installation/`:

    *   On a Mac, it can be installed using `$ brew install kompose`

    *   On Windows, use `$ choco install kubernetes-kompose`

4. Run the `kompose` tool as follows:

    ```
    $ kompose convert
    ```

    The tool should create four files:

    *   `db-deployment.yaml`

    *   `pets-data-persistentvolumeclaim.yaml`

    *   `web-deployment.yaml`

    *   `web-service.yaml`

5. Open the `web-service.yaml` file and after line 11 (the `spec` entry), add the `NodePort` entry type so that it looks as follows:

    ```
    ...
    spec:
      type: NodePort
      ports:
        - name: "3000"
    ...
    ```

6. Now we can use `kubectl` to deploy these four resources to our Kubernetes cluster:

    ```
    $ kubectl apply -f '*.yaml'
    ```

    We should see this:

    ```
    deployment.apps/db created
    persistentvolumeclaim/pets-data created
    deployment.apps/web created
    service/web created
    ```

7. We need to find out to which host port Kubernetes has mapped the 3000 service port. Use the following command for this:

```
$ kubectl get service
```

You should see something similar to this:

```
NAME        TYPE       CLUSTER-IP     EXTERNAL-IP PORT(S)       AGE
kubernetes  ClusterIP  10.96.0.1      <none>          443/TCP    10d
web         NodePort   0.111.98.154   <none>     3000:32134/
TCP    5m33s
```

In my case, we can see that the service web has the 3000 port mapped to the 32134 host (or node) port. In the following command, I have to use that port. In your case, the number likely will be different. Use the number you are getting from the previous command!

8. We can test the application using curl:

```
$ curl localhost:32134/pet
```

We will see that it is running as expected:

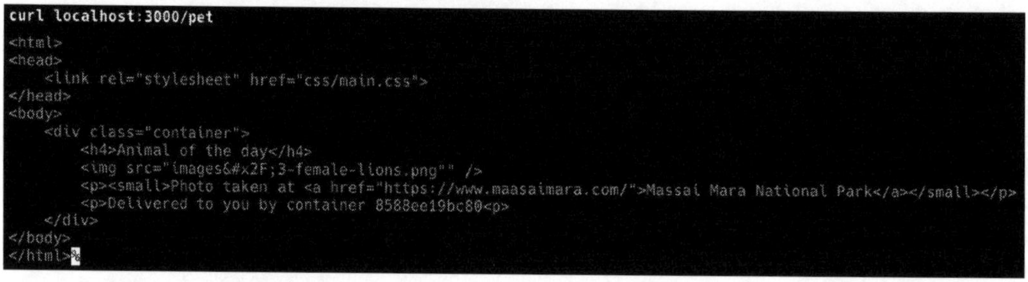

Figure 16.9 – Pets application running in Kubernetes on Docker Desktop

Now, let's see exactly what resources we have on Kubernetes after the previous Deployment.

9. We can use kubectl to find out:

```
$ kubectl get all
```

This gives us this output:

```
kubectl get all
NAME                          READY   STATUS    RESTARTS        AGE
pod/db-ccb5655f5-tw6bd        1/1     Running   0               9m27s
pod/web-66744486f5-65x2s      1/1     Running   1 (8m51s ago)   9m27s

NAME                  TYPE        CLUSTER-IP      EXTERNAL-IP   PORT(S)          AGE
service/kubernetes    ClusterIP   10.96.0.1       <none>        443/TCP          10d
service/web           NodePort    10.111.98.154   <none>        3000:32134/TCP   9m27s

NAME                     READY   UP-TO-DATE   AVAILABLE   AGE
deployment.apps/db       1/1     1            1           9m27s
deployment.apps/web      1/1     1            1           9m27s

NAME                                    DESIRED   CURRENT   READY   AGE
replicaset.apps/db-ccb5655f5            1         1         1       9m27s
replicaset.apps/web-66744486f5          1         1         1       9m27s
```

Figure 16.10 – Listing all Kubernetes objects created by Docker stack deploy

Docker created a Deployment for the web service and db service. It also automatically created a Kubernetes service for web so that it can be accessed inside the cluster.

This is pretty cool, to say the least, and tremendously decreases friction in the development process for teams targeting Kubernetes as their orchestration platform.

10. Before you continue, please remove the stack from the cluster:

```
$ kubectl delete -f '*.yaml'
```

Now that we have had an introduction to the tools we can use to develop applications that will eventually run in a Kubernetes cluster, it is time to learn about all the important Kubernetes objects that are used to define and manage such an application. We will start with pods.

Introduction to pods

Contrary to what is possible in Docker Swarm, you cannot run containers directly in a Kubernetes cluster. In a Kubernetes cluster, you can only run pods. **Pods** are the atomic units of Deployment in Kubernetes. A pod is an abstraction of one or many co-located containers that share the same kernel namespaces, such as the network namespace. No equivalent exists in Docker SwarmKit. The fact that more than one container can be co-located and shared with the same network namespace is a very powerful concept. The following diagram illustrates two pods:

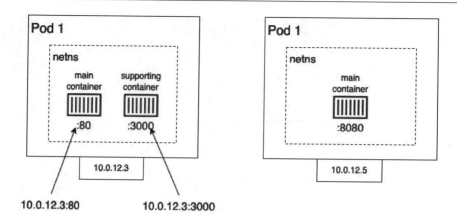

Figure 16.11 – Kubernetes pods

In the preceding diagram, we have two pods, **Pod 1** and **Pod 2**. The first pod contains two containers, while the second one only contains a single container. Each pod gets an IP address assigned by Kubernetes that is unique in the whole Kubernetes cluster. In our case, these are the following IP addresses: 10.0.12.3 and 10.0.12.5. Both are part of a private subnet managed by the Kubernetes network driver.

A pod can contain one or many containers. All those containers share the same Linux kernel namespaces, and in particular, they share the network namespace. This is indicated by the dashed rectangle surrounding the containers. Since all containers running in the same pod share the network namespace, each container needs to make sure to use its own port since duplicate ports are not allowed in a single network namespace. In this case, in Pod 1, the main container is using the 80 port while the supporting container is using the 3000 port.

Requests from other pods or nodes can use the pod's IP address combined with the corresponding port number to access the individual containers. For example, you could access the application running in the main container of Pod 1 through 10.0.12.3:80.

Comparing Docker container and Kubernetes pod networking

Now, let's compare Docker's container networking and Kubernetes pod networking. In the following diagram, we have Docker on the left-hand side and Kubernetes on the right-hand side:

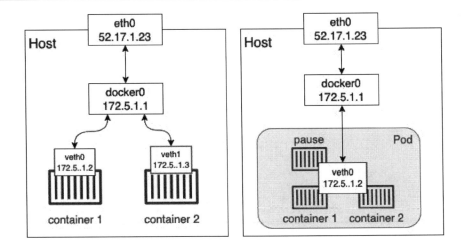

Figure 16.12 – Containers in a pod sharing the same network namespace

When a Docker container is created and no specific network is specified, then Docker Engine creates a virtual ethernet (`veth`) endpoint. The first container gets `veth0`, the next one gets `veth1`, and so on. These virtual ethernet endpoints are connected to the Linux bridge, `docker0`, that Docker automatically creates upon installation. Traffic is routed from the `docker0` bridge to every connected `veth` endpoint. Every container has its own network namespace. No two containers use the same namespace. This is on purpose, to isolate applications running inside the containers from each other.

For a Kubernetes pod, the situation is different. When creating a new pod, Kubernetes first creates a so-called `pause` container, the purpose of which is to create and manage the namespaces that the pod will share with all containers. Other than that, it does nothing useful; it is just sleeping. The `pause` container is connected to the `docker0` bridge through `veth0`. Any subsequent container that will be part of the pod uses a special feature of Docker Engine that allows it to reuse an existing network namespace. The syntax to do so looks like this:

```
$ docker container create --net container:pause ...
```

The important part is the `--net` argument, which uses `container:<container name>` as a value. If we create a new container this way, then Docker does not create a new `veth` endpoint; the container uses the same one as the pause container.

Another important consequence of multiple containers sharing the same network namespace is the way they communicate with each other. Let's consider the following situation: a pod containing two containers, one listening at the `80` port and the other at the `3000` port:

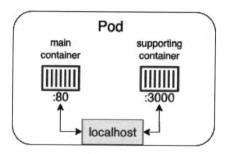

Figure 16.13 – Containers in pods communicating via localhost

When two containers use the same Linux kernel network namespace, they can communicate with each other through localhost, similarly to how, when two processes are running on the same host, they can communicate with each other through localhost too.

This is illustrated in the preceding diagram. From the main container, the containerized application inside it can reach out to the service running inside the supporting container through http://localhost:3000.

Sharing the network namespace

After all this theory, you might be wondering how a pod is actually created by Kubernetes.

Kubernetes only uses what Docker provides. So, how does this network namespace share work? First, Kubernetes creates the so-called pause container, as mentioned previously.

This container has no other function than to reserve the kernel namespaces for that pod and keep them alive, even if no other container inside the pod is running. Let's simulate the creation of a pod, then. We start by creating the pause container and use Nginx for this purpose:

```
$ docker container run –detach \
    --name pause nginx:alpine
```

Now we add a second container called main and attach it to the same network namespace as the pause container:

```
$ docker container run --name main \ -d -it \
    --net container:pause \
    alpine:latest ash
```

Since the pause and sample containers are both parts of the same network namespace, they can reach each other through localhost. To show this, we have to exec into the main container:

```
$ docker exec -it main /bin/sh
```

Now we can test the connection to Nginx running in the pause container and listening on the 80 port. The following is what we get if we use the wget utility to do so:

```
/ # wget -qO - localhost
```

Doing so gives us this output:

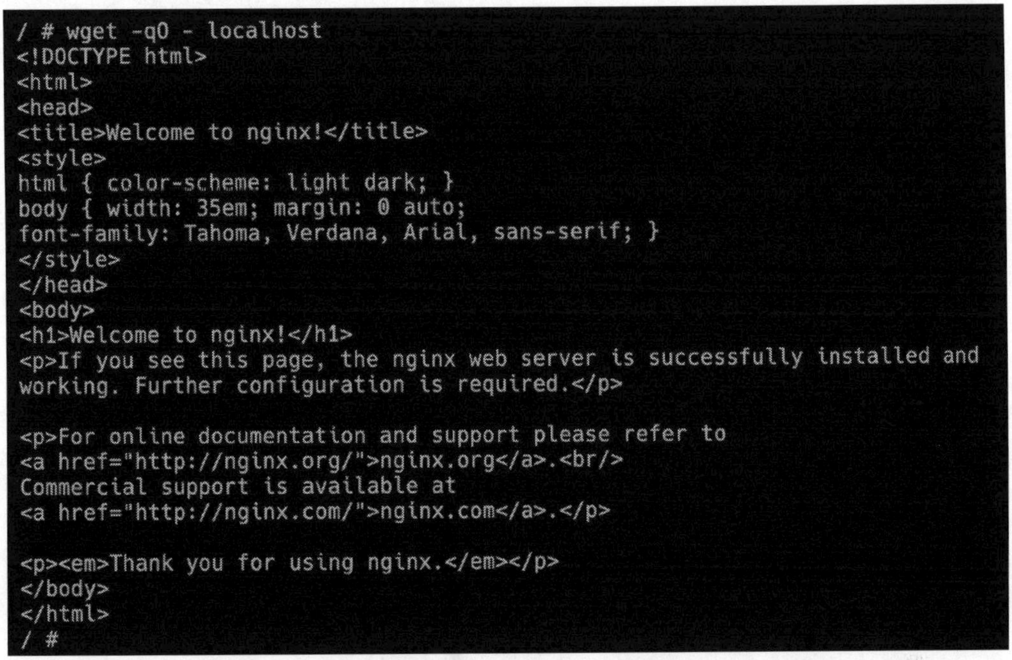

```
/ # wget -qO - localhost
<!DOCTYPE html>
<html>
<head>
<title>Welcome to nginx!</title>
<style>
html { color-scheme: light dark; }
body { width: 35em; margin: 0 auto;
font-family: Tahoma, Verdana, Arial, sans-serif; }
</style>
</head>
<body>
<h1>Welcome to nginx!</h1>
<p>If you see this page, the nginx web server is successfully installed and
working. Further configuration is required.</p>

<p>For online documentation and support please refer to
<a href="http://nginx.org/">nginx.org</a>.<br/>
Commercial support is available at
<a href="http://nginx.com/">nginx.com</a>.</p>

<p><em>Thank you for using nginx.</em></p>
</body>
</html>
/ #
```

Figure 16.14 – Two containers sharing the same network namespace

The output shows that we can indeed access Nginx on localhost. This is proof that the two containers share the same namespace. If that is not enough, we can use the ip tool to show eth0 inside both containers and we will get the exact same result, specifically, the same IP address, which is one of the characteristics of a pod; all its containers share the same IP address:

```
/ # ip a show eth0
```

This will show the following output:

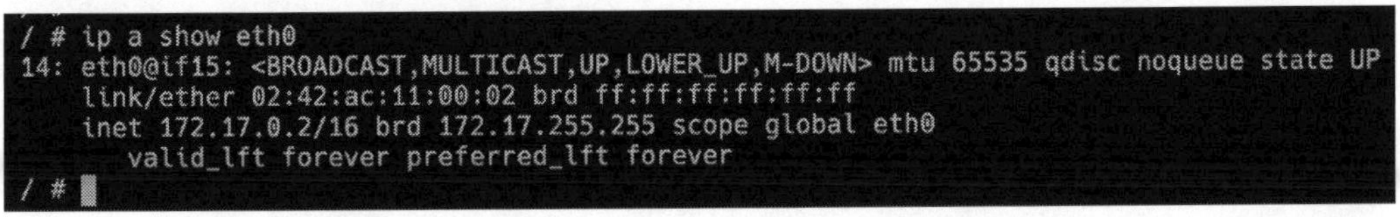

```
/ # ip a show eth0
14: eth0@if15: <BROADCAST,MULTICAST,UP,LOWER_UP,M-DOWN> mtu 65535 qdisc noqueue state UP
    link/ether 02:42:ac:11:00:02 brd ff:ff:ff:ff:ff:ff
    inet 172.17.0.2/16 brd 172.17.255.255 scope global eth0
        valid_lft forever preferred_lft forever
/ #
```

Figure 16.15 – Displaying the properties of eth0 with the ip tool

We inspect the `bridge` network with the following:

```
$ docker network inspect bridge
```

After that, we can see that only the pause container is listed:

```
[
    {
        "Name": "bridge",
        "Id": "c7c30ad64...",
        "Created": "2023-05-18T08:22:42.054696Z",
        "Scope": "local",
        "Driver": "bridge",
        ...
        "Containers": {
            "b7be6946a9b...": {
                "Name": "pause",
                "EndpointID": "48967fbec...",
                "MacAddress": "02:42:ac:11:00:02",
                "IPv4Address": "172.17.0.2/16",
                "IPv6Address": ""
            }
        },
        ...
    }
]
```

The preceding output has been shortened for readability.

The main container didn't get an entry in the `Containers` list since it is reusing the `pause` container's endpoint.

Before you continue, please remove the two `pause` and `main` containers:

```
$ docker container rm pause main
```

Next, we will be looking at the pod life cycle.

Pod life cycle

Earlier in this book, we learned that containers have a life cycle. A container is initialized, run, and ultimately exited. When a container exits, it can do this gracefully with an exit code zero or it can terminate with an error, which is equivalent to a non-zero exit code.

Similarly, a pod has a life cycle. Because a pod can contain more than one container, this life cycle is slightly more complicated than that of a single container. The life cycle of a pod can be seen in the following diagram:

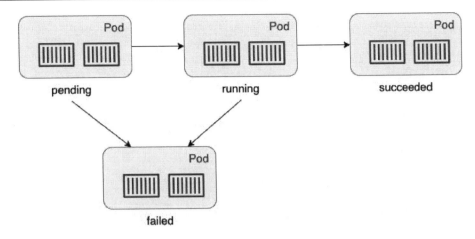

Figure 16.16 – The life cycle of Kubernetes pods

When a pod is created on a cluster node, it first enters the *pending* status. Once all the containers of the pod are up and running, the pod enters the *running* status. The pod only enters into this state if all its containers run successfully. If the pod is asked to terminate, it will request all its containers to terminate. If all containers terminate with exit code zero, then the pod enters into the *succeeded* status. This is the happy path.

Now, let's look at some scenarios that lead to the pod being in a *failed* state. There are three possible scenarios:

- If, during the startup of the pod, at least one container is not able to run and fails (that is, it exits with a nonzero exit code), the pod goes from the *pending* state into the failed state.

- If the pod is in the *running* status and one of the containers suddenly crashes or exits with a nonzero exit code, then the pod transitions from the *running* state into the *failed* state.

- If the pod is asked to terminate and, during the shutdown, at least one of the containers, exits with a nonzero exit code, then the pod also enters into the *failed* state.

Now let's look at the specifications for a pod.

Pod specifications

When creating a pod in a Kubernetes cluster, we can use either an imperative or a declarative approach. We discussed the difference between the two approaches earlier in this book but, to rephrase the most important aspect, using a declarative approach signifies that we write a manifest that describes the end state we want to achieve. We'll leave out the details of the orchestrator. The end state that we want to achieve is also called the desired state. In general, the declarative approach is strongly preferred in all established orchestrators, and Kubernetes is no exception.

Thus, in this chapter, we will exclusively concentrate on the declarative approach. Manifests or specifications for a pod can be written using either the YAML or JSON formats. In this chapter, we will concentrate on YAML since it is easier to read for us humans. Let's look at a sample specification. Here is the content of the `pod.yaml` file, which can be found in the `ch16` subfolder of our `labs` folder:

```
apiVersion: v1
kind: Pod
metadata:
  name: web-pod
spec:
  containers:
  - name: web
    image: nginx:alpine
    ports:
    - containerPort: 80
```

Each specification in Kubernetes starts with the version information. Pods have been around for quite some time and thus the API version is `v1`. The second line specifies the type of Kubernetes object or resource we want to define. Obviously, in this case, we want to specify a pod. Next follows a block containing metadata. At a bare minimum, we need to give the pod a name. Here, we call it `web-pod`. The next block that follows is the `spec` block, which contains the specification of the pod. The most important part (and the only one in this simple sample) is a list of all containers that are part of this pod. We only have one container here, but multiple containers are possible. The name we chose for our container is `web` and the container image is `nginx:alpine`. Finally, we define a list of ports the container is exposing.

Once we have authored such a specification, we can apply it to the cluster using the Kubernetes CLI, `kubectl`:

1. Open a new terminal window and navigate to the `ch16` subfolder:

    ```
    $ cd ~/The-Ultimate-Docker-Contianer-Book/ch16
    ```

2. In this example, we're going to use Docker Desktop's Kubernetes cluster. Thus, make sure that you are using the right context for the `kubectl` CLI:

    ```
    $ kubectl config use-context docker-desktop
    ```

    This will switch the context to our Kubernetes cluster provided by Docker Desktop.

3. In this folder, create a new file called `pod.yml` and add the mentioned pod specification to it. Save the file.

4. Execute the following command:

    ```
    $ kubectl create -f pod.yaml
    ```

This will respond with `pod "web-pod" created`.

5. We can then list all the pods in the cluster:

```
$ kubectl get pods
```

Doing so will provide us with this output:

NAME	READY	STATUS	RESTARTS	AGE
web-pod	1/1	Running	0	2m

As expected, we have one of one pod in the `Running` state. The pod is called `web-pod`, as defined.

6. We can get more detailed information about the running pod by using the `describe` command:

```
$ kubectl describe pod/web-pod
```

This gives us something similar to this:

```
kubectl describe pod/web-pod
Start Time:        Thu, 18 May 2023 17:26:28 +0200
Labels:            <none>
Annotations:       <none>
Status:            Running
IP:                10.1.0.10
IPs:
  IP:  10.1.0.10
Containers:
  web:
    Container ID:   docker://a68c8244cfa89fe9c6f305da9984707212af2fa962ddecc7dd9e179f131d19a7
    Image:          nginx:alpine
    Image ID:       docker-pullable://nginx@sha256:02ffd439b71d9ea9408e449b568f65c0bbbb94bebd8750f1d80231ab6496008e
    Port:           80/TCP
    Host Port:      0/TCP
    State:          Running
      Started:      Thu, 18 May 2023 17:26:34 +0200
    Ready:          True
    Restart Count:  0
    Environment:    <none>
    Mounts:
      /var/run/secrets/kubernetes.io/serviceaccount from kube-api-access-8rmv7 (ro)
Conditions:
  Type              Status
  Initialized       True
  Ready             True
  ContainersReady   True
  PodScheduled      True
Volumes:
  kube-api-access-8rmv7:
    Type:                    Projected (a volume that contains injected data from multiple sources)
    TokenExpirationSeconds:  3607
    ConfigMapName:           kube-root-ca.crt
    ConfigMapOptional:       <nil>
    DownwardAPI:             true
QoS Class:                   BestEffort
Node-Selectors:              <none>
Tolerations:                 node.kubernetes.io/not-ready:NoExecute op=Exists for 300s
                             node.kubernetes.io/unreachable:NoExecute op=Exists for 300s
Events:
  Type    Reason     Age     From               Message
  ----    ------     ----    ----               -------
  Normal  Scheduled  2m16s   default-scheduler  Successfully assigned default/web-pod to docker-desktop
  Normal  Pulling    2m15s   kubelet            Pulling image "nginx:alpine"
  Normal  Pulled     2m10s   kubelet            Successfully pulled image "nginx:alpine" in 5.366771503s (5.366774878s including waiting)
  Normal  Created    2m10s   kubelet            Created container web
  Normal  Started    2m10s   kubelet            Started container web
```

Figure 16.17 – Describing a pod running in the cluster

Note

The `pod/web-pod` notation in the previous section includes the `describe` command. Other variants are possible. For example, `pods/web-pod`, `po/web-pod`, `pod`, and `po` are aliases of `pods`.

The `kubectl` tool defines many aliases to make our lives a bit easier.

The `describe` command gives us a plethora of valuable information about the pod, not the least of which is a list of events that happened and affected this pod. The list is shown at the end of the output.

The information in the `Containers` section is very similar to what we find in a `docker container inspect` output.

We can also see a `Volumes` section with a `Projected` entry type. It contains the root certificate of the cluster as a secret. We will discuss Kubernetes secrets in the next chapter. Volumes, on the other hand, will be discussed next.

Pods and volumes

In the chapter about containers, we learned about volumes and their purpose: accessing and storing persistent data. Since containers can mount volumes, pods can do so as well. In reality, it is really the containers inside the pod that mount the volumes, but that is just a semantic detail. First, let's see how we can define a volume in Kubernetes. Kubernetes supports a plethora of volume types, so we won't delve into too much detail about this.

Let's just create a local volume implicitly by defining a `PersistentVolumeClaim` claim called `my-data-claim`:

1. Create a file called `volume-claim.yaml` and add the following specification to it:

    ```
    apiVersion: v1
    kind: PersistentVolumeClaim
    metadata:
      name: my-data-claim
    spec:
      accessModes:
      - ReadWriteOnce
      resources:
        requests:
          storage: 2Gi
    ```

    We have defined a claim that requests 2 GB of data.

2. Let's create this claim:

    ```
    $ kubectl create -f volume-claim.yaml
    ```

This will resulting in the following output:

```
persistentvolumeclaim/my-data-claim created
```

3. We can list the claim using `kubectl` (pvc is a shortcut for `PersistentVolumeClaim`) with the following:

```
$ kubectl get pvc
```

This gives us this output:

Figure 16.18 – List of PersistentStorageClaim objects in the cluster

In the output, we can see that the claim has implicitly created a volume called `pvc-<ID>`.

4. Remove the pod before you continue:

```
$ kubectl delete pod/web-pod
```

Alternatively, use the original file defining the pod with the following command:

```
$ kubectl delete -f pod.yaml
```

We are now ready to use the volume created by the claim in a pod. Let's use a modified version of the pod specification that we used previously:

1. Create a file called `pod-with-vol.yaml` and add the following specification to it:

```
apiVersion: v1
kind: Pod
metadata:
  name: web-pod
spec:
  containers:
  - name: web
    image: nginx:alpine
    ports:
    - containerPort: 80
    volumeMounts:
    - name: my-data
      mountPath: /data
  volumes:
  - name: my-data
    persistentVolumeClaim:
      claimName: my-data-claim
```

In the last four lines, in the `volumes` block, we define a list of volumes we want to use for this pod. The volumes that we list here can be used by any of the containers of the pod. In our particular case, we only have one volume. We specify that we have a volume called `my-data`, which is a persistent volume claim whose claim name is the one we just created.

Then, in the container specification, we have the `volumeMounts` block, which is where we define the volume we want to use and the (absolute) path inside the container where the volume will be mounted. In our case, we mount the volume to the `/data` folder of the container filesystem.

2. Let's create this pod:

```
$ kubectl create -f pod-with-vol.yaml
```

We can also use the declarative way:

```
$ kubectl apply -f pod-with-vol.yaml
```

3. Then, we can `exec` into the container to double-check that the volume has mounted by navigating to the `/data` folder, creating a file there, and exiting the container using:

```
$ kubectl exec -it web-pod -- /bin/sh
/ # cd /data
/data # echo "Hello world!" > sample.txt
/data # exit
```

If we are right, then the data in this container must persist beyond the life cycle of the pod.

4. Thus, let's delete the pod:

```
$ kubectl delete pod/web-pod
```

5. Then, we'll recreate it:

```
$ kubectl create -f pod-with-vol.yaml
```

6. We'll then `exec` into the container of the pod:

```
$ kubectl exec -it web-pod  -- ash
```

7. Finally, we output the data:

```
/ # cat /data/sample.txt
```

This is the output produced by the preceding command:

```
Hello world!
```

It is what we expected.

8. Exit the container by pressing *Ctrl + D*.

9. Delete the pod and the persistent volume claim before you continue. By now, you should know the command to do so. Otherwise, have a look back at *step 4*.

Now that we have a good understanding of pods, let's investigate how those pods are managed with the help of ReplicaSets.

Kubernetes ReplicaSets

A single pod in an environment with high availability requirements is insufficient. What if the pod crashes? What if we need to update the application running inside the pod but cannot afford any service interruption? These questions and more indicate that pods alone are not enough, and we need a higher-level concept that can manage multiple instances of the same pod. In Kubernetes, the ReplicaSet is used to define and manage such a collection of identical pods that are running on different cluster nodes. Among other things, a ReplicaSet defines which container images are used by the containers running inside a pod and how many instances of the pod will run in the cluster. These properties and many others are called the **desired state**.

The ReplicaSet is responsible for reconciling the desired state at all times if the actual state ever deviates from it. Here is a Kubernetes ReplicaSet:

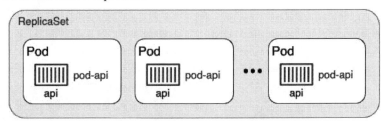

Figure 16.19 – Kubernetes ReplicaSet

In the preceding diagram, we can see a ReplicaSet that governs a number of pods. The pods are called `pod-api`. The ReplicaSet is responsible for making sure that, at any given time, there is always the desired number of pods running. If one of the pods crashes for whatever reason, the ReplicaSet schedules a new pod on a node with free resources instead. If there are more pods than the desired number, then the ReplicaSet kills superfluous pods. With this, we can say that the ReplicaSet guarantees a self-healing and scalable set of pods. There is no limit to how many pods a ReplicaSet can hold.

ReplicaSet specification

Similar to what we have learned about pods, Kubernetes also allows us to either imperatively or declaratively define and create a ReplicaSet. Since the declarative approach is by far the most recommended one in most cases, we're going to concentrate on this approach. Let's work with a sample specification for a Kubernetes ReplicaSet:

1. Create a new file called `replicaset.yaml` and add the following content to it:

```
apiVersion: apps/v1
kind: ReplicaSet
```

```
metadata:
  name: rs-web
spec:
  selector:
    matchLabels:
      app: web
  replicas: 3
  template:
    metadata:
      labels:
        app: web
    spec:
      containers:
      - name: nginx
        image: nginx:alpine
        ports:
        - containerPort: 80
```

This looks an awful lot like the pod specification we introduced earlier. Let's concentrate on the differences, then. First, on line 2, we have the kind, which was a pod, and is now `ReplicaSet`. Then, on lines 6–8, we have a selector, which determines the pods that will be part of the ReplicaSet. In this case, it is all the pods that have `app` as a label with the value `web`. Then, on line 9, we define how many replicas of the pod we want to run; three, in this case. Finally, we have the `template` section, which first defines the metadata, and then the spec, which defines the containers that run inside the pod. In our case, we have a single container using the `nginx:alpine` image and exporting `80` port.

The really important elements are the number of replicas and the selector, which specifies the set of pods governed by the ReplicaSet.

2. Let's use this file to create the ReplicaSet:

```
$ kubectl create -f replicaset.yaml
```

This results in the following:

```
replicaset "rs-web" created
```

3. Now we list all the ReplicaSets in the cluster (`rs` is a shortcut for ReplicaSet):

```
$ kubectl get rs
```

We get the following:

NAME	DESIRED	CURRENT	READY	AGE
rs-web	3	3	3	51s

In the preceding output, we can see that we have a single ReplicaSet called `rs-web`, the desired state of which is three (pods). The current state also shows three pods and tells us that all three pods are ready.

4. We can also list all the pods in the system:

    ```
    $ kubectl get pods
    ```

    This results in the following output:

NAME		READY	STATUS	RESTARTS	AGE
rs-web-nbc8m	1/1	Running	0		4m
rs-web-6bxn5	1/1	Running	0		4m
rs-web-1qhm5	1/1	Running	0		4m

    Here we can see our three expected pods. The names of the pods use the `ReplicaSet` name with a unique ID appended for each pod. In the READY column, we can see how many containers have been defined in the pod and how many of them are ready. In our case, we only have a single container per pod and, in each case, it is ready. Thus, the overall status of the pod is `Running`. We can also see how many times each pod had to be restarted. In our case, we don't have any restarts.

Next, let's see how the ReplicaSet helps us with self-healing.

Self-healing

Now, let's test the magic powers of the self-healing ReplicaSet by randomly killing one of its pods and observing what happens:

1. Let's delete the first pod from the previous list. Make sure to replace the name of the pod (`rs-web-nbc8m`) with the name you have in your own example:

    ```
    $ kubectl delete po/rs-web-nbc8m
    ```

    The previous command produces the following output:

    ```
    pod "rs-web-nbc8m" deleted
    ```

2. Now, let's list all the pods again. We expect to see only two pods, right? You're wrong:

NAME		READY	STATUS	RESTARTS	AGE
rs-web-4r587	1/1	Running	0		5s
rs-web-6bxn5	1/1	Running	0		4m30s
rs-web-1qhm5	1/1	Running	0		4m30

    OK. Evidently, the first pod in the list has been recreated, as we can see from the AGE column. This is auto-healing in action.

3. Let's see what we discover if we describe the ReplicaSet:

```
$ kubectl describe rs
```

This will give us this output:

```
kubectl describe rs
Name:           rs-web
Namespace:      default
Selector:       app=web
Labels:         <none>
Annotations:    <none>
Replicas:       3 current / 3 desired
Pods Status:    3 Running / 0 Waiting / 0 Succeeded / 0 Failed
Pod Template:
  Labels:  app=web
  Containers:
   nginx:
    Image:          nginx:alpine
    Port:           80/TCP
    Host Port:      0/TCP
    Environment:    <none>
    Mounts:         <none>
  Volumes:          <none>
Events:
  Type    Reason            Age    From                   Message
  ----    ------            ---    ----                   -------
  Normal  SuccessfulCreate  9m4s   replicaset-controller  Created pod: rs-web-nbc8m
  Normal  SuccessfulCreate  9m4s   replicaset-controller  Created pod: rs-web-6bxn5
  Normal  SuccessfulCreate  9m4s   replicaset-controller  Created pod: rs-web-lqhm5
  Normal  SuccessfulCreate  3m3s   replicaset-controller  Created pod: rs-web-4r587
```

Figure 16.20 – Describe the ReplicaSet

And indeed, we find an entry under Events that tells us that the ReplicaSet created a new pod called rs-web-4r587.

4. Before you continue, please delete the ReplicaSet:

```
$ kubectl delete rs/rs-web
```

Now it's time to talk about the Kubernetes Deployment object.

Kubernetes Deployments

Kubernetes takes the single-responsibility principle very seriously. All Kubernetes objects are designed to do one thing and one thing only, and they are designed to do this one thing very well. In this regard, we must understand Kubernetes ReplicaSets and Deployments. A ReplicaSet, as we have learned, is responsible for achieving and reconciling the desired state of an application service. This means that the ReplicaSet manages a set of pods.

A **Deployment** augments a ReplicaSet by providing rolling updates and rollback functionality on top of it. In Docker Swarm, the Swarm service incorporates the functionality of both a ReplicaSet and Deployment. In this regard, SwarmKit is much more monolithic than Kubernetes. The following diagram shows the relationship of a Deployment to a ReplicaSet:

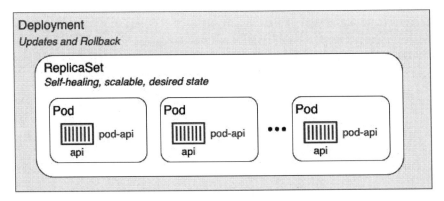

Figure 16.21 – Kubernetes Deployment

In the preceding diagram, the ReplicaSet defines and governs a set of identical pods. The main characteristics of the ReplicaSet are that it is self-healing, scalable, and always does its best to reconcile the desired state. The Kubernetes Deployment, in turn, adds rolling updates and rollback functionality to this. In this regard, a Deployment is a wrapper object for a ReplicaSet.

We will learn more about rolling updates and rollbacks in *Chapter 17, Deploying, Updating, and Securing an Application with Kubernetes.*

In the next section, we will learn more about Kubernetes services and how they enable service discovery and routing.

Kubernetes Services

The moment we start to work with applications consisting of more than one application service, we need service discovery. The following diagram illustrates this problem:

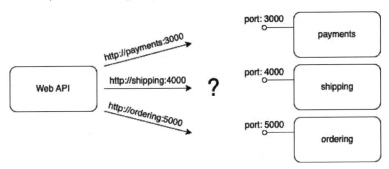

Figure 16.22 – Service discovery

In the preceding diagram, we have a `Web API` service that needs access to three other services: `payments`, `shipping`, and `ordering`. The `Web API` service should never have to care about how and where to find those three services. In the API code, we just want to use the name of the service we want to reach and its port number. A sample would be the following URL, `http://payments:3000`, which is used to access an instance of the `payments` service.

In Kubernetes, the payments application service is represented by a ReplicaSet of pods. Due to the nature of highly distributed systems, we cannot assume that pods have stable endpoints. A pod can come and go on a whim. But that's a problem if we need to access the corresponding application service from an internal or external client. If we cannot rely on pod endpoints being stable, what else can we do?

This is where **Kubernetes Services** come into play. They are meant to provide stable endpoints to ReplicaSets or Deployments, as follows:

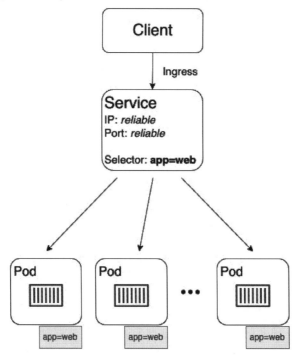

Figure 16.23 – Kubernetes service providing stable endpoints to clients

In the preceding diagram, in the center, we can see such a Kubernetes Service. It provides a reliable cluster-wide IP address, also called a **virtual IP** (**VIP**), as well as a reliable Port that's unique in the whole cluster. The pods that the Kubernetes Service is proxying are determined by the Selector defined in the service specification. Selectors are always based on labels. Every Kubernetes object can have zero to many labels assigned to it. In our case, the Selector is `app=web`; that is, all pods that have a label called `app` with a value of `web` are proxied.

In the next section, we will learn more about context-based routing and how Kubernetes alleviates this task.

Context-based routing

Often, we want to configure context-based routing for our Kubernetes cluster. Kubernetes offers us various ways to do this. The preferred and most scalable way currently is to use IngressController. The following diagram tries to illustrate how this ingress controller works:

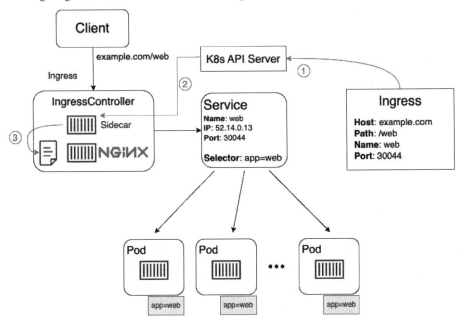

Figure 16.24 – Context-based routing using a Kubernetes ingress controller

In the preceding diagram, we can see how context-based (or layer 7) routing works when using an IngressController, such as Nginx. Here, we have the Deployment of an application service called web. All the pods of this application service have the following label: app=web. Then, we have a Kubernetes Service called web that provides a stable endpoint to those pods. The Service has a VIP of 52.14.0.13 and exposes a 30044 port. That is, if a request comes to any node of the Kubernetes cluster for the name web and 30044 port, then it is forwarded to this Service. The Service then load balances the request to one of the pods.

So far, so good, but how is an ingress request from a client to the `http[s]://example.com/web` URL routed to our web service? First, we must define routing from a context-based request to a corresponding `<service name>/<port>` request. This is done through an Ingress object:

1. In the Ingress object, we define the Host and Path as the source and the (service) name, and the port as the target. When this Ingress object is created by the Kubernetes API server, then a process that runs as a sidecar in IngressController picks up this change.

2. The configuration file of the Nginx reverse proxy is modified.

3. By adding the new route, Nginx is then asked to reload its configuration and thus, will be able to correctly route any incoming requests to `http[s]://example.com/web`.

In the next section, we are going to compare Docker SwarmKit with Kubernetes by contrasting some of the main resources of each orchestration engine.

Comparing SwarmKit with Kubernetes

Now that we have learned a lot of details about the most important resources in Kubernetes, it is helpful to compare the two orchestrators, SwarmKit and Kubernetes, by matching the important resources. Let's take a look:

SwarmKit	Kubernetes	Description
Swarm	Cluster	Set of servers/nodes managed by the respective orchestrator.
Node	Cluster member	Single host (physical or virtual) that's a member of the Swarm/cluster.
Manager node	Master	Node managing the Swarm/cluster. This is the control plane.
Worker node	Node	Member of the Swarm/cluster running application workload.
Container	Container**	An instance of a container image running on a node. **Note: In a Kubernetes cluster, we cannot run a container directly.
Task	Pod	An instance of a Service (Swarm) or ReplicaSet (Kubernetes) running on a node. A task manages a single container while a Pod contains one to many containers that all share the same network namespace.
Service	ReplicaSet	Defines and reconciles the desired state of an application service consisting of multiple instances.

SwarmKit	Kubernetes	Description
Service	Deployment	A Deployment is a ReplicaSet augmented with rolling updates and rollback capabilities.
Routing mesh	Service	The Swarm Routing Mesh provides L4 routing and load balancing using IPVS. A Kubernetes Service is an abstraction that defines a logical set of pods and a policy that can be used to access them. It is a stable endpoint for a set of pods
Stack	Stack**	The definition of an application consists of multiple (Swarm) services. **Note: While stacks are not native to Kubernetes, Docker's tool, Docker Desktop, will translate them for Deployment onto a Kubernetes cluster
Network	Network policy	Swarm **software-defined networks (SDNs)** are used to firewall containers. Kubernetes only defines a single flat network. Every pod can reach every other pod and/or node unless network policies are explicitly defined to constrain inter-pod communication

This concludes our introduction to Kubernetes, currently the most popular container orchestration engine.

Summary

In this chapter, we learned about the basics of Kubernetes. We took an overview of its architecture and introduced the main resources that are used to define and run applications in a Kubernetes cluster. We also introduced minikube and Kubernetes support in Docker Desktop.

In the next chapter, we're going to deploy an application into a Kubernetes cluster. Then, we're going to be updating one of the services of this application using a zero-downtime strategy. Finally, we're going to instrument application services running in Kubernetes with sensitive data using secrets. Stay tuned!

Further reading

Here is a list of articles that contain more detailed information about the various topics that we discussed in this chapter:

- *The Raft Consensus Algorithm*: https://raft.github.Io/
- *Kubernetes Documentation*: https://kubernetes.io/docs/home/

Questions

Please answer the following questions to assess your learning progress:

1. What is the high-level architecture of a Kubernetes cluster?

2. Explain in a few short sentences what the role of a Kubernetes master is.

3. List the elements that need to be present on each Kubernetes (worker) node.

4. We cannot run individual containers in a Kubernetes cluster.

   A. True

   B. False

5. What are the three main characteristics of a Kubernetes pod?

6. Explain the reason why the containers in a pod can use `localhost` to communicate with each other.

7. What is the purpose of the so-called `pause` container in a pod?

8. Bob tells you, "Our application consists of three Docker images: `web`, `inventory`, and `db`. Since we can run multiple containers in a Kubernetes pod, we are going to deploy all the services of our application in a single pod." List three to four reasons why this is a bad idea.

9. Explain in your own words why we need Kubernetes ReplicaSets.

10. Under what circumstances do we need Kubernetes Deployments?

11. What are the main responsibilities of a Kubernetes Service?

12. List at least three types of Kubernetes Services and explain their purposes and their differences.

13. How do you create a Kubernetes Service to expose an application service internally within the cluster?

Answers

Here are some sample answers to the questions presented in this chapter:

1. A Kubernetes cluster consists of a control plane (Kubernetes Master) and several worker nodes. The control plane is responsible for maintaining the desired state of the cluster, such as which applications are running and which container images they use. Worker nodes are the servers where applications are deployed and run.

2. The Kubernetes master is responsible for managing the cluster. All requests to create objects, reschedule pods, manage ReplicaSets, and more happen on the master. The master does not run the application workload in a production or production-like cluster.

3. On each worker node, we have the kubelet, the proxy, and container runtime.

4. The answer is *A. True*. You cannot run standalone containers on a Kubernetes cluster. Pods are the atomic units of Deployment in such a cluster.

5. A Kubernetes pod is the smallest deployable unit in Kubernetes. It can run one or multiple co-located containers. Here are three main characteristics:

    A. A pod can encapsulate multiple containers that are tightly coupled and need to share resources.

    B. All containers in a pod share the same network namespace, meaning they can communicate with each other using `localhost`.

    C. Each pod has a unique IP address within the cluster.

6. All containers running inside a pod share the same Linux kernel network namespace. Thus, all processes running inside those containers can communicate with each other through `localhost` in a similar way to how processes or applications directly running on the host can communicate with each other through `localhost`.

7. The `pause` container's sole role is to reserve the namespaces of the pod for containers that run in it.

8. This is a bad idea since all containers of a pod are co-located, which means they run on the same cluster node. Also, if multiple containers run in the same pod, they can only be scaled up or down all at once. However, the different components of the application (that is, `web`, `inventory`, and `db`) usually have very different requirements concerning scalability or resource consumption. The `web` component might need to be scaled up and down depending on the traffic and the `db` component, in turn, has special requirements regarding storage that the others don't have. If we do run every component in its own pod, we are much more flexible in this regard.

9. We need a mechanism to run multiple instances of a pod in a cluster and make sure that the actual number of pods running always corresponds to the desired number, even when individual pods crash or disappear due to network partitions or cluster node failures. The ReplicaSet is the mechanism that provides scalability and self-healing to any application service.

10. We need Deployment objects whenever we want to update an application service in a Kubernetes cluster without causing downtime to the service. Deployment objects add rolling updates and rollback capabilities to ReplicaSets.

11. A Kubernetes Service is an abstract way to expose an application running on a set of pods as a network service. The main responsibilities of a Kubernetes service include the following:

    A. Providing a stable IP address and DNS name to the set of pods, helping in the discovery, and allowing for load balancing

    B. Routing network traffic to distribute it across a set of pods provides the same functionality

    C. Allowing for the exposure of services to external clients if necessary

12. Kubernetes Service objects are used to make application services participate in Service discovery. They provide a stable endpoint to a set of pods (normally governed by a ReplicaSet or a Deployment). Kube services are abstractions that define a logical set of pods and a policy regarding how to access them. There are four types of Kube Services:

   - **ClusterIP**: Exposes the service on an IP address that's only accessible from inside the cluster; this is a **VIP**.

   - **NodePort**: Publishes a port in the range of 30000 to 32767 on every cluster node.

   - **LoadBalancer**: This type exposes the application service externally using a cloud provider's load balancer, such as ELB on AWS.

   - **ExternalName**: Used when you need to define a proxy for a cluster's external service such as a database.

13. To create a Kubernetes Service, you typically create a service configuration file (YAML or JSON) that specifies the desired service type (e.g., ClusterIP for internal communication), and selector labels to identify the target pods and the ports for network traffic. This file is then applied using the kubectl apply command. This creates a service that routes traffic across the set of pods matching the selector labels.

17

Deploying, Updating, and Securing an Application with Kubernetes

In the previous chapter, we learned about the basics of the container orchestrator known as Kubernetes. We got a high-level overview of the architecture of Kubernetes and learned a lot about the important objects used by Kubernetes to define and manage a containerized application.

In this chapter, we will learn how to deploy, update, and scale applications into a Kubernetes cluster. We will also explain how zero-downtime deployments are achieved to enable disruption-free updates and rollbacks of mission-critical applications. Finally, we will introduce Kubernetes secrets as a means to configure services and protect sensitive data.

This chapter covers the following topics:

- Deploying our first application
- Defining liveness and readiness
- Zero-downtime deployments
- Kubernetes secrets

After working through this chapter, you will be able to do the following:

- Deploy a multi-service application into a Kubernetes cluster
- Define a liveness and readiness probe for your Kubernetes application service
- Update an application service running in Kubernetes without causing downtime
- Define secrets in a Kubernetes cluster
- Configure an application service to use Kubernetes secrets

Technical requirements

In this chapter, we're going to use Docker Desktop on our local computer. Please refer to *Chapter 2, Setting Up a Working Environment*, for more information on how to install and use Docker Desktop.

The code for this chapter can be found here: `main/sample-solutions/ch17`.

Please make sure you have cloned this book's GitHub repository, as described in *Chapter 2*.

In your Terminal, navigate to the `~/The-Ultimate-Docker-Container-Book` folder and create a subfolder called `ch17` and navigate to it:

```
$ mkdir ch17 & cd ch17
```

Deploying our first application

We will take our pets application, which we first introduced in *Chapter 11, Managing Containers with Docker Compose*, and deploy it into a Kubernetes cluster. Our cluster will be Docker Desktop, which, as you know, is offering us a single node Kubernetes cluster. However, from the perspective of deployment, it doesn't matter how big the cluster is and whether the cluster is located in the cloud, in your company's data center, or on your workstation.

Deploying the web component

Just as a reminder, our application consists of two application services: the Node-based web component and the backing PostgreSQL database. In the previous chapter, we learned that we need to define a Kubernetes Deployment object for each application service we want to deploy. We'll do this for the web component first. As always in this book, we will choose the declarative way of defining our objects:

1. We will use our local Kubernetes single-node cluster provided by Docker Desktop. Make sure Kubernetes is turned on for your Docker Desktop installation:

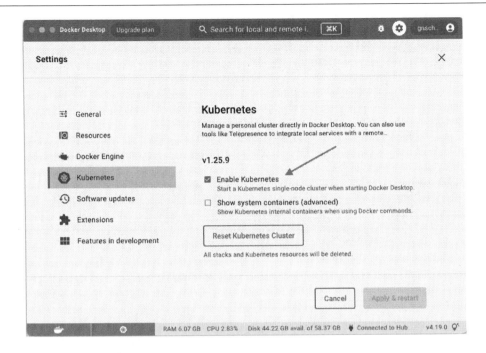

Figure 17.1 – Kubernetes on Docker Desktop

2. To your code subfolder (ch17), add a file called web-deployment.yaml with the following content:

Figure 17.2 – Kubernetes deployment definition for the web component

The preceding deployment definition can be found in the `web-deployment.yaml` file in the `sample-solutions/ch17` subfolder. It contains the instructions necessary to deploy the web component. The lines of code are as follows:

- Line 7: We define the name for our `Deployment` object as `web`.

- Line 9: We declare that we want to have one instance of the `web` component running.

- Lines 11 to 13: Through `Selector`, we define which pods will be part of our deployment, namely those that have the `app` and `service` labels with values of `pets` and `web`, respectively.

- Line 14: In the template for the pods starting at line 11, we define that each pod will have the `app` and `service` labels applied to them.

- Lines 20 onward: We define the single container that will be running in the pod. The image for the container is our well-known `fundamentalsofdocker/ch11-web:2.0` image and the name of the container will be `web`.

- Lines 23 and 24: It is worth noting that we declare that the container exposes port `3000` to incoming traffic.

3. Please make sure that you have set the context of `kubectl` to Docker Desktop. See *Chapter 2, Setting Up a Working Environment*, for details on how to do that. Use the following command:

```
$ kubectl config use-context docker-desktop
```

You will receive the following output:

```
Switched to context "docker-desktop".
```

4. We can deploy this `Deployment` object using the following command:

```
$ kubectl create -f web-deployment.yaml
```

The preceding command outputs the following message:

```
deployment.apps/web created
```

5. We can double-check that the deployment has been created again using our Kubernetes CLI:

```
$ kubectl get all
```

We should see the following output:

```
kubectl get all
NAME                          READY   STATUS      RESTARTS   AGE
pod/web-6dd7f94ff6-9kggq      1/1     Running     0          93s

NAME                 TYPE        CLUSTER-IP   EXTERNAL-IP   PORT(S)   AGE
service/kubernetes   ClusterIP   10.96.0.1    <none>        443/TCP   6h26m

NAME                   READY   UP-TO-DATE   AVAILABLE   AGE
deployment.apps/web    1/1     1            1           93s

NAME                             DESIRED   CURRENT   READY   AGE
replicaset.apps/web-6dd7f94ff6   1         1         1       93s
```

Figure 17.3 – Listing all the resources running in Kind

In the preceding output, we can see that Kubernetes created three objects – the deployment, a pertaining ReplicaSet, and a single pod (remember that we specified that we want one replica only). The current state corresponds to the desired state for all three objects, so we are fine so far.

6. Now, the web service needs to be exposed to the public. For this, we need to define a Kubernetes Service object of the NodePort type. Create a new file called web-service.yaml and add the following code to it:

```
1   apiVersion: v1
2   kind: Service
3   metadata:
4     labels:
5       app: pets
6       service: web
7     name: web
8   spec:
9     type: NodePort
10    ports:
11      - name: "3000"
12        port: 3000
13        targetPort: 3000
14    selector:
15      app: pets
16      service: web
17
```

Figure 17.4 – Definition of the Service object for our web component

Once again, the same file can be found in the web-service.yaml file in the sample-solutions/ch17 subfolder.

The preceding lines of code are as follows:

- Line 7: We set the name of this `Service` object to web.

- Line 9: We define the type of `Service` object we're using. Since the web component has to be accessible from outside of the cluster, this cannot be a `Service` object of the `ClusterIP` type and must be of the `NodePort` or `LoadBalancer` type. We discussed the various types of Kubernetes services in the previous chapter, so will not go into further detail about this. In our example, we're using a `NodePort` type of service.

- Lines 10 to 13: We specify that we want to expose port `3000` for access through the TCP protocol. Kubernetes will map container port `3000` automatically to a free host port in the range of 30,000 to 32,768. Which port Kubernetes effectively chooses can be determined using the `kubectl get service` or `kubectl describe` command for the service after it has been created.

- Lines 14 to 16: We define the filter criteria for the pods that this service will be a stable endpoint for. In this case, it is all the pods that have the app and `service` labels with the `pets` and web values, respectively.

7. Now that we have this specification for a `Service` object, we can create it using `kubectl`:

    ```
    $ kubectl apply -f web-service.yaml
    ```

8. We can list all the services to see the result of the preceding command:

    ```
    $ kubectl get services
    ```

    The preceding command produces the following output:

    ```
    kubectl get services
    NAME          TYPE        CLUSTER-IP      EXTERNAL-IP   PORT(S)          AGE
    kubernetes    ClusterIP   10.96.0.1       <none>        443/TCP          6h38m
    web           NodePort    10.96.195.255   <none>        3000:30319/TCP   87s
    ```

    Figure 17.5 – The Service object that was created for the web component

    In the preceding output, we can see that a service called web has been created. A unique `ClusterIP` value of `10.96.195.255` has been assigned to this service, and container port `3000` has been published on port `30319` on all cluster nodes.

9. If we want to test this deployment, we can use `curl`:

    ```
    $ curl localhost:30319/
    ```

    This will result in the following output:

    ```
    Pets Demo Application
    ```

As we can see, the response is `Pets Demo Application`, which is what we expected. The web service is up and running in the Kubernetes cluster. Next, we want to deploy the database.

Deploying the database

A database is a stateful component and has to be treated differently from stateless components, such as our web component. We discussed the difference between stateful and stateless components in a distributed application architecture in detail in *Chapter 9, Learning about Distributed Application Architecture*, and *Chapter 3, Introducing Container Orchestration*.

Kubernetes has defined a special type of `ReplicaSet` object for stateful components. This object is called `StatefulSet`. Let's use this kind of object to deploy our database.

1. Create a new file called `db-stateful-set.yaml` and add the following content to it:

```yaml
1   apiVersion: apps/v1
2   kind: StatefulSet
3   metadata:
4     name: db
5   spec:
6     selector:
7       matchLabels:
8         app: pets
9         service: db
10    serviceName: db
11    template:
12      metadata:
13        labels:
14          app: pets
15          service: db
16      spec:
17        containers:
18          - image: fundamentalsofdocker/ch08-db:1.0
19            name: db
20            ports:
21              - containerPort: 5432
22            volumeMounts:
23              - mountPath: /var/lib/postgresql/data
24                name: pets-data
25    volumeClaimTemplates:
26      - metadata:
27          name: pets-data
28        spec:
29          accessModes:
30            - ReadWriteOnce
31          resources:
32            requests:
33              storage: 100Mi
```

Figure 17.6 – A StatefulSet object for the DB component

The definition can also be found in the `sample-solutions/ch17` subfolder.

OK; this looks a bit scary, but it isn't. It is a bit longer than the definition of the deployment for the web component since we also need to define a volume where the PostgreSQL database can store the data. The volume claim definition is on lines 25 to 33.

We want to create a volume called `pets-data` that has a maximum size equal to 100 MB. On lines 22 to 24, we use this volume and mount it into the container at `/var/lib/postgresql/data`, where PostgreSQL expects it. On line 21, we also declare that PostgreSQL is listening at port `5432`.

2. As always, we use `kubectl` to deploy our `StatefulSet`:

```
$ kubectl apply -f db-stateful-set.yaml
```

3. Now, if we list all the resources in the cluster, we will be able to see the additional objects that were created:

```
kubectl get all
NAME                                   READY   STATUS    RESTARTS   AGE
pod/db-0                               1/1     Running   0          3m48s
pod/web-deployment-9d66cd994-wq8px     1/1     Running   0          57m

NAME                  TYPE        CLUSTER-IP      EXTERNAL-IP   PORT(S)          AGE
service/kubernetes    ClusterIP   10.96.0.1       <none>        443/TCP          12d
service/web           NodePort    10.100.174.92   <none>        3000:30976/TCP   57m

NAME                             READY   UP-TO-DATE   AVAILABLE   AGE
deployment.apps/web-deployment   1/1     1            1           57m

NAME                                        DESIRED   CURRENT   READY   AGE
replicaset.apps/web-deployment-9d66cd994    1         1         1       57m

NAME                      READY   AGE
statefulset.apps/db       1/1     3m48s
```

Figure 17.7 – The StatefulSet and its pod

Here, we can see that `StatefulSet` and a pod have been created. For both, the current state corresponds to the desired state and thus the system is healthy, but that doesn't mean that the web component can access the database at this time. Service discovery won't work. Remember that the web component wants to access the db service under the name db. We hardcoded the db hostname in the `server.js` file.

4. To make service discovery work inside the cluster, we have to define a Kubernetes `Service` object for the database component too. Since the database should only ever be accessible from within the cluster, the type of `Service` object we need is `ClusterIP`.

Create a new file called db-service.yaml and add the following specification to it. It can be found in the sample-solutions/ch17 subfolder:

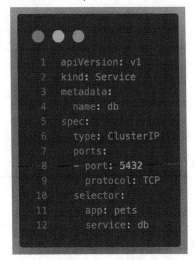

```
1    apiVersion: v1
2    kind: Service
3    metadata:
4      name: db
5    spec:
6      type: ClusterIP
7      ports:
8        - port: 5432
9          protocol: TCP
10     selector:
11       app: pets
12       service: db
```

Figure 17.8 – Definition of the Kubernetes Service object for the database

The database component will be represented by this Service object. It can be reached by the name db, which is the name of the service, as defined on line 4. The database component does not have to be publicly accessible, so we decided to use a Service object of the ClusterIP type. The selector on lines 10 to 12 defines that this service represents a stable endpoint for all the pods that have the necessary labels defined – that is, app: pets and service: db.

5. Let's deploy this service with the following command:

```
$ kubectl apply -f db-service.yaml
```

6. Now, we should be ready to test the application. We can use the browser this time to enjoy the beautiful animal images from the Maasai Mara national park in Kenya:

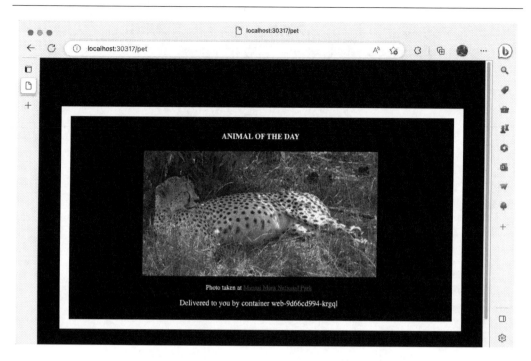

Figure 17.9 – Testing the pets application running in Kubernetes

In this case, port number 30317 is the number that Kubernetes automatically selected for my web Service object. Replace this number with the port that Kubernetes assigned to your service. You can get the number by using the kubectl get services command.

With that, we have successfully deployed the pets application to a single-node Kubernetes cluster provided by Docker Desktop. We had to define four artifacts to do so, which are as follows:

- Deployment and Service objects for the web component
- StatefulSet and Service objects for the database component

To remove the application from the cluster, we can use the following small script:

```
kubectl delete svc/web
kubectl delete deploy/web
kubectl delete svc/db
kubectl delete statefulset/db
kubectl delete pvc/pets-data-db-0
```

Please note the last line in this script. We are deleting the persistent volume claim that Kubernetes automatically created as part of the db deployment. When we delete the db deployment, this claim is not automatically deleted! Persistent volume claims are a bit similar (but not the same, mind you) as Docker volumes.

Use the `kubectl get pvc` command to get a list of all claims on your machine.

Next, we will optimize the deployment.

Streamlining the deployment

So far, we have created four artifacts that needed to be deployed to the cluster. This is only a very simple application, consisting of two components. Imagine having a much more complex application. It would quickly become a maintenance nightmare. Luckily, we have several options as to how we can simplify the deployment. The method that we are going to discuss here is the possibility of defining all the components that make up an application in Kubernetes in a single file.

Other solutions that lie outside the scope of this book include using a package manager, such as Helm (`https://helm.sh/`), or Kustomize (`https://kubernetes.io/docs/tasks/manage-kubernetes-objects/kustomization/`), the native Kubernetes solution.

If we have an application consisting of many Kubernetes objects, such as `Deployment` and `Service` objects, then we can keep them all in a single file and separate the individual object definitions by three dashes. For example, if we wanted to have the `Deployment` and `Service` definitions for the `web` component in a single file, this would look as follows:

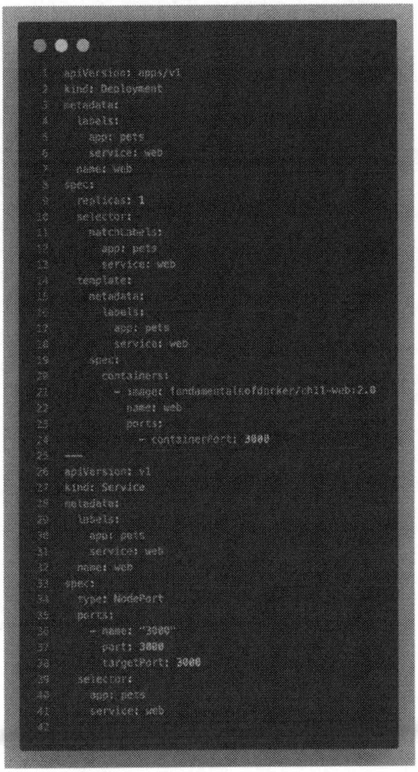

```yaml
apiVersion: apps/v1
kind: Deployment
metadata:
  labels:
    app: pets
    service: web
  name: web
spec:
  replicas: 1
  selector:
    matchLabels:
      app: pets
      service: web
  template:
    metadata:
      labels:
        app: pets
        service: web
    spec:
      containers:
        - image: fundamentalsofdocker/ch11-web:2.0
          name: web
          ports:
            - containerPort: 3000
---
apiVersion: v1
kind: Service
metadata:
  labels:
    app: pets
    service: web
  name: web
spec:
  type: NodePort
  ports:
    - name: "3000"
      port: 3000
      targetPort: 3000
  selector:
    app: pets
    service: web
```

Figure 17.10 – Deployment and Service for web in a single file

You can find this file in `sample-solutions/ch17/install-web.yaml`.

Next, we collected all four object definitions for the pets application in the `sample-solutions/ch17/install-pets.yaml` file, and we can deploy the application in one go:

```
$ kubectl apply -f install-pets.yaml
```

This will give us this output:

```
deployment "web" created
service "web" created
deployment "db" created
service "db" created
```

Similarly, we created a script called `sample-solutions/ch17/remove-pets.sh` to remove all the artifacts of the pets application from the Kubernetes cluster. Note that the file was made executable with `chmod +x ./remove-pets.sh` first. Now, we can use the following command:

```
$ ./remove-pets.sh
```

This will result in an output like is:

```
deployment.apps "web" deleted
service "web" deleted
statefulset.apps "db" deleted
service "db" deleted
persistentvolumeclaim "pets-data-db-0" deleted
```

Alternatively, you can use the following command:

```
$ kubectl delete -f install-pets.yaml
```

This will delete all the resources except the persistent volume claim, which you still need to delete by hand:

```
$ kubectl delete pvc/pets-data-db-0
```

With this, we have taken the pets application we introduced in *Chapter 11, Managing Containers with Docker Compose*, and defined all the Kubernetes objects that are necessary to deploy this application into a Kubernetes cluster. In each step, we made sure that we got the expected result, and once all the artifacts existed in the cluster, we showed the running application.

Defining liveness and readiness

Container orchestration systems such as Kubernetes and Docker Swarm make it significantly easier to deploy, run, and update highly distributed, mission-critical applications. The orchestration engine automates many cumbersome tasks, such as scaling up or down, asserting that the desired state is maintained at all times, and more.

However, the orchestration engine cannot just do everything automatically. Sometimes, we developers need to support the engine with some information that only we can know about. So, what do I mean by that?

Let's look at a single application service. Let's assume it is a microservice and let's call it service A. If we run service A containerized on a Kubernetes cluster, then Kubernetes can make sure that we have the five instances that we require in the service definition running at all times. If one instance crashes, Kubernetes can quickly launch a new instance and thus maintain the desired state. But what if an instance of the service does not crash, but is unhealthy or just not ready yet to serve requests? Kubernetes should know about both situations. But it can't, since good or bad health from an application service perspective is outside of the knowledge of the orchestration engine. Only we application developers can know when our service is healthy and when it is not.

The application service could, for example, be running, but its internal state could have been corrupted due to some bug, it could be in an endless loop, or it could be in a deadlock situation.

Similarly, only we application developers know whether our service is ready to work, or whether it is still initializing. Although it is highly recommended to keep the initialization phase of a microservice as short as possible, it often cannot be avoided if a significant time span is needed by a particular service so that it's ready to operate. Being in this state of initialization is not the same thing as being unhealthy, though. The initialization phase is an expected part of the life cycle of a microservice or any other application service.

Thus, Kubernetes should not try to kill our microservice if it is in the initialization phase. If our microservice is unhealthy, though, Kubernetes should kill it as quickly as possible and replace it with a fresh instance.

Kubernetes has the concept of probes to provide the seam between the orchestration engine and the application developer. Kubernetes uses these probes to find out more about the inner state of the application service at hand. Probes are executed locally, inside each container. There is a probe for the health – also called liveness – of the service, a startup probe, and a probe for the readiness of the service. Let's look at them in turn.

Kubernetes liveness probes

Kubernetes uses the liveness probe to decide when a container needs to be killed and when another instance should be launched instead. Since Kubernetes operates at a pod level, the respective pod is killed if at least one of its containers reports as being unhealthy.

Alternatively, we can say it the other way around: only if all the containers of a pod report to be healthy is the pod considered to be healthy.

We can define the liveness probe in the specification for a pod as follows:

```
apiVersion: v1
kind: Pod
metadata:
  ...
spec:
  containers:
  - name: liveness-demo
    image: postgres:12.10
  ...

    livenessProbe:
      exec:
        command: nc localhost 5432 || exit -1
      initialDelaySeconds: 10
      periodSeconds: 5
```

The relevant part is in the `livenessProbe` section. First, we define a command that Kubernetes will execute as a probe inside the container. In our case, we have a `PostreSQL` container and use the `netcat` Linux tool to probe port 5432 over TCP. The `nc localhost 5432` command is successful once Postgres listens to it.

The other two settings, `initialDelaySeconds` and `periodSeconds`, define how long Kubernetes should wait after starting the container until it first executes the probe and how frequently the probe should be executed thereafter. In our case, Kubernetes waits for 10 seconds before executing the first probe and then executes a probe every 5 seconds.

It is also possible to probe an HTTP endpoint instead of using a command. Let's assume we're running a microservice from an image, `acme.com/my-api:1.0`, with an API that has an endpoint called `/api/health` that returns status `200 (OK)` if the microservice is healthy, and `50x (Error)` if it is unhealthy. Here, we can define the liveness probe as follows:

```
apiVersion: v1
kind: Pod
metadata:
  ...
spec:
  containers:
  - name: liveness
    image: acme.com/my-api:1.0
  ...
```

```
    livenessProbe:
      httpGet:
        path: /api/health
        port: 3000
      initialDelaySeconds: 5
      periodSeconds: 3
```

In the preceding snippet, I defined the liveness probe so that it uses the HTTP protocol and executed a GET request to the /api/health endpoint on port 5000 of localhost. Remember, the probe is executed inside the container, which means I can use localhost.

We can also directly use the TCP protocol to probe a port on the container. But wait a second – didn't we just do that in our first example, where we used the generic liveness probe based on an arbitrary command? Yes, you're right, we did, but we had to rely on the presence of the netcat tool in the container to do so. We cannot assume that this tool is always there. Thus, it is favorable to rely on Kubernetes to do the TCP-based probing for us out of the box. The modified pod spec looks like this:

```
apiVersion: v1
kind: Pod
metadata:
  ...
spec:
  containers:
  - name: liveness-demo
    image: postgres:12.10
  ...

    livenessProbe:
      tcpSocket:
        port: 5432
      initialDelaySeconds: 10
      periodSeconds: 5
```

This looks very similar. The only change is that the type of probe has been changed from exec to tcpSocket and that, instead of providing a command, we provide the port to probe.

Note that we could also use failureThreshold here with Kubernetes' livenessProbe. The livenessProbe failure threshold in Kubernetes is the minimum number of consecutive failures that must occur before the container is restarted. The default value is 3. The minimum value is 1. If the handler returns a failure code, kubelet kills the container and restarts it. Any code greater than or equal to 200 and less than 400 indicates success. Any other code indicates failure.

Let's try this out:

1. Copy the `probes` subfolder from the `sample-solutions/ch17` folder to your `ch17` folder.

2. Build the Docker image with the following command:

    ```
    $ docker image build -t demo/probes-demo:2.0 probes
    ```

3. Use `kubectl` to deploy the sample pod that's defined in `probes-demo.yaml`:

    ```
    $ kubectl apply -f probes/probes-demo.yaml
    ```

4. Describe the pod and specifically analyze the log part of the output:

    ```
    $ kubectl describe pods/probes-demo
    ```

    During the first half minute or so, you should get the following output:

    ```
    Events:
      Type    Reason     Age  From               Message
      ----    ------     ---  ----               -------
      Normal  Scheduled  26s  default-scheduler  Successfully assigned default/probes-demo to docker-desktop
      Normal  Pulled     25s  kubelet            Container image "demo/probes-demo:2.0" already present on machine
      Normal  Created    25s  kubelet            Created container probes-demo
      Normal  Started    25s  kubelet            Started container probes-demo
    ```

    Figure 17.11 – Log output of the healthy pod

5. Wait at least 30 seconds and then describe the pod again. This time, you should see the following output:

    ```
    Events:
      Type     Reason     Age              From               Message
      ----     ------     ---              ----               -------
      Normal   Scheduled  99s              default-scheduler  Successfully assigned default/probes-demo to docker-desktop
      Warning  Unhealthy  53s (x3 over 63s) kubelet           Liveness probe failed: cat: /app/healthy: No such file or directory
      Normal   Killing    53s              kubelet            Container probes-demo failed liveness probe, will be restarted
      Normal   Pulled     23s (x2 over 98s) kubelet           Container image "demo/probes-demo:2.0" already present on machine
      Normal   Created    23s (x2 over 98s) kubelet           Created container probes-demo
      Normal   Started    23s (x2 over 98s) kubelet           Started container probes-demo
    ```

    Figure 17.12 – Log output of the pod after it has changed its state to Unhealthy

    The marked lines indicate the failure of the probe and the fact that the pod is going to be restarted.

6. If you get the list of pods, you will see that the pod has been restarted several times:

    ```
    $ kubectl get pods
    ```

    This results in this output:

    ```
    NAME              READY  STATUS   RESTARTS      AGE
    probes-demo  1/1       Running  5 (49s ago)   7m22s
    ```

7. When you're done with the sample, delete the pod with the following command:

    ```
    $ kubectl delete pods/probes-demo
    ```

Next, we will have a look at the Kubernetes readiness probe.

Kubernetes readiness probes

Kubernetes uses a readiness probe to decide when a service instance – that is, a container – is ready to accept traffic. Now, we all know that Kubernetes deploys and runs pods and not containers, so it only makes sense to talk about the readiness of a pod. Only if all containers in a pod report as ready is the pod considered to be ready itself. If a pod reports as not ready, then Kubernetes removes it from the service load balancers.

Readiness probes are defined the same way as liveness probes: just switch the `livenessProbe` key in the pod spec to `readinessProbe`. Here is an example using our prior pod spec:

```
...
spec:
  containers:
  - name: liveness-demo
    image: postgres:12.10

  ...

    livenessProbe:
      tcpSocket:
        port: 5432
      failureThreshold: 2
      periodSeconds: 5
    readinessProbe:
      tcpSocket:
        port: 5432
      initialDelaySeconds: 10
      periodSeconds: 5
```

Note that, in this example, we don't need an initial delay for the liveness probe anymore since we now have a readiness probe. Thus, I have replaced the initial delay entry for the liveness probe with an entry called `failureThreshold`, which indicates how many times Kubernetes should repeat probing in case of a failure until it assumes that the container is unhealthy.

Kubernetes startup probes

It is often helpful for Kubernetes to know when a service instance has started. If we define a startup probe for a container, then Kubernetes does not execute the liveness or readiness probes, so long as the container's startup probe does not succeed. Once again, Kubernetes looks at pods and starts executing liveness and readiness probes on its containers if the startup probes of all the pod's containers succeed.

When would we use a startup probe, given the fact that we already have the liveness and readiness probes? There might be situations where we have to account for exceptionally long startup and initialization times, such as when containerizing a legacy application. We could technically configure the readiness or liveness probes to account for this fact, but that would defeat the purpose of these probes. The latter probes are meant to provide quick feedback to Kubernetes on the health and availability of the container. If we configure for long initial delays or periods, then this would counter the desired outcome.

Unsurprisingly, the startup probe is defined the same way as the readiness and liveness probes. Here is an example:

```
spec:
  containers:
...
    startupProbe:
      tcpSocket:
        port: 3000
      failureThreshold: 30
      periodSeconds: 5
...
```

Make sure that you define the `failureThreshold` * `periodSeconds` product so that it's big enough to account for the worst startup time.

In our example, the max startup time should not exceed 150 seconds.

Zero-downtime deployments

In a mission-critical environment, the application must be always up and running. These days, we cannot afford downtime anymore. Kubernetes gives us various means of achieving this. Performing an update on an application in the cluster that causes no downtime is called a **zero-downtime deployment**. In this section, we will present two ways of achieving this. These are as follows:

- Rolling updates
- Blue-green deployments

Let's start by discussing rolling updates.

Rolling updates

In the previous chapter, we learned that the Kubernetes `Deployment` object distinguishes itself from the `ReplicaSet` object in that it adds rolling updates and rollbacks on top of the latter's functionality. Let's use our web component to demonstrate this. We will have to modify the manifest or description of the deployment for the web component.

We will use the same deployment definition as in the previous section, with one important difference – we will have **five replicas** of the web component running. The following definition can also be found in the `sample-solutions/ch17/web-deployment-rolling-v1.yaml` file:

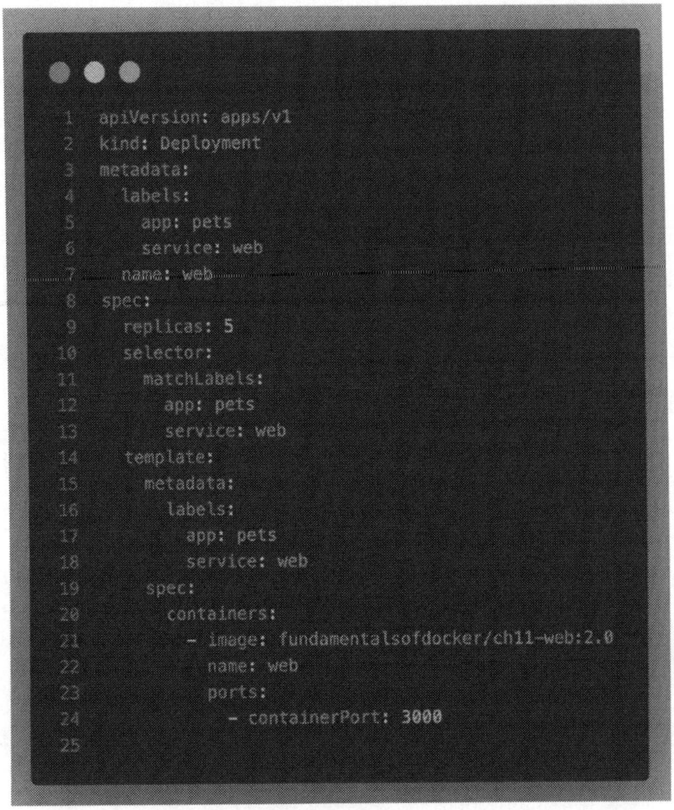

```
1   apiVersion: apps/v1
2   kind: Deployment
3   metadata:
4     labels:
5       app: pets
6       service: web
7     name: web
8   spec:
9     replicas: 5
10    selector:
11      matchLabels:
12        app: pets
13        service: web
14    template:
15      metadata:
16        labels:
17          app: pets
18          service: web
19      spec:
20        containers:
21          - image: fundamentalsofdocker/ch11-web:2.0
22            name: web
23            ports:
24              - containerPort: 3000
25
```

Figure 17.13 – Deployment for the web component with five replicas

Now, we can create this deployment as usual and also, at the same time, the service that makes our component accessible:

```
$ kubectl apply -f web-deployment-rolling-v1.yaml
$ kubectl apply -f web-service.yaml
```

Once we have deployed the pods and the service, we can test our web component. First, we can get the assigned node port with this command:

```
$ PORT=$(kubectl get svc/web -o jsonpath='{.spec.ports[0].nodePort}')
```

Next, we can use the $PORT environment variable in our curl statement:

```
$ curl localhost:${PORT}/
```

This provides the expected output:

```
Pets Demo Application
```

As we can see, the application is up and running and returns the expected message, Pets Demo Application.

Our developers have created a new version, 2.1, of the web component. The code of the new version of the web component can be found in the sample-solutions/ch17/web folder, and the only change is located on line 12 of the server.js file:

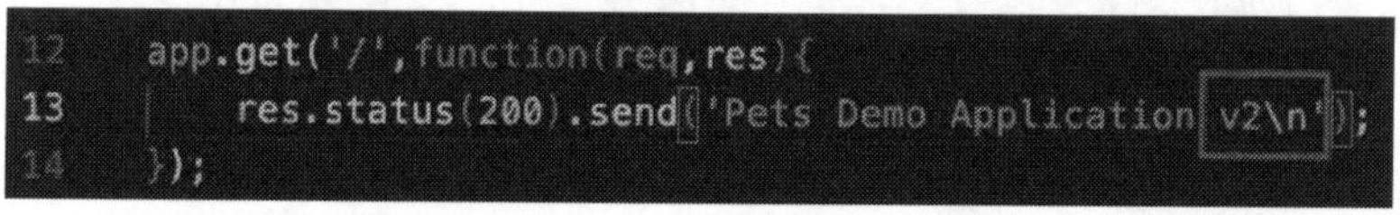

```
12    app.get('/',function(req,res){
13        res.status(200).send('Pets Demo Application v2\n');
14    });
```

Figure 17.14 – Code change for version 2.0 of the web component

We can now build the new image as follows (replace demo with your GitHub username):

```
$ docker image build -t demo/ch17-web:2.1 web
```

Subsequently, we can push the image to Docker Hub, as follows (replace demo with your GitHub username):

```
$ docker image push demo/ch17-web:2.1
```

Now, we want to update the image that's used by our pods that are part of the web Deployment object. We can do this by using the set image command of kubectl:

```
$ kubectl set image deployment/web \
    web=demo/ch17-web:2.1
```

If we test the application again, we'll get a confirmation that the update has indeed happened:

```
$ curl localhost:${PORT}/
```

The output indicates that we now have version 2 installed:

```
Pets Demo Application v2
```

Now, how do we know that there hasn't been any downtime during this update? Did the update happen in a rolling fashion? What does rolling update mean at all? Let's investigate. First, we can get a confirmation from Kubernetes that the deployment has indeed happened and was successful by using the `rollout status` command:

```
$ kubectl rollout status deploy/web
```

The command will respond as follows:

```
deployment "web" successfully rolled out
```

If we describe the web deployment object with `kubectl describe deploy/web`, we will get the following list of events at the end of the output:

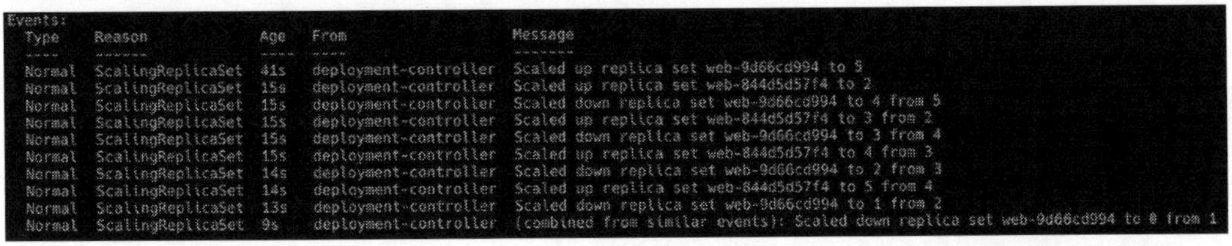

```
Events:
  Type    Reason             Age  From                   Message
  ----    ------             ---- ----                   -------
  Normal  ScalingReplicaSet  41s  deployment-controller  Scaled up replica set web-9d66cd994 to 5
  Normal  ScalingReplicaSet  15s  deployment-controller  Scaled up replica set web-844d5d57f4 to 2
  Normal  ScalingReplicaSet  15s  deployment-controller  Scaled down replica set web-9d66cd994 to 4 from 5
  Normal  ScalingReplicaSet  15s  deployment-controller  Scaled up replica set web-844d5d57f4 to 3 from 2
  Normal  ScalingReplicaSet  15s  deployment-controller  Scaled down replica set web-9d66cd994 to 3 from 4
  Normal  ScalingReplicaSet  15s  deployment-controller  Scaled up replica set web-844d5d57f4 to 4 from 3
  Normal  ScalingReplicaSet  14s  deployment-controller  Scaled down replica set web-9d66cd994 to 2 from 3
  Normal  ScalingReplicaSet  14s  deployment-controller  Scaled up replica set web-844d5d57f4 to 5 from 4
  Normal  ScalingReplicaSet  13s  deployment-controller  Scaled down replica set web-9d66cd994 to 1 from 2
  Normal  ScalingReplicaSet  9s   deployment-controller  (combined from similar events): Scaled down replica set web-9d66cd994 to 0 from 1
```

Figure 17.15 – List of events found in the output of the deployment description of the web component

The first event tells us that, when we created the deployment, a `ReplicaSet` object called `web-769b88f67` with five replicas was created. Then, we executed the `update` command. The second event in the list tells us that this meant creating a new `ReplicaSet` object called `web-55cdf67cd` with, initially, one replica only. Thus, at that particular moment, six pods existed on the system: the five initial pods and one pod with the new version. But, since the desired state of the `Deployment` object states that we want five replicas only, Kubernetes now scales down the old `ReplicaSet` object to four instances, which we can see in the third event.

Then, again, the new `ReplicaSet` object was scaled up to two instances, and, subsequently, the old `ReplicaSet` object was scaled down to three instances, and so on, until we had five new instances and all the old instances were decommissioned. Although we cannot see any precise time (other than 3 minutes) when that happened, the order of the events tells us that the whole update happened in a rolling fashion.

During a short period, some of the calls to the web service would have had an answer from the old version of the component, and some calls would have received an answer from the new version of the component, but at no time would the service have been down.

We can also list the `ReplicaSet` objects in the cluster and get confirmation of what I said in the preceding section:

```
kubectl get rs
NAME              DESIRED   CURRENT   READY   AGE
web-844d5d57f4    5         5         5       92s
web-9d66cd994     0         0         0       118s
```

Figure 17.16 – Listing all the ReplicaSet objects in the cluster

Here, we can see that the new `ReplicaSet` object has five instances running and that the old one has been scaled down to zero instances. The reason that the old `ReplicaSet` object is still lingering is that Kubernetes provides us with the possibility of rolling back the update and, in that case, will reuse that `ReplicaSet`.

To roll back the update of the image in case some undetected bug sneaked into the new code, we can use the `rollout undo` command:

```
$ kubectl rollout undo deploy/web
```

This outputs the following:

```
deployment.apps/web rolled back
```

We can test whether the rollback was successful like so:

```
$ curl localhost:${PORT}/
```

As we can see, the output shows us that this is the case:

```
Pets Demo Application
```

If we list the `ReplicaSet` objects, we will see the following output:

```
kubectl get rs
NAME              DESIRED   CURRENT   READY   AGE
web-844d5d57f4    0         0         0       5m5s
web-9d66cd994     5         5         5       5m31s
```

Figure 17.17 – Listing the ReplicaSet objects after rolling back

This confirms that the old ReplicaSet (web-9d66cd994) object has been reused and that the new one has been scaled down to zero instances.

Before continuing, please delete the deployment and the service:

```
$ kubectl delete deploy/web
$ kubectl delete service/web
```

Sometimes, though, we cannot, or do not want to, tolerate the mixed state of an old version coexisting with the new version. We want an all-or-nothing strategy. This is where blue-green deployments come into play, which we will discuss next.

Blue-green deployment

If we want to do a blue-green style deployment for our web component of the pets application, then we can do so by using labels creatively. First, let's remind ourselves how blue-green deployments work. Here is a rough step-by-step guide:

1. Deploy the first version of the web component as blue. We will label the pods with a label of color: blue to do so.

2. Deploy the Kubernetes service for these pods with the color: blue label in the selector section.

3. Now, we can deploy version 2 of the web component, but, this time, the pods have a label of color: green.

4. We can test the green version of the service to check that it works as expected.

5. Now, we can flip traffic from blue to green by updating the Kubernetes service for the web component. We will modify the selector so that it uses the color: green label.

Let's define a `Deployment` object for version 1, `blue`:

```
1   apiVersion: apps/v1
2   kind: Deployment
3   metadata:
4     labels:
5       app: pets
6       service: web
7       color: blue
8     name: web-blue
9   spec:
10    replicas: 5
11    selector:
12      matchLabels:
13        app: pets
14        service: web
15        color: blue
16    template:
17      metadata:
18        labels:
19          app: pets
20          service: web
21          color: blue
22      spec:
23        containers:
24          - image: fundamentalsofdocker/ch11-web:2.0
25            name: web
26            ports:
27              - containerPort: 3000
28
```

Figure 17.18 – Specification of the blue deployment for the web component

The preceding definition can be found in the `sample-solutions/ch17/web-deployment-blue.yaml` file.

Please take note of line 8, where we define the name of the deployment as `web-blue` to distinguish it from the upcoming deployment, `web-green`. Also, note that we have added the `color: blue` label on lines 7, 15, and 21. Everything else remains the same as before.

Now, we can define the `Service` object for the web component. It will be the same as the one we used before but with a minor change, as shown in the following screenshot:

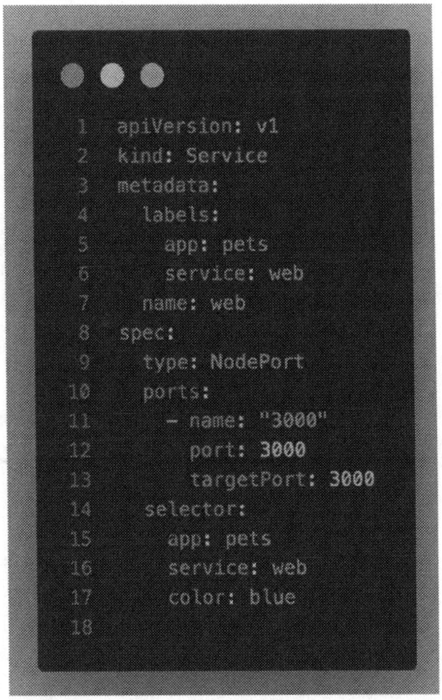

Figure 17.19 – Kubernetes service for the web component supporting blue-green deployments

The only difference regarding the definition of the service we used earlier in this chapter is line 17, which adds the `color: blue` label to the selector. We can find the preceding definition in the `sample-solutions/ch17/web-service-blue-green.yaml` file.

Then, we can deploy the blue version of the web component with the following command:

```
$ kubectl apply -f web-deploy-blue.yaml
```

We can deploy its service with this command:

```
$ kubectl apply -f web-service-blue-green.yaml
```

Once the service is up and running, we can determine its IP address and port number and test it:

```
$ PORT=$(kubectl get svc/web -o jsonpath='{.spec.ports[0].nodePort}')
```

Then, we can access it with the `curl` command:

```
$ curl localhost:${PORT}/
```

This gives us what we expect:

```
Pets Demo Application
```

Now, we can deploy the green version of the web component. The definition of its Deployment object can be found in the sample-solutions/ch17/web-deployment-green.yaml file and looks as follows:

```
 1  apiVersion: apps/v1
 2  kind: Deployment
 3  metadata:
 4    labels:
 5      app: pets
 6      service: web
 7      color: green
 8    name: web-green
 9  spec:
10    replicas: 5
11    selector:
12      matchLabels:
13        app: pets
14        service: web
15        color: green
16    template:
17      metadata:
18        labels:
19          app: pets
20          service: web
21          color: green
22      spec:
23        containers:
24          - image: demo/ch11-web:2.1
25            name: web
26            ports:
27              - containerPort: 3000
28
```

Figure 17.20 – Specification of the green deployment for the web component

The interesting lines are as follows:

- Line 8: Named web-green to distinguish it from web-blue and allow for parallel installation
- Lines 7, 15, and 21: Have the color green
- Line 24: Now using version 2.1 of the web image we built earlier in this chapter

Do not forget to change "demo" to your own GitHub username on line 24.

Now, we're ready to deploy this green version of the service. It should run separately from the blue service:

```
$ kubectl apply -f web-deployment-green.yaml
```

We can make sure that both deployments coexist like so:

```
kubectl get deploy
NAME        READY   UP-TO-DATE   AVAILABLE   AGE
web-blue    5/5     5            5           14m
web-green   5/5     5            5           17s
```

Figure 17.21 – Displaying the list of Deployment objects running in the cluster

As expected, we have both blue and green running. We can verify that blue is still the active service:

```
$ curl localhost:${PORT}/
```

We should still receive the following output:

```
Pets Demo Application
```

Now comes the interesting part: we can flip traffic from blue to green by editing the existing service for the web component. To do so, execute the following command:

```
$ kubectl edit svc/web
```

Change the value of the label color from blue to green. Then, save and quit the editor. The Kubernetes CLI will automatically update the service. Now, when we query the web service again, we'll get this:

```
$ curl localhost:${PORT}/
```

This time, we should get the following output:

```
Pets Demo Application v2
```

This confirms that the traffic has indeed switched to the green version of the web component (note v2 at the end of the response to the curl command).

> **Note**
>
> If we wanted to stick to the declarative form, it would be better to update the web-service-blue-green.yaml file and apply the new version so that the desired state is still present in a file, avoiding potential mismatch in reality and the file. However, for illustration, the presented way is fine.

If we realize that something went wrong with our green deployment and the new version has a defect, we can easily switch back to the blue version by editing the web service again and replacing the value of the color label with blue. This rollback is instantaneous and should always work. Then, we can remove the buggy green deployment and fix the component. Once we have corrected the problem, we can deploy the green version once again.

Once the green version of the component is running as expected and performing well, we can decommission the blue version:

```
$ kubectl delete deploy/web-blue
```

When we're ready to deploy a new version, 3.0, this one becomes the blue version. We must update the `ch17/web-deployment-blue.yaml` file accordingly and deploy it. Then, we must flip the web service from green to blue, and so on.

With that, we have successfully demonstrated, with our web component of the pets application, how blue-green deployment can be achieved in a Kubernetes cluster.

Next, we are going to learn how to deal with secrets used by applications running on Kubernetes.

Kubernetes secrets

Sometimes, services that we want to run in the Kubernetes cluster have to use confidential data such as passwords, secret API keys, or certificates, to name just a few. We want to make sure that this sensitive information can only ever be seen by the authorized or dedicated service. All other services running in the cluster should not have any access to this data.

For this reason, Kubernetes secrets were introduced. A secret is a key-value pair where the key is the unique name of the secret, and the value is the actual sensitive data. Secrets are stored in etcd. Kubernetes can be configured so that secrets are encrypted at rest – that is, in etcd – and in transit – that is, when the secrets are going over the wire from a master node to the worker nodes that the pods of the service using this secret are running on.

Manually defining secrets

We can create a secret declaratively in the same way as we can create any other object in Kubernetes. Here is the YAML for such a secret:

```
apiVersion: v1
kind: Secret
metadata:
  name: pets-secret
type: Opaque
data:
  username: am9obi5kb2UK
  password: cOVjcmVOLXBhc1N3MHJECg==
```

The preceding definition can be found in the `sample-solutions/ch17/pets-secret.yaml` file. Now, you might be wondering what the values are. Are these the real (unencrypted) values? No, they are not. And they are also not encrypted values, but just base64-encoded values.

Thus, they are not really secure, since base64-encoded values can easily be reverted to cleartext values. How did I get these values? That's easy – follow these steps:

1. Use the base64 tool as follows to encode the values:

    ```
    $ echo "john.doe" | base64
    ```

    This will result in the following output:

    ```
    am9obi5kb2UK
    ```

    Also, try the following:

    ```
    $ echo "sEcret-pasSw0rD" | base64
    ```

    This will give us the following output:

    ```
    c0VjcmV0LXBhc1N3MHJECg==
    ```

2. Using the preceding values, we can create the secret:

    ```
    $ kubectl create -f pets-secret.yaml
    ```

    Here, the command outputs this:

    ```
    secret/pets-secret created
    ```

3. We can describe the secret with the following command:

    ```
    $ kubectl describe secrets/pets-secret
    ```

    The output of the preceding command looks like this:

Figure 17.22 – Creating and describing the Kubernetes secret

4. In the description of the secret, the values are hidden and only their length is given. So, maybe the secrets are safe now. No, not really. We can easily decode this secret using the kubectl get command:

    ```
    $ kubectl get secrets/pets-secret -o yaml
    ```

The output looks like this:

```
kubectl get secrets/pets-secret -o yaml
apiVersion: v1
data:
  password: c0VjcmV0LXBhc1N3MHJECg==
  username: am9obi5kb2UK
kind: Secret
metadata:
  creationTimestamp: "2023-05-21T18:26:59Z"
  name: pets-secret
  namespace: default
  resourceVersion: "77600"
  uid: 44d96436-c881-4b4f-b2e5-267060685804
type: Opaque
```

Figure 17.23 – Kubernetes secret decoded

As we can see in the preceding screenshot, we have our original secret values back.

5. Decode the values you got previously:

```
$ echo "c0VjcmV0LXBhc1N3MHJECg==" | base64 –decode
```

This will result in the following output:

```
sEcret-pasSw0rD
```

Thus, the consequence is that this method of creating a Kubernetes secret is not to be used in any environment other than development, where we deal with non-sensitive data. In all other environments, we need a better way to deal with secrets.

Creating secrets with kubectl

A much safer way to define secrets is to use kubectl. First, we must create files containing the base64-encoded secret values, similar to what we did in the preceding section, but, this time, we must store the values in temporary files:

```
$ echo "sue-hunter" | base64 > username.txt
$ echo "123abc456def" | base64 > password.txt
```

Now, we can use kubectl to create a secret from those files, as follows:

```
$ kubectl create secret generic pets-secret-prod \
    --from-file=./username.txt \
    --from-file=./password.txt
```

This will result in this output:

```
secret "pets-secret-prod" created
```

The secret can then be used the same way as the manually created secret.

Why is this method more secure than the other one, you might ask? Well, first of all, no YAML defines a secret, and it is stored in some source code version control system, such as GitHub, which many people have access to, so they can see and decode the secrets.

Only the admin that is authorized to know the secrets ever sees their values and uses them to directly create the secrets in the (production) cluster. The cluster itself is protected by role-based access control so that no unauthorized persons have access to it, nor can they possibly decode the secrets defined in the cluster.

Now, let's see how we can use the secrets that we have defined.

Using secrets in a pod

Let's say we want to create a `Deployment` object where the web component uses our secret, `pets-secret`, which we introduced in the preceding section. We can use the following command to create the secret in the cluster:

```
$ kubectl apply -f pets-secret.yaml
```

In the `sample-solutions/ch17/web-deployment-secret.yaml` file, we can find the definition of the `Deployment` object. We had to add the part starting from line 23 to the original definition of the `Deployment` object:

```
1   apiVersion: apps/v1
2   kind: Deployment
3   metadata:
4     labels:
5       app: pets
6       service: web
7     name: web
8   spec:
9     replicas: 1
10    selector:
11      matchLabels:
12        app: pets
13        service: web
14    template:
15      metadata:
16        labels:
17          app: pets
18          service: web
19      spec:
20        containers:
21          - image: fundamentalsofdocker/ch11-web:2.0
22            name: web
23            ports:
24              - containerPort: 3000
25            volumeMounts:
26              - name: secrets
27                mountPath: "/etc/secrets"
28                readOnly: true
29        volumes:
30          - name: secrets
31            secret:
32              secretName: pets-secret
33
```

Figure 17.24 – The Deployment object for the web component with a secret

On lines 29 through 32, we define a volume called `secrets` from our secret, `pets-secret`. Then, we use this volume in the container, as described on lines 25 through 28.

We mount the secrets in the container filesystem at `/etc/secrets` and mount the volume in read-only mode. Thus, the secret values will be available to the container as files in said folder. The names of the files will correspond to the key names, and the content of the files will be the values of the corresponding keys. The values will be provided in unencrypted form to the application running inside the container.

Apply the deployment with the following command:

```
$ kubectl apply -f web-deployment-secret.yaml
```

In our case, since we have the username and password keys in the secret, we will find two files, named `username` and `password`, in the `/etc/secrets` folder in the container filesystem. The `username` file should contain the `john.doe` value and the `password` file should contain the `sEcret-pasSw0rD` value. Let's confirm this:

- First, we will get the name of the pod:

```
$ kubectl get pods
```

This will give us the following output:

```
kubectl get pods

NAME                   READY    STATUS     RESTARTS    AGE
web-b7b6fcc99-xh4hc    1/1      Running    0           3m59s
```

Figure 17.25 – Looking for the name of the pod

- Using the pod's name, we can execute the commands shown in the following screenshot to retrieve the secrets:

```
kubectl exec -it web-b7b6fcc99-xh4hc -- /bin/sh

/app # cd /etc/secrets/
/etc/secrets # ls -al
total 4
drwxrwxrwt    3 root     root           120 May 21 18:39 .
drwxr-xr-x    1 root     root          4096 May 21 18:39 ..
drwxr-xr-x    2 root     root            80 May 21 18:39 ..2023_05_21_18_39_01.3846062839
lrwxrwxrwx    1 root     root            32 May 21 18:39 ..data -> ..2023_05_21_18_39_01.3846062839
lrwxrwxrwx    1 root     root            15 May 21 18:39 password -> ..data/password
lrwxrwxrwx    1 root     root            15 May 21 18:39 username -> ..data/username
/etc/secrets # cat username && cat password
john.doe
sEcret-pasSw0rD
```

Figure 17.26 – Confirming that secrets are available inside the container

On line 1 of the preceding output, we `exec` into the container where the `web` component runs. Then, on lines 2 to 5, we list the files in the `/etc/secrets` folder, and, finally, on the last 3 lines, we show the content of the two files, which, unsurprisingly, shows the secret values in clear text.

Since any application written in any language can read simple files, this mechanism of using secrets is very backward-compatible. Even an old Cobol application can read clear text files from the filesystem.

Before leaving, please delete the Kubernetes deployment:

```
$ kubectl delete deploy/web
```

Sometimes, though, applications expect secrets to be available in environment variables.

Let's look at what Kubernetes offers us in this case.

Secret values in environment variables

Let's say our web component expects the username in the PETS_USERNAME environment variable and the password in the PETS_PASSWORD environment variable. If this is the case, we can modify our deployment YAML file so that it looks as follows:

```
1  apiVersion: apps/v1
2  kind: Deployment
3  metadata:
4    labels:
5      app: pets
6      service: web
7    name: web
8  spec:
9    replicas: 1
10   selector:
11     matchLabels:
12       app: pets
13       service: web
14   template:
15     metadata:
16       labels:
17         app: pets
18         service: web
19     spec:
20       containers:
21       - image: fundamentalsofdocker/ch11-web:2.0
22         name: web
23         ports:
24         - containerPort: 3000
25         env:
26         - name: PETS_USERNAME
27           valueFrom:
28             secretKeyRef:
29               name: pets-secret
30               key: username
31         - name: PETS_PASSWORD
32           valueFrom:
33             secretKeyRef:
34               name: pets-secret
35               key: password
36
```

Figure 17.27 – Deployment mapping secret values to environment variables

On lines 25 through 35, we define the two environment variables, PETS_USERNAME and PETS_PASSWORD, and map the corresponding key-value pair of pets-secret to them.

Apply the updated deployment:

```
$ kubectl apply -f web-deployment-secret.yaml
```

Note that we don't need a volume anymore; instead, we directly map the individual keys of pets-secret to the corresponding environment variables that are valid inside the container. The following sequence of commands shows that the secret values are indeed available inside the container in the respective environment variables:

```
k exec -it web-5446f87bdc-68xtc -- /bin/sh
/app # echo $PETS_USERNAME && echo PETS_PASSWORD
john.doe
PETS_PASSWORD
```

Figure 17.28 – The secret values have been mapped to environment variables

In this section, we have shown you how to define secrets in a Kubernetes cluster and how to use those secrets in containers running as part of the pods of a deployment. We have shown two variants of how secrets can be mapped inside a container – using files and using environment variables.

Summary

In this chapter, we learned how to deploy an application into a Kubernetes cluster and how to set up application-level routing for this application. Furthermore, we learned how to update application services running in a Kubernetes cluster without causing any downtime. Finally, we used secrets to provide sensitive information to application services running in the cluster.

In the next chapter, we are going to learn about different techniques that are used to monitor an individual service or a whole distributed application running on a Kubernetes cluster. We will also learn how we can troubleshoot an application service that is running in production without altering the cluster or the cluster nodes that the service is running on. Stay tuned.

Further reading

Here are a few links that provide additional information on the topics that were discussed in this chapter:

- *Performing a rolling update*: https://bit.ly/2o2okEQ
- *Blue-green deployment*: https://bit.Ly/2r2IxNJ
- *Secrets in Kubernetes*: https://bit.ly/2C6hMZF

Questions

To assess your learning progress, please answer the following questions:

1. You have an application consisting of two services, the first one being a web API and the second one being a database, such as MongoDB. You want to deploy this application into a Kubernetes cluster. In a few short sentences, explain how you would proceed.

2. What are liveness and readiness probes in the context of a Kubernetes application service?

3. Describe in your own words what components you need to establish layer 7 (or application-level) routing for your application.

4. List the main steps needed to implement a blue-green deployment for a simple application service. Avoid going into too much detail.

5. Name three or four types of information that you would provide to an application service through Kubernetes secrets.

6. Name the sources that Kubernetes accepts when creating a secret.

7. How do you configure an application service to use Kubernetes secrets?

Answers

Here are the answers to this chapter's questions:

1. Assuming we have a Docker image in a registry for the two application services – the web API and MongoDB – we need to do the following:

   I.   Define a deployment for MongoDB using a `StatefulSet` object; let's call this deployment `db-deployment`. The `StatefulSet` object should have one replica (replicating MongoDB is a bit more involved and is outside the scope of this book).

   II. Define a Kubernetes service called `db` of the `ClusterIP` type for `db-deployment`.

   III. Define a deployment for the web API; let's call it `web-deployment`.

   IV. Let's scale this service to three instances.

   V.   Define a Kubernetes service called `api` of the `NodePort` type for `web-deployment`.

   VI. If we are using secrets, then define those secrets directly in the cluster using `kubectl`.

   VII. Deploy the application using `kubectl`.

2.   Liveness and readiness probes are health checks provided by Kubernetes for containers. A liveness probe checks whether a container is still running, and if not, Kubernetes automatically restarts it. A readiness probe checks whether a container is ready to serve requests. If a container fails the readiness check, it is not removed, but it does not receive incoming requests until it passes the readiness probe.

3.   To implement layer 7 routing for an application, we ideally use `IngressController`. This is a reverse proxy such as Nginx that has a sidecar listening on the Kubernetes Server API for relevant changes and updating the reverse proxy's configuration and restarting it if such a change has been detected. Then, we need to define ingress resources in the cluster that define the routing, for example, from a context-based route such as `https://example.com/pets` to `<a service name>/<port>` or a pair such as `api/32001`. The moment Kubernetes creates or changes this `Ingress` object, the sidecar of `IngressController` picks it up and updates the proxy's routing configuration.

4.   Assuming this is a cluster internal inventory service, then we do the following:

   I.   When deploying version 1.0, we define a deployment called `inventory-deployment-blue` and label the pods with a label of `color:blue`.

   II.   We deploy the Kubernetes service of the `ClusterIP` type called `inventory` for the preceding deployment with the selector containing `color:blue`.

   III. When we're ready to deploy the new version of the `payments` service, we define a deployment for version 2.0 of the service and call it `inventory-deployment-green`. We add a label of `color:green` to the pods.

   IV.   We can now smoke-test the "green" service and when everything is OK, we can update the inventory service so that the selector contains `color:green`.

5.   Some forms of information that are confidential and thus should be provided to services through Kubernetes secrets include passwords, certificates, API key IDs, API key secrets, and tokens.

6.   Sources for secret values can be files or base64-encoded values.

7.   To configure an application to use a Kubernetes secret, you must create a `Secret` object with the sensitive data. Then, you must modify your `Pod` specification so that it includes a reference to the `Secret` object. This reference can be made as an environment variable in the container specification or as a volume mount, allowing the secret data to be used by your application.

18

Running a Containerized Application in the Cloud

In the previous chapter, we learned how to deploy, update, and scale applications into a Kubernetes cluster. We discovered how zero-downtime deployments are achieved to enable disruption-free updates and rollbacks of mission-critical applications. Finally, we were introduced to Kubernetes secrets as a means to configure services and protect sensitive data.

In this chapter, we will give an overview of the three most popular ways of running containerized applications in the cloud. We will explore each of the hosted solutions and discuss their pros and cons.

Here are the topics we will be discussing in this chapter:

- Why choose a hosted Kubernetes service?
- Running a simple containerized application on **Amazon Elastic Kubernetes Service (Amazon EKS)**
- Exploring Microsoft's **Azure Kubernetes Service (AKS)**
- Understanding **Google Kubernetes Engine (GKE)**

After reading this chapter, you will be able to do the following:

- Reason about the pros and potential cons of a hosted Kubernetes service compared to a self-managed Kubernetes cluster
- Deploy and run a simple distributed application in Amazon EKS
- Deploy and run a simple distributed application on Microsoft's AKS
- Deploy and run a simple distributed application on GKE

Technical requirements

We are going to use **Amazon Web Services** (**AWS**), Microsoft Azure, and Google Cloud in this chapter; therefore, it is necessary to have an account for each platform. If you do not have an existing account, you can ask for a trial account for all of these cloud providers.

We'll also use the files in the `~/The-Ultimate-Docker-Container-Book/sample-solutions/ch18` folder of our lab's repository from GitHub at `https://github.com/PacktPublishing/The-Ultimate-Docker-Container-Book/tree/main/sample-solutions/ch18`.

Prepare the folder where you will put your own code. For this, first, navigate to the source folder, as follows:

```
$ cd ~/The-Ultimate-Docker-Container-Book
```

Then, create a `ch18` subfolder and navigate to it, like so:

```
$ mkdir ch18 & cd ch18
```

Why choose a hosted Kubernetes service?

Currently, the three most popular cloud providers, AWS, Microsoft Azure, and Google Cloud each have a managed Kubernetes offering, as outlined here:

- **Amazon EKS**: Amazon EKS is a managed service that makes it easy for you to run Kubernetes on AWS without needing to install, operate, and maintain your own Kubernetes control plane or nodes.

- **AKS**: AKS is Microsoft's managed Kubernetes offering. It offers developer productivity with **continuous integration and continuous deployment** (**CI/CD**) capabilities and Kubernetes tools integration. It also has an Azure DevOps project for a complete container CI/CD platform.

- **GKE**: Google was the original creator of Kubernetes, and GKE was the first managed Kubernetes service available on the market. It offers advanced cluster management features, as well as integration with Google Cloud services.

Other providers also offer **Kubernetes as a service** (**KaaS**), such as IBM Cloud Kubernetes Service, Oracle Container Engine for Kubernetes, and **DigitalOcean Kubernetes** (**DOKS**). It's always a good idea to check the latest offerings and their features since the cloud market evolves rapidly.

Managing a Kubernetes cluster, either on-premises or in the cloud, involves considerable operational complexity and requires expertise. Here are a few reasons why using a hosted Kubernetes service is often the preferred solution:

- **Ease of setup and management**: Hosted Kubernetes services handle the underlying infrastructure, reducing the operational burden of managing a Kubernetes cluster. They automatically take care of the provisioning, upgrades, patching, and scaling of the Kubernetes control plane.

- **High availability (HA) and high scalability**: Hosted services often offer out-of-the-box HA and high scalability for your applications. They handle the orchestration necessary to distribute applications across different nodes and data centers.

- **Security and compliance**: Hosted services often include built-in security features such as network policies, **role-based access control** (**RBAC**), and integration with cloud provider **Identity & Access Management** (**IAM**) services. They also handle security updates to the Kubernetes software itself.

- **Monitoring and diagnostics**: Hosted Kubernetes services typically include integration with monitoring and logging services, making it easier to observe and troubleshoot your applications.

- **Cost**: While there is a cost associated with using a managed service, it can often be less than the cost of the dedicated personnel and infrastructure required to operate a Kubernetes cluster efficiently and securely.

- **Support**: When using a hosted Kubernetes service, you'll have access to support from the cloud provider. This can be particularly valuable if you're running production workloads and need fast resolution of any issues that arise.

In contrast, running your own Kubernetes clusters involves significant setup and maintenance work. You're responsible for everything, from the installation and configuration of Kubernetes to the ongoing tasks of cluster upgrades, security patching, node provisioning, and scaling, as well as setting up monitoring and alerting.

While managing your own clusters provides more control and flexibility, it requires a substantial investment in time, resources, and expertise. For many organizations, the benefits of a managed service far outweigh the increased control of self-managing their clusters.

Running a simple containerized application on Amazon EKS

In this section, we want to create a fully managed Kubernetes cluster on Amazon EKS using Fargate. The process of creating a new cluster is well described in the AWS documentation, and we will refer to the respective pages to not duplicate too much information. That said, let us start with the following steps.

> **What is Fargate?**
>
> AWS Fargate is a serverless compute engine for containers provided by AWS. It removes the need to manage the underlying servers and allows you to focus on designing and building your applications. Fargate handles the deployment, scaling, and management of containers, enabling you to launch applications without worrying about the infrastructure.

Let us first get a few prerequisites out of the way, as follows:

1. Make sure you have access to an AWS account. If not, you can get a free 1-year trial account here: `https://aws.amazon.com/free`.

2. Log in to your AWS account.

3. Create a new *access key* and *access key secret* pair for your account, which you will use to configure your AWS CLI so that you can access your account from the command line.

4. Locate your profile at the top right of the screen, and from the dropdown, select **Security credentials**.

    Select **Access keys** (access key ID and secret access key) and then click **Create access key**:

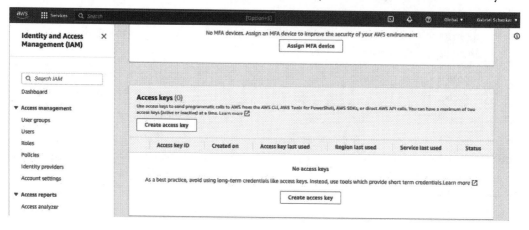

Figure 18.1 – Note down the access key ID and secret pair in a safe place

5. Open a new terminal.

6. Make sure you have the AWS CLI installed.

    On a Mac, use the following command:

    ```
    $ brew install awscli
    ```

    On Windows, use this command:

    ```
    $ choco install awscli
    ```

7. In both cases, test the installation with the following command:

    ```
    $ aws --version
    ```

8. Configure your AWS CLI. For this, you need your *AWS access key ID* and *AWS secret access key* that you created in preceding *step 3*, as well as your default *region*.

    Then, use the following command:

    ```
    $ aws configure
    ```

    Enter the appropriate values when asked. For the default output format, select JSON, as shown here:

    ```
    aws configure
    AWS Access Key ID [None]: AKIA5LXL546QSNJJMN2R
    AWS Secret Access Key [None]:
    Default region name [None]: eu-central-1
    Default output format [None]: JSON
    ```

    Figure 18.2 – Configuring the AWS CLI

9. Try accessing your account with a command such as the following:

    ```
    $ aws s3 ls
    ```

    This should list all the **Simple Storage Service** (**S3**) buckets defined for your account. Your list may be empty. The important thing here is that the command succeeds.

10. Finally, double-check that you have kubectl installed by running the following command:

    ```
    $ kubectl version
    ```

Now, we are ready to create the Amazon EKS cluster. Follow these steps:

1. Define a few environment variables for later use, as follows:

    ```
    $ export AWS_REGION=eu-central-1
    $ export AWS_STACK_NAME=animals-stack
    $ export AWS_CLUSTER_ROLE=animals-cluster-role
    ```

    Make sure to replace eu-central-1 with the AWS region closest to you.

2. You can now create the necessary AWS stack consisting of VPC, private and public subnets, and a security group, using the following command, which—to simplify things—uses a sample YAML file from AWS:

    ```
    $ aws cloudformation create-stack --region $AWS_REGION \
        --stack-name $AWS_STACK_NAME \
    ```

```
    --template-url https://s3.us-west-2.amazonaws.com/amazon-
eks/cloudformation/2020-10-29/amazon-eks-vpc-private-subnets.
yaml
```

Please take a moment to download and inspect the preceding YAML file to understand what exactly the command is provisioning.

3. In the next few steps, you need to define the right settings to grant the necessary access rights to the cluster:

    I.   Start by creating an IAM role with this command:

```
$ aws iam create-role \
    --role-name $AWS_CLUSTER_ROLE \
    --assume-role-policy-document file://"eks-cluster-
role-trust-policy.json"
```

    II.   Proceed by attaching the necessary Amazon EKS-managed IAM policy to the role just created with this command:

```
$ aws iam attach-role-policy \
    --policy-arn arn:aws:iam::aws:policy/
AmazonEKSClusterPolicy \
    --role-name $AWS_CLUSTER_ROLE
```

4. Now, we continue with some interactive steps using the Amazon EKS console at `https://console.aws.amazon.com/eks/home#/clusters`.

> **Note**
>
> Make sure that the AWS Region shown in the upper right of your console is the AWS Region in which you want to create your cluster in (for example, **Frankfurt** (`eu-central-1`) in the author's case). If it's not, select the dropdown next to the AWS Region name and choose the AWS Region that you want to use.

5. To create your cluster, choose the **Add cluster** command and then choose **Create**. If you don't see this option, choose **Clusters** in the left navigation pane first.

6. On the **Configure cluster** page, do the following:

    I.   **Name**: Enter an appropriate name for your cluster; we propose `animals-cluster`.

    II.   **Cluster Service Role**: You should see the previously defined role here called `animals-cluster-role`. Please select it.

    III. All the other settings can be left as their default values.

    IV.   Choose **Next**.

7. On the **Specify networking** page, do the following:

    I.   Choose the ID of the VPC that you created in *step 2* from the **VPC** drop-down list. It should be something like `vpc-00x0000x000x0x000` | `animals-stack-VPC`. Note the postfix of the name, indicating it is the one we defined just a moment ago.

    II.   Once again, you can leave the remaining settings at their default values.

    III.   Choose **Next** to continue.

8. We do not need to change anything on the **Configure logging** page, so choose **Next**.

9. The same applies for the **Select add-ons** page; thus, choose **Next**.

10. And once again, on the **Configure selected add-ons** settings page, there is nothing to do, so choose **Next**.

11. Finally, on the **Review and create** page, choose **Create**.

12. To the right of the cluster's name, the cluster status is **Creating** for several minutes until the cluster provisioning process completes, as shown in the following screenshot. Don't continue to the next step until the status is **Active**:

Figure 18.3 – Creating an EKS cluster

13. Sadly, we are not done yet. We need to create a trust policy and attach it to our cluster. To do this, proceed as follows:

    I.   Start by creating a `pod-execution-role-trust-policy.json` file and add the following content to it:

```
{
  "Version": "2012-10-17",
  "Statement": [
    {
      "Effect": "Allow",
      "Condition": {
        "ArnLike": {
```

```
        "aws:SourceArn": "arn:aws:eks:<region-
code>:<account-no>:fargateprofile/animals-cluster/*"
      }
    },
    "Principal": {
      "Service": "eks-fargate-pods.amazonaws.com"
    },
    "Action": "sts:AssumeRole"
  }
 ]
}
```

In the preceding code, replace <region-code> with the code for your AWS region (eu-central-1 in my case) and <account-no> with the number of your account. You can find the latter under your profile in the upper left of the AWS console.

II.   Using the trust policy just provisioned, create a **Pod execution IAM role** with this command:

```
$ aws iam create-role \
    --role-name AmazonEKSFargatePodExecutionRole \
    --assume-role-policy-document file://"pod-
execution-role-trust-policy.json"
```

III.   Finally, connect the required role and policy with each other using this command:

```
$ aws iam attach-role-policy \
    --policy-arn arn:aws:iam::aws:policy/
AmazonEKSFargatePodExecutionRolePolicy \
    --role-name AmazonEKSFargatePodExecutionRole
```

14. On the **Clusters** page, choose the animals-cluster cluster.

15. On the animals-cluster page, do the following:

I.   Select the **Compute** tab.

II.   Under **Fargate Profiles**, choose **Add Fargate Profile**.

III.   On the **Configure Fargate Profile** page, do the following:

i.   For **Name**, enter a unique name for your Fargate profile, such as animals-profile.

ii.   For **Pod execution role**, choose the AmazonEKSFargatePodExecutionRole role that you created in a previous step.

iii.   Choose the **Subnets** dropdown and deselect any subnet with **Public** in its name. Only private subnets are supported for Pods that are running on Fargate.

iv.   Choose **Next**.

16. On the **Configure Pod** selection page, do the following:

    I.   For **Namespace**, enter `default`.

    II.   Then choose **Next**.

17. On the **Review and create page**, review the information for your Fargate profile and choose **Create**.

18. After a few minutes, the status in the **Fargate Profile configuration** section will change from **Creating** to **Active**. Don't continue to the next step until the status is **Active**.

19. If you plan to deploy all Pods to Fargate (none to Amazon EC2 nodes), do the following to create another Fargate profile and run the default name resolver (CoreDNS) on Fargate.

> **Note**
> If you don't do this, you won't have any nodes at this time.

20. On the **Fargate Profile** page, choose `animals-profile`.

21. Under **Fargate profiles**, choose **Add Fargate Profile**.

22. In the **Name** field, enter **CoreDNS**.

23. For **Pod execution role**, choose the `AmazonEKSFargatePodExecutionRole` role that you created in *step 13*.

24. Click the **Subnets** dropdown and make sure to deselect any subnet with `Public` in its name. Fargate only supports Pods on private subnets.

25. Choose **Next**.

26. In the **Namespace** field, enter `kube-system`.

27. Choose **Match labels**, and then choose **Add label**.

28. Enter `k8s-app` for **Key** and `kube-dns` for **Value**. This is necessary for the default name resolver (CoreDNS) to deploy to Fargate.

29. Choose **Next**.

30. On the **Review and create** page, review the information for your Fargate profile and choose **Create**.

31. Run the following command to remove the default `eks.amazonaws.com/compute-type : ec2` annotation from the CoreDNS Pods:

```
kubectl patch deployment coredns \
    -n kube-system \
    --type json \
    -p='[{"op": "remove", "path": "/spec/template/metadata/
annotations/eks.amazonaws.com~1compute-type"}]'
```

> **Note**
>
> The system creates and deploys two nodes based on the Fargate profile label you added. You won't see anything listed in **Node groups** because they aren't applicable to Fargate nodes, but you will see the new nodes listed in the **Compute** tab.

For a more detailed explanation, you can follow the step-by-step instructions at the following link to create your cluster:

`https://docs.aws.amazon.com/eks/latest/userguide/getting-started-console.html` (*Getting started with Amazon EKS – AWS Management Console and AWS CLI*)

When your cluster is ready, you can then continue with the following steps:

1. Configure `kubectl` to access your new cluster on AWS, as follows:

    ```
    $ aws eks update-kubeconfig --name animals-cluster
    ```

    The response should be similar to the following:

    ```
    Added new context arn:aws:eks:eu-central-...:cluster/animals-
    cluster to /Users/<user-name>/.kube/config
    ```

    Here, `<user-name>` corresponds to your username on the machine you're working on.

2. Double-check that `kubectl` is using the correct context—the one that was just created for the cluster on AWS and added to your `~/.kube/config` file:

    ```
    $ kubectl config current-context
    ```

    The answer should look similar to the following:

    ```
    arn:aws:eks:eu-central-...:cluster/animals-cluster
    ```

    In case another context is the active one, use the `kubectl config use-context` command in combination with the correct AWS context.

3. Use `kubectl` to list all the resources on your cluster, like so:

    ```
    $ kubectl get all
    ```

    The answer at this time should look like this:

    Figure 18.4 – Amazon EKS – kubectl get all

4. To see the nodes of your cluster, use the following command:

    ```
    $ kubectl get nodes
    ```

You should then see something like this:

```
kubectl get nodes
NAME                                                  STATUS   ROLES    AGE    VERSION
fargate-ip-192-168-198-47.eu-central-1.compute.internal   Ready    <none>   111s   v1.26.3-eks-f4dc2c0
fargate-ip-192-168-207-95.eu-central-1.compute.internal   Ready    <none>   111s   v1.26.3-eks-f4dc2c0
```

Figure 18.5 – List of nodes in the EKS cluster

5. Navigate to the ch18 folder of this chapter, create an aws-eks subfolder, and then navigate to it:

```
$ cd ~/The-Ultimate-Docker-Container-Book/ch18
$ mkdir aws-eks && cd aws-eks
```

6. In this subfolder, create a deploy-nginx.yaml file with the following content:

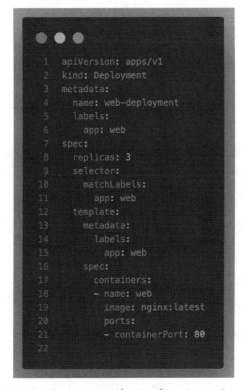

```
1   apiVersion: apps/v1
2   kind: Deployment
3   metadata:
4     name: web-deployment
5     labels:
6       app: web
7   spec:
8     replicas: 3
9     selector:
10      matchLabels:
11        app: web
12    template:
13      metadata:
14        labels:
15          app: web
16      spec:
17        containers:
18        - name: web
19          image: nginx:latest
20          ports:
21          - containerPort: 80
22
```

Figure 18.6 – Deployment specification for nginx on Amazon EKS

7. Use kubectl to deploy our deployment to the cluster, as follows:

```
$ kubectl apply -f deploy-nginx.yaml
```

8. Observe the creation of the Pods with the following command:

```
$ kubectl get pods -w
```

And wait until they are ready:

```
kubectl get pods -w
NAME                             READY   STATUS    RESTARTS   AGE
web-deployment-ddc9c846c-2vsrl   0/1     Pending   0          10s
web-deployment-ddc9c846c-4jwsl   0/1     Pending   0          10s
web-deployment-ddc9c846c-ld27m   0/1     Pending   0          10s
```

Figure 18.7 – Listing the Pods of the deployment to AWS

9. Wait until their value in the **READY** column is 1/1.

10. In the AWS console, navigate to your cluster.

11. In the **Resources** tab, observe that three web Pods and two coredns Pods were created.

12. In the **Compute** tab, observe that multiple Fargate nodes have been created.

13. Drill down to a node to see the Pod that has been deployed to it.

14. Drill further down to the Pod and observe the list of events shown in its **Details** view.

Congratulations—you have created a fully hosted Kubernetes cluster on AWS and created a first Deployment on it using kubectl! As you will know, this is quite an achievement. It turns out that of all the discussed cloud providers, AWS requires by far the most steps to get a Kubernetes cluster up and running.

Before you leave, and to avoid unexpected costs, make sure you clean up all the resources that you have created during this exercise. For this, follow the next steps:

1. Use kubectl to delete the previous deployment:

```
$ kubectl delete -f deploy-nginx.yaml
```

2. Locate your animals-cluster cluster and select it.

3. In the **Compute** tab, scroll down to the **Fargate profiles** section. Select the animals-profile and CoreDNS profiles and delete them.

4. When both profiles are deleted—which may take a few minutes—then click the **Delete cluster** button to get rid of the cluster.

5. Delete the VPC AWS CloudFormation stack that you created.

6. Open the **AWS CloudFormation** console at https://console.aws.amazon.com/cloudformation.

7. Choose the animals-stack stack, and then choose **Delete**.

8. In the **Delete animals-stack** confirmation dialog box, choose **Delete stack**.

9. Delete the IAM roles that you created.

10. Open the IAM console at `https://console.aws.amazon.com/iam/`.

11. In the left navigation pane, choose **Roles**.

12. Select each role you created from the list (`myAmazonEKSClusterRole`, as well as `AmazonEKSFargatePodExecutionRole` or `myAmazonEKSNodeRole`). Choose **Delete**, enter the requested confirmation text, then choose **Delete**.

Alternatively, follow the steps in the *Step 5: Delete resources* section in the AWS documentation:

`https://docs.aws.amazon.com/eks/latest/userguide/getting-started-console.html`

This was quite an achievement! Creating and managing an EKS cluster requires more intimate knowledge of details than we would want. We will see that other providers are more user-friendly in that regard.

Now that we have a rough understanding of what Amazon EKS offers, let us have a look at what the second-biggest cloud provider has in its portfolio.

Exploring Microsoft's AKS

To experiment with Microsoft's container-related offerings in Azure, we need an account on Azure. You can create a trial account or use an existing account. You can get a free trial account here: `https://azure.microsoft.com/en-us/free/`.

Microsoft offers different container-related services on Azure. The easiest one to use is probably Azure Container Instances, which promises the fastest and simplest way to run a container in Azure, without having to provision any **virtual machines** (**VMs**) and without having to adopt a higher-level service. This service is only really useful if you want to run a single container in a hosted environment. The setup is quite easy. In the Azure portal (`https://portal.azure.com`), you first create a new resource group and then create an Azure container instance. You only need to fill out a short form with properties such as the name of the container, the image to use, and the port to open. The container can be made available on a public or private IP address and will be automatically restarted if it crashes. There is a decent management console available, for example, to monitor resource consumption such as CPU and memory.

The second choice is **Azure Container Service** (**ACS**), which provides a way to simplify the creation, configuration, and management of a cluster of VMs that is preconfigured to run containerized applications. ACS uses Docker images and provides a choice between three orchestrators: Kubernetes, Docker Swarm, and the **Distributed Cloud Operating System** (**DC/OS**) (powered by Apache Mesos). Microsoft claims that its service can be scaled to tens of thousands of containers. ACS is free, and you are only charged for computing resources.

In this section, we will concentrate on the most popular offering, based on Kubernetes. It is called AKS and can be found here: `https://azure.microsoft.com/en-us/services/kubernetes-service/`. AKS makes it easy for you to deploy applications in the cloud and run them on Kubernetes. All the difficult and tedious management tasks are handled by Microsoft, and you can concentrate fully on your applications. What that means is that you will never have to deal with tasks such as installing and managing Kubernetes, upgrading Kubernetes, or upgrading the operating system of the underlying Kubernetes nodes. All this is handled by the experts at Microsoft Azure. Furthermore, you will never have to deal with `etc` or Kubernetes master nodes. This is all hidden from you, and the only things you will interact with are the Kubernetes worker nodes that run your applications.

Preparing the Azure CLI

That said, let's start. We assume that you have created a free trial account or that you are using an existing account on Azure. There are various ways to interact with your Azure account. We will use the Azure CLI running on our local computer. We can either download and install the Azure CLI natively on our computer or run it from within a container running on our local version of Docker Desktop. Since this book is all about containers, let's select the latter approach.

The latest version of the Azure CLI can be found on Docker Hub. Let's pull it:

```
$ docker image pull mcr.microsoft.com/azure-cli:latest
```

We will run a container from this CLI and executing all subsequent commands from within the shell running inside this container. Now, there is a little problem we need to overcome—this container will not have a Docker client installed. But we will also run some Docker commands, so we must create a custom image derived from the preceding image, which contains a Docker client. The Dockerfile that's needed to do so can be found in the `sample-solutions/ch18` subfolder and has this content:

```
FROM mcr.microsoft.com/azure-cli:latest
RUN apk update && apk add docker
```

On *line 2*, we are just using the Alpine package manager, `apk`, to install Docker. We can then use Docker Compose to build and run this custom image. The corresponding `docker-compose.yml` file looks like this:

```
version: "2.4"
services:
  az:
    image: fundamentalsofdocker/azure-cli
    build: .
    command: tail -F anything
    working_dir: /app
```

```
volumes:
  - /var/run/docker.sock:/var/run/docker.sock
  - .:/app
```

> **Note**
>
> The `tail -F anything` command is used to keep the container running, as well as for the mounting of the Docker socket and the current folder in the `volumes` section.

> **Tip**
>
> If you are running Docker Desktop on Windows, then you need to define the `COMPOSE_CONVERT_WINDOWS_PATHS` environment variable to be able to mount the Docker socket. Use `export COMPOSE_CONVERT_WINDOWS_PATHS=1` from a Bash shell or `$Env:COMPOSE_CONVERT_WINDOWS_PATHS=1` when running PowerShell. Please refer to the following link for more details: `https://github.com/docker/compose/issues/4240`.

Now, let's build and run this container, as follows:

```
$ docker compose up --build -d
```

Then, let's execute into the `az` container and run a Bash shell in it with the following command:

```
$ docker compose exec az /bin/bash
```

You should get an output like this:

```
376f1e715919:/app #
```

Note that your hash code (`376f1e...`) representing the hostname inside the container will be different. To simplify the reading, we will omit this hash code in subsequent commands.

As you may have noted, we find ourselves running in a Bash shell inside the container. Let's first check the version of the CLI:

```
# az --version
```

This should result in an output like this:

```
azure-cli                          2.49.0

core                               2.49.0
telemetry                           1.0.8

Dependencies:
```

```
msal                                 1.20.0
azure-mgmt-resource                  22.0.0

Python location '/usr/local/bin/python'
Extensions directory '/root/.azure/cliextensions'

Python (Linux) 3.10.11 (main, May 11 2023, 23:59:31) [GCC 12.2.1
20220924]

Legal docs and information: aka.ms/AzureCliLegal

Your CLI is up-to-date.
```

OK—we're running on version 2.49.0. Next, we need to log in to our account. Execute this command:

```
# az login
```

You will be presented with the following message:

```
To sign in, use a web browser to open the page https://microsoft.com/
devicelogin and enter the code <code> to authenticate.
```

Follow the instructions and log in through the browser. Once you have successfully authenticated your Azure account, you can go back to your terminal and you should be logged in, as indicated by the output you'll get:

```
[
  {
    "cloudName": "AzureCloud",
    "id": "<id>",
    "isDefault": true,
    "name": "<account name>",
    "state": "Enabled",
    "tenantId": "<tenant-it>",
    "user": {
      "name": <your-email>,
      "type": "user"
    }
  }
]
```

Now, we are ready to first move our container images to Azure.

Creating a container registry on Azure

First, we create a new resource group named `animal-rg`. In Azure, resource groups are used to logically group a collection of associated resources. To have an optimal cloud experience and keep latency low, it is important that you select a data center located in a region near you. Follow these steps:

1. You can use the following command to list all regions:

    ```
    # az account list-locations
    ```

    The output should look like this:

    ```
    [
      {
        "displayName": "East Asia",
        "id": "/subscriptions/186760.../locations/eastasia",
        "latitude": "22.267",
        "longitude": "114.188",
        "name": "eastasia",
        "subscriptionId": null
      },
      ...
    ]
    ```

    This will give you a rather long list of all possible regions you can select from. Use the name— for example, `eastasia`—to identify the region of your choice. In my case, I will select `westeurope`. Please note that not all locations listed are valid for resource groups.

2. The command to create a resource group is simple; we just need a name for the group and the location, as demonstrated here:

    ```
    # az group create --name animals-rg --location westeurope
    {
      "id": "/subscriptions/186.../resourceGroups/animals-rg",
      "location": "westeurope",
      "managedBy": null,
      "name": "animals-rg",
      "properties": {
        "provisioningState": "Succeeded"
      },
      "tags": null,
      "type": "Microsoft.Resources/resourceGroups"
    }
    ```

    Make sure that your output shows `"provisioningState": "Succeeded"`.

> **Note**
>
> When running a containerized application in production, we want to make sure that we can freely download the corresponding container images from a container registry. So far, we have always downloaded our images from Docker Hub, but this is often not possible. For security reasons, the servers of a production system often have no direct access to the internet and thus are not able to reach out to Docker Hub. Let's follow this best practice and assume the same for our Kubernetes cluster that we are going to create in an instant.

So, what can we do? Well, the solution is to use a container image registry that is close to our cluster and that is in the same security context. In Azure, we can create an **Azure Container Registry (ACR)** instance and host our images there, so here's what we'll do:

1. Let's first create such a registry, as follows:

    ```
    # az acr create --resource-group animals-rg \
        --name <acr-name> --sku Basic
    ```

    Note that <acr-name> needs to be unique. In my case, I have chosen the name gnsanimalsacr. The (shortened) output looks like this:

    ```
    Registration succeeded.
    {
      "adminUserEnabled": false,
      "creationDate": "2023-06-04T10:31:14.848776+00:00",
    ...
      "id": "/subscriptions/186760ad...",
      "location": "westeurope",
      "loginServer": "gnsanimalsacr.azurecr.io",
      "name": " gnsanimalsacr ",
    ...
      "provisioningState": "Succeeded",
    ```

2. After successfully creating the container registry, we need to log in to that registry using the following command:

    ```
    # az acr login --name <acr-name>
    ```

    The response to the preceding command should be this:

    ```
    Login Succeeded
    ```

Once we are successfully logged in to the container registry on Azure, we need to tag our containers correctly so that we can then push them to ACR. Tagging and pushing images to ACR will be described next.

Pushing our images to ACR

Once we have successfully logged in to ACR, we can tag our images such that they can be pushed to the registry. For this, we need to know the URL of our ACR instance. It is as follows:

```
<acr-name>.azurecr.io
```

We now use the preceding URL to tag our images:

```
# docker image tag fundamentalsofdocker/ch11-db:2.0 \
    <acr-name>.azurecr.io/db:2.0
# docker image tag fundamentalsofdocker/ch11-web:2.0 \
    <acr-name>.azurecr.io/web:2.0
```

Then, we can push them to our ACR instance:

```
# docker image push <acr-name>.azurecr.io/db:2.0
# docker image push <acr-name>.azurecr.io/web:2.0
```

To double-check that our images are indeed in our ACR instance, we can use this command:

```
# az acr repository list --name <acr-name> --output table
```

This should give you the following output:

```
Result
--------
Db
web
```

Indeed, the two images we just pushed are listed.

With that, we are ready to create our Kubernetes cluster.

Creating a Kubernetes cluster

Once again, we will be using our custom Azure CLI inside the Docker container to create a Kubernetes cluster. We will have to make sure that the cluster can access the ACR instance that we just created; this is where our container images reside. So, the command to create a cluster named animals-cluster with two worker nodes looks like this:

```
# az aks create \
    --resource-group animals-rg \
    --name animals-cluster \
    --node-count 2 \
    --generate-ssh-keys \
    --attach-acr <acr-name>
```

This command takes a while, but after a few minutes, we should receive some JSON-formatted output with all the details about the newly created cluster.

To access the cluster, we need kubectl. We can easily get it installed in our Azure CLI container using this command:

```
# az aks install-cli
```

Having installed kubectl, we need the necessary credentials to use the tool to operate on our new Kubernetes cluster in Azure. We can get the necessary credentials with this:

```
# az aks get-credentials --resource-group animals-rg \
    --name animals-cluster
```

The command should respond with the following:

```
Merged "animals-cluster" as current context in /root/.kube/config
```

After the success of the preceding command, we can list all the nodes in our cluster, like so:

```
# kubectl get nodes
```

This provides us with the following list:

```
NAME STATUS ROLES AGE VERSION
aks-nodepool1-12528297-vmss000000 Ready agent 4m38s v1.25.68
aks-nodepool1-12528297-vmss000001 Ready agent 4m32s v1.25.68
```

As expected, we have two worker nodes up and running. The version of Kubernetes that is running on those nodes is v1.25.68.

We are now ready to deploy our application to this cluster. In the next section, we are going to learn how we can deploy our application to Kubernetes.

Deploying our application to the Kubernetes cluster

To deploy the application, we can use the kubectl apply command:

```
# kubectl apply -f animals.yaml
```

The output of the preceding command should look similar to this:

```
deployment.apps/web created
service/web created
deployment.apps/db created
service/db created
```

Now, we want to test the application. Remember that we created a service of type `LoadBalancer` for the web component. This service exposes the application to the internet.

This process can take a moment as AKS, among other tasks, needs to assign a public IP address to this service. We can observe this with the following command:

```
# kubectl get service web --watch
```

Please note the `--watch` parameter in the preceding command. It allows us to monitor the progress of the command over time. Initially, we should see output like this:

NAME	TYPE	CLUSTER-IP	EXTERNAL-IP	PORT(S)	AGE
web	LoadBalancer	10.0.38.189	\<pending\>	3000:32127/TCP	5s

The public IP address is marked as `pending`. After a few minutes, that should change to this:

```
1d7d8116dd2f:/app# kubectl get service web --watch
NAME     TYPE           CLUSTER-IP     EXTERNAL-IP    PORT(S)          AGE
web      LoadBalancer   10.0.38.189    20.76.160.79   3000:32127/TCP   35s
```

Figure 18.8 – The LoadBalancer service for the animals application on Microsoft's AKS

Our application is now ready at the IP address 20.76.160.79 and port number 3000.

Note that the load balancer maps the internal port 32127 to the external port 3000; this was not evident to me the first time.

Let's check it out. In a new browser tab, navigate to http://20.76.160.79:3000/pet and you should see our familiar application:

Figure 18.9 – Our sample application running on AKS

With that, we have successfully deployed our distributed application to Kubernetes hosted in Azure. We did not have to worry about installing or managing Kubernetes; we could concentrate on the application itself.

Note that you can also manage your Azure resource group, your container registry, and your cluster via the Azure portal at `https://portal.azure.com/`. It will look similar to this:

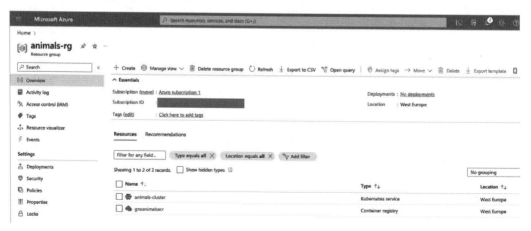

Figure 18.10 – Microsoft Azure portal showing the animals resource group

Please make yourself familiar with the portal and try to drill down into the cluster, its nodes, and deployments.

Now that we are done experimenting with the application, we should not forget to delete all resources on Azure to avoid incurring unnecessary costs. We can delete all resources created by deleting the resource group as follows:

```
# az group delete --name animal-rg --yes --no-wait
```

Azure has a few compelling offerings regarding the container workload, and the lock-in is not as evident as it is on AWS since Azure does mainly offer open source orchestration engines, such as Kubernetes, Docker Swarm, DC/OS, and Rancher.

Technically, we remain mobile if we initially run our containerized applications in Azure and later decide to move to another cloud provider. The cost should be limited.

> **Note**
>
> It is worth noting that when you delete your resource group, the **Azure Active Directory** (**AAD**) service principal used by the AKS cluster is not removed.

Refer to the online help page for details on how to delete the service principal. You can find this information here: `https://learn.microsoft.com/en-us/powershell/module/azuread/remove-azureadserviceprincipal?view=azureadps-2.0`.

Next on the list is Google with its GKE service.

Understanding GKE

Google is the inventor of Kubernetes and, to this date, the driving force behind it. You would therefore expect that Google has a compelling offering around hosted Kubernetes.

Let's have a peek into it now. To continue, you need to either have an existing account with Google Cloud or create a test account here: `https://console.cloud.google.com/freetrial`. Proceed with the following steps:

1. In the main menu, select **Kubernetes Engine**. The first time you do that, it will take a few moments until the Kubernetes engine is initialized.

2. Next, create a new project and name it `massai-mara`; this may take a moment.

3. Once this is ready, we can create a cluster by clicking on **Create Cluster** in the popup.

4. On the **Cluster basics** tab, enter the cluster name as `animals-cluster` and select the region closest to you. In the author's case, this is `europe-west1`. Then click **NEXT: NETWORKING**.

5. Leave all settings at their default values and click **NEXT: ADVANCED SETTINGS**.

6. Once again, leave all settings at their default values and click **NEXT: REVIEW AND CREATE**.

7. Review your cluster settings and if everything looks OK, then click on **CREATE CLUSTER**, as illustrated in the following screenshot:

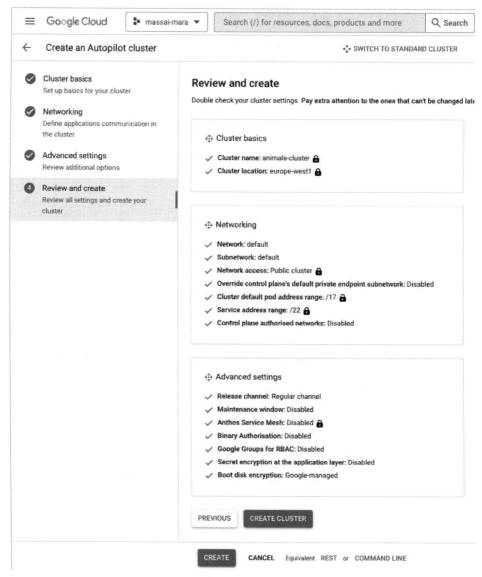

Figure 18.11 – The Review and create view of the GKE cluster creation wizard

It will again take a few moments to provision the cluster for us.

8. Once the cluster has been created, we can open Cloud Shell by clicking on the shell icon in the upper-right corner of the view. This is how it should look:

Figure 18.12 – The first Kubernetes cluster ready and Cloud Shell open in GKE

9. We can now clone our lab's GitHub repository to this environment with the following command:

```
$ git clone https://github.com/PacktPublishing/The-Ultimate-
Docker-Container-Book.git ~/src
```

10. Switch to the correct folder where you'll find the sample solution:

```
$ cd ~/src/sample-solutions/ch18/gce
```

You should now find an `animals.yaml` file in the current folder, which you can use to deploy the `animals` application into our Kubernetes cluster.

11. Have a look at the file by running the following command:

```
$ less animals.yaml
```

It has pretty much the same content as the same file we used in the previous chapter. The two differences are these:

- We use a service of type `LoadBalancer` (instead of `NodePort`) to publicly expose the web component. Note we did the same on Azure AKS.

- We do not use volumes for the PostgreSQL database since configuring `StatefulSet` correctly on GKE is a bit more involved than in a product such as Minikube or Docker Desktop. The consequence of this is that our `animals` application will not persist the state if the db Pod crashes. How to use persistent volumes on GKE lies outside the scope of this book.

Also, note that we are not using **Google Container Registry** (**GCR**) to host the container images but are instead directly pulling them from Docker Hub. It is very easy—and similar to what we learned in the section about AKS—to create such a container registry in Google Cloud.

12. Before we can continue, we need to set up `gcloud` and `kubectl` credentials. Here's the code we need to execute:

```
$ gcloud container clusters \
    get-credentials animals-cluster --zone <zone>
```

Please replace `<zone>` with the same zone you selected in *step 5* when you created the cluster.

The response of the preceding command should be this:

```
Fetching cluster endpoint and auth data.
kubeconfig entry generated for animals-cluster.
```

13. Let's have a look at which nodes for the cluster were created by running the following command:

```
$ kubectl get nodes
```

You should see something like this:

```
gnschenker@cloudshell:~/src/sample-solutions/ch17/gce (massai-mara-388809)$ kubectl get nodes
NAME                                             STATUS   ROLES    AGE     VERSION
gk3-animals-cluster-default-pool-7ce2cf80-qtfq   Ready    <none>   5m23s   v1.25.8-gke.500
gk3-animals-cluster-default-pool-b0a15d01-b2sw   Ready    <none>   5m23s   v1.25.8-gke.500
gnschenker@cloudshell:~/src/sample-solutions/ch17/gce (massai-mara-388809)$ 
```

Figure 18.13 – Cluster nodes on GCE

We can see that two nodes were created in our cluster, and the version of Kubernetes deployed is apparently `v1.25.8`.

14. Having done that, it's time to deploy the application, so run the following command:

```
$ kubectl apply -f animals.yaml
```

The output should look like this:

```
gnschenker@cloudshell:~/src/sample-solutions/ch17/gce (massai-mara-388809)$ kubectl create -f animals.yaml
Warning: Autopilot set default resource requests for Deployment default/web, as resource requests were not s
pecified. See http://g.co/gke/autopilot-defaults
deployment.apps/web created
service/web created
Warning: Autopilot set default resource requests for Deployment default/db, as resource requests were not sp
ecified. See http://g.co/gke/autopilot-defaults
deployment.apps/db created
service/db created
```

Figure 18.14 – Deploying the application on GKE

15. Once the objects have been created, we can observe the `LoadBalancer` web service until it is assigned a public IP address, as follows:

```
$ kubectl get svc/web –watch
```

The preceding command yields this output:

```
NAME TYPE CLUSTER-IP EXTERNAL-IP PORT(S) AGE
web LoadBalancer 10.57.129.72 <pending> 3000: 32384/TCP 32s
web LoadBalancer 10. 57.129.72 35.195.160.243 3000: 32384/TCP
39s
```

The second line in the output is showing the situation while the creation of the load balancer is still pending, and the third one gives the final state. Press *Ctrl* + *C* to quit the –watch command. Apparently, we got the public IP address 35.195.160.243 assigned and the port is 3000.

16. We can then use this IP address and navigate to `http://<IP address>:3000/pet`, and we should be greeted by the familiar animal image.

17. Take a moment and use the various `kubectl` commands you know to analyze what's going on in the GKE cluster.

18. Also, take a moment to use the web portal of GCE and drill down into the details of your cluster. Specifically, have a look into the **OBSERVABILITY** tab of the cluster.

19. Once you are done playing with the application, delete the cluster and the project in the Google Cloud console to avoid any unnecessary costs.

20. You can use the `gcloud` CLI in the Cloud Shell to delete the cluster, as follows:

```
$ gcloud container clusters delete animals-cluster
```

This will take a moment. Alternatively, you can do the same from the web portal.

21. Next list all your projects, like so:

```
$ gcloud projects list
```

22. Next, you can use this command to delete the project you created earlier:

```
$ gcloud projects delete <project-id>
```

Here, you should get the correct <project-id> value from the previous list command.

We have created a hosted Kubernetes cluster in GKE. We then used Cloud Shell, provided through the GKE portal, to first clone our lab's GitHub repository and then the `kubectl` tool to deploy the `animals` application into the Kubernetes cluster.

When looking into a hosted Kubernetes solution, GKE is a compelling offering. It makes it very easy to start your projects, and since Google is the main driving force behind Kubernetes, we can rest assured that we will always be able to leverage the full functionality of Kubernetes.

Summary

In this chapter of the book, you first got an introduction to how to create a fully managed Kubernetes cluster on Amazon EKS using Fargate and how to deploy a simple application on this cluster. Then, you learned how to create a hosted Kubernetes cluster in Azure AKS and run the `animals` application on it, followed by doing the same for Google's own hosted Kubernetes offering, GKE.

Are you ready to unlock the secrets of keeping your production environment in peak health? In the next chapter, we will dive into the exciting realm of monitoring and troubleshooting an application running in production. We'll explore diverse techniques for instrumenting and overseeing both individual services and entire distributed applications operating on a Kubernetes cluster. But it doesn't stop there—you'll also learn about creating alerts based on crucial metrics. And when things go awry, we'll guide you on how to troubleshoot live applications without disrupting the cluster or its nodes. Stay tuned, because this final chapter promises to arm you with the tools you need to confidently maintain your applications at scale.

Questions

To assess your knowledge, please answer the following questions:

1. List a few reasons why you would select a hosted Kubernetes offering, such as Amazon EKS, Microsoft's AKS, or Google's GKE, to run your applications on Kubernetes.

2. Name two reasons when using a hosted Kubernetes solution, such as Amazon EKS, Azure AKS, or Google GKE, to consider hosting your container images in the container registry of the respective cloud provider.

Answers

Here are some sample answers to the chapter questions:

1. Here are a few reasons to consider a hosted Kubernetes offering:

    *   You do not want to or do not have the resources to install and manage a Kubernetes cluster

    *   You want to concentrate on what brings value to your business, which in most cases is the applications that are supposed to run on Kubernetes and not Kubernetes itself

    *   You prefer a cost model where you pay only for what you need

    *   The nodes of your Kubernetes cluster are automatically patched and updated

    *   Upgrading the version of Kubernetes with zero downtime is easy and straightforward

2.   The two main reasons to host container images on the cloud provider's container registry (such as ACR on Microsoft Azure) are these:

- The images are geographically close to your Kubernetes cluster, and thus the latency and transfer network costs are minimal

- Production or production-like clusters are ideally sealed from the internet, and thus the Kubernetes cluster nodes cannot access Docker Hub directly

19

Monitoring and Troubleshooting an Application Running in Production

In the previous chapter, we got an overview of the three most popular ways of running containerized applications in the cloud – AWS EKS, Azure AKS, and Google GKE. We then explored each of the hosted solutions and discussed their pros and cons.

This chapter looks at different techniques used to instrument and monitor an individual service or a whole distributed application running on a Kubernetes cluster. You will be introduced to the concept of alerting based on key metrics. The chapter also shows how one can troubleshoot an application service that is running in production without altering the cluster or the cluster nodes on which the service is running.

Here is a list of topics we are going to discuss in this chapter:

- Monitoring an individual service

- Using OpenTracing for distributed tracing

- Leveraging Prometheus and Grafana to monitor a distributed application

- Defining alerts based on key metrics

- Troubleshooting a service running in production

After reading this chapter and following the exercises carefully, you will have acquired the following skills:

- Instrumenting your services with OpenTracing

- Configuring application-level monitoring for a service

- Using Prometheus to collect and centrally aggregate relevant application metrics

- Using Grafana to monitor the application

- Defining and wiring alerts triggered based on rules defined for key metrics

- Troubleshooting a service running in production using a special tools container

Without further ado, let's dive into the chapter.

Technical requirements

We are going to use Docker Desktop and its single-node Kubernetes cluster in this chapter. Make sure you have Docker Desktop installed and properly configured as described in *Chapter 2, Setting Up a Working Environment.*

We'll also use the files in the `~/The-Ultimate-Docker-Container-Book/sample-solutions/ch19` folder of our labs repository from GitHub, at `https://github.com/PacktPublishing/The-Ultimate-Docker-Container-Book/tree/main/sample-solutions/ch19`.

Monitoring an individual service

Effective monitoring of distributed, mission-critical applications is crucial, akin to the instrumentation in a nuclear power plant or airplane cockpit. Our application services and infrastructure need "sensors" that collect important data, functioning similarly to the sensors monitoring the temperature or flow rate in complex systems.

These "sensors" collect values – or metrics – to provide insight into our application's performance. Metrics can be both functional, which provide business-relevant data, and non-functional, which give insight into system performance irrespective of the application's business type.

Functional metrics might include the rate of checkouts per minute on an e-commerce platform or the five most streamed songs in the last 24 hours for a music streaming service. Non-functional metrics could show the average latency of a web request, the number of 4xx status codes returned, or resource usage such as RAM or CPU cycles.

In a distributed system, a centralized service is needed to aggregate these metrics. This is similar to how an airplane cockpit consolidates all necessary readings, eliminating the need for pilots to inspect each part of the plane during a flight.

Prometheus, an open source project donated to the **Cloud Native Computing Foundation (CNCF)**, is a popular service for metrics exposure, collection, and storage. It integrates well with Docker containers, Kubernetes, and many other systems. We will use Prometheus to demonstrate metric instrumentation for a service in this chapter.

Using OpenTracing for distributed tracing

OpenTracing is an open standard for distributed tracing that provides a vendor-neutral API and instrumentation for distributed systems. In OpenTracing, a trace tells the story of a transaction or workflow as it propagates through a distributed system. The concept of the trace borrows a tool from the scientific community called a **directed acyclic graph** (**DAG**), which stages the parts of a process from a clear start to a clear end.

Distributed tracing is a way to track a single request and log a single request as it crosses through all of the services in our infrastructure. It can help us understand how long each service takes to process the request and identify bottlenecks in our system. It can also help us identify which service is causing an issue when something goes wrong.

Using OpenTracing for distributed tracing can help us gain visibility into our distributed system and understand how requests are flowing through it. It can also help us identify performance issues and troubleshoot problems more quickly.

A Java example

Let's create the simplest possible Java example with a Spring Boot example that uses OpenTracing:

1. Start by navigating to your source code folder:

    ```
    $ cd ~/The-Ultimate-Docker-Container-Book
    ```

2. Then create a subfolder, ch19, and navigate to it:

    ```
    $ mkdir ch19 && cd ch19
    ```

3. Go to https://start.spring.io/ to create a SpringBoot application.

4. Use Gradle - Groovy as the project and Java as the language.

5. Leave all the other defaults.

6. Create the application and download the ZIP file.

7. Extract it into the ch19/java subfolder.

8. Modify your `build.gradle` file such that it looks like this one:

```gradle
plugins {
    id 'java'
    id 'org.springframework.boot' version '2.5.0'
    id 'io.spring.dependency-management' version '1.0.11.RELEASE'
}

group = 'com.example'
version = '0.0.1-SNAPSHOT'
sourceCompatibility = '17'

repositories {
    mavenCentral()
}

dependencies {
    implementation 'org.springframework.boot:spring-boot-starter-web'
    implementation 'io.opentracing.contrib:opentracing-spring-web-starter:0.4.1'
    implementation 'io.opentracing.contrib:opentracing-spring-jaeger-web-starter:3.1.0'
    implementation 'io.opentracing.contrib:opentracing-spring-jaeger-cloud-starter:3.1.0'
    implementation 'io.opentracing.contrib:opentracing-spring-web-autoconfigure:0.4.1'
    implementation 'io.jaegertracing:jaeger-client:1.7.0'
    testImplementation 'org.springframework.boot:spring-boot-starter-test'
}

tasks.named('test') {
    useJUnitPlatform()
}
```

Figure 19.1 – build.gradle file when using OpenTracing

9. Modify your `DemoApplication.java` file such that it looks like this:

```java
1   package com.example.demo;
2
3   import org.springframework.beans.factory.annotation.Autowired;
4   import org.springframework.boot.SpringApplication;
5   import org.springframework.boot.autoconfigure.SpringBootApplication;
6   import org.springframework.web.bind.annotation.GetMapping;
7   import org.springframework.web.bind.annotation.RestController;
8
9   import io.opentracing.Span;
10  import io.opentracing.Tracer;
11
12  @SpringBootApplication
13  @RestController
14  public class DemoApplication {
15
16      @Autowired
17      private Tracer tracer;
18
19      public static void main(String[] args) {
20          SpringApplication.run(DemoApplication.class, args);
21      }
22
23      @GetMapping("/")
24      public String hello() {
25          Span span = tracer.buildSpan("hello").start();
26          String message = "Hello, World!";
27          span.finish();
28          return message;
29      }
30  }
31
```

Figure 19.2 – DemoApplication.java file demoing OpenTracing

10. Run the application by clicking on the **Run** (or **Debug**) link decorating the main method of the DemoApplication class.

11. In a terminal window, use curl to hit the http://localhost:8080 endpoint. The response should be Hello, World!.

12. Observe the output in the Terminal window of VS Code. You should see something like this:

Figure 19.3 – OpenTracing used in a simple Java and Spring Boot application

This shows that a span has been created and reported.

Next, let's see how we can instrument a Node.js service.

Instrumenting a Node.js-based service

In this section, we will learn how to instrument a microservice authored in Node.js by following these steps:

1. Navigate to your source code folder:

    ```
    $ cd ~/The-Ultimate-Docker-Container-Book/ch19
    ```

2. Create a new folder called `node` and navigate to it:

    ```
    $ mkdir node && cd node
    ```

3. Run `npm init` in this folder, and accept all defaults except the entry point, which you change from the `index.js` default to `server.js`.

4. We need to add `express` to our project with the following:

    ```
    $ npm install --save express
    ```

> **Note**
>
> As of npm 5.0.0, you no longer need to use this option. Now, npm saves all installed packages as dependencies by default.

5. Now we need to install the Prometheus adapter for Node Express with the following:

    ```
    $ npm install --save prom-client
    ```

6. Add a file called `server.js` to the folder with this content:

    ```
    const app = require("express")();

    app.get('/hello', (req, res) => {
        const { name = 'World' } = req.query;
        res.json({ message: `Hello, ${name}!` });
    });

    app.listen(port=3000, () => {
        console.log('Example api is listening on http://
    localhost:3000');
    });
    ```

This is a very simple Node Express app with a single endpoint – `/hello`.

7. To the preceding code, after line 1, add the following snippet to initialize the Prometheus client:

```
const client = require("prom-client");
const register = client.register;
const collectDefaultMetrics =
    client.collectDefaultMetrics;
collectDefaultMetrics({ register });
```

8. Next, add an endpoint to expose the metrics. You can add it right after the definition of the `/hello` endpoint:

```
app.get('/metrics', (req, res) => {
    res.set('Content-Type', register.contentType);
    res.end(register.metrics());
});
```

9. Now let's run this sample microservice:

```
$ npm start
```

You should see an output similar to this:

```
> node@1.0.0 start
> node server.js
Example api is listening on http://localhost:3000
```

We can see in the preceding output that the service is listening on port 3000.

10. Let's now try to access the metrics at the `/metrics` endpoint, as we defined in the code. For this, open a new terminal window and use this command:

```
$ curl localhost:3000/metrics
```

You should see output similar to this:

```
# HELP process_cpu_user_seconds_total Total user CPU time spent
in seconds.
# TYPE process_cpu_user_seconds_total counter
process_cpu_user_seconds_total 0.081801
# HELP process_cpu_system_seconds_total Total system CPU time
spent in seconds.
# TYPE process_cpu_system_seconds_total counter
process_cpu_system_seconds_total 0.02082
# HELP process_cpu_seconds_total Total user and system CPU time
spent in seconds.
# TYPE process_cpu_seconds_total counter
process_cpu_seconds_total 0.102621
...
```

Note that the preceding output has been shortened for readability. What we get as output is a pretty long list of metrics, ready for consumption by a Prometheus server.

This was pretty easy, wasn't it? By adding a Node package and adding a few trivial lines of code to our application startup, we have gained access to a plethora of system metrics.

Now let's define our own custom metric. We will make it a `counter` object:

1. Add the following code snippet to `server.js` to define a custom counter called `my_hello_counter`:

```
const helloCounter = new client.Counter({
    name: 'my_hello_counter',
    help: 'Counts the number of hello requests',
});
```

2. To our existing `/hello` endpoint, add code to increase the counter. The modified endpoint should look like this:

```
app.get('/hello', (req, res) => {
    helloCounter.inc();
    const name = req.query.name || 'World';
    res.json({ message: `Hello, ${name}!` });
});
```

3. Rerun the application with `npm start`.

4. To test the new counter, let's access our `/hello` endpoint twice:

```
$ curl localhost:3000/hello?name=Sue
$ curl localhost:3000/hello?name=Marc
```

5. We will get this output when accessing the `/metrics` endpoint:

```
$ curl localhost:3000/metrics
```

Analyze the output generated by the preceding command and look for something like this toward the end of the output:

```
...
# HELP my_hello_counter Counts the number of hello requests
# TYPE my_hello_counter counter
my_hello_counter 2
...
```

The counter we defined in the code clearly works and is output with the HELP text we added.

Now that we know how to instrument a Node Express application, let's do the same for a .NET-based microservice.

Instrumenting a .NET service

Let's start by creating a simple .NET microservice based on the Web API template:

1. Navigate to your source code folder:

```
$ cd ~/The-Ultimate-Docker-Container-Book/ch19
```

2. Create a new `dotnet` folder, and navigate to it:

```
$ mkdir dotnet && cd dotnet
```

3. Use the `dotnet` tool to scaffold a new microservice called `sample-api`:

```
$ dotnet new webapi --output sample-api
```

4. We will use the Prometheus adapter for .NET, which is available to us as a NuGet package called `prometheus-net.AspNetCore`. Add this package to the `sample-api` project with the following command:

```
$ dotnet add sample-api package prometheus-net.AspNetCore
```

5. Open the project in your favorite code editor; for example, when using VS Code, execute the following:

```
$ code .
```

6. Locate the `Program.cs` file, and open it. At the beginning of the file, add a `using` statement:

```
using Prometheus;
```

7. Then, in the code of the file, right after the `app.MapControllers()` command, add the `app.MapMetrics()` command. Your code should look as follows:

```
...
app.UseAuthorization();
app.MapControllers();
app.MapMetrics();
app.Run();
```

Note that the preceding is valid for version 7.x of .NET or newer. If you're on an earlier version, the configuration might look slightly different. Consult the repo for more details, at `https://github.com/prometheus-net/prometheus-net`.

8. With this, the Prometheus component will start publishing the request metrics of ASP.NET. Let's try it. First, start the application with the following:

```
$ dotnet run --project sample-api
```

The output of the preceding command should look like this:

```
Building...
info: Microsoft.Hosting.Lifetime[14]
      Now listening on:
info: Microsoft.Hosting.Lifetime[0]
      Application started. Press Ctrl+C to shut down.
info: Microsoft.Hosting.Lifetime[0]
      Hosting environment: Development
info: Microsoft.Hosting.Lifetime[0]
      Content root path: /Users/.../ch19/dotnet/sample-api
...
```

The preceding output tells us that the microservice is listening at `http://localhost:5204`.

9. We can now use `curl` to call the metrics endpoint of the service:

```
$ curl http://localhost:5204/metrics
```

The (shortened) output of the preceding command looks similar to this:

```
# HELP process_private_memory_bytes Process private memory size
# TYPE process_private_memory_bytes gauge
process_private_memory_bytes 55619584
# HELP process_virtual_memory_bytes Virtual memory size in
bytes.
# TYPE process_virtual_memory_bytes gauge
process_virtual_memory_bytes 2221930053632
# HELP process_working_set_bytes Process working set
# TYPE process_working_set_bytes gauge
process_working_set_bytes 105537536
...
prometheus_net_metric_families{metric_type="histogram"} 0
prometheus_net_metric_families{metric_type="summary"} 0
prometheus_net_metric_families{metric_type="counter"} 3
prometheus_net_metric_families{metric_type="gauge"} 12
```

What we get is a list of system metrics for our microservice. That was easy: we only needed to add a NuGet package and a single line of code to get our service instrumented!

What if we want to add our own (functional) metrics? This is equally straightforward. Assume we want to measure the number of concurrent accesses to the `/weatherforecast` endpoint that .NET scaffolding created for us. To do this, we define a gauge and use it to wrap the logic in the appropriate endpoint with this gauge.

> **Metric types**
>
> Prometheus supports four types of metrics:
>
> - **Counter**: A cumulative metric that represents a single monotonically increasing counter whose value can only increase or be reset to zero on restart.
> - **Gauge**: A metric that represents a single numerical value that can arbitrarily go up and down. Gauges are typically used for measured values such as temperatures or current memory usage.
> - **Histogram**: A metric that samples observations (usually things such as request durations or response sizes) and counts them in configurable buckets. It also provides a sum of all observed values.
> - **Summary**: Similar to a histogram, a summary samples observations. While it also provides a total count of observations and a sum of all observed values, it calculates configurable quantiles over a sliding time window.

We can define our own gauge by following these steps:

1. Locate the `WeatherForecastController.cs` class in the `Controllers` folder.

2. Add `using Prometheus;` to the top of the file.

3. Define a private instance `callsInProgress` variable of the `Gauge` type in the `WeatherForecastController` class:

```
private static readonly Gauge callsInProgress = Metrics
    .CreateGauge("myapp_calls_in_progress",
    "Number of weather forecast operations ongoing.");
```

4. Wrap the logic of the `Get` method with a `using` statement:

```
[HttpGet]
public IEnumerable<WeatherForecast> Get()
{
    using(callsInProgress.TrackInProgress())
    {
        // code of the Get method
    }
}
```

5. Restart the microservice.

6. Call the `/weatherforecast` endpoint a couple of times using `curl`:

```
$ curl http://localhost:5204/weatherforecast
```

7. Use `curl` to get the metrics, as done earlier in this section:

```
$ curl http://localhost:5204/metrics
```

You should see an output similar to the following one (shortened):

```
...
# HELP myapp_calls_in_progress Number of weather forecast
operations ongoing.
# TYPE myapp_calls_in_progress gauge
myapp_weather_forecasts_in_progress 0
...
```

You will notice that there is now a new metric called `myapp_weather_forecasts_in_progress` available in the list. Its value will be zero since, currently, you are not running any requests against the tracked endpoint, and a gauge-type metric only measures the number of ongoing requests.

Congratulations, you have just defined your first functional metric! This is only a start; many more sophisticated possibilities are readily available to you.

Node.js- or .NET-based application services are by no means special. It is just as straightforward and easy to instrument services written in other languages, such as Kotlin, Python, or Go.

Having learned how to instrument an application service so that it exposes important metrics, let's now have a look at how we can use Prometheus to collect and aggregate those values to allow us to monitor a distributed application.

Leveraging Prometheus and Grafana to monitor a distributed application

Now that we have learned how to instrument an application service to expose Prometheus metrics, it's time to show how we can collect the metrics and forward them to a Prometheus server where all metrics will be aggregated and stored. We can then either use the (simple) web UI of Prometheus or a more sophisticated solution such as Grafana to display important metrics on a dashboard.

Unlike most other tools that are used to collect metrics from application services and infrastructure components, the Prometheus server takes the load of work and periodically scrapes all the defined targets. This way, applications and services don't need to worry about forwarding data. You can also describe this as pulling metrics, versus pushing them.

This makes Prometheus servers an excellent fit for our case. We will now discuss how to deploy Prometheus to Kubernetes, followed by our two sample application services. Finally, we will deploy Grafana to the cluster, and use it to display our custom metrics on a dashboard.

Architecture

Let's have a quick overview of the architecture of the planned system. As mentioned before, we have our microservices, the Prometheus server, and Grafana. Furthermore, everything will be deployed to Kubernetes. The following diagram shows the relationships:

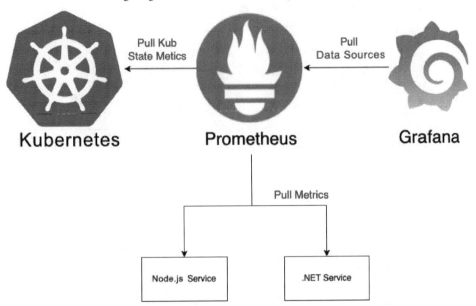

Figure 19.4 – High-level overview of an application using Prometheus and Grafana for monitoring

At the top center of the diagram, we have Prometheus, which periodically scrapes metrics from Kubernetes, shown on the left. It also periodically scrapes metrics from the services, in our case from the Node.js and .NET sample services we created and instrumented in the previous section. Finally, on the right-hand side of the diagram, we have Grafana, which pulls data periodically from Prometheus to then display it on graphical dashboards.

Deploying Prometheus to Kubernetes

As indicated, we start by deploying Prometheus to Kubernetes. Let's first define the Kubernetes YAML file that we can use to do so. First, we need to define a Kubernetes Deployment that will create a ReplicaSet of Prometheus server instances, and then we will define a Kubernetes service to expose Prometheus to us, so that we can access it from within a browser tab, or so that Grafana can access it. Let's do it:

1. Navigate to the source folder:

```
$ cd ~/The-Ultimate-Docker-Container-Book/ch19
```

2. Create a kube folder, and navigate to it:

```
$ mkdir -p ch19/kube && cd ch19/kube
```

3. Add a file called prometheus.yaml to this folder.

4. Add the following code snippet to this file; it defines a Deployment for Prometheus:

```yaml
1  apiVersion: apps/v1
2  kind: Deployment
3  metadata:
4    name: prometheus-deployment
5    labels:
6      app: prometheus
7      purpose: monitoring-demo
8  spec:
9    replicas: 2
10   selector:
11     matchLabels:
12       app: prometheus
13       purpose: monitoring-demo
14   template:
15     metadata:
16       labels:
17         app: prometheus
18         purpose: monitoring-demo
19     spec:
20       containers:
21       - name: prometheus
22         image: prom/prometheus
23         volumeMounts:
24         - name: config-volume
25           mountPath: /etc/prometheus/prometheus.yml
26           subPath: prometheus.yml
27         ports:
28         - containerPort: 9090
29       volumes:
30       - name: config-volume
31         configMap:
32           name: prometheus-cm
```

Figure 19.5 – Deployment for Prometheus

We are defining a ReplicaSet with two instances of Prometheus. Each instance is assigned two labels, app: prometheus and purpose: monitoring-demo, for identification purposes. The interesting part is in the volumeMounts section of the container spec. There, we mount a Kubernetes ConfigMap object called prometheus-cm, containing the Prometheus configuration, in the container at the location where Prometheus expects its configuration file(s) to be. The volume of the ConfigMap type is defined in the last four lines of the preceding code snippet.

Note that we will define the ConfigMap later on.

5. Now let's define the Kubernetes service for Prometheus. Append this snippet to the previous file:

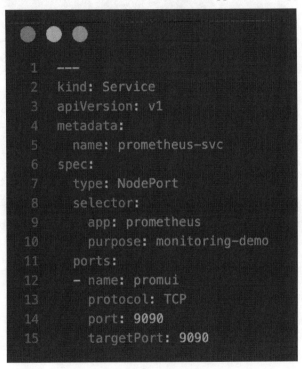

```
1   ---
2   kind: Service
3   apiVersion: v1
4   metadata:
5     name: prometheus-svc
6   spec:
7     type: NodePort
8     selector:
9       app: prometheus
10      purpose: monitoring-demo
11    ports:
12    - name: promui
13      protocol: TCP
14      port: 9090
15      targetPort: 9090
```

Figure 19.6 – Service for Prometheus

Please note the three dashes (- - -) at the beginning of the snippet are needed to separate individual object definitions in our YAML file.

We call our service prometheus-svc and make it NodePort (and not just a service of the ClusterIP type) to be able to access the Prometheus web UI from the host.

6. Now we can define a simple configuration file for Prometheus. This file basically instructs the Prometheus server which services to scrape metrics from and how often to do so. First, create a ch19/kube/config subfolder:

```
$ mkdir config
```

7. Add a file called `prometheus.yml` to the `config` folder, and add the following content to it:

```
 1  scrape_configs:
 2      - job_name: 'prometheus'
 3        scrape_interval: 5s
 4        static_configs:
 5        - targets: ['localhost:9090']
 6      - job_name: dotnet
 7        scrape_interval: 5s
 8        static_configs:
 9        - targets: ['dotnet-api-svc:80']
10      - job_name: node
11        scrape_interval: 5s
12        static_configs:
13        - targets: ['node-api-svc:3000']
14          labels:
15            group: 'production'
```

Figure 19.7 – Prometheus configuration

In the preceding file, we define three jobs for Prometheus:

- The first one, called `prometheus`, scrapes metrics every five seconds from the Prometheus server itself. It finds those metrics at the `localhost:9090` target. Note that, by default, the metrics should be exposed on the `/metrics` endpoint.

- The second job, called `dotnet`, scrapes metrics from a service found at `dotnet-api-svc:80`, which will be our .NET Core service that we defined and instrumented previously.

- Finally, the third job does the same for our Node service. Note that we have also added a group `'production'` label to this job. This allows further grouping of jobs or tasks.

8. Now we can define the `ConfigMap` object in our Kubernetes cluster with the next command. From within the `ch19/kube` folder, execute the following:

```
$ kubectl create configmap prometheus-cm \
--from-file config/prometheus.yml
```

What is a Kubernetes ConfigMap?

A Kubernetes ConfigMap is an API object used to store non-confidential configuration data in key-value pairs. This can include settings such as environment-specific URLs, command-line arguments, or any other parameters your applications need to run.

The main advantage of ConfigMaps is that they allow you to decouple configuration details from your application code. This can help make your applications more portable and easier to scale.

ConfigMaps can be consumed by Pods in a variety of ways: as environment variables, as command-line arguments for a container, or as configuration files in a volume. This flexibility allows developers to choose the most suitable method for their use case.

---

9. We can now deploy Prometheus to our Kubernetes server with the following:

```
$ kubectl apply -f prometheus.yaml
```

This gives this response:

```
deployment.apps/prometheus-deployment created
service/prometheus-svc created
```

10. Let's double-check that the deployment succeeded:

```
$ kubectl get all
```

Here is the output of the preceding command:

```
kubectl get all
NAME                                          READY   STATUS    RESTARTS   AGE
pod/prometheus-deployment-64d99cf5f7-nvgwn    1/1     Running   0          87s
pod/prometheus-deployment-64d99cf5f7-p82kv    1/1     Running   0          87s

NAME                     TYPE        CLUSTER-IP      EXTERNAL-IP   PORT(S)          AGE
service/kubernetes       ClusterIP   10.96.0.1       <none>        443/TCP          33d
service/prometheus-svc   NodePort    10.106.160.105  <none>        9090:31421/TCP   87s

NAME                                    READY   UP-TO-DATE   AVAILABLE   AGE
deployment.apps/prometheus-deployment   2/2     2            2           87s

NAME                                              DESIRED   CURRENT   READY   AGE
replicaset.apps/prometheus-deployment-64d99cf5f7  2         2         2       87s
```

Figure 19.8 – The Prometheus resources created on the Kubernetes cluster

Keep a close eye on the list of Pods, and make sure they are all up and running. Please also note the port mapping of the prometheus-svc object. In the author's case, the 9090 port is mapped to the 31421 host port. In your case, the latter may be different, but it will also be in the 3xxxx range.

11. We can now access the web UI of Prometheus. Open a new browser tab, and navigate to `http://localhost:<port>/targets` where `<port>` in the author's case is `31421`. You should see something like this:

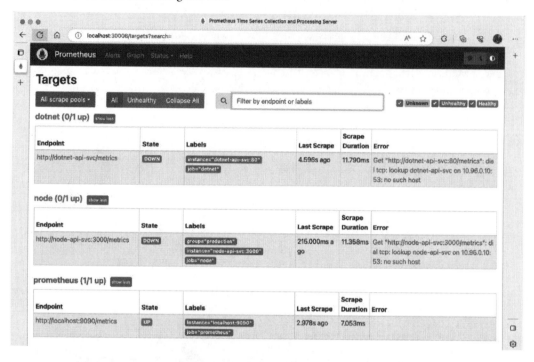

Figure 19.9 – Prometheus web UI showing the configured targets

In the previous screenshot, we can see that we defined three targets for Prometheus. Only the third one in the list is up and accessible by Prometheus. It is the endpoint we defined in the configuration file for the job that scrapes metrics from Prometheus itself. The other two services are not running at this time, and thus their state is down.

12. Now navigate to **Graph** by clicking on the respective link in the top menu of the UI.

13. Start typing in the search box and a list of known metrics will appear in a list. Inspect all the listed metrics that Prometheus found. In this case, it is only the list of metrics defined by the Prometheus server itself:

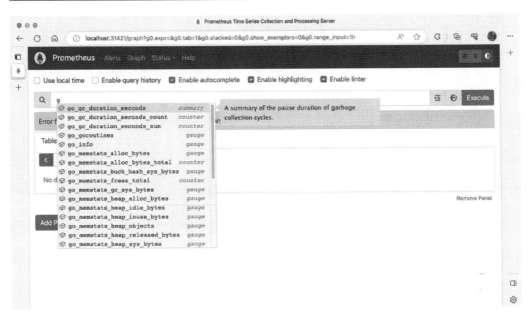

Figure 19.10 – Prometheus web UI showing available metrics

With that, we are ready to deploy the .NET and Node sample services we created earlier to Kubernetes.

Deploying our application services to Kubernetes

Before we can use the sample services we created earlier and deploy them to Kubernetes, we must create Docker images for them and push them to a container registry. In our case, we will just push them to Docker Hub.

Let's start with the .NET Core sample:

1. Add a Dockerfile with the following content to the ch19/dotnet/sample-api project folder:

```
FROM mcr.microsoft.com/dotnet/sdk:7.0 AS build-env
WORKDIR /app
COPY *.csproj ./
RUN dotnet restore
COPY . ./
RUN dotnet publish -c Release -o out
FROM mcr.microsoft.com/dotnet/aspnet:7.0
WORKDIR /app
COPY --from=build-env /app/out .
ENTRYPOINT ["dotnet", "sample-api.dll"]
```

2. Create a Docker image by using this command from within the `dotnet/sample-api` project folder:

    ```
    $ docker image build -t fundamentalsofdocker/ch19-dotnet-api:2.0
    .
    ```

    Note that you may want to replace `fundamentalsofdocker` with your own Docker Hub username in the preceding and subsequent commands.

3. Make sure you are logged in to Docker. If not, use this command to do so:

    ```
    $ docker login
    ```

4. Push the image to Docker Hub:

    ```
    $ docker image push fundamentalsofdocker/ch19-dotnet-api:2.0
    ```

Now we do the same with the Node sample API:

1. Add a Dockerfile with the following content to the `ch19/node` project folder:

    ```
    FROM node:lts
    WORKDIR /app
    COPY package.json ./
    RUN npm ci --only=production
    COPY . .
    EXPOSE 3000
    CMD ["node", "server.js"]
    ```

2. Create a Docker image by using this command from within the `ch19/node` project folder:

    ```
    $ docker image build -t fundamentalsofdocker/ch19-node-api:2.0 .
    ```

    Note once again that you may want to replace `fundamentalsofdocker` with your own Docker Hub username in the preceding and subsequent commands.

3. Push the image to Docker Hub:

    ```
    $ docker image push fundamentalsofdocker/ch19-node-api:2.0
    ```

With this, we are ready to define the necessary Kubernetes objects for the deployment of the two services. The definition is somewhat lengthy and can be found in the `sample-solutions/ch19/kube/app-services.yaml` file in the repository.

Please open that file and analyze its content.

Let's use this file to deploy the services:

1. Make sure you are in the `kube` subfolder.

2. Use the following command to deploy the two services:

```
$ kubectl apply -f app-services.yaml
```

This is the output:

```
deployment.apps/dotnet-api-deployment created
service/dotnet-api-svc created
deployment.apps/node-api-deployment created
service/node-api-svc created
```

3. Double-check that the services are up and running using the `kubectl get all` command. Make sure all the Pods of the Node and .NET sample API services are up and running.

4. List all Kubernetes services to find out the host ports for each application service:

```
$ kubectl get services
```

The output looks like this:

```
kubectl get services

NAME             TYPE        CLUSTER-IP       EXTERNAL-IP   PORT(S)           AGE
dotnet-api-svc   NodePort    10.104.213.192   <none>        80:30211/TCP      14s
kubernetes       ClusterIP   10.96.0.1        <none>        443/TCP           33d
node-api-svc     NodePort    10.98.105.103    <none>        3000:30663/TCP    14s
prometheus-svc   NodePort    10.99.238.198    <none>        9090:30008/TCP    5m13s
```

Figure 19.11 – Output of kubectl get services

In the author's case, the .NET API is mapped to port `30211`, and the Node API to port `30663`. Your ports may differ.

5. Use `curl` to access the `/metrics` endpoint for the .NET service:

```
$ curl localhost:30211/metrics
```

The output should look like this:

```
# HELP process_cpu_seconds_total Total user and system CPU time
spent in seconds.
# TYPE process_cpu_seconds_total counter
process_cpu_seconds_total 0.4
# HELP prometheus_net_meteradapter_instruments_connected Number
of instruments that are currently connected to the adapter.
# TYPE prometheus_net_meteradapter_instruments_connected gauge
prometheus_net_meteradapter_instruments_connected 0
# HELP prometheus_net_exemplars_recorded_total Number of
exemplars that were accepted into in-memory storage in the
```

```
prometheus-net SDK.
# TYPE prometheus_net_exemplars_recorded_total counter
prometheus_net_exemplars_recorded_total 0
...
```

6. Now do the same for the Node service:

```
$ curl localhost:30663/metrics
```

This time, the output looks like this:

```
# HELP process_cpu_user_seconds_total Total user CPU time spent
in seconds.
# TYPE process_cpu_user_seconds_total counter
process_cpu_user_seconds_total 1.0394399999999997 1578294999302
# HELP process_cpu_system_seconds_total Total system CPU time
spent in seconds.
# TYPE process_cpu_system_seconds_total counter
process_cpu_system_seconds_total 0.3370890000000001
1578294999302
...
```

7. Double-check the /targets endpoint in Prometheus to make sure the two microservices are now reachable:

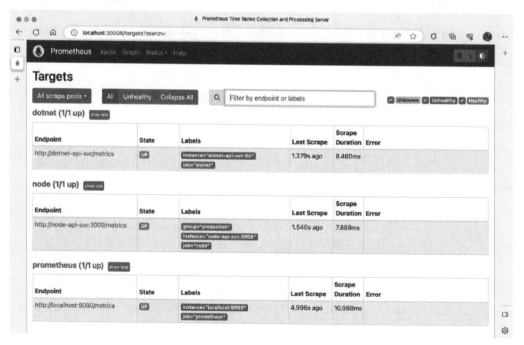

Figure 19.12 – Prometheus showing all targets are up and running

8. To make sure the custom metrics we defined for our Node.js and .NET services are defined and exposed, we need to access each service at least once. Thus use `curl` to access the respective endpoints a few times:

```
# access the /weatherforecast endpoint in the .NET service
$ curl localhost:30211/weatherforecast


# and access the /hello endpoint in the Node service
$ curl localhost:30663/hello
```

9. We can also see the two metrics in the Prometheus Graph view:

Figure 19.13 – Custom metrics in Prometheus

The last step is to deploy Grafana to Kubernetes so that we have the ability to create sophisticated and graphically appealing dashboards displaying key metrics of our application services and/or infrastructure components.

Deploying Grafana to Kubernetes

Now let's also deploy Grafana to our Kubernetes cluster, so that we can manage this tool the same way as all the other components of our distributed application. As the tool that allows us to create dashboards for monitoring the application, Grafana can be considered mission-critical and thus warrants this treatment.

Deploying Grafana to the cluster is pretty straightforward. Let's do it as follows:

1. Add a new file called `grafana.yaml` to the `ch19/kube` folder.

2. To this file, add the definition for a Kubernetes Deployment for Grafana:

```
1  apiVersion: apps/v1
2  kind: Deployment
3  metadata:
4    name: grafana-deployment
5    labels:
6      app: grafana
7      purpose: monitoring-demo
8  spec:
9    replicas: 1
10   selector:
11     matchLabels:
12       app: grafana
13       purpose: monitoring-demo
14   template:
15     metadata:
16       labels:
17         app: grafana
18         purpose: monitoring-demo
19     spec:
20       containers:
21         - name: grafana
22           image: grafana/grafana
```

Figure 19.14 – The content of the grafana.yaml file

If you prefer not to type the code yourself, then the file can be found in the `sample-solutions/ch19/kube` subfolder of your repo.

There are no surprises in that definition. In this example, we are running a single instance of Grafana, and it uses the `app` and `purpose` labels for identification, similar to what we used for Prometheus. No special volume mapping is needed this time since we are only working with defaults.

3. We also need to expose Grafana, and thus append the following snippet to the preceding file to define a service for Grafana:

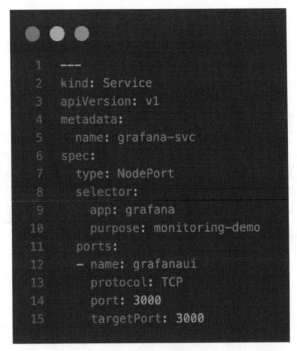

```
1    ---
2    kind: Service
3    apiVersion: v1
4    metadata:
5      name: grafana-svc
6    spec:
7      type: NodePort
8      selector:
9        app: grafana
10       purpose: monitoring-demo
11     ports:
12     - name: grafanaui
13       protocol: TCP
14       port: 3000
15       targetPort: 3000
```

Figure 19.15 – The Kubernetes service for Grafana

Once again, we are using a service of the NodePort type to be able to access the Grafana UI from our host.

4. We can now deploy Grafana with this command:

    ```
    $ kubectl apply -f grafana.yaml
    ```

    This results in this output:

    ```
    deployment.apps/grafana-deployment created
    service/grafana-svc created
    ```

5. Let's find out what the port number will be, over which we can access Grafana:

    ```
    $ kubectl get services/grafana-svc
    ```

    This gives us this:

```
kubectl get services/grafana-svc
NAME          TYPE       CLUSTER-IP     EXTERNAL-IP   PORT(S)          AGE
grafana-svc   NodePort   10.99.110.17   <none>        3003:32736/TCP   5m40s
```

Figure 19.16 – Get details of the Grafana service

6.   Open a new browser tab and navigate to `http://localhost:<port>`, where `<port>` is the port you identified in the previous step, and in my case is `32736`. You should see something like this:

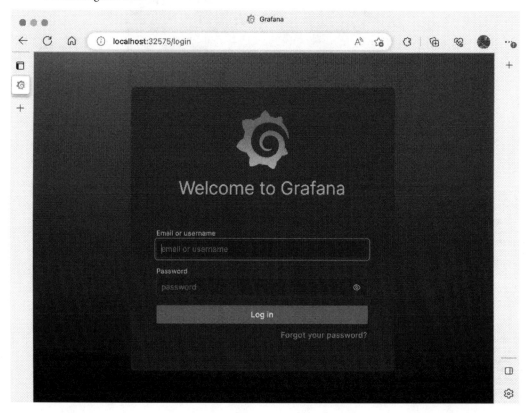

Figure 19.17 – Login screen of Grafana

7.   Log in with the default username `admin`, and the password is also `admin`. When asked to change the password, click the **Skip** link for now. You will be redirected to the **Home** dashboard.

8.   On the **Home** dashboard, click on **Create your first data source**, and select **Prometheus** from the list of data sources.

9.   Add `http://prometheus-svc:9090` for the URL to Prometheus, and click the green **Save & Test** button.

10. In Grafana, navigate back to the **Home** dashboard, and then select the **New dashboard** link.

11. Click **Add query**, and then from the **Metrics** drop-down menu, select the custom metric we defined in the .NET sample service:

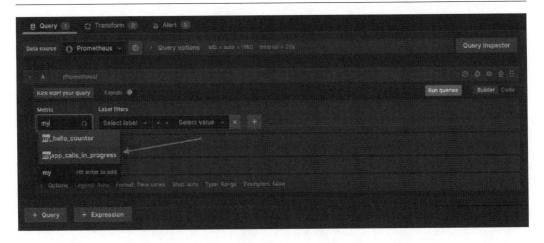

Figure 19.18 – Selecting the .NET custom metric in Grafana

12. Change the value of **Relative time** from **1h** to **5m** (5 minutes).

13. Change the dashboard refresh rate, found in the upper-right corner of the view, to **5s** (5 seconds).

14. Repeat the same for the custom metric defined in the Node sample service, so that you will have two panels on your new dashboard.

15. Modify the dashboard and its panels to your liking by consulting the documentation at `https://grafana.com/docs/grafana/latest/guides/getting_started/`.

16. Use `curl` to access the two endpoints of the sample services, and observe the dashboard. It may look like this:

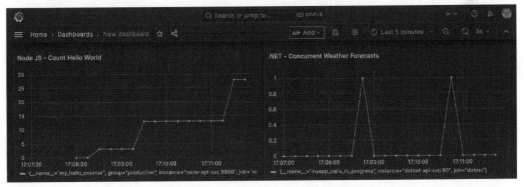

Figure 19.19 – Grafana dashboard with our two custom metrics

To summarize, we can say that Prometheus is a good fit to monitor our microservices because we just need to expose a metrics port, and thus don't need to add too much complexity or run additional services. Prometheus then is in charge of periodically scraping the configured targets, so that our services don't need to worry about emitting them.

Defining alerts based on key metrics

You will be let down if you believe that gathering logs and metrics and showing them in attractive dashboards is sufficient. If we just use dashboards, some support staff will need to be stationed in front of a large number of monitors constantly, round the clock, every day of the year, just in case. To put it mildly, this job is tedious. What happens if the person nods off? We must adjust our approach. Let's start by defining what metrics are.

Metrics

Metrics are used as input values in the rules on which alerts are based. Critical metrics must be identified, and if they surpass a predetermined value repeatedly or for an extended period of time, an alert is required. For illustration, consider CPU usage.

Defining alerts based on key metrics is an important part of monitoring and maintaining the health of our Docker and Kubernetes systems. Alerts allow us to define conditions based on metrics and to send notifications when those conditions are met, allowing us to quickly respond to potential issues.

In Kubernetes, we can use tools such as Prometheus to define alerting rules based on PromQL expressions. These rules allow us to specify conditions based on metrics collected from our cluster and send notifications to an external service when those conditions are met. For example, we could define an alert that triggers when CPU or memory utilization on cluster nodes exceeds a certain threshold.

In Docker, we can use tools such as cAdvisor or Docker stats to collect metrics from our containers, and then use a monitoring and alerting tool to define alerts based on those metrics. For example, we could define an alert that triggers when the number of running containers exceeds a certain threshold.

When defining alerts, it's important for us to follow best practices to ensure that our alerts are effective and actionable. Some best practices for alerting on Kubernetes include the following:

- **Alerting on symptoms**: Alerts should be based on symptoms that have a noticeable impact, rather than unexpected values in metrics

- **Alerting on the host or Kubernetes node layer**: Monitor the health of your hosts and nodes to ensure that your cluster is running smoothly

- **Alerting on the Kubernetes infrastructure**: Monitor the health of the Kubernetes control plane and other internal services

- **Alerting on services running on Kubernetes**: Monitor the health of your applications running on Kubernetes

- **Alerting on application layer metrics**: Monitor application-specific metrics to ensure that your applications are running smoothly

Now let's talk about alerting when an exceptional situation occurs.

Alerts

Let's define alerts, which are sent out when something unusual occurs. We may alert in different ways. If you are on duty, it may be a pager message, a text message, an email, or even the activation of an alarm sound and some blinking alert lights. Everything hinges on the use case. Let's just state that the author has contributed to several programs that have employed all of the aforementioned methods of alerting users.

For illustration, consider CPU use. When a Kubernetes cluster node's CPU use exceeds 95% for a period of more than a minute, the **System Reliability Engineer** (**SRE**) needs to be notified.

But who must establish the guidelines, you might wonder? Operations – or, more precisely, the SREs – are responsible for determining what non-functional metrics are significant and when they wish to be notified, even in the middle of the night. The company must specify the functional metrics as well as the tolerance levels or other criteria that will cause an alert for each measure.

Defining alerts

It is not sufficient to merely gather and display metrics, whether they pertain to infrastructure or the business. In order to develop **Service-Level Objectives** (**SLOs**) and **Service-Level Agreements** (**SLAs**) for those metrics, we must first determine the crucial indicators that truly define the state of the system. Following that, we establish guidelines for how frequently and for how long a measured metric may exceed the appropriate SLO or SLA. We send out an alert if one of these rules is broken.

Let's define a few potential alert candidates to get a sense of this. The first sample is a system-level statistic, whereas the second is a functional, or business-relevant, metric. Can you distinguish between them?

- We define the percentage of the total CPU utilized in a banking application as a statistic. *The proportion should not exceed 99%* could be the SLO. The rule might be that an alert should be sent out if the CPU percentage rises above 99% for more than 50% of a minute.

- We may designate the amount of time it takes to generate a quote for a customer interested in a quote as a critical statistic in an application providing life insurance. The SLA for this metric may then be that 99% of all quote requests must be processed within 50 milliseconds. No request can take more than 1,000 milliseconds. If the SLA is breached more than three times in a single hour, an alert should be sent, according to a rule for alerts.

The former is a infrastructure metric, whereas the latter is an commercial metric.

The chosen target individuals, such as SREs or developers, can then get alerts via a variety of channels, including email, text messages, automated phone calls, Slack messages, audio alarms, optical alarms, and others.

Service employees can now conduct other activities instead of actively monitoring the system once we have created and wired such alarms. They are guaranteed to be informed if anything significant or unusual occurs to which they must respond.

Runbooks

Say that an alert has been raised. What follows? Runbooks can help in this situation. A runbook outlines for each alert who must be notified, what this person must do to remedy the underlying problem, and to whom the problem must be escalated if it cannot be resolved. Runbook creation is a difficult process that shouldn't be taken lightly. However, they are a crucial tool for businesses. An SRE is only capable of so much. Some production problems are so serious that the C-level management must be notified. Imagine, for instance, that you run an online store and that there are no payments coming in because your **Payment Service Provider** (**PSP**) is down, making it impossible to process payments on your platform. This indicates that your application is now devoid of a crucial requirement. In essence, you are unable to conduct business until the problem is fixed; don't you think your CTO should be aware of this?

Let's talk about a current hot topic: problems occurring with a production system. We need to swiftly identify the underlying cause of the problem.

Troubleshooting a service running in production

It is a recommended best practice to create minimal images for production that don't contain anything that is not absolutely needed. This includes common tools that are usually used to debug and troubleshoot an application, such as `netcat`, `iostat`, `ip`, and others. Ideally, a production system only has container orchestration software such as Kubernetes installed on a cluster node with a minimal OS, such as CoreOS. The application container in turn ideally only contains the binaries absolutely necessary to run. This minimizes the attack surface and the risk of having to deal with vulnerabilities. Furthermore, a small image has the advantage of being downloaded quickly, using less space on disk and in memory, and showing faster startup times.

But this can be a problem if one of the application services running on our Kubernetes cluster shows unexpected behavior and maybe even crashes. Sometimes we are not able to find the root cause of the problem just from the logs generated and collected, so we might need to troubleshoot the component on the cluster node itself.

We may be tempted to SSH into the given cluster node and run some diagnostic tools. But this is not possible since the cluster node only runs a minimal Linux distro with no such tools installed. As a developer, we could now just ask the cluster administrator to install all the Linux diagnostic tools we intend to use. But that is not a good idea. First of all, this would open the door for potentially vulnerable software now residing on the cluster node, endangering all the other pods that run on that node, and would also open a door to the cluster itself, which could be exploited by hackers. Furthermore, it is always a bad idea to give developers direct access to nodes of a production cluster, no matter how much you trust them. Only a limited number of cluster administrators should ever be able to do so.

A better solution is to have the cluster admin run a so-called bastion container on behalf of the developers. This bastion or troubleshooting container has all the tools installed that we need to pinpoint the root cause of the bug in the application service. It is also possible to run the bastion container in the host's network namespace; thus, it will have full access to all the network traffic of the container host.

The netshoot container

Nicola Kabar, a former Docker employee, created a handy Docker image called `nicolaka/netshoot` that field engineers at Docker use all the time to troubleshoot applications running in production on Kubernetes or Docker Swarm. The purpose of this container, in the words of the creator, is as follows:

> *"Purpose: Docker and Kubernetes network troubleshooting can become complex. With proper understanding of how Docker and Kubernetes networking works and the right set of tools, you can troubleshoot and resolve these networking issues. The netshoot container has a set of powerful networking troubleshooting tools that can be used to troubleshoot Docker networking issues."*

> *- Nicola Kabar*

To use this container for debugging purposes, we can proceed as follows:

1. Spin up a throwaway bastion container for debugging on Kubernetes, using the following command:

   ```
   $ kubectl run tmp-shell --rm -i --tty \
       --image nicolaka/netshoot
   ```

   You will be greeted by this prompt:

   ```
   bash-5.0#
   ```

2. You can now use tools such as `ip` from within this container:

   ```
   bash-5.0# ip a
   ```

On my machine, this results in an output similar to the following if the pod is run on Docker Desktop:

```
kubectl run tmp-shell --rm -i --tty --image nicolaka/netshoot
If you don't see a command prompt, try pressing enter.
                      dP             dP                         dP
                      88             88                         88
88d888b. .d8888b. d8888P .d8888b. 88d888b. .d8888b. .d8888b. d8888P
88'  `88 88ooood8   88   Y8ooooo. 88'  `88 88'  `88 88'  `88   88
88    88 88.  ...   88         88 88    88 88.  .88 .88 88.  .88   88
dP    dP `88888P'   dP   `88888P' dP    dP `88888P' `88888P'   dP

Welcome to Netshoot! (github.com/nicolaka/netshoot)
Version: 0.11




tmp-shell ⟩⟩⟩   ip a
1: lo: <LOOPBACK,UP,LOWER_UP> mtu 65536 qdisc noqueue state UNKNOWN group default qlen 1000
    link/loopback 00:00:00:00:00:00 brd 00:00:00:00:00:00
    inet 127.0.0.1/8 scope host lo
       valid_lft forever preferred_lft forever
2: tunl0@NONE: <NOARP> mtu 1480 qdisc noop state DOWN group default qlen 1000
    link/ipip 0.0.0.0 brd 0.0.0.0
3: ip6tnl0@NONE: <NOARP> mtu 1452 qdisc noop state DOWN group default qlen 1000
    link/tunnel6 :: brd :: permaddr c6ff:c17c:362c::
4: eth0@if219: <BROADCAST,MULTICAST,UP,LOWER_UP> mtu 1500 qdisc noqueue state UP group default
    link/ether 2a:2b:2b:0a:75:f8 brd ff:ff:ff:ff:ff:ff link-netnsid 0
    inet 10.1.0.131/16 brd 10.1.255.255 scope global eth0
       valid_lft forever preferred_lft forever
```

Figure 19.20 – Output of the ip a command using the netshoot container

3.   To leave this troubleshooting container, just press *Ctrl + D* or type exit and then hit *Enter*.

4.   If we need to dig a bit deeper and run the container in the same network namespace as the Kubernetes host, then we can use this command instead:

```
$ kubectl run tmp-shell --rm -i --tty \
    --overrides='{"spec": {"hostNetwork": true}}' \
    --image nicolaka/netshoot
```

5.   If we run ip again in this container, we will see everything that the container host sees too, for example, all the veth endpoints.

The netshoot container has all the usual tools installed that an engineer ever needs to troubleshoot network-related problems. Some of the more familiar ones are ctop, curl, dhcping, drill, ethtool, iftop, iperf, and iproute2.

Summary

In this last chapter of the book, we have looked at different techniques used to instrument and monitor an individual service or a whole distributed application running on a Kubernetes cluster. You have been introduced to the concept of alerting based on key metrics. Furthermore, you have been shown how one can troubleshoot an application service that is running in production without altering the cluster or the cluster nodes on which the service is running.

As we come to the end of this book, we would like to thank you for your interest and for persisting till the end. We hope that the information and examples provided have been helpful in deepening your understanding of Docker and Kubernetes. These technologies are powerful tools for building and deploying modern applications, and we hope that this book has given you the knowledge and confidence to use them effectively. Thank you again for reading, and we wish you all the best in your future endeavors!

Questions

To assess your learning progress, please answer the following questions:

1. Why is it important to instrument your application services?

2. Can you describe to an interested layperson what Prometheus is?

3. Exporting Prometheus metrics is easy. Can you describe in simple words how you can do this for a Node.js application?

4. You need to debug a service running on Kubernetes in production. Unfortunately, the logs produced by this service alone don't give enough information to pinpoint the root cause. You decide to troubleshoot the service directly on the respective Kubernetes cluster node. How do you proceed?

Answers

Here are sample answers to the preceding questions:

1. We cannot do any live debugging on a production system for performance and security reasons. This includes interactive or remote debugging. Yet application services can show unexpected behavior in response to code defects or other infrastructure-related issues such as network glitches or external services that are not available. To quickly pinpoint the reason for the misbehavior or failure of a service, we need as much logging information as possible. This information should give us a clue about, and guide us to, the root cause of the error. When we instrument a service, we do exactly this – we produce as much information as is reasonable in the form of log entries and published metrics.

2. Prometheus is a service that is used to collect functional or non-functional metrics that are provided by other infrastructure services and, most importantly, by application services. Since Prometheus itself pulls those metrics periodically from all configured services, the services themselves do not have to worry about sending data. Prometheus also defines the format in which the metrics are to be presented by the producers.

3. To instrument a Node.js-based application service, we need to take the following four steps:

    I. Add a Prometheus adapter to the project. The maintainers of Prometheus recommend a library called `siimon/prom-client`.

    II. Configure the Prometheus client during the startup of the application. This includes the definition of a metrics registry.

    III. Expose an HTTP GET endpoint/metrics where we return the collection of metrics defined in the metrics registry.

    IV. Finally, define custom metrics of the counter, gauge, or histogram type, and use them in our code; for example, we increase a metric of the counter type each time a certain endpoint is called.

4. Normally, in production, a Kubernetes cluster node only contains a minimal OS to keep its attack surface as limited as possible and to not waste precious resources. Thus, we cannot assume that the tools typically used to troubleshoot applications or processes are available on the respective host. A powerful and recommended way to troubleshoot is to run a special tool or troubleshoot container as part of an ad hoc pod. This container can then be used as a bastion from which we can investigate network and other issues with the troubled service. A container that has been successfully used by many Docker field engineers at their customers' sites is `nicolaka/netshoot`.

Index

Packtpub.com

Subscribe to our online digital library for full access to over 7,000 books and videos, as well as industry leading tools to help you plan your personal development and advance your career. For more information, please visit our website.

Why subscribe?

- Spend less time learning and more time coding with practical eBooks and Videos from over 4,000 industry professionals

- Improve your learning with Skill Plans built especially for you

- Get a free eBook or video every month

- Fully searchable for easy access to vital information

- Copy and paste, print, and bookmark content

Did you know that Packt offers eBook versions of every book published, with PDF and ePub files available? You can upgrade to the eBook version at Packtpub.com and as a print book customer, you are entitled to a discount on the eBook copy. Get in touch with us at customercare@packtpub.com for more details.

At www.packtpub.com, you can also read a collection of free technical articles, sign up for a range of free newsletters, and receive exclusive discounts and offers on Packt books and eBooks.

Other Books You May Enjoy

If you enjoyed this book, you may be interested in these other books by Packt:

A Developer's Essential Guide to Docker Compose

Emmanouil Gkatziouras

ISBN: 978-1-80323-436-6

- Create multi-container applications using Docker Compose
- Use Docker Compose for daily development
- Connect microservices leveraging Docker network fundamentals
- Add monitoring to services leveraging Prometheus
- Deploy to production using Docker Compose
- Translate Compose files to Kubernetes deployments

Learn Docker - Fundamentals of Docker 19.x - Second Edition

Gabriel N. Schenker

ISBN: 978-1-83882-747-2

- Containerize your traditional or microservice-based applications
- Develop, modify, debug, and test an application running inside a container
- Share or ship your application as an immutable container image
- Build a Docker Swarm and a Kubernetes cluster in the cloud
- Run a highly distributed application using Docker Swarm or Kubernetes
- Update or rollback a distributed application with zero downtime
- Secure your applications with encapsulation, networks, and secrets
- Troubleshoot a containerized, highly distributed application in the cloud

Packt is searching for authors like you

If you're interested in becoming an author for Packt, please visit `authors.packtpub.com` and apply today. We have worked with thousands of developers and tech professionals, just like you, to help them share their insight with the global tech community. You can make a general application, apply for a specific hot topic that we are recruiting an author for, or submit your own idea.

Share Your Thoughts

Now you've finished *The Ultimate Docker Container Book*, we'd love to hear your thoughts! Scan the QR code below to go straight to the Amazon review page for this book and share your feedback or leave a review on the site that you purchased it from.

`https://packt.link/r/1804613983`

Your review is important to us and the tech community and will help us make sure we're delivering excellent quality content.

Download a free PDF copy of this book

Thanks for purchasing this book!

Do you like to read on the go but are unable to carry your print books everywhere? Is your eBook purchase not compatible with the device of your choice?

Don't worry, now with every Packt book you get a DRM-free PDF version of that book at no cost.

Read anywhere, any place, on any device. Search, copy, and paste code from your favorite technical books directly into your application.

The perks don't stop there, you can get exclusive access to discounts, newsletters, and great free content in your inbox daily

Follow these simple steps to get the benefits:

1. Scan the QR code or visit the link below

https://packt.link/free-ebook/9781804613986

1. Submit your proof of purchase
2. That's it! We'll send your free PDF and other benefits to your email directly

Made in the USA
Columbia, SC
20 September 2024

42678168R00341